PSYCHOLOGY RESEARCH METHODS

Comprehensive, engaging, and punctuated with humor, this undergraduate textbook provides an interesting introduction to research methodology. *Psychology Research Methods* allows students to become familiar with the material through examples of research relevant to their lives. The textbook covers every major research approach in psychology. Students will learn how to evaluate and conduct the different varieties of descriptive research and experimental research. They will learn all steps of the research process from developing a research idea to writing about and presenting what they did. Each chapter contains suggestions for journal article readings and activities relevant to the topics covered. The textbook also includes a chapter on how to conduct research online and an appendix with an annotated manuscript keyed to the current edition of the *Publication Manual of the American Psychological Association*.

WENDY HEATH earned a doctorate in Experimental Psychology in 1992 with a focus on cognitive and social psychology and was the recipient of Rider University's Iorio Faculty Research Prize in 2015. She has enjoyed teaching research methods to and conducting research with undergraduates for over 20 years. Dr. Heath has also shown her support for student research by creating the American Psychology-Law Society Award for the Best Undergraduate Research Paper, awarded annually since 2006. She is a member of the American Psychological Association, the Society for the Teaching of Psychology, and the Association for Psychological Science.

PSYCHOLOGY
RESEARCH METHODS

Connecting Research to Students' Lives

WENDY HEATH
Rider University, New Jersey

CAMBRIDGE
UNIVERSITY PRESS

University Printing House, Cambridge CB2 8BS, United Kingdom

One Liberty Plaza, 20th Floor, New York, NY 10006, USA

477 Williamstown Road, Port Melbourne, VIC 3207, Australia

314–321, 3rd Floor, Plot 3, Splendor Forum, Jasola District Centre,
New Delhi - 110025, India

79 Anson Road, #06–04/06, Singapore 079906

Cambridge University Press is part of the University of Cambridge.

It furthers the University's mission by disseminating knowledge in the pursuit of
education, learning, and research at the highest international levels of excellence.

www.cambridge.org
Information on this title: www.cambridge.org/9781107461116
DOI: 10.1017/9781316105566

First published 2018

Printed in the United States of America by Sheridan Books, Inc.

A catalogue record for this publication is available from the British Library

Library of Congress Cataloging-in-Publication data
Names: Heath, Wendy, 1960– author.
Title: Psychology research methods: connecting research to students' lives /
Wendy Heath, Rider University, New Jersey.
Description: New York : Cambridge University Press, 2018 | Includes
bibliographical references and index.
Identifiers: LCCN 2017023081 | ISBN 9781107461116 (alk. paper)
Subjects: LCSH: Psychology – Research – Methodology.
Classification: LCC BF76.5 .H424 2017 | DDC 150.72/1 – dc23
LC record available at https://lccn.loc.gov/2017023081

ISBN 978-1-107-46111-6 Paperback

Contents

List of Figures

List of Tables

Preface

Why I Wrote This Textbook

Every year one of my social psychology lectures holds my students' attention more than any other. My students are rapt, at times laughing, at times seemingly astounded at the story I am telling. What is this lecture about? The topic is Clark and Hatfield's (1989) article on receptivity to sexual offers. In this experiment, Clark and Hatfield had research assistants approach students of the opposite sex on campus and randomly ask one of three questions: "Would you go out tonight?" "Will you come over to my apartment?" or "Would you go to bed with me?" Clark and Hatfield found that a majority of men but not a single woman agreed to have a "sexual liaison" with the person who approached them (p. 39). I will admit that my students do not act in quite the same way for all my lectures. Why is this lecture different? Developing a relationship is something that virtually all have experienced or want to experience. This research is relevant to the students' lives, and it is exciting. I found myself wondering: Why not make all of this early research exposure relevant and exciting?

Thus, this textbook uses research relevant to students' lives to illustrate research methodology. Every major research approach in psychology is covered. Students will learn how to evaluate and use different varieties of descriptive research and experimental research methods. They will learn all steps of the research process from coming up with a research idea to writing about and presenting what they did. Through it all, the one constant is that information is presented within the confines of the familiar: the students' own lives.

This textbook is likely to be of interest to instructors who teach undergraduate research methodology courses that are not discipline-specific. The students and instructor potentially will have a range of discipline interests, but all of the students likely have the "student life" interest in common. This textbook could also be of interest to instructors in research methods courses that focus on social psychology, for many of the research examples come from the social psychology discipline.

Audience

Who is the intended audience for this textbook? This textbook is intended for use in undergraduate research methods classes. The text provides an introduction to all aspects of research methodology, and thus no prerequisite knowledge is needed. Students both new to and familiar with the world of research will appreciate the clarity of presentation and the use of research examples relevant to their lives.

Features

Pedagogy
- Learning objectives are provided at the beginning of every chapter. Key terms are provided in bold in the text and are defined both in the text

and in a glossary. To help students review the material, review questions covering the main topics of each chapter are presented at the end of each chapter.

Style

- The chapters are written with a clear, conversational style with touches of humor, which will appeal to an undergraduate audience.

Content

- This text provides an introduction to a wide variety of research methods, both experimental and non-experimental.
- The first four chapters cover topics relevant to whatever research approach one decides to consider. Chapter 1 includes a description of the goals of science, a review of the steps in the research process, and an explanation of why knowledge of research methodology is important (even to those who will not ultimately be researchers). Chapter 2 describes a variety of ways to come up with a research idea. Chapter 3 describes research ethics, and Chapter 4 considers measurement issues including reliability and validity.
- The next seven chapters concern different research approaches. Chapter 5 covers descriptive approaches such as naturalistic observation and archival research. Chapter 6 focuses on correlations, and Chapter 7 covers survey research. Chapter 8 covers experimentation with one independent variable while Chapter 9 considers factorial designs. Comprehensive coverage of quasi-experimental design and small-*N* research is provided using separate chapters for each (Chapters 10 and 11 respectively). Other texts often combine these two topics in one chapter.

- The next two chapters again concern areas relevant to research in general: Chapter 12 is a consideration of external validity while Chapter 13 is on the topic of online research, an increasingly popular technique used for collecting data. Step-by-step instructions help students learn how to create surveys and experiments for online data collection. Students are taught how to launch online research studies for little to no money.
- Chapter 14 covers "Writing about and Presenting your Research." This chapter is keyed to the current (6th) edition of the *Publication Manual of the American Psychological Association* (APA).
- Appendix A provides a sample manuscript annotated with information from the APA *Publication Manual* and tips on writing.
- In virtually all cases, research examples pertinent to students' lives are used to explain the different methods; this is a new and exciting way to teach students about research.
- This is not a statistics text, although statistics are occasionally presented within the context of a research study. In those situations statistics are discussed conceptually in easy-to-understand language. Instructors can easily choose to eliminate coverage of this information if they wish.

Articles as Illustration

- Journal article citations are provided at the end of each chapter. These articles have been chosen because they provide good examples of the concepts discussed in the chapter. Questions follow each suggested article.

Suggested Activities

- Each chapter contains suggestions for activities relevant to the topics covered.

Chapter Flexibility

- The chapters are relatively independent and thus can be taught out of order. Instructors can choose to include all chapters on their syllabi or choose to eliminate whole chapters or even portions of chapters.

Reviewers

I am grateful to those who provided detailed reviews of this text: Dennis Rodriguez, Indiana University; Diane Byrd, Fort Valley State University; Efthalia Esser, Minot State University; Erin Dupuis, Loyola University New Orleans; Jonathan Weaver, Michigan State University; Justin Purl, Ohio University; Katherine Hughes, Florida Atlantic University; Kevin Keating, Florida Atlantic University; Kimberly Rios, Ohio University; Leah Zinner Gottesman, Oglethorpe University; Lisa Elliott, Missouri Western State University; Michael C. Hout, New Mexico State University; Nakia Gordon, Marquette University; Nicole Bies-Hernandez, Northern Arizona University; Peggy Zoccola, Ohio University; Sara Peters, Newberry College.

Acknowledgments

I'd like to thank David Repetto, Senior Editor at Cambridge University Press, for his guidance throughout this entire process. Dave, working with you really helped to make writing this book a very pleasant experience. I also want to thank Cambridge University Press staff members Brianda Reyes, Development Editor, and Alexandra Poreda, Senior Editorial Assistant, for their aid along the way. In addition, I would like to acknowledge Charles Howell of Cambridge University Press for his skill in managing the content of this text, Neil Wells for preparing the index, and Frances Brown for her very capable copy-editing. A very special thank you goes to Elisa Adams, a Development Editor who helped me shape the content and the presentation of this textbook. Elisa, I really enjoyed working with you. This is a much better text because of your involvement.

I also want to thank Rider University for the support I received while I worked on this project. Rider's support was multi-faceted; I was provided with a research leave, summer fellowships, supportive colleagues, and quick access to interlibrary loan services. I am also thankful that my course load has included research methods courses for almost 25 years. I thoroughly enjoy teaching this content and watching students gain an understanding of and even an enthusiasm for research. I consider myself very fortunate to have found an academic home at Rider.

On a more personal level, I want to thank my friends for understanding that I had to work on this book even during scrapbooking get-togethers. Finally, I want to thank my husband, Stephen Kaplan for his support during this project. Thank you Stephen, for all you do for our daughter Jenny and for muting the TV during commercials (sorry advertisers!).

I dedicate this textbook to the teachers in my life. Your positive influence cannot be overstated.

Wendy P. Heath

1 Introduction to Research Methodology

LEARNING OBJECTIVES

- Explain why an understanding of research methods is important.
- Describe the four goals of science.
- Describe the steps of the research process.
- Identify four characteristics of science.

Consider the following questions:

- Is a relationship more exciting when you keep it a secret?
- What is your prospective employer likely to think of your new tattoo?
- Does drinking alcohol affect the extent of our self-disclosure?
- Are people more likely to lie for a friend or a stranger?
- Does the amount of sleep you get affect your test performance the next day?

FIGURE 1.1 Would this person's body modifications affect his chance of being hired?

Research can answer questions like these. In fact, each of the above questions is addressed somewhere in this textbook, which is designed to teach you how to understand research. I'll use this chapter to give you a brief introduction to research and an introduction to many of the topics you'll encounter in this book.

Why Do I Need to Know about Research Methods?

Early in my college career, I read a newspaper headline that said, "Peanut butter causes cancer." This really worried me because I ate peanut butter multiple times a week. Was this report true, I wondered? Now that I know how to be a critical consumer of research, I realize I didn't have much to worry about. The statement that peanut butter *caused* cancer was very much an overstatement. In fact, the investigation of peanut butter and cancer relied on what we call correlational research, and you cannot determine causation from correlational research. (We'll talk more about correlational research in Chapter 6.)

Why is it important to understand research? Well, for one thing, without that understanding, I would have missed out on an additional 30 years of peanut butter. But there are other reasons. For one, the media often provide us with research results, and it's important that we understand how to evaluate them. For example, as I was writing this, I took a look at the Yahoo website and found the following headlines:

1. "This ground-breaking high fat diet could combat diabetes and promote weight loss" (Lewis, March 4, 2016)
2. "Chimpanzees believe in God, research suggests" (Dicker, March 4, 2016)
3. "Dogs have a very special way of seeing human faces" (Freeman, March 4, 2016).

Do I just accept these findings? Should I start eating a lot of fat and rethink any interactions I have with chimps and dogs? Not necessarily. If I had just accepted that media report about peanut butter, I would have missed eating a lot of it. If you learn how to critically evaluate the way the researchers did their research, you will be able to decide whether the conclusions they put forth and/or the media reports of the research are warranted.

Understanding research methods can also help you in your work as a college student. Throughout your college career, you'll learn a lot about what scholars have discovered in your field. How do they know all they know? Research! It's important to distinguish a well-executed study from one that is severely flawed so you will know when to accept and when to question the research findings you learn about.

You may also have opportunities to conduct some research yourself. Then, of course, it is important that you know what you are doing so you can understand which methods are appropriate for your particular investigation and so you can arrive at the appropriate conclusions.

Understanding research methods can also help you as a consumer. For example, I am currently in the market for a new car. How should I choose my new car? I could just talk with my friend who has the type of car I want and see what she thinks of her car. However, someone who is familiar with research methods would know that, under typical circumstances, getting the view of just one person is not likely to provide you with the information you need. You might want to know, for example, how reliable the car is. What if your friend is particularly hard on her car, careening around corners and jumping curbs? She might need more service on her car than those who treat their cars more gently. What likely is more helpful is to know how reliable this vehicle *typically* is. To know this, you need to go to a source (such as *Consumer Reports*) that has collected data from a larger sample, ideally a representative sample. A **representative sample** is one that has the same characteristics as the population of interest. A **population** consists of the members of an identifiable group – in this case the population is defined as all the people

FIGURE 1.2 Teachers use research too!

who drive the car you are interested in. You'll learn more about **sampling**, or choosing a portion of the population as study participants for research, in Chapter 7.

Finally, understanding research methods can help you in your future career. Many careers require using research methods and/or evaluating research findings in some way. For example, you could be a market researcher, determining what people think of a particular toothpaste, politician, or radio station. You could be a teacher, evaluating which teaching techniques to use and assessing how well your students are doing. You could work in the mental health industry, selecting the best treatment method given your client's particular needs. You could be a human resources executive, evaluating and implementing ways to enhance employee performance and morale as well as increase employees' participation in healthy activities. There are so many ways a knowledge of research methodology can become a part of your life.

The Goals of Science

Scientific research has four general goals: (1) to **describe** the phenomenon of interest, (2) to **explain** the phenomenon of interest, (3) to **predict** when the observed phenomenon will occur again, and (4) to

The Four Goals of Science

- Describe
- Explain
- Predict
- Control

FIGURE 1.3 The four goals of science.

control the phenomenon of interest. I'll talk about each of these goals below. (See Figure 1.3.)

Description

One of the main goals of scientists is to describe phenomena. For scientists who study psychology, this often means describing observable behavior. **Observable behaviors** are behaviors that can be seen, such as the amount of time students spend texting while walking between two buildings on campus, the number of alcoholic beverages people drink on the day they turn 21, or the number of M&Ms eaten while watching a movie with friends. We can observe activities like these in a systematic manner and document the results of our observations. To be systematic means to develop a plan for what exactly we are going to look for, striving to make these observations as objective as possible so we can generate accurate descriptions of the phenomena of interest.

For example, McCormick and Jones (1989) conducted an observation study to investigate differences in nonverbal flirtation in men and women. They were interested in the following behaviors: "gaze, movement, posture, facial expression, grooming, and touch" (p. 273). According to McCormick and Jones, each of these behaviors could be used to bring about two possible outcomes when you are interacting with someone – you could be trying to increase closeness ("escalation") or to reduce it ("deescalation"). Thus the researchers used a

checklist with 12 options (Table 1.1), and they checked these options off as they saw them while observing couples in a bar. At the end of their observation study, McCormick and Jones were able to describe the frequency of the nonverbal flirtation behaviors they observed.

Psychologists also can describe factors that are less readily observable, such as how many times a week people remember their dreams, how anxious people feel when speaking in front of an audience, or how people feel after working out. We typically can't get the answers to these questions by observing people, but we *can* get them by asking. Basow and Kobrynowicz (1993) found that women were seen as more appealing by a sample of college students when they were shown eating fewer rather than more calories. How did Basow and Kobrynowicz know this? They asked. (By the way, I'm not happy about this finding, but it doesn't matter whether I am happy or even whether Basow and Kobrynowicz are happy. These are the results that were obtained; the way a researcher feels about them does not matter.) You'll learn more about how to observe behavior in Chapter 5 and how to describe thoughts and attitudes in Chapter 7.

FIGURE 1.4 In order to learn how people feel after working out, we can ask them.

Table 1.1   McCormick and Jones' (1989) twelve categories of nonverbal flirtation behavior.

Behavior	Purpose*	Definition
Gaze toward	Escalation	Establishing or holding eye contact; mutual gaze
Gaze away	Deescalation	Looking away; avoiding partner's eyes
Move closer	Escalation	Positioning body closer to partner
Move away	Deescalation	Increasing distance between self and partner
Open posture	Escalation	Relaxed stance, e.g., open legs, open arms, trunk easily visible; pivoting toward or facing partner
Closed posture	Deescalation	Arms and/or legs crossed and held tightly against body, closing off body; pivoting away from partner; shifting to shoulder-to-shoulder position
Positive facial expression	Escalation	Smiling, laughing, and grinning
Negative facial expression	Deescalation	Frowning, yawning, and grimacing
Grooming	Escalation	Enhancing appearance: smoothing hair, tightening abdomen, most self-touching; arched back, chest thrusting, stretching; lip licking
Brief touching	Escalation	Placing fingertips on or making fleeting physical contact with partner's shoulder, hair, arm, leg, face, or hand for a few seconds
Continuous touching	Escalation	Ongoing touching; holding hands, placing arm around partner, leaning against partner, touching legs; one partner rests against the other's head or shoulder
Intimate touching	Escalation	Touching two or more parts of partner's body or sexual areas; kissing, hugging, placing hand on partner's buttocks, breast, or genitals; rubbing against partner

* Escalation behaviors attempt to increase intimacy or attract another person; deescalation behaviors attempt to decrease intimacy or reject another person.
Source: McCormick, N. B. & Jones, A. J. (1989). Gender differences in nonverbal flirtation. *Journal of Sex Education & Therapy, 15,* 271–282.

Explanation

Scientists also want to explain the phenomena of interest. Often this means that we wish to determine *why* something happens. In other words, we want to find out what causes the phenomena of interest.

Scientists will often look at the pattern of data from research on a particular topic and propose a theory to account for why the data appear as they do. More formally: a **theory** is a statement that organizes, summarizes, and explains available information about a phenomenon and serves as a basis for formulating testable predictions about the phenomenon. Let's look at an example.

Have you ever glanced through a magazine at a store, decided to buy it, but then put it back and chosen a "fresh" one from the back of the display? Argo, Dahl, and Morales (2006) were interested in investigating how consumers react to products they think were touched by others. In this case, the products of interest were t-shirts, and Argo et al. tested what people thought about three possible contamination cues: how close the item was to the location where it was presumably touched by someone (proximity to contact), how long it has been since someone presumably touched the item, and how many people were believed to have touched the item. With regard to proximity, they found that evaluations of the t-shirts were less favorable when, for example, the t-shirt was reported as discarded in a dressing room as opposed to hanging on a rack; however, this lowered evaluation occurred only when participants thought others had more recently touched the item. Contamination effects seemed to wear off with time. Participants also rated the t-shirt less favorably when they believed many people had touched it as opposed to only one.

Thus Argo et al. found that if consumers thought a product had recently come into contact with one or more other customers, they saw it as less appealing. When Argo et al. asked their study participants a series of questions to determine why they felt the way they did about the t-shirt, they found that the responses were driven by disgust. Argo et al. then proposed a *theory of consumer contamination* motivated by disgust to explain why people feel as they do about products that have been touched. Consumers are believed to contaminate products simply by having contact with them. Think about this the next time you're in a fitting room.

Once a scientific phenomenon has been described and a theory has been put forth to explain the phenomenon, we can attempt the next goal of science: prediction.

Prediction

Forming hypotheses is the third purpose of scientific research. **Hypotheses** are predictions, our expectations for our results, and they often are developed from theories. To illustrate, let's look at a specific theory and a specific hypothesis derived from that theory. Duval and Wicklund's (1972) theory of objective self-awareness claims that when people are self-aware, they tend to focus on what behavior is expected in a particular setting and evaluate how well their behavior matches that standard. Now let's look at how a team of researchers used this theory to generate a hypothesis.

Diener and Wallbom (1976) gave their study participants an "intelligence test" requiring them to solve a series of anagrams in the allotted time (p. 109). Some participants were first made self-aware by the experience of seeing themselves in a mirror and hearing a recording of their voice, while others were not made self-aware. Diener and Wallbom hypothesized that if being self-aware leads us

FIGURE 1.5 A mirror is often used in research to make someone self-aware.

to think about standards of behavior appropriate to the setting, then those who are self-aware will be less likely to act in a deviant manner, in this case by cheating on a test. Consistent with this hypothesis, they found that college students were less likely to cheat on a test if they were self-aware as opposed to not self-aware.

Once we have formed our hypotheses, we can test them to find out how accurately they predict events. If the results are as we predicted, we need to relay that information to our audience. There are specific ways to say this. Each of the following is appropriate:

- the data support the hypothesis
- the data are consistent with the hypothesis.

If the results are not as we predicted, we say:

- the data did not support the hypothesis, or
- the data are not consistent with the hypothesis.

If the data were not consistent with the hypotheses, and the hypotheses were derived from a theory, then the theory likely needs to be modified. We could then modify the theory, generate new hypotheses, and test again. That's how science works. Each time our hypotheses are supported (the results come out as we expected), we gain confidence in the theory. We'll talk more about hypotheses in Chapter 2.

Notice, however, that we never use any version of the word "prove" when talking about theories or hypotheses (do not say "my hypothesis was proven!"). The reason for this is that, as scientists continue to explore a particular topic, they may find disconfirming evidence, a case in which the theory does not fully account for the observed pattern of results or a case in which a hypothesis is not supported. It is always possible that new information may require researchers to modify current ideas.

Control

After we have described and explained a scientific phenomenon and made predictions about what we expect to occur, it's time to talk about control, the fourth purpose of scientific research. For many psychologists, learning how to influence or even control attitudes and behavior is the goal. For example, many researchers are trying to determine how to curb racism, discrimination, and aggression, to name a few. Let's look at a more specific example.

Emile Bruneau is a cognitive neuroscientist who has spent years investigating groups around the world that have historically been in conflict (such as Democrats and Republicans, Israelis and Palestinians). How can we stop or at least lessen the likelihood of these conflicts? Many have suggested solutions, each designed to increase people's positive attitudes toward those who oppose them. Bruneau's approach is to use brain scans in an effort to see how our brains react when we empathize or fail to empathize with someone outside our group (empathy is thought to play a role in conflict resolution). The hope is that we'll be able to identify the parts of the brain responsible for empathy and then learn how to increase empathy for those outside the group (see Interlandi, 2015). Again, learning how to minimize conflict is an example of the kind of influence or control a psychological researcher might have as an overall goal.

The Goals of Science in Action

Let's take a look at a research example to illustrate the goals of description, explanation, prediction, and control. First, picture the following. You're a star of the track team preparing for a big meet. Under which conditions are you likely to run your fastest: alone or with other runners? Those with experience running on a track team are likely to say: I run faster when other runners are present. Now picture another situation. You are about to perform your first monologue

FIGURE 1.6 Members of a track team tend to run faster when they are running with others as opposed to alone.

in acting class. You practice in front of the mirror repeatedly until you feel you are pretty good. Then it's finally time to perform in front of the class. You slowly walk up to the front of the class and prepare to speak. But you start to shake and stutter. And you realize you are not giving nearly the same level of performance you gave in the mirror.

These two scenarios both describe a performance in front of others. In one case the performer is better in front of others, while in the other the performer is worse. Early researchers were often perplexed by similar outcomes, sometimes seeing better performance with an audience (for example Weston & English, 1926) and sometimes worse (see Pessin, 1933). Why the difference? Researchers wanted to create a theory that accounted for both outcomes, and Robert Zajonc (rhymes with "science") did just

that. In 1965, Zajonc used the theory of social facilitation to explain why the presence of others sometimes improves performance and sometimes inhibits it. He explained that when someone is just learning a task, that person's responses are likely the wrong responses (wrong responses are dominant). However, when the task is well learned, the dominant responses are likely correct responses. Zajonc postulated that the presence of others increases physiological arousal, and that arousal enhances the presence of dominant responses. In other words, according to Zajonc's depiction of social facilitation, when others are present, people will tend to do better on simple or well-learned tasks and worse on complex or poorly learned tasks. (See Figure 1.7.)

So Zajonc's theory of social facilitation did a good job of explaining the data. This theory then could be used to generate hypotheses. For example, Kotzer (2007) used Zajonc's theory to predict what will happen when expert and novice basketball players attempt free throws in front of an audience and alone. As hypothesized, Kotzer found that those who were relatively experienced at playing basketball made more free throws when being watched by an audience than when alone. On the other hand, those who were relatively inexperienced made more free throws when alone than with an audience. This is consistent with what Zajonc's theory of social facilitation would predict.

Now that the phenomenon of performance differences has been described and explained through

SOCIAL FACILITATION

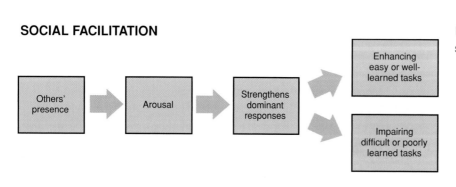

FIGURE 1.7 Zajonc's (1965) social facilitation hypothesis.

theory and predictions have been made, let's take a look at how researchers could use social facilitation research to influence or control attitudes and/or behavior. Yu and Wu (2015) considered how the presence of observers would affect those performing baggage x-ray screening tasks. Would the presence of an audience enhance simple x-ray screening tasks and impair difficult x-ray screening tasks, as the theory of social facilitation predicts? The researchers brought the screening task into the laboratory and trained college students to look for knives in x-ray images of baggage. After the training, these students were tested on an additional 400 images, 200 of which had a knife. For half the images an observer watched the student complete the screening; for the other half, the students performed the screening task while alone. What happened? The presence of an observer did have an influence; when the screening task was relatively easy, those being watched performed it faster. When it was relatively difficult, those being watched slowed down. The presence of an audience did not affect response accuracy, however.

How did Yu and Wu use this research to influence or control the phenomenon of interest? After seeing their results, they made recommendations for the security industry. They suggested that if the task is simple, such as detecting threats in small bags (what you likely would find people carrying on the subway), the security screeners should be performing their tasks while being watched. On the other hand, if the task is complex, such as detecting threats in large bags (what you likely would find people carrying in the airport), they should be performing their tasks while alone. The researchers also suggested that small bags and large bags be screened separately, with an observer present only for those screening small bags. According to Yu and Wu, these policies would optimize the performance of those detecting threats to security. With these recommendations, Yu and Wu are seeking to influence the way x-rays of baggage are screened.

Note that even though the theory of social facilitation could explain many research findings by focusing on the complexity of the task, science didn't stop there. Researchers have continued to conduct research to determine *why* people have such reactions to the presence of others. There are currently three major categories of explanations for the social facilitation effects researchers have found. As Aiello and Douthitt (2001) noted in their review of social facilitation, researchers have continued to investigate Zajonc's assertion that the presence of others increases arousal levels. Researchers have also considered the possibility that people are affected by the presence of others because they are worried about being evaluated, or because they are distracted. So, as you can see, while Zajonc's theory of social facilitation was an important development in explaining why performance sometimes improves and sometimes falters when people are watched, researchers have continued to refine the theory with additional research.

The Steps in the Research Process

How do scientists accomplish their four goals of description, explanation, prediction, and control? In this section we'll go over the general steps you take when you conduct research. We'll discuss all these steps in more detail later in the textbook.

(Step 1) Develop a Research Idea

The first thing you need to do is come up with a research idea. There are lots of ways to do this. This textbook was designed to provide you with research examples that are generally pertinent to students' lives, and one of the things you can do is to look at the experiences in your own life to come up with ideas.

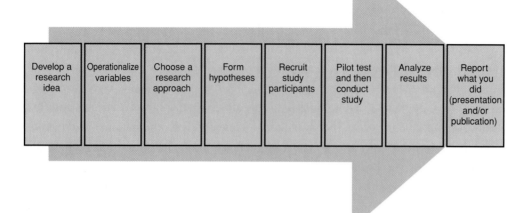

| Develop a research idea | Operationalize variables | Choose a research approach | Form hypotheses | Recruit study participants | Pilot test and then conduct study | Analyze results | Report what you did (presentation and/or publication) |

FIGURE 1.8 The steps in the research process.

Let's take an example. Let's say you find yourself completely obsessed with texting on your cell phone, even in very odd places like the shower and at very odd times such as during intimate moments. You wonder, "Am I the only one doing this?" You now have an idea for research. You can develop a survey and ask your respondents to indicate under what conditions they text.

As you'll see in Chapter 13, Harrison and Gilmore (2012) did this. They were interested in why and when college students text. So they created an online survey presenting 29 social situations and asked a sample of students at their university to indicate whether they texted in such situations. They found that almost 30% of the respondents had texted while in the shower, and 13% while having sex! In Chapter 7, you will learn how to create a survey to address your own research questions, and in Chapter 13 you'll learn how to create and administer a survey online.

Thinking about your own life is just one of many ways to come up with an idea for your research. You can also get ideas from the need to solve practical problems, from previous research, and from

FIGURE 1.9 Where do you do your texting?

theories. Chapter 2 will elaborate on each of these ways to generate research ideas.

There is another way to think about research ideas. Psychological research can generally be considered as either basic or applied. **Basic research** attempts to answer fundamental questions about a phenomenon, without much focus on how the information could be applied in the real world.

Let's look at a memory task as an example. Many researchers have demonstrated that it is more difficult to recognize a face when it is presented upside-down than right side up (see Valentine, 1988 for a review of this "face-inversion effect"). For example, Rakover (2012) considered how removal of the eyebrows affects memory for upright versus inverted faces. Why is it important to study how well people remember inverted faces, with or without their eyebrows? As you'll find with many basic research studies, the potential application of this work is not necessarily obvious, perhaps even to the researchers themselves. The researchers and, if the work is published, the research community will learn something about facial recognition that adds to our general body of knowledge about memory for faces. Perhaps one day, our knowledge of how facial stimuli are processed by the brain will have an application in the real world, such as aiding those who have difficulty processing such stimuli.

Applied research, on the other hand, is conducted with a practical, real-world issue in mind. Let's say a researcher is interested in investigating ways in which restaurant employees can improve their ability to remember food and drink orders accurately without writing the orders down. In fact, Bekinschtein, Cardozo, and Manes (2008) conducted an applied research study on this general topic. They did their work in Buenos Aires, Argentina, where restaurant workers never write down food and drink orders, so having a good memory for the orders taken is imperative. They found that expert waiters' memory for drink orders was superior when the patrons remained in their original seats versus when they changed locations. These expert waiters later revealed that they were linking the drink orders to both the patrons' features (faces and outfits) and their location. When the location changed, memory accuracy decreased.

A group of novice waiters tested in a laboratory setting did not use this feature/location strategy and often delivered drinks to the wrong people, even when the patrons had not changed seats. Making this comparison between expert waiters and novices allowed the researchers to isolate a strategy that worked to maximize memory accuracy in those taking drink orders. Thus, Bekinschtein et al. recommended that wait staff use a feature/location strategy to aid their memory. As you can see, while both the face recognition work and the drink order

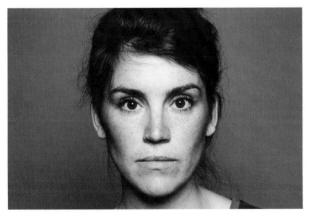

FIGURE 1.10 Which face would you find easier to recognize?

FIGURE 1.11 How does a restaurant server remember all those drink orders?

research concern memory issues, the drink order research is more applied, because it seeks to address an identified real-world concern.

Basic research often provides a foundation for later applied research. For example, basic information about the way people process faces can certainly be helpful when investigating a related memory issue in the real world, such as the facial recognition capabilities of an eyewitness to a crime. Ultimately both types of research, basic and applied, are necessary to advance knowledge and aid society.

(Step 2) Operationalize Your Variables

Once you have your research idea, you are ready to specify the variables you are going to study. A **variable** is any characteristic that can take on different values. One way to think about this is to remember they are called variables because they can vary. For example, IQ is a variable, a measure of intelligence that for most people yields a test score somewhere between 70 and 130 (Neisser et al., 1996). Quantifying other variables is perhaps less intuitive, but we can still measure them. For example, shyness can be a variable; someone can be more shy or less shy, and we can use a shyness test to measure this (for example, Jones & Russell, 1982). Anything that

can vary, such as gender, socioeconomic status, or food type, can be a variable in a research study.

When you are planning your research, you should always **operationalize your variables**. This means you specify the precise meaning of a variable in terms of the specific procedures to be performed. You'll learn more about operationalizing your variables in Chapter 4, but for now let's go over a brief example.

To operationalize your variables it's not enough to say, "I'm studying aggression." I would ask you, "What do you mean by that? How will you measure aggression? Will you ask your study participants how aggressive they feel on a scale of 1 to 10? Will you count the number of times someone throws a punch in a bar?" Scientists are precise. Take the work of Reifman, Larrick, and Fein (1991) as an example. These researchers looked at a random sample of major league games in an effort to investigate the relationship between temperature and aggression in professional baseball. How did they operationalize aggression? They identified it as the act of hitting batters while they are on home plate, and they counted the number of batters hit by the ball per game. This operational definition of aggression is appropriate given Reifman et al.'s

FIGURE 1.12 What is the relationship between temperature and aggression in professional baseball?

research question. They found that as the temperature increased, there tended to be more players hit by pitches.

(Step 3) Choose a Research Approach

There are lots of different ways to conduct research and you need to decide which approach you are going to take. One of your most fundamental decisions is whether you will use experimental or descriptive research methods. We'll start by looking at what it means to conduct an experiment.

FIGURE 1.13 Does listening to music while exercising affect your mood?

The Experimental Research Approach. The experiment is our most influential research approach because it is the only one that allows us to establish cause and effect. In the simplest kind of experiment, researchers manipulate (vary) one variable, called the **independent variable**, and observe the effects of that manipulation on a response measure called the **dependent variable**. The independent variable is considered the "cause," and the dependent variable is considered the "effect." Let's look at an example.

Have you ever wondered whether music can affect people's mood? Campbell and White (2015) wondered whether music would affect undergraduates' mood if they were exposed to music during exercise. In their experiment, Campbell and White tested two groups of undergraduates; one group exercised while listening to music and the other group exercised without listening to music. Music was Campbell and White's independent variable. They wanted to see whether music would cause a change in their participants' mood. Mood was what they were measuring; this was one of their dependent variables. Another way to think of this is that mood was expected to *depend* on the presence or absence of music.

When you are conducting an experiment, the goal is to keep everything the same between your groups except for your independent variable(s). So Campbell and White had everyone do the same kind of exercise (moderately intense walking) for the same amount of time (20 minutes). You might think, "Well, how about fitness level? Maybe everyone wasn't equally fit and that affected their mood?" That's a reasonable question. To ensure that all things besides the independent variable were held constant across groups, Campbell and White randomly determined which participants heard the music and which did not. When we use **random assignment** to place people into groups, all characteristics of the participants are theoretically distributed across groups in approximately equal proportions. So the two groups were theoretically equivalent in fitness level and in all other ways too.

What did Campbell and White find? Those who listened to music while exercising reported a more pleasant mood than those who did not. We know it was music that caused the difference because its presence was the only thing that differed between the two groups. When you can conclude that your independent variable caused the change in your dependent variable, your experiment is said to have high internal validity. In other words, **internal validity** is the degree to which the results of an experiment can be attributed to the manipulation of the independent variable.

This example described a relatively simple experiment, with just one independent variable. You will learn more about experiments with one independent variable in Chapter 8, and we'll consider experiments with more than one independent variable in Chapter 9.

The Small-N Design Approach. The experimental approach described above involved testing groups of people, summarizing the responses for each group, and then comparing one group's responses to the other group's responses. Testing just a single individual could have yielded a response that was unusual, perhaps exceedingly large or small. Testing larger groups tends to provide a fuller range of responses and allows us to see what the typical response is for the group overall. Thus much experimental research involves testing large groups.

One experimental research approach, however, typically involves testing just one or a few participants. We call this the **small-N design** approach. "*N*" refers to the number of people in your study, so "small-*N* design" means you are doing research with a small number of study participants. When you use a small-*N* design, you consider the results for each individual separately and do not combine them with the results for other individuals. Small-*N* designs are often used in applied settings to examine whether a particular treatment works to alter a behavior you want to change in a *particular* person. To achieve this, the researcher needs to assess the behavior of interest before and after the treatment. Let's take a look at an example.

Wack, Crosland, and Miltenberger (2014) were interested in finding out whether the act of setting goals and getting individualized feedback would help five female runners on a college campus increase

their weekly running distances. First the researchers measured how far each student was running without setting any goals. This is called determining the **baseline** level of performance; it took 2 to 4 weeks to determine the baseline for each runner, how far each generally ran.

The researchers then met with each runner to decide on a long-term goal (for example, "When this study is over in 20 weeks, how far do you want to be running each time you run?"). In addition, a researcher met with each runner once a week to set a short-term goal for the upcoming week (such as, "Each time you run next week, how far do you want to run?"). Participants were expected to run at least three times a week and were allowed to increase their distance goals as the weeks progressed if they were meeting earlier goals as scheduled. At their weekly meetings, each runner got feedback from a researcher on whether the weekly goal had been accomplished.

What happened? Although the five women had varying levels of achievement, all increased their running distance over their baseline levels of performance. Thus, with a small-*N* design, Wack et al. demonstrated that goal setting and performance feedback worked to increase the running distance for each of the five participants. You can read more about small-*N* designs in Chapter 11.

Although goal setting and feedback improved the running distances in these five individuals, we cannot jump to the conclusion that the same treatment will work for all who want to increase their running distance. The question here – "Do these results hold for others?" – is one of external validity. **External validity** refers to the generalizability of the results to other persons, places, or times. Replicating these results with additional respondents from a different type of sample can help us know just how generalizable these findings are. You can read more about external validity in Chapter 12.

The Quasi-Experimental Approach. Another experimental research approach is the **quasi-experimental approach**. "Quasi" means "resembling," and **quasi-experimental research** is research that resembles experimentation but is missing one of the key components of experimentation: random assignment. In a quasi-experiment, the participants are already in pre-formed groups, so the groups are not considered equivalent. This means, of course, that we cannot definitively establish cause and effect with a quasi-experiment. Let's look at an example.

Livingston, Testa, Hoffman, and Windle (2010) wondered whether there was a relationship between parents allowing their high school children to drink at home and the likelihood that those children would abuse alcohol when they got to college. To investigate this, they divided a sample of female high school seniors into three groups: (1) girls who were not allowed to drink alcohol, (2) girls who were allowed to drink alcohol during family meals, and (3) girls who were allowed to drink alcohol at home with friends. Livingston et al. then assessed how much drinking these girls did in high school and during their first semester of college. When they compared the three groups, they found that those who were not allowed to drink in high school drank the least in college, significantly less than those who had been allowed to drink during family meals. Those who had been permitted to drink at home with friends while in high school reported the most drinking in high school and in college.

What can we say about Livingston et al.'s data? We can say that a greater level of parental permissiveness was associated with more drinking. What can't we say? We cannot say that this greater permissiveness *caused* the increase in drinking. We cannot state cause and effect in this case because parental permissiveness was not randomly assigned to groups. In other words, the researchers didn't determine who would allow their daughters not to drink, to drink with meals, or to drink at home with friends. The parents determined that for themselves. Because the groups were not randomly determined, there could have also been other differences between them besides permissiveness, such as parents who are problem drinkers or an older sibling who drinks, and these could be the reasons for the daughters' drinking habits in college.

When researchers use quasi-experimental design, they often strive to increase the internal validity of their research by ruling out known threats to it. For example, Livingston et al. could attempt to assess the percentage of drinking siblings in each group. If they found, for example, that these percentages did not differ across groups, they could rule out the influence of older siblings' drinking as a possible reason for their results. In this way, they could make a stronger argument for the internal validity of their research findings. When a threat to internal validity cannot be ruled out in a quasi-experimental design, the researchers have to acknowledge that an alternative explanation for their findings exists. Thus, again, due to the lack of random assignment (in other words, a lack of equivalent groups) we cannot use quasi-experimental research to definitively state cause and effect. We'll talk more about quasi-experimental research in Chapter 10.

The Descriptive Research Approach. All descriptive research methods have one thing in common; they are *non-experimental* methods. That means we cannot use descriptive methods to establish cause and effect. We are only observing and describing what we see; we do not have an independent variable to manipulate. Since we are only observing and not controlling what our participants experience, we cannot determine what is causing their behavior. There are various types of descriptive research methods, as you'll see in Chapters 5, 6, and 7. I'll give a couple of brief examples here.

FIGURE 1.14 Danger! Do not text while crossing the street.

You've already read about one descriptive research study, the work by McCormick and Jones (1989) on gender differences in nonverbal flirtation. McCormick and Jones observed people in a variety of bars. I referred to this study earlier as an observational study; to be more specific, the type of research McCormick and Jones did is called a **naturalistic observation** study. In naturalistic observation we observe people (or animals) in their natural settings (such as a school, park, mall, bar) and systematically record their behavior.

Before I give you another example, let me ask you whether you use a cell phone while you walk. If so, do you think you are putting yourself in potential danger? Researchers have recently considered whether using a phone while walking is hazardous. Let's take a look at this naturalistic observation research.

Hatfield and Murphy (2007) observed people crossing the street; some were looking at a cell phone (talking or texting) and others were not. They found, for example, that at intersections with a traffic light,

females who crossed the street while talking on their cell phone moved more slowly and were less likely to look for traffic than those who were not talking on their cell phones. At intersections without a traffic light, males talking on the phone were observed to be moving more slowly than those who were not on their phone. Hatfield and Murphy speculated that those crossing the street while talking on the phone were distracted by their phones.

We can indeed speculate that the use of the phone affected walking speed and a tendency to look for traffic, but we cannot conclude that the use of the phone caused these behaviors. Why not? Because the researchers merely observed what was happening in their surroundings. They did not have control over who crossed or whether those pedestrians were on their phones. The reason we can't conclude that a cause and effect relationship exists in Hatfield and Murphy's work is because other reasons could exist that explain the observed relationship. Maybe those who happened to be walking with phones also happened to be slower people!

What we did learn from Hatfield and Murphy's work is that people generally moved more slowly while crossing the street when they had a phone. This can certainly be important information to know; we just can't be sure whether the presence of the phones *caused* the slower movement. Thus, we don't really know whether the staircase that Utah Valley University created in jest (see Figure 1.15) is really necessary!

Another type of descriptive research technique you'll encounter is correlational research. **Correlational research** is a descriptive research technique in which we measure two or more variables to see whether there is a relationship between or among them. Again, because it is a descriptive technique, we cannot use correlational research to determine whether one thing causes another. We are merely observing our study participants, without

FIGURE 1.15 All those texting stay to the right please!

FIGURE 1.16 Are you one of the many who enjoy an occasional cat video?

influencing them at all. Merriam-Webster's online dictionary definition of correlation sums this up well: it is "the relationship between things that happen or occur together."

Let's look at a brief example, and again I'll start with a question. Are you one of the millions of people who watch cat videos on the Internet? Myrick (2015) wondered about the characteristics of people who watch Internet cats. Remember that in correlational research there is no independent variable. Nothing gets manipulated. Researchers only measure variables in correlational research, and that's what Myrick did. She asked an online sample of those who acknowledged viewing online cat videos or photos to answer questions about themselves. For example, she asked how often they viewed online cat videos and/or photos as well as how many hours a day they spent online overall. She also asked them a series of questions to assess factors such as their level of shyness and emotional well-being. What did she find? Many of these variables were correlated; in other words, there was a relationship between them. For example, those

who spent more time online overall were more likely to view cat videos and photos, were more likely to own a cat, and were also more likely to be classified as shy.

Remember that correlation does not imply causation. For example, viewing cat videos and photos likely didn't cause people to be shy, and being shy likely didn't cause people to view cats doing funny things on the Internet. Just because variables are correlated does not mean that one causes another. We'll talk about this more when we discuss correlational research in Chapter 6.

Finally, have you ever wondered who likely falls in love first in a relationship between a man and a woman? Who do you think would say "I love you" first? Do you think others would agree with you? One way to find out more about this is to conduct a survey. When you conduct a **survey**, you are attempting to estimate the opinions, characteristics, and/ or behaviors of a particular population by asking some of the people in that population to respond to questions. Again, this is non-experimental research; there is no independent variable manipulation, so you cannot state cause and effect. However, you can find out what people think and how they feel about your topic of interest. Let's take a look at what

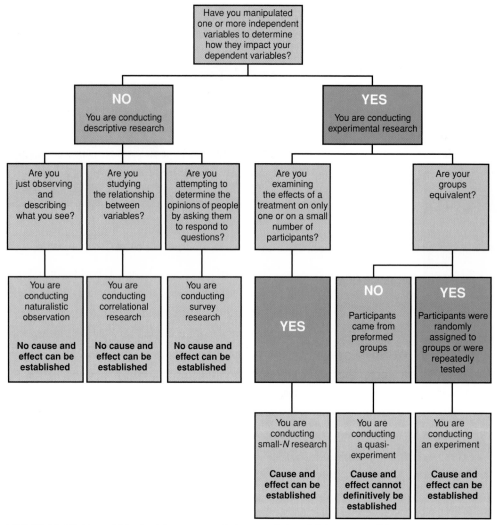

FIGURE 1.17 Use of this decision tree can help you distinguish between different types of research methods.

two researchers interested in the topic of romantic heterosexual love found out.

Harrison and Shortall (2011) surveyed a sample of heterosexual college students in the northeastern United States and asked them a series of questions about their experiences and beliefs about love. Approximately 88% of respondents thought a woman would fall in love first, and 75% thought a woman would be first to say "I love you." Harrison and Shortall found that males and females alike generally felt this way. Is this what you thought too?

Harrison and Shortall took their research a step further. They asked study participants to indicate what had happened in their most recent romantic relationship. For example, they asked how long it was before respondents realized they were in love, and they gave them a series of responses to choose from ("I am not in love," "immediately," "a few days," "a few weeks," "a few months," "a year," "more than a year"). In addition, they asked who actually said "I love you" first. Harrison and Shortall summarized the answers for males and for females and found that, surprisingly, the males said they fell in love more quickly than the females (on average, males said they fell in love somewhere between a few weeks and a few months into the relationship, while females said they fell in love, on average, in a few months). In relationships in which someone said it first, the males were quicker than the females to say "I love you!" These data suggest that females are slower to fall in love and to express that love than is commonly believed.

As you can see, survey research can be informative, although it does have limitations. For example, the study participants were asked to remember what had happened in a previous romantic relationship. It is certainly possible that they were not accurately reporting what happened, perhaps because they did not want to or perhaps because they couldn't remember. You will read more about creating surveys as well as the advantages and potential limitations of this kind of research in Chapter 7. (See Figure 1.17 for a summary of all the research methods discussed in this chapter.)

(Step 4) Form Hypotheses

Once you have selected your research idea, operationalized your variables, and selected your research approach, you are ready to form your hypotheses. As we noted earlier, hypotheses are your predictions for the outcome(s) of your research. Recall Reifman et al.'s investigation of the potential relationship between temperature and aggression on the baseball field. Prior to conducting their research study, Reifman et al. expected that aggression would increase as temperature increased initially and then decrease as players weakened. This hypothesis was only partially supported, because they found that aggression did increase as the temperature increased, but the expected decrease did not occur. You will read more about forming hypotheses in Chapter 2.

(Step 5) Recruit Study Participants

After you have decided what kind of study you are going to conduct, you need to decide who to recruit as research participants. Think about who your ideal participants would be. Community citizens? Children? Shoppers at the mall? It all depends on your research question. You might decide, as many in psychology do, to test undergraduates at their college or university. This type of sample is known as a **convenience sample** because it's so convenient. That's one advantage of testing a sample like this.

There is, however, a disadvantage: Your results may not generalize to a different type of population. Undergraduate students are generally different in some ways from the general population. They tend to be relatively young and also have a relatively advanced educational background (Sears, 1986). Ultimately, the differences between your ideal population of interest and undergraduates means you should indicate to those presented with your research findings that the results may not generalize to the population of interest. As I mentioned earlier, you can read more about the issue of generalizability (also known as external validity) in Chapter 12.

FIGURE 1.18 How are these college students likely different from the general population, and how would those differences limit our ability to generalize our results if we chose them to be our research participants?

These days researchers often recruit online participants for their research. Although the practice is still relatively new, researchers generally find that data collected online do not differ significantly from data collected from more traditional sources (for example, Lutz, 2016). You can learn more about collecting data online in Chapter 13. Of course, no matter who your study participants are, you have a responsibility to treat them ethically. You'll learn more about these responsibilities in Chapter 3.

(Step 6) Pilot Test and then Conduct Your Study

Before you actually conduct your study, you need to conduct a pilot test. A **pilot test** is a series of practice sessions run during the initial stages of research that allow us to determine whether the procedure is running as intended. At the end of these practice sessions, you will ask your participants for their feedback: Were the task instructions and the questions you asked clearly understood? Your pilot test will also allow you to determine how long the actual testing session will take. And practicing gives you experience running the study so you get comfortable with the procedure. Note that you should not include the data you generate from the pilot study in your final dataset.

Once your pilot test has been completed, you will conduct your study as planned and record your data for later analysis. That brings us to the next step.

(Step 7) Analyze the Results of Your Study

After you have collected your data, it's time to analyze your results. One of the first steps researchers typically take after collecting their data is to calculate **descriptive statistics** to summarize the data they collected. In many cases, they then use **inferential statistics** to determine whether the mean responses for the groups were significantly different

from each other. Inferential statistics theoretically enable researchers to make conclusions about a population after studying just a sample of that population. After analyzing the results, we interpret the findings and draw conclusions from what we see. We will talk more about what statistics enable us to do in Chapters 8 and 9.

(Step 8) Report What You Did

As suggested above, researchers share what they did by presenting and/or publishing their research. You will read more about preparing your work for presentation and publication in Chapter 14. In addition, a sample manuscript is provided in Appendix A so you can see how to prepare a research paper for publication.

(Step 9) Starting the Whole Process All Over Again

I've included Step 9 just to indicate that the scientific process is cyclical. Every study we run will likely answer some questions but also will likely lead us to ask additional ones. And researchers tend not to stop after just doing one study. We continue to investigate the topics that interest us, and with each study we gain more knowledge.

Characteristics of Science

All kinds of scientists, including psychologists, biologists, chemists, physicists, and sociologists, learn about science by collecting data in systematic ways and drawing conclusions about those data. A main goal of this textbook is to provide you with information about the systematic ways in which data are collected. Scientists use the **scientific method** when conducting research; it is a basic set of rules and procedures that govern the way research is to be conducted.

Note that although it sounds like the scientific method is just *one* method, that's not the case. In fact, as you saw above, there are many different strategies a scientist can use to answer research questions. But in any case, use of the scientific method means that scientists typically follow this general pattern: they formulate a hypothesis, test that hypothesis, revise the hypothesis as needed, and test again until they ultimately form a conclusion. Both individual scientists and the scientific community as a whole use this pattern of hypothesis formulation and testing. On an individual level, scientists can formulate a hypothesis, test that hypothesis, and form a conclusion. They may then choose to test a revised hypothesis or just make recommendations for future researchers regarding how the hypothesis should be revised. They will often publish their findings so others can use this information when creating their own hypotheses. In this way, the scientific community works together to come closer to the truth.

Regardless of the strategy you use to investigate your research question, science has certain common characteristics: It is empirical, objective, replicable, and public. We'll now discuss these important characteristics.

Science Is Empirical

Scientists rely on **empirical data**, evidence collected from the systematic observation or measurement of relevant information. We do not accept that something is true just because we've always known it to be true, or just because it is intuitive, or just because it is told to us by an authority, or just because it makes sense. We need evidence.

Suppose you were wondering whether having a cell phone ring during class would affect how well people do when tested on the class material. This is an empirical question. An **empirical question** can be answered using systematic observations and techniques. Let's take a look at how one set of researchers chose to answer this question.

End, Worthman, Mathews, and Wetterau (2010) decided to use an experiment to investigate whether a ringing cell phone could cause impaired academic performance. Participants were shown a video and later were tested on the material in it. They were each randomly assigned to one of two groups; one group heard a ringing phone interrupt the video and the other group did not. The phone, which rang at predetermined times during the video, belonged to a confederate who was also in the room. A **confederate** is an accomplice of the experimenter. So the independent variable in End et al.'s experiment was the ringing of the phone, and there were two levels of variation (presence of a ringing phone, absence of a ringing phone). The dependent variable was the score on a test of the information shown in the video. What did End et al. find? Participants who watched a video interrupted by a ringing phone performed worse on the test than those whose video was not interrupted by a ringing phone.

End et al. used an experiment to answer the question of whether a ringing phone in the middle of a lecture could impact academic performance. Their approach is considered empirical because they used systematic observations (the phone rang at predetermined times for only one of the two groups) and a measurement of relevant information (test performance). They collected evidence; they didn't just rely on their intuition or ask a few friends what they thought.

Science Is Objective

Science is objective; it is free of our personal biases. Let me give you an example of what *not* to do when you need to be objective.

A student of mine wanted to do a research study that would enable her to test what people thought of a prospective employee with tattoos as opposed to one without tattoos. She did a good job of reviewing the research in this area; researchers have consistently found that those with tattoos are viewed more negatively than those without (see for example, Resenhoeft, Villa, & Wiseman, 2008). The student then hypothesized that the prospective employee who was tattooed would receive more favorable ratings than the prospective employee who was not tattooed.

Can you see the problem here? While none of the previous researchers had done the exact same study my student was planning, their results should have led her to hypothesize that the tattooed individual would be seen *less* favorably, not more. Why didn't she come to this conclusion? Would you be surprised to learn that my student was tattooed and felt pretty positive about her tattoos? She had injected her personal values into the work. We need instead to consider what the data tell us. The results from previous research typically help us form the expectations for our own work.

Science Can Be Replicated

Sometimes researchers will repeat a study to try to replicate the research findings. To **replicate** the findings means to discover a pattern of results similar to that obtained before. Each time we replicate our findings, we gain confidence in them. If our findings are not replicated, we have reason to question their validity.

In recent years, some psychologists have instituted a "mass replication effort" with the goal of determining whether prominent research findings can be replicated (see Bohannon, 2015, p. 910). While many findings have not been replicated, researchers acknowledge that attempting replication is an important part of the scientific process; it allows us to ultimately get at the truth (Open Science Collaboration, 2015).

Science Is Public

After conducting a research study, a scientist typically tells the scientific world about it by presenting the results at a scientific conference and/or publishing them in a scientific journal. However, in most cases, before a study is presented or published, other scientists familiar with the topic will first carefully evaluate the research. This process is called **peer review**. Those conducting the review decide whether the work should be accepted for presentation or publication. This process helps to ensure that research studies with major flaws do not become part of the scientific literature.

Evaluation of researchers' work can continue even after a study has been published. For example, in the journal *American Psychologist*, those who view the evidence differently or otherwise dispute something that has been recently published in that journal can send in a comment for publication. If an editor accepts a comment for publication, he or she will likely invite the original authors of the published piece to respond to the comment and then publish both pieces. This open discourse is another way in which science progresses.

In addition, in the literature review researchers conduct for their own work, they will refer to earlier studies and may, for example, point out a flaw or omission. Fixing this flaw or considering the missing information can be the motivation for the current work. In this way, researchers can build upon previous work in order to make further research advances.

Let's take a look at an example. Bushman and Bonacci (2002) had participants watch either a violent, a sexually explicit, or a neutral television program; there were 6 programs of each kind and each participant was randomly assigned to watch one program. Each program was accompanied by 9 advertisements. Participants were then asked about the ads both immediately after viewing and after a

FIGURE 1.19 Does the type of program you are watching affect how well you remember the ads?

24-hour delay. Would the type of television program watched affect how well participants remembered the ads?

Bushman and Bonacci found that those who saw the violent or sexually explicit ads as opposed to the neutral ads had poorer memory both immediately and after the delay. In fact, Bushman and Bonacci recommended that advertisers refrain from placing ads within programs with violent or sexual content because viewers are less likely to remember them.

However, Fried and Johanson (2008) questioned Bushman and Bonacci's conclusions due to what they cite as "methodological shortcomings" (p. 1719). They pointed out that the content of Bushman and Bonacci's programs was not well controlled. For example, some that were specified as sexual in nature were also comedies, while some of the violent programs were dramas, and the neutral programs tended to be "light family fare" (p. 1720). Fried and Johanson argued that it is unclear whether the intentionally manipulated content was really responsible for differences in memory. The cause could have been these other differences in content.

In their article, Fried and Johanson pointed out the flaw they saw in Bushman and Bonacci's work and then described a study in which they had revised the methodology to eliminate it. They standardized the programming so that the *only* thing that differed was the type of program: only violent content, only sexual content, only violent and sexual content (this was a condition Bushman and Bonacci didn't have), or only neutral content. Everything else participants viewed was the same for all. After this change in methodology, were Bushman and Bonacci's results replicated? No. The type of program watched did not affect participants' memory of the ads. Fried and Johanson concluded that the differences in memory obtained by Bushman and Bonacci were caused not by the sexual and violent nature of the programs they used, but likely by the other variations in that programming. So fixing Bushman and Bonacci's methodological flaw was the motivation for Fried and Johanson's work, and through it, we now have a better understanding of the relationship between program content and memory for advertising.

SUMMARY

An understanding of research methods can aid you whether you need to know how scholars obtained knowledge in your field or you choose to conduct your own research. It will also help you evaluate media reports of research findings.

The four general goals of science are description, explanation, prediction, and control. Scientists often develop a theory to explain what they observe and then hypothesize what will occur under similar conditions. Then they are often interested in learning how to influence or control the phenomenon of interest.

The research process contains a series of common steps that begin with the development of a research idea. The researcher must operationalize the variables of interest by specifying precisely how they are to be manipulated and/or measured. A fundamental decision is whether to use experimental or descriptive research methods. Only a true experiment allows us to establish cause and effect. Once researchers have formed a hypothesis they will recruit study participants, pilot test, and then conduct the research. The final steps are analyzing the data and reporting the findings.

Researchers use the scientific method when investigating their phenomenon of interest. They formulate a hypothesis, test, revise as needed, and test again until they form a conclusion. Scientists must rely on empirical data and remain objective. Science can be replicated; each time we replicate our findings, we gain confidence in them. Science is also a public endeavor. We share our results with the research community and with the public by presenting and/or publishing those results, typically after a peer review process.

GLOSSARY

Applied research – research conducted with a practical, real-world issue in mind.

Baseline – the level of performance a study participant is exhibiting prior to treatment in a small-N design.

Basic research – attempts to answer fundamental questions about a phenomenon, without much focus on how the information could be applied in the real world.

Confederate – an accomplice of the experimenter.

Convenience sample – a group of study participants who are obtained with relative ease, usually college students.

Correlational research – a descriptive research approach in which two or more variables are measured to determine the relationship between or among them.

Dependent variable – response measure used by the researcher to assess the effect of an experiment's independent variable.

Descriptive statistics – summarize the data collected.

Empirical data – evidence collected from observation or measurement.

Empirical question – a question that can be answered using systematic observations and techniques.

Experiment – a research approach that allows for a cause and effect conclusion. In an experiment researchers manipulate (vary) one or more variables (independent variables), and then observe the effects of that manipulation on a response measure called the dependent variable.

External validity – generalizability of results to other persons, places, and times.

Hypotheses – stated expectations for the results.

Independent variable – the variable that is manipulated in an experiment. This variable is expected to influence the dependent variable.

Inferential statistics – statistics that enable researchers to make conclusions about a population after studying just a sample of that population.

Internal validity – the degree to which the results of an experiment can be attributed to the manipulation of the independent variable.

Naturalistic observation – a descriptive research approach in which researchers observe people (or animals) in natural settings and systematically record their behavior. Cause and effect cannot be determined.

Observable behavior – behaviors that can be seen.

Operationalization – specification of the precise meaning of a variable in terms of the specific procedures to be performed.

Peer review – before a study is presented or published, other scientists familiar with the topic carefully evaluate the research.

Pilot test – practice sessions run during the initial stages of research allow one to determine whether the procedure is running as intended.

Population – the members of an identifiable group.

Quasi-experimental research – a research approach that does not use random assignment and cannot definitively establish cause and effect.

Random assignment – a technique used when distributing people into different groups such that all characteristics of the participants are theoretically distributed across groups in approximately equal proportions.

Replicate – obtain a similar pattern of results to earlier research.

Representative sample – a selection of study participants that have the same characteristics as the population of interest.

Sampling – choosing a portion of the population as study participants for research.

Scientific method – a basic set of rules and procedures that govern the way research is to be conducted.

Small-N design – an experimental research approach that involves testing one or just a few participants. Often used in applied settings.

Survey – asking people to answer questions in an effort to estimate the opinions, characteristics, and/or behaviors of a particular population.

Theory – a statement that organizes, summarizes, and explains available information about a phenomenon and works as a basis for formulating testable hypotheses.

Variable – any characteristic that can take on different values.

1   Identify five reasons why it is important for people to have an understanding of research methods.
2   Name and describe the four goals of science.
3   Describe the steps in the research process.
4   Differentiate between basic and applied research.
5   Define the term "variable" and explain what it means to operationalize your variable.
6   An experiment is considered the most influential research approach because it is the one approach that allows you to establish cause and effect. Explain why an experiment allows for this conclusion. Use the following terms in your explanation: independent variable, dependent variable, random assignment.
7   Explain what a small-N design is and when it is likely to be used.
8   Describe how a quasi-experimental design differs from an experimental design, and how this difference limits what you can conclude with a quasi-experimental design.
9   Compare experimental and descriptive research approaches.
10 Explain what a naturalistic observation study is.
11 Explain what correlation research is.
12 Describe why it is important to run a pilot test.
13 Define internal and external validity.
14 Identify and explain the characteristics of science.

ARTICLES AS ILLUSTRATION

1   Bohannon, J. (2015). Many psychology papers fail replication test. *Science, 349(6251),*

910–911. doi:http://dx.doi.org/10.1126/science.349.6251.910.

Van Bavel, J. (2016, May 27). Why do so many studies fail to replicate? *The New York Times.* Retrieved from www.nytimes.com

Read the article by Bohannon to get a glimpse of the "mass replication effort" that has recently begun in psychology (p. 910). Then read the op-ed piece by Van Bavel. Answer the following questions.

a. Describe the replication effort that began in 2011. What percentage of the studies in this effort replicated?

b. Why, according to Van Bavel, did many of the research studies likely not replicate? What evidence does Van Bavel give to support his reasoning?

2 Glick, P., Larsen, S., Johnson, C., & Branstiter, H. (2005). Evaluations of sexy women in low- and high-status jobs. *Psychology of Women Quarterly, 29*, 389–395. doi:http://dx.doi.org/10.1111/j.1471–6402.2005.00238.x.

Wookey, M. L., Graves, N. A., & Corey Butler, J. (2009). Effects of a sexy appearance on perceived competence of women. *Journal of Social Psychology, 149(1),* 116–118. doi:http://dx.doi.org/10.3200/SOCP.149.1.116–118

Wookey et al. (2009) attempted a replication of the research of Glick et al. (2005). Read both articles and then answer the following questions:

a. What were Glick et al.'s (2005) hypotheses? What were the reasons for these hypotheses?

b. How were Wookey et al.'s and Glick et al.'s studies different?

c. Did Wookey et al. (2009) replicate Glick et al.'s (2005) findings?

3 Bearinger, L. H., Taliaferro, L., & Given, B. (2010). When R & R is not rest & recovery, but revise & resubmit. *Research in Nursing & Health, 33*, 381–385.

Science is a public endeavor, and peer review is part of the process that controls whether an article goes into publication. This peer review process can be tough, but the end result, a better paper for the scientific literature, is well worth the work. Bearinger et al. discuss peer review in the area of nursing and health, but the lessons provided are relevant to virtually all who undergo the process. Answer the following questions.

a. According to Bearinger et al. what is the best course of action to take when you get a "revise and resubmit" decision from a journal?

b. What should you do when reviewers disagree with each other?

4 The following articles are covered briefly in this chapter. Read one or more of them to see examples of research approaches presented here. Questions are presented after each of the readings.

A survey:
Harrison, M. A., & Gilmore, A. L. (2012). U txt when? College students' social contexts of text messaging. *Social Science Journal, 49(4),* 513–518. doi:http://dx.doi.org/10.1016/j.soscij.2012.05.003

a. Describe the sample.

b. How did the researchers assess the importance of texting to their sample?

c. What six categories did Harrison and Gilmore use as reasons for texting? Give an example of a result in each of these categories.

A naturalistic observation study:

Hatfield, J., & Murphy, S. (2007). The effects of mobile phone use on pedestrian crossing behavior at signalised and unsignalised intersections. *Accident Analysis and Prevention, 39*, 197–205. doi:http://dx.doi.org/10.1016/j. aap.2006.07.001

a. Why is this study considered a naturalistic observation study as opposed to an experiment?

b. Describe the procedure.

c. Describe the main results.

An experiment:
End, C. M., Worthman, S., Mathews, M. B., & Wetterau, K. (2010). Costly cell phones: the impact of cell phone rings on academic performance. *Teaching of Psychology, 37*, 55–57. doi:10.1080/00986280903425912

a. What was the independent variable?

b. What was the dependent variable?

c. Describe the procedure.

d. Describe the main results.

SUGGESTED ACTIVITIES

1 This chapter lists a variety of ways in which people use research methods and/or evaluate research findings. Can you think of other ways in which research methods and/or research findings are already a part of your life?

2 Description is one of the main goals of scientists, and we differentiated between describing observable behavior (such as the average number of M&Ms eaten when watching a movie with a friend) and describing phenomena you must ask people about rather than observe (such as how many times a week people remember their dreams). Give two additional examples each of observable behaviors and behaviors that are less observable.

3 Find an article in the popular press (newspaper, magazine, online) that describes a psychological science research study. You can use the following "Psychological Science in the News" link from the Association for Psychological Science to help you find an article: www.psychologicalscience.org/index.php/news?type = items
Once you've found an article you like, answer the following questions:

a. What kind of study was described?

b. Who were the study participants?

c. What were the author's/authors' conclusions?

4 In the following research descriptions, identify the independent variable and the dependent variable. The first one is done for you.

a. Azar, Yosef, and Bar-Eli (2015) wondered how receiving too much change after paying their restaurant bill would affect the size of the tips restaurant patrons left. The patrons received approximately either $3 or $12 in extra change. The average tip was higher for those who received a larger amount of extra change. Independent variable: the amount of extra change ($3, $12).
Dependent variable: *the average amount of tip*

b. Ford, Boyer, Menachemi, and Huerta (2014) were interested in whether a towel dispenser set up to present a towel automatically would increase the percentage of people washing their hands after using a public restroom. The towel dispenser was set up to provide a towel either with or without activation by the user. When towels were presented automatically, use of both towel and soap increased.

Independent variable:

Dependent variables (there are two!):

c. Peetz and Soliman (2016) examined whether varying the size of an image of money would vary the way people perceived that money. They presented study participants with an image of money that was either actual size or enlarged by 15%. Participants were asked to imagine the cash was their own. Those presented with the larger-size money reported feeling more wealthy than those presented with smaller, actual size money.

Independent variable:

Dependent variable:

REFERENCES

Aiello, J. R., & Douthitt, E. A. (2001). Social facilitation from Triplett to electronic performance monitoring. *Group Dynamics: Theory, Research, and Practice*, 5, 163–180. doi:http://dx.doi.org/10.1037/1089-2699.5.3.163

Argo, J. J., Dahl, D. W., & Morales, A. C. (2006). Consumer contamination: How consumers react to products touched by others. *Journal of Marketing*, 70 (2), 81–94. doi:http://dx.doi.org/10.1509/jmkg.70.2.81

Azar, O. H., Yosef, S., & Bar-Eli, M. (2015). Restaurant tipping in a field experiment: How do customers tip when they receive too much change? *Journal of Economic Psychology*, 50, 13–21. doi:http://dx.doi.org/10.1016/j.joep.2015.06.007

Basow, S. A., & Kobrynowicz, D. (1993). What is she eating? The effects of meal size on impressions of a female eater. *Sex Roles*, 28, 335–344. doi:http://dx.doi.org/10.1007/BF00289889

Bearinger, L. H., Taliaferro, L., & Given, B. (2010). When R & R is not rest & recovery, but revise & resubmit. *Research in Nursing & Health*, 33, 381–385.

Bekinschtein, T. A., Cardozo, J., & Manes, F. F. (2008). Strategies of Buenos Aires waiters to enhance memory capacity in a real-life setting. *Behavioural Neurology*, 20, 65–70. doi:http://dx.doi.org/10.1155/2008/621964

Bohannon, J. (2015). Many psychology papers fail replication test. *Science*, 349, 910–911. doi:http://dx.doi.org/10.1126/science.349.6251.910

Bushman, B. J., & Bonacci, A. M. (2002). Violence and sex impair memory for television ads. *Journal of Applied Psychology*, 87, 557–564. doi:http://dx.doi.org/10.1037/0021-9010.87.3.557

Campbell, C. R., & White, K. R. G. (2015). Working it out: Examining the psychological effects of music on moderate-intensity exercise. *Psi Chi Journal of Psychological Research*, 20, 73–79.

Dicker, R. (2016, March 4). Chimpanzees believe in God, research suggests. Retrieved from www.usnews.com/news/articles/2016-03-04/new-behavior-suggests-chimpanzees-may-believe-in-god

Diener, E., & Wallbom, M. (1976). Effects of self-awareness on antinormative behavior. *Journal of Research in Personality*, 10, 107–111. doi:http://dx.doi.org/10.1016/0092-6566(76)90088-X

Duval, S., & Wicklund, R. A. (1972). *Objective self-awareness*. Oxford: Academic Press.

End, C. M., Worthman, S., Mathews, M. B., & Wetterau, K. (2010). Costly cell phones: The impact of cell phone rings on academic performance. *Teaching of Psychology*, 37, 55–57. doi:10.1080/00986280903425912

Ford, E. W., Boyer, B. T., Menachemi, N., & Huerta, T. R. (2014). Increasing hand washing compliance with a simple visual cue. *American Journal of Public Health*, 104, 1851–1856. doi:http://dx.doi.org/10.2105/AJPH.2013.301477

Freeman, D. (2016, March 4). Dogs have a very special way of seeing human faces. Retrieved from www.huffingtonpost.com/entry/dog-perception-human-faces_us_56d8a654e4b0000de403d313

Fried, C. B., & Johanson, J. C. (2008). Sexual and violent media's inhibition of advertisement memory: Effect or artifact? *Journal of Applied Social Psychology*, 38, 1716–1735. doi:http://dx.doi.org/10.1111/j.1559-1816.2008.00366.x

Glick, P., Larsen, S., Johnson, C., & Branstiter, H. (2005). Evaluations of sexy women in low- and high-status jobs. *Psychology of Women Quarterly*, 29, 389–395. doi:http://dx.doi.org/10.1111/j.1471-6402.2005.00238.x

Harrison, M. A., & Gilmore, A. L. (2012). U txt when? College students' social contexts of text messaging. *Social Science Journal, 49,* 513–518. doi:http://dx.doi.org/10.1016/j.soscij.2012.05.003

Harrison, M. A., & Shortall, J. C. (2011). Women and men in love: Who really feels it and says it first? *Journal of Social Psychology, 151,* 727–736. doi:http://dx.doi.org/10.1080/00224545.2010.522626

Hatfield, J., & Murphy, S. (2007). The effects of mobile phone use on pedestrian crossing behavior at signalised and unsignalised intersections. *Accident Analysis and Prevention, 39,* 197–205. doi:http://dx.doi.org/10.1016/j.aap.2006.07.001

Interlandi, J. (2015, March 22). The brain's empathy gap: Can mapping neural pathways help us make friends with our enemies? Retrieved from www.nytimes.com

Jones, W., & Russell, D. (1982). The social reticence scale: An objective instrument to measure shyness. *Journal of Personality Assessment, 46,* 629–631. doi:http://dx.doi.org/10.1207/s15327752jpa4606_12

Kotzer, R. D. (2007). The social facilitation effect in basketball: Shooting free throws. *Huron University College Journal of Learning and Motivation, 45,* 124–142.

Lewis, M. (2016, March 4). This ground-breaking high fat diet could combat diabetes and promote weight loss. Retrieved from www.yahoo.com/news/groundbreaking-high-fat-diet-could-161400121.html?ref=gs

Livingston, J. A., Testa, M., Hoffman, J. H., & Windle, M. (2010). Can parents prevent heavy episodic drinking by allowing teens to drink at home? *Addictive Behaviors, 35,* 1105–1112. doi:http://dx.doi.org/10.1016/j.addbeh.2010.08.005

Lutz, J. (2016). The validity of crowdsourcing data in studying anger and aggressive behavior: A comparison of online and laboratory data. *Social Psychology, 47,* 38–51. doi:http://dx.doi.org/10.1027/1864-9335/a000256

McCormick, N. B., & Jones, A. J. (1989). Gender differences in nonverbal flirtation. *Journal of Sex Education and Therapy, 15,* 271–282.

Myrick, J. G. (2015). Emotion regulation, procrastination, and watching cat videos online: Who watches Internet cats, why, and to what effect? *Computers in Human Behavior, 52,* 168–176. doi:http://dx.doi.org/10.1016/j.chb.2015.06.001

Neisser, U., Boodoo, G., Bouchard, T. J., Boykins, A. W., Brody, N., Ceci, S. J., Halpern, D. F., Loehlin, J. C., Perloff, R., Sternberg, R. J., & Urbina, S. (1996). Intelligence: Known and unknowns. *American Psychologist, 51,* 77–101. doi:http://dx.doi.org/10.1037/0003-066X.51.2.77

Open Science Collaboration (2015). *Science, 349,* 1–8.

Peetz, J., & Soliman, M. (2016). Big money: The effect of money size on value perceptions and saving motivation. *Perception, 45,* 631–641. doi:http://dx.doi.org/10.1177/0301006616629033

Pessin, J. (1933). The comparative effects of social and mechanical stimulation on memorizing. *American Journal of Psychology, 45,* 263–270. doi:http://dx.doi.org/10.2307/1414277

Rakover, S. S. (2012). A feature-inversion effect: Can an isolated feature show behavior like the face-inversion effect? *Psychonomic Bulletin & Review, 19,* 617–624. doi:http://dx.doi.org/10.3758/s13423-012-0264-4

Reifman, A. S., Larrick, R. P., & Fein, S. (1991). Temper and temperature on the diamond: The heat-aggression relationship in major league baseball. *Personality and Social Psychology Bulletin, 17,* 580–585. doi:http://athena.rider.edu:2082/10.1177/0146167291175013

Resenhoeft, A., Villa, J., & Wiseman, D. (2008). Tattoos can harm perceptions: A study and suggestions. *Journal of American College Health, 56,* 593–595. doi:http://dx.doi.org/10.3200/JACH.56.5.593-596

Sears, D. O. (1986). College sophomores in the laboratory: Influences of a narrow data base on social psychology's view of human nature. *Journal of Personality and Social Psychology, 51,* 515–530. doi:http://dx.doi.org/10.1037/0022-3514.51.3.515

Valentine, T. (1988). Upside-down faces: A review of the effect of inversion upon face recognition. *British Journal of Psychology, 79,* 471–491. doi:http://dx.doi.org/10.1111/j.2044-8295.1988.tb02747.x

Van Bavel, J. (2016, May 27). Why do so many studies fail to replicate? *The New York Times.* Retrieved from www.nytimes.com

Wack, S. R., Crosland, K. A., & Miltenberger, R. G. (2014). Using goal setting and feedback to increase weekly running distance. *Journal of Applied Behavior Analysis, 47*, 181–185. doi:http://dx.doi.org/10.1002/jaba.108

Weston, S. B., & English, H. B. (1926). The influence of the group of psychological test scores. *American Journal of Psychology, 27*, 600–601. doi:http://dx.doi.org/10.2307/1414922

Wookey, M. L., Graves, N. A., & Corey Butler, J. (2009). Effects of a sexy appearance on perceived competence of women. *Journal of Social Psychology, 149*, 116–118. doi:http://dx.doi.org/10.3200/SOCP.149.1.116–118

Yu, R., & Wu, X. (2015). Working alone or in the presence of others: Exploring social facilitation in baggage x-ray security screening tasks. *Ergonomics, 58*, 857–865. doi:http://dx.doi.org/10.1080/00140139.2014.993429

Zajonc, R. B. (1965). Social facilitation. *Science, 149*, 269–274. doi:http://dx.doi.org/10.1126/science.149.3681.269

2 Developing Research Ideas and Hypotheses

LEARNING OBJECTIVES

- Identify four sources of research ideas.

- Describe ways to find literature relevant to your research topic.

- Identify the basic components of a journal article.

- Explain what it means to generate a hypothesis.

When I was a first-year graduate student, I had to write a research proposal for one of my psychology classes. I was supposed to propose something original, something no one had ever done before (since most of the research that gets published is original, my professor thought I should get used to thinking of these kinds of ideas). I had a very difficult time choosing a topic to study. It seemed that all the original ideas were taken!

I've since realized that if you want to do original research, you don't need to find a *big* new idea; you just need to do something that's at least a *little* bit different from what's been done before (although big new ideas are good too!). In this chapter I'll

Sources of research ideas

- **Real life**
- **Practical problems**
- **Previous research**
- **Theory**

FIGURE 2.1 Sources of research ideas.

tell you how to generate research ideas. We'll begin by exploring the following potential sources of research ideas as shown in Figure 2.1:(1) real life, (2) practical problems, (3) previous research, and (4) theory.

Sources of Research Ideas

Have you ever come across an item in the news or in your own life that made you wonder about why things happen? Perhaps you won't be surprised that real life is a primary source of ideas for research.

Real Life

I recently read a story about two girls in Australia who got stuck in a storm drain. Luckily they had their cell phones with them, but instead of calling the police or someone they knew, they updated their Facebook status! Someone finally saw it and called the police.

FIGURE 2.2 Is social media use so prevalent among young people that they would likely rely on Facebook as a way to reach out to others instead of just making a phone call?

Thankfully the girls were not injured, but a police officer later acknowledged that they would have been helped much sooner had they called the police directly (Malkin, 2009). This story led me to wonder: Is social media use so prevalent among young people that they would likely rely on that as a way to reach out to others instead of just making a phone call? At this point we have the beginning of a research idea: Use a survey to ask people about their social media use (see Chapter 7 for more information on surveys). But before you go and conduct this study, or any study actually, you need to find out what researchers already know about the topic. As I mentioned before, researchers tend to do original research so they can add to the body of knowledge that already exists on a topic. So you need to gather information about what's already been done, and then propose something that's at least slightly different.

For example, let's say researchers have already considered the prevalence of young Facebook users in Australia. You might wonder whether the results for young people in the United States would be the same. In fact, there are a lot of questions regarding Facebook usage you could address: Do people of different ages differ in how much they use Facebook? Do females use the site more than males? These questions are relevant to the issue of external validity. External validity refers to our ability to generalize our findings to other people, settings, and times. Here I am asking the question: Are the results you get with one population similar to the results you're likely to see with other types of people? You might want to investigate why people use Facebook, and whether people of different ages, sexes, or ethnic groups tend to use it for different reasons. These are just a few examples; the possibilities are virtually limitless.

Let's look at a specific example. Thompson and Lougheed (2012) wanted to investigate gender differences in undergraduates' use of Facebook. To do so, they surveyed college students and asked them questions about their use of the site. They found that although males and females spent approximately the same amount of time on Facebook per day, females were more likely to report spending a longer period of time than they intended, and to report often losing sleep because of it. Females more than males also reported that Facebook use caused them to experience stress, and half the sample of females (versus 22% of the males) selected "strongly agree" or "agree" when asked whether they sometimes feel they are addicted to the site. Although positive emotions were also associated with Facebook, the negative emotions cited in this sample are a cause for concern, perhaps especially for women (see Table 2.1).

Thompson and Lougheed (2012) suggested that future researchers may wish to determine whether their results hold for other young adults beyond their university (a question of external validity); they also suggested ideas to help decrease stress that may develop as a result of Facebook use.

As I hope you can see from this brief example, the real world is full of possibilities for research ideas. In the next section I will describe practical problems as a potential source of research ideas.

Practical Problems

Sometimes researchers are motivated to conduct research on a particular topic because of the need to solve a problem in the world. Let's take one such problem and see how a researcher sought to provide information that could help solve it. The problem in this case is that heterosexual undergraduates' sexual experiences can put them at risk of becoming infected with sexually transmitted diseases (STDs) such as human immunodeficiency virus (HIV) (Lewis, Malow, & Ireland, 1997). Consistent use of condoms is known to be effective in decreasing that risk (Pinkerton & Abramson, 1997), but many

undergraduates use condoms inconsistently or not at all (Wendt & Solomon, 1995).

Civic (2000) focused on this inconsistency of use and wondered whether there were systematic reasons for a change in condom use once students became involved in long-term relationships. She thought that if the reasons for discontinuing condoms in a long-term relationship could be identified, programs could be designed to educate college students about the accuracy of their reasoning. Thus she asked heterosexual undergraduates in long-term relationships (of at least 1.5 years' duration) to answer a survey.

Civic found that consistent condom use did decrease over time, with 50% of the undergraduates reporting consistent use during the first month of the relationship, and only 34% reporting consistent use later in the relationship. Why the change? The two most frequently stated reasons were that (1) the couple started using a different method of birth control, and (2) they had discussed their sexual histories and felt their partner was safe. The problem with this reasoning is that (1) despite the use of a different form of birth control, condoms are still needed for prevention of STDs, and (2) knowledge of a partner's sexual history is not enough of a safeguard because people do lie about their histories (Cochran & Mays, 1990); actually viewing the more objective measure of HIV/STD test results is preferable to taking someone at his or her word.

Once armed with this information, Civic recommended that those educating college students about HIV/STD prevention should emphasize the importance of knowing a partner's HIV/STD testing results, and of recognizing that condoms may still be needed even if alternative forms of birth control are used. Thus, Civic saw a problem (the risk of HIV and other STDs in college students) and used research to try and find a solution (specific improvements in preventive education).

Table 2.1 Thompson and Lougheed's (2012) survey results regarding undergraduates' use of Facebook ($N = 252$).

Survey item	All % Strongly agree or agree	Male % Strongly agree or agree	Female
Facebook is part of my everyday activity.	80.24	71.2	88.1
I feel out of touch when I haven't logged into Facebook for a while.	43.9	30.5	55.56
I am sometimes on Facebook for longer amounts of time than I intend to be.	64.3	50.0	76.9
Sometimes I lose sleep because of the time I spend on Facebook.	18.7	12.1	24.4
I need to make sure that I have access to my Facebook page on vacations.	17.9	12.8	22.4
Facebook helps me make friends.	25.5	26.1	24.8
I feel closer with my friends on Facebook than my friends I see every day.	6.8	4.3	9.0
I like spending time on Facebook more than actual time with my friends.	4.0	4.3	3.7
The pictures others post on Facebook give me a negative self body image.	5.6	7.6	9.6
Facebook usage sometimes causes me to feel stressed.	15.9	11.1	20.0
If I cannot access Facebook I feel anxious and upset.	10.7	7.7	13.3
I wish I didn't have the "need" to be on Facebook.	20.3	11.9	27.8
I wouldn't use Facebook as much if my friends didn't.	48.4	48.7	48.1
I think Facebook positively influences my health.	11.1	10.4	12.0
Being on Facebook causes me to feel excited and energized.	13.9	11.0	16.4
I feel a lack of control over checking my profile and posting things on Facebook.	12.0	12.0	12.0
I feel an irresistible pull to get on Facebook.	24.1	19.5	28.1
Sometimes I feel like I am addicted to Facebook.	35.7	22.03	47.76
I know someone who is addicted to Facebook.	75.4	69.2	80.7
I would rather talk on Facebook with people than face-to-face.	6.7	4.2	8.9
Facebook helps me to express my feelings easier.	21.4	18.8	23.7
Facebook gives me more confidence.	9.9	7.6	11.8
Other's Facebook postings have caused me to feel discomfort about my life.	13.8	9.3	17.8
I wish others didn't post everything on the wall so everyone could read it.	32.8	28.0	37.0
The thought of getting off Facebook leaves me really stressed.	4.4	5.1	3.7

Source: Adapted from Thompson, S. H. & Lougheed, E. (2012). Frazzled by Facebook? An exploratory study of gender differences in social network communication among undergraduate men and women. *College Student Journal, 46*, 88–98.

Previous Research

Many researchers come up with an idea for research by reading what others have done in an area they find interesting. If you don't have any idea at all about what you want to study, open a textbook and find a topic that's appealing. Once you do have a general topic you are interested in, go to a library database that provides coverage of the relevant literature, type in a few selected key terms, and start searching through titles of literature sources (I'll say more on how to search the literature later in this chapter). When you find a title that sounds like something you want to investigate further, read the abstract. The **abstract** is a short summary of the research report. Does it still sound appealing? If so, locate the entire document so you can learn more.

Once you find a journal article that appeals to you, consider reading more articles on the same general topic so you can get a better sense of what researchers have done relevant to your topic of interest. Newer articles will tend to give you a more up-to-date view of what researchers know about your topic. Review articles are also good for getting an overall view of the previous research on the topic. When preparing a review article, a researcher reads through the existing literature, evaluates it, and summarizes it. Thus, a **review article** provides a comprehensive summary regarding what's been done on a topic, but without including a full research report for any of the research projects it covers.

For example, Henry, West, and Jackson (2010) recently provided a review of research showing the effects of the hip-hop culture on the identity of Black female college students. More specifically, this review compiled information regarding how hip-hop has influenced a variety of areas including fashion choices, self-perception, and social activism.

Another potential source of information about a topic is a meta-analysis. When conducting a **meta-analysis**, the researcher uses statistical

FIGURE 2.3 How does hip-hop culture affect the attitudes and feelings of young Black women?

procedures to combine the results of multiple studies on the same topic. Instead of just relying on the researcher's evaluation of the literature, a meta-analysis allows the researcher to determine, statistically, what conclusions can be made overall.

Let's look at an example. Steinka-Fry, Tanner-Smith, and Grant (2015) conducted a meta-analysis to determine whether an intervention targeting college students turning 21 reduced the amount of 21st birthday drinking. After a search for relevant literature, Steinka-Fry et al. found nine research studies to include in their meta-analysis. Intervention was operationalized in different ways in these nine studies. For example, some emailed while others mailed a card; some messages were educational information about alcohol, while others told a story about a student who died from drinking too much alcohol. But for each research study, the goal was to determine whether those with upcoming birthdays who had received information regarding alcohol would drink less to celebrate than those who did not receive such information.

The overall result was that although those who received the intervention had a slightly lower blood alcohol content (BAC) than those who did not, there was no difference in the amount of alcohol consumed. Why was the BAC affected while the amount of alcohol consumed was not? Steinka-Fry et al. thought that perhaps study participants ate more food while drinking or spaced their drinking over a longer period of time. Thus, with the aid of this meta-analysis, Steinka-Fry et al. concluded that these types of interventions have, at best, only minimal effects on the alcohol consumption of those celebrating their 21st birthdays. Even though a variety of methods were used to ask the same basic question, a meta-analysis was able to reveal an overall conclusion regarding the magnitude and the generality of the intervention. Steinka-Fry et al. urged researchers to continue to work on developing interventions to target risky 21st birthday celebration behavior.

Let's say you've completed your literature search. Now that you have some familiarity with your topic, you can start thinking about what you want to do. Consider choosing one article you like and thinking about the next step that would be reasonable to take; in fact, most articles include ideas for future research in their discussion. Feel free to consider those ideas as you plan your own research. Recognize, of course, that it's possible other researchers were similarly inspired – you can check on this by using a library database to see who else has cited your article of interest.

Another possibility you might want to pursue is to take an article or a set of articles you like and tackle the same idea but a little bit differently. If we get similar findings when studying the same topic in different ways, it gives us confidence in the generalizability of the findings. Below are some ideas about what you can do (ideally, you should have a good rationale for making any of these choices).

Vary an Independent Variable Differently. Recall that in an experiment you present different groups with different stimuli or different experiences (the independent variables), and then you examine

whether those variations had an impact on whatever it is you are measuring (the dependent variables). Sometimes when designing original research, researchers choose to vary their independent variables in a way that others in the field have not done before. Here's an example. Have you ever been attracted to someone else's boyfriend or girlfriend? If you acted on those feelings, you would be doing what is known as "mate poaching." The idea behind mate poaching is that someone in a committed relationship is appealing because someone else has pre-screened this person and found desirable qualities in him or her. Some researchers have considered this phenomenon, although not all have found the expected relationship (stronger feelings of attraction for one in a committed relationship).

For example, Uller and Johansson (2003) had female undergraduates interact with two men, one of whom was randomly assigned to wear a wedding ring. In this case, the women did not find the attached man to be more attractive. Parker and Burkley (2009) decided to look at this issue slightly differently; they looked at mate poaching in both males and females and varied something they thought might influence the likelihood of mate poaching: the relationship status of the poacher. Parker and Burkley's consideration of the relationship status of both male and female potential poachers was certainly something unique they added to the literature, but the point I want to make is that Parker and Burkley and Uller and Johansson varied relationship status in different ways. Instead of using live interactions with two different individuals as Uller and Johansson did, Parker and Burkley had single and attached male and female undergraduates view a photo of someone of the opposite sex after learning that this person had been matched to them based on their answers to a questionnaire asking about their ideal mate. In each case in Parker and Burkley's research, participants read that the person pictured was either "single or in a current romantic relationship" (p. 1017). Unlike Uller and Johansson, Parker and Burkley found evidence for mate poaching; they found that only single women were more interested in the attached male than the unattached male.

Let's take a closer look at how Parker and Burkley and Uller and Johansson each varied relationship status; each method had its advantages and disadvantages. Parker and Burkley's independent variable manipulation was well controlled; all women, for example, looked at a photo of the *same* man – the only thing about him that varied was his relationship status. We could argue that evaluating your preference for a man in a photograph is not the same as evaluating your preference for a man you're interacting with (although in today's computer dating scene, evaluating someone from a photo *is* commonplace!). See Table 2.2 for a comparison of the methodologies used in Uller and Johansson's and Parker and Burkley's works.

Uller and Johansson had women interact with two *different* men, each of whom had his own unique charms and faults (in fact, one of the men was seen as generally more attractive than the other, so the researchers analyzed the data for each man separately). While a live interaction is probably more realistic, perhaps the scripted nature of this interaction made for a less than natural interaction (although the men did note that the interactions "worked well" (p. 269)). So why did Uller and Johansson not find evidence for mate poaching, while Parker and Burkley did? It is difficult to say, since there can be many different reasons for the absence of significant findings (for instance, sometimes the sample isn't big enough). Understandably and appropriately, Uller and Johansson did wonder why they did not find evidence of mate poaching. For example, they wondered whether men who actually are engaged (and are not pretending to be, as the men in their study were) somehow act

differently toward women, doing something that makes them more attractive. Future research can of course attempt to uncover the answer to this and other relevant questions.

Change the Way You Measure Something. Another change you can make when designing your research is to measure the variable of interest differently than others have done (recall that we measure variables within both experimental and non-experimental studies; within the context of an experiment, the measured variable is called the dependent variable). Take the following non-experimental examples: Winstock, Griffiths, and Stewart (2001) were interested in examining drug use patterns among those who frequent dance clubs in the United Kingdom. In their effort to do this, they put an anonymous questionnaire about drug use in a dance music magazine, and people could choose to self-report about their drug use and send in the questionnaire. They found out, for example, that almost all in the sample (96% of 1,151 respondents) had used ecstasy, often in combination with alcohol or other drugs, risky because of the likelihood of severe health consequences.

Now, in terms of methodology, Winstock et al.'s (2001) technique had its advantages. Think about it this way; where can you find large numbers of illicit drug users, and how do you get them to report honestly about their drug usage? Placing a questionnaire in a dance music magazine enabled the researchers to reach a large number of potential users, and the anonymity likely increased the response rate (many respondents could be at risk of legal trouble if police investigators became aware of their drug purchasing and use). This technique also had its disadvantages. People were able to choose whether to answer the questionnaire. Perhaps those who answered were somehow different from those who did not. Thus, as Winstock et al. acknowledge,

Table 2.2   A comparison of methodologies.

	Uller and Johansson (2003)	Parker and Burkley (2009)
Study participants	Female undergraduates	Single and attached male and female undergraduates (relationship status and gender of the participant were additional independent variables)
Target of attention – how was attachment varied? (an independent variable)	Participants each interacted with two males, one at a time. One of the males was wearing a wedding ring.	Participants each were presented with a photo of an opposite-sex person who had reportedly been matched to them based on their answers to a questionnaire asking about their ideal partner. The person in the photo was presented as either single or currently involved in a romantic relationship.
Examples of dependent variables	What was your impression of the man at first sight regarding his physical attractiveness? How willing would you be to start a serious relationship with him?	How attractive is the target? How likely would you be in initiating a relationship with this person?
Main result	No evidence of mate poaching. Females did not find the attached male to be more attractive.	Evidence for mate poaching was revealed only for single females. Single females were more interested in the attached males than in the unattached males.

their results do not necessarily reflect the typical experience of those in the UK dance scene or of people in general.

There are also limitations to the self-report technique Winstock et al. used. Whenever you use self-report, you have to rely on what people remember or what they say they remember, and both, quite frankly, can be wrong. Ramsey et al. (2001) recognized the limitations of the self-report of drug use, so they decided to try a new way of examining drug use among young people at dance clubs in the UK. They analyzed all the drugs collected in an "amnesty bin" at a London dance club over the course of a year. Drugs were deposited in this bin either because

patrons were required to discard illicit drugs when entering the club, or because security staff obtained the drugs during a search. Thus, these researchers did not rely on self-report. They were able to get information regarding drug use in dance clubs in the UK by measuring the variable of interest (the amount and type of drugs) differently. Instead of asking people what they have been taking via a self-report, they essentially had people empty their pockets!

This "empty your pockets" technique has its limitations too. For example, while Ramsey et al.'s technique gives us information about the types of drugs available to users, it does not tell us anything about the pattern of usage (such as, the usual dosages). Also, many patrons may have swallowed, snorted, or injected their drug(s) of choice prior to entering the club, or perhaps they did not willingly give up their stash and the security staff did not find it. For our purposes, note that in both cases – Winstock et al., 2001 and Ramsey et al., 2001 – the researchers sought to find out about the drug use of those associated with dance clubs; both teams obtained important information, but they did it in different ways.

Extend the External Validity. As mentioned above, external validity refers to our ability to generalize our findings to other people, settings, and times. In other words, we are asking the following questions: Will we get similar results with other people, in other kinds of places, and are these results likely to be similar over time? While we will delve into this area more in Chapter 12, I will talk about external validity briefly here because the desire to extend the external validity of a given piece of research can be a reason to conduct a new study.

My first example describes an attempt to extend the external validity of findings to another time. Before I describe this research, let me tell you about the conversation that started it all. Russ Clark was teaching a course in experimental social psychology, and he and his students were discussing Pennebaker et al.'s (1979) study "Don't the girls get prettier at closing time" (see more on this study below). In this study, Pennebaker et al. investigate whether members of the opposite sex are seen as more attractive as the time to interact with them diminishes. This led to a discussion in Clark's class of men's and women's receptivity to sexual offers. Clark ventured an opinion that "a woman … good looking or not, doesn't have to worry about timing in searching for a man. Arrive at *any* time. All she has to do is point an inviting finger at any man, whisper 'Come on 'a my place,' and she's made a conquest" (Clark &

Hatfield, 2003, p. 228). When the women in Clark's class disagreed with his assessment, he replied, "It's an empirical question. Let's design a field experiment to see who's right" (Clark & Hatfield, 2003, p. 228). (This is a perfect response for a researcher! I invite you to incorporate this set of phrases into your collection of conversational choices!)

Clark and his class then designed a simple experiment. He had research assistants approach students of the opposite sex on campus (whom they did not know) and randomly ask one of three questions: "Would you go out tonight?," "Will you come over to my apartment?" or "Would you go to bed with me?" The reason I'm mentioning this study here is that this study was actually conducted three times. The first study, in 1978, revealed that while men and women were equally receptive to the offer of a date, there were striking sex differences in receptivity to the other offers: 69% of men and only 6% of women were willing to go to the apartment of someone they just met. How about the offer of sex? No woman was willing to take the man up on that offer, but 75% of men said yes. Beyond saying "yes" or "no," the males provided responses such as, "Why do we have to wait until tonight?" or "I cannot tonight, but tomorrow would be fine," while the females' responses included statements such as, "What is wrong with you? Leave me alone." Clearly there were differences in receptivity to offers of a liaison.

Just four years later, Clark ran the study again (Clark & Hatfield, 1989) to test whether similar results would be obtained (see Clark & Hatfield, 2003). Then the study was run a third time (Clark, 1990, Experiment I). Why the subsequent testing? One reason was that AIDS was now a part of the social climate, first recognized by the Centers for Disease Control and Prevention in 1981 (www.aids.gov/hiv-aids-basics/hiv-aids-101/aids-timeline/). Would the presence of a potentially deadly sexually

FIGURE 2.4 Would you be willing to accept a date with, go to the apartment of, or sleep with someone you just met?

transmitted disease change the way people respond to the offer of a night with a stranger?

It didn't. The results were basically the same. (In the third study, only one person, a female, said anything about sexually transmitted diseases when explaining a refusal.) The subsequent testing extended this study's external validity; the results generalized to other times. If the results are similar each time the study is conducted, you can have more confidence in the generality of the findings.

Others have attempted to extend the external validity of Clark and Hatfield's (e.g., 1989) work in other ways. For example, Guéguen (2011) ran Clark's basic study in France to discover whether the results would hold in another culture (generalizing to other people). The results were essentially

the same. Men were much more willing to have a sexual relationship with someone they didn't know than women were. These results give us confidence that these results will likely generalize to others in similar cultures.

Clark's original research (e.g., Clark & Hatfield, 1989) was conducted on a college campus in the United States, while Guéguen's (2011) study was conducted in a pedestrian zone of a medium-sized town in France (generalizing to other settings). The similarity in results obtained in two different kinds of settings gives us further confidence in the generalizability of the results. In other words, we can state that the external validity of this work appears to be high.

Theory

Sometimes research is conducted to test a particular theory. First I'll remind you what a theory is and does, and then I'll provide an example. A theory is a set of ideas that explains a particular phenomenon. More specifically, a theory will summarize an existing body of knowledge about a particular phenomenon, provide a coherent explanation for that body of knowledge, and help to generate predictions about the phenomenon of interest. A good theory must be **parsimonious**. This means it should explain the phenomenon of interest in the simplest way possible. What this means in practical terms is this: If more than one theory is proposed to explain a phenomenon, scientists will prefer the theory that makes the fewest assumptions and explains the data in the simplest terms.

A good theory must also be testable. If the research conducted to test the theory provides data that we expect, given the theory, our confidence in that theory grows. If the research does not provide data that we expect given the theory, the theory will need to be modified so it can better account for the data.

For example, take the research reported by Clark and Hatfield (1989) presented earlier. Clark and Hatfield used sociobiological theory to make a prediction. They cited the work of Symons (1979), who argued that individuals are motivated to produce as many surviving children as possible so their genetic material is passed on to as much of the next generation as possible. Females have a 9-month commitment to a single pregnancy, so they have to be very selective in the choice of mates. Males don't have the same time investment. They generally father a large number of children, so for them the optimal strategy for spreading their genetic material is to impregnate as many females as possible.

Clark and Hatfield used this sociobiological theory to generate a prediction for males' and females' receptivity to sexual offers from strangers. Because men have the evolution-based goal of wanting sex with a lot of women, and women have the evolution-based goal of holding back in an effort to discover whether a man is a good genetic choice, Clark and Hatfield predicted that men will be more likely to accept an offer of a sexual encounter with a stranger than women will. This expectation or prediction is Clark and Hatfield's hypothesis. Hypotheses are predictions about the relationship that exists among the variables of interest, and they are often developed from theories as you saw here and in Chapter 1 (you'll read more about hypotheses later in this chapter). As you recall, Clark and Hatfield's hypothesis was indeed supported.

One More Point about Generating Research Ideas

As researchers, we aim to do meaningful research, research that ultimately provides explanations for phenomena we experience in the world around us. As you saw above, the ideas for research come from a variety of sources. However, no matter what the source of your research idea is, feel free to think about creative ways to test your hypotheses. I'll use one of my favorite examples from Wegner's lab to illustrate.

Did you ever have a relationship or even a crush that you had to keep secret? Maybe you wanted to keep knowledge of it from your parents, or your friends, or your employer, or the object of the crush itself. Wegner, Lane, and Dimitri (1994) decided to study the "allure of secret relationships" (p. 287); they wondered whether a secret relationship is more exciting *because of* its secrecy. Now I think this topic is inherently interesting, but the creative way Wegner et al. studied it using an experiment makes it especially compelling. Simply put, Wegner et al. used a game of "footsie" to create secret "relationships" between study participants.

Groups of four unacquainted participants (two coed pairs) would come to the lab to play a "Communication" card game. Each coed pair received a randomly determined set of instructions. Specifically, in each group of four, one of the coed pairs were told that while they were playing cards, they should touch their partner's feet with their feet and try to find some pattern of nonverbal communication to help them win the game. In some cases, these "footsie" pairs were to keep this touching secret, while in other cases, the nonverbal communication taking place under the table was known to all four players.

After 10 minutes of playing cards, the study participants separated, and then each filled out a questionnaire to determine how attracted each participant was to each opposite-sex team member. As Wegner et al. predicted, those who had touched their partner's feet secretly reported more attraction to that partner than those who either touched without secrecy or did not touch at all (attraction measures taken after the teams were formed but before the game was played revealed no differences – there were differences only after the game was played).

So Wegner et al. were able to demonstrate that playing a secret game of footsie can lead to increased attraction for the footsie partner, and it is the secretive nature of the game that is crucial; there was significantly less attraction for the partner who played footsie, but didn't keep it a secret. What a creative way to demonstrate a fascinating part of the human experience!

Finding Relevant Literature

No matter what kind of research you do and no matter where you get your research idea, you should investigate what others have written about the topic. Why do a literature review? There are many reasons. This information helps you develop your hypotheses (more on this point below), and it also gives you information about what has already been done so you can make an educated decision as to what would be a good addition to the literature.

You don't have to read everything written on your topic since the invention of the printing press, but you do need to become familiar with the *current* state of knowledge on your topic; recent articles will be more helpful for this than older ones. As mentioned previously, review articles and meta-analyses are good sources too. And the introduction sections of research articles on your topic will also tell you what others have done that's relevant. Another reason to do a literature review is to learn from others' experiences; perhaps other authors experienced a methodological problem you can avoid. That sort of information will likely be discussed in the relevant journal articles.

Oftentimes no one has done *exactly* what you're planning on doing; in that case you need to review the research most relevant to what you're doing. Here's an example. Seiter (2007) wanted to know whether complimenting restaurant patrons on their dinner choices led to higher tips than not complimenting them. No one had considered this question before, but others had studied the sorts of things that can affect restaurant tipping behavior (such as Strohmetz, Rind, Fisher, & Lynn, 2002), and some had studied the effects of ingratiation techniques such as complimenting people (see, for example, Gordon, 1996). So Seiter reviewed relevant literature from both of these areas, and this helped him develop his hypothesis that food servers will collect a higher tip percentage when they compliment their customers than when they do not. His hypothesis was supported.

PsycINFO

To locate sources relevant to your topic, you'll likely use *PsycINFO*. *PsycINFO* is a computerized database that provides citations, abstracts, and in some cases the full text of journal articles, as well as information about books on all topics relevant to behavioral and social science research. You probably have access to *PsycINFO* through your university or college library (other access options are available: for example, it is possible to buy access to *PsycINFO* as an individual on a 24-hour or yearly basis). While the look of *PsycINFO* may be slightly different from institution to institution, the basic information I provide here will generally be available in the version you see. For updates to *PsycINFO*, please visit www.apa.org/pubs/databases/psycinfo/.

Each entry in *PsycINFO* includes bibliographic information for a particular source (see Figure 2.5). For example, in the case of a journal article, you will see the title of the article, the name or names of the author or authors, the title of the journal, the volume number, and the year of publication. Each entry will also include an abstract. You can often decide whether you want to read the article by reviewing the title and reading the abstract.

The **allure** of **secret relationships.**

Authors: Wegner, Daniel M.. U Virginia, Dept of Psychology, Charlottesville, US
Lane, Julie D.
Dimitri, Sara

Source: Journal of Personality and Social Psychology, Vol 66(2), Feb, 1994. pp. 287-300.

NLM Title Abbreviation: J Pers Soc Psychol

Page Count: 14

Publisher: US : American Psychological Association

ISSN: 0022-3514 (Print)
1939-1315 (Electronic)

Language: English

Keywords: role of secrecy in attraction to **relationships**, college students to 92 yr olds

Abstract: Two surveys and a laboratory experiment examined the role of secrecy in attraction to **relationships**. In the 1st survey, respondents reported that past **relationships** they currently continued to think about were more likely to have been **secret** than ones they no longer pondered. In the 2nd survey, those respondents who indicated that a past **relationship** had been **secret** also reported that it continued to be a target of their obsessive preoccupation. The laboratory experiment explored attraction between mixed-sex couples who were induced to play footsie under a table in the presence of another couple. When this was **secret**, greater attraction for the partner was reported than when it was not. (PsycINFO Database Record (c) 2016 APA, all rights reserved)

Document Type: Journal Article

Subjects: *Male Female Relations; *Secrecy

PsycINFO Classification: Group & Interpersonal Processes (3020)

Population: Human

Age Group: Adulthood (18 yrs & older)
Aged (65 yrs & older)
Very Old (85 yrs & older)

Methodology: Empirical Study

Format Covered: Print

Publication Type: Journal; Peer Reviewed Journal

Publication History: Accepted: Jul 29, 1993; Revised: Jun 20, 1993; First Submitted: Dec 12, 1991

Release Date: 19940801

Copyright: American Psychological Association. 1994

Digital Object Identifier: http://dx.doi.org/10.1037/0022-3514.66.2.287

FIGURE 2.5 A sample listing from *PsycINFO*.

PsycINFO contains information about a variety of different types of sources, but most of the citations refer to journal articles, books, and book chapters. Most journal articles are primary sources of information. Most books are secondary sources. A **primary source** is a complete research report about a particular study or studies the author or authors conducted (it will include sections on participants, method, and results). A **secondary source** does not provide the complete research report of a study or studies; it provides only summaries of the cited works. The textbook you're reading is an example of a secondary source; it is a secondary source for all the different research studies I summarize in these pages. To prepare this text, I read the primary sources of those research studies (journal articles) so that I could be sure to get all the details I needed.

It is important to read primary sources when you are preparing a literature review and not just trust what secondary sources tell you. Secondary sources do not always depict a study accurately. Landy and Aronson (1969) provided an early example of how characteristics of both defendants and victims could affect the sentencing of a defendant. More specifically, they varied the character of the defendant and victim; the character was presented as either "attractive" (for example, gave to charity), "unattractive" (for example, was a criminal), or "neutral" (p. 141). They found, for example, that when a defendant was portrayed as an unattractive rather than a neutral or an attractive character, he was sentenced to a longer period of time in prison. However, some researchers have mistakenly indicated that Landy and Aronson varied the physical characteristics (presumably misled by the "unattractive" and "attractive" labels), and not the character, of the defendant and the victim. If we had consulted only these secondary sources, we would have been led to believe something that was not true.

Does this mean you should never consult secondary sources? No. Books, as secondary sources, can give you ideas about what primary sources you'll want to investigate further. Books are also generally good sources if you want an overview of an area, but most of the sources you'll likely use in your research are journal articles that are primary sources. You'll want to see the entire research report, to know how the authors developed their hypotheses and to learn the details of their methodology. Obtain the primary sources of research that interest you, so you'll have access to details about what those researchers actually did.

FIGURE 2.6 Interested in finding out the potential health benefits of community yoga? Try using the phrase *yoga and health* in your search of the literature in *PsycINFO* and then narrow your search from there.

Search Terms. Once you have decided what your topic of interest is, it's time to do a search for relevant literature using *PsycINFO*. You'll first need to choose appropriate search terms. This can entail some trial and error. You'll want your search to be specific enough to generate some relevant hits, but not so general that you end up with a list of sources that have little to do with your topic. Typically you'll want to use standard psychology terms. *PsycINFO* has a thesaurus that can help you identify what these are. For example, let's say you're interested in doing some research on eating disorders, but you aren't quite sure exactly what search terms to use. Go to the *PsycINFO* thesaurus, type in "eating disorders," and check off relevancy rating, click "Browse," and the thesaurus will give you a variety of search terms for finding information about eating disorders (such as "eating disorders," "purging," "binge eating," "bulimia").

***How to Narrow Your Search in* PsycINFO.** Let me give you an example of how to narrow your search. Let's say you are interested in reading about the relationship between alcohol abuse and aggressive behavior. The key terms here are "alcohol abuse" and "aggressive behavior" (I found these terms in the *PsycINFO* thesaurus). *PsycINFO* uses Boolean operators (the words "and," "or," "not") to expand or narrow a search (note that some databases require their Boolean operators to be capitalized). For example, the Boolean operator "and" can narrow a search. In this case, I would search for "alcohol abuse and aggressive behavior." The word "and" narrows the search because adding it means each retrieved source must include *both* "alcohol abuse" and "aggressive behavior" in the title, abstract, subject, or keyword fields.

However, it is possible that when I do a search for "alcohol abuse and aggressive behavior," I end up with a lot of irrelevant references. When this happens I want to narrow the search further, and there are many ways to do that in *PsycINFO*.

For example, since you'll want to use mostly primary sources, one search option is to ask *PsycINFO* to limit your search to "All Journals" (listed under "Publication Type"). Let's also say you're interested in alcohol abuse and aggressive behavior in adolescents. With *PsycINFO*'s advanced search capabilities, you can limit a search to citations that consider only the age range of interest. *PsycINFO* gives you age group choices; just click the box you want (for example, adulthood is 18 years and older, young adulthood is 18–29, adolescence is 13–17).

Another way to narrow your search is to use a "population" limiter. Say I want to focus on the relationship between alcohol abuse and aggressive behavior in females. I can narrow my search by population and choose "females." This means that the search will only produce hits that include females. When I did this search using all the search limiters noted above, the retrieved result was 64 relevant journal articles. That is a manageable number to peruse. You can see how I narrowed my search, step by step, in Figure 2.7. Recognize that since *PsycINFO* adds about 4,000 records to the database every week,

the number of retrieved records for this and other searches will likely increase as time goes by.

There are still additional options for narrowing a search. Consider visiting www.apa.org/pubs/databases/training/search-guides.aspx for more information regarding designing an efficient search for relevant literature.

***How to Broaden Your Search in* PsycINFO.** Now let's say you want to broaden your search. Suppose you're interested in whether alcohol use increases the likelihood of sexting. So you start out with the search terms "sexting and alcohol." Unfortunately, that doesn't generate many hits. You want to broaden your search. One thing you can do is to use the Boolean operator "or." I've looked up "sexting" in *PsycINFO*'s thesaurus and found the term "cybersex" so I will include that in my search phrase. So now the search phrase is "sexting or cybersex and alcohol." Now that generates far more hits. See Figure 2.8 for more on this particular search and the citations retrieved.

Note that I didn't suggest "sexting and cybersex and alcohol," because that would provide only a very short list of the sources that use *all* those terms in their title, abstract, subject line, or keywords. After your search, take a look at how relevant the citations are, and decide whether to broaden or narrow the search from there.

Another technique to broaden a search is to use truncation. Let's say you are still looking for articles on aggression. *PsycINFO* recommended "aggressive behavior" as a search phrase; however, it is possible you'll want to capture sources that have just the term "aggression" in a search field (it's worth a try!). You can search using a truncated term, meaning you use an asterisk to stand in for the different ways a particular word can end. In this case, if you search using the term "aggress*" you'll get any word that begins with

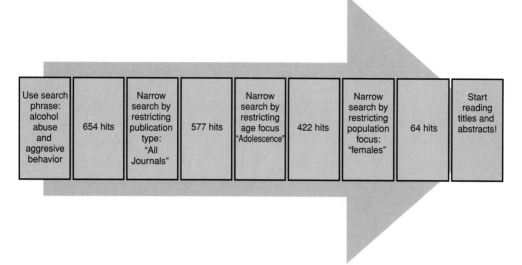

FIGURE 2.7 How to narrow a search using *PsycINFO*.

"aggress," regardless of how it ends – aggression, aggressive.

You do need to be careful how you use truncation; think about all the different ways the word of interest could end. For example, when trying to broaden a search on dating behavior I used "dat*" because I thought that would give me "date," "dates," and "dating." However, this search was not a good choice, because I also ended up with a lot of sources on my generated list that had the word "data" in the title and/or abstract, and they had nothing to do with the topic of interest.

There are other options for broadening a search. Again, you may choose to visit www.apa.org/pubs/

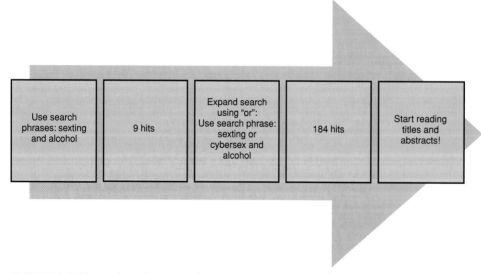

FIGURE 2.8 How to broaden a search using *PsycINFO*.

databases/training/search-guides.aspx for more information.

Once you find some sources that will work for you, there is another good *PsycINFO* technique to use. For each citation listing, *PsycINFO* will provide both a list of the references cited within that source (click on "cited references"), and a list of the other sources that have cited your source of interest (click on "times cited in this database"). You may choose to find out more about these additional sources, because they may also be helpful in your search for information about your topic of interest.

***Full-Text Articles in* PsycINFO.** In some but not all cases, *PsycINFO* will include the full text of the article (available as a PDF file in which the content maintains proper formatting and appearance, or as an HTML file that does not have formatting). In these cases, you can download, email, and/or print the article directly from *PsycINFO*. In other cases, *PsycINFO* will not have the full text of the article available; if you want to read beyond the title and the abstract, you'll have to get the article in another way. It might be shelved at your university or college library, or you may have to go through a process called interlibrary loan. **Interlibrary loan** is a system in which libraries lend and borrow from each other. A librarian at your library should be able to help you with this request.

Although it is possible to limit your search to articles that have the full text attached, I do not recommend this. It may be that great articles for your topic exist, but *PsycINFO* does not have the full text available for them. If you limit your search to only full-text articles, you'll never know about their existence.

Other Databases

PsycINFO is often the database of choice for those in psychology and related fields. However, sometimes researchers do not have access to *PsycINFO*. Your school library might instead have the Web of Science, which allows you to search for journal articles and conference proceedings in science, social science, arts, and the humanities. Or you may have access to Scopus, which is a database that has journal article and book information in the sciences, social sciences, arts, humanities, technology, and medicine.

If you do not have access to any of the above noted databases, you can instead use the easily accessible Google Scholar (https://scholar.google.com) to search for relevant literature. You use Google Scholar just like you use Google; type your key words into the search box. Google Scholar then returns a list of sources including journal article citations and book information, which you can sort by relevance or by date. For each retrieved entry, Google Scholar will provide information regarding who has cited the article and provide a list of related articles. Sometimes you can even obtain the full text of articles through Google Scholar. Obtaining primary sources is important, so if the database doesn't provide you with the primary sources you want, you can work with your school library to obtain them.

The Basic Components of a Journal Article

Now that you have found sources relevant to your topic, it's time to start reading. Since much of what you'll likely read is primary source journal articles, this section presents the basic components of a journal article (see Figure 2.9) so you will generally know what to expect. We'll discuss journal articles in more detail in Chapter 14 when we talk about how to write up your own research.

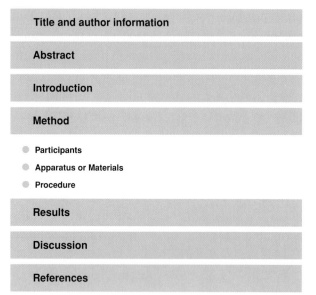

FIGURE 2.9 The basic components of a journal article.

Title and Author Information

A well-written title will give you a good idea of what the article is about. This initial part of the article will also typically list the authors, their affiliations, and contact information for the lead author.

Abstract

The abstract is a one-paragraph summary of the article. The abstract will typically provide information regarding the purpose of the research, the number and type of participants, the methodology, a summary of the results, and the implications of the findings. Because it provides an overview of the entire article, reading the abstract is a good way to determine whether the article is a good fit for your needs.

Introduction

The purpose of the introduction is to provide information regarding past research and theories relevant to the topic of interest, develop a rationale for doing the present research, and provide information regarding the purpose of the present research. The researchers' expectations (hypotheses) for the

results of the current study are presented in the introduction too.

Method

The Method section is typically divided into subsections as noted in Figure 2.9. Thus, there is a Participants subsection in which the details regarding the sample are provided (such as the number of participants as well as their gender, age, and how they were selected). Older articles usually refer to this section as a Subjects section.

The second subsection in the Method section is generally a Materials or an Apparatus subsection. Researchers usually use a Materials section if they need to describe material such as the scenarios and/ or questionnaires presented to study participants. An apparatus subsection is included if the researchers need to describe equipment they used to test the participants.

The third subsection in the Method section is usually a Procedure section. Here the researchers provide the essential details of the steps that the participants completed. This section often includes information regarding ethical issues (such as informed consent and debriefing).

The Method section provides the details you will need if you choose to replicate the study. You can usually assume the article you are reading is a primary source if it has a Method section.

Results

The Results section describes the statistical tests the researchers used to analyze the data, and the outcomes of those tests are provided. Tables and Figures (for example, graphs) are sometimes included to further illustrate the results.

Discussion

The Discussion usually begins with a statement of whether the data supported the hypotheses. Then the researchers discuss the results in light of previous research. Were the results consistent with what others have found? If not, the researchers will speculate about why not. The discussion section will also typically include information about the limitations of the present research as well as ideas for future research.

References

The Reference section provides a list of all the sources referred to in the article. This section can be a wonderful resource because the sources cited in an article of interest may also be of interest to you.

Generating Hypotheses

No matter what kind of research you do, and no matter what the source of your research idea is, you will need to generate one or more hypotheses *before* you conduct the research. As mentioned above, hypotheses are your expectations or predictions about the relationship that exists among the variables of interest. Earlier I gave an example of generating a hypothesis from theory. Hypotheses are also often derived from previous research. For an example, let's look at the research of Jacob, Guéguen, and Boulbry (2010). They were interested in finding out whether music with prosocial lyrics would affect tipping behavior in a restaurant, and previous research led them to the hypothesis that it would. Specifically, previous researchers such as Greitemeyer (2009) had found that people who heard music with prosocial lyrics were more likely to donate money to a nonprofit organization than those who listened to music with neutral lyrics. Thus Greitemeyer (2009) found that listening to prosocial lyrics increased a form of helping behavior in the lab.

Now let's bring this back to the work of Jacob et al. Jacob et al. saw tipping as a form of helping behavior (it certainly helps the waitstaff!), and they knew that under the well-controlled circumstances of the lab, where study participants listen to the presented songs without any distractions, helping behavior increases after people hear prosocial lyrics. This knowledge led Jacob et al. to hypothesize that results in the natural setting would show a similar pattern. The data were indeed consistent with their hypothesis. The restaurant patrons tipped more when the music had prosocial versus neutral lyrics. So if you are working in a restaurant and your salary is at least partially dependent on tips, you may wish to suggest that management play music with a prosocial theme (such as "Heal the World" by Michael Jackson).

Once you have a research idea and literature relevant to your topic, you need to create a research hypothesis or hypotheses. There are a few guidelines to follow. First your hypothesis must be testable; you must state your hypothesis so that it is possible to design a study to test it. You must also state your hypothesis as something you *expect* to happen, not something that *will* happen. Since hypotheses are stated before a study has been conducted, if you state what will happen, you'll inappropriately sound like some all-knowing being.

Let's look at another example of a hypothesis. Consider the study conducted by Byington and Schwebel (2013). They were interested in whether mobile devices play a role in college students' pedestrian accidents. To investigate, they had college students participate in a virtual pedestrian task while either undistracted or distracted by their cell phones. Before conducting the study, Byington and Schwebel stated the following, "We hypothesized that participants would take greater risks and be less attentive to traffic while distracted by mobile Internet in the virtual pedestrian environment" (p. 79). Another way to write this hypothesis is to use an "if … then" format: If pedestrians are distracted, as opposed to not distracted, by mobile Internet in a virtual pedestrian environment, then they are hypothesized to take greater risks and be less attentive to traffic. (This hypothesis was supported.)

Regardless of the format used to convey Byington and Schwebel's hypothesis, note that the hypothesis not only says differences are expected between those distracted and those not distracted; it also predicts the direction of the outcome – that those on the phone will take *greater* risks and be *less* attentive. Researchers typically do expect to obtain differences between groups (although note that researchers can state that they expect differences between all groups or specify explicitly that they expect differences between just some of the tested groups), and they often are able to indicate an expected direction for the outcome because the previous literature has led them to that expectation. If there is a lack of previous research on your topic, however, you can state a nondirectional hypothesis, such as that those who are distracted are expected to display a different amount of risk and attention to traffic than those who are undistracted, or no hypothesis at all. In the latter case, you should state that because of the lack of previous research, no hypotheses will be provided.

SUMMARY

Researchers can get their research ideas from real-life experiences, from a need to solve practical problems, from reading previous research, and from a knowledge of theory. They often conduct original research, building on work that has been done previously; thus it is important that before starting your own investigation you become familiar with the topic by conducting a literature search using a library database, such as *PsycINFO*.

While secondary sources such as books, review articles, and meta-analyses can help to give overviews of topic areas, primary sources are important because they provide the details of how a study was conducted. Journal articles are typically primary sources. Reading the abstract is a good way to determine whether the article is a good fit for your needs.

No matter what the source of your research idea is, you will need to generate one or more hypotheses *before* you conduct the research. Hypotheses are typically generated from results obtained in previous research and/or from theory; thus the literature search is important to this process as well.

GLOSSARY

Abstract – a short summary of the research report.

Interlibrary loan – a system in which libraries lend and borrow from each other.

Meta-analysis – a procedure that uses statistical procedures to combine the results of multiple studies on the same topic.

Parsimonious – the characteristic of a theory that explains the phenomenon of interest in the simplest way possible.

Primary source – a complete research report about a particular study or studies the author or authors conducted.

Review article – a comprehensive summary regarding what's been done on a topic.

Secondary source – a source that provides only summaries of the cited works, not the complete research report of a study or studies.

REVIEW QUESTIONS

1   Identify four sources of research ideas.
2   Differentiate between a review article and a meta-analysis.

3 State three general ways you can modify previous research.

4 Differentiate between a primary source and a secondary source. What kind of information can you obtain from each kind of source?

5 Describe how to locate sources relevant to your research topic.

6 Identify the basic components of a journal article.

7 List some guidelines for creating a hypothesis.

ARTICLES AS ILLUSTRATION

The three articles mentioned immediately below provide an extended example of how some researchers got the ideas for their work. In the first example, a favorite of mine, James Pennebaker and his colleagues (1979) got an idea for a study by listening to a country and western song presumably based on someone's real-life experiences: "Don't the girls get prettier at closing time?" An interesting idea for research certainly, but how to test it? They decided to do an experiment to investigate, for both sexes, whether members of the opposite sex are seen as more attractive as the time to interact with them diminishes. Pennebaker et al. had study participants rate the attractiveness of those of the opposite sex at three different times during the night (9:00 p.m., 10:30 p.m., and midnight). Then they examined whether those ratings changed significantly over the course of the evening. I'll let you read the article to find out what happened!

The other two articles mentioned here show how researchers can use previous research to get their ideas. Specifically, at the end of Pennebaker et al.'s article, the authors wrote about possible reasons for their results, reasons that future researchers might be inclined to investigate (Pennebaker's research was not designed to isolate the reasons for their findings). Gladue and Delaney (1990) read Pennebaker's work and decided to investigate a possible reason for their findings (here's a hint: beer goggles!). Again, I'll let you read the article to discover what they found.

In the third article mentioned below, Madey and his colleagues (1996) also read Pennebaker et al.'s (1979) article and investigated whether there is a limitation on its results – a situation in which Pennebaker et al.'s results do not hold. In this case, the title reveals the answer to the question they ask with their research: "They do get more attractive at closing time, but only when you are not in a relationship."

The questions for each of these three articles will help you focus on the important points of the articles. In addition, see how one article leads to the next and how together they tell a story.

1 Pennebaker, J. W., Dyer, M. A., Caulkins, R. S., Litowitz, D. L., Ackerman, P. L., Anderson, D. B., & McGraw, K. M. (1979). Don't the girls get prettier at closing time: a country and western application to psychology. *Personality and Social Psychology Bulletin, 5*, 122–125. doi:10.1177/014616727900500127.

   a. What was Pennebaker et al.'s hypothesis? How did Pennebaker et al. come to develop this hypothesis?

   b. What does it mean to say that individuals exhibit greater liking for threatened behaviors, and how does this greater liking apply to Pennebaker et al.'s work?

   c. Describe Pennebaker's methodology, including dependent and independent variable(s).

   d. How did Pennebaker et al. choose their study participants?

   e. Pennebaker et al. tested their hypothesis at three different bars. Why do you think they went to three bars as opposed to only one?

   f. What were Pennebaker et al.'s results?

g. What do Pennebaker et al. propose as possible reasons for their results?

2 Gladue, B. A., & Delaney, H. J. (1990). Gender differences in perception of attractiveness of men and women in bars. *Personality and Social Psychology Bulletin, 16,* 378–391. doi:10.1177/0146167290162017.

    a. Where did Gladue and Delaney get their idea to do this research?

    b. Describe Gladue and Delaney's methodology, including dependent and independent variable(s).

    c. Why did Gladue and Delaney ask their study participants to rate both patrons at a bar and those in photos?

    d. What were Gladue and Delaney's results?

3 Madey, S. F., Simo, M., Dillworth, D., Kemper, D., Toczynski, A., & Perella, A. (1996). They do get more attractive at closing time, but only when you are not in a relationship. *Basic and Applied Social Psychology, 18,* 387–393. doi:10.1207/s15324834basp1804_2.

    a. Where did Madey et al. get their idea to do this research?

    b. Describe Madey et al.'s methodology, including dependent and independent variable(s).

    c. What were Madey et al.'s results?

SUGGESTED ACTIVITIES

1 Do a search for a journal article that you find appealing. Read the article and then propose your own idea for a follow-up study to this research.

2 Do a search for literature on a topic you find interesting. Try narrowing and broadening your search.

3 Do a search for a journal article, locate the entire article (the primary source), and summarize briefly each of the major sections.

4 Propose a research study to study a real-life issue relevant for your campus. One possibility is to propose a survey to assess what people would think about a particular change on campus (I recently wondered what people think about students living with pets in their dorm rooms – what campus change can you think of?). Do a literature search on the topic and use this literature to help you generate a hypothesis.

REFERENCES

Byington, K. W., & Schwebel, D. C. (2013). Effects of mobile Internet use on college student pedestrian injury risk. *Accident Analysis and Prevention, 51,* 78–83. doi:http://dx.doi.org/10.1016/j.aap.2012.11.001

Civic, D. (2000). College students' reasons for nonuse of condoms within dating relationships. *Journal of Sex & Marital Therapy, 26,* 95–105. doi:http://dx.doi.org/10.1080/009262300278678

Clark, R. D. (1990). The impact of AIDS on gender differences in willingness to engage in casual sex. *Journal of Applied Social Psychology, 20,* 771–782. doi:http://dx.doi.org/10.1111/j.1559–1816.1990.tb00437.x

Clark, R. D., & Hatfield, E. (1989). Gender differences in receptivity to sexual offers. *Journal of Psychology & Human Sexuality, 2*(1), 39–55. doi:http://dx.doi.org/10.1300/J056v02n01_04
(2003). Love in the afternoon. *Psychological Inquiry, 14,* 227–231. doi:http://dx.doi.org/10.1207/S15327965PLI1403&4_8

Cochran, S. D., & Mays, V. M. (1990). Sex, lies and HIV. *New England Journal of Medicine, 322,* 774. doi:http://dx.doi.org/10.1056/NEJM199003153221111

Gladue, B. A., & Delaney, H. J. (1990). Gender differences in perception of attractiveness of men and women in bars. *Personality and Social Psychology Bulletin, 16,* 378–391. doi:http://dx.doi.org/10.1177/0146167290162017

Gordon, R. A., (1996). Impact of ingratiation on judgments and evaluations: A meta-analytic investigation. *Journal of Personality and Social Psychology, 71,* 54–70. doi:http://dx.doi.org/10.1037/0022–3514.71.1.54

Greitemeyer, T. (2009). Effects of songs with prosocial lyrics on prosocial thoughts, affect, and behavior. *Journal of Experimental Social Psychology*, *45*, 186–190. doi:http://dx.doi.org/10.1016/j.jesp.2008.08.003

Guéguen, N. (2011). Effects of solicitor sex and attractiveness on receptivity to sexual offers: A field study. *Archives of Sexual Behavior*, *40*, 915–919. doi:http://dx.doi.org/10.1007/s10508-011-9750-4

Henry, W. J., West, N. M., & Jackson, A. (2010). Hip-hop's influence on the identity development of Black female college students: A literature review. *Journal of College Student Development*, *51*, 237–251. doi:http://dx.doi.org/10.1353/csd.0.0135

Jacob, C., Guéguen, N., & Boulbry, G. (2010). Effects of songs with prosocial lyrics on tipping behavior in a restaurant. *International Journal of Hospitality Management*, *29*, 761–763. doi:http://dx.doi.org/10.1016/j.ijhm.2010.02.004

Landy, D., & Aronson, E. (1969). The influence of the character of the criminal and his victim on the decisions of simulated jurors. *Journal of Experimental Social Psychology*, *5*, 141–152. doi:http://dx.doi.org/10.1016/0022-1031(69)90043-2

Lewis, J. E., Malow, R. M., & Ireland, S. J. (1997). HIV/AIDS in heterosexual college students: A review of a decade of literature. *Journal of American College Health*, *45*, 147–158. doi:http://dx.doi.org/10.1080/07448481.1997.9936875

Madey, S. F., Simo, M., Dillworth, D., Kemper, D., Toczynski, A., & Perella, A. (1996). They do get more attractive at closing time, but only when you are not in a relationship. *Basic and Applied Social Psychology*, *18*, 387–393. doi:http://dx.doi.org/10.1207/s15324834basp1804_2

Malkin, B. (2009, September 8). Trapped girls update Facebook instead of calling police. Retrieved from Telegraph.co.uk

Parker, J., & Burkley, M. (2009). Who's chasing whom? The impact of gender and relationship status on mate poaching. *Journal of Experimental Social Psychology*, *45*, 1016–1019. doi:http://dx.doi.org/10.1016/j.jesp.2009.04.022

Pennebaker, J. W., Dyer, M. A., Caulkins, R. S., Litowitz, D. L., Ackerman, P. L., Anderson, D. B., & McGraw, K. M. (1979). Don't the girls get prettier at closing time: A country and western application to psychology. *Personality and Social Psychology Bulletin*, *5*, 122–125. doi:http://dx.doi.org/10.1177/014616727900500127

Pinkerton, S. D., & Abramson, P. R. (1997). Effectiveness of condoms in preventing HIV transmission. *Social Science & Medicine*, *44*, 1303–1312. doi:http://dx.doi.org/10.1016/S0277-9536(96)00258-4

Ramsey, J. D., Butcher M. A., Murphy, M. F., Lee, T., Johnston, A., & Holt, D. W. (2001). A new method to monitor drugs at dance venues. *British Medical Journal*, *323*, 603. doi:http://dx.doi.org/10.1136/bmj.323.7313.603

Seiter, J. S. (2007). Ingratiation and gratuity: The effect of complimenting customers on tipping behavior in restaurants. *Journal of Applied Social Psychology*, *37*, 478–485. doi:http://dx.doi.org/10.1111/j.1559-1816.2007.00169.x

Steinka-Fry, K., Tanner-Smith, E. E., & Grant, S. (2015). Effects of 21st birthday brief interventions on college student celebratory drinking: A systematic and meta-analysis. *Addictive Behaviors*, *50*, 13–21. doi:http://dx.doi.org/10.1016/j.addbeh.2015.06.001

Strohmetz, D. B., Rind, B., Fisher, R., & Lynn, M. (2002). Sweetening the till: The use of candy to increase restaurant tipping. *Journal of Applied Social Psychology*, *32*, 300–309. doi:http://dx.doi.org/10.1111/j.1559-1816.2002.tb00216.x

Symons, D. (1979). *The evolution of human sexuality*. Oxford: Oxford University Press.

Thompson, S. H., & Lougheed, E. (2012). Frazzled by Facebook? An exploratory study of gender differences in social network communication among undergraduate men and women. *College Student Journal*, *46*, 88–98.

Uller, T., & Johansson, L. C. (2003). Human mate choice and the wedding ring effect: Are married men more attractive? *Human Nature*, *14*, 267–276. doi:http://dx.doi.org/10.1007/s12110-003-1006-0

Wegner, D. M., Lane, J. D., & Dimitri, S. (1994). The allure of secret relationships. *Journal of Personality and Social Psychology*, *66*, 287–300. doi:http://dx.doi.org/10.1037/0022-3514.66.2.287

Wendt, S. J., & Solomon, L. J. (1995). Barriers to condom use among male and female college students. *Journal of American College Health, 44,* 105–110. doi:http://dx.doi.org/10.1080/07448481.1995.9939102

Winstock, A. R., Griffiths, P., & Stewart, D. (2001). Drugs and the dance music scene: A survey of current drug use patterns among a sample of dance music enthusiasts in the UK. *Drug and Alcohol Dependence, 64,* 9–17. doi:http://dx.doi.org/10.1016/S0376-8716(00)00215-5

3 Ethics

LEARNING OBJECTIVES

- Summarize the history of research ethics.
- List the five general principles of the APA Ethics Code.
- Discuss the ethical standards of the APA Ethics Code with regard to research.
- Discuss the ethical standards of the APA Ethics Code with regard to publication.
- Discuss how the ethical standards of the APA Ethics Code pertain to research on the Internet.

When I was an undergraduate and taking a research methods course, I was stunned to learn about a study conducted by Middlemist, Knowles, and Matter (1976). What did Middlemist et al. do? They wondered whether invading people's personal space in a college men's room would cause arousal and in turn affect the timing of the observed men's urination (how long before they started urinating, and how long they spent urinating).

So they set up a situation in which males would enter a public restroom with three urinals and be forced to use the urinal on the left. This allowed for a situation in which there was a confederate either at the urinal right next to the study participant or one urinal away (a control condition was also used in which no one was present at a urinal when the participant entered the restroom). An observer positioned in a stall used a periscopic prism to view the stream of urine. Upon hearing of the periscope, I remember thinking, "Wait, what?! Can they do that?"

Sure, the results were interesting: invading people's personal space in the bathroom did affect how long it was before the men started urinating, and it affected the amount of time they spent urinating. But was this study ethical? Welcome to the chapter on ethics, where we'll review the specifics that govern

FIGURE 3.1 Can we conduct research in a men's room?

researchers' ethical responsibilities and answer the question, "Can they do that?"

A Brief History of Research Ethics

History is unfortunately littered with examples of research in which humans were subjected to gross mistreatment. Many suffered and even died as a result of such mistreatment. We'll consider a couple of these cases in an effort to illustrate how research ethics have evolved over time.

The Nuremberg Code

After World War II, physicians who had worked for the Nazis went on trial in Nuremberg, Germany for crimes committed against prisoners of war. The details of these crimes were horrific as these physicians deliberately tested the limits of human endurance. For example, they placed people in ice water to see how long it would take them to freeze to death. They shot people with poison bullets. They placed them in chambers that allowed the Nazis to test people's responses to high-altitude conditions (Harvard Law School Library: Nuremberg Trials Project). More specifically, according to the Nuremberg Medical Case Transcripts (1946), four experiments concerning high altitude conditions were conducted:

> a. slow descent without oxygen b. slow descent with oxygen c. falling without oxygen d. falling with oxygen. The latter two tests were designed to simulate a free fall from an airplane before the parachute opens. Several tests from time to time were conducted on the same experimental subject. (p. 156)

During this trial, the physicians' actions were condemned as unethical. Most of the physicians were sentenced to either death by hanging or life in prison. After the trial, a group of three judges who helped

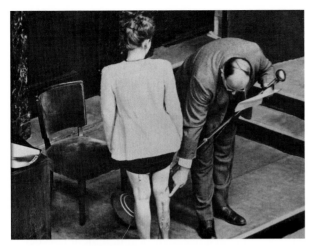

FIGURE 3.2 Nuremberg Trials, 1946: Dr. Leo Alexander presents an example of the effects of medical experimentation conducted on concentration camp prisoners.

The Nuremberg Code

1. The voluntary consent of the human subject is absolutely essential. This means that the person involved should have legal capacity to give consent; should be so situated as to be able to exercise free power of choice, without the intervention of any element of force, fraud, deceit, duress, overreaching, or other ulterior form of constraint or coercion; and should have sufficient knowledge and comprehension of the elements of the subject matter involved as to enable him to make an understanding and enlightened decision. This latter element requires that before the acceptance of an affirmative decision by the experimental subject there should be made known to him the nature, duration, and purpose of the experiment; the method and means by which it is to be conducted; all inconveniences and hazards reasonably to be expected; and the effects upon his health or person which may possibly come from his participation in the experiment.
    The duty and responsibility for ascertaining the quality of the consent rests upon each individual who initiates, directs or engages in the experiment. It is a personal duty and responsibility which may not be delegated to another with impunity.
2. The experiment should be such as to yield fruitful results for the good of society, unprocurable by other methods or means of study, and not random and unnecessary in nature.
3. The experiment should be so designed and based on the results of animal experimentation and a knowledge of the natural history of the disease or other problem under study that the anticipated results will justify the performance of the experiment.
4. The experiment should be so conducted as to avoid all unnecessary physical and mental suffering and injury.
5. No experiment should be conducted where there is an a priori reason to believe that death or disabling injury will occur; except, perhaps, in those experiments where the experimental physicians also serve as subjects.
6. The degree of risk to be taken should never exceed that determined by the humanitarian importance of the problem to be solved by the experiment.
7. Proper preparations should be made and adequate facilities provided to protect the experimental subject against even remote possibilities of injury, disability, or death.
8. The experiment should be conducted only by scientifically qualified persons. The highest degree of skill and care should be required through all stages of the experiment of those who conduct or engage in the experiment.
9. During the course of the experiment the human subject should be at liberty to bring the experiment to an end if he has reached the physical or mental state where continuation of the experiment seems to him to be impossible.
10. During the course of the experiment the scientist in charge must be prepared to terminate the experiment at any stage, if he has probable cause to believe, in the exercise of the good faith, superior skill, and careful judgment required of him, that a continuation of the experiment is likely to result in injury, disability, or death to the experimental subject.

FIGURE 3.3 The ten principles of the Nuremberg Code.

to prosecute the Nazi physicians worked together to create the Nuremberg Code (Shuster, 1997). The **Nuremberg Code**, drafted in 1947, is a set of ten ethical principles that must be fulfilled before medical experimentation can take place (Figure 3.3).

As you can see in principle 1 from the Nuremberg Code, consent to be a participant in experimentation must be voluntary, and the decision to consent must be made with knowledge of what the experimental procedure entails. This is what we refer to as **informed consent**. You will see evidence of this principle and others of the Nuremberg Code echoed in later ethics codes.

The Tuskegee Syphilis Study

The United States was not innocent of the mistreatment of research participants. A particularly egregious example began in Alabama in 1932. Six hundred poor Black men were recruited to be part of a research study run by the US Public Health Service and the Tuskegee Institute. Four hundred of the men had syphilis, a sexually transmitted disease that can cause a variety of symptoms including deafness, blindness, and heart disease. They were not told

they had syphilis, nor were they treated. Why not? The researchers wanted to learn about the short- and long-term effects of the disease, so they lied about the true purpose of the study … for 40 years. Even after a cure for syphilis became available, the men were not treated (Heller, 1972).

It wasn't until 1972 that the world at large became aware of the Tuskegee syphilis study. It had not been kept a secret; reports of the study had been in the medical literature, but information about it was not well known outside the medical community (Roberts, 2015). The study did have at least one early critic. Dr. Irwin Schatz read a 1964 article about the study and wrote to the article's author to register his objection. His letter read:

I am utterly astounded by the fact that physicians allow patients with potentially fatal disease to remain untreated when effective therapy is available. I assume you feel that the information which is extracted from observation of this untreated group is worth their sacrifice. If this is the case, then I suggest the United States Public Health Service and those physicians associated with it in this study need to re-evaluate their moral judgments in this regard.

Dr. Schatz's letter was never answered, but it was found by the *Wall Street Journal* years later, and news of the study started spreading through the popular media in 1972. In 2009, Dr. Schatz was awarded a Distinguished Alumni Award from the Mayo Clinic because of his willingness to take a stand against what he perceived to be a morally unjust investigation.

Knowledge of the Tuskegee Syphilis Study was a motivation behind another ethics code that was soon developed: The Belmont Report.

The Belmont Report

The **Belmont Report**, published in 1979, is particularly relevant to our discussion because it covers both biomedical and behavioral research (see the Report at or.org/pdf/BelmontReport.pdf). Developed by the National Commission for the Protection of Human Subjects of Biomedical and Behavioral Research (NCPHSBBR), the Belmont Report identified three primary ethical principles: (1) respect for persons, (2) beneficence, and (3) justice.

Respect for persons means individuals should be treated as "autonomous agents" (NCPHSBBR, 1979, p. 6). People who have **autonomy** are capable of considering and making a decision about whether to participate in research. The Belmont Report recognizes that some people have "diminished autonomy," and thus deserve protection (NCPHSBBR,

1979, p. 6). How do we determine how much protection is needed? We must weigh potential harm against potential benefits to research participants. There are no easy answers here. The protection needed can vary from person to person and from situation to situation.

Beneficence, the second principle in the Belmont Report, describes the act of doing good for others. In terms of research, this means the work should deliver benefits to individuals and/or to society as a whole. Beneficence is considered an obligation. Researchers must use their best judgment in order to maximize benefits and minimize harms. If the risk of harm is too great, the benefits should be forsaken.

Justice, the third principle, means fairness. In terms of research, who should benefit from research and who should "bear its burdens" (NCPHSBBR, 1979, p. 8)? The Belmont Report explicitly cites examples of the prisoners of war in Nazi Germany and the study participants in the Tuskegee Syphilis Study as examples of injustice. They bore the burden without reaping any of the benefits.

As you'll see in a moment, principles emphasized in the Belmont Report are also present in the American Psychological Association (APA) Ethics Code. We'll turn to this next.

General Principles of the American Psychological Association's Ethics Code

The American Psychological Association (APA) published its first set of ethics guidelines in 1953, just a few years after the Nuremberg Code was formulated. The APA code has been revised multiple times since then, and in it you'll recognize the spirit of both the Nuremberg Code and the Belmont Report. We'll pay special attention to this set of guidelines, for it is the one used most often by psychologists.

The APA set of guidelines for ethics is entitled "Ethical Principles of Psychologists and Code of

Conduct" (see APA, 2002; hereafter referred to as the "APA Ethics Code"). It contains five general principles as well as a set of ethical standards.

The general principles of the APA Ethics Code are "aspirational," not obligatory; their "intent is to guide and inspire psychologists toward the very highest ethical ideals of the profession" (APA, 2002, p. 1062). Let's briefly go over the essence of these principles. While I will pay special attention to their relevance to psychologists as researchers, recognize that we have a responsibility to be ethical in all our interactions, regardless of their nature.

Principle A: Beneficence and Nonmaleficence

"Psychologists strive to benefit those with whom they work and take care to do no harm" (APA, 2002, p. 1062).

As mentioned above, beneficence refers to doing good things for others, while **nonmaleficence** refers to not harming others. As researchers we must do what we can to ensure that we minimize the likelihood of harm and maximize the likelihood that our study participants and/or society members will benefit from our research. Psychologists also have opportunities to work with others as teachers and as clinicians, for example. This principle specifies that, for each of the groups we serve and for society as a whole, we should strive to help and not hurt.

Principle B: Fidelity and Responsibility

"Psychologists establish relationships of trust with those with whom they work. They are aware of their professional and scientific responsibilities to society and to the specific communities in which they work" (APA, 2002, p. 1062).

Fidelity refers to the idea that psychologists should behave in a trustworthy manner, being careful not to exploit or harm those with whom they come into contact. Fulfilling our responsibility to

give to society and to the communities in which we work can include giving a portion of our time to our field without any expectation of compensation. For example, a researcher can serve on the editorial board of a journal, review submissions for conferences, and evaluate applications for research grants.

Principle C: Integrity

"Psychologists seek to promote accuracy, honesty, and truthfulness in the science, teaching, and practice of psychology" (APA, 2002, p. 1062).

The principle of **integrity** dictates that psychologists need to be honest in all we do. We must not falsify or otherwise misrepresent our data. When it has been determined that researchers have falsified their data, publications that used these data are often withdrawn from the scientific literature (Jha, 2012). Any discussion of honesty must include a mention of the deception sometimes used in our research. This deception must be justified, and we have the responsibility to undo any harm that may come from the use of deception. We will have more to say about the role of deception in research later in the chapter.

Principle D: Justice

"Psychologists recognize that fairness and justice entitle all persons to access to and benefit from the contributions of psychology and to equal quality in the processes, procedures, and services being conducted by psychologists" (APA, 2002, p. 1062).

Those who conduct research in psychology often seek ways to help people lead better lives. Certainly, all people should have access to this knowledge so they can benefit from it. Glance at the APA's homepage online, for instance, and you'll see how the organization works to communicate knowledge to all those who seek it out (you might start at the lists of "topics" on this web page – see Figure 3.4). APA

All Psychology Topics

- Abortion
- Addictions
- ADHD
- Aging
- Alzheimer's
- Anger
- Anxiety
- Autism
- Bipolar Disorder
- Bullying
- Children
- Death & Dying
- Depression
- Disability
- Disasters
- Eating Disorders
- Education
- Emotional Health
- Environment
- Ethics

- Hate Crimes
- Health Disparities
- HIV & AIDS
- Human Rights
- Hypnosis
- Immigration
- Intelligence
- Kids & the Media
- Law & Psychology
- Learning & Memory
- Lesbian, Gay, Bisexual, Transgender
- Marriage & Divorce
- Miltary
- Money
- Obesity
- Pain
- Parenting
- Personality

- Post-traumatic Stress Disorder
- Race
- Safety & Design
- Schizophrenia
- Sex
- Sexual Abuse
- Shyness
- Sleep
- Socioeconomic Status
- Sport and Exercise
- Stress
- Suicide
- Teens
- Testing Issues
- Therapy
- Trauma
- Violence
- Women & Men
- Workplace Issues

FIGURE 3.4 The American Psychological Association's website provides the public with information on many psychology topics.

also has a Press Office that operates a newswire and puts out press releases pertaining to psychology topics of interest. Research findings from APA members are promoted through media outlets such as Facebook and Twitter. Even with all this outreach, psychological research benefits are likely not available to all. Some communities do not have easy access to the Internet or to clinicians who can aid them. The principle of justice calls upon psychologists to continue to work to make psychology and its benefits available to all.

Principle E: Respect for People's Rights and Dignity

"Psychologists respect the dignity and worth of all people, and the rights of individuals to privacy, confidentiality, and self-determination. Psychologists are aware that special safeguards may be necessary to protect the rights and welfare of persons or communities whose vulnerabilities impair autonomous decision making. Psychologists are aware of and respect cultural, individual, and role differences, including those based on age, gender, gender identity, race, ethnicity, culture, national origin, religion, sexual orientation, disability, language, and socioeconomic status, and consider these factors when working with members of such groups. Psychologists try to eliminate the effect on their work of biases based on those factors, and they do not knowingly participate in or condone activities of others based upon such prejudices" (APA, 2002, p. 1063).

This principle emphasizes the fact that all people have worth and the right to determine the course of their lives. With regard to research, this means people have the right to choose whether to participate in a research study, and if they do, to be able to be sure of privacy and confidentiality. We must not disclose any information about our study participants that could put them at risk or damage their reputation. Researchers also need to take special steps to honor the rights of those whose ability to make their own decisions is limited (such as children and prisoners).

As you can see, according to the General Principles of the APA Ethics Code, those working within the field of psychology are expected to exemplify the highest standards of professional behavior (Fig. 3.5).

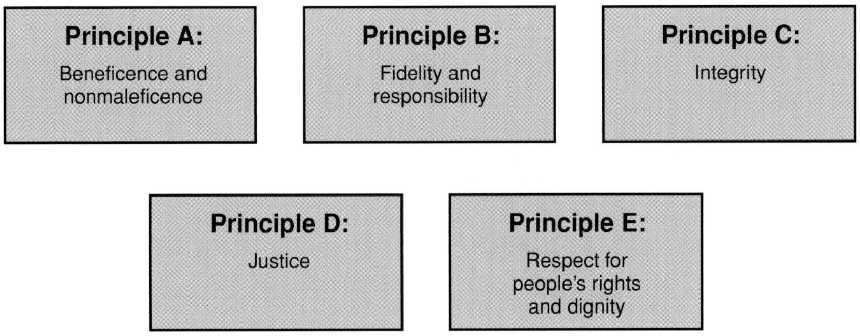

Principle A:	Principle B:	Principle C:
Beneficence and nonmaleficence	Fidelity and responsibility	Integrity

Principle D:	Principle E:
Justice	Respect for people's rights and dignity

FIGURE 3.5 General principles of the American Psychological Association's Ethics Code.

Ethical Standards of the American Psychological Association's Ethics Code: Research

Unlike the General Principles of the APA Ethics Code, the APA Ethical Standards are not merely aspirational; these are specific and mandatory rules of conduct. Being a student affiliate or a member of the APA means you must comply with these Standards for all your professional activities. Violation can mean a public announcement of the termination of your APA membership, with far-reaching consequences. Below I'll tell you what you need to know to do your research responsibly and within the guidelines of the APA Ethics Code. Note that the APA Ethics Code also considers many topics beyond the scope of this text (such as record keeping).

Obtain Institutional Approval

Virtually every university or college has at least one **Institutional Review Board** (IRB) responsible for reviewing all the research conducted by the people at that institution (an IRB may be university- or college-wide, or different departments may have their own IRBs). Any college, university, or other type of organization receiving federal funding for research *must* have an IRB. Before any research project begins, the researcher has to submit information about the proposed research to the relevant IRB and obtain the

board's approval. The IRB can approve, disapprove, or ask for modifications to a project. What kind of information do you submit to the IRB? Typically, you will provide a description of the proposed research project, information about how you will recruit study participants, and what you will tell participants prior to their participation (your informed consent form).

The members of the IRB will examine all your materials and evaluate whether the benefits of the study outweigh the physical, psychological, or other risk to your participants. If there is little or no risk to your study participants (as with anonymous questionnaires), your research is likely to be granted an expedited review or considered exempt from review.

Avoid Harm

According to the current APA Ethics Code, "psychologists take reasonable steps to avoid harming their clients/patients, students, supervisees, research participants, organizational clients, and others with whom they work, and to minimize harm when it is foreseeable and unavoidable" (APA, 2002, p. 1065).

To illustrate how we think about harm today, let's first look at a little history in the field of psychology. As mentioned above, the APA published its first Ethics Code in 1953, when the potential for harm was presented differently than it is today. For example, the 1958 Code said the following: "Only when a problem is significant and can be investigated in no other way is the psychologist justified in giving misinformation to research subjects or exposing research subjects to physical or emotional stress. When the possibility of serious aftereffects exists, research is conducted only when the subject or their responsible agents are fully informed of this possibility and volunteer nevertheless" (APA, 1958, p. 271). So you can see that, historically, exposing research participants (they used to be called "subjects") to physical or emotional stress was considered potentially justifiable.

About a decade after the first APA Ethics Code was developed, Stanley Milgram conducted a study on obedience that challenged some people's views of what could reasonably be done in the name of psychological science. Let's take a look at Milgram's (1963) work, and then we'll look at a current-day variation on it (Burger 2009) to see how one researcher changed an investigative approach to stay in line with current ethical standards.

Milgram (1963) began his investigation into people's willingness to obey authority in part because he was attempting to understand the Holocaust and how millions of people could have been murdered on command. But obedience is an issue that confronts us all. We are socialized to respond to the commands of those in authority: parents, teachers, and law enforcement officers, to name a few. So Milgram decided to study the issue systematically, to see just how far people would go as a result of the commands of another.

In each study session of his first experiment, a male participant was teamed up with a male confederate, and through a rigged drawing the participant was always assigned the role of "teacher" and the confederate the role of "learner." Both were told the research was designed as a study of the "effects of punishment on memory" (p. 372). The teacher was to test the learner on a series of word association lists and for each wrong answer administer an increasingly more severe electric shock. The learner was then led to an adjoining room where the teacher

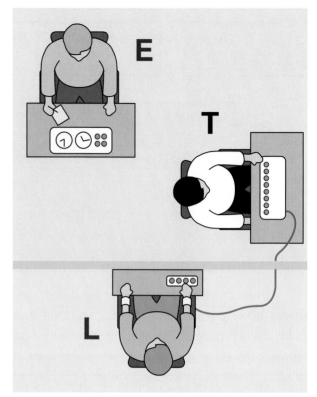

FIGURE 3.6 In this version of Milgram's experiment, the teacher (T) and the experimenter (E) are in one room, while the learner (L) is in another.

watched as the learner was seated and had his arms fastened down and his wrist attached to an electrode. Both the teacher and the learner were then told that "although the shocks can be extremely painful, they cause no permanent tissue damage" (p. 373). The test began, and the learner, now out of the teacher's sight, could be heard from the adjoining room, complaining bitterly when shocked.

However, unknown to the teacher, the errors were preplanned and the *learner never received a shock.* The learner had slipped the shock generator apparatus off as soon as the teacher exited the room, and a tape player was providing standardized auditory responses, so that every study participant heard the same responses from the learner.

If at any point the teacher expressed an interest in stopping the delivery of shocks, the researcher (another confederate) urged the teacher to continue. The researcher, in fact, made a series of "prods" (such as, "It is absolutely essential that you continue") each time the teacher expressed unwillingness. The study session was terminated early only if the teacher refused to obey after being prodded four times. How many of the 40 participants in this study delivered the severest shock (450 volts)? Sixty-five percent. Milgram (1974) later did a study with 40 females and found the results were the same.

Milgram provided additional information about this study in his 1974 book on obedience. For example, he indicated that the learner did not voice any discomfort until the 75-volt shock was delivered. The vocal response increased in intensity with each shock delivery such that, by 150 volts, the teacher could hear the learner screaming, "Experimenter, get me out of here! I won't be in the experiment any more! I refuse to go on!" (p. 23). At 300 volts, the learner screamed that he would stop responding to the test questions. The researcher informed the teacher that no response from the learner was considered a wrong answer, and the teacher was told to continue to shock the learner for wrong answers. At 315 volts the learner just screamed. After 330 volts, the learner no longer responded in any way. He no longer pounded on the wall, grunted, screamed, or complained about his heart problem.

Picture yourself in this situation. The learner in the next room has been complaining with each shock and now he is no longer making a sound. What would you think had happened? I would probably believe I had killed him or at least rendered him unconscious.

The reason I'm bringing up Milgram's work is to talk about physical and psychological harm. In fact, the participants who were playing the role of learner seemed quite distressed over the delivery of the shocks. Milgram's (1963) words summarize this distress well:

In a large number of cases the degree of tension reached extremes that are rarely seen in sociopsychological laboratory studies. Subjects were observed to sweat, tremble, stutter, bite their lips, groan, and dig their fingernails into their flesh ... Full-blown, uncontrollable seizures were observed for 3 subjects. On one occasion we observed a seizure so violently convulsive that it was necessary to call a halt to the experiment. (p. 375)

Think about what these participants experienced. Would you consider this physical harm? Psychological harm? Some certainly did; in fact, Milgram was criticized for the harm inflicted using these procedures (see Baumrind, 1964). From the early 1960s until the early 1970s, Milgram went on to complete many studies of obedience using this basic procedure (Milgram, 1974). However, things were about to change.

In 1973, the APA published an Ethics Code that covered research issues more comprehensively. Now harm was considered differently, as you can see in the following passage:

The ethical investigator protects participants from physical and mental discomfort, harm and danger. If the risk of such consequences exists, the investigator is required to inform the participant of that fact, to secure consent before proceeding, and to take all possible measures to minimize distress. A research procedure may not be used if it is likely to cause serious and lasting harm to participants. (APA, 1973, p. 79)

After the 1973 publication of the APA Ethics Code, use of Milgram's research procedure dropped off (Blass, 2009). That is, until Burger (2009) came up with a clever way to use the same approach in an ethically appropriate manner. Burger realized that a majority (79%) of the participants in Milgram's (1963) study who went beyond the 150-volt shock continued all the way to the 450-volt maximum shock. Thus, in Burger's (2009) study, participants did not have the option to go beyond the 150-volt shock. Instead Burger assumed that those who delivered a 150-volt shock would likely have delivered a 450-volt shock under Milgram's conditions.

This means Burger's participants experienced only a minimal amount of stress, quite different from that documented by Milgram (1963). As an additional safeguard, Burger had his study participants pre-screened to help ensure that those prone to anxiety and depression would not be a part of the sample.[1]

Given the similarities between Burger's and Milgram's procedures, we can compare their results. So what was the outcome of Burger's study? Think about it for a moment. Do you think study participants would be just as likely to obey authority now as they were in the 1960s? In fact, Burger's results were basically the same as Milgram's. In addition, just as Milgram found, there were no significant differences between the obedience rates for males and females. Thus, both researchers answered very important questions. Milgram demonstrated that humans have a very powerful tendency to obey authority, and that ordinary people are capable of hurting others when commanded to do so. Burger's work, in line with the current-day Ethics Code, minimized the amount of harm to which his participants were exposed while demonstrating that Milgram's results are not limited to the time in which he did his work.

The APA Ethics Code has changed over time with regard to the consideration of harm. Milgram's original procedure could not be used today because of the potential physical and psychological harm to its participants. However, Burger demonstrated that it is possible to use an altered version of Milgram's procedure to study obedience while allowing for the protection of research participants.

Maintain Confidentiality

"Psychologists have a primary obligation and take reasonable precautions to protect confidential information obtained through or stored in any medium" (APA, 2002, p. 1066).

Confidentiality means the identity of participants will not be released without their consent, and their study responses will not be linked to their identities. Your participants may have provided information they do not want those outside the research team to know, and if you do not protect their confidentiality you may be putting them at risk. Consider, for example, the research conducted by White, Becker-Blease, and Grace-Bishop (2006). They were interested in finding out about potential abuse of stimulants among college students at their University. They found that over 16% of respondents indicated they misused or abused stimulants (typically Ritalin), in that they had not been diagnosed with a disorder requiring this medication nor did they have a prescription for the drug. You can imagine these participants would not want parents, employers, or law enforcement officers to know about their abuse of medication. The authors were thus appropriately careful to protect their participants. The surveys

---

1 You might be wondering whether it is appropriate to compare Burger's (2009) study and Milgram's (1963) study in light of the fact that Burger prescreened and then excluded some participants who might be prone to depression and anxiety. It is a reasonable question. Perhaps the results would have been different in Burger's study had he not excluded these participants. It was ethically responsible for Burger to exclude them, however, and while it is difficult to know for sure whether including them would have changed the results, it appears the answer is no. For example, these participants did answer several questions before they were excluded, and Burger compared this information to answers from his final sample. He found no differences between those excluded and those included in terms of various demographic variables (gender, education, age) or personality variables (empathic concern). The similarities between those excluded and those included in the sample suggest the results would likely have been the same.

were answered anonymously, and the participants' **anonymity** meant that even the researchers did not know a participant's identity. In this case, the authors even removed from the dataset the Internet provider (IP) addresses of all online responses, so there was no way to identify the computer that sent them.

In summary, you must protect your participants' confidential information either by refraining from asking for identifying information, or at least by keeping all identifying information separate from the research data.

Obtain Informed Consent

In almost all cases (except in circumstances such as those discussed below), psychological researchers have to obtain informed consent from their participants before the study can begin. By giving it, participants acknowledge they have been provided with enough information about the study to make a decision about whether to participate. Usually they read over an informed consent form, which must be written in clearly understandable language, and sign it. The APA Ethics Code details exactly what information needs to be provided on the form.

When obtaining informed consent …
psychologists inform participants about (1)
the purpose of the research, expected duration,
and procedures; (2) their right to decline to
participate and to withdraw from the research
once participation has begun; (3) the foreseeable
consequences of declining or withdrawing;
(4) reasonably foreseeable factors that may
be expected to influence their willingness to
participate such as potential risks, discomfort,
or adverse effects; (5) any prospective research
benefits; (6) limits of confidentiality; (7)
incentives for participation; and (8) whom to
contact for questions about the research and
research participants' rights. (APA, 2002, p. 1069)

As you can see from the sample in Figure 3.7, the current APA Ethics Code is fairly specific about the type of information you need to include in your informed consent form. However, you do have some leeway in the *level* of specificity. For example, you need to provide information about the purpose of your study, but you can phrase this in very general terms. Let's go over a specific example.

Olson, Barefoot, and Strickland (1976) told their study participants they were interested in "impression formation in surveillance situations" (p. 585). This was indeed true, but it was a very general statement of their interests. Here's what the researchers did. They had male college students follow a female around in public, telling some of the males that the female was randomly selected to be followed and was unaware of being watched ("covert surveillance"). They told others that the female was a confederate who knew she was being watched ("overt surveillance"). A third group of males just watched a videotape of the female ("inactive") as she completed preplanned public activities. In all cases, however, the female was a confederate completing preplanned public activities.

Now while impression formation of the person under surveillance was indeed of interest, what the researchers did not reveal until the experimental session was over was that the nature of the surveillance was expected to influence the participants' impression of the woman being watched. Specifically, they hypothesized that secretive surveillance would be experienced as exciting and positive, while observers who thought the woman knew she was being watched would experience more negative emotions; in both cases, these emotions were expected to influence the observers' impressions of their targets.

Olson et al.'s hypotheses were not part of the informed consent form. We typically do not reveal our hypotheses to participants before the research, because that information may affect their thoughts,

FIGURE 3.7 Sample informed consent form.

You are being invited to participate in research being conducted by Dr. Wendy Heath of Rider University.

Purpose of the study:
This study is designed to study juror decision making.

Risks involved in the study:
There are no known risks involved in participating in this research. This study received approval from the Rider University Human Subjects Committeee in September, 2016.

Benefits involved in the study:
This brief questionnaire will help us understand how individual jurors view someone who is on trial.

What will be asked of you:
You will be asked to read a brief scenario and to answer a series of questions. Overall, participation in this study should take no more than twenty minutes.

Your rights as a participant:
Your participation is completely voluntary, and you may choose to end the study at any time without penalty. If you have any questions or concerns you may contact: Dr Wendy Heath at heath@rider.edu.

Confidentiality and anonymity:
Your identity will remain anonymous. Your responses will never be matched to your identity, and no one will know how you personally chose to answer any of the questions.

Incentive:
In exchange for your participation in this study, you will receive extra credit for a Rider University psychology class of your choice.

I understand the above stated procedure, and I agree to participate in this study.

Signature _____ Date: _____

feelings, and/or behaviors. Participants may act the way they think you want them to, but this isn't what we want; we want natural behavior. If we reveal our hypotheses prior to the study, we may risk the presence of demand characteristics. **Demand characteristics** are cues in the study that inform the participants about its true purpose and hypotheses. We often conceal our hypotheses until the debriefing at the end of the study session so that we can avoid demand characteristics (more about debriefing below).

So what did Olson et al. find? The participants in the three different conditions did indeed experience different emotions. Those who just watched a videotape of the female's behavior reported being bored, while those taking part in the overt-surveillance task felt uneasy. The participants who covertly watched a female found the process relatively high in both thrill and aversion. Participants' impressions of the person being observed were affected too; the woman was seen more negatively when she was overtly watched.

Olson et al. gave participants a vague purpose statement prior to the start of their study. Sometimes researchers will not just be vague but will provide a misleading statement about the purpose of the study prior to the start of the study session. This kind of statement is a form of deception known as a **cover story**. You would use a cover story if providing the true purpose of the study is likely to change people's behavior; we'll discuss this further when we talk about deception below. You can provide a misleading statement of your purpose as long as you are not leaving out details that would be important to someone's decision to participate. You still need to give people enough information so they can make an informed decision.

In some situations psychological researchers will not obtain informed consent from their study participants. Picture a situation in which you are conducting a naturalistic observation study of hand-washing at a college men's room. Now imagine that before walking into that college restroom, your study participants were met at the door and asked whether they would be willing to participate in a study in which they would be monitored to see whether they wash their hands after using the bathroom. What do you think would happen? If anyone chooses to stay and use the facilities, his knowledge that he is being watched might likely affect the results. So that's not ideal. Therefore, should informed consent be collected in this case? What does the current APA Ethics Code say about this?

Psychologists may dispense with informed consent only (1) where research would not reasonably be assumed to create distress

or harm and involves (a) the study of normal educational practices, curricula, or classroom management methods conducted in educational settings; (b) only anonymous questionnaires, naturalistic observations, or archival research for which disclosure of responses would not place participants at risk of criminal or civil liability or damage their financial standing, employability, or reputation, and confidentiality is protected. (APA, 2002, pp. 1069–1070)

Let's consider my example given these guidelines. Could this hand-washing study reasonably be assumed to cause distress or harm? It is difficult to imagine how knowing whether college students wash their hands could cause distress or harm. In addition, this naturalistic observation study would likely not put the students at risk for legal action or damage their financial standing, employability, or reputation, especially given that their identities were not known. Thus, it seems feasible that obtaining informed consent is not necessary in this situation.

Sometimes you may wish to work with people who are not able to give valid consent to participate in your study. Children are not legally allowed, and are not considered cognitively able, to make such decisions. In this situation, informed consent must be obtained from the participants' parents or legal guardians. In addition, minors who can read can also sign a form to consent to research; the agreement by a minor is called **assent**. The language on a research assent form is much simpler (2nd–3rd grade level) than the language on an informed consent form (6th–8th grade level). For more information about ethical guidelines relevant to work with children, consult the Society for Research in Child Development (SRCD) (see www.srcd.org/about-us/ethical-standards-research). The SRCD's guidelines include many of the concepts considered in this chapter.

FIGURE 3.8 Before children can participate in psychological research, informed consent must be obtained from their parents or legal guardians. In addition, children who can read can sign an assent form to consent to their participation.

Respect Client/Patient, Student, and Subordinate Research Participants

A portion of the APA Ethics Code addresses research participation from a different perspective:

1. *When psychologists conduct research with client/patients, students, or subordinates as participants, psychologists take steps to protect the prospective participants from adverse consequences of declining or withdrawing from participation.*
2. *When research participation is a course requirement or an opportunity for extra credit, the prospective participant is given the choice of equitable alternative activities.* (APA, 2002, p. 1069)

As you can see, our prospective research participants have the right to decline participation or withdraw from participation at any point during the study without being penalized. This information is typically included in the informed consent form.

The second prong of this section of the Code acknowledges that research is often conducted with psychology undergraduates who are seeking to fulfill a class requirement or earn extra credit for a psychology class. These students should be given a reasonable substitute (such as summarizing a journal article) if they choose not to participate and should not be penalized in any way.

Offer Inducements for Research Participation

The APA Ethics Code recognizes that study participants can be offered inducements (extra class credit, money) but advises that "psychologists make reasonable efforts to avoid offering excessive or inappropriate financial or other inducements for research participation when such inducements are likely to coerce participation" (APA, 2002, p. 1070).

Think about it this way. If a researcher is offering $600 in exchange for your participation in a one-hour research study, you might find it difficult to turn this offer down. The inducement would be considered excessive and thus coercive. In this situation you would not likely give careful consideration to the details in the informed consent form (such as the potential risks involved in the research). All you would concentrate on is that money. We can offer money or extra credit in exchange for participation, but the amount should not be excessive.

Handle Deception Appropriately

The use of deception in research is controversial; some believe it should never be practiced (for example, see Ortmann & Hertwig, 1997). But in fact, a lot of social research does include deception in some form (see Sieber, Iannuzzo, & Rodriguez, 1995), research participants don't seem to mind the deception (Christensen, 1988), and deception is allowed by the APA Ethics Code as long as you adhere to certain guidelines. Using a confederate and presenting a cover story are two relatively common forms of deception. Basically, if you withhold some information from your study participants (lying by omission) or you intentionally deceive them (lying by commission), you are using deception.

Let's talk more about using a confederate in research. Both Middlemist et al. (1976) and Olson et al. (1976) used confederates in their work. For Middlemist et al. the confederate just stood at a randomly selected urinal. For Olson et al., the confederate conducted some pre-planned activities while being observed. In both cases, the confederates followed scripts, providing the experimental situation with the needed actions, but they did not interact with the study participants. In many cases, however (such as Milgram's study), confederates do. Let's go over another example now.

Swim and Hyers (1999) investigated how women would react when they encountered sexism. They asked groups to discuss who would be best suited for survival on a deserted island, but in each group, only one woman was a true study participant. The other group members were male or female confederates (some groups had three male confederates, while other groups had two female confederates and one male confederate). In each group, one of the male confederates either made three sexist remarks (such as "I think we need more women on the island to keep the men satisfied") or three non-sexist remarks ("I think we need more entertainers on the island to keep everyone happy" p. 73). The other confederates did not respond to these remarks. Would the true study participant object to the sexist remarks? In fact, 45% of the women confronted the "sexist" male in some way, although only 16% directly addressed the inappropriateness of the comment (in the non-sexist condition, only 14% of target remarks drew comments).

In all the research we've reviewed that incorporated confederates, their use had definite advantages. If you want to know how study participants will react to the words and behaviors of others in a live interaction, the only way to standardize the words and behavior of others is to use confederates. Think of the research Olson et al. conducted. Olson et al. expected that the manner in which the confederate was watched (covertly, overtly, on tape) would affect participants' feelings about the experience and in turn their impression about the person being watched. But imagine that one person being watched goes shopping while another visits a grave site. These two situations might reasonably affect the thoughts and feelings of the observer differently. The only way to ensure that each participant experiences the same sequence of events is to plan it ahead of time with an experimenter's accomplice.

Let's also spend a few moments talking about deception in the form of a cover story. When researchers are concerned that participants' knowledge of the true purpose of a study could alter the results of the study, they'll often use a cover story to mask that true purpose. We saw that Milgram (1963) used a cover story in his work on obedience. He claimed he was interested in "what effect different people have on each other as teachers and learners, and also what effect punishment will have on learning" (p. 373). Milgram felt a cover story was necessary to explain why electric shock needed to be administered. If his study participants had known his true purpose was to determine how far someone would go to obey the commands of another, their responses may likely have been different.

Here's another example of researchers using a cover story. Hermans, Engles, Larsen, and Herman (2009) were interested in whether the number of M&Ms undergraduate women would eat could be influenced by how much someone else in the room (a confederate) eats and by how sociable that someone else is. Clearly, it would not be advisable to inform the study participants, prior to their participation, that the purpose of the experiment was to observe how much they ate. So Hermans et al. used

Table 3.1   The average number of M&Ms consumed by participants in Hermans et al.'s (2009) experiment.

	Low-intake confederate	High-intake confederate
	Mean	Mean
Sociable confederate	6.58	5.68
Unsociable confederate	2.14	10.63

Source: Adapted from Hermans, R. C. J., Engels, R. C. M. E., Larsen, J. K., & Herman, C. P. (2009). Modeling of palatable food intake. The influence of quality of social interaction. *Appetite, 52*, 801–804. doi:http://dx.doi.org/10.1016/j.appet.2009.03.008.

a cover story, telling the study participants they were there to evaluate movie trailers. After meeting the experimenter and the confederate, participants were instructed to individually evaluate three movie trailers, and then the participant and confederate took a break together in a room. It was during this break that the confederate socialized (or didn't socialize) with the study participant, while eating a lot or a few M&Ms (notice that evaluating the movie trailers didn't matter at all). So what happened? The research participants ate more when exposed to a confederate who ate more, but only when the confederate was antisocial. See Table 3.1.

What does the APA Ethics Code say about the use of deception?

1. *Psychologists do not conduct a study involving deception unless they have determined that the use of deceptive techniques is justified by the study's significant prospective scientific, educational, or applied value and that effective nondeceptive alternative procedures are not feasible.*

2. *Psychologists do not deceive prospective participants about research that is reasonably*

expected to cause physical pain or severe emotional distress.

3. *Psychologists explain any deception … as early as feasible, preferably at the conclusion of their participation, but not later than at the conclusion of the data collection, and permit participants to withdraw their data. (APA, 2002, p. 1070)*

Let's consider each of these points in turn. The APA Ethics Code indicates that psychologists do not use deception unless they have determined its use is justified. Thus, researchers and the IRB have the responsibility of weighing the costs of deception against the potential benefits of the research.

Middlemist, Knowles, and Matter (1977) provided a wonderful glimpse into the process of a cost-benefit analysis when they wrote about this for their 1976 experiment (in response to Koocher's [1977] criticism of their study). In order to evaluate the potential for distress or harm in their experiment, Middlemist et al. conducted a pilot test. As you recall from Chapter 1, a pilot test is a trial run of a study, conducted prior to the start of the actual study. In their pilot test, Middlemist et al. informed a small sample of men that a confederate had recorded their urine activity in the restroom. When questioned, the participants revealed that they were not bothered by this at all because urinating next to others in a public space is commonplace. Middlemist et al. thus concluded that their study (including the deception) would not cause their participants distress or harm. Thus, the costs here seemed low.

And the benefits? The authors saw merit in adding to the literature a well-controlled field study of the effects of personal space violations on arousal and its impact on a bodily function. Ultimately, it is up to the researchers and their IRB to weigh the benefits and the costs against each other when deciding whether to proceed with research (though the results of this analysis are not often provided in the resulting publication, especially in the amount of detail given by Middlemist et al., 1977).

The first prong of the APA Ethics Code's notes on deception indicates that deception can be used if justified (as described above) and if effective nondeceptive alternative procedures are not feasible. We address this next.

Some have proposed that the use of alternate procedures is preferable to deceiving study participants (for example, Baumrind, 1985). One suggested procedure is role-playing (see Miller, 1972). In this method, the researcher describes a situation to participants and then asks, "If you were in this situation, how would you react?"

Take Olson et al.'s study on surveillance as an example and substitute role-playing for deception. Recall that participants who covertly watched a female found the process relatively high in both thrill and aversion. Would they have known how they truly would feel without actually experiencing the situation of interest? Perhaps they wouldn't expect the process to be thrilling; maybe the thrilling nature of the experience came as a surprise to those who actually experienced it.

Many researchers do not consider role-playing a reasonable substitute for deception. It can be difficult to know how you would react to a situation, and just thinking about it probably won't affect you as much as actually experiencing it. And if the researcher is not using deception, the true purpose of the study and its hypotheses are more likely to be obvious. Then participants may just say what they think the researcher wants to hear. Again, as researchers we don't want people to tell us what they think we want to hear; we want to know how they would really respond given the situation in question.

The second prong of the APA Ethics Code with regard to deception indicates that "psychologists do not deceive prospective participants about research that is reasonably expected to cause physical pain or severe emotional distress" (APA, 2002, p. 1070). This is self-explanatory; you cannot use deception to hide information that could reasonably affect someone's willingness to participate.

The third prong of the APA Ethics Code with regard to deception refers to researchers' responsibility to explain why deception was used. This is part of the debriefing process (explained below). The APA Ethics Code recommends that debriefing occur as early as possible, and that participants be given an opportunity to remove their responses from the dataset if they prefer.

In summary, psychologists do sometimes use deception, when they have determined it is justified and when there is no reasonable alternative. Debriefing, which we turn to next, gives us the needed opportunity to "come clean" with our participants and reveal why the deception was necessary.

Debrief

Here is what the APA Ethics Code has to say about debriefing:

1. *Psychologists provide a prompt opportunity for participants to obtain appropriate information about the nature, results, and conclusions of the research, and they take reasonable steps to correct any misconceptions that participants may have of which the psychologists are aware.*
2. *If scientific or humane values justify delaying or withholding this information, psychologists take reasonable measures to reduce the risk of harm.*
3. *When psychologists become aware that research procedures have harmed a participant, they take reasonable steps to minimize the harm. (APA, 2002, p. 1070)*

As you can see from the APA Ethics Code, we have a responsibility to debrief our study participants. During **debriefing**, you reveal the true purpose of the study and your hypotheses. You also give participants an opportunity to ask any questions they may have. This is an opportunity to educate.

If there was deception in the study, you need to reveal its nature and explain why it was necessary. In addition, you should assess whether the study participants "bought" the deception. For example, if there was a cover story or if confederates were part of your study, determine if the participants suspected that they were being deceived. If so, this perception may have altered their behavior, and for this reason data from suspicious participants are typically not included in the final dataset. For example, in Olson et al.'s surveillance study, one of the participants "voiced suspicion of the randomness of the choice of target," so the data from this participant was discarded (p. 584). This was a reasonable thing to do because his feelings about the task may have been affected by his suspicions. Note that it would be inappropriate to look at this person's responses in order to decide whether to discard them – you must decide without knowledge of the data.

If you use deception in your work, you should also take the time to make sure your study participants do not feel bad for falling for your deception. Explain why you designed the study the way you did and reassure your participants that others responded as they did.

Another potential component of the debriefing is to swear your participants to secrecy. This is especially important when you have used deception in your research and you are testing participants who may know each other (such as undergraduates at the same school). Explain to your participants that knowledge of the study's true purpose before taking part in the study could affect someone's responses,

FIGURE 3.9 Researcher debriefing a participant.

and thus you are asking them to keep the details of the study from others who might also be participants. Diener, Matthews, and Smith (1972) found that most of the participants who were sworn to secrecy did, in fact, comply. An alternative to this approach is to choose to debrief all participants after the entire study has been completed, as opposed to debriefing individuals after each session.

The APA Ethics Code says if you become aware that your research has harmed someone, you need to take reasonable steps to minimize this harm. Make sure you are prepared in case this happens. You can provide a debriefing sheet with contact information for a therapist, sexual abuse counselor, or other professional (depending on the topic of your study), in addition to the contact information for the researcher in charge of the study. Your study participants should leave feeling as good as or better than when they arrived. Milgram (1963) appreciated this need in his obedience study; he stated that "procedures were undertaken to assure that the subject would leave the laboratory in a state of well-being" (p. 374).

Finally, there are situations in which debriefing is not recommended. Let's look at a study by Monk-Turner et al. (2005) as an illustration. Monk-Turner et al. observed people's hand-washing behavior in three restrooms at a large university. They wondered

FIGURE 3.10 If the participants' behavior is public and within the realm of their everyday experiences (such as hand washing in a public restroom), then debriefing is not necessary.

whether this behavior would vary by race, gender, and whether anyone else was present. Here's how it worked. For a three-week period, the researchers collected data. All those who came into a target restroom and used the toilet were observed to see whether and for how long they washed their hands (and whether they used soap).

Monk-Turner et al. did not expect to find differences in hand-washing behavior as a function of race, nor did they. However, they did expect and did find that more females (89%) washed their hands than males (69%); women also used soap more often than men. On the other hand, very few people overall washed their hands for the 15 seconds or more recommended by the Centers for Disease Control and Prevention. Having an observer present made no difference in the percentage of participants who washed their hands.

Now let's examine the question of debriefing. What do you think? Should Monk-Turner et al.'s research participants have been debriefed? In fact, they were not. Why not? If your debriefing would cause distress (perhaps participants would have been embarrassed that they did not wash their hands), and if the participants' behavior is within the realm of their everyday experiences (hand-washing in a public restroom is a common activity), then debriefing is not necessary.

Treat Research Animals Humanely

While the research covered in this text has humans as its focus, I do want to take a moment to talk about animals. According to the APA Committee on Animal Research and Ethics, only about 7–8% of psychology research involves animals, mostly rats, mice, and pigeons. For some researchers the goal is to learn about the capabilities of other species. For example, a few decades ago, there was a heightened quest to determine whether animals were capable of language (see Hixon, 1998 for a review). For others, the goal is to study animals in an effort to shed light on how to improve the human experience. For example, consider the recent review by Kumar, Aakriti, and Gupta (2016) on the use of animals in the search for effective therapies for those who have suffered a stroke.

The APA Ethics Code also has guidelines for humane animal care and use. Specifically, this Ethics Code covers how animals should be treated; all reasonable efforts are made to "minimize the discomfort, infection, illness and pain of animal subjects" (p. 11). Furthermore, animals are not subjected to any discomfort unless an alternative procedure is not feasible and the goal of the research is justified. The APA Ethics Code also acknowledges the importance of specific training for those working with animals.

Ethical Standards of the American Psychological Association's Ethics Code: Publication

Report Research Results

So far we've discussed the ethics pertinent to conducting research. The APA Ethics Code also covers the reporting of research results.

1. *Psychologists do not fabricate data …*
2. *If psychologists discover significant errors in their published data, they take reasonable steps to correct such errors in a correction, retraction, erratum, or other appropriate publication means. (APA, 2002, p. 1070)*

Again, this is pretty self-explanatory. We do not make up data, and if we find that we've made a significant error in something that has already been published, we inform the editor of the journal that published the article. The editor may then publish a very brief follow-up piece to identify and correct the error.

Avoid Plagiarism

The APA Ethics Code states the following: "psychologists do not present portions of another's work or data as their own, even if the other work or data source is cited occasionally" (APA, 2002, p. 1070).

There are many different ways to plagiarize, but they all have one feature in common: They consist of presenting another person's work as your own. Let's go over a couple of examples.

If you copy someone else's work directly by using his or her exact words without giving the author credit for that work, you are plagiarizing. How do you fix this so that you are not plagiarizing? You use quotation marks around your source's exact words and give credit to the source (list the original source's author(s) and year the material was published, and for exact quotes the page number(s) where the information is located).

For example, let's say I am writing a paper on how violations of personal space can affect biological functions, and I want to cite the purpose of Middlemist et al.'s (1976) work. Middlemist et al. wrote as follows: "The following experiment was conducted to test the hypothesis that decreases in interpersonal distance lead to arousal as evidenced by increases in micturition delay and decreases in micturition

persistence" (Middlemist et al., 1976, p. 543). Note that I did not plagiarize this work. I used quotation marks to indicate that the words were not mine, *and* I cited the source of this information (authors' last names, year of publication, and the page number where you can find these exact words).

In general, you want to use quoted material sparingly. Why? Think about it this way. Picture a student who is so fearful of plagiarism that she puts virtually her entire paper in quotes, each time citing the sources of the material. She hasn't actually written the paper; in essence, she's taken a typing test ("let's see how well I can copy this material"). So only quote someone when the words in the original source are so special that you can't think of another way to express the thought or when you decide for another reason to maintain the exact words (I'm doing the latter when I quote from the APA Ethics Code in this chapter because I think it is important for you to know exactly how the APA Ethics Code represents the issues of interest). In all other cases, the ideal situation is to **paraphrase**, that is, to put the information in your own words *and* cite the source of the information.

Now let's take Middlemist et al.'s (1976) example from above and paraphrase it. Again, here are Middlemist et al.'s exact words: "The following experiment was conducted to test the hypothesis that decreases in interpersonal distance lead to arousal as evidenced by increases in micturition delay and decreases in micturition persistence." When you want to paraphrase, you must put the information in your own words, not just substitute a few words here and there. So to paraphrase the above sentence, I have decided to write: *In a field observation study, Middlemist et al. (1976) sought to determine whether decreases in personal space in a men's restroom can create arousal in people. They measured the effects of arousal by timing how long it takes for urination to begin and how long the urination process lasts.*

Table 3.2 Examples of original sources and acceptable paraphrasing.

Source of the information	Original source's exact words	Paraphrase
Schwab, Cullum, and Harton, 2016	"The tendency to acquire similar beliefs and behaviors from our larger social network is well documented within social psychology."	Social psychologists have demonstrated that people often have attitudes and actions that are consistent with those of their friends and family.
Williams, Vik, and Wong, 2015	"Students who endorsed drinking heavily alone were more likely to have higher distress intolerance scores and more coping motives than their social-drinking peers."	Students who tended to drink to excess when they were by themselves were more prone to have trouble tolerating distress and more motivation to drink in an effort to cope than those who just drank socially.
Xu, Wang, and David, 2016	"A large body of research has established that media multitasking during cognitive activities, such as reading and studying, produces negative consequences."	Researchers have consistently found that attending to multiple media sources while reading or studying has a negative impact.

With these last two sentences, I've essentially said what Middlemist et al. (1976) said, but I've put the information in my own words. Note that I still need to cite Middlemist et al. because the ideas were theirs, not mine. But also note that the quotation marks and the page number citation are no longer necessary, because I am no longer using Middlemist et al.'s exact words. So the bottom line is, keep exact quotes to a minimum; for everything else, put the information in your own words and cite your sources. See Table 3.2 for other examples of acceptable paraphrasing.

Give Publication Credit

The APA Ethics Code says the following about publication credit:

1. *Psychologists take responsibility and credit, including authorship credit, only for work they have actually performed or to which they have substantially contributed.*

2. *Principal authorship and other publication credits accurately reflect the relative scientific or professional contributions of the individuals involved, regardless of their relative status. Mere possession of an institutional position, such as department chair, does not justify authorship credit. Minor contributions to the research or to the writing for publications are acknowledged appropriately, such as in footnotes or in an introductory statement.*

3. *Except under exceptional circumstances, a student is listed as principal author on any multiple-authored article that is substantially based on the student's doctoral dissertation. Faculty advisors discuss publication credit with students as early as feasible and throughout the research and publication process as appropriate. (APA, 2002, p. 1070)*

Publication credit is typically considered an important issue for those who conduct research. For many professors, for example, the number and quality of the publications are considered during the job promotion process, with first-author status given more weight than the other options.

As you can see, there are pretty specific rules regarding publication credit. You may have opportunities to conduct research with a professor; recognize that these guidelines exist so you'll generally know what to expect.

Avoid Duplicate Publication of Data

"Psychologists do not publish, as original data, data that have been previously published. This does not preclude republishing data when they are accompanied by proper acknowledgment" (APA, 2002, p. 1071).

As noted above, during the job promotion process for researchers, employers often consider how many articles a researcher has published. Thus, it's important that each publication represent a separate piece of scholarship, and that the number of publications is not artificially inflated.

It is also worth thinking about this from another point of view. When you are searching the literature, aren't you glad to know each article you find will represent a different study or group of studies? Imagine that a researcher could publish the same study over and over again. It certainly would be a lot more difficult to do an efficient search of the literature. With this rule, you can rest assured that the articles you do find will be unique contributions to a review of your topic's literature.

Ethics and Research on the Internet

Many researchers now use the Internet to collect data. There are a variety of ways to do this (see Gosling & Johnson, 2010; Mason & Suri, 2012), but in each case, you must still abide by an ethics code even though many ethics codes (such as the APA Ethics Code) do not specifically address online research. Most of the ethical guidelines we've discussed are still applicable. For example, you are still responsible for submitting your research plans to the IRB. You still need to protect your study participants from harm, use deception only when deemed necessary, get participants' informed consent, and debrief.

Doing research on the Internet can bring special challenges (see Kraut et al., 2004). For example, while it is easy to include an informed consent form for your online participants (there is usually a button that says "click if you consent" at the bottom of the informed consent form), you are not there to answer questions for online participants. The researcher's absence can also be a concern for the debriefing, which under typical offline circumstances is an interactive question-and-answer period.

Another possible concern for those doing online research is the psychologist's obligation to protect participant confidentiality. Certainly one thing you can do to lessen the risk to your participants when you are collecting data online (or offline) is to refrain from asking for identifying information (participants' names, email addresses, and so on) (Kraut et al., 2004). We'll discuss this and other ethical concerns for research on the Internet in Chapter 13.

SUMMARY

History provides us with examples of research in which humans were subjected to gross mistreatment; these abuses helped shape the ethics codes that are present today.

The current APA Ethics Code contains a set of five aspirational general principles: beneficence and nonmaleficence, fidelity and responsibility, integrity, justice, and respect for people's rights and dignity.

The APA Ethics Code also includes Standards or specific and mandatory rules of conduct. Prior to conducting research, our research studies need to be approved by an IRB. We need to protect our study participants from psychological and physical harm, only use deception when it is justified and there is no viable alternative, provide them enough information to enable them to give informed consent, and, in most cases, debrief them, typically when the study session comes to an end. We must respect our study participants' right to privacy and confidentiality.

The APA Ethics Code also provides us with Standards pertaining to publication. We must not falsify our data, plagiarize, or publish the same data more than once.

Most of the ethical guidelines we've discussed are also applicable when we conduct our research online. For example, you are still responsible for submitting your research plans to the IRB. You still need to protect your study participants from harm, use deception only when deemed necessary, get participants' informed consent, and debrief.

GLOSSARY

Anonymity – the condition in which a participant's identity is not known.

Assent – agreement by a minor to participate in a research study.

Autonomy – the ability to consider and make a decision regarding whether or not to participate in research.

Belmont Report – an ethics code that covers biomedical and behavioral research.

Beneficence – the act of doing good things for others.

Confidentiality – the promise that the identity of participants will not be released without their consent, and their study responses will not be linked to their identities.

Cover story – a misleading statement about the purpose of a research study.

Debriefing – an event after a study in which researchers inform participants about the true purpose of the research study and provide information about the hypotheses. Any deception that was used is also explained.

Deception – the withholding of details of a study from participants (omission) or actively lying to participants (commission). Using a cover story or using a confederate are both forms of deception.

Demand characteristics – cues in the study that inform the participants about the study's true purpose and hypotheses.

Fidelity – trustworthiness.

Informed consent – participants' agreement to participate in a research study after being provided with adequate information to allow them to knowingly consent.

Institutional Review Board – a committee responsible for reviewing research before it is conducted to ensure that it does not violate ethical standards.

Integrity – honesty.

Justice – fairness.

Nonmaleficence – the goal of not harming others.

Nuremberg Code – a set of ten ethical principles that must be fulfilled before medical experimentation can take place. This ethics code was formulated in response to the Nazi war crimes trials after World War II.

Respect for persons – the idea that individuals should be treated as "autonomous agents."

REVIEW QUESTIONS

1 Explain why the Tuskegee Syphilis Study was important to the evolution of research ethics.

2 Summarize the principles of the Belmont Report.

3 Describe the five general aspirational principles of the APA Ethics Code.

4 Explain what it means to obtain institutional approval for research.

5 Describe the history of the APA Ethics Code in terms of "avoiding harm." Use Milgram's research in your answer.

6 Differentiate between confidentiality and anonymity.

7 Explain what it means to obtain informed consent.

8 Explain how to obtain consent when your study participants are minors.

9 Identify what the APA Ethics Code says about research participation as a course requirement.

10 Describe the approved form of inducements for research participation.

11 Explain when deception is allowed according to the APA Ethics Code.

12 Summarize what debriefing is and when it is conducted.

13 Summarize the APA Ethics Code with regard to publication.

14 Identify the ethics issues pertinent to conducting research on the Internet.

ARTICLES AS ILLUSTRATION

1 Read through the following sources to see how people have responded to a recent ethics controversy; answer the questions that follow.

Kramer, A. D. I., Guillory, J. E., & Hancock, J. T. (2014). Experimental evidence of massive-scale emotional contagion through social networks. Proceedings of the National Academy of Sciences, 111, 8788–8790.

LaFrance, A. (2014, June 29). Even the editor of Facebook's mood study thought it was creepy. The Atlantic. Retrieved from www.theatlantic.com/technology/archive/2014/06/even-the-editor-of-facebooks-mood-study-thought-it-was-creepy/373649/.

Lanier, J. (2014, June 30). Should Facebook manipulate users? The New York Times. Retrieved from www.nytimes.com/2014/07/01/opinion/jaron-lanier-on-lack-of-transparency-in-facebook-study.html.

Here is a brief summary of the controversy. Kramer et al. (2014) collected data from almost 700,000 randomly selected Facebook users that revealed that when Facebook manipulated what their users saw (positive versus negative) over a one-week period, the content of the posts affected their moods. The observed users were more likely to post mood-matching content; in other words, they showed "emotional contagion" (p. 8788). The reasons for the controversy? One reason was that these Facebook users did not give their informed consent in the traditional way as discussed above. When they initially signed up for Facebook, the agreed-to terms included Facebook's being able to access user-generated data on the site (for the current Facebook policy on data use, see www.facebook.com/about/privacy/your-info). Another reason for the controversy was concern about whether this study had undergone an IRB review (see LaFrance, 2014 for more on this issue).

In the days that followed the release of this article, many provided their thoughts. For example, LaFrance (2014) of *The Atlantic* noted "the idea that Facebook is altering what you see to find out if it can make you feel happy or sad seems in some ways cruel" (para. 12). Lanier (2014) of *The New York Times* voiced concern about the negative manipulation of the newsfeed of Facebook posts for those who are at risk (e.g., "an estimated 60 percent of suicides are preceded by a mood disorder," para. 5). He urged "all of us engaged in research over networks must commit to finding a way to modernize the process of informed consent" (para. 11).

a. Should this study have been done? Do the potential risks outweigh the benefits?

b. Should Facebook change the way it obtains informed consent?

2 Read through Middlemist et al.'s article and the correspondence that followed and then answer the question that follows.

Middlemist, R. D., Knowles, E. S., & Matter, C. F. (1976). Personal space invasions in the lavatory: Suggestive evidence for arousal. *Journal of Personality and Social Psychology, 33*, 541–546. doi:http://dx.doi.org/10.1037/0022–3514.33.5.541.

Koocher, G. P. (1977). Bathroom behavior and human dignity. *Journal of Personality and Social Psychology, 35*, 120–121. doi:http://dx.doi.org/10.1037/0022–3514.35.2.120

Middlemist, R. D., Knowles, E. S., & Matter, C. F. (1977). What to do and what to report: A reply to Koocher. *Journal of Personality and Social Psychology, 35*, 122–124. doi:http://dx.doi.org/10.1037/0022–3514.35.2.122.

Given that you are now familiar with both sides of this issue, do you think this research should have been conducted?

3 Read through the following article and answer the questions that follow.

West, S. G., Gunn, S. P., & Chernicky, P. (1975). Ubiquitous Watergate: An attributional analysis. *Journal of Personality and Social Psychology, 32*, 55–65. doi:http://dx.doi.org/10.1037/h0076858.

In the first experiment in this article, West and his colleagues randomly selected a group of criminology undergraduates at Florida State University. Each then met with a known private investigator and was offered an opportunity to participate in a burglary (with varying rationales). The plans for this burglary were elaborate (it was portrayed as a professional job with little chance of being caught), and they were presented to the participants in great detail over two meetings. Participants were given an opportunity to ask questions and then come to a final planning meeting. The investigators were interested in whether the participants agreed to commit this illegal act, and what their reasons were for their decisions. No burglary took place and the participants were debriefed after they made their choice and stated the reason for their decision.

West et al. (1975) used this and a second study to investigate what is known as "attribution theory" (see Watson, 1982 for a review); that is, they were particularly interested in how people attribute causes to their behavior.

a. Is there a risk to the study participants who were offered a burglary job even though there never really was an opportunity to commit a burglary?

b. Do you think the participants learned something about themselves that they might not have wanted to know?

c. Do you think this study should have been done? Why or why not?

4 Read through the following article and answer the questions that follow.

Smith, B. J., Sanford, F., & Goldman, M. (1977). Norm violations, sex, and the "blank stare." *Journal of Social Psychology, 103*, 49–55. doi:http://dx.doi.org/10.1080/00224545.1977.9713295.

How do you feel when someone is blankly staring at you? Is this pleasant or aversive? Smith et al. (1977) decided to find out how people generally feel under these conditions. They had confederates blankly stare at 16 males and 16 females who were each sitting alone in university libraries (in each case a person seated nearby served as a control). Ignoring any attempts at interaction by the person being watched, the confederates stared for 15 minutes or until the person being stared at left. At the end of the 15 minutes or when the participant got up to leave, he or she was debriefed (told the purpose of the study). The researchers found that females left earlier than males, especially when being stared at by a male confederate.

a. Do you think this study should have been conducted? Why or why not?

b. Was debriefing appropriate in this situation? Why or why not?

SUGGESTED ACTIVITIES

1 Have a class debate regarding whether deception should be used in research. See the following for ideas:
Elms, A. C., & Baumrind, D. (2007). Is deception of human participants ethical? In J. Nier (ed.), *Taking sides: Clashing views in social psychology* (pp. 2–27). New York: McGraw-Hill.

2 Take a published article and write an informed consent form for the research. See the information in the "Informed Consent" section above regarding the content of your consent form.

REFERENCES

American Psychological Association. (1958). Standards of ethical behavior for psychologists: Report of the Committee on ethical standards of psychologists. *American Psychologist, 13*, 266–271. doi:http://dx.doi.org/10.1037/h0039809

(1973). Ethical principles in the conduct of research with human participants. *American Psychologist, 28*, 79–80. doi:http://dx.doi.org/10.1037/h0038067

(2002). Ethical principles of psychologists and code of conduct. *American Psychologist, 57*, 1060–1073. doi:http://dx.doi.org/10.1037/0003–066X.57.12.1060

Baumrind, D. (1964). Some thoughts on ethics of research: After reading Milgram's "Behavioral Study of Obedience." *American Psychologist, 19*, 421–423. doi:http://dx.doi.org/10.1037/h0040128

(1985). Research using intentional deception: Ethical issues revisited. *American Psychologist, 40*, 165–174. doi:http://dx.doi.org/10.1037/0003–066X.40.2.165

Blass, T. (2009). From New Haven to Santa Clara: A historical perspective on the Milgram obedience experiments. *American Psychologist, 64*, 37–45. doi:http://dx.doi.org/10.1037/a0014434

Burger, J. M. (2009). Replicating Milgram: Would people still obey today? *American Psychologist, 64*, 1–11. doi:http://dx.doi.org/10.1037/a0010932

Christensen, L. (1988). Deception in psychological research: When is its use justified? *Personality and Social Psychology Bulletin, 14*, 664–675. doi:http://dx.doi.org/10.1177/0146167288144002

Diener, E., Matthews, R., & Smith, R. E. (1972). Leakage of experimental information to potential future subjects by debriefed subjects. *Journal of Experimental Research in Personality, 6*, 264–267.

Elms, A. C., & Baumrind, D. (2007). Is deception of human participants ethical? In J. Nier (ed.), *Taking sides: Clashing views in social psychology* (pp. 2–27). New York: McGraw-Hill.

Gosling, S. D., & Johnson, J. A. (eds.). (2010). *Advanced methods for conducting online behavioral research.* Washington, DC: American Psychological Association.

Harvard Law School Library. (1946, December 10) Nuremberg trials project: A digital document collection. *Medical case transcript.* Retrieved from http://nuremberg.law.harvard.edu/NurTranscript/TranscriptPages/195_156.html

Heller, J. (1972, July 26). Syphilis victims in U.S. study went untreated for 40 years. *The New York Times*, A1, A8.

Hermans, R. C. J., Engels, R. C. M. E., Larsen, J. K., & Herman, C. P. (2009). Modeling of palatable food intake. The influence of quality of social interaction. *Appetite, 52*, 801–804. doi:http://dx.doi .org/10.1016/j.appet.2009.03.008

Hixon, M. D. (1998). Ape language research: A review and behavioral perspective. *Analysis of Verbal Behavior, 15*, 17–39.

Jha, A. (2012, September 13). False positives: Fraud and misconduct are threatening scientific research. *The Guardian*. Retrieved from www.theguardian.com

Koocher, G. P. (1977). Bathroom behavior and human dignity. *Journal of Personality and Social Psychology, 35*, 120–121. doi:http://dx.doi.org/10.1037/0022–3514.35.2.120

Kramer, A. D. I., Guillory, J. E., & Hancock, J. T. (2014). Experimental evidence of massive-scale emotional contagion through social networks. *Proceedings of the National Academy of Sciences, 111*, 8788–8790. doi:http://dx.doi.org/10.1073/ pnas.1320040111

Kraut, R., Olson, J., Banaji, M., Bruckman, A., Cohen, J., & Couper, M. (2004). Psychological research online: Report of Board of Scientific Affairs' Advisory Group on the conduct of research on the Internet. *American Psychologist, 59*, 105–117. doi:http://dx.doi .org/10.1037/0003–066X.59.2.105

Kumar, A., Aakriti, & Gupta, V. (2016). A review on animal models of stroke: An update. *Brain Research Bulletin, 122*, 35–44. doi:http://dx.doi.org/10.1016/ j.brainresbull.2016.02.016

LaFrance, A. (2014, June 29). Even the editor of Facebook's mood study thought it was creepy. *The Atlantic*. Retrieved from www.theatlantic.com

Lanier, J. (2014, June 30). Should Facebook manipulate users? *The New York Times*. Retrieved from www .nytimes.com

Mason, W., & Suri, S. (2012). Conducting behavioral research on Amazon's Mechanical Turk. *Behavior Research Methods, 44*, 1–23. doi:https://doi. org/10.3758/s13428-011-0124-6

Middlemist, R. D., Knowles, E. S., & Matter, C. F. (1976). Personal space invasions in the lavatory: Suggestive evidence for arousal. *Journal of Personality*

and Social Psychology, 33, 541–546. doi:http://dx.doi .org/10.1037/0022–3514.33.5.541

(1977). What to do and what to report: A reply to Koocher. *Journal of Personality and Social Psychology, 35*, 122–124. doi:http://dx.doi.org/10.1037/0022– 3514.35.2.122

Milgram, S. (1963). Behavioral study of obedience. *Journal of Abnormal and Social Psychology, 67*, 371–378. doi:http://dx.doi.org/10.1037/h0040525 (1974). *Obedience to authority: An experimental view.* New York: Harper & Row.

Miller, A. G. (1972). Role playing: An alternative to deception? A review of the evidence. *American Psychologist, 27*, 623–636. doi:http://dx.doi. org/10.1037/h0033257

Monk-Turner, E., Edwards, D., Broadstone, J., Hummel, R., Lewis, S., & Wilson, D. (2005). Another look at hand-washing behavior. *Social Behavior and Personality, 33*, 629–634. doi:http://dx.doi.org/ 10.2224/sbp.2005.33.7.629

National Commission for the Protection of Human Subjects of Biomedical and Behavioral Research (1979). *The Belmont Report: Ethical principles and guidelines for the protection of human subjects of research.* Retrieved from or.org/pdf/Belmont Report.pdf

Olson, J. M., Barefoot, J. C., & Strickland, L. H. (1976). What the shadow knows: Person perception in a surveillance situation. *Journal of Personality and Social Psychology, 34*, 583–589. doi:http://dx.doi .org/10.1037/0022–3514.34.4.583

Ortmann, A., & Hertwig, R. (1997). Is deception acceptable? *American Psychologist, 52*, 746–747. doi:http://dx.doi.org/10.1037/0003–066X.52.7.746

Roberts, S. (2015, April 18). Irwin Schatz, 83, rare critic of Tuskegee syphilis study, is dead. Retrieved from www.nytimes.com

Schwab, N. G., Cullum, J. C., & Harton, H. C. (2016). Clustering of worry appraisals among college students. *Journal of Social Psychology, 156*, 413–421. doi:http:// dx.doi.org/10.1080/00224545.2015.1115387

Shuster, E. (1997). Fifty years later: The significance of the Nuremberg Code. *New England Journal of Medicine, 337*, 1436–1440.

Sieber, J. E., Iannuzzo, R., & Rodriguez, B. (1995). Deception methods in psychology: Have they changed in 23 years? *Ethics and Behavior*, *5*, 67–85. doi:http://dx.doi.org/10.1207/s15327019eb0501_5

Smith, B. J., Sanford, F., & Goldman, M. (1977). Norm violations, sex, and the "blank stare." *Journal of Social Psychology*, *103*, 49–55. doi:http://dx.doi.org/10.1080/00224545.1977.9713295

Swim, J. K., & Hyers, L. L. (1999). Excuse me – what did you just say?! Women's public and private responses to sexist remarks. *Journal of Experimental Social Psychology*, *35*, 68–88. doi:http://dx.doi.org/10.1006/jesp.1998.1370

Watson, D. (1982). The actor and the observer: How are their perceptions of causality divergent? *Psychological Bulletin*, *92*, 682–700. doi:http://dx.doi.org/10.1037/0033-2909.92.3.682

West, S. G., Gunn, S. P., & Chernicky, P. (1975). Ubiquitous Watergate: An attributional analysis. *Journal of Personality and Social Psychology*, *32*, 55–65. doi:http://dx.doi.org/10.1037/h0076858

White, B. P., Becker-Blease, K. A., & Grace-Bishop, K. (2006). Stimulant medication use, misuse, and abuse in an undergraduate and graduate student sample. *American College Health*, *54*, 261–268. doi:http://dx.doi.org/10.3200/JACH.54.5.261–268

Williams, C. L., Vik, P. W., & Wong, M. M. (2015). Distress tolerance in social versus solitary college student drinkers. *Addictive Behaviors*, *50*, 89–95. doi:http://dx.doi.org/10.1016/j.addbeh.2015.06.025

Xu, S., Wang, Z., & David, P. (2016). Media multitasking and the well-being of university students. *Computers in Human Behavior*, *51(Part A)*, 242–250. doi:http://dx.doi.org/10.1016/j.chb.2015.08.040

4 Defining and Measuring Variables

LEARNING OBJECTIVES

- Explain what it means to operationally define an independent (manipulated) variable and a measured variable.

- Describe the four scales of measurement.

- Define reliability and validity and ways of assessing them.

- Differentiate between internal and external validity.

Do you ever drink something with caffeine in it to help you stay awake? Does it help? Anderson and Horne (2008) wondered whether just *thinking* you've ingested caffeine would be enough to give the desired boost. They compared two groups that both drank a decaffeinated liquid; participants in one group believed their drink was highly caffeinated, while the other knew their drink was not. Anderson and Horne found that just believing you've ingested caffeine (when you haven't) is enough to affect performance on a reaction-time task.

In addition to revealing a fascinating result, Anderson and Horne, like all researchers, were responsible for defining and measuring their variables of interest. For example, they needed to provide details about how they got their study participants to believe they ingested caffeine when they didn't, and to define the way they measured the effects of that imaginary caffeine intake. These details are an important part of the research process. In this chapter we'll go over how to define and measure variables. We'll start with a discussion of how to define your variables.

FIGURE 4.1 Anderson and Horne (2008) found that thinking you've ingested caffeine when you haven't is enough to boost performance on a reaction-time task.

Operational Definitions

As mentioned in Chapter 1, a variable is any characteristic that can take on different values. In other words, a variable is something that varies, so it must have at least two values or levels. In addition, every variable that is part of a research study must be operationally defined. Recall that to operationally define a variable means to specify the precise meaning of the variable in terms of the specific procedures to be performed. The operational definition for an independent variable manipulation is the specific method used to *manipulate* the variable and an operational definition for a dependent variable is the specific method used to *measure* the variable.

Let's look at some examples. We'll start with operational definitions of independent variables. Recall that when researchers conduct an experiment, they manipulate (vary) one or more independent variables to find out how these will affect one or more response measures called dependent variables. Let's talk about using anger as an independent variable. We need to indicate specifically the different ways we will induce anger in our

study participants. There are many different ways to induce anger. Lobbestael, Arntz, and Wiers (2008) used four in their research, so let's take a look at how they induced anger. Participants in Lobbestael et al.'s work were either: (1) shown a film, (2) interviewed, (3) subjected to punishment, or (4) subjected to harassment.

(1)   Film: Participants were shown a segment from the film *My Bodyguard* in which a child is bullied and blackmailed at school.

(2)   Stress interview: Participants were asked to describe a past event that generated a strong feeling of anger.

(3)   Punishment: Participants were asked to complete a frustrating computer task, rigged to yield a mediocre performance, and they received feedback on their performance. The feedback was provided as a red "X" on the computer screen and a loud irritating tone played through headphones.

(4)   Harassment: Participants were asked to take a rigged "intelligence test" in which they do not do well. An experimenter posing as another study participant who had been asked to supervise the session harassed the participant as he or she completed the task.

Lobbestael et al. compared these procedures to see which was the best at inducing anger. Thus, this independent variable can be labeled "techniques used to induce anger" and in the experiment it had four levels. The details about these four ways to induce anger represent the operational definition for the anger induction.

Researchers have also operationalized anger as an independent variable in other ways. For example, Shields, Moons, Twell, and Yonelinas (2016) induced anger (and compared it to induced anxiety and a neutral mood) by having students write about an

Table 4.1 Examples of operational definitions of independent (manipulated) variables.

What was manipulated? (independent variable)	How was it manipulated? (operational definition)	Who conducted this research?
Type of animal being petted during a stressful situation (a tarantula was present)	Participants were randomly assigned to pet a rabbit, a turtle, a toy rabbit, a toy turtle, or nothing	Shiloh, Sorek, and Terkel (2003)
Type of odor	Synthetic odors of disinfectant, beeswax, summer air, burnt smell, vomit, musty smell, and odorless water on sniffing strips presented in random order	Glass, Lingg, and Heuberger (2014)
Use of expletives by sports coach	Participants were randomly assigned to read a halftime speech in which a high school coach spoke with expletives or not	Howell and Giuliano (2011)
Compliments offered by food servers in restaurants	Food servers either paid compliments or not on patrons' food choices (randomly determined)	Seiter and Weger (2010)
Sexual history of potential date	Participants read about a potential date randomly described as having had only one sexual partner, a few partners, or several partners.	Epstein, Klinkenberg, Scandell, Faulkner, and Claus (2007)

unresolved situation in their lives that made them angry. Fairclough and Spiridon (2012) had participants take part in a simulated driving task in which traffic jams made it impossible to complete the journey in the allotted time (participants thought they would have to forfeit compensation if the journey was not completed). The timing of the traffic jams induced different levels of anger in the participants. Plaisier and Konijn (2013) used a game to induce anger. They had adolescents play a video game of catch in which they were supposed to throw a ball to two other participants. However, the other participants were not real but computer-generated to either include the true participant in the game one-third of the time ("peer acceptance") or to represent "peer rejection" by keeping the ball away for most of the game (p. 1167). Those who were rejected showed more anger than those who were accepted.

So as you see, there are many ways to operationalize anger as an independent variable. How anger is operationalized is up to the researcher and his or her research goals. For example, Fairclough and Spiridon wanted to view anger in a driving context so they used the presence of traffic jams to get people angry. Whatever it is you are operationalizing, it is a good idea to become familiar with the ways researchers before you have operationalized similar variables. In science, we learn from each other (giving everyone proper credit for their ideas, of course). Table 4.1 shows operational definitions of some other independent variables.

Now let's look at the operational definitions of dependent variables. In an experiment, we use dependent variables to measure the impact of the independent variable manipulation. Operational definitions specify *how* we will measure the

Table 4.2 Examples of operational definitions of measured variables.

What was measured?	How was it measured? (Operational definition)	Who conducted this research?
Personal space	The distance between two chairs as arranged by each participant before an expected interaction	Vaidis and Oberlé (2014)
Sleepiness over the past six months	Epworth Sleepiness Scale: Participants' indication on a 3-point scale the likelihood of falling asleep during various activities (1 = would never doze; 3 = high chance of dozing)	Lund, Reider, Whiting, and Prichard (2010)
School engagement	The number of sports and extra-curricular activities listed by participants	Bentley-Edwards and Chapman-Hilliard (2015)
Professor's likeability	Participants' rating of how much they like their professor (1 = do not like at all) (7 = like very much)	Gurung and Vespia (2007)
Frequency of tanning salon use in the past 12 months	Participants stated frequency of visits to a tanning salon in the past 12 months (never, fewer than 5 times, 5+ times)	Basch, Hillyer, Basch, and Neugut (2012)

variables of interest. In nonexperimental research, we still need to operationally define what we are measuring, but we call these variables *measured variables* rather than dependent variables. I will use the term *measured variables* in this chapter to refer to whatever we are measuring (within an experimental or non-experimental context). So let's look at a few examples of how measured variables can be operationally defined.

Lobbestael et al. used a variety of ways to measure anger so let's take a closer look at how they operationally defined their measurements of anger. Specifically, they asked their participants to rate their emotional state shortly after the anger manipulation. Participants provided a self-report with regard to a variety of different emotions, including anger. Physiological responses including blood pressure and heart rate were also assessed as indices of anger. And Lobbestael et al. used two ways of measuring palm sweat gland activity: skin conductance level (SCL) and skin conductance response (SCR).

So they used five different operational definitions of measuring anger: self-report, blood pressure, heart rate, SCL, and SCR.

Researchers have also operationalized anger as a measured variable in other ways. For example, Herrero, Gadea, Rodrigues-Alarcón, Espert, and Salvador (2010) measured testosterone, cortisol levels, and changes in brain symmetry as indicators of anger in addition to using self-report and cardiovascular measures like blood pressure and heart rate. Table 4.2 lists examples of operational definitions of some other measured variables.

Sometimes researchers decide to use more than one operational definition to measure a particular variable, in an effort to obtain converging evidence. **Converging evidence** is present if we use different operational definitions of a variable (that is, we measure the same construct in different ways) and yet we come to the same overall conclusion about that variable's role in the research. For example, Herrero et al. found that an anger induction led to both self-reported mood changes and physiological changes. Thus, Herrero et al. were able to present a more complete picture of what happens when people get angry.

Sometimes psychological researchers are interested in studying concepts that are relatively abstract, such as intelligence, self-esteem, love, happiness, shame, stress, shyness, and depression, that cannot generally be directly observed or easily measured. We call these concepts constructs. **Constructs** are psychological concepts that we cannot identify by observation but instead infer from measurable behaviors or outcomes. Although we cannot directly observe constructs, we still need to operationally define them when they are variables in our research. When you are precise in your description of what you've manipulated and/or measured, it enables other researchers to better understand your work and, when desired, to try and replicate it.

Scales of Measurement

It is important not only to define your variables of interest, but also to know and understand the limits of the scale of measurement you are using. There are four scales of measurement: nominal, ordinal, interval, and ratio. Your choice will determine the type of information you can describe from your data and what statistical analyses you can do with the data you generate. Let's look at the four scales.

Nominal

A **nominal scale** is the most basic form of measurement. These scales are characterized by the placement of information into categories. If any numbers are associated with nominal scales, they do not have numerical meaning; you can only count the number of items that are placed into each category. Here's an example – the variable "clothing" uses a nominal scale. There are different types of clothing: shirts,

FIGURE 4.2 The variable "clothing" uses a nominal scale. We can place clothing into categories (such as shirts, pants etc.), but one type of clothing is not numerically greater than another.

pants, hats, skirts and so on, but one type of clothing is not greater than another.

We often use nominal variables when describing a sample of participants. For example, we can ask our respondents to indicate their ethnicity and ask them to choose from a variety of response options (such as African American, Asian American, Caucasian, Hispanic, Native American). We can then report what percentage chose each response.

Sometimes researchers will rename the values of a nominal variable using numbers. So for example, researchers asking participants to indicate their political party might assign numeric codes to these responses, such as 1 = Democrat and 2 = Republican. Remember these numeric codes are arbitrary; in nominal scales the numbers have no real meaning and are only identification labels. However, as suggested above, you can count the number of cases falling into each exemplar category and use math to summarize that information. For example, you could report that 56% of your sample identified as Democrat. But that is essentially the limit of what you can do numerically with nominal scales.

The next three kinds of scales – ordinal, interval, ratio – are different from nominal scales because they use meaningful numbers. Thus, they are known as quantitative variables. Let's talk about ordinal scales first.

Ordinal

We use an **ordinal scale** when we want to rank-order the levels of the variable we are studying. We often see ordinal scales in use in the real world. For example, *US News and World Report* ranks colleges on their academic quality. *Consumer Reports* ranks almost everything consumers can buy, including bacon, beer, and bike helmets. Let's take a closer look at rankings in an example from the psychological research literature.

Quiles (2003) asked university students in Puerto Rico and New Jersey to answer the following question: "What do you consider to be romantic behaviors or acts of romantic courtship?" (p. 356). He presented these study participants with 15 items and asked each to rank the items from 1 (most romantic) to 15 (least romantic). He then compared the answers for males and females in both locations (see Table 4.3 for Quiles' rankings). Quiles found

Table 4.3   Rankings of romantic behaviors among male and female university students in New Jersey and in Puerto Rico.

Romantic behaviors	Puerto Rico		New Jersey	
	Ranking for males	Ranking for females	Ranking for males	Ranking for females
Kissing	1	1	1	6
Making love	2	5	2	9
Flowers (receive/send)	3	2	10	5
Saying "I love you"	4	4	8	2
Hugging	5	3	5	3
Candlelight Dinner	6	6	6	7
Slow Dancing	7	7	7	10
Cuddling	8	8	4	1
Love cards/letters	9	9	9	4
Holding Hands	10	11	3	8
Going out (movies)	11	12	13	11
Taking walks	12	10	12	14
Sitting by fireplace	13	14	11	13
Surprise gifts	14	13	14	12
Phone calls	15	15	15	15

Note: Ranking scale: #1 = most romantic, #15 = least romantic.
Source: Adapted from Quiles, J. A. (2003). Romantic behaviors of university students: A cross-cultural and gender analysis in Puerto Rico and the United States. *College Student Journal, 37(3)*, 354–366.

FIGURE 4.3 Which activity do you see as more romantic?

that in Puerto Rico males and females generally agreed on how romantic individual items were. Both males and females, for example, saw "kissing" as the most romantic item. On the other hand, males and females in New Jersey had different ideas about what is romantic. Males saw "kissing" as most romantic, but females chose "cuddling." Quiles suggested that overall in New Jersey, items males identified as ranking higher in romantic behavior included physical actions (such as making love, holding hands, slow dancing), while those identified by females expressed emotional connectivity (such as sending or receiving flowers and love cards or letters). The activity everyone in both New Jersey and Puerto Rico agreed was least romantic was "phone calls," so perhaps you should note this if romance is what you're after.

Notice that when we are working with ordinal data, we can't tell whether the intervals between the rankings are equal. For example, in Quiles' New Jersey sample, females ranked "cuddling" as the most romantic item, while "saying I love you" was the second most romantic item, and "hugging" was third. These rankings indicate only more or less of something; we cannot say *how much* more romantic "cuddling" is than "saying I love you." Furthermore,

the amount of difference between the first- and second-ranked items is not necessarily the same as the difference between the second- and third-ranked items and so on. In other words, for New Jersey females in Quiles' sample, "cuddling" may be *much* more romantic than "saying I love you," but "saying I love you" may be only a *little* more romantic than "hugging." This ranking does indicate that "cuddling" for this sample is more romantic than both "saying I love you" and "hugging," but since this is an ordinal scale, it doesn't tell us whether the amount of difference between rankings is equivalent.

Interval

In an **interval scale**, there are equal intervals between the scale values. For instance, temperature uses an interval scale. The difference between 40 and 50 degrees is the same as the difference between 80 and 90 degrees. In addition, we can do standard arithmetic with interval scales, such as calculating averages. This has certainly helped me plan summer vacations. Since I do not like hot weather, I look for places whose average temperature doesn't go above 60 degrees.

The other important feature of an interval scale is that, although you can have a zero value (for

Pets should be allowed in dorm rooms.						
Strongly disagree	Disagree	Somewhat disagree	Neutral	Somewhat agree	Agree	Strongly agree
1	2	3	4	5	6	7

FIGURE 4.4 Example of a Likert scale item.

example, a zero-degree temperature is very cold), this scale does not have a *true* zero. Think about it this way – there is no such thing as the absence of temperature. The lack of a true zero also means you cannot state that someone with, say, an IQ of 160 is twice as intelligent as someone with an IQ of 80. The reason is that a person who scores zero on the IQ test likely doesn't have zero intelligence. Again, the zero in an interval scale is not a true zero.

Researchers often include rating scales on questionnaires and treat them as interval scales. For example, Likert scales (Likert, 1932) provide a statement and ask respondents how much they agree or disagree with it. See Figure 4.4 for an example.

For any rating scale to be *unequivocally* classified as an interval scale, the distance between adjacent numbers ideally should reflect equal amounts. So if you are asking participants how much they agree with the idea that pets should be allowed in dorm rooms, the change in the intensity of feeling between "disagree" and "strongly disagree" should be the same as the change in the intensity of feeling between "agree" and "strongly agree." But is it really? Probably not. So some have argued that Likert-type scales are really providing ordinal data (see, for example, Jamieson, 2004). On the other hand, research has supported the assumption that Likert-type rating scales reflect an interval scale of measurement (Carifio & Perla, 2008), and many researchers do consider their Likert-type rating scales to be interval data. Making this assumption is an important research decision; we'll see why after

discussing one more measurement scale: the ratio scale.

Ratio

A **ratio scale** has all the qualities of an interval scale but has a true zero, which means whatever is being measured *can also be absent*. Time and distance are examples of ratio variables. Think of it this way: It is possible in an experiment that no time has elapsed and you have not gained any distance (that is, you haven't moved). The advantage of the true zero means that when measuring distance, for example, we can say that a distance of 4 miles is twice the length of 2 miles.

So that's an overview of the four types of measurement scales. Why is it important to know which scale you are using? The scale helps determine the kinds of statistical procedures you will use to

FIGURE 4.5 When we quantify a runner's distance and time we are using ratio scales.

analyze your data. You are most limited, statistically speaking, when you are using nominal and ordinal measurement scales (as I've indicated above). Interval and ratio scales have the edge; more types of statistical analyses are available for interval and ratio variables, and these types of analyses tend to be more powerful.

Characteristics of Good Measurement

As I've already suggested, psychologists often have to measure something in the research that they do. They may create one or more items (questions, statements) and put these together to develop a measurement tool designed to assess a specific psychological characteristic such as shyness, intelligence, or an online gaming addiction. We can refer to a set of items created to measure information about the same topic as a scale or test (here we are using the term *scale* to refer to a collection of items designed to measure a topic of interest as opposed to a *scale of measurement* which refers to the four levels of measurement described earlier); I'll be using this language in the remainder of this chapter.

In Chapter 7, we'll go over how to write different types of items. In this next section, we're going to discuss something else you need to know when you create a series of items designed to measure the same issue; your tests need to have both reliability and validity. These are two very important characteristics of good measures.

Reliability

The **reliability** of a measure is its ability to produce consistent results each time we use it. I'll provide a simple example, but first a confession: I weigh myself on my bathroom scale every morning. Now let's say I decided to get a little more excessive about this, and started to weigh myself three times each morning. Say I step on the scale three times one morning, and I saw the same weight reading each time. That consistency is an indicator of the high reliability of the measure. If, on the other hand, I obtained different readings during each morning ritual, we would say my scale is less reliable. The more variability in the readings, the less reliable the measurement instrument is. Another way to think about this is that if there is variation in the measurements, there is **measurement error** in the measurement device.

There are two kinds of measurement error. Let's say my scale routinely displays a reading 30 pounds lower than my true weight. This is an example of systematic error. **Systematic error** is a constant amount of error present each time a measurement is taken, and its presence affects the accuracy of the reading. If you are aware that your measurement is giving you a systematic error, you need to do what is necessary to fix the problem. Get a new scale or attempt to correctly calibrate this scale. You can, for example, make sure the scale is set to zero when nothing is on it, and then check it for accuracy by weighing something with a known weight such as a 5-pound bag of sugar.

The other type of measurement error is **random error**, a nonsystematic fluctuation in the measurement. Say that sometimes when I weigh myself three times in the morning, it doesn't show the same three readings. Sometimes it's a little up, sometimes a little down. Why do I have this random error? It's difficult to say. Perhaps the scale is not lying flat on the floor sometimes; perhaps I am standing on the scale on my tiptoes other times. In any case, the scale is not giving me consistent output so I have to be concerned with its reliability. The more random error you have, the less reliable your measurement instrument is.

How do we assess the reliability of measurement in our research? There are a few ways to do this. We'll start by talking about test–retest reliability.

−1.00   0   +1.00

FIGURE 4.6 The number line of the Pearson r gives us information about both the strength and the direction of a relationship.

Test–Retest Reliability. We assess **test–retest reliability** by administering the same test to the same people at two different times under equivalent test conditions. The results should be the same or very similar each time. We look for test–retest reliability when measuring something we expect to be stable over time, such as personality or intelligence, for instance, but not hunger.

Ideally we administer the test and retest at least a week apart. Then we use a statistical analysis to determine how well the scores at the two testing sessions match. Specifically, we calculate a correlation coefficient. We'll talk more about correlation coefficients in Chapter 6, but here is a brief introduction.

We calculate a correlation with the Pearson product–moment correlation coefficient. The abbreviation for this numerical value is "Pearson r" or just r. It is a numerical value that ranges from −1.00 to +1.00, and it gives us information about both the strength and the direction of the relationship between the two variables we are measuring.

Picture a number line going from −1.00 to +1.00 (Figure 4.6).

Let's talk about the strength of the relationship first. We want the two things we are measuring (scores at Time 1 and scores at Time 2) to have a relationship, preferably a strong relationship. The closer a correlation coefficient is to either +1.00 or −1.00 (and the further away from zero), the stronger the correlation is.

However, we must also consider the direction of the relationship. The sign of the correlation, either positive or negative, provides information regarding the direction of the relationship. A positive correlation (indicated by a plus sign or no sign at all in the correlation coefficient) means the scores move in the same direction – when the scores are high on the first variable (Time 1), they are high on the second variable (Time 2). Similarly, when the scores are low on the first variable (Time 1), they are low on the second variable (Time 2). On the other hand, a negative correlation (indicated by the negative sign in the correlation coefficient) means the scores move in opposite directions – high scores on one of the variables are associated with low scores on the other variable.

What kind of correlation coefficient do we want when we are assessing the reliability of a measure? Ideally, we want the scores from Time 1 to be very similar to the scores from Time 2. We want to see a *strong positive* relationship between the scores from the two testing sessions. If one score is high, we want the other score to be consistent with that. If one score is low, we want the other score to be consistent with that. So we would like the Pearson r to be close to +1.00. Let's look at an example from the literature in which researchers sought to determine the test–retest reliability of their measurement instrument.

Sato, Harman, Adams, Evans, and Coolsen (2013) were interested in assessing how much college students relied on their phones for both making calls and texting. Cell phone usage certainly seems prevalent – Beaver, Knox, and Zusman (2010) actually found that approximately 94% of the students at their university used a cell phone regularly. But how much do students actually rely on their phones? To address this question Sato et al. created a test called a Cell Phone Reliance Scale (CPRS) asking participants to respond to statements such as "I feel more attached to my phone than to most other things I own." Once the test had been created, the researchers wanted to determine how reliable it was. In other words, would scores be reasonably consistent over time? So here's what they did. They had university students complete the CPRS two times, three weeks apart. Then they computed a Pearson *r*. They found that the correlation between the two testing sessions was .93. That's a strong, positive correlation, indicating that this scale is highly reliable.

The advantage of using the test–retest check on reliability is that it is relatively easy to do. The disadvantage is that it's possible for people taking the test a second time to remember how they answered the first time and to respond in the same way in an effort to appear consistent. Under these circumstances, reliability will be overestimated. It's also possible that people taking the test a second time are just quickly skimming it because they are not pleased at having to do it again. Quickly running through the test and not taking it seriously may lead people to respond in ways that don't truly reflect how they think or feel. In this case, reliability may be underestimated. This is why it's a good idea to separate the two testing sessions by enough time to lessen the likelihood of these problems. Or you might want to choose other methods of checking on your test's reliability. Let's talk about these other methods now.

Internal Consistency Reliability. Since administering the test twice has some potential disadvantages, as noted above, some researchers chose a technique that instead can assess reliability even though the test has only been taken once. In other words, instead of checking for consistency over time, we can check for the *internal* consistency in a test. A test has **internal consistency reliability** if all the items on it are related, measuring the same underlying attribute. So if you are creating a test to measure anxiety, all the items on your test should address anxiety in some way. There are a few ways to check for internal consistency.

One way is to check for split-half reliability. **Split-half reliability** is the correlation between the total score on one half of the test with the total score on the other half. You can test for split-half reliability by dividing the test items in half and performing a correlation calculation called the **Spearman-Brown split-half reliability coefficient**. Why don't we use a Pearson *r*? Reliability coefficients are typically higher when you are working with more items. If we split our items in half to do a split-half reliability check, then your reliability estimate will go down just because you are using only half the number of items to compute your estimate. The Spearman Brown coefficient corrects for this and increases the estimate upwards (Vogt, 2005). Let's look at how one set of researchers obtained a split-half reliability estimate.

Lawson, Jordan-Fleming, and Bodle (2015) developed an updated version of the Psychological Critical Thinking Exam to measure psychology students' ability to think critically about basic principles of psychological science (for example, knowing not to draw causal conclusions from correlational data). The test they created was a 14-item test, with two questions to measure each of seven critical thinking issues. To perform a split-half reliability test, they split the test in two so that one question on each half measured each of the seven critical thinking issues. They then compared one half of the test to the other. Their Spearman-Brown split-half reliability coefficient of .88 revealed that each half of their test was a close match to the other.

Incidentally, after establishing the reliability of their test, Lawson et al. (2015) administered the test to various groups. They found, as expected, that senior psychology majors did well, scoring higher than junior psychology majors, introductory psychology students, senior biology majors, and senior art majors. This was happy news – it suggested that by the time psychology majors are seniors, they are gaining the critical thinking skills they need.

The Spearman-Brown split-half reliability coefficient was used for many years, but there were recognized problems with it. Different ways of splitting a test can yield different reliability coefficients (Beckstead, 2013). Cronbach (1951) created a solution: calculate all possible split-half correlations in a test and average them together. This calculation yields **Cronbach's α (alpha) coefficient**; it is now a commonly used way to calculate internal consistency. Scores for Cronbach's α range from 0 (unreliable) to 1.00 (reliable), and scores above .70 indicate that the test items are measuring the same construct (Vogt, 2005).

There is one more way of measuring internal reliability. Remember that when you create a test, all the items on that test should be measuring the same general issue. Before you decide on the final version of the test, you can compute **item-to-total correlations**. First create your test and give it to a sample of participants. Then calculate the correlations between the score on each of the individual items and the total score (excluding the score for the item you are checking). Items that are not strongly correlated with the total score can be dropped from the scale, leaving a group of items that work well together to measure the same thing.

Inter-rater Reliability. So far, we have talked about reliability in terms of self-report tests. People are responding to items on a test, reporting on themselves and the way they think and feel. In addition, the test items we have been discussing have been closed-ended items. Closed-ended items have response options provided, such as numbers on a rating scale, and participants just need to choose among them. It is easy for us to summarize their responses – we can add up the ratings to get a score or indicate what percentage of respondents chose a particular response option.

However, sometimes we ask our participants open-ended questions for which they have to generate the answers themselves. There are no options to choose from. As we'll discuss more in Chapter 7, when you are analyzing the responses to open-ended questions, you need to perform a content analysis. In this process, you read through all the responses and then create categories for them that will help you summarize the content. Since researchers have to decide which response belongs in which category and they could make mistakes, we typically have more than one person make these decisions and then we compare their responses. We want to see consistency in those judgments; thus, reliability is an important issue in this kind of situation too. **Inter-rater reliability** is the level of internal consistency between two or more judges. In this type of case, researchers use a statistic known as **Cohen's kappa** (κ) to indicate the measure of agreement among the judges. Kappa ranges from 0, which means the judges do not agree at all, to +1.00 which signals they are in perfect agreement. We'll discuss kappa further in Chapter 5; for now, let's take a look at one research team's use of kappa to indicate the level of inter-rater reliability in their research.

Wickens, Wiesenthal, Hall, and Roseborough (2013) were interested in what makes drivers angry, so they completed a content analysis of the complaints registered at www.RoadRagers.com. Between 1999 and 2007, there were 5,315 complaints eligible for inclusion in the study. Two researchers independently read them and placed each complaint into a category or sub-category; this action is called coding (see Table 4.4 for an abbreviated version of Wickens et al.'s coding scheme). The two coders were generally consistent in their categorization; when they were not, a third coder made the coding decision. In the 28 cases where no one initially agreed, the three coders discussed the placement to

Table 4.4 An abbreviated version of Wickens et al.'s coding scheme.

(A) Improper speed	
(i) Speeding/racing	Speed greater than the posted limit or too high for the current road conditions
(ii) Unnecessary slow driving	Such a slow rate of speed as to impede the normal movement of traffic
(iii) Sporadic speeds	Continuously changing or unpredictable speeds
(B) Tailgating	Following a vehicle more closely than is reasonable
(C) Lane usage	
(i) Improper lane usage	Has not driven within a single lane, has passed another vehicle by driving outside a single lane and onto the shoulder of the roadway, or has violated the legally prescribed use of a lane
(ii) Weaving through traffic/cutting off/sideswiping	Has moved from one lane to another or has entered a lane from a side road without due regard for whether that movement can be made safely
(D) Improperly equipped/unsafe vehicle	
(i) No turn signal	Failed to use a flashing light signal for turn or lane change
(ii) All other forms of improperly equipped/unsafe vehicle	Has operated a vehicle that is improperly equipped (such as improper display of license plate and lack of headlight/tail light) or is in such an unsafe condition as to potentially endanger others (for example mechanical error and overloading)
(E) Disobedience of traffic signs/signals	Failed to obey a traffic control sign (such as red light, yield sign, and pedestrian crossing)
(F) Erratic/improper braking	Sudden and unnecessary braking without due regard for other vehicles
(G) Blocking	Preventing other vehicles from merging or passing
(H) Perceived driver displays of hostility or violence	
(i) Perceived hostile driver displays	Such as yelling, gesturing, horn honking, and flashing high beams
(ii) Perceived violent driver displays	Behavioral displays of discontent that are more intense than verbal commentary or gestures that are not included elsewhere in the coding scheme (such as chasing/following, getting out of the vehicle to verbally or physically argue, waving a firearm/blunt instrument/weapon, and throwing threatening objects)

Table 4.4 (*cont.*)

(I) Driver inattention	
(i) Cell phone use	Inattention associated with cell phone use
(ii) Other or unspecified distraction	Source of inattention not specified, or associated with anything but a cell phone
(J) Hazardous road conditions not attributable to driver behavior	Such as people/hitchhikers on the road, disabled/abandoned vehicle, and debris on the road
(K) Cannot be classified	Cannot be placed in any of the above categories

Source: Wickens, C. M., Wiesenthal, D. L., Hall, A., & Roseborough, J. E. W. (2013). Driver anger on the information superhighway: A content analysis of online complaints of offensive driver behavior. *Accident Analysis and Prevention, 51,* 84–92. doi:http://dx.doi.org/10.1016/j.aap.2012.10.007.

come to an agreement. The level of inter-rater reliability for this research, the kappa, was reported to be .85.

We can also assess inter-rater reliability when a research team is making observations. We'll continue with the driver theme for this next example. First a question: Where do you put your hands when you are driving? I can still remember my driver's education teacher in high school screaming, "Ten and two!" to indicate the proper hand placement on the top of the steering wheel. Fourie, Walton, and Thomas (2011) wondered where drivers put their hands on the steering wheel while driving, and whether their hand positions varied as a function of other variables such as the speed of the vehicle. How did they find out?

Two members of the research team stood by the side of the road; one member randomly identified an oncoming car as a target, and then both independently wrote down the position of the driver's hands. Specifically, hand placement was coded as the number of hands (0, 1, 2) on the steering wheel between a 3 o'clock and a 9 o'clock position. The researchers recorded hand placement in 100 cars before assessing inter-rater reliability. For both slower vehicles (those travelling in a 50 kph zone (about 31 mph)) and faster vehicles (those in a

FIGURE 4.7 Fourie et al. (2011) wondered whether drivers use proper hand placement on the wheel while driving.

100 kph zone (about 62 mph)), inter-rater reliability was high (slower: kappa = .90; faster: kappa = .88). Interestingly, drivers who placed two hands at the top half of the wheel drove more slowly than those who didn't.

After finding their reliability was high after 100 cars, the researchers decided to continue recording data as planned. It is reasonable to assume that had reliability not been at an adequate level, the research team members would have undergone additional training to improve their level of coding consistency.

Table 4.5   Types of reliability.

Test–retest reliability	How consistent is the test over time?
Internal consistency reliability	How interrelated are the individual items in the test; are they measuring the same underlying attribute?
Inter-rater reliability	What is the degree of consistency between two or more judges?

In conclusion, reliability is a consideration of two overall concepts: stability and equivalence (Beckstead, 2013). When we talked about test–retest reliability, we were asking whether test results would be stable over time. When we talked about internal consistency issues (split-half, Cronbach's α, and item-to-total correlations), we were looking at equivalence among the items on a test. Finally, when we talked about inter-rater reliability, we were talking about equivalence again, but this time how consistently members of a research team make judgments. See Table 4.5 for a review of the different types of reliability.

When deciding what measures are appropriate to use, researchers must consider reliability. However, that is not all. They also have to consider validity. We'll turn to that next.

Validity

The **validity** of a measure is the degree to which it measures what you intend it to measure. Before we talk about different kinds of validity and how it is assessed, let's differentiate validity from reliability with a frivolous example. Let's say I want to know whether the height of the pile of papers on someone's desk is a good measure of intelligence. I measure the tallest pile on someone's desk and find it is 14 inches tall. To check for test–retest reliability, I measure again. Again, I get a measurement of 14 inches. So the measurements are consistent; I have good test–retest reliability. But is my measure of a paper stack on a desk a good measure of intelligence? That's a question of validity.

FIGURE 4.8 Is the height of papers on a desk a sign of intelligence?

Validity can be divided into two general categories: construct validity and criterion validity. Let's talk about construct validity first.

Construct Validity. **Construct validity** is the degree to which a test actually measures the construct it is designed to measure. There are a variety of ways to assess construct validity: face validity, content validity, convergent validity, and discriminant validity. We will consider each of these in turn.

Face validity tells us how well a measure, on the face of it, *appears* to measure what it was designed to measure. This is a subjective judgment. For example, if you are trying to measure someone's ability to do algebra and the test you give doesn't ask about algebra, this test would appear to have low face validity. While experts are usually the ones to assess whether an item has face validity, those taking the test could also reasonably have a judgment about it. Those taking what they thought was an algebra

FIGURE 4.9 Is it possible to determine your age from your vocabulary?

test might wonder why there were no algebra questions on their test, for instance. This lack of face validity could affect their willingness to take the test seriously.

Face validity is the most superficial of ways to assess validity. Just because a test has face validity does not make it a valid measure. Let's take a look at a website quiz called "Can we guess your age by your vocabulary?" (www.sun-gazing.com/quiz-can-we-guess-your-age-by-your-vocabulary/) as an example.

The questions on this quiz are vocabulary questions, such as the following:

Choose a synonym for "wise"
Politic
Insightful
Enlightened
Perspicacious
Intelligent
Sagely

This test seems to have face validity for the topic "Can we guess your age by your vocabulary" because it has questions about vocabulary, but again, that doesn't mean that the test is doing a good job of measuring one's age.

In other words, in order to be considered valid, a test needs to have more than face validity. Another issue is that sometimes you do not want your test to have high face validity, such as when you want to disguise what you are trying to assess. Let's look at an example.

Turner (2014) conducts research on the feeling of shame. This can be a difficult area to study, because those who are feeling shame may not wish to admit it. So Turner developed the Experiential Shame Scale, which allows her to assess people's shame experiences without asking them directly whether they are feeling shame. For example, the scale asks respondents whether they are experiencing distress and a desire not to talk to others. After establishing that her scale does measure people's experience of shame, Turner conducted a study in which she gave the scale to respondents and asked, "What do you think this scale is measuring?" (p. 594). Virtually all the participants who ventured a guess were incorrect. Overall, Turner's work demonstrated that the Experiential Shame Scale does provide a valid assessment of the experience of shame; however, it is low in face validity. Thus, face validity is neither a necessary feature of a scale nor sufficient on its own.

Let's talk about content validity next. **Content validity** is the degree to which the items on the test adequately reflect *all* components of the construct you are measuring. Let's take a look at an example.

Latner, Mond, Kelly, Haynes, and Hay (2014) wanted to create a test to assess loss-of-control eating, which they defined as

the subjective perception of being compelled to eat or unable to resist or stop eating, resulting in initiating eating when not intended, and/

or eating more than originally intended, and/ or difficulty stopping eating. The loss of control over eating often involves subjective distress and/ or eating past the point of fullness. It can occur irrespective of the weight or size of the person eating, and irrespective of the amount or type of food eaten. (p. 651)

As you can see, there are a lot of components to this definition, and the degree of content validity in the Loss of Control over Eating Scale is the degree to which it addresses *all* of them. How did the researchers assess this? While developing the items for the scale, they consulted with experts and those previously diagnosed with this problem to ensure that scale items were fully covering the construct being measured.

Another type of construct validity is **convergent validity**, the degree to which a measure is related to other tests designed to measure the same general construct. Let's look at an example.

Komnenić, Filipović, and Vukosavljević-Gvozden (2015) were interested in online gaming, a popular

FIGURE 4.10 Tests have been created to measure the extent of an online gaming addiction. The degree to which one test is related to other tests designed to measure the same general construct is a measure of construct validity.

pastime of many who frequent the Internet. Specifically, they wanted to assess whether those who participate in online gaming experience "maladaptive cognitions" (p. 131). You can think of maladaptive cognitions as thinking of experiences like loneliness and depression. In order to assess the presence of this type of thinking with regard to online gaming, Komnenić et al. modified a scale called the Online Cognitions Scale. This scale had originally been created to measure the cognitive components of problematic Internet use in general (not just during gaming). They then assessed the convergent validity of their scale by correlating it with the Game Addiction Scale, which assesses the existence of primarily behavioral symptoms in those with an online gaming addiction. Thus, both scales were designed to assess whether someone has an online gaming addiction. The two scales were highly correlated, indicating the new scale had high convergent validity.

Another type of construct validity is **discriminant validity**, or **divergent validity**, which is the degree to which a measure is *not* associated with measures of different constructs. The following example should make this clear. Romaniuk and Khawaja (2013) assessed the validity of the University Student Depression Inventory, which is a short test that measures the presence of depression in university students. In order to check the discriminant validity of this test, they also gave their participants a test called the Life Satisfaction Scale. Think about it this way. Would someone who is depressed score the same way on both the University Student Depression Inventory and the Life Satisfaction Scale? They certainly do not sound like they are measuring the same constructs to me. You would expect a depressed student to score high on the University Student Depression Inventory but low on the Life Satisfaction Scale, because a depressed person is likely not satisfied with life. So if you are testing the discriminant validity of the University Student

Depression Inventory, you would expect a low or even a negative correlation between this test and the Life Satisfaction Scale. Romaniuk and Khawaja in fact found a strong negative correlation between the two tests, suggesting that the University Student Depression Inventory was *not* measuring life satisfaction. In this way, they have established the test's discriminant validity.

So in summary, face validity, content validity, and convergent validity all help researchers assess the extent to which a test measures what it is designed to measure; they are all measures designed to assess construct validity. Discriminant validity is also a way to assess construct validity, but it assesses the extent to which a test is unrelated to measures designed to measure different constructs. Now let's talk about the other general type of validity, criterion validity.

Criterion Validity. **Criterion validity** refers to the idea that the measure in question is related to a specific relevant outcome. There are two types of criterion validity: predictive validity and concurrent validity.

Predictive validity tells us whether a test can accurately predict a particular future behavior. Let's take a look at an example of researchers seeking to determine whether their test has predictive validity.

Amirkhan, Urizar, and Clark (2015) were interested in assessing the predictive validity of a stress measure called the Stress Overload Scale. Theories of stress tend to focus on both the demands made on individuals and the extent of their compromised resources. In addition, the experience of stress at times when resources are compromised has long been connected with illness (see Folkman, 2011). The Stress Overload Scale was designed to measure both the demands made on an individual and the extent to which coping resources are available to meet those demands. But would the Stress Overload

Scale be able to predict who is likely to get sick in the near future?

Amirkan et al. decided to find out. They tested undergraduates who were all experiencing the stress of finals. The undergraduates filled out the Stress Overload Scale and then were given a health survey and told to wait one month before filling it out and sending it back. What happened? The Stress Overload Scale scores predicted who got ill. For example, those in the high-risk group reported more illness frequency and more severe symptoms than those in the lowest-risk group. Thus, Amirkan et al. demonstrated that the Stress Overload Scale had predictive validity.

Another type of criterion validity is concurrent validity. **Concurrent validity** is present when scores on a test correlate with an already validated measure given at the same time (concurrently). Let's take a look at an example.

Meerkerk, Van Den Eijnden, Vermulst, and Garrestsen (2009) wanted to develop a short and valid test to measure the severity of compulsive Internet use. Yes, apparently it is possible to be on the Internet too much! (I just spent 6 hours online finding this out.) So Meerkerk et al. developed a test called the Compulsive Internet Use Scale, a 14-item test with a 5-point scale (0 = never to 4 = very often) that asked questions such as, "Do you neglect your daily obligations (work, school, or family life) because you prefer to go on the Internet?" To establish concurrent validity, Meerkerk et al. compared the scores on the Compulsive Internet Use Scale to scores on an already validated but much longer test called the Online Cognition Scale (a shorter test is often preferable because it requires less time commitment from respondents). The scores on the two tests were highly correlated, which suggested they were measuring the same construct. Thus the researchers established the concurrent validity of the Compulsive Internet Use Scale.

Table 4.6   Types of validity.

Construct validity – The degree to which a test actually measures the construct it is designed to measure.	Face validity	Does the test *appear* to be measuring what it was designed to measure?
	Content validity	Do the items on the test adequately reflect *all* components of the construct being measured?
	Convergent validity	To what degree is the test related to other tests designed to measure the *same* construct?
	Discriminant validity	To what degree is the test related to other tests designed to measure *other* constructs?
Criterion validity – Is the measure in question related to a specific relevant outcome?	Predictive validity	Does the test accurately predict a particular future behavior?
	Concurrent validity	Do scores on a test correlate with an already validated measure given at the same time?

One More Point about Creating Scales and Tests

We have looked at separate examples of assessments of reliability and validity. However, keep in mind that a research team will often assess *both* the reliability and the validity of a test, often including an assessment of multiple forms of each. For example, Romaniuk and Khawaja assessed both the reliability and the validity of the University Student Depression Inventory. More specifically, they tested reliability using a test–retest assessment and Cronbach's α. As for validity, they tested discriminant validity as described above, and they also tested for convergent validity by calculating the correlation between the University Student Depression Inventory and the Depression Anxiety Stress Scale (as expected, these two tests appear to be measuring similar constructs). Thus, reliability and validity are important concepts to both those who develop tests (developers should assess the reliability and validity of their tests) and those who use tests that others develop (look for evidence of reliability and validity before using tests that others have developed). See Table 4.6 for a review of the different types of validity relevant to test development.

Internal Validity and External Validity

Two additional types of validity you will encounter are internal and external validity. Let's go back momentarily to the definition of validity. The validity of a measure is the degree to which it measures what you intend it to measure. To put it another way, does the measure do what it's supposed to do? Internal validity asks the same question about an experiment: Does it do what it's supposed to do? More formally, internal validity asks the question: To what extent can I conclude that my independent variable caused my dependent variable responses? When you can confidently state that your independent variable caused the difference observed in your dependent variable, your experiment is said to have high internal validity. Internal validity is thus an assessment of whether we can determine cause and effect; thus, the term internal validity is relevant only for experimentation.

When you conduct a well-controlled experiment, the only difference between the groups is the variation in the independent variable(s), the variables you have purposely manipulated. Everything else is held constant. In other words, researchers hold all extraneous variables constant. Extraneous variables are all the uncontrolled variables that are not purposely manipulated but that could theoretically affect your results.

Let's go over a simple example. Let's say I want to know whether wearing a red shirt will affect the likelihood of a female's getting help from male study participants (there is a lot of research demonstrating the power of red in social interaction – see for example, Elliot & Niesta, 2008). In this case, my independent variable is the color of the shirt (red, black), and I have randomly assigned study participants to groups. The color of the shirt is the only thing I want to be different between my two groups. Everything else should be the same in all cases: the female confederate, the other clothes she wears, the environmental conditions (such as noise and lighting).

But now say that sometimes the confederate wears high heels and sometimes she wears flat shoes when a study session occurs – the height of her heel could affect whether she receives help (see Guéguen & Stefan, 2015). Heel height is now an extraneous variable that could be affecting my results. We do not want extraneous variables to affect our participants' responses, so we eliminate their impact by keeping as much as possible constant across groups. In short, the confederate should look the same, with the exception of the independent variable, the shirt color, every time an experimental session occurs.

The most troublesome kind of extraneous variable is a confound, an extraneous variable that varies systematically with the independent variable. When a confound is present, we can no longer state with certainty that the independent variable caused our results. Suppose, for instance, that every time the confederate wore a red shirt she also wore heels, and every time she wore a black shirt, she wore flats. In this case, the color of the shirt is

FIGURE 4.11 Guéguen and Stefan (2015) found that the height of a woman's heel can affect the likelihood of her receiving help. So unless you are intentionally studying how heel height affects participants' responses to a confederate, keep confederates' heels constant! You do not want your results to be caused by variables that you did not intentionally vary (extraneous variables).

systematically varying with the heel height. We have no way of knowing whether it is the shirt color that is affecting helping behavior or the heel height or both. We cannot state cause and effect with any certainty when a confound is present. Thus, the presence of a confound decreases internal validity. We'll talk about internal validity in more detail in Chapter 10 when we discuss specific threats to internal validity.

External validity is the extent to which you can generalize your results to other persons, places, and times. Let's return to an example from earlier in this chapter. Recall Lawson et al.'s Psychological Critical Thinking Exam, designed to measure psychology students' ability to think critically about basic principles of psychological science. I initially gave information regarding Lawson et al.'s investigation of the reliability of this test. They found that the test was reliable in that consistent results were obtained on each half of the test. However, Lawson et al. also considered the validity of the Psychological Critical Thinking Test. They found that senior psychology majors did well on this test, better than any other groups tested. These results do suggest that, at least at the university where the students were tested, psychology students were obtaining the desired critical thinking skills. So Lawson et al. had determined that this test was measuring what it was supposed to measure; the test was determined to be valid. But do these results hold for other psychology students at other learning institutions? That's a question of external validity, and only additional testing will enable the research community to know whether Lawson et al.'s results are generalizable to others. We consider external validity in depth in Chapter 12.

SUMMARY

Every variable in a research study must be operationally defined. When we operationally define an independent variable, we state the specific method used to manipulate the variable; for a dependent variable, we state the specific method used to measure the variable.

It is important not only to define your variables of interest, but also to understand the limits of the scale of measurement you are using. Nominal scales are the most basic form of measurement, characterized by the placement of information into categories. Numbers have no real meaning in nominal scales. Ordinal scales rank-order the levels of a variable. The intervals between the rankings are not necessarily equal; rankings indicate only more or less of something. Interval scales have equal intervals between the scale values but no true zero. Ratio scales also have equal intervals between scale values, but they have a true zero, which means whatever is being measured can also be absent.

Reliability is the ability of a measure to produce consistent results. You can assess reliability by administering the test twice to the same group of people and comparing the scores. You can also assess a test's internal consistency, such as by splitting the test in half and comparing scores on each half. A measure of inter-rater reliability called Cohen's kappa assesses consistency in judgments made by the research team.

Validity is the degree to which a test measures what you intend it to measure. Construct validity – the degree to which a test actually measures the construct it is designed to measure – can be assessed by a test's face validity (does the test superficially appear to be measuring what it's supposed to be measuring?), content validity (is the test assessing *all* the components of the construct of interest?), convergent validity (is it correlated with other tests designed to measure the same thing?), and discriminant validity (is it correlated with tests designed to measure something different?). Criterion validity of a test tells us whether the measure in question is related to a specific relevant outcome. For predictive validity the outcome is a future behavior. For concurrent validity, the outcome is a different but already validated test measuring the same general construct administered at the same time.

Your experiment has high internal validity if you can say conclusively that the change in your dependent variable was caused by your independent variable manipulation. External validity asks whether the results obtained with your research will hold for other persons, places, and times.

GLOSSARY

Cohen's kappa (κ) – a statistic that indicates the measure of agreement among judges.

Concurrent validity – present when scores on a test correlate with an already validated measure given at the same time (concurrently).

Constructs – psychological concepts that we cannot identify by observation but instead infer from measurable behaviors or outcomes.

Construct validity – the degree to which a test actually measures the construct it is designed to measure.

Content validity – the degree to which items on a test adequately reflect *all* components of the construct being measured.

Convergent validity – the degree to which a measure is related to other tests designed to measure the same general construct.

Converging evidence – if we use different operational definitions of a variable and we come to the same overall conclusion about that variable's role in the research, we have established converging evidence.

Criterion validity – refers to a consideration of whether the measure in question is related to a specific relevant outcome.

Cronbach's α (alpha) coefficient – used to assess internal consistency in a measure by calculating all possible split-half correlations in a test and averaging them together.

Discriminant validity (divergent validity) – the degree to which a measure is *not* associated with measures of different constructs.

Face validity – a test has face validity if, on the face of it, it *appears* to measure what it was designed to measure.

Internal consistency reliability – a measure is internally reliable if all the items on it are related, measuring the same underlying attribute.

Inter-rater reliability – the level of internal consistency between two or more judges.

Interval scale – a scale of measurement that has equal intervals between the scale values. Although you can have a zero value, this scale does not have a *true* zero.

Item-to-total correlations – used to assess internal consistency. Calculate the correlations between the score on each of the individual items and the total score (excluding the score for the item you are checking). Items not strongly correlated with the total score can be dropped from the scale, leaving a group of items that work well together to measure the same thing.

Measurement error – variation in measurement.

Nominal scale – the most basic scale of measurement, characterized by the placement of information into categories. Nominal variables reflect different *types* rather than different *quantities*. Numbers have no meaning in nominal scales.

Ordinal scale – a scale of measurement used when we want to rank-order the levels of the variable we are studying. In ordinal scales, the intervals between the rankings are not necessarily equal.

Predictive validity – indicates whether a test can accurately predict a particular future behavior.

Random error – a nonsystematic fluctuation in measurement.

Ratio scale – a scale of measurement that has equal intervals between the scale values. This scale has a true zero, which means whatever is being measured can also be absent.

Reliability – the ability of a measure to produce consistent results each time we use it.

Spearman-Brown split-half reliability coefficient – used to assess internal consistency in a measure when performing a split-half reliability check.

Split-half reliability – assessing reliability by determining the correlation between the total score on one half of the test with the total score on the other half.

Systematic error – a constant amount of error present each time a measurement is taken.

Test–retest reliability – assesses consistency of a measure by administering the same test to the same people at two different times under equivalent test conditions.

Validity – the degree to which a test measures what you intend it to measure.

REVIEW QUESTIONS

1 Explain what it means to operationally define an independent (manipulated) variable and a measured variable. Give an example of each.
2 Define construct.
3 Describe the four scales of measurement.
4 Differentiate between systematic error and random error.
5 Define reliability and describe ways of assessing it.
6 Describe the various types of validity and how they are assessed.
7 Differentiate between internal and external validity.
8 Differentiate between extraneous variables and confounds.

ARTICLES AS ILLUSTRATION

The articles presented below provide opportunities for you to use your knowledge of topics covered in this chapter. The questions that follow will help you focus on the pertinent points.

For each of the following articles, provide answers to the following:
  a. What is the research question?
  b. Name each independent variable and indicate how it was operationalized.
  c. What were the dependent variables and how were they operationalized?
  d. For each dependent variable, name the measurement scale used.
1 Guéguen, N. (2011). "Say it with flowers": The effect of flowers on mating attractiveness and behavior. *Social Influence, 6(2)*, 105–112. doi:http://dx.doi.org/10.1080/15534510.2011561556 (Note that this article contains two experiments. You can address the issues above for each experiment.)
2 Guéguen, N. (2014). Effect of an interviewer's tactile contact on willingness to disclose voting choice. *Social Behavior and Personality, 42*, 1003–1006. doi:http://dx.doi.org/10.2224/sbp.2014.42.6.1003

SUGGESTED ACTIVITIES

1 Identify the scale of measurement used with each of the variables noted below:
  a. American Film Institute's top 100 films of all time
  b. Time that it takes to spit out disgusting food
  c. Types of languages
  d. Grade point average
  e. Number of answers correct on a math test
  f. *Consumer Reports'* ranking of chocolate bars

g. Types of pets

h. Age

2 Name the four scales of measurement and provide your own example of each.

3 Choose a construct that you would like to know more about. Conduct a search of the literature to find information on a measure of that construct in which the authors assessed reliability and/or validity (include "reliability" or "validity" as search terms). Describe how the authors tested the reliability and/or validity of the test.

4 Describe how you would test the predictive validity of the SAT.

REFERENCES

Amirkhan, J. H., Urizar Jr., G. G., & Clark, S. (2015). Criterion validation of a stress measure: The Stress Overload Scale. *Psychological Assessment*, *27*, 985–996. doi:http://dx.doi.org/10.1037/pas0000081

Anderson, C., & Horne, J. A. (2008). Placebo response to caffeine improves reaction time performance in sleepy people. *Human Psychopharmacology*, *23*, 333–336. doi:http://dx.doi.org/10.1002/hup.931

Basch, C. H., Hillyer, G. C., Basch, C. E., & Neugut, A. I. (2012). Improving understanding about tanning behaviors in college students: A pilot study. *Journal of American College Health*, *60*, 250–256. doi:http://dx.doi.org/10.1080/07448481.2011.596872

Beaver, T., Knox, D., & Zusman, M. E. (2010). "Hold the phone!": Cell phone use and partner reaction among university students. *College Student Journal*, *44*, 629–632.

Beckstead, J. W. (2013). On measurements and their quality: Paper 1: Reliability-history, issues and procedures. *International Journal of Nursing Studies*, *50(7)*, 968–973. doi:http://dx.doi.org/10.1016/j.ijnurstu.2013.04.005

Bentley-Edwards, K. L., & Chapman-Hilliard, C. (2015). Doing race in different places: Black racial cohesion on Black and White college campuses. *Journal of Diversity in Higher Education*, *8*, 43–60. doi:http://dx.doi.org/10.1037/a0038293

Carifio, J., & Perla, R. (2008). Resolving the 50-year debate around using and misusing Likert scales. *Medical Education*, *42*, 1150–1152. doi:http://dx.doi.org/10.1111/j.1365-2923.2008.03172.x

Cronbach, L. J. (1951). Coefficient alpha and the internal structure of tests. *Psychometrika*, *16*, 297–334. doi:http://dx.doi.org/10.1007/BF02310555

Elliot, A. J., & Niesta, D. (2008). Romantic red: Red enhances men's attraction to women. *Journal of Personality and Social Psychology*, *95*, 1150–1164. doi:http://dx.doi.org/10.1037/0022-3514.95.5.1150

Epstein, J., Klinkenberg, W. D., Scandell, D. J., Faulkner, K., & Claus, R. (2007). Perceived physical attractiveness, sexual history, and sexual intentions: An Internet study. *Sex Roles*, *56*, 23–31. doi:http://dx.doi.org/10.1007/s11199-006-9169-x

Fairclough, S. H., & Spiridon, E. (2012). Cardiovascular and electrocortical markers of anger and motivation during a simulated driving task. *International Journal of Psychophysiology*, *84(2)*, 188–193. doi:http://dx.doi.org/10.1016/j.ijpsycho.2012.02.005

Folkman, S. (2011). Stress, health, and coping: An overview. In S. Folkman (ed.), *The Oxford Handbook of Stress, Health and Coping* (pp. 3–11). Oxford: Oxford University Press.

Fourie, M., Walton, D., & Thomas, J. A. (2011). Naturalistic observation of drivers' hands, speed and headway. *Transportation Research Part F*, *14*, 413–421. doi:http://dx.doi.org/10.1016/j.trf.2011.04.009

Glass, S. T., Lingg, E., & Heuberger, E. (2014). Do ambient urban odors evoke basic emotions? *Frontiers in Psychology*, *5*, 1–11.

Guéguen, N. (2011). "Say it with flowers": The effect of flowers on mating attractiveness and behavior. *Social Influence*, *6(2)*, 105–112. doi:http://dx.doi.org/10.1080/15534510.2011561556

(2014). Effect of an interviewer's tactile contact on willingness to disclose voting choice. *Social Behavior and Personality*, *42*, 1003–1006. doi:http://dx.doi.org/10.2224/sbp.2014.42.6.1003

Guéguen, N., & Stefan, J. (2015). Men's judgment and behavior toward women wearing high heels. *Journal of Human Behavior in the Social Environment*, *25*,

416–425. doi:http://dx.doi.org/10.1080/10911359.2014.976697

Gurung, R. A. R., & Vespia, K. M. (2007). Looking good, teaching well? Linking liking, looks, and learning. *Teaching of Psychology*, 34, 5–10. doi:http://dx.doi.org/10.1080/00986280709336641

Herrero, N., Gadea, M., Rodriguez-Alarcon, G., Espert, R., & Salvador, A. (2010). What happens when we get angry? Hormonal, cardiovascular and asymmetrical brain responses. *Hormones and Behavior*, 57(3), 276–283. doi:http://dx.doi.org/10.1016/j.yhbeh.2009.12.008

Howell, J. L., & Giuliano, T. A. (2011). The effect of expletive use and team gender perceptions of coaching effectiveness. *Journal of Sport Behavior*, 34, 69–81.

Jamieson, S. (2004). Likert scales: How to (ab)use them. *Medical Education*, 38, 1212–1218. doi:http://dx.doi.org/10.1111/j.1365-2929.2004.02012.x

Komnenić, D., Filipović, S., & Vukosavljević-Gvozden, T. (2015). Assessing maladaptive cognitions related to online gaming: Proposing an adaptation of online cognitions scale. *Computers in Human Behavior*, 51(Pt. A), 131–139. doi:http://dx.doi.org/10.1016/j.chb.2015.04.051

Latner, J. D., Mond, J. M., Kelly, M. C., Haynes, S. N., & Hay, P. J. (2014). The Loss of Control over Eating Scale: Development and psychometric evaluation. *International Journal of Eating Disorder*, 47, 647–659. doi:http://dx.doi.org/10.1002/eat.22296

Lawson, T. J., Jordan-Fleming, M. K., & Bodle, J. H. (2015). Measuring psychological critical thinking: An update. *Teaching of Psychology*, 42, 248–253. doi:http://dx.doi.org/10.1177/0098628315587624

Likert, R. (1932). A technique for the measurement of attitudes. *Archives of Psychology*, 22(140), 55.

Lobbestael, J., Arntz, A., & Wiers, R. W. (2008). How to push someone's buttons: A comparison of four anger-induction methods. *Cognition and Emotion*, 22, 353–373. doi:http://dx.doi.org/10.1080/02699930701438285

Lund, H. G., Reider, B. D., Whiting, A. B., & Prichard, J. R. (2010). Sleep patterns and predictors of disturbed sleep in a large population of college students. *Journal of Adolescent Health*, 46, 124–132. doi:http://dx.doi.org/10.1016/j.jadohealth.2009.06.016

Meerkerk, G. J., Van Den Eijnden, R. J. J. M., Vermulst, A. A., & Garretsen, H. F. L. (2009). The Compulsive Internet Use (CIUS): Some psychometric properties. *CyberPsychology & Behavior*, 12, 1–6. doi:http://dx.doi.org/10.1089/cpb.2008.0181

Plaisier, X. S., & Konijn, E. A. (2013). Rejected by peers – attracted to antisocial media content: Rejection-based anger impairs moral judgment among adolescents. *Developmental Psychology*, 49, 1165–1173. doi:http://dx.doi.org/10.1037/a0029399

Quiles, J. A. (2003). Romantic behaviors of university students: A cross-cultural and gender analysis in Puerto Rico and the United States. *College Student Journal*, 37, 354–366.

Romaniuk, M., & Khawaja, N. G. (2013). University student depression inventory (USDI): Confirmatory factor analysis and review of psychometric properties. *Journal of Affective Disorders*, 150(3), 766–775. doi:http://dx.doi.org/10.1016/j.jad.2013.02.037

Sato, T., Harman, B. A., Adams, L. T., Evans, J. V., & Coolsen, M. K. (2013). The cell phone reliance scale: Validity and reliability. *Individual Differences Research*, 11(3), 121–132.

Seiter, J. S., & Weger Jr., H. (2010). The effect of generalized compliments, sex of server, and size of dining party on tipping behavior in restaurants. *Journal of Applied Social Psychology*, 40, 1–12. doi:http://dx.doi.org/10.1111/j.1559-1816.2009.00560.x

Shields, G. S., Moons, W. G., Tewell, C. A., & Yonelinas, A. P. (2016). The effect of negative affect on cognition: Anxiety, not anger, impairs executive function. *Emotion*, 16, 792–797. doi:http://dx.doi.org/10.1037/emo0000151

Shiloh, S., Sorek, G., & Terkel, J. (2003). Reduction of state-anxiety by petting animals in a controlled laboratory experiment. *Anxiety, Stress, & Coping: An International Journal*, 16, 387–395. doi:http://dx.doi.org/10.1080/1061580031000091582

Turner, J. E. (2014). Researching state shame with the Experiential Shame Scale. *Journal of Psychology*, 148, 577–601. doi:http://dx.doi.org/10.1080/00223980.2013.818927

Vaidis, D. C., & Oberlé, D. (2014). Approaching opponents and leaving supporters: Adjusting physical proximity to reduce cognitive dissonance. *Social Behavior and Personality, 42*, 1091–1098. doi:http://dx.doi.org/10.2224/sbp.2014.42.7.1091

Vogt, W. P. (2005). *Dictionary of statistics & methodology: A nontechnical guide for the social sciences*. (3rd ed.). Thousand Oaks, CA: Sage.

Wickens, C. M., Wiesenthal, D. L., Hall, A., & Roseborough, J. E. W. (2013). Driver anger on the information superhighway: A content analysis of online complaints of offensive driver behavior. *Accident Analysis and Prevention, 51*, 84–92. doi:http://dx.doi.org/10.1016/j.aap.2012.10.007

5 Descriptive Research Methods

LEARNING OBJECTIVES

- Describe naturalistic observation and its advantages and disadvantages.

- Describe participant observation and its advantages and disadvantages.

- Describe archival research and its advantages and disadvantages.

- Describe the case study approach and its advantages and disadvantages.

In the first chapter you were introduced to different types of research methodologies. In an experiment, as you'll recall, you vary what you present to different groups of study participants, and then you see how the different groups are affected by your manipulation. But in some situations, it would be extremely difficult or even unethical to do an experiment. So instead of manipulating what our study participants see or experience, we observe them in their natural environments and describe what we see.

Let's consider an example. What if I were interested in the behavior of people who are saying goodbye to each other at an airport? Could I reasonably study this within the laboratory? That would certainly be difficult; airport behavior is probably best studied in the airport with a form of descriptive research. That's what we are going to discuss in this chapter: descriptive research methodology.

All descriptive research methods have one thing in common; they are *non-experimental* methods.

We are observing and describing what we see; we are not manipulating anything. Since we do not have control over what our participants experience, we cannot draw definitive conclusions about what is influencing their behavior. Thus, none of these descriptive methods gives us the ability to establish cause and effect.

Despite their inability to help us establish cause and effect, descriptive research methods can be an effective way to explore a topic researchers do not yet know much about. Once our observations allow us to become more familiar with the topic, we can work toward making predictions and developing a theory to explain our observations.

In this chapter we will cover four types of descriptive research methods: (1) naturalistic observation, (2) participant observation, (3) archival research, and (4) case studies. We'll start with naturalistic observation.

Naturalistic Observation

In naturalistic observation you observe people (or animals) in their natural settings and systematically record their behavior. In fact, there are many natural settings for people. Just think about where you are during your everyday life: school, library, gym, park, office, restaurant, stores. Observing people in their natural settings can provide important information about the way they behave.

Let's go over an example of naturalistic observation. Young, Mizzau, Mai, Sirisegaram, and Wilson (2009) were interested in whether the food choices of students in a university cafeteria were influenced by students' gender and by the number and gender of their companions. Consider this for a moment. Do you think people generally eat differently because of whom they're with? Do you think men and women have the same response in this situation? To investigate these questions, Young et al. observed students during meals in three cafeterias at the same university. Like many campus eateries, these had a vast selection of food choices. Those being observed were free to select whatever foods they wanted in whatever quantities they wanted. In addition, they were free to sit wherever and with whomever they wished.

The observers watched from a distance and recorded the types of food in front of each person. They also recorded the gender of each person, and the number of the people in each dining group. For each person, the observer made a rough estimate of the caloric count of the selected foods (the university dining services provided caloric information for most of the available foods).

What did the researchers find? Males generally had more calories on their plates than females (Young et al. did not consider whether the food was consumed). Most people ate in groups of two, and females chose food with fewer calories when they were eating with a male as opposed to a female.

Why Use Naturalistic Observation?

Let's talk about why Young et al. (2009) chose naturalistic observation as their research method. Earlier laboratory research regarding social influences on food choices had typically offered participants "highly constrained" options in the very non-natural setting of the laboratory (p. 269). This is quite different from participants' typical eating experiences. Eating in the laboratory, and knowing someone may be watching you eat (even if there is a cover story suggesting you are in the lab for other reasons), can alter your food choices.

Points to Consider when Conducting Naturalistic Observation

There are a few things to know before you conduct a naturalistic observation study. Let's turn to these now.

Follow Systematic Procedures for Recording Observations. What does it mean to systematically record behavior? Well, first you should have clear definitions of the behaviors of interest. This is important for a few reasons. If you have more than one observer, each needs to understand exactly what to look for in the people he or she is observing. When you write about your study, your clear definitions will also enable your readers to understand specifically what you did. Finally, having clear definitions can help you avoid **observer bias**, which can occur when the observer has a preconceived notion of how the person being observed is likely to act. This expectation can affect the behaviors the researcher notices as well as the way he or she interprets them. If the behaviors you are looking for are well defined, observer bias is less likely to drive decisions about what to look at or how to interpret it.

Let's take a look at an example. Suppose you are interested in learning about displays of public affection among college students on campus, so you and your research team decide to conduct a naturalistic observation study and watch male–female pairs. Now let's pretend the lead researcher on the research team told you and the other observers just to watch for "public displays of affection." You all went out and watched people and then returned with the following comments.

1. "I saw a man tousle a woman's hair. Does that count?"
2. "I didn't see that, but I saw a woman wipe food off a man's cheek. Does that count?"
3. "I saw her cleaning the man's cheek, but I didn't know if that was really affectionate so I didn't count it. I did, however, count the people I saw holding hands. How about that?"

This example suggests that the term "public displays of affection" was not defined specifically enough, since the observers were not sure what to look for.

Researchers often talk about creating operational definitions of the behavior of interest. When we create an operational definition for something that we are measuring, we are defining it by stating *exactly* what is to be observed and measured. Thus, to take our earlier example, if you wish to measure public displays of affection, you would need to decide what behaviors constitute public displays of affection (observing a sample of people before making your formal observations can help you decide what behaviors you will watch for). So let's say you and your team decide specifically that hand holding, walking arm in arm, hugging, and kissing are the ways you will define public displays of affection (and you will ignore all tousling of hair and wiping of faces!).

Also note that when you conduct a naturalistic observation study, you may need a **coding system** so you can categorize your data for later analysis. Researchers often develop their coding system before they start their formal observations (again note that you may need to observe sample research participants for a while in order to help you develop the coding system). Let's consider an example.

Fraley and Shaver (1998) were interested in investigating the behaviors that couples display in the airport. To develop their coding system, they first observed and took notes on the behaviors and emotions of 13 couples in a small airport. A sample of these notes appears in Table 5.1.

After making these observations, Fraley and Shaver identified the specific behaviors they were going to watch for – they created operational definitions of the behaviors of interest – and then they designed a coding sheet to use for later observations. As you can see in Table 5.2, the behaviors noted in the initial observations were placed in categories on the coding sheet. Furthermore, Fraley and Shaver decided that, for each person watched, they would rate each of the behaviors using a scale from 1 (not

Table 5.1   A sampling of Fraley and Shaver's observed behaviors.

Brief hug
Before boarding, he reads the newspaper and she leans her head on his shoulder
Massages her inner thigh
Kissed several times when she tries to leave
Both hold each other for approximately 5 minutes
When they separated, neither turned around to take "one last look" at the other
Eye-to-eye contact
Extended hug and stroking (lasts for about 5 minutes)
She stands on her tip-toes to give him a kiss
Tears in eyes; both members wipe the other's tears away
She goes back to the window and watches the plane leave
Holding hands
Petting other's head
She is still at the window 20 minutes after the plane leaves
Looks at wristwatch
Crying
At departure, she is the last to board the plane
She gives him money to buy coffee
Extended hand stretch
He leaves before she boards the plane but watches her from a distance without her knowledge
Intimate kiss
He waves goodbye when boarding plane
He kisses her head several times
He leaves quickly
She walks away crying
Long hug; both are crying
Sitting close
She whispers "I love you" to him as she boards
Prolonged hug at the gate
She, in a comforting manner, strokes his face

Source: Fraley, R. C. & Shaver, P. R. (1998). Airport separations: A naturalistic study of adult attachment dynamics in separating couples. *Journal of Personality and Social Psychology, 75(5),* 1198–1212. doi:http://dx.doi.org/10.1037/0022-3514.75.5.1198.

Table 5.2 Fraley and Shaver's coding sheet of operationally defined behaviors.

Contact Seeking	Avoidance
Kissing	Looking elsewhere (not directly at partner)
Watching from window after partner has boarded	Turning away
Embracing the partner	Trying to hurry the separation
Interrupted leaving (leaving, then coming back; turning back; looking at plane)	Breaking off contact
Contact Maintenance	**Sexuality**
Contact duration	Sexual touching
Hugging	Sexual caressing (hand on inner thigh)
Unwillingness to let go	Intimate kissing
Clinging, kneading, and so forth	**Sadness**
Eye-to-eye contact	Tears, crying
Being near the end of line at boarding	Facial expressions of sadness
"Extended hand stretch"	**Resistance**
Hands held or body held	Wanting to embrace or be held, but also resisting contact
Caregiving	Signs of anger, annoyance, or pouting
Petting, stroking	
Caregiving, reassurance	
Silent whisper ("I love you")	
Embracing the other to comfort	

Source: Fraley, R. C. & Shaver, P. R. (1998). Airport separations: A naturalistic study of adult attachment dynamics in separating couples. *Journal of Personality and Social Psychology, 75(5)*, 1198–1212. doi:http://dx.doi.org/10.1037/0022–3514.75.5.1198.

at all) to 4 (a lot). So if the person being watched did not display any intimate kissing, then the rating for that person under "intimate kissing" would be 1. (Note that the researchers could have decided to just use the list of behaviors as a checklist and check off behaviors as they see them.)

When conducting a naturalistic observation study you also have to have a plan for deciding which participants to observe. For example, there are a lot of people in an airport. How did Fraley and Shaver decide whom to watch?

In the second phase of their research, a member of the research team approached couples waiting in airport gate lobbies and asked whether they would fill out a short questionnaire that included questions about their relationship length, attachment style, and demographics. After the couples had filled out their questionnaires, another member of the research team sitting nearby began the observations and continued observing until the couple left the gate area (either the couple boarded a plane together or one boarded and one later left the gate area alone).

In some cases, you may choose to be very specific about whom you are going to observe. For example, Sommer and Steele (1997) were interested in watching people at restaurants to see whether there was a relationship between how many people were in a group and how long they stayed. Sommer and Steele decided that observers would take a seat in the restaurant and then record information for the next three people who came into the restaurant alone and the next three people who came in with groups (one person in each group was arbitrarily designated as the person to be watched). They used this specific rule in each of their 27 visits to 5 coffee shops and 30 visits to 20 restaurants.

Notice that the observers did not get to the restaurant, sit down, and then think, "Now whom should I watch? Oh, that person coming in looks interesting! I'll watch that person." This approach is not ideal because there might be something inherently different about the people who draw your attention, and you don't want the thing that makes them different to influence your results. Specifying a rule to follow ahead of time takes the question out of whom to watch. Just follow the rule. By the way, you might be interested to know that groups did spend a longer period of time in restaurants and coffee shops than did those who were alone.

Make reliable observations. Researchers conducting naturalistic observation should also be concerned about the reliability of their observations, that is, we want our observations to be consistent. In addition, sometimes more than one researcher is observing the same information. Under these conditions, the observers need to be consistent with each other. As we discussed in Chapter 4, inter-rater reliability (also known as inter-observer reliability) is the degree to which independent observers agree in their observations. There are various ways to determine inter-rater reliability. One way is to calculate the correlation of observations between two observers (see Chapter 6 for a discussion of correlation).

Another way is to use Cohen's kappa, which is the proportion of observed agreement between two judges beyond what we would expect to occur by chance. In this case the observers have to be using

a nominal scale, which means they put their observations into mutually exclusive categories such as "Democrat" & "Republican" (Cohen, 1960; Watkins and Pacheco, 2000). As you saw in Chapter 4, Cohen's kappa is easy to interpret. Its value ranges from −1.00 to +1.00. A value of +1.00 means you have total agreement between your two observers (that's great!). A value less than 0 means you have less than chance agreement between your two observers (that's not good). Several researchers have developed guidelines for Cohen's kappa that indicate the degree of agreement suggested by the values. For example, Cicchetti and Sparrow (1981) proposed that a kappa between .60 and .74 is good and between .75 and 1.00 is excellent (see Watkins & Pacheco for more regarding how to calculate Cohen's kappa).

If inter-observer reliability is not high enough (if you don't have a kappa of at least .60), ask yourself the following questions: Are there clear definitions about what behavior is to be observed? Are the observers adequately trained and have they had enough practice? Discuss discrepancies in the observation judgments so observers can come to an understanding of what to look for when observing. Once you have established a high level of reliability, the observers can continue with independent observations, checking only periodically to ensure that reliability remains high.

Fraley and Shaver were appropriately concerned with the reliability of their airport observations. Since their goal was to have one researcher code the behaviors of all those observed, they needed to first ensure the reliability of the behavior coding. In other words, they needed to know whether two people who saw the same behaviors would likely code them in the same way? If the answer is "yes," then it is ok to have just one person code an individual's behaviors. If the answer is "no," then further training is needed.

So here's how Fraley and Shaver took care of reliability in their observations. For training purposes, the research team watched 10 couples at the airport and discussed how the various behaviors observed should be coded, using the form shown in Table 5.2. Then they needed to test the adequacy of the coding training. So they had pairs of coders watch and code the behaviors of 21 people. They then calculated the inter-rater reliability for each of the categories shown in Table 5.2 (such as "Caregiving"). They found that the correlations were high, ranging from .80 to .95 depending on the behavioral category. Thus they determined that the training had worked well, and from then on only one person coded the behaviors of each observed study participant.

Be unobtrusive. Another consideration for those conducting naturalistic observation is that researchers should be unobtrusive during their observations. For example, in Young et al.'s study of University students in the cafeteria, students were observed from at least 32 feet away. In two of the monitored cafeterias, tables were viewed from a mezzanine, so the observers in this case were out of sight (the third cafeteria was said to be sparsely populated). The goal in each case is to ensure that research participants do not know they are being watched. If they do know, that knowledge may affect their behavior in an effect called **reactivity**.

The low likelihood of reactivity was one reason Fraley and Shaver (1998) chose the airport for their observations. In addition to being sites of freely expressed emotional and affectionate behaviors, airports are public spaces with many people engaged in different types of tasks like reading, writing, texting, eating, and talking, and they may or may not be watching those around them. The researchers could easily blend into this busy environment without making it obvious that they were watching those around them and taking notes.

As you can see, sometimes it is not possible to be completely out of sight when conducting a naturalistic study. Fraley and Shaver's observers weren't out of sight, but they found a way to make it work: they just blended into the bustling environment of an airport. Another option you might want to consider is to have your study participants habituate to your presence. **Habituation** means people gradually get used to the observer's presence and reduce their attention and responsiveness to him or her. This option is often a reasonable alternative when you are observing young children or animals; they are often not likely to notice or care if you and/or your camera equipment are present. Again, you want to make sure, as best as you can, that your presence does not affect the behavior of those you are observing. Once your research participants are accustomed to your presence, they are less likely to feel self-conscious and you are more likely to see natural behavior.

Let's look at an example in which the individuals in a naturalistic observation research project knew they were being observed. Stutts et al. (2005) were interested in the distractions drivers encounter and how they affect driving. Ever eat while you're driving? Well, that's one of the situations Stutts et al. considered. To look at the many possible distractions, Stutts et al. installed camera equipment in the cars of volunteers. The volunteers, who agreed to drive with the cameras for a week, were told a cover story: that the researchers wanted to learn "how traffic and roadway conditions affect driving behavior" (p. 1095). This is still naturalistic observation, but since the participants knew the cameras were there, we certainly have to be concerned about participant reactivity.

In fact, it is not clear whether the people in Stutts et al.'s study were able to habituate to the camera, since they were observed for only one week. Indeed approximately 22% reported that the presence of the cameras in their cars altered their driving

FIGURE 5.1 If we put cameras in people's cars, will they be as likely to engage in distracting behaviors?

in some way (about half said they became "more safety conscious or more aware of their driving" (p. 1096)). Even so, the results overall suggested that driver distractions do occur; almost 15% of the total time spent *moving* was also spent doing something defined as distracting (eating and drinking were the most common activities). There was also some evidence that these distractions could affect driving performance, because there were indeed times that drivers had no hands on the steering wheel, had their eyes on something inside the car instead of on the road, or had their vehicles drift.

Advantages and Disadvantages of Naturalistic Observation

Naturalistic observational research does have its advantages. Most importantly, since you are observing people in their natural environments, you typically can have confidence that you are seeing true behavior. However, naturalistic observation has disadvantages too. Let's consider one of Young et al.'s results again. Young et al. found that females chose food with fewer calories when they were eating with a male rather than a female. Because Young et al. did not do an experiment, they cannot establish cause and effect. In other words, we do not know why the females had fewer calories on their plates

when dining with a male. Were these females trying to control the impression they made on their male dining companions? Possibly, but we have no way of knowing this from the observations that Young et al. made.

One more possible disadvantage is the potential for ethical dilemmas to occur during naturalistic observation. Recall from Chapter 3 that we do not typically obtain informed consent from those being watched (due to potential reactivity), nor do we typically debrief them (which could cause distress); these procedures are in line with the APA Ethics Code (2002). However, some may well feel uneasy about observing people who do not know they are being watched. To defend naturalistic observation as a viable approach, I will note that what we observe is, in the vast majority of cases, public behavior within the realm of participants' everyday experiences. And of course, in line with APA Ethics Code, we "do not place participants at risk of criminal or civil liability or damage their financial standing, employability, or reputation, and confidentiality is protected" (APA, 2002, pp. 1069–1070). Therefore, some researchers decide that, despite its inability to establish cause and effect, naturalistic observation can be a helpful technique when it would be difficult to study the behavior of interest in a laboratory.

Participant Observation

Another type of descriptive research methodology is participant observation. **Participant observation** is what it sounds like; the researcher is observing, as in naturalistic observation, but in this case he or she is also participating in the observed activities, in some cases interacting with the study participants. The researcher conducting participant observation often works undercover, however, because, as we have seen, knowledge of being watched by a researcher can, in fact, change someone's behavior. And as always, we want to be observing people's true behaviors, not behaviors people put on because they know we're watching them.

I want to illustrate participant observation by telling you about a classic social psychology study. This example of participant observation was designed to investigate the theory of *cognitive dissonance* (Festinger, Riecken, & Schacter, 1956). Psychologists have discovered that our thoughts and our behaviors have to be consistent with each other or else we feel uncomfortable. That discomfort is cognitive dissonance. Here's an example. Let's say I think getting a tattoo is disgusting, but on a whim one night, I do it; I get a tattoo. In this case, my thought ("tattoos are disgusting") does not match my behavior (I got a tattoo!). This mismatch makes me feel uncomfortable, and thus I am motivated to change something, either my thought (well, it is kind of a pretty butterfly) or my behavior (I guess it's time to go to get that butterfly removed). Once my thought and behavior are in line with each other, I feel comfortable again.

Back to our classic study. Festinger et al. (1956) designed a participant observation study in order to investigate cognitive dissonance in the real world. Its focus was people who thought the world was about to end.

Throughout history, many small groups of people have believed the world is coming to an end. For example, in the 1970s Marshall Applewhite started a group called Heaven's Gate. Applewhite and his 38 followers all committed suicide in 1997 because they believed the earth was about to be "recycled" (Secter, 1997, para 6). They thought their souls would be taken to a higher level of being by a spacecraft traveling behind an incoming comet. In another example, as the year 2000 approached, some people feared our computer systems would not be able to handle switching from 1999 to 2000 and chaos

FIGURE 5.2 If I get a tattoo and I think that tattoos are disgusting, I likely will experience cognitive dissonance and will be motivated to change either my thought or behavior in order to feel comfortable again.

would ensue, yielding a society incapable of functioning. A CNN poll revealed that as a result of what was called the "Y2K bug," 38% of respondents were expecting riots and 9% thought the world was going to end ("Poll: Many foresee Y2K," 1999, para. 1). Thankfully, these predictions were unfounded.

Festinger and his colleagues (1956) had been considering historical examples of groups organized around the prediction of future events such as the end of the world. Specifically, they looked at what happened when predicted events did not occur. Often they found, in line with their hypothesis, that people were motivated to change their thoughts to eliminate the dissonance. More specifically, thinking and acting like the world was going to end, and then seeing that it does not, could make someone feel like a fool. And feeling like a fool is quite uncomfortable.

Those who believed the world was to end would likely be motivated to lessen this dissonance. They could stop believing the world will end and stop all behaviors that prepared for that ending. This is tough to do because followers typically believed so strongly in the idea that the world was going to end that stopping would be difficult and uncomfortable. Think about how tough it would be to say, "I was wrong about everything I believed." Another possibility according to Festinger et al. is that believers would come up with a reason that fits within their belief system and explains why the world did not end. This reasoning can be especially effective if the others in the group believe it too. So Festinger et al. predicted that spreading the word of a group's beliefs, "proselytizing," would increase when the group's predictions did not come true, and they provided a variety of historical examples to support this point (p. 28).

When Festinger et al. learned about a woman in the midwestern United States who, along with her followers, believed the world was soon coming to an end, they realized they had a unique opportunity. They didn't just have to rely on historical documents to understand the actions of those who believe the world is going to end. They could observe this woman ("Marian Keech") and her followers to see what they thought and did when the world didn't end.

Festinger et al. hired a few college students they called "observers" and all of them, students and researchers, joined the group as followers of Keech. My account below includes some details from Festinger et al.'s book describing this observation.

Keech said she had received messages from a planet she referred to as "Clarion." According to her, beings from Clarion had visited the earth, seen evidence in the earth's formation that indicated disaster was to arrive at midnight on December 21st, and selected Keech to relay these messages of disaster.

Keech and her followers believed they would be safe from the impending disaster because flying saucers would be arriving to rescue them. Keech instructed her followers how to prepare for their upcoming journey. She said metal was not allowed on the saucer ("contact with metal would produce severe burns"), so all took off their watches and glasses, cut out their zippers, and removed their belts (Festinger et al., 1956, p. 109). Each follower also received a passport for the saucer (a blank piece of paper and a stamped envelope) and learned the password to enter the saucer ("I left my hat at home") (Festinger et al., 1956, p. 126). Many even received an assigned seat number for the saucer trip.

They prepared and then waited for a spaceman to arrive at midnight on December 21st to take them to the flying saucer. But at the appointed hour, nothing happened. By 2:00 a.m., one of the followers, a high school student, was told to call his mother and say he was on his way home (he was assured that the spacemen would find him wherever he was, but since his mother had warned that she would call the police if he were not home by 2:00 a.m., his going home was a way to avoid getting the police involved). Then at 4:45 a.m., after many in the group were reduced to tears of disappointment, Keech received a message from the extraterrestrial beings: God had spared the earth because of the faith of this group.

What would Keech and her followers do when faced with the knowledge that the world was not ending? Well, prior to the predicted date of doom, Keech did not seek out publicity and was often very hesitant to talk to outsiders. Now, with this new message, the group had an explanation for why the saucer didn't arrive, and they were thrilled. They had saved the world! And now they wanted publicity. By 6:30 a.m. on that fateful day, Keech and two of her most devoted followers had contacted all the local newspapers and wire services to spread the word of their achievements. Only a few followers began to doubt the truth of what Keech had said; most of those who had been firmly committed to the idea of the world's ending remained steadfast in their devotion. As the theory of cognitive dissonance predicted, "proselyting increased meteorically following disconfirmation" (Festinger et al., 1956, p. 212). In other words, group members' encouraging of others to believe as they did increased substantially after the saucer failed to appear, because any other action would cause discomfort or dissonance.

Why Use Participant Observation?

Let's talk about why Festinger et al. chose participant observation for this research. Festinger and his colleagues were interested in observing the behavior of those who think the world is coming to an end. As researchers, they could not just go up to this group and say, "Hi. We'd like to watch your reaction when the world doesn't end. Could we just hang out with you a while?" The group might well be offended that the researchers didn't share their belief that the world would end and would very likely have refused permission. This is also not a good approach for research purposes because knowing they were being watched could certainly alter the behavior of the observed. So the best approach in this type of situation is to use participant observation. The researchers went undercover, pretending they too believed that the world was going to end, and they joined the group.

Participant observation is still used today in situations in which gaining information about a phenomenon would be difficult for a non-participating observer. For example, participant observation has been used to learn about college Republicans

(Kidder, 2015) and about the psychological support provided by those in a "pro-ana" (pro-anorexia) online support group (Brotsky & Giles, 2007). In each of these cases, the researchers would not have been privy to those in these environments without participating.

It is reasonable to question the ethics of participant observation in which the researchers are undercover; we do not know whether Festinger et al.'s study could be done today due to potential ethical concerns. As with all research, the researchers and the IRB have the responsibility of weighing the costs of the deception (covert observations) against the potential benefits of the research. Brotsky and Giles' work is relevant here because one of the authors pretended to be pro-anorexia in order to be admitted into these online communities. The research team presented the ethical dilemma of this covert examination in the following way:

> We were fully aware that our study contravened certain ethical research principles, at least those pertinent to offline, conventional social science research. Traditionally, when ethical guidelines are breached, it is necessary for researchers to defend their behavior in relation to the importance of the research. In this instance, was deception justified? We believe that it was, given the charges laid against the pro-ana community (that they are effectively sanctioning self-starvation), and the potential benefit of our findings to the eating disorders clinical field. (Brotsky & Giles, 2007, p. 96)

Note that not all participant observation research studies include researchers participating undercover. In some cases, researchers identify themselves as researchers and are given permission to be present. For example, in Kidder's study of college Republicans, he indicates that he was truthful about his identity as a researcher, and although he tried to blend in while attending a variety of their meetings over the course of three years, he never represented himself as a Republican. In a situation like this where someone's identity as a researcher is known, habituation is relevant; those being observed may habituate to the presence of the observers over time.

Points to Consider when Conducting Participant Observation

Before you conduct a participant observation study, here are a few things to know.

Use Systematic Procedures for Recording Observations. As in naturalistic observation, you should have clear definitions of the behaviors of interest in participant observations so each observer knows what to look for. Clear definitions also help researchers avoid observer bias. In Festinger et al.'s work, all observers were trained and given specific instructions about the kinds of information to obtain. For example, they were to get information about all members in the group, most of whom were college students, about how much each was convinced of the beliefs (beyond Keech, 8 were very committed and 7 less committed), about what each had done or not done because of these beliefs such as quitting jobs, saying goodbye to family and friends, or giving away belongings, and about how much they had tried to convince others to agree with their belief system. The observers were also told to take note of what the members of the group did as the proposed end of the world date drew near. For example, anticipating the flood said to accompany the end, one member gave her young son his Christmas presents in early December.

Try not to influence the study participants. As researchers conducting an observational research study, you do not want to influence the people you are watching. But being a participant in a group

makes this difficult. Here's an example of how this sort of thing was handled by Festinger's group. One night Marian Keech ordered one of the researchers to lead a meeting. How does someone lead without influencing? The researcher cleverly suggested that the group sit silently and meditate and wait for inspiration.

In other situations, not being an influence was more difficult. For example, all in the group were pressured to leave their jobs. The researchers were understandably reluctant to make such a commitment, and delayed making any such announcement as long as possible. Festinger et al. acknowledged that "evasion of these requests and their failure to quit their jobs at once were not only embarrassing to them and threatening to their rapport with the group, but also may have had the effect of making the members who had quit their jobs less sure that they had done the right thing" (p. 241). Festinger et al. acknowledged that, "as members, the observers could not be neutral – any action had consequences" (p. 241).

Another example of a researcher's influence on a follower came shortly before the proposed saucer's arrival, when one of the researchers informed the crowd that he had neglected to remove the zipper from his pants (remember the "no metal on the saucer" rule?). Here is Festinger et al.'s account of this occurrence.

> *This knowledge produced a near panic reaction. He was rushed into the bedroom where Dr. Armstrong [a follower who was a physician], his hands trembling and his eyes darting to the clock every few seconds, slashed out the zipper with a razor blade and wrenched its clasps free with wire cutters". (p. 162)*

Record observations secretly. Festinger et al. could not freely write anything down without arousing suspicion. This meant they often wrote their notes while in the restroom or dictated them into tape recorders off-site. When possible, they recorded information verbatim, such as a phone conversation, but sometimes it was only a summary of what was said and recorded only after a delay.

Keeping up with note taking was a very demanding task. The observers were with the group for about a month before the predicted end. On some days their contact was brief, only an hour or two, but on other days, observers were present up to 14 hours. One student observer even moved into the home of two of the followers and often cared for their children while the followers took overnight trips. There were all-night meetings and lack of sleep was acknowledged as a problem. Festinger et al. indicated that participant observation was indeed exhausting work.

Advantages and Disadvantages of Participant Observation

The advantages and disadvantages of participant observation mostly parallel those for naturalistic observation. On the plus side, you are likely to be observing true behavior, since those being observed often do not know you are watching them. A disadvantage is that, as with naturalistic observation, you cannot definitively establish cause and effect. And you run the risk of influencing your study participants as a result of interacting with them. We saw examples of this in Festinger et al.'s work. Unfortunately, this can be difficult to avoid.

We should not leave this topic without discussing the ethics of participant observation. Like naturalistic observation, participant observation does not typically include informed consent and debriefing. However, it might actually make you privy to behavior that is not what we traditionally think of as "public" behavior. Most of the information regarding Keech's group would have been difficult to obtain

had the researchers not infiltrated it. Does this mean the witnessed behavior is "private" behavior or just a different kind of public behavior? Participant observation also involves deception because we are concealing our identity. These are all important ethical issues that need to be addressed. Ultimately, it is up to you, as the researcher, and your IRB to decide what is appropriate.

Therefore, as with naturalistic observation, despite the inability to establish cause and effect, there are clearly some situations in which participant observation would be a logical choice.

Archival Research

Another descriptive research technique is archival research. When a researcher does **archival research**, he or she is using the data from existing documents to answer research questions. Archival data are data collected by someone else and then saved so others could access the data. Let's look at some examples.

Some institutions have a repository of data specifically available to those who want access to data that have already been collected. A good example of this kind of "survey archive" is the large repository at University of Michigan's Interuniversity Consortium for Political and Social Research (ICPSR) (go to www.icpsr.umich.edu). You can browse these data by subject, by geographical location, and by time period. I encourage you to wander around this site and explore.

Let's look at a few examples of data housed in the ICPSR survey archive. In 1993, Henry Wechsler of the Harvard School of Public Health conducted a "College Alcohol Study" (CAS) in which a national sample of college students were asked various demographic questions and about their use of alcohol. The same basic questionnaire was later answered by different samples of students in 1997, 1999, and 2001. These datasets are all available at ICPSR, and various researchers have accessed them to answer their own questions of interest (because there is confidential information in the dataset, researchers have to apply for access to these data). Just to get a feel for some of the different ways in which these data have been used, let's look at some examples.

Chauvin (2012) accessed the 2001 CAS dataset to look at binge drinking and the motives for binge drinking among college students, comparing those in Greek organizations (fraternities and sororities) with those not. (Binge drinking in the CAS dataset was defined as the consumption of at least 5 drinks at a sitting for men or 4 drinks at a sitting for women during the 2 weeks before the survey – Wechsler, Davenport, Dowdall, Moeykens, & Castillo, 1994.) First Chauvin found that those in Greek organizations reported binge drinking at higher rates than those who were not in Greek organizations. Further comparison of the two groups revealed different social motives for their binge drinking. For those in Greek organizations, the answer to the question, "How important is it for you to participate in parties at college?" was a strong predictor of binge drinking (p. 265). In other words, Greek students who thought parties were important were more likely to binge drink than were those who didn't think so.

The answer to this question was also a motive for those not in fraternities or sororities; however, this latter sample also had other motives for binge drinking, such as the degree to which students at their school are said to approve of having six drinks at a party. When those around them approved, non-Greek students were more likely to binge. Chauvin suggests that the CAS dataset may not fully capture the motives of those who are binge drinking within the Greek system and recommend that future researchers consider collecting additional data.

Abu-Ras, Ahmed, and Arfken (2010) accessed the same CAS (2001) dataset and focused on alcohol use among American Muslim students. All students who answered "Islam" in response to the question, "In what religion were you raised?" were compared to those who provided every other available answer – "None," "Catholicism," "Judaism," "Protestantism," or "Other" (p. 209). The researchers found that approximately 47% of Muslim students at the US colleges included in this CAS dataset indicated they had consumed alcohol within the past year, while approximately 80% of non-Muslim students did (see Table 5.3).

Abu-Ras et al. noted that the rate of drinking for Muslim students sampled in the CAS dataset is

Table 5.3 Abu-Ras et al.'s findings regarding religion and drinking: alcohol use in prior year by religious heritage.

Level of alcohol use	Islam (N = 131)	Protestantism (N = 3,936)	Catholicism (N = 3,565)	Judaism (N = 275)	Other (N = 701)	None (N = 1,503)
No alcohol	53.4%	26.1%	11.1%	7.3%	30.0%	17.1%
Alcohol but no heavy, episodic drinking	27.5%	35.1%	36.3%	36.3%	41.5%	38.0%
Heavy, episodic drinking	19.1%	38.7%	52.7%	58.9%	28.5%	44.9%

Source: Adapted from Abu-Ras, W., Ahmed, S., & Arfken, C. L. (2010). Alcohol use among U.S. Muslim college students: Risk and protective factors. *Journal of Ethnicity in Substance Abuse, 9(3),* 206–220. doi:http://dx.doi.org/10.1080/15332640.2010.500921.

higher than often found for Muslims, so they were interested in what other factors might be influencing this drinking rate. They found that parental approval of drinking was a risk factor. They also found that the Muslim students who did not consume alcohol were more likely to see participation in religious activities as very important; thus they identified religiosity as "protective against drinking" (p. 206). They suggested that future researchers examine this latter relationship more closely, since the CAS dataset did not delve much into the religiosity issue.

Now let's consider one more research study that used the CAS dataset from 2001. Kuo, Wechsler, Greenberg, and Lee (2003) considered how the marketing of beer can influence the binge drinking of college students. These researchers combined the data from the 2001 CAS dataset with an examination of how beer is marketed in the communities where the colleges of interest were located; they considered places that sold beer within a 2-mile radius of the colleges. Specifically, they were looking to see how the nearby communities advertised and sold their beer, such as whether they offered volume discounts. They found, for example, that colleges in communities with more places offering larger volumes of beer for sale, such as kegs, also had higher binge drinking rates.

All the researchers described above were able to use the 2001 CAS dataset because it contained questions relevant to each of the research questions of interest. The different focuses of the research teams determined what each pulled out of the dataset.

A survey archive repository is only one option for accessing archived data. Another approach is to use written historical or contemporary documents that have been archived, whether electronically or not. Typically we analyze these documents using a technique called content analysis. **Content analysis** is a systematic analysis of documents or participant

responses that results in a summary of the available information. In content analysis, you read through all the available information and then create a coding system that will help you to summarize and make sense of the content. Let's review a few examples, beginning with an analysis of historical documents.

Cho, Hall, Kosmoski, Fox, and Mastin (2010) were interested in what popular magazines targeting females had to say about tanning and skin cancer. In addition, they wanted to assess whether the rising incidence of skin cancer was associated with an increase in the magazines' coverage of skin cancer issues. Thus they took a historical perspective and looked at magazines spanning a recent 10-year period.

Tanning has been associated with a risk of skin cancer (for example, see Ting, Schultz, Cac, Peterson, & Walling, 2007). Unfortunately, many see tanning as beneficial because they believe those with a tan appear more attractive (Pettijohn, Pettijohn & Geschke, 2009). To assess how well popular magazines communicate the dangers of tanning, Cho et al. examined eight magazines targeting audiences from adolescent girls to older women. Within these eight magazines, they used search terms such as "skin cancer," "tan," and "tanning beds" to look for articles that had appeared within their predefined period of 10 years. Once they had obtained the articles, they then used the coding system they had developed to identify whether the articles covered tanning consequences ("aged skin"), tanning benefits ("healthy glow"), skin cancer prevention ("long-sleeved shirts"), and skin cancer detection ("how to perform a skin examination") (pp. 3–4).

Cho et al. found 250 articles on relevant topics published during the 10-year period. Coverage of the consequences of tanning, the benefits of tanning, and the methods of skin cancer detection and prevention had increased over time. While the authors were pleased that magazines were increasingly

FIGURE 5.3 With the use of a content analysis, Cho et al. (2010) found that magazines targeting females were increasingly providing information regarding the risks of tanning while still providing information about tanning "benefits."

warning their readers of the dangers of tanning, the persistent coverage of tanning "benefits" was a concern.

Cho et al. thus analyzed a set of documents and took a historical view, though a relatively recent one. Sometimes researchers examine archived written documents from long ago.

Let's take a look at an example. Freudenmann, Öxler, and Bernschneider-Reif (2006) were curious about a statement often put forth in the medical literature, that the drug company Merck originally created the drug ecstasy as an appetite suppressant. Freudenmann et al. noted that there were few details available in the literature about this history, so they decided to investigate the validity of this statement. To look into this, they traveled to Germany and went through Merck's archives. Some documents were available electronically and others were not, so as part of their research process Freudenmann et al. digitized all obtained documents so other researchers would then have access to them. Through a systematic analysis of all available and relevant documents from 1900 to 1960, including laboratory records, patents, and

interviews, they found that ecstasy had *not* been developed as an appetite suppressant. This information likely came to light only because these researchers took the time to comb through the archived documents.

Now let's look at an analysis of written documents that doesn't have that historical focus. Huffman, Tuggle, and Rosengard (2004) were interested in whether campus media outlets cover sports for male and female athletes equally. The impetus for this investigation was the recognition that it had been approximately 30 years since Title IX required gender equity for all, including athletes, by banning sex discrimination in education. Huffman et al. acknowledged that since the passage of Title IX more females were participating in sports, but they wondered whether, on the college level, campus media coverage of these events was equal to the coverage of sporting events for males. To investigate this, they began by creating a list of the colleges and universities that produce television newscasts. Then they contacted faculty at each school and requested a copy of the student television newscast and the campus newspaper from within a specific, contemporary time period.

FIGURE 5.4 Huffman et al. (2004) found there was more campus media coverage of male than female athletes, although the quality of coverage was similar.

Huffman et al. used their research questions to guide their development of a coding system for analyzing the materials. For example, to answer the question "What is the ratio in campus media of stories featuring women's sports to men's sports?" the authors assessed the number and length of the stories found in the submissions (p. 480). They found that the newspaper articles and television programs provided more coverage of male than female athletes, although the quality of coverage was similar. For instance, stories about both genders were just as likely to include color photos.

Why Use Archival Research?

Sometimes, especially in survey archives, the data in archived datasets were obtained from large, nationally representative samples. Few researchers have the financial resources to obtain such samples themselves (often the original dataset was obtained with the help of grant money); thus access to these archived datasets can be wonderfully helpful to their research plans.

Points to Consider when Conducting Archival Research

One consideration when evaluating whether to use a particular dataset is that the data available might not address all the questions you want to address. Since you didn't collect the data, you were not able to specify exactly what questions you wanted to ask of the study participants. We saw examples of this. In some cases, researchers mined the data for what was relevant to their research questions, noted what was missing from the collected data, and then recommended that future researchers consider additional data collection. Abu-Ras et al.'s study of alcohol use among US Muslim students fits into this category. The researchers found that religiosity acted as protection against drinking and recommended that future researchers look specifically at this issue.

Another approach when the archived dataset doesn't address all that you need is to supplement the dataset with some complementary information. For example, think about the study by Kuo et al. as discussed above. The team were interested in whether binge drinking was associated with particular forms of marketing of beer in the communities surrounding the campuses of interest. The CAS did have the information about binge drinking Kuo et al. wanted, but it did not have information about retail outlets that sold beer in the neighborhood communities. Thus Kuo et al. supplemented the CAS data with data of their own. There are even more ways to use archived data when you are able to expand it with data you collect yourself.

Advantages and Disadvantages of Archival Research

An advantage of using any type of archival data is that you do not have to expend the time, money, or energy to collect the data yourself. Another advantage is that, in many cases, the archived data are available electronically and so are already in an easy-to-analyze spreadsheet format. It's also a good procedure to use when you have questions about historical trends; you saw a glimpse of this with Cho et al.'s research on tanning as represented in magazines over a 10-year period.

One possible disadvantage of using archival data is that sometimes obtaining access is not as easy as you would like. For example, some survey repositories require that your college or university be a member of their network. In other cases, you may have to request special permission to access the desired information. While obtaining access can vary in difficulty, the end result can certainly be worth your time. Finally, the biggest disadvantage is that since archival research, like all the techniques in this chapter, is a non-experimental technique, we cannot use it to establish cause and effect.

Case Studies

A case study is usually an in-depth study of an individual, although sometimes it can be an in-depth study of an event or an organization. Researchers in psychology typically use case studies when they want to provide an in-depth analysis of a specific person who is unusual in some way, perhaps because of a special ability or a disorder.

Let's first consider a case study of someone with a special ability. Jambor and Weekes (1996) provided an in-depth analysis of a 36-year-old woman in college sports. Most college students are between 18 and 24 years old (US Department of Education, 2010), and while plenty of college students are older than the traditional age, few of them play college sports. Recognizing that this woman's experience was unusual, Jambor and Weekes asked her to participate in a case study. The athlete agreed, and the researchers proceeded to interview her, and sometimes her coach, once or twice a week over the course of 9 weeks. Of particular interest to the researchers was how the athlete's experiences on the track team were affected by her life circumstances (she was married and had two children), and how her experiences differed from those of traditional college athletes. Here are a few observations from the case study that resulted.

Jambor and Weekes found that their study participant was highly motivated to do well and had a high level of self-esteem, characteristics similar to those of other college athletes. On the other hand, she was different because of the many roles she had to fill – athlete, student, wife, and mother. For example, because of her family responsibilities, her coach let her train in her own time instead of with the team. Jambor and Weekes also reported that their observed athlete did not have the typical social support often found on college teams. The other team members saw her as a leader and looked to her for support (presumably because of her age and her role as mother to an 18-year-old daughter), but she did not look for support from her teammates. However, she did have the support of her husband, who often ran with her, and of her children and her coach (her parents were not supportive of her work on the track team). Jambor and Weekes concluded that, with the help of a coach who was flexible in his training requirements, this athlete was able to compete successfully despite her differences.

As suggested above, case studies are also used in psychology to document information about someone who has a psychological disorder. The researchers in this type of situation would likely ask questions of the client (I'll refer to the participant here as the "client" due to the clinical nature of the study) to get a history and establish his or her current level of functioning. They may assess the client using various psychological measures, such as intelligence tests and neuropsychological tests that can help diagnose issues in brain functioning. They may describe the techniques used to treat the client, and the clinical outcome. A case study like this will be informative to those who may have clients in similar situations.

Let's take a look at an example. Cardi et al. (2012) worked with a 21-year-old female with anorexia nervosa, an eating disorder. This client suffered from intense anxiety with regard to food. She had tried various treatments, but they had not been successful. Cardi et al. decided to use virtual reality exposure in conjunction with cognitive behavioral treatment in an effort to ease the client's anxious feelings about food.

Psychologists have often treated fear responses using a technique called "systematic desensitization," in which a person relaxes while imagining a series of increasingly anxiety-evoking situations (see Wolpe, Brady, Serber, Agras, & Liberman, 1973). The client does not proceed to a new object until no longer fearful of the previous object. In virtual

FIGURE 5.5 Cardi et al. (2012) used virtual reality and cognitive behavioral treatment in an effort to ease a client's anxious feelings about food. They described their technique in a case study.

reality treatment, all the presentations of the feared objects are virtual – seen on a computer – rather than imagined.

So Cardi et al. had the goal of eliminating their client's fear of food. They presented her with a virtual kitchen with virtual cupboards that contained virtual food. The client was gradually exposed to the foods in this virtual kitchen, starting with her least-feared (salad) and ending with her most-feared (lasagna, for one). Each virtual bite was accompanied by the sound of biting and chewing, making the experience quite realistic.

As part of the case study, Cardi et al. also gathered data about their client using a variety of scales to assess the magnitude of her eating disorder as well as her experience of anxiety and depression. The researchers assessed this information both before and after the treatment, a comparison that allowed them to see whether the treatment was helpful. Cardi et al. reported that the client gradually became more comfortable with foods; her anxiety dissipated, and her symptoms were reduced.

Why Use Case Studies?

As you can see from these examples, case studies provide in-depth documentation of a person who is unusual in some respect. The client in Cardi et al.'s work was unusual in having an eating disorder that was not responding to traditional methods of treatment, so she began virtual reality treatment in combination with cognitive behavior therapy. The virtual reality treatment reported here was a relatively new technique, and information about it was reported in Cardi et al.'s article in detail so other therapists could utilize the method if they choose.

Points to Consider when Conducting Case Studies

Recall that observer bias can occur when an observer has expectations about the person being observed. This bias is a concern with case studies because researchers typically create an in-depth description at least partially developed as a result of observing the participant. However, a feature of some case studies makes this technique especially subject to the risk of observer bias. Specifically, in some of the more clinically oriented case studies, the researchers may be using a therapeutic technique they themselves developed, and understandably they have a vested interest in the client's being helped by it. Researchers must not let that personal investment in the treatment influence their observations and interpretation of the data.

Advantages and Disadvantages of Case Studies

One advantage of using the case study method is that you generate a wealth of information about an unusual person. Another advantage is that the case study method can document the application of new therapeutic techniques to treat someone (as we saw in Cardi et al.'s study of a woman with anorexia). This wealth of information in turn gives you another advantage: you might be able to generate some ideas about how the person came to be unusual.

Case studies do have disadvantages, however. For one, while you may speculate about what caused someone's behavior, you cannot draw clear causal conclusions. No matter how reasonable the explanation you offer for the individual's behavior, with a case study you would not be able to rule out other explanations. Therefore, your inability to state cause and effect is a limitation of the case study method (and of all descriptive methods in this chapter).

Another disadvantage of a case study is that, since you are studying only one individual, you cannot know whether what you see is also what you would see with others who are similarly unusual. In other words, you cannot generalize from your case study observations. For example, recall that Jambor and Weekes found that the 36-year-old athlete they studied did not look to her track teammates for support. Would other non-traditional college athletes take a similar approach? You can know this only by studying others.

SUMMARY

Naturalistic observation, participant observation, archival research, and case studies are all descriptive, *non-experimental* research methods. With each of these descriptive research methods we are observing and describing what we see; we are not manipulating anything. Since we do not have control over what our participants experience, we cannot establish cause and effect with these methods.

In naturalistic observation researchers observe study participants in their natural settings and systematically record their behavior without interacting with them or interfering in any way. In participant observation the researchers systematically record their observations while participating in the observed activities (sometimes their identity as researchers is not disclosed). While those conducting participant observation sometimes interact with their study participants, they try not to influence them.

When researchers conduct archival research, they use data from existing documents to answer research questions. The type of document and the period of time they cover vary depending on the nature of the research question.

A case study is an in-depth study of an individual, an event, or an organization. Researchers in psychology typically use case studies when they want to provide an in-depth analysis of a person who is unusual in some way, perhaps because of a special ability or a disorder.

Despite their inability to help us establish cause and effect, descriptive research methods can provide important information about study participants and their experiences.

GLOSSARY

Archival research – research that uses data from existing documents to answer research questions.

Case study – an in-depth study of an individual, an event, or an organization.

Coding system – a categorization plan for organizing data.

Content analysis – systematic analysis of documents or participant responses that results in a summary of the information.

Habituation – process by which people gradually get used to an observer's presence and reduce their attention and responsiveness to him or her.

Observer bias – an observer's preconceived notion of how the person being observed is likely to act.

Participant observation – a researcher participates in the observed activities, sometimes including interacting with the study participants.

Reactivity – a change in behavior as a result of knowing one is being watched.

REVIEW QUESTIONS

1 Describe the naturalistic observation research approach.
2 Explain why researchers would use a naturalistic research approach.
3 State what it means to systematically record observations.
4 Define observer bias.
5 Explain why it is important to be unobtrusive when conducting a naturalistic observation study.
6 Identify advantages and disadvantages of the naturalistic observation approach.
7 Describe the participant observation research approach.
8 Explain why we would use a participant research approach.
9 Identify advantages and disadvantages of the participant observation approach.
10 Explain what habituation is and why it is important in naturalistic and participant observation.
11 Describe the archival research approach.
12 Identify possible sources of archival data.
13 Explain why we would use archival data.

14 Identify the advantages and disadvantages of using archival data.
15 Explain what it means to conduct a case study.
16 Explain why someone would conduct a case study.
17 Identify the advantages and disadvantages of case studies.

ARTICLES AS ILLUSTRATION

The articles presented below provide examples of the four types of descriptive research covered in this chapter: (1) naturalistic observation, (2) participant observation, (3) archival research, and (4) case study. The questions that follow each of the articles will help you focus on the important points of each.

1 The following article is an example of a naturalistic observation study.

Bungum, T. J., Day, C., & Henry, L. J. (2005). The association of distraction and caution displayed by pedestrians at a lighted crosswalk. *Journal of Community Health, 30,* 269–279. doi:http://dx.doi.org/10.1007/s10900-005-3705-4

a. What was the purpose of this research? Why was naturalistic observation a good choice for this research?
b. Were the researchers unobtrusive? Was this important? If so, why? If not, why not?
c. What were the hypotheses?
d. Describe the procedure. Include information about the way the authors defined a "cautious pedestrian" and a "distracted pedestrian." How did the authors decide which pedestrians to watch?
e. Discuss the authors' approach to inter-rater reliability.
f. What were the main results? Were the hypotheses supported?

2 The following article is an example of a participant observation study.

Montemurro, B., Bloom, C., & Madell, K. (2003). Ladies night out: A typology of women patrons of a male strip club. *Deviant Behavior: An Interdisciplinary Journal, 24*, 333–352. doi:http://dx.doi.org/10.1080/713840221

a. What was the purpose of this research? Why was participant observation a good choice for this research?

b. Provide a summary of the observed patrons.

c. Describe the procedure.

d. What were the main results?

3 The following article is an example of a study that used the archival CAS dataset discussed earlier in this chapter.

Wechsler, H., Lee, J. E., Nelson, T. F., & Lee, H. (2003). Drinking and driving among college students: The influence of alcohol-control policies. *American Journal of Preventive Medicine, 25*, 212–218. doi:http://dx.doi.org/10.1016/S0749-3797(03)00199-5

a. What was the purpose of this research?

b. Describe the sample.

c. Which of the questions in the archived dataset were used for this project?

d. Did the archived dataset have all the data needed for this project, or did the authors have to collect additional data? If so, what did they need and how did they obtain it?

e. What were the main results?

f. Did the authors find that the anti-drinking and driving campaigns were generally working? Explain your answer.

g. One of Wechsler et al.'s major findings is that 20% of the sampled college students were passengers in cars driven by drivers who were high or drunk. As the authors point out, it is not illegal to ride with an intoxicated driver; however, it is tremendously risky. Can you think of ways to educate college students about this risk?

4. The following article is an example of a case study.

Grassick, P. (1990). The fear behind the fear: A case study of apparent simple injection phobia. *Journal of Behavior Therapy and Experimental Psychiatry, 21*, 281–287. doi:http://dx.doi.org/10.1016/0005-7916(90)90030-O

a. Why was a case study approach a good choice for this research?

b. Describe the client. Why was the client referred for treatment?

c. What were the individual steps in her treatment?

d. Did it appear there was a connection between her different phobias? How did the author explain this possibility?

e. Was the client's phobia eliminated? Describe her level of functioning after the treatment.

SUGGESTED ACTIVITIES

1 Design a naturalistic observation study and present a summary of what you did and what you found to your class. Below are some ideas. Feel free to use one of these or develop your own!

a. Observe people using a piece of equipment at the gym and calculate the percentages of males versus females who wipe down the equipment after they use it.

b. Observe people walking past a mirrored wall and calculate the percentage of males versus females who glance at their reflection.

c. Observe drivers as they drive past you and calculate the percentage that have a cell phone in their hands.

2 Conduct an archival research study. One possibility is to obtain a sample of personal ads from an archive of personal ads (you can find personal ads in some newspapers and/or at online sites such as www.pof.com) and conduct a content analysis of them. You can analyze the ads for demographic information (such as gender, race, age, occupation, marital status, sexual orientation) and other characteristics (such as interests). Consider comparing the ads placed by different types of people (such as males versus females). Below are some suggestions for articles using this general approach:

Koestner, R., & Wheeler, L. (1988). Self-presentation in personal advertisements: The influence of implicit notions of attraction and role expectations. *Journal of Social and Personal Relationships, 5,* 149–160. doi:http://dx.doi.org/10.1177/026540758800500202

Smith, C. A., & Stillman, S. (2002). What do women want? The effects of gender and sexual orientation on the desirability of physical attributes in the personal ads of women. *Sex Roles, 46,* 337–342. doi:http://dx.doi.org/10.1023/A:1020280630635

3 Another way to learn more about archival research is to visit a survey repository and explore. For example, visit ICPSR (www.icpsr.umich.edu), the repository discussed earlier, find a dataset that interests you, and then look up articles that have used it (recall that you can browse these datasets by subject, by geographical location, and by time period; articles that have used each dataset are also

listed at this website). You can then put together a summary of articles that have used the same dataset. Your instructor may also choose to have you analyze data obtained from a survey repository.

REFERENCES

Abu-Ras, W., Ahmed, S., & Arfken, C. L. (2010). Alcohol use among U.S. Muslim college students: Risk and protective factors. *Journal of Ethnicity in Substance Abuse, 9,* 206–220. doi:http://dx.doi.org/10.1080/15332640.2010.500921

American Psychological Association. (2002). Ethical principles of psychologists and code of conduct. *American Psychologist, 57,* 1060–1073. doi:http://dx.doi.org/10.1037/0003-066X.57.12.1060

Brotsky, S. R., & Giles, D. (2007). Inside the "pro-ana" community: A covert online participant observation. *Eating Disorders, 15,* 93–109. doi:http://dx.doi.org/10.1080/10640260701190600

Bungum, T., J., Day, C., & Henry, L. J. (2005). The association of distraction and caution displayed by pedestrians at a lighted crosswalk. *Journal of Community Health, 30,* 269–279. doi:http://dx.doi.org/10.1007/s10900-005-3705-4

Cardi, V., Krug, I., Perpiña, C., Mataix-Cols, D., Roncero, M., & Treasure, J. (2012). The use of a nonimmersive virtual reality programme in anorexia nervosa: A single case-report. *European Eating Disorders Review, 20,* 240–245. doi:http://dx.doi.org/10.1002/erv.1155

Chauvin, C. D. (2012). Social norms and motivations associated with college binge drinking. *Sociological Inquiry, 82,* 257–281. doi:http://dx.doi.org/10.1111/j.1475-682X.2011.00400.x

Cho, H., Hall, J. G., Kosmoski, C., Fox, R. L., & Mastin, T. (2010). Tanning, skin cancer risk and prevention: A content analysis of eight popular magazines that target female readers, 1997–2006. *Health Communication, 25,* 1–10. doi:http://dx.doi.org/10.1080/10410230903265938

Cicchetti, D. V., & Sparrow, S. S. (1981). Developing criteria for establishing interrater reliability of specific items: Applications to assessment of adaptive behavior. *American Journal of Mental Deficiency*, *86*, 127–137.

Cohen, J. (1960). A coefficient of agreement for nominal scales. *Educational and Psychological Measurement*, *20*, 37–46. doi:http://dx.doi.org/10.1177/001316446002000104

Festinger, L., Riecken, H. W., & Schachter, S. (1956). *When prophecy fails*. New York: Harper Torchbooks.

Fraley, R. C., & Shaver, P. R. (1998). Airport separations: A naturalistic study of adult attachment dynamics in separating couples. *Journal of Personality and Social Psychology*, *75*, 1198–1212. doi:http://dx.doi.org/10.1037/0022-3514.75.5.1198

Freudenmann, R. W., Öxler, F., & Bernschneider-Reif, S. (2006). The origin of MDMA (ecstasy) revisited: The true story reconstructed from the original documents. *Addiction*, *101*, 1241–1245. doi:http://dx.doi.org/10.1111/j.1360-0443.2006.01511.x

Grassick, P. (1990). The fear behind the fear: A case study of apparent simple injection phobia. *Journal of Behavior Therapy and Experimental Psychiatry*, *21*, 281–287. doi:http://dx.doi.org/10.1016/0005-7916(90)90030-O

Huffman, S., Tuggle, C. A., & Rosengard, D. S. (2004). How campus media cover sports: The gender-equity issue, one generation later. *Mass Communication & Society*, *7*, 475–489. doi:http://dx.doi.org/10.1207/s15327825mcs0704_6

Jambor, E. A., & Weekes, E. M. (1996). The nontraditional female athlete: A case study. *Journal of Applied Sport Psychology*, *8*, 146–159. doi:http://dx.doi.org/10.1080/10413209608406473

Kidder, J. L. (2015). College Republicans and conservative social identity. *Sociological Perspectives*, *59*, 177–200. doi:http://dx.doi.org/10.1177/0731121415583104

Koestner, R., & Wheeler, L. (1988). Self-presentation in personal advertisements: The influence of implicit notions of attraction and role expectations. *Journal of Social and Personal Relationships*, *5*, 149–160. doi:http://dx.doi.org/10.1177/026540758800500202

Kuo, M., Wechsler, H., Greenberg, P., & Lee, H. (2003). The marketing of alcohol to college students: The role of low prices and special promotions. *American Journal of Preventive Medicine*, *25*, 204–211.

doi:http://dx.doi.org/10.1016/S0749-3797(03)00200-9

Montemurro, B., Bloom, C., & Madell, K. (2003). Ladies night out: A typology of women patrons of a male strip club. *Deviant Behavior: An Interdisciplinary Journal*, *24*, 333–352. doi:http://dx.doi.org/10.1080/713840221

Pettijohn, T. F. II, Pettijohn, T. F., & Geschke, K. S. (2009). Changes in sun tanning attitudes and behaviors of U.S. college students from 1995 to 2005. *College Student Journal*, *43*, 161–165.

Poll: Many foresee Y2K cash crunch, few fear doomsday (1999, January 10). Retrieved from cnn.com

Secter, B. (1997, March 28). The deadly riddle of Heaven's Gate: Ideology merged science fiction, religion. *Chicago Tribune*. Retrieved from http://articles.chicagotribune.com

Smith, C. A., & Stillman, S. (2002). What do women want? The effects of gender and sexual orientation on the desirability of physical attributes in the personal ads of women. *Sex Roles*, *46*, 337–342. doi:http://dx.doi.org/10.1023/A:1020280630635

Sommer, R., & Steele, J. (1997). Social effects on duration in restaurants. *Appetite*, *29*, 25–30. doi:http://dx.doi.org/10.1006/appe.1996.0062

Stutts, J., Feaganes, J., Reinfurt, D., Rodgman, E., Hamlett, C., Gish, K., & Staplin, L. (2005). Driver's exposure to distractions in their natural driving environment. *Accident Analysis and Prevention*, *37*, 1093–1101. doi:http://dx.doi.org/10.1016/j.aap.2005.06.007

Ting, W., Schultz, K., Cac, N. N., Peterson, M., & Walling, H. W. (2007). Tanning bed exposure increases the risk of malignant melanoma. *International Journal of Dermatology*, *46*, 1253–1257. doi:http://dx.doi.org/10.1111/j.1365-4632.2007.03408.x

US Department of Education (2010, Spring). National Center for Education Statistics, *Integrated Postsecondary Education Data Systems (IPEDS), Enrollment component*. Retrieved from nces.ed.gov

Watkins, M. W., & Pacheco, M. (2000). Interobserver agreement in behavioral research: Importance and calculation. *Journal of Behavioral*

Education, 10(4), 205–212. doi:http://dx.doi.org/10.1023/A:1012295615144

Wechsler, H. (1993). *Harvard School of Public Health College Alcohol Study*. ICPSR06577-v3. Ann Arbor, MI: Inter-university Consortium for Political and Social Research [distributor], 2005–11–14. http://doi.org/10.3886/ICPSR06577.v3

(1997). *Harvard School of Public Health College Alcohol Study*. ICPSR03163-v3. Ann Arbor, MI: Inter-university Consortium for Political and Social Research [distributor], 2005–11–22. http://doi.org/10.3886/ICPSR03163.v3

(1999). *Harvard School of Public Health College Alcohol Study*. ICPSR03818-v2. Ann Arbor, MI: Inter-university Consortium for Political and Social Research [distributor], 2005–11–22. http://doi.org/10.3886/ICPSR03818.v2

(2001). *Harvard School of Public Health College Alcohol Study*. ICPSR04291-v2. Ann Arbor, MI: Inter-university Consortium for Political and Social Research [distributor], 2008–02–05. http://doi.org/10.3886/ICPSR04291.v2

Wechsler, H., Davenport, A., Dowdall, G., Moeykens, B., & Castillo, S. (1994). Health and behavioral consequences of binge drinking in college: A national survey of students at 140 campuses. *Journal of the American Medical Association, 272*, 1672–1677. doi:http://dx.doi.org/10.1001/jama.272.21.1672

Wechsler, H., Lee, J. E., Nelson, T. F., & Lee, H. (2003). Drinking and driving among college students: The influence of alcohol-control policies. *American Journal of Preventive Medicine, 25*, 212–218. doi:http://dx.doi.org/10.1016/S0749-3797(03)00199-5

Wolpe, J., Brady, J. P., Serber, M., Agras, W. S., & Liberman, R. P. (1973). The current status of systematic desensitization. *American Journal of Psychiatry, 130*, 961–965. doi:http://dx.doi.org/10.1176/ajp.130.9.961

Young, M. E., Mizzau, M., Mai, N. T., Sirisegaram, A., & Wilson, M. (2009). Food for thought: What you eat depends on your sex and eating companions. *Appetite, 53*, 268–271. doi:http://dx.doi.org/10.1016/j.appet.2009.07.021

6 Correlational Research

LEARNING OBJECTIVES

- Explain the differences between experimentation and correlation research.

- Describe how a correlation coefficient provides information about the strength and direction of a relationship between variables.

- Explain how scatterplots and correlation matrices can visually represent correlational relationships.

- Describe factors that can affect the strength of a correlation coefficient: nonlinearity and range restriction.

- Explain when to use several common statistical procedures.

- Explain why correlation does not indicate causation.

- Discuss how a partial correlation analysis addresses the third-variable problem.

In Chapter 5, you saw that sometimes, instead of manipulating what our study participants see and experience, we use non-experimental methods; we just observe our participants in their natural environments without influencing them at all. In these cases, we are using descriptive research methods. The lack of control in descriptive research methods means that we do not have the ability to establish cause and effect.

The correlational research approach, a popular research method, is another non-experimental research approach. In correlational research, we measure different variables to see whether there is a relationship between or among them. In other words, you would have a relationship between measured variables if they vary systematically together (as intelligence rises, does academic performance rise as well?). I'll explain more about this below. Before we go on, remember that since correlational research is another descriptive research technique, we cannot use it to investigate whether one variable causes another.

The Basic Differences between Experimentation and Correlational Research

Before we talk about the details of correlational research, I'd like to explain the basic methodological differences between experimentation and correlational research.

Experimentation

Consider the simplest kind of experiment. It has one independent variable with two levels represented by two groups with different people in each group. Here are the steps we take in a simple experiment:

1. We randomly *assign* participants to the two groups.

2. We *manipulate* (vary) an independent variable. Say we give one group 2 oz. of caffeine and the other group 10 oz.

3. We *measure* a dependent variable, say performance on a math test.

There are indeed advantages to doing experimental research; number one is the ability to establish cause and effect (as explained in Chapter 1). Unfortunately, there are times when we cannot do highly controlled experiments due to practical or ethical concerns. Take the following example:

- Does illegal drug use during their college years increase students' risk of having difficulties in college?

We cannot *randomly* put study participants into two groups, and give one group illegal drugs and not give illegal drugs to the other group; this would be unethical. Whether a student takes illegal drugs is not a decision that is up to experimenters. To investigate these types of questions, researchers instead often turn to correlational research.

Correlational Research

There are different approaches to doing correlational research. The simplest is to determine if there is a relationship between two variables. Let's take a closer look at the steps in this approach.

1. We *measure* one variable, say the number of hours spent studying for a social psychology exam

2. We *measure* a second variable, say performance on the social psychology exam

3. We determine whether there is a *relationship* between the two variables.

Take a closer look at the methodology of the experiment as opposed to the correlation research as I've illustrated it. Notice that in correlational research there is no independent variable (nothing gets manipulated) and there is no random assignment to groups. In correlation research we are only measuring variables as they exist in the real world. In this case, the two variables of interest were measured: the number of hours spent studying for a social psychology exam and performance. Certainly, people differ in terms of how much they study for any given exam, and we can measure how much studying they did. An experiment would be inappropriate here because it should not be up to a researcher to determine the amount of time people study for a real exam. That is a choice students should make for themselves.

Methodology Indicates the Type of Study

To identify whether a particular study is an experiment or a correlational study, look at the steps the researchers take when conducting their research (as in the examples above). You can find this information in the method section of any primary research source. Are there manipulated variables? In other words, did the experimenter vary what was presented to the participants? Then it's an experiment. Are variables only measured and not manipulated? Then it's a correlational study.

Thus far we've discussed correlation research as a method. However, researchers can also talk about correlations as statistical analyses. **Statistics** are mathematical methods used to systematically analyze data. It's possible, for example, for researchers who have conducted an experiment to decide to include a correlational analysis when they are computing their results. Because they did an experiment, they can potentially determine that their independent variable caused the change in their dependent variable. However, if as part of a statistical analysis of their results they conduct a correlational analysis to determine whether there is a relationship between selected variables, they could not establish cause and effect between *those* variables used in the correlational analysis. Let's look at an example.

Have you ever worked as a server in a restaurant and wondered how to increase your tips? Rind and his colleagues have conducted a series of studies to identify what can increase restaurant tipping. For example, in one of these studies, Rind and Strohmetz (2001) investigated whether placing a message about future weather conditions on the back of the check would increase tip percentage. So they had a female server randomly provide information about different types of forecasts. She provided either a good forecast ("The weather is supposed to be really good tomorrow! I hope you enjoy the day!"), an unfavorable forecast ("The weather is supposed to be not so good tomorrow. I hope you enjoy the day anyway!"), or no forecast at all. The researcher found that the average tip percentage was higher when the patrons were given a favorable forecast as opposed to an unfavorable forecast or no forecast at all. Rind and Strohmetz also conducted a correlation analysis; they looked at the relationship between the size of the dining party and the percentage of tip and found that the two were not correlated.

So let's say you were asked: What kind of study did Rind and Strohmetz (2001) conduct? To find out, you look at their study method (not at the kind of statistical analyses they conducted). Rind and Strohmetz randomly varied what was written on the back of the check; they wrote about either a favorable forecast, an unfavorable forecast, or no forecast at all. The type of forecast (favorable, unfavorable, none) was their independent variable. So even though they included a correlation in their results section, we still say that they completed an experiment and that they can conclusively state the presence of the favorable forecast on the check (over an unfavorable forecast or no forecast at all) caused the

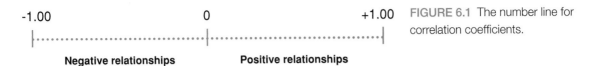

FIGURE 6.1 The number line for correlation coefficients.

tip percentage increase. However, even if they had found a significant correlation between dining party size and tip percentage, they could not state that one of these variables caused the other – we cannot establish cause and effect when you are referring to a correlational relationship.

The Correlation Coefficient

It is important to distinguish between the correlational research approach and correlational analyses. As you saw above, in correlational research variables are measured, not manipulated. Correlational analyses, on the other hand, use statistical analyses to investigate the relationships that exist between or among your variables.

Let's begin with a closer look at the statistical side of correlation. We usually represent a correlational relationship with a **correlation coefficient**, a numerical value that ranges from –1.00 to +1.00 as shown in Figure 6.1. Each correlation coefficient gives us information about the relationship between two variables. More specifically, it tells us about the *direction* and the *strength* of that relationship.

Most correlation coefficients are the result of an analysis called a **Pearson product–moment analysis**. This is a statistical analysis that identifies the direction and strength of the linear relationship between two variables measured on an interval or ratio scale. A **linear relationship** is a relationship that can be approximated with a straight line on a graph (more on this later). The abbreviation for a Pearson product–moment analysis is "Pearson r" or just "r" as you'll see later in this chapter. Let's continue this with a closer look at correlation coefficients.

The Direction of a Correlation

Correlation coefficients are either positive or negative, as you can see in Figure 6.1. You'll know whether you have a positive or a negative correlation by the presence of a plus or minus sign in front of it; if there is no sign, the correlation is positive. This positive or negative sign indicates the direction of the correlation. Let's now talk about what that means.

Positive Correlations. When you have a **positive correlation** between two variables, it means those variables tend to move in the same direction. Higher scores of one variable tend to be associated with higher scores on the other variable. Lower scores of one variable tend to be associated with lower scores on the other variable. They move together.

Let's consider an example. Bina, Graziano, and Bonino (2006) were interested in whether adolescents who drive in a risky manner also tend take part in other risky behaviors. They asked Italian males and females, aged 14–17, to answer a questionnaire about their traffic offenses such as speeding within the last two months and about a variety of their other lifestyle choices. They found that risky driving was positively correlated with a variety of other risky behaviors such as abusing alcohol ($r = .30$ for males and $r = .32$ for females). What this means is that those who committed *more* traffic offenses were *more* likely to abuse alcohol. More of one thing was associated with more of the other thing. Do you see how both measured activities tended to move in the same direction? That is a positive correlation.

We can represent Bina et al.'s positive correlation in another way. Males and females who committed

FIGURE 6.2 Bina et al. (2006) found that risky driving in adolescents was positively correlated with other risky behaviors such as abusing alcohol.

fewer traffic offenses were *less* likely to abuse alcohol. Again, both variables tended to move in the same direction. When two variables tend to move in the same direction (both moving up together or both moving down together), you have a positive correlation.

Bina et al. found that other risks were positively correlated with risky driving. Let's take a look at some of these other correlations. For consistency, I'll represent all these correlations with both variables increasing.

- Those who committed more traffic offenses were more likely to smoke cigarettes (males: $r = .41$; females: $r = .28$)
- Those who committed more traffic offenses were more likely to smoke marijuana (males: $r = .40$; females: $r = .27$)
- Those who committed more traffic offenses were more likely to take part in antisocial activities (for example, vandalism) (males: $r = .57$; females: $r = .45$)

Thus, as you can see from the list of positive correlations shown above, Bina et al. found that the adolescents who were more likely to display risky

driving practices were also more likely to engage in the other risky behaviors stated above.

Negative Correlations. When you have a **negative correlation**, it means the two variables of interest tend to move in opposite directions. Higher scores of one variable tend to be associated with lower scores on the other variable. Let's look at another research example.

Ballard, Gray, Reilly, and Noggle (2009) were interested in examining the correlations between video game screen time and physical activity in adult males. Specifically, they asked university males about their frequency and level of physical activity, as well as how often and for how long they did sedentary activities like playing video games or reading. They found that the frequency of video game playing was negatively correlated with the amount of time exercising ($r = -.21$). In other words, those who played video games *more* often tended to spend *less* time exercising. More of one thing was associated with less of the other thing. Do you see how the measured activities tended to move in opposite directions? That is a negative correlation.

Ballard et al. found that other accessed behaviors were negatively correlated with the time spent video gaming. Let's take a look at some of these other correlations.

- Those who spent more time playing video games exercised less frequently ($r = -.21$)
- Those who spent more time playing video games walked less frequently ($r = -.22$)
- Those who spent more time spent playing "massively-multiplayer online role-playing games" exercised less often ($r = -.49$) (p. 163)

No Correlation. We've talked about positive correlations (two variables move in the same direction) and negative correlations (two variables move in opposite directions). Let's now go back to that number line shown in Figure 6.1. In the middle of the number line is a zero that represents the absence of a correlation, a correlation that is neither positive nor negative. Sometimes you measure two variables and find that the two variables are not correlated. Ballard et al.'s work on video game play did reveal that some variables were not correlated. For example, the number of years spent playing video games was not significantly correlated with the males' body fat percentage ($r = .03$). Notice I said "not significantly correlated." This means the researchers analyzed the correlations they obtained and found them to be not significantly different from zero. This brings us to a discussion of the strength of a correlation – another component that is part of the correlation coefficient.

The Strength of a Correlation

Do you remember when I said that the correlation coefficient gives us information about the *direction* and the *strength* of the relationship between two variables? When we discussed positive and negative correlations, we discussed the "direction" of the relationships. Now we'll discuss the "strength" of the relationship.

In Figure 6.3 we revisit the number line shown in Figure 6.1 with a few additions. Notice first that the number line has two anchor points or "poles" – one pole is marked "−1.00" and one pole is marked "+1.00." These poles are also labeled as "perfect." The −1.00 pole is labeled as a "perfect negative correlation" and the +1.00 pole is labeled as a "perfect positive correlation." A **perfect correlation** means

that the two variables in question vary together perfectly. In fact, the closer a correlation coefficient is to either pole (and the further away from zero), the stronger the correlation is. So +.42 is a stronger correlation than +.25 because +.42 is closer to the right-hand pole, and −.42 is a stronger correlation than −.25 because −.42 is closer to the left-hand pole.

Which do you think describes a stronger correlation, −.74 or +.52? The answer is −.74, because it is closer to its respective pole than +.52. If you prefer, you can answer the question of which is stronger by considering the absolute values of the two correlation coefficients. **Absolute values** have no positive or negative sign. In other words, ignore the positive and negative signs for the moment and simply see which is the larger number. That correlation will be the stronger correlation.

Also note that it is possible to calculate a probability value (*p*-value) to determine whether any given correlation is significantly different from zero (the calculations themselves are beyond the scope of this text). A **probability value** refers to the statistical likelihood that a result is due simply to chance. Remember a correlation coefficient of zero means the two variables of interest are not correlated. Having a significant positive or significant negative relationship between two variables means you can predict a person's score on one measured variable when you know his or her score on the other measured variable. If the correlation is not significant, the correlation coefficient will not give you the information that you need to predict one score from another. So the bottom line is: When two variables are significantly correlated, it means you can predict one

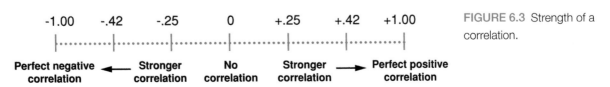

FIGURE 6.3 Strength of a correlation.

from another; the stronger the correlation, the better the prediction.

A Visual Representation of a Correlation: Scatterplots

Sometimes researchers decide to examine correlation data visually by creating a scatterplot. A **scatterplot** (or scattergram) is a graph of the relationship between two variables. The horizontal axis (the *x* axis) indicates the possible scores for one of the variables, and the vertical axis (the *y* axis) indicates the possible scores for the other. Each point on the scatterplot represents the intersection of an individual's scores on the two variables.

Sample scatterplots are shown in Figure 6.4. As you can see from the scatterplot on the far left, if you have a strong positive correlation, the plotted data will generally take the form of a diagonal line, going from the bottom left to the upper right of the graph at a 45-degree angle (Fig. 6.4a). When the positive correlation is weaker, the diagonal from the bottom left to the upper right of the graph will not be as easy to visualize (Fig. 6.4b).

If you have a strong negative correlation, you'll see a clear diagonal going from the bottom right to the upper left of the graph (Fig. 6.4e). When the negative correlation is weaker, the diagonal from the bottom right to the upper left of the graph will not be as easy to visualize (Figure 6.4d).

As previously mentioned, when the relationship between the variables on the scatterplot can be easily approximated with a straight line, the variables are said to represent a linear relationship. This can be a positive (upward-sloping) linear relationship or a negative (downward-sloping) linear relationship, depending on the direction of the diagonal as suggested above.

Sometimes, as we discussed above, there is no relationship between the two variables. In this case a scatterplot will show a pattern that looks random (Figure 6.4c). When two variables are not correlated, they are independent of one another and we cannot use one variable to predict the other.

A Visual Representation of Many Correlations: A Correlation Matrix

We often use a **correlation matrix** to present information about the correlations of many variables with each other. Let's take a look at an example from the literature.

Have you ever been the target of verbal abuse from someone you don't know? I certainly hope not. It's not common, but, unfortunately, sometimes people do verbally abuse strangers. Ickes, Park, and Robinson (2012) were interested in "predicting the propensity to verbally abuse strangers" (p. 75). They conducted an online survey asking people to provide demographic information, respond to personality

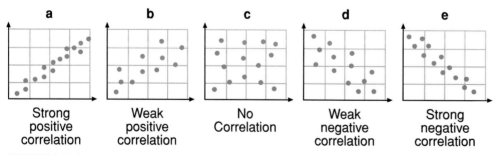

FIGURE 6.4 Sample scatterplots.

Table 6.1 Zero-order intercorrelations of the personality predictors, the demographic variables, and the rudeness measure.

Measure	1	2	3	4	5	6	7	8	9
1. Rudeness	–								
2. Impulsivity	.25**	–							
3. Aggression	.37**	.33**	–						
4. Social desirability	−.33**	−.32**	−.42**	–					
5. Ego defensiveness	.38**	.21**	.42**	−.38**	–				
6. Conventional morality	−.52**	−.31**	−.52**	.50**	−.37**	–			
7. Affect intensity for anger and frustration	.34**	.24**	.61**	−.36**	.39**	−.32**	–		
8. Gender	.14*	.06	.25***	.08	.03	.39***	.02	–	
9. Race	.10	.12	.20*	.06	.17❖	.09	.22*	nt[a]	–

[a] Not tested as a correlation (both variables are categorical)

❖ $p < .10$. *$p < .05$. **$p < .01$. ***$p < .001$.

Source: Ickes, W., Park, A., & Robinson, R. L. (2012). F#!%ing rudeness: Predicting the propensity to verbally abuse strangers. *Journal of Language and Social Psychology, 3(1)*, 75–94. doi:http://dx.doi.org/10.1177/0261927X11425036.

measures (measuring, for example, participants' level of impulsivity), and indicate, on a "Rudeness Scale," how they would respond to a series of 10 situations. Here is one of those situations as an example:

Not noticing a trash receptacle near the exit to the fast-food restaurant, you open the car door and set the trash in your fast-food bag down on the curb. A store employee sees you do this, points to the trash receptacle, and tells you to put it there. Which of the following would be your most likely response?

1. *I would apologize and do what he said.*
2. *I would say, "I'll tell you where you can put it."*
3. *I would give him a dirty look and then drive off.*
4. *I would pretend that I didn't hear him.*
   (p. 89)

Ickes et al. first calculated correlations among the measures and found that the personality measures were all correlated with the participants' scores on the Rudeness Scale. For example, the tendency to be verbally rude was positively correlated with impulsivity ($r = .25$) and aggression ($r = .37$), while the tendency to be verbally abusive was negatively correlated with conventional morality ($r = −.52$) and social desirability ($r = −.33$). Ickes et al. presented these and other zero-order correlations in a correlation matrix (Table 6.1). **Zero-order correlations** are correlations involving two variables.

As you can see from Table 6.1, each variable ("measure") is assigned a number from 1 to 9 and these numbers are located on the left side of the table and across the top. Rudeness is number 1, impulsivity is number 2, and so on. To see how two variables in the matrix are correlated, go to the variable on the left that you're interested in, and move to the right in that row until you get to the column that corresponds to the other variable of interest. For example, the correlation between aggression (measure 3 on the left) and impulsivity (measure 2 on the top) is .33.

If you try to find out from the table how a variable correlates with itself, you'll just find a dash in the correlation matrix. In fact, the correlation of a variable with itself is the perfect correlation of 1.00. Some researchers put a 1.00 along the diagonal to represent this, while others put a dash. You may also notice that the correlation matrix is symmetrical. If all the spaces were filled in, each of the correlations above the diagonal would be the same as the correlations below it. For that reason most researchers present either the upper or the lower portion of the matrix. Finally, you may have noticed that some of the correlations have asterisks. The explanation for these is below the table, where you can see that some of the correlations are significant at less than a .05 level ($p < .05$). This means there is less than a 5% probability that the coefficient is this large by chance. Other correlations in this matrix are significant at less than .01 level or less than .001 level. Again this means that there is less than a 1% probability or less than a .1% probability respectively that the coefficient's size is due to chance.

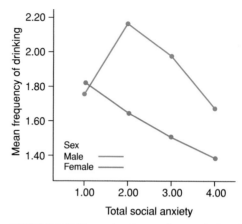

FIGURE 6.5 Example of a nonlinear relationship.

Factors Affecting the Strength of a Correlation Coefficient

We use correlation coefficients to see whether two variables have a relationship (vary systematically together). However, statistical tests can sometimes lead us to believe that the variables in question are not correlated or are only weakly correlated. Under these conditions, further testing can reveal a relationship. These special cases will be discussed below.

Nonlinearity

When a correlation coefficient reveals that two variables are not correlated, it could mean that the relationship between them is not linear. It could be curvilinear. A **curvilinear relationship** is present when changes in the value of one variable are accompanied by both increases and decreases in the other variable. Let's look at an example of a curvilinear relationship. Strahan, Panayiotou, Clements, and Scott (2011) wanted to look at the relationship between fear of social situations and alcohol consumption in male and female college students in the United States and Cyprus. In Figure 6.5, which combines data for US and Cypriot students, you can see an example of a curvilinear relationship. Specifically, Strahan et al. found an inverted U-shaped relationship between social anxiety and drinking for males (curvilinear relationships can be a U-shape or an inverted U-shape). As you can see along the red curve, the highest levels of alcohol consumption for males occurred at moderate levels of social anxiety. Males tended to drink less when they were very anxious or not at all anxious. (Strahan et al. found that the relationship between drinking and social anxiety for females, the green curve in the figure, was not significant.) The point is that if you have a curvilinear relationship such as that shown in Figure 6.5 for males, your correlation coefficient will not be significant.

Range Restriction

The strength of a correlation coefficient can be reduced if range restriction exists in the data. **Range**

FIGURE 6.6 Researchers have questioned how well GRE scores predict success in graduate school. Range restriction has been blamed for inconsistent results.

restriction occurs when most of the participants in a sample have similar scores for one of the measured variables in the correlation; that is, the range of scores for one of the variables is restricted. Let's take a look at an example. When deciding whether to admit an applicant, many graduate schools consider his or her score on the Graduate Record Exam (GRE) along with other factors like GPA. Researchers have questioned how well GRE scores predict success in graduate school, and tested correlations between GRE scores and indices of graduate school success have varied (see Sternberg & Williams, 1997).

One of the reasons that have been cited for the inconsistent results obtained in GRE validation studies is range restriction (see Chernyshenko & Ones, 1999). In other words, it is possible that the size of the obtained correlation is reduced because researchers are only using the GRE scores of those who had been *accepted* into graduate school, and these people likely have mostly high GRE scores. Of course if researchers want to consider factors such as the GPA from students' first year of graduate school, then they have to restrict their sample to accepted students. So the range of GRE scores has typically been restricted, and this restriction acts to lower the obtained correlation coefficient. Note that it is possible to use a formula to compute a correlation that corrects for range restriction; when this is accomplished, the correlation indicating the validity of the GRE vastly improves (Chernyshenko & Ones, 1999).

Statistical Assessments of Relationships

We've talked generally about what a correlation coefficient means. Now let's get a little more specific about the kinds of analyses you can do to assess relationships between or among variables. Since this is not a statistics textbook, we won't actually calculate any analyses, but we will go over the concepts so you generally understand correlational analyses when you see them in the literature. If you want to learn how to calculate any of the statistics we talk about here, consult virtually any introductory statistics textbook.

When you are assessing the relationship between two variables, you are calculating **bivariate correlations** ("bi" stands for two). There are a few types of bivariate correlations you can use. I'll talk about three of the main types: (1) the Pearson product–moment correlation, (2) the Spearman correlation for ranked data, and (3) the point–biserial correlation. As you'll see, it's the type of data you are considering that determines which type of correlation technique you will use. Each type of correlation technique yields a correlation coefficient that falls along the same –1 to +1 number line we've seen before, and they are all interpreted in the manner we discussed above.

Pearson Product–Moment Correlation

One type of test for bivariate correlations is the **Pearson product–moment correlation** (also known as the Pearson *r* as noted above). A Pearson product–moment correlation identifies the degree to which scores on two variables show a linear relationship.

FIGURE 6.7 We can only calculate a Pearson *r* when we are using continuous variables. Temperature is a continuous variable because it can take on any value between two numbers. Here the temperature is likely somewhere between 10 and 20 degrees Fahrenheit.

FIGURE 6.8 After a sample of college students from three ethnic groups rank ordered the characteristics they wanted to see in counselors, Atkinson et al. (1989) used Spearman correlations to reveal that these groups generally agreed on the characteristics they want to see.

The closer the Pearson *r* is to –1.00 or +1.00, the more linear the scores are, the more they approximate a straight line on a graph. Note that the scores we use when calculating Pearson's *r* have to be continuous variables, meaning they can take on any value between two numbers, such as temperature for example (that is, it can be 80 degrees or 81 degrees in a room and anything in between). So far in this chapter we have focused on Pearson product–moment correlations (for example, Ballard et al.'s work). There are other ways to assess the relationship between and among variables. Let's turn to these now.

Spearman Correlation for Ranked Data

Another type of test for bivariate correlations is the **Spearman correlation for ranked data**, in which data are ordinal. This means the data are ranked in order, from say least to most preferred. Let's look at an example. Atkinson, Poston, Furlong, and Mercado (1989) were wondering what characteristics college students of different ethnicities would look for in a counselor. So they asked Asian-American, Mexican-American, and Caucasian-American students to

answer a series of questions. Each question started with, "If you were going to see a counselor to discuss a personal problem, would you prefer to see a counselor who is …" (p. 69). This question stem was followed by a series of forced choice options, meaning respondents had to choose one of two presented options. The options were counselor characteristics such as "dissimilar to you in attitudes and values" and "similar to you in ethnicity" (p. 69). Atkinson et al. then calculated the percentage of respondents in each ethnic group who expressed a preference for each counselor characteristic. Finally, they put the characteristics in rank order from most to least preferred for each ethnic group.

Atkinson et al. found their Spearman rank-order correlations revealed a high level of similarity in the results. The preferences stated by each ethnic group were highly correlated with those stated by all other ethnic groups tested (all Spearman correlations were over .95). Specifically, all three groups studied preferred a counselor who was older and more educated, with a personality and attitudes similar to theirs, and rated these preferences as more important than shared ethnicity. So Spearman correlations revealed that the participants in these three ethnic groups generally agreed on the characteristics they want to see in counselors.

The Point–Biserial Correlation

You can use the **point–biserial correlation** (r_{pb}) when you want to calculate a correlation between one **dichotomous variable** – a variable with two choices like Republican or Democrat – and one continuous variable. Let's look at an example.

Many colleges and universities allow students to take part in psychological research (see Arnett, 2008 for an example from the field of social psychology). Students usually have options as to when they sign up to participate over the course of the semester, and inevitably some students sign up earlier than others. Cooper, Baumgardner, and Strathman (1991) wondered whether there were differences between those who sign up early in the semester and those who sign up later. Some of the questions of interest required the researchers to calculate point–biserial correlations because, for example, they wanted to see whether there was a significant correlation between gender (used as a dichotomous variable – male versus female) and the point in the semester at which students signed up for research (a continuous variable coded from day 1 of the semester to day 98). They found that females signed up to participate in research earlier than males ($r_{pb} = .26$). They also used a point–biserial correlation to reveal that first-year students signed up earlier than those more advanced in their college career ($r_{pb} = .23$). For this, they created a dichotomous variable: first-year students versus sophomores, juniors, and seniors combined.

Simple Regression

As you saw, a correlation coefficient can indicate whether there is a relationship between two variables. Once you know that variables are significantly correlated, you may choose to do a regression analysis, which allows you to predict one variable when you know the other. More specifically, when you do this analysis, you get a regression equation. A **regression equation** allows one to make the best possible prediction of scores. The variable you are predicting is the **criterion variable** (also known as the y variable or the outcome variable), while the variable you know is the **predictor variable** (also known as the x variable). The ability to predict the criterion variable is a big advantage of conducting regression analyses.

When you use two variables in a regression analysis, the analysis is called **simple regression**, because we are still concerned with only two variables. You may also hear people refer to a two-variable regression as **simple linear regression**. This refers to a regression analysis that is linear; in other words, when you plot the data points on a scatterplot, they cluster around a straight line.

Think about simple regression with a GRE example. If GRE scores correlate with grades in the first year of graduate school (as we discussed earlier), then we can use GRE as a predictor of graduate school success. Once we have conducted a regression analysis on a tested sample using GRE scores and first-year grades – the predictor and criterion variables, respectively – we can use the resulting equation to predict the first-year grades of prospective students. It is likely that graduate school admission offices already think along these lines; they use the GRE scores of graduate school applicants when deciding whether to admit them.

Let's next turn to a more complex case, a case with more than two variables.

Multiple Regression

Sometimes we decide to consider more than just two variables. Why? Think about our last example. The GRE has been found to predict first-year grades in graduate school, although not perfectly (see Kuncel, Hezlett, & Ones, 2001). Other potentially influential factors include motivation and the amount of time spent studying. In these cases, we often turn to a multivariate statistical technique. **Multivariate statistics** are data analysis procedures that are designed to analyze three or more variables at one time. We'll next consider one of these techniques.

Multiple regression analysis is a statistical technique that allows us to look at the relationship between a number of predictor variables and a single criterion variable. A multiple regression analysis tells us if the predictor variables are positively or negatively correlated with the criterion variable. The analysis also tells us the relative importance of each variable in determining the behavior of interest. Let's go over another example.

Suppose it's the middle of the semester and there's a test coming up. Would you prefer the exam to be given before the break (so you can party during the break) or after the break (so you can study during the break)? To investigate whether grades would be affected by the decision to give an exam before or after a semester break, O'Connor (2013) had students in different sections of an undergraduate educational psychology class take the midterm exam either before a 5-day semester break or after it.

In an effort to measure the impact of the semester break on exam performance O'Connor conducted a multiple regression analysis. The predictor variables were the students' scores on the first and last exams during the same semester (all first exams were taken on the same day and all final exams were taken on the same day), a break condition (exam before or after the break), and the single-criterion outcome variable was the scores students earned for the midterm exam. O'Connor's question was whether the first and final exam scores and the timing of the break could predict the midterm exam scores.

The multiple regression analysis allows you to determine how *all* the predictor variables combined (first exam, final exam, and the timing of the break) relate to the outcome variable (midterm exam scores). When you conduct a multiple regression analysis, you will get a multiple correlation coefficient. The **multiple correlation coefficient** is symbolized by R (comparable to Pearson r), and it refers to the correlation between the combined predictors and the outcome variable. If each of the predictor variables is correlated with the outcome variable, then your ability to predict the outcome variable will often be even greater when you use all the predictor variables together in the same analysis.

A multiple regression analysis will also give you a multiple coefficient of determination. The **multiple coefficient of determination**, symbolized by R^2, refers to the amount of variation in the outcome variable that can be accounted for by all the predictors taken together. In this case, O'Connor determined that, taken together, the three predictors did predict performance on the midterm exam and explained almost 43% of the amount of variation in this outcome variable. This means the first and final exam and the timing of the break explained some but not all of the influences on that midterm exam score. That also means that 57% of the variability in the midterm scores is unexplained (100% total − 43% explained). What else is potentially influencing those midterm scores? There are likely many other possible influences such as the intelligence level of the students, how much the students slept the night before, and how anxious they were during testing. If O'Connor had information about these other variables for his sample, possibly he could account for more of the variability in the scores.

The multiple regression analysis also allows us to determine the relative importance of each predictor variable to the outcome variable. You'll see

FIGURE 6.9 Would you prefer to have an exam before or after spring break? You may have a preference, however, O'Connor (2013) found that whether the break occurs before or after your exam is not a good predictor of that exam grade.

these statistics referred to as standardized regression coefficients or beta weights. **Standardized regression coefficients** or **beta weights** are statistics that indicate the relationship between one of the predictor variables and the outcome variable. You can interpret beta weights, symbolized by β, just the way you would interpret a correlation, and you can also test them for statistical significance just as you do with a correlation. For example, the beta weight for the first exam in O'Connor's research was .24 ($p < .05$), and the beta weight for the final exam was .51 ($p < .01$). So both the first and the final exams made significant contributions to predicting performance on the midterm, and because the beta weight for the final exam was stronger than the beta weight for the first exam, this indicates that the final exam was a better predictor than the first exam. On the other hand, when O'Connor considered the relative importance of the break condition variable (was the break before or after the exam?), he found it did not make a significant contribution to the prediction of the midterm exam scores ($\beta = -.07$, p > .05).

So O'Connor concluded that only the scores on the first and final exams significantly predicted midterm grades. The timing of the break did not make a significant contribution to the prediction of the midterm exam scores. So don't worry. Whether the break occurs before or after your exam is not a good predictor of that exam grade. You'll likely do about as well on that exam as you have on the others, regardless of when you take it.

Correlation and Causality

Say we find that two variables, X and Y, are significantly correlated. We cannot conclude that one of the variables causes the other for two reasons: (1) the **bidirectionality problem** – we don't know whether X has caused Y or Y has caused X; and (2) the **third-variable problem** – a third variable may be causing both variables of interest. Let's take a break from the statistics and discuss each of these problems next.

The Bidirectionality Problem

If you're like my students (and me), you spend a lot of time texting. Would you expect higher levels of texting to be associated with higher or lower levels of well-being? Klein Murdock (2013) expected that "high levels of texting would be associated with the

FIGURE 6.10 Klein Murdock (2013) found that the more students texted, the more problems they had sleeping. Is frequent texting causing sleep problems or are sleep problems causing frequent texting? This is a bidirectionality problem.

have no way of knowing whether either of these is true.

In some relationships bidirectionality is not a problem. It all depends on what variables you are studying. Let's take a look at another correlation, one in which bidirectionality is not an issue. The relationship of interest here is between heat and aggression, a topic that has long intrigued researchers. One research team was interested in looking at the heat–aggression relationship as it plays out in professional baseball. Specifically, Reifman et al. (1991) looked at a random sample of major league games over a 3-year span, consulting newspapers for temperature readings for the relevant days. They also consulted statistics on the number of batters hit in each game (that is, hitting batters while they are on the plate was operationalized as an indicator of aggression).

They found a weak but significant positive correlation ($r = .11$, $p < .002$) between temperature and the number of players hit by a pitch. In other words, as the temperature increased, there tended to be more players hit by pitches. Bidirectionality is not

poorest functioning among students" (p. 210). She tested this idea with a sample of first-year undergraduates. I'll just focus on one of Klein Murdock's results. She found that the number of daily texts was positively correlated with sleep problems, a measure of well-being. In other words, the more students texted, the more problems they had sleeping.

We cannot know, from this result, whether one of these things, number of daily texts or sleep problems, is causing the other. Specifically, bidirectionality is a problem here. In other words, the question is: Is frequent texting causing the sleep problems (I'm texting so much that I have no time to sleep), or are the sleep problems causing frequent texting (I can't sleep so I will text all my friends and tell them)? We

FIGURE 6.11 Reifman et al. (1991) found a positive correlation between temperature and the number of baseball players hit by a pitch. Why isn't bidirectionality a problem here?

an issue here. Why not? Because if there is causality, it can run in only one direction. Specifically, we can say it is possible that heat causes pitchers to hit batters with baseballs, but I assure you that under no circumstances does hitting batters with a pitch cause the air temperature to rise.

Does that mean we can state a cause-and-effect relationship for the obtained correlation between heat and the number of players hit by a baseball pitch? No, because it is still possible it wasn't the heat at all but some other variable that caused the pitchers to be more aggressive. Because the researchers didn't control everything potentially affecting those pitchers (as you would in an experiment), you cannot state cause and effect. This brings us to the second issue noted above: the third-variable problem.

The Third-Variable Problem

It is possible that X and Y, while correlated, are not causally linked in any way and that a third variable is affecting both. To show you what I mean, I'll use an often-cited example (see Peters, 2013). There is a positive correlation between the number of ice cream cones sold and the number of murders committed. Are ice cream cones causing people to murder? Is committing murder causing people to crave ice cream cones?

It is likely that neither of these statements reflects what is truly occurring, so let's think about it another way. Can you think of a third variable that might be responsible for both an increase in the sale of ice cream cones and an increase in murders? One possibility is the temperature. It is possible that when the temperature rises, more ice cream cones are sold. It is also possible that when the temperature rises, more people are murdered. This is an example of the third-variable problem. The third variable of heat could plausibly be responsible for causing an increase in both the number of murders and the number of ice cream cones sold.

You might be wondering why I wasn't allowing for a causality statement to be made with regard to heat and aggression earlier when we talked about baseball, yet now I seem to be supporting a heat and aggression causality argument to explain murder. The reason is that I was just using the heat and aggression relationship as an example of how a third variable could be responsible for the relationship we see, but I could be wrong about heat as the third variable causing the murder rate to rise and ice cream cones to sell. The point is that when variables are merely measured and not controlled as in an experiment, we cannot know what is causing what. So maybe it isn't heat that is causing an increase in either ice cream cones or murders. Maybe it's something else, something I can't even think of. The third-variable problem is a recognition that other variables may be responsible for the observed relationship between two variables. Thus, X and Y may be correlated, but there may be no causal link between them at all; the correlation can be explained by a third variable.

Let's take a look at another third-variable example. Vogt (2005) cites a positive relationship between the hair length of students and their test scores. In other words, those with longer hair get higher test scores. Are the higher grades causing people's hair to grow? Not likely. Is longer hair causing higher grades? Should I recommend that you grow your hair long so your grades will go up? Or is there another reason for this positive correlation between hair length and grades? Ah yes, that third-variable problem. What could that third variable be? Well, one possibility is gender. Females tend to have longer hair than males, and females in the tested class were also the ones who tended to get the higher grades. Vogt also suggests that perhaps student rank in college is that third variable. Maybe those further along in college got better grades and they are also the ones with longer hair. The point is that we do not know what is responsible for the relationship between hair length and grades.

When researchers are interpreting a significant correlation between two variables, they should always consider the possibility of a third variable.

Partial Correlations: A Statistical Technique for Controlling Third Variables

Sometimes researchers try to remove the influence of possible third variables by measuring them when the data are collected and then calculating **partial correlations**, which statistically control for those variables in the analysis by "partialing out" or removing the third variable from the analysis.

Let's take a look at an example we reviewed earlier. Recall that Strahan et al. considered the relationship between social anxiety and alcohol use. Although I didn't mention it before, they also found a significant negative correlation between anxiety and the frequency of drinking ($r = -.12$). In other words, those with more social anxiety drank less. Why did they find that those who are more socially anxious drank less? Is a higher level of social anxiety causing some people to stay away from alcohol? Is staying away from alcohol causing a higher level of social anxiety? We cannot state cause and effect when we are dealing with correlations, so we cannot know the answer to these questions. Another possibility is that perhaps those with social anxiety drink less because they just do not tend to go to places where alcohol is served.

So "lack of alcohol exposure" is a possible third variable, and Strahan et al. decided to investigate this possibility using a partial correlation analysis. While they were collecting data on social anxiety and drinking, they also collected data on participants' exposure to alcohol by asking them how many times per week they go to a place where alcohol is served (1 = never, 5 = 4 or more times per week). Then they ran a partial correlation analysis to look at the relationship between anxiety and alcohol use with alcohol exposure controlled. Remember that the relationship between anxiety and the frequency of drinking was initially negative? Now, with alcohol exposure controlled, the correlation between these two variables is no longer significant. The fact that the correlation between social anxiety and frequency of alcohol use became non-significant when alcohol exposure was controlled suggests that the negative correlation observed between social anxiety and alcohol use is likely due to participants' lack of exposure to places that serve alcohol.

Here's a question for you. Let's pretend that when Strahan et al. did their partial correlation analysis and controlled alcohol exposure, the result was that the original correlation between social anxiety and frequency of alcohol use was unchanged; it was still a significant negative correlation. So in this pretend situation, we would know that the correlation between social anxiety and alcohol use was likely not due to a lack of exposure to places that serve alcohol. Now could we conclude that social anxiety and frequency of alcohol use are causally related? No, we could not. Even though we have the ability to use partial correlation techniques to control the influence of a suspected third variable, we can never fully account for all possible third variables that might be influencing our correlations.

SUMMARY

When researchers conduct correlational research they measure variables to see whether there is a relationship between or among them. Correlational research is particularly useful when practical or ethical considerations prevent us from manipulating variables as we do in experiments.

Correlation coefficients are numerical values that indicate the strength and direction of a relationship between two variables. Correlation coefficients can be positive – indicating that the variables move in the same direction – or negative – indicating that the variables move in opposite directions. Possible values of correlation coefficients range from –1.00 to +1.00, with values closer to –1.00 or +1.00 representing stronger correlations and those closer to zero representing weaker correlations. Correlation coefficients are often visually presented using scatterplots or matrices.

When a correlation coefficient reveals that two variables are not correlated, it could mean that the relationship between them is not linear, but it could be curvilinear. A curvilinear relationship exists when changes in the value of one variable are accompanied by both increases and decreases in the other variable. The strength of a correlation can also be impacted by range restriction in the dataset. Range restriction exists in the data if most participants in a sample have similar scores for one of the measured variables in the correlation.

A variety of statistical techniques are available to assess relationships between or among variables. The Pearson product–moment correlation is used when you have two variables and both use interval or ratio scales. The Spearman correlation for ranked data is a statistical test used when you have two variables that are ordinal (ranked). The point–biserial correlation is used to calculate a correlation between one dichotomous variable and one continuous variable. Simple regression is used to predict one variable (criterion variable) from the other (predictor variable). Multiple regression analysis allows us to look at the relationships between a number of predictor variables and a single criterion variable.

Regardless of the correlation technique used, we cannot use correlation to establish cause and effect. There are two important reasons for this limitation. When two variables are correlated, we do not know which is the cause and which is the effect (the bidirectionality problem). We also do not know if a third variable is causing the variables in our correlation to move (the third-variable problem). We can try to remove the influence of possible third variables by measuring them and then calculating partial correlations. However, we can never fully account for all possible third variables that might be influencing our correlations.

In the next chapter we will continue our examination of non-experimental techniques with a closer look at survey research.

GLOSSARY

Absolute values – numbers that have no positive or negative sign.

Bidirectionality problem – an inability to ascertain the direction of causality in a correlation.

Bivariate correlations – a relationship between two variables ("bi" stands for two).

Correlation coefficient – a numerical value that ranges from –1.00 to +1.00 that describes the strength and direction of a relationship between variables.

Correlation matrix – a table in which information about the correlations of many variables with each other are presented.

Criterion variable – the variable in a regression analysis that is predicted based upon an individual's score on another variable (the predictor variable).

Curvilinear relationship – a nonlinear relationship in which changes in the values of the first variable are accompanied by both increases and decreases in the values of another variable and thus cannot be described with a straight line.

Dichotomous variable – a variable with two choices (for example, Republican or Democrat).

Linear relationship – a relationship between two variables that can be approximated with a straight line.

Multiple coefficient of determination (R^2) – the amount of variation in the outcome variable in a multiple regression analysis that can be accounted for by all the predictors taken together.

Multiple correlation coefficient (R) – the correlation between the combined predictors and the outcome variable.

Multiple regression analysis – a statistical technique that allows us to look at the relationship between a number of predictor variables and a single criterion variable.

Multivariate statistics – data analysis procedures that are designed to analyze three or more variables at the same time.

Negative correlation – the two variables of interest tend to move in opposite directions. Higher scores of one variable tend to be associated with lower scores on the other variable.

Partial correlations – researchers try to remove the influence of possible third variables by controlling for them in an analysis.

Pearson product–moment correlation – a statistic that identifies the direction and strength of the linear relationship between two variables measured on an interval or ratio scale.

Perfect correlation – the two variables in question vary together perfectly.

Point–biserial correlation (r_{pb}) – a correlation between one dichotomous variable and one continuous variable.

Positive correlation – two variables tend to move in the same direction. Higher scores of one variable are associated with higher scores on the other variable. Lower scores of one variable are associated with lower scores on the other variable.

Predictor variable – the variable in a regression analysis that is used to make a prediction of an individual's score on another variable (the criterion variable).

Probability value (p-value) – the statistical likelihood that a result is due simply to chance.

Range restriction – occurs when most of the participants in a sample have similar scores for one of the measured variables in the correlation.

Regression equation – the equation that makes the best-possible prediction of scores on the outcome variables using scores on one or more predictor variables.

Scatterplot (scattergram) – a graph of the relationship between two variables.

Simple regression (simple linear regression) – a statistical method of describing the relationship between two variables by calculating a "best-fitting" straight line on a graph.

Spearman correlation for ranked data – a statistical test for the linear relationship between ranked (ordinal) variables.

Standardized regression coefficients (beta weights) – statistics that indicate the relationship between one of the predictor variables and the outcome variable in a multiple regression analysis.

Statistics – mathematical methods used to systematically analyze data.

Third-variable problem – a variable that exists as a plausible alternative explanation for a correlation between two variables.

Zero-order correlations – correlations involving two variables.

REVIEW QUESTIONS

1 Explain the differences between experimentation and correlation research.
2 Explain what a correlation coefficient is.
3 Differentiate between a positive and a negative correlation.
4 Explain what it means to say two variables are not correlated.
5 Identify where stronger correlation coefficients are on a number line.
6 Explain how scatterplots represent strong and weak, negative and positive correlations.
7 Explain how to read a correlation matrix.
8 Describe how nonlinearity and range restriction can affect the strength of a correlation coefficient.
9 Explain when the following statistical procedures will be used: Pearson product–moment correlation, Spearman correlation for ranked data, the point–biserial correlation, simple regression, and multiple regression.
10 Explain how the bidirectionality problem and the third-variable problem keep us from establishing causality with correlational data.
11 Explain why a partial correlation analysis would be helpful to address a third-variable problem but still does not allow for a cause and effect statement between correlated variables.

ARTICLES AS ILLUSTRATION

The articles presented below provide examples of topics covered in this chapter, like correlation analyses and multiple regression. The questions that follow each of the articles will help you focus on the important points of each.

1 Björkqvist, K., Båtman, A., & Åman-Back, S. (2004). Adolescents' use of tobacco and alcohol: Correlations with habits of parents and friends.

Psychological Reports, 95, 418–420. doi:http://dx.doi.org/10.2466/PR0.95.6.418–420

Björkqvist, Båtman, and Åman-Back (2004) considered the relationship between adolescents' use of alcohol and tobacco and the use of these substances by friends and parents.

a. Describe the sample and methodology.
b. Look at the correlations relevant to adolescents' use of alcohol. For girls, was this use significantly correlated with the use of alcohol by their fathers and mothers? If so, were the correlations positive or negative? Was the adolescents' use of alcohol significantly correlated with the use of alcohol by their friends? If so, was this correlation positive or negative? Report on the analogous findings for boys.
c. Now consider the correlations relevant to adolescents' use of tobacco. For girls, was this use significantly correlated with the tobacco use of their fathers and their mothers? If so, were the correlations positive or negative? Was the use of tobacco in adolescents significantly correlated with the use of tobacco by friends? If so, was this correlation positive or negative? Report on the analogous findings for boys.
d. Was adolescent tobacco use significantly correlated with the alcohol use of friends and parents? Describe any significant relationship present in Björkqvist's et al.'s data.
e. Was adolescent alcohol use significantly correlated with the tobacco use of friends and parents? Describe any significant relationship present in Björkqvist et al.'s data.
f. What are Björkqvist et al.'s conclusions?
g. Björkqvist et al. are correct in noting that their correlations do not indicate a cause-and-effect relationship, and they suggest that

other variables may influence the relationship between adolescents' use of alcohol and tobacco and the use of these substances by their parents and friends. Can you think of possible third variables in this situation?

2 Greenberg, J. L., Lewis, S. E., & Dodd, D. K. (1999). Overlapping addictions and self-esteem among college men and women. *Addictive Behaviors, 24(4)*, 565–571. doi:http://dx.doi.org/10.1016/S0306–4603(98)00080-X

Greenberg, Lewis and Dodd (1999) wondered whether college students had a tendency to become addicted to multiple substances/activities.

a. Describe the sample and methodology.
b. Explain why a measure of self-esteem was included in the analyses and what the authors found with regard to this variable.
c. Explain why gender was included in the analyses and what the authors found with regard to this variable.
d. Describe the correlations among the different substances and activities. Was there a tendency for the sampled college students to become addicted to multiple substances or activities?

3 Odaci, H., & Çelik, C. B. (2013). Who are problematic Internet users? An investigation of the correlations between problematic Internet use and shyness, loneliness, narcissism, aggression and self-perception. *Computers in Human Behavior, 29*, 2382–2387. doi:http://dx.doi.org/10.1016/j.chb.2013.05.026

Odaci and Çelik (2013) investigated the relationship between problematic internet use in university students and shyness, loneliness, narcissism, aggression, and self-perception.

a. Describe the sample and methodology.
b. Describe any significant correlations between problematic Internet use and levels of shyness, narcissism, loneliness, aggression, and self-perception.
c. Odaci and Çelik also ran a multiple regression analysis. What percentage of the variation in problematic Internet use is accounted for by a combination of the variables of shyness, narcissism, loneliness, aggression, self-perception, and gender? In addition, which specific variables made significant contributions to problematic Internet use (look at Table 6.2 and check for p values less than .05)?

SUGGESTED ACTIVITIES

1 Take a correlation matrix from the literature and summarize each of the presented correlations. As an example, consider the work by Panek (2014) discussed below, which provides an example of research with a correlation matrix you can summarize. More specifically, Panek wanted to examine the degree to which popular media act as a distraction for those in college. He had university students answer questions regarding their use of media (hours watching online video, DVDs, and TV, and visiting social networking sites [SNS]), questions about their self-control (ability to keep from acting on impulse), questions about the amount of guilt they feel when they use media sources, and questions about the amount of schoolwork participants did each day. Panek presented bivariate correlations of these variables. See Table 6.2 for Panek's correlation matrix. I purposely picked a correlation matrix that has some positive correlations, some negative correlations, and some correlations that are not significant at all. Describe each correlation in two sentences. Here's an example: *Panek (2014) found the amount of time participants*

Table 6.2   Pearson correlation statistics.

	Social networking sites	DVR	DVD	TV	Self-control	Guilt	School work
Social networking sites	–						
DVR	.03	–					
DVD	−.05	.34**	–				
TV	.09	.17**	.11*	–			
Self-control	−.25**	−.01	−.03	.06	–		
Guilt	.21**	.08	.06	.03*	−.32**	–	
School work	−.06	.05	−.03	.02	.23**	−.05	–

Note: *p < .05, **p < .01.
Source: Adapted from Panek, E. (2014). Left to their own devices: College students' "guilty pleasure" media use and time management. *Communication Research, 41(4)*, 561–577. doi:http://dx.doi.org/10.1177/0093650213499657.

spent on social networking sites was positively correlated with the amount of guilt they felt (r = .21). In other words, participants felt more guilt when they spent more time on social networking sites. I'll leave the rest of the summarizing to you!

2   Can you think of possible third variables that could account for the following correlations?

a. The weight of children at a local elementary school is positively correlated with their reading level.

b. Income level is positively correlated with the height of local business people.

c. The number of shoppers at the mall is negatively correlated with the number of days left in the year.

d. The number of parks is positively correlated with the number of movie theaters in a local town.

e. The number of hours spent on Facebook is negatively correlated with grade point averages.

f. The number of students in class on a given day is negatively correlated with the number of car accidents in the area.

REFERENCES

Arnett, J. J. (2008). The neglected 95%: Why American psychology needs to become less American. *American Psychologist, 63*, 602–614. doi:http://dx.doi.org/10.1037/14805–008

Atkinson, D. R., Poston, W. C., Furlong, M. J., & Mercado, P. (1989). Ethnic group preferences for counselor characteristics. *Journal of Counseling Psychology, 36*, 68–72. doi:http://dx.doi.org/10.1037/0022–0167.36.1.68

Ballard, M., Gray, M., Reilly, J., & Noggle, M. (2009). Correlates of video game screen time among males: Body mass, physical activity, and other media use. *Eating Behaviors, 10*, 161–167. doi:http://dx.doi.org/10.1016/j.eatbeh.2009.05.001

Bina, M., Graziano, F., & Bonino, S. (2006). Risky driving and lifestyles in adolescence. *Accident Analysis and Prevention, 38*, 472–481. doi:http://dx.doi.org/10.1016/j.aap.2005.11.003

Björkqvist, K., Båtman, A., & Åman-Back, S. (2004). Adolescents' use of tobacco and alcohol: Correlations with habits of parents and friends. *Psychological Reports*, *95*, 418–420. doi:http://dx.doi.org/10.2466/PR0.95.6.418-420

Chernyshenko, O. S., & Ones, D. S. (1999). How selective are psychology graduate programs? The effect of the selection ratio on GRE score validation. *Educational and Psychological Measurement*, *59*, 951–961. doi:http://dx.doi.org/10.1177/00131649921970279

Cooper, H., Baumgardner, A. H., & Strathman, A. (1991). Do students with different characteristics take part in psychology experiments at different times of the semester? *Journal of Personality*, *59*, 109–127. doi:http://dx.doi.org/10.1111/j.1467-6494.1991.tb00770.x

Greenberg, J. L., Lewis, S. E., & Dodd, D. K. (1999). Overlapping addictions and self-esteem among college men and women. *Addictive Behaviors*, *24*(4), 565–571. doi:http://dx.doi.org/10.1016/S0306-4603(98)00080-X

Ickes, W., Park, A., & Robinson, R. L. (2012). F#!%ing rudeness: Predicting the propensity to verbally abuse strangers. *Journal of Language and Social Psychology*, *3*, 75–94. doi:http://dx.doi.org/10.1177/0261927X11425036

Klein Murdock, K. (2013). Texting while stressed: Implications for students' burnout, sleep and well-being. *Psychology of Popular Media Culture*, *2*, 207–221. doi:http://dx.doi.org/10.1037/ppm0000012

Kuncel, N. R., Hezlett, S. A., & Ones, D. S. (2001). A comprehensive meta-analysis of the predictive validity of the graduate record examinations: Implications for graduate student selection and performance. *Psychological Bulletin*, *127*, 162–181. doi:http://dx.doi.org/10.1037/0033-2909.127.1.162

O'Connor, K. J. (2013). Should I give the exam before or after the break? *Teaching of Psychology*, *41*, 63–65. doi:http://dx.doi.org/10.1177/0098628313514180

Odaci, H., & Çelik, C. B. (2013). Who are problematic internet users? An investigation of the correlations between problematic internet use and shyness, loneliness, narcissism, aggression and self-perception. *Computers in Human Behavior*, *29*, 2382–2387. doi:http://dx.doi.org/10.1016/j.chb.2013.05.026

Panek, E. (2014). Left to their own devices: College students' "guilty pleasure" media use and time management. *Communication Research*, *41*, 561–577. doi:http://dx.doi.org/10.1177/0093650213499657

Peters, J. (2013, July 9). When ice cream sales rise, so do homicides. Coincidence or will your next cone murder you? Slate. Retrieved from www.slate.com

Reifman, A. S., Larrick, R. P., & Fein, S. (1991). Temper and temperature on the diamond: The heat–aggression relationship in major league baseball. *Personality and Social Psychology Bulletin*, *17*, 580–585. doi:http://dx.doi.org/10.1177/0146167291175013

Rind, B., & Strohmetz, D. (2001). Effect of beliefs about future weather conditions on restaurant tipping. *Journal of Applied Social Psychology*, *31*, 2160–2164. doi:http://dx.doi.org/10.1111/j.1559-1816.2001.tb00168.x

Sternberg, R. J., & Williams, W. M. (1997). Does the graduate record examination predict meaningful success in the graduate training of psychologist? A case study. *American Psychologist*, *52*, 630–641. doi:http://dx.doi.org/10.1037/0003-066X.52.6.630

Strahan, E. Y., Panayiotou, G., Clements, R., & Scott, J. (2011). Beer, wine, and social anxiety: Testing the "self-medication hypothesis" in the US and Cyprus. *Addiction Research and Theory*, *19*, 302–311. doi:http://dx.doi.org/10.3109/16066359.2010.545152

Vogt, W. P. (2005). *Dictionary of statistics & methodology: A nontechnical guide for the social sciences*. Thousand Oaks, CA: Sage.

7 Survey Research

LEARNING OBJECTIVES

- Describe the different types of survey questions.

- Identify six question-writing guidelines.

- Describe different ways of administering a survey.

- Describe the three response biases.

- Explain why a non-response bias is a concern for researchers.

- Differentiate between probability and nonprobability sampling.

- Explain what influences whether you can generalize from a sample to a population.

- Describe ways to select the appropriate sample size.

It may not surprise you to learn that researchers have recently reported that a substantial percentage of college students do not sleep well. How do we know this? Lund, Reider, Whiting, and Prichard (2010) conducted a survey; they asked over a thousand students at a midwestern university questions about their sleep habits.

When you conduct a survey, you are attempting to estimate the opinions, characteristics, and/or behaviors of a particular population by asking a sample to respond to questions. A population (sometimes called a **target population** or a **population of interest**) is a defined group of individuals, and it can be very large (such as all

FIGURE 7.1 Lund et al. (2010) surveyed college students about their sleep habits. Many reported that they didn't sleep well. How about you?

American adults) or it can be more specific (such as all female Democrats in the Princeton, NJ area). A **sample** is a subset of individuals chosen from a population.

Many of us have been exposed to surveys. For example, during political campaigns, you may have been asked for your views on the candidates. According to one Gallup poll, shortly before the 2008 election, almost 40% of 18- to 29-year-olds had been contacted by either the Obama or the McCain campaign (Newport, Jones, & Saad, 2008).

The same Gallup poll asked respondents whether they were registered to vote, whether they were giving a lot of thought to the election, and what was their chance of voting. These measures were used as voter turn-out indicators. With these numbers in hand, researchers were able to predict the likely turn-out of the youngest US voters on election day.

To survey a population, you need to know what kinds of questions to ask, how to write effective ones, and how to obtain and contact your participant sample. These topics will each be covered in this chapter.

Survey Questions

In this section we will discuss different types of question content (demographic versus topical) as well as different types of question formats (open- versus closed-ended questions).

Demographic Questions

Most surveys include questions designed to assess the characteristics of the respondents, such as their age, gender, marital status, occupation, income, and education level. These types of questions are called **demographic questions**. When you include these types of questions in your survey, you can identify how different subsets of your sample answered your questions. For example, Harris, Hoekstra, Scott, Sanborn, and Dodds (2004) asked undergraduates to recall a romantic movie they had seen on a date. Then they asked the students to imagine they could stand in for one of the central characters in a scene from the movie. Which type of scene would they choose to be a part of – a sex scene, a romantic scene, a daring rescue scene, an intimate conversation scene, or another type?

FIGURE 7.2 Collecting demographic data – in this case, the gender of the study participants – enabled Harris et al. (2004) to determine that males and females would choose to be part of different types of movie scenes.

Would you be surprised to learn that males and females answered this question differently? Females chose a romantic scene significantly more often (56%) than males did (40%). In addition, 21% of the males said they would like to imagine themselves in a sex scene, while only 3% of females felt this way. Collecting demographic data – in this case, the gender of the study participants – allowed the researchers to make these comparisons.

Topical Questions

A survey generally needs more than just demographic questions; you have to include items that relate to your topic of interest. So if you're interested in predicting who will win an upcoming election, you would make sure to include at least one item in your questionnaire to specifically measure people's candidate preferences.

Topical questions can address a lot of different goals. For example, you can ask people questions about what they believe, what they would do, what they have done, and how they feel. Let's look at a specific survey example.

Sheldon and Bryant (2016) were interested in investigating college students' use of Instagram, a social network site that allows users to modify and then share photos and videos. Specifically, Sheldon and Bryant wanted to identify students' motives for using Instagram and how their feelings about their lives, their social activities, and any narcissistic tendencies they have influence that use. So Sheldon and Bryant asked their respondents a series of questions regarding their life satisfaction (for example, "I am very content and satisfied with my life"), social activities (such as "I often travel, vacation, or take trips with others"), and interpersonal interactions (for example, "I get to see my friends as often as I would like") (p. 91). Each of these questions was answered using a 5-point scale (1 = strongly disagree; 5 = strongly agree).

To assess the presence of narcissism in their study participants Sheldon and Bryant asked participants to indicate their level of agreement (1 = strongly disagree; 5 = strongly agree) with items such as "I can become entirely absorbed in thinking about my personal affairs, my health, my cares, or my relations to others" (p. 91). They also asked participants to indicate how much they have used Instagram (number of hours/minutes per day) and to rate how often they used Instagram (1 = never, 5 = always) for a series of presented reasons (such as "to depict my life through photos" p. 92). Through the use of these and other topical questions, Sheldon and Bryant determined that, for example, the more active students were socially, the more they used Instagram to document their lives. In addition, those who were rated higher in narcissism were more likely to use Instagram to "appear cool" (p. 93).

Open-Ended Questions

Let's talk about the different types of question formats. One type is the **open-ended question** format, which does not have fixed answers but allows the respondent to answer in any way. Think of it like an essay question on an exam. For example, "What do you like best about college?" is an open-ended question.

An advantage to asking an open-ended question is that respondents may give you important information you had not considered before. It may show you a new way of understanding the issue being investigated. A drawback is that respondents may not understand what you're looking for and give you an answer that really isn't helpful given your research goals. For example, if you ask people what they like best about college and anticipate answers like academics, sports, and social life experiences, it is probably not very helpful if someone tells you "My favorite thing about college is the lovely carpeting in the classrooms."

In any case, when you are analyzing the responses to open-ended questions, you need to do a content analysis by reading through all the responses and then creating categories that will help you summarize and make sense of them.

Let's go over an example of a content analysis of an open-ended question. Kulick and Rosenberg (2000) asked university students to explain why they choose to drive or not drive after four recent episodes of drinking. For the purposes of this example, let's just consider one of these open-ended questions: What were your reasons for driving after drinking? After reading through all the answers that the students gave in response to this question, Kulick and Rosenberg used content analysis to categorize the students' responses, grouping together similar types of responses. They found that the most commonly offered reason for driving after drinking was that the student needed or wanted to go on to a new destination. Many also noted that they saw themselves as minimally intoxicated, that others in their drinking party were perceived to be too intoxicated to be driving, or that they drank less than their drinking companions. Kulick and Rosenberg found the results of this content analysis to be informative and thought the results would help to guide researchers in their efforts to prevent college students from driving under the influence. For example, students could be taught that self-assessment of intoxication can be inaccurate, and just because you drank less than everyone in your party doesn't mean you are sober enough to drive.

Closed-Ended Questions

Another type of question format is the **closed-ended question** (also known as a **restricted** or **fixed-alternative question**). In this case people are asked to respond by choosing one or more answers from a set of offered options. Think of a closed-ended question as a multiple-choice exam question. Answer options can be as simple as "yes or no," or they can get more complicated. For example, take the work of Judson and Langdon (2009). To investigate the illegal use of prescription stimulants among undergraduates, they asked a sample of undergraduates a series of closed-ended questions. One was, "Have you ever used Ritalin, Concerta, Metadate, Methylin, Dexedrine, Adderall, Desoxyn, Cyclert, or any other stimulant medication without a prescription?" The answer options for this closed-ended question were simply "yes or no." For those who responded "yes," Judson and Langdon also assessed the motives for using these drugs illegally, and again students were given options to choose from: (1) to help concentrate, (2) to help increase alertness/stay awake, (3) to counteract the effects of other drugs, (4) to give a high, (5) to lose weight, (6) to control appetite, and (7) to enhance appetite. Using these closed-ended questions, Judson and Langdon were able to determine, for example, that 20% of the students in their sample did use stimulants without a prescription, most often to improve concentration (29%) and to increase alertness/stay awake (23%).

You may have noticed that it is much easier to summarize the results of closed-ended than open-ended questions. You usually just report the percentage that chose each option.

One of the best-known closed-ended question formats is the Likert scale. The **Likert scale** provides study participants a way to indicate their level of agreement or disagreement with a statement (Likert, 1932). For an example, let's take a look at the work of Stone and Baker-Eveleth (2013), who were interested in whether college students who had used

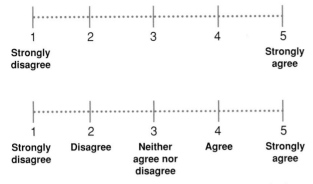

FIGURE 7.3 A 5-point Likert scale with just the endpoints labeled (top) and a 5-point Likert scale with each numbered option labeled" (bottom).

electronic textbooks would elect to continue to use them. The researchers asked a sample of university students to respond to a web-based questionnaire that included statements such as the following: "In the future, I plan to use an electronic textbook." The rating scale was a 5-point Likert scale with 1 = strongly disagree; 2 = disagree; 3 = neither agree or disagree; 4 = agree and 5 = strongly agree (p. 987).

Stone and Baker-Eveleth could have provided the scale with just the endpoints labeled (top of Fig. 7.3) instead of labeling each numbered option (bottom of Fig. 7.3). When only the endpoints are labeled, the researchers are relying on the respondents to decide the meaning of the non-named response options.

It is possible to include more than one type of rating scale in the same questionnaire. For example, Stone and Baker-Eveleth also asked people to respond to rating questions such as: "When I compare my grade in a course using an electronic textbook to my grade in a course using a traditional textbook, in general my grade in the course using an electronic textbook is ...," and the presented scale was a different 5-point scale (p. 987). This time the rating scale ranged from 1 = much worse; 2 = worse; 3 = about the same; 4 = better, and 5 = much better. Note that this scale is not officially a Likert scale (it

is not asking respondents to indicate their degree of agreement); some would refer to it as a Likert-type scale.

One of the reasons to point out Stone and Baker-Eveleth's use of two types of question formats is that researchers need to be sure the response options for each question make sense given the presented statement. In other words, it would be inappropriate to ask students to respond to, "In the future, I plan to use an electronic textbook" with the rating scale that ranged from 1 = much worse to 5 = much better. Always check to make sure that your statement and its response options work well together.

In both cases, Stone and Baker-Eveleth's scales follow an often-used pattern (see Figure 7.4). Their rating scales have at least 5 points (see Friedman & Weiser Friedman, 1986) with higher numbers indicating more of the characteristic of interest. Friedman and Weiser Friedman recommend that a maximum of 11 points can be used for a rating scale. Scales also often provide an odd number of response options so participants can select a neutral midpoint if they choose.

Rating scale guidelines

Design your scale so that higher ratings indicate more of the characteristic being measured.

Provide an odd number of response options so that respondents can choose a midpoint.

Create rating scales that have between 5 and 11 points.

Make sure that the statement and its response options work well together.

FIGURE 7.4 Rating scale guidelines.

Binge Drinking

Unenjoyable ___ ___ ___ ___ ___ ___ Enjoyable

FIGURE 7.5 Example of a semantic differential scale.

Sometimes researchers use another type of closed-ended question format called a **semantic differential scale** to provide respondents with response options that are paired adjectives that are opposites of each other (Friedman & Weiser Friedman, 1986). For example, when Johnston and White (2002) wanted to assess how college students feel about binge drinking, they used five semantic differential scales: unenjoyable/enjoyable, bad/good, favorable/unfavorable, unpleasant/pleasant, and satisfying/unsatisfying. Respondents could indicate the point on each rating scale that corresponded to their attitude toward the activity (Figure 7.5).

Another possible closed-ended format uses pictures as response options. For example, Maldonado, Bentley, and Mitchell (2004) created the pictorial sleepiness scale shown in Figure 7.6 to use to ask preschool children or those with "limited education" how sleepy they were feeling (p. 544).

Note that you can combine open- and closed-ended questions in a single questionnaire item. For example,

Who is your favorite male movie star?

1. Channing Tatum
2. Leonardo DiCaprio
3. Denzel Washington
4. Bradley Cooper

5. Ryan Gosling
6. Other: _____

You can also combine open- and closed-ended questions in a questionnaire by asking an open-ended question and then following it up with a closed-ended question. Here is an example:

If you have done something within the last year that upset your parents, what was it?

————————————————————

Within the last year, have you done any of the following?

1. got into a fight
2. lied
3. stole something
4. cheated on an exam

When you provide open-ended questions followed by closed-ended questions, it is called **funneling** because you are placing the broader question first and the narrower (more specific) question later. If you're going to have both types of questions on the same topic in the same questionnaire, you will want to be sure people answer the open-ended questions first. Giving the closed-ended question first could change someone's answer to the open-ended question. In the example above, if I put the closed-ended question first, it's quite possible people would answer the open-ended question with one of the options from the closed-ended question (got into a fight, lied, stole something, cheated on an exam). But perhaps respondents did something else that upset their parents, such as failing a course or getting into a car accident. These response alternatives

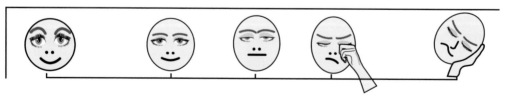

FIGURE 7.6 Example of a pictorial scale used by Maldonado et al. (2004).

Question writing guidelines
Use easy-to-understand language.
Avoid writing questions that have negative wording.
Avoid writing double-barreled questions, which ask two questions in one.
Make sure your response options are mutually exclusive.
Avoid writing questions that contain emotionally charged language.
Consider providing your respondents with an "I don't know" response option.

FIGURE 7.7 Question writing guidelines.

might not occur to the respondent because the earlier closed-ended question creates a mindset consisting of the answer choices provided.

Question-Writing Guidelines

There are general guidelines to follow when you are writing questions (see Figure 7.7). No matter what type of questions you are writing, they should be clear and in easy-to-understand language. Avoid writing questions that have negative wording, such as, "Do you agree that people should not hitchhike?" People might miss the "not" or be confused by the idea that agreeing with this question means disagreeing with the idea of hitchhiking.

Avoid writing double-barreled questions, which ask two questions in one. For example, if you ask respondents, "Would you be willing to get a tattoo or get your tongue pierced?" and they say "yes," you don't know whether they are willing to get a tattoo or a tongue piercing or both. Ask only one question at a time: "Are you willing to get a tattoo?" and then separately, "Are you willing to get your tongue pierced?"

Response options also must be mutually exclusive. For example, it would be inappropriate to ask people to choose a category that represents their age and provide the following categories:

1. 18–34
2. 34–50
3. 50–65
4. 65 +

Can you see why this is inappropriate? What response should a 34-year-old choose? Make sure your response options do not overlap.

Also avoid writing questions that contain emotionally charged language. For example, you don't want to ask someone how much they agree with a statement like this: "Those over 18 should be able to get an immoral sentiment tattooed on their body if they so choose." Even if respondents think people should be able to tattoo themselves with anything they want, they may be influenced by the negative implications of the word "immoral." If instead you ask people how much they agree with the statement, "Those over 18 should be able to get any type of sentiment tattooed on their body they choose," you're likely to get a different level of agreement.

One assumption we make when asking people questions – which is after all a means of collecting self-report data – is that they will provide truthful answers. However, people are not always truthful and will even give their opinion on topics they know nothing about. A funny example was seen in a segment from the television show *Jimmy Kimmel Live* ("Lie Witness News") in which a *Kimmel* show staff member interviews attendees at the Coachella Valley Music and Arts Festival (an annual multi-band event in California). The staffer asks those entering the venue for their thoughts on particular bands that do not actually exist. For example,

Interviewer: "One of my favorite things today, straight out of Williamsburg, is The Chelsea Clintons."

Respondent: "Oh yea, I have heard of them actually. I don't know if I'm going to see them or not, but I do know of their music."

Interviewer:	"What did you hear about them?"
Response:	"They're just fun."
Interviewer:	"What's fun about The Chelsea Clintons?"
Response:	"I think they just give off that energy. You can just tell that they're doing it from a good place."

It sounds like this respondent knows her music, right? Except The Chelsea Clintons is not a real band. People will indeed express views about things they couldn't possibly know about. However, I hesitate to rely on a segment of *Jimmy Kimmel Live* to make a research methodology point, so I will provide you with more solid evidence. Graeff (2003) found that respondents will in fact provide answers to questions about which they are "uninformed" (p. 643).

You may wonder why I am willing to accept Graeff's word that people will provide uninformed responses and not the word of the staff of *Jimmy Kimmel Live*. There are many reasons. We don't know the details of the way Kimmel's staff collected the "data." How many people did they approach who refused to answer? Did Kimmel's staff have to talk with 100 people before getting one uninformed response? If so, then having only 1% of people provide an uninformed response is not really noteworthy (although it can still be funny).

Graeff, on the other hand, reported in his journal article, that he called 1,854 people and an impressive 72% agreed to be interviewed. When they had the option of saying "I don't know" in response to a question, 49% gave uninformed responses. When "I don't know" was not an option, over 95% gave uninformed responses. Now we have noteworthy information. What's the moral of this story (besides that you shouldn't trust Jimmy Kimmel for your scientific information)? People will indeed provide uninformed answers to questions, and the

likelihood of an uninformed response decreases significantly when respondents have the option of saying "I don't know." This is a good reason to provide your respondents with an "I don't know" response option.

Administering the Survey

You've written your survey questions so it's almost time to administer your survey. There's just one more thing to do before you start collecting data. You need to pilot your survey. That means doing a practice run with a few people from your target population, so you can make sure the instructions and questions are easy to understand (which you can ascertain during a thorough debriefing of the pilot group), and that you are asking the questions you want to ask. You can also use this time to become comfortable with running the study. Time these sessions so you can give your final sample an estimate of the time needed to be a part of the study. Finally, do not include the data from your pilot in your final analysis. Since we consider the pilot to be practice, use this time to make sure that everything is working as planned before collecting data.

How are you going to administer your survey? You have choices to make here too. You can conduct a face-to-face interview or a telephone interview. You can instead choose to email or mail questions to your study participants or direct your participants to an online questionnaire. Each technique has advantages and disadvantages.

Face-to-Face Interviews

In a **face-to-face interview** you interview people in person. This type of technique does have some advantages. You can often judge immediately whether the respondent understands the question. If he or she doesn't, you're there to clear it up. Or,

FIGURE 7.8 One way to administer a survey is to conduct a face-to-face interview.

FIGURE 7.9 What's it like to be an only child? Roberts and White Blanton (2001) interviewed a sample of young adults raised as only children and then used a content analysis to summarize their responses.

if someone doesn't give you a complete answer, you can prompt for a fuller response.

One disadvantage of the face-to-face interview is that it is a relatively time-consuming and expensive approach to gathering information, since you do have to meet in person. Also, the interviewer can actually bias the results, either consciously or unconsciously. For example, say an interviewer feels more comfortable talking with women than with men and thus probes more when interviewing women. Now the responses from women are more in-depth purely as a function of the interviewer's technique, not because there is an inherent difference between the male and female respondents. This interviewer has biased the results.

Another concern is that people might give different answers in a face-to-face interview than if they were not in the presence of the researcher. That's a real risk when you're questioning people about very personal information. Most are probably more likely to reveal this type of information in an anonymous questionnaire than in a face-to-face interview.

Sometimes it is necessary for researchers to conduct a content analysis of the material obtained from face-to-face interviews. Let's look at an example. In an article cleverly entitled "I always knew Mom and Dad loved me best: experiences of only children," Roberts and White Blanton (2001) reported the results of a study they conducted to investigate what it's like to be raised as an only child. After 45- to 75-minute face-to-face interviews with 20 young adults raised as single children were completed, they were transcribed. The researchers then read them all and organized the content into four categories: (1) having no sibling relationship, (2) closeness of the parent–child relationship, (3) being treated like a small adult, and (4) implications for the future (Roberts and White Blanton decided that each of the categories could contain both positive and negative comments).

After categorizing each of the responses, the researchers were able to summarize how their respondents generally felt about being an only child. They found that most did not mind being without siblings and liked being the sole recipients of their parents' attention. On the other hand, because they had spent so much time with adults, many had difficulty connecting with people their own age. Many were also worried about having to care for aging parents in the future, and some felt pressure to provide grandchildren for their parents. Almost half indicated that they too wanted to have only one child. Thus, as a result of these interviews, these researchers have provided information about the experiences of only children and shown perceived advantages and disadvantages of the experience.

Telephone Surveys

For a more cost-effective method of surveying than face-to-face, you could choose to conduct your interviews by phone (land line or cell phone). Telephone interviews are useful in that you can often develop rapport (as you can in a face-to-face interview) and clarify questions as well as prompt for additional responses if there's a need.

In addition to having a live person conduct a telephone interview, researchers can now ask respondents either to use their touch-tone telephones or to provide verbal responses to prerecorded questions. Despite these conveniences, telephone interviewing may be losing favor. In 2003, the Federal Trade Commission implemented a "do not call registry" giving consumers the right to limit the number of phone calls received by telemarketers (www.consumer.ftc.gov/articles/0108-national-do-not-call-registry). While phone calls made for the purpose of conducting a survey are not covered under the "do not call" rules, people may be less likely to answer phone surveys given their expectation that they should not be receiving unsolicited calls.

Another disadvantage is that some people are giving up their landlines and using only cell phones. If researchers target only landlines or only cellphones, they may not be able to generalize the results from one group of people to the other (see Keeter, Christian, & Dimock, 2010). People also often use their cell phones differently from their landlines, such as while in a public space, and that could affect their responses (www.people-press.org/methodology/collecting-survey-data/cell-phone-surveys/).

Internet Surveys

You can also administer a questionnaire via the Internet, using web sites like www.surveymonkey.com to create and store your survey, before contacting people and directing them to it. You can also include your questionnaire in a list of online research opportunities (for example, see Hanover College's list at http://psych.hanover.edu/Research/exponnet.html). Then those interested in participating in research can find your questionnaire and answer it. Internet surveys can be relatively cost-effective, although some survey creation websites do charge a fee. An added bonus is that survey responses can immediately be sent to you in database form ready for analysis. A disadvantage of administering your survey online is that the dropout rate tends to be relatively high for online surveys – this can mean that there is a possibility of a non-response bias, which we will discuss below. (See Chapter 13 for more about conducting research online.)

Mail Surveys

Another option is to send a questionnaire to potential respondents through e-mail or regular postal mail. It is relatively cost-effective, especially compared to a face-to-face interview. An often-cited disadvantage, however, is that there are usually some people who will not return the questionnaire. This disadvantage can also lead to a non-response bias.

Response Biases

Respondents can exhibit a variety of response biases. In each case, they are *not* providing answers that indicate how they really think and/or feel. For example, respondents may respond in a particular way because they fear their true response will not make a favorable impression on the observers. This phenomenon, termed the **social desirability effect** (Edwards, 1957), occurs because people want to portray themselves in a positive or socially desirable light. If you are attempting to ask people about sensitive topics such as drug abuse or sexual behavior, for example, you may not get truthful answers. One way to get around this problem is to ensure participant anonymity. If you must collect participants' identifying information, let them know that their responses are confidential, that only group data will be disseminated and not individual data, and that their names will not be connected to their data in any way.

Sometimes survey respondents do not take the time to answer the survey questions thoughtfully; instead, they just have the tendency to mark responses without regard for item content. These biases come in a variety of forms as you'll see below.

One example of this type of response bias is called **acquiescence** or **yea-saying**. As the name suggests, this bias is present when people repeatedly choose the response option "yes" or "strongly agree" regardless of item content. One reason for acquiescence is the result of respondents' desire to quickly answer the items without exerting the cognitive effort necessary to respond thoughtfully, and one way to control for this bias is to reverse some, perhaps all, of the items (Lavrakas, 2008). For example, "Students should be allowed to keep pets in their dorm room" can be reversed to "Students should *not* be allowed to keep pets in their dorm room."

Reverse wording items can lead to respondents needing to slow down to in order to think more carefully about how they wish to respond. However, as Lavrakas has noted, there are potential disadvantages to having two versions of each question. For one thing, the redundancy may be annoying to respondents. For another, disagreeing with a negative statement can be confusing for participants. If respondents do agree with each statement despite the reverse wording, the series of responses will not make sense when considered together (for example, you can't be both for and against pets in dorm rooms). If you find a respondent shows this pattern of responding, you can eliminate this respondent's data from your data set.

Some respondents will show a tendency to disagree with all statements; this is called **nay-saying**. Nay-saying can be the result of a wish to move through the items quickly, or it can be caused by "excessive modesty or reserve, or an antagonism toward the researcher" (Tellis & Chandrasekaran, 2010, p. 332). Reverse wording items can help you detect this response pattern too.

Another response bias is **fence sitting**, which occurs when respondents choose a response in the middle of the scale (this is possible when there is an odd number of response options). In some cases this response is warranted; a person may choose a middle response to indicate that they are taking a neutral position. However, it is also possible that someone has a position on an issue but is unwilling to make that position known, perhaps because the issue is sensitive, personal, or controversial. Researchers can try alleviating this problem by ensuring the participants' anonymity or by removing the neutral option from the array of responses, forcing respondents to take a more extreme position (see Nowlis, Kahn, & Dhar, 2002). Researchers have to consider which is the preferred option for their particular project.

Non-response Bias

When a large proportion of your sample fails to return a completed questionnaire, you run the risk of having a non-response bias. A **non-response bias** is an error that occurs if the respondents who fail to return the questionnaire differ in significant ways from those who do return it, such that your survey yields answers that do not represent the attitudes of the target population.

The potential for non-response bias can occur in all kinds of surveys. You might phone potential respondents who, for whatever reason, refuse to talk with you. As mentioned above, you might contact people to complete your Internet or mailed questionnaire who neglect to finish and/or return it. Even people you interview face-to-face could decide not to finish the session. Whenever a portion of respondents fail to finish the presented questions, you need to consider the possibility of a non-response bias.

Let's look back at Stone and Baker-Eveleth's research and use it as an example. Stone and Baker-Eveleth wanted to know what students generally thought of electronic textbooks, so they sent an email to their entire university student population of 11,957 people. Almost 12% of the students responded to an emailed invitation to complete a questionnaire. We can reasonably wonder whether those who neglected to respond had a different view of electronic textbooks. It is difficult to know for sure; however, there are ways to assess this. The researchers could, for example, expend extra effort to collect data from initial non-responders and then compare data from early versus later responders, equating late responders to non-responders (Groves, 2006).

Some researchers have indeed directly focused on considering whether a non-response bias may be affecting data. For example, some have used the technique of asking those participating in research to answer a follow-up questionnaire. Inevitably, some will answer the follow-up while others will not, and characteristics of these two groups can be compared. Barchielli and Balzi (2002) used this technique, for example, to determine that non-responders had higher smoking rates and higher mortality rates than responders. This result suggests that researchers assessing smoking rates may be obtaining biased estimates of smoking behavior.

Remember that while the size of a non-response rate is not a good predictor of the size of a potential bias, some have put forth estimates regarding what a good response rate is (rates range from 50% to 85% depending on source, see Groves, 2006). The **response rate** is the percentage of people who complete the study; certainly a high response rate is an ideal goal, so researchers often include an incentive for returning the questionnaire (like being entered in a raffle with an enticing prize).

Sampling from a Population

Sampling is the process of selecting respondents for your study. There are two main types of sampling, and we'll discuss each one below. First, some general principles about both kinds.

As mentioned, when researchers are interested in assessing the attitudes, characteristics, and/or behaviors of a particular group of individuals, which we call a population, they typically ask questions of just a small portion of that group, called a sample. Sometimes the population in which you are interested is very small; in that case, you might choose to study *all* the members of that population rather than taking a sample. For instance, suppose I want to see what the 25 students in my new course, "Wrongful Conviction," think about it. The size of my population of interest is quite manageable, and I could just survey all of them. The survey data I gather in this instance could be very informative, but the results would not be relevant for any course but this one. In other words, the results I get from surveying students about this course will not generalize to other students or other courses.

Much of the time, however, the population of interest is not that small, and surveying everyone in it is impractical. In these cases, we take a sample of

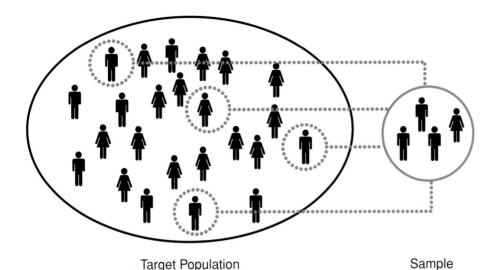

Target Population   Sample

the population and ask questions just of that smaller group (see Figure 7.10).

Probability Sampling

Now let's look at the two major sampling techniques. The first one is **probability sampling**, in which each study participant has a known probability of being included in the sample. How do we know? If we use a well-defined target population that can be quantified (for example, all full-time undergraduates at Rider University), we can determine how likely it is for each individual in that population to be a part of the sample (one divided by the number in the target population). We'll discuss three ways to conduct probability sampling: simple random sampling, stratified sampling, and cluster sampling.

Simple Random Sampling. One way to select participants for your study is to do what is known as **simple random sampling**. Let's look closer at this issue using an example. Suppose you wanted to find out how students at your educational institution feel about the food on campus. You could question them all, but there are probably too many to make

this a reasonably sized project. Instead, you can just ask questions of a representative sample of the total student population. A **representative sample** is one that has the same relevant characteristic(s) as the population of interest – in this case, that means being a student on your campus.

How do you make your sample representative of the population? By making it a **random sample**, one in which every person in the entire population of interest has an equal chance of being selected. Thus if you wanted to ask questions of a random group of students on your campus, you could get a list of students from the registrar (thus we know the number of people in the population) and randomly choose from that list. Let's talk about how to do this.

Say you have a target population of 500 people and you have a list of all their names. Go down the list and assign a number to each person in turn, from 0 to 500. Your goal is to draw a random sample from this target population. Go to a table of random numbers (see Appendix B). Choose a starting place on the page of random numbers (just close your eyes and point). Since we need three-digit numbers in this example (because the number 500 has three digits), we will read three-digit numbers down the

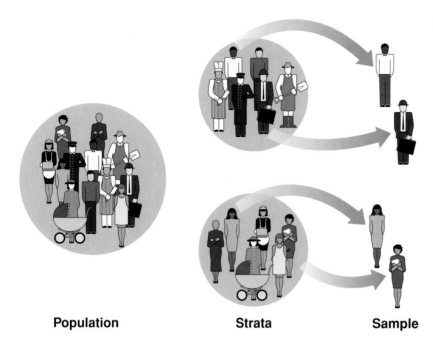

FIGURE 7.11 A stratified sample.

Population   **Strata**   **Sample**

page from our starting point. In the random numbers table in the Appendix, if I started from the top of column c, I would read the following numbers: 016, 488, 114 ... (numbers that begin with one or two zeros would be read as numbers less than 100 while numbers above 500 would be ignored). Then each person on the list that corresponds to those numbers would be considered "randomly chosen" for the study. Your next step would be to obtain survey responses from the randomly selected people; the goal again is to achieve as high a response rate as possible.

If you wish, instead of using a random numbers table you can use a randomizer available online. For example, you can consult www.randomizer.org for a list of numbers, randomly generated according to your specifications (for example, indicate how many numbers you want). Once you have obtained the list of random numbers, then, as above, each person on your list who corresponds to one of those numbers is considered to be randomly chosen for the study.

If you sample randomly from your target population, in theory you can infer that your obtained results hold for the rest of the target population. If you do not collect data from a sample representative of the entire population of interest, your ability to generalize beyond your sample is limited. For instance, if you ask only the commuters on campus to report on the campus food, you cannot say your results reflect what *all* students on your campus think about the food. You didn't take a random sample of your target population, so your sample was not representative.

Stratified sampling. You may also obtain a representative sample using another probability sampling technique called a **stratified sample**. First you divide your population of interest into segments called strata (the singular form is stratum). Each stratum represents a group of people who have one or more characteristics of interest. For example, you could divide your target population of college students into groups of males and groups of females. Once you divide the population of interest into strata, then you choose a random sample from each of the segments (see Figure 7.11).

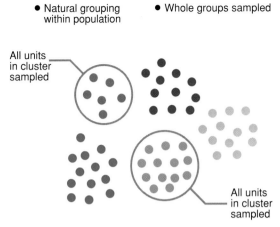

FIGURE 7.12 Cluster sampling.

Let's take a look at an example. Sutfin et al. (2012) were interested in determining whether student health centers on college campuses were screening for tobacco use and encouraging students to quit smoking. To do this, they used a stratified random sample. They wanted to obtain responses from freshmen, sophomores, juniors, and seniors from each of eight North Carolina universities. So they obtained enrollment lists from the eight universities, separated into strata by academic year. They then randomly selected students from the enrollment lists and encouraged them to answer a survey (the overall response rate was approximately 23% so a non-response bias was a concern that the authors addressed). The result was a sample of 3,800 students, ranging from freshmen to seniors, from all eight universities; this allowed the researchers to compare the results across the different years and schools.

They found, for example, that overall 62% of the students were screened for tobacco use. Screening rates varied by school and by year and were lower among freshmen and sophomores than among seniors. For those asked about their use of tobacco, only 50% reported that the campus health care center staff recommended they quit or reduce their smoking (again, the reported rate differed across schools).

According to Sutfin et al., this research suggests that student health center staff are missing opportunities to: (1) screen for smoking, and (2) offer intervention for those who smoke. For our purposes, I hope you can see how using stratified sampling helps ensure that you obtain data from those who have particular characteristics of interest.

Cluster sampling. I started this section on sampling by talking about getting a list of students from the registrar and then randomly choosing your sample from that list. But what if the registrar is not cooperating? What if privacy laws do not allow him or her to give you a list of all students? Then what do you do?

When a list of those in your population of interest is not available, you can use **cluster sampling**. In this technique, the researcher identifies clusters of individuals, then randomly samples the clusters to decide which ones to use. Once the clusters to be used have been identified, *all* participants within the chosen clusters are surveyed (see Figure 7.12). An example will help illustrate this.

Cerrito and Levi (1999) were interested in determining why students at their university were often not doing well in their entry-level math courses. The rule of thumb, announced at the beginning of the semester, was that students should spend 2–3 hours studying for each hour of class time. But were they studying the recommended amount? Instead of asking about the study habits of all their students in entry-level math courses (likely too many to be practical), or asking a random selection of these students (likely a risk of a large non-response bias), the researchers used cluster sampling. They randomly selected instructors who taught entry math courses at their institution and asked them to give a one-week diary survey to *all* the students in their classes. Thus for one week, these students were to report all their study, work, and leisure activities. Were they studying the recommended amount?

FIGURE 7.13 Cerrito and Levi (1999) used cluster sampling in their study of how much students in entry-level math classes were studying at their university. They randomly selected instructors who taught these classes and asked them to give a one-week diary survey to *all* the students in their classes.

Students were generally found to be studying more for their math courses than for their other courses; however, the amount of time they reported studying math was much lower than the recommended amount, although there was wide variation in study times among the different instructors. What did Cerrito and Levi recommend? Although they could not conclude that more studying causes better math performance (because they didn't do an experiment), they did recommend that students use some of their leisure time to study more math. Given that many students were not doing well in these classes, you're probably not surprised to hear this.

Nonprobability Sampling

As I've suggested, randomly selecting your study participants is an ideal situation, but it cannot always be easily done. When random sampling is not possible,

researchers often use a form of nonprobability sampling. **Nonprobability sampling** literally means the researchers will not know the probability of an individual's being selected for the study. In practical terms, the use of nonprobability sampling means your sample is not random; thus it is not representative of the population, and you need to be cautious about generalizing from the sample to the population of interest. The two types of nonprobability sampling are convenience sampling and quota sampling.

Convenience Sampling. One type of nonprobability sampling is referred to as convenience sampling (also known as **haphazard sampling**). As its name suggests, **convenience sampling** allows researchers to survey participants who are conveniently available. This could mean, for example, sampling commuters at the train station, factory workers in the factory, or people strolling in a park. The most common type of convenience sample is a college student sample (you may even have been part of a convenience sample for research on your own campus). For example, Sears (1986) found that 75% of the articles in mainstream social psychology journals tested undergraduate students from the United States (see Arnett, 2008 for a comparable finding in a more recent analysis).

Quota Sampling. Quota sampling is another type of nonprobability sampling. **Quota sampling** starts with a convenience sample, but in this case the researcher wants to ensure that certain types of participants are selected in particular proportions.

Let's take a look at an example. McKetin, Chalmers, Sunderland, and Bright (2014) wanted to investigate whether taking recreational drugs, specifically stimulants and marijuana, was related to simultaneous binge drinking. To conduct this study, they needed to find people who were taking part in these activities. How did they find the people they

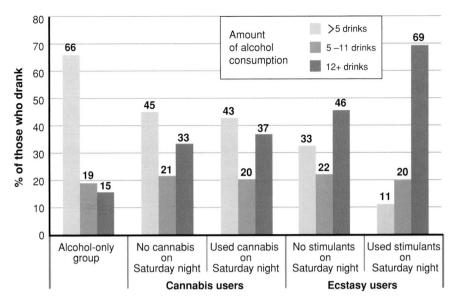

FIGURE 7.14 Reported alcohol consumption for a previous Saturday night for ecstasy users, cannabis users or those who had not used either in the past year (alcohol only). McKetin et al., (2014) found that those who took Ecstacy, not marijuana, were more likely to binge drink.

needed? They worked with a market research panel in Australia that had study participants available for research opportunities. Once they got access to this panel, they used quota sampling. To be eligible, participants had to be between the ages of 18 and 30 and to have used alcohol within the last year. But there was more. Let's look at how McKetin et al. explained their sampling procedure:

Quota sampling was used to recruit equal numbers of men and women who had either: (i) used ecstasy in the past year (ecstasy users); (ii) used cannabis but not ecstasy in the past year (cannabis users); or (iii) who had not used either cannabis or ecstasy in the past year (alcohol only). Recruitment was discontinued when the number of completed surveys reached 400 for men and 400 for women in each of these categories, or when the number of new recruits fell to below five per week. (p. 437)

Once they had obtained their sample, McKetin et al. asked participants to report what drugs they had taken the previous Saturday night. Ultimately they determined that those who took stimulants, not marijuana, were more likely to binge drink (see

Figure 7.14). As you can see, McKetin et al. needed study participants with specific characteristics to answer their research question, and quota sampling was a good way to get the sample they needed.

I was *almost* a part of a quota sample once. I was with a friend at a train station in Washington, DC, and a researcher approached my friend wanting to assess her thoughts about the trailer for an upcoming Charlie Sheen movie called *The Chase* (yes, *that* Charlie Sheen) (see Figure 7.15). My friend watched the trailer and provided her ratings while I excitedly waited my turn. (I probably get more excited about surveys than most people, but it is part of what I do for a living, and I like to see the questions other researchers use.) But when my friend had completed the survey, the researcher began to walk away.

I called after her, "Wait, don't you want responses from me?"

"No," she said, "I've filled my quota of females." And that's how I was almost in a quota sample.

Clearly, this researcher was getting a convenience sample (just walking up to people who were available at the train station) with quotas for participant gender. It is likely the movie studio was anticipating an equal proportion of males and females

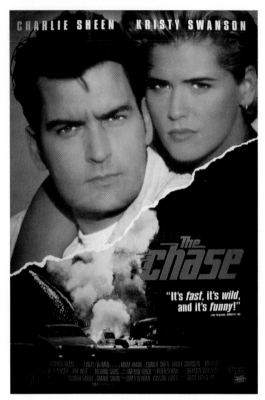

FIGURE 7.15 I almost got to be part of a quota sample to rate the trailer for this movie.

would be the target audience for this movie, and so the researcher wanted to obtain responses from an equal proportion of male and female participants. The number of responses she needed was set before she started collecting data. Were the responses she obtained representative of the US movie-going audience? With quota sampling, or indeed with *any* kind of convenience sampling, you just do not know. The responses you obtain can still be informative and interesting, but they may not be the same as you would get from the target population. Let's turn to this issue more formally next.

Generalizing from the Sample to the Population

As noted above, if you randomly select your study participants from the population of interest, then your sample is representative, and you can generalize from the sample to the population (the extent to which research results can be generalized is referred to as external validity, which you'll learn more about in Chapter 9).

When you do not randomly select your sample from the population, you are limited in your ability to generalize from the sample to the population. Let's talk about this issue with regard to the most often tested convenience sample: college students. Are the results obtained with college student samples generalizable to others? College student samples are not representative of people in general; they are considered biased samples because they have certain characteristics that people in general likely do not share in the same proportions. For example, undergraduate samples tend to be young relative to the general population, with a relatively advanced educational background. In addition, "social and political attitudes tend to be considerably less crystallized" in younger adults (Sears, 1986, p. 521), suggesting, of course, that information about attitudes you collect from a college student population is unlikely to reflect the attitudes of the general population. Research conducted with this convenience sample can be interesting, but because the sample is not a representative one (it wasn't selected randomly), researchers who choose it are limited in their ability to generalize their results.

Understandably, behavioral scientists are often interested in exploring how humans in general think, feel, and behave. They might be so bold as to wish their obtained results held for all beings, that all people would show the same pattern of beliefs or behaviors. We recognize the limitations of using convenience samples. In recent years, there has also been a call for researchers to make more effort to recognize cultural differences. For example, Arnett (2008) reviewed the samples tested in 6 major US journals and noted that, given its narrow focus on

FIGURE 7.16 Results obtained with American college student samples are not necessarily generalizable to others.

people in the United States, there are "doubts of how well American psychological research can be said to represent humanity" (p. 602).

Henrich, Heine, and Norenzayan (2010) noted that psychological research in the world's top journals tends to be based on WEIRD samples (**W**estern, **E**ducated, **I**ndustrialized, **R**ich, and **D**emocratic); the world's people certainly cannot all be classified in this manner. In support of this argument, Henrich et al. reviewed multiple areas of research (such as people's motivation to conform), comparing results from the WEIRD samples to those from other cultures, and they often found differences. In fact, they found evidence that WEIRD samples are "highly unrepresentative of the species," living lives that are quite unusual compared with the way the rest of the world lives (p. 19). Thus, with this work, Henrich et al. explicitly challenge those who assume college students are appropriate samples from which to make claims about human psychological processes, and they encourage researchers to tap into more diverse populations.

Ideally, your research question should influence your choice of what population to sample (Gächter, 2010). Consider, for example, research discussed at the beginning of this chapter. Lund et al. (2010) were interested in the sleep habits of students and

reported on these habits from a convenience sample of students at a midwestern US university. Since the research question presumably concerns the sleep habits of students in general, we should ask: Do Lund et al.'s results generalize to students at other US universities? Do these results generalize to students at universities in other countries? Replicating the research can be an answer here. Obtaining similar results with other university student samples can help researchers know how generalizable their results are. And if you want to generalize to all humanity, then you need to reach beyond the WEIRD.

Reaching beyond the WEIRD is a challenging task, but researchers have begun to find ways to accomplish it. Certainly an ideal is to accumulate comparative data across diverse populations (Henrich et al., 2010). The Internet can help here; there is accumulating evidence that sampling online can lead one to relatively diverse populations. For example, Gosling, Sandy, John, and Potter (2010) collected online data from over half a million study participants and then compared them to the WEIRD samples discussed by Henrich et al. Gosling et al.'s online sample was impressively non-WEIRD (66% of participants were not of the typical college age). The bottom line is: However your research is conducted, you'll need to recognize the limitations of the work and include a discussion of its generalizability in your write-up.

Sample Size

Finally, how large should your sample for your survey be? There are a couple of points you need to consider when making this decision. Let's look at it conceptually so you understand the thoughts behind the decision.

You want the sample to be large enough to represent the population adequately, so you need to have a sense of how much diversity there is in your

FIGURE 7.17 This group of people could be considered homogeneous, which means its members are very similar to each other.

population.[1] Let's take a ridiculous example. Say we want to know the average height of females, but *all* females are exactly 5 feet 4 inches; in other words, there is no diversity. If all females are 5 feet 4, then it doesn't take a large sample to find this out – one female should be enough. This population is **homogeneous**, which means its members are all very similar to each other. With a homogeneous population, your sample doesn't need to be large to capture a good range of responses.

When your population has variability, however, or in other words when it is **heterogeneous**, your sample needs to be larger to represent that population adequately. So, in my pretend world, if the height of females can vary from say 4 feet to 7 feet, then I need to test the height of more females to capture this variability. This larger sample will allow me to gather data that are more representative of my diverse population. This leads us to a general rule of thumb: Larger samples generally represent populations better than smaller samples. In addition, if you want to divide the sample according to particular characteristics such as gender, you will need

to collect data from enough participants to fill your desired groups.

A second issue in selecting sample size is the accuracy of the information we obtain with our sample. That is, we need to identify how much error we are willing to tolerate in our results. You might be familiar with "margin of error" statements from hearing survey results in the news media. For example, according to a recent Gallup poll, 61% of US adults now favor same-sex marriage. This information was based on a telephone survey of people in all 50 states and the District of Columbia, in which numbers were randomly dialed and a quota of 60% cell phone and 40% landline respondents was met. For this sample of 1,025 adults, Gallup proclaims to have 95% confidence that the margin of sampling error is ± (plus or minus) 4 percentage points (McCarthy, 2016). The **margin of sampling error** acknowledges that there may be some measurement error when you look at only a sample of the population as opposed to the whole population. In other words, Gallup claims to have 95% confidence that the actual percentage of US adults in favor of same-sex marriage likely ranges from 57% to 65% (subtract 4% points from the 61% stated at the beginning of this paragraph and also add 4% points to 61%).

The actual computation of sample size can be determined with a mathematical formula, which is beyond the scope of this text but is discussed in many statistics textbooks. Note that once you have obtained a recommendation for a sample size, you should plan on asking more respondents to answer your survey than you need, because unfortunately some will likely refuse to answer or will not complete it. As suggested earlier, a small incentive can help increase your response rate and limit concerns about potential non-response bias.

---

1 One way to determine how much variability exists in your population is to see what others studying your general topic have found. You could also do a pilot study in which you test a small portion of your population in an effort to determine how much variability exists. In either case, a standard deviation is a good measure of variability to use.

SUMMARY

When you conduct a survey, you are attempting to estimate the opinions, characteristics, and/or behaviors of a particular population by asking a sample to respond to questions. Most surveys include demographic questions designed to assess the characteristics of the respondents and topical questions that ask people what they believe, what they would do, what they have done, and/or how they feel.

Open-ended questions do not have fixed answers but allow the respondent to answer in any way, while in closed-ended questions (such as Likert scales), people are asked to respond by choosing one or more answers from a set of offered options. No matter what type of question you write, make sure you use easy-to-understand language with response options that are mutually exclusive, and avoid negative wording, double-barreled questions, and emotionally charged language.

After piloting, it's time to administer your survey. You can conduct a face-to-face or a telephone interview. You can email or mail questions to your potential respondents or direct them to an online questionnaire.

Some participants may exhibit response biases. Perhaps they responded in a particular way because they fear their true response will not make a favorable impression (social desirability effect). Sometimes participants repeatedly choose the response option "yes" or "strongly agree" regardless of item content (acquiescence) or "no" or "strongly disagree" regardless of item content (nay-saying). A non-response bias can occur when the respondents who fail to return the questionnaire differ in significant ways from those who do return it.

Two major sampling techniques are: (1) probability sampling in which each respondent has a known probability of being included in the sample (examples are simple random sampling, stratified sampling, and cluster sampling), and (2) nonprobability sampling in which researchers do not know the probability of an individual being selected for the study (examples are convenience sampling and quota sampling). The use of nonprobability sampling means your sample is not random, so you are limited in your ability to generalize from the sample to the population. In any case, remember larger samples generally represent populations better than smaller samples.

GLOSSARY

Acquiescence (yea-saying) – a survey response bias present when people choose the response option "yes" or "strongly agree" regardless of item content.

Closed-ended questions (restricted or fixed-alternative questions) – questions in which people are asked to respond by choosing one or more answers from a set of offered options.

Cluster sampling – a probability sampling technique in which the researcher identifies clusters of individuals, then randomly samples the clusters to decide which ones to use. Once the clusters to be used have been identified, *all* participants within the chosen clusters are surveyed.

Convenience sampling (haphazard sampling) – a type of nonprobability sampling in which researchers survey participants who are conveniently available, such as college students.

Demographic questions – questions designed to assess the characteristics of the respondents, such as their age, gender, marital status, occupation, income, and education level.

Face-to-face interview – interview someone in person.

Fence sitting – a response bias in which respondents choose a response in the middle of the scale.

Funneling – refers to the organization of a survey in which open-ended questions are followed by closed-ended questions.

Heterogeneous – different, high amount of variability as in "members of this target population are heterogeneous."

Homogeneous –same or similar as in "members of this target population are homogeneous."

Likert scale – a survey question format in which participants indicate their level of agreement or disagreement with a statement.

Margin of sampling error – acknowledgment of the presence of measurement error when you consider only a sample of the population as opposed to the whole population.

Nay-saying – a survey response bias in which respondents show a tendency to disagree with statements regardless of the item content.

Nonprobability sampling – the researchers do not know the probability of an individual's being selected for the study.

Non-response bias – an error that occurs if the respondents who fail to return the questionnaire differ in significant ways from those who do return it, such that your survey yields answers that do not represent the attitudes of the target population.

Open-ended questions – questions that do not have fixed answers but allow the respondent to answer in any way.

Population (target population, population of interest) – a defined group of individuals from which a sample is drawn.

Probability sampling – each study participant has a known probability of being included in the sample.

Quota sampling – a type of nonprobability sampling in which a researcher chooses participants who have particular characteristics, characteristics selected in particular proportions, usually intended to match their proportions in the target population.

Random sample – a sample in which every person in the entire population of interest has an equal chance of being selected.

Representative sample – a sample that has the same characteristic(s) as the population of interest.

Response rate – the percentage of people who complete the study.

Sample – a subset of individuals chosen from a population.

Sampling – the process of selecting respondents for a study.

Semantic differential scale – a type of rating scale in which respondents indicate their views using response options that are opposites.

Simple random sampling – a probability sampling technique in which the researcher randomly selects a sample of individuals from a population of interest.

Social desirability effect – people may not be truthful when questioned because they want to portray themselves in a positive or socially desirable light.

Stratified sample – a probability sampling technique in which the population of interest is divided into segments called strata (the singular form is stratum). Each stratum represents a group of people who have one or more characteristics of interest. Once divided, you choose a random sample from each of the segments.

1 Differentiate between demographic and topical survey questions. Provide examples of each.
2 Explain the difference between open- and closed-ended questions. Provide an example of an open-ended question as well as an example of a question that uses a Likert scale and a question that uses a semantic differential scale.
3 Identify six question-writing guidelines.
4 Describe different ways of administering a survey.
5 Explain the three different response biases.
6 Summarize what a non-response bias is and state why it is a concern for researchers.
7 Differentiate between probability and nonprobability sampling.
8 Describe simple random sampling, stratified sampling, and cluster sampling.
9 Differentiate between convenience sampling and quota sampling.
10 Explain what influences whether you can generalize from a sample to a population.
11 Explain how the following concepts relate to a survey's sample size: variability, margin of error.

ARTICLES AS ILLUSTRATION

The following cited articles provide examples of survey research. For each, obtain the article and answer the questions provided to learn more about how survey research is conducted.

1 Armstrong, Roberts, Owen, & Koch (2004) surveyed students with and without body piercing and then summarized the differences between them.

Armstrong, M. L., Roberts, A. E., Owen, D. C., & Koch, J. R. (2004). Contemporary college students and body piercing. *Journal of Adolescent Health, 35*, 58–61. doi:http://dx.doi.org/10.1016/j.jadohealth.2003.08.012

a. Describe the details of Armstrong et al.'s sample.
b. What kinds of questions (demographic, open-ended, closed-ended) did Armstrong et al. use in their research? List the types of questions used, and for each type provide an example.
c. What were Armstrong et al.'s major findings?
d. Comment on the generalizability of Armstrong et al.'s results in light of what we know about their sample.

2 Herold and Milhausen (1999) investigated college women's views of "nice guys." Do undergraduate women want to date nice guys? Are nice guys viewed as more or less sexually successful than guys who are less nice? What do you think? See Herold and Milhausen's article for results from both closed- and open-ended questions designed to determine what university women think of nice guys.

Herold, E. S., & Milhausen, R. R. (1999). Dating preferences of university women: An analysis of the nice guy stereotype. *Journal of Sex and Marital Therapy, 25*, 333–343. doi:http://dx.doi.org/10.1080/00926239908404010

a. What did Herold and Milhausen learn from their closed-ended questions?
b. Describe the results of Herold and Milhausen's content analysis.
c. Do you think "nice guys" are likely to be pleased or not pleased with the results of Herold and Milhausen's work? Explain your answer.

3 Lambert, Kahn, and Apple (2003) describe a study in which college students answer questions regarding "hooking up" (engaging

in sexual behavior without a commitment). They found evidence in their sample for a phenomenon known as pluralistic ignorance; this refers to the idea that people in a group do what the group is doing, but privately they each feel conflicted and they think no one else feels this way (for example Allport, 1924). With regard to hooking up, Lambert et al. found that both males and females thought others were more comfortable with various hooking up behaviors ("petting above the waist, petting below the waist, oral sex and sexual intercourse") than they themselves are. Lambert et al. also found differences between males and females with regard to hooking up.

Lambert, T. A., Kahn, A. S., & Apple, K. J. (2003). Pluralistic ignorance and hooking up. *Journal of Sex Research, 40*, 129–133. doi:http://dx.doi.org/10.1080/00224490309552174

a. Describe the details of Lambert et al.'s sample. How were the study participants obtained? Are there any advantages and disadvantages to obtaining study participants in this way?

b. What kinds of questions (demographic, open-ended, closed-ended) did Lambert et al. use in their research? List the types of questions used, and for each type provide an example.

c. What were Lambert et al.'s major findings? Be sure to differentiate any differences between men and women in your answer.

SUGGESTED ACTIVITIES

1 Create a questionnaire. Select a topic, and then write demographic questions as well as a series of open- and closed-ended questions that pertain to your topic. Administer this questionnaire to a convenience sample on your campus. Summarize the responses (you'll need to do a content analysis for the open-ended questions) and present the work to the class.

2 An alternative to creating your own questionnaire is to seek out a published questionnaire on a topic of interest and administer it to your population of choice. Many questionnaires are available in Robinson, Shaver, and Wrightsman's (1991) *Measures of social psychological attitudes*. In addition, sometimes questionnaires are published in the appendices of a journal article. For an example, consider Jay, King, and Duncan's (2006) questionnaire assessing memories of being punished for cursing. Was your mouth ever washed out with soap when you cursed as a child? Jay et al. found that 20% of their sample said their mothers had taken this disciplinary action, although most of this sample admitted they continued to curse!

3 Conduct a content analysis of existing information to investigate an issue of interest. Here are some possibilities: (1) analyze issues of your college newspaper for gender bias in sport reporting (see Huffman et al. for an example of this type of work), (2) analyze women's fitness magazines for information about the health consequences of tanning (see Cho et al. for an example), and (3) analyze students' comments about their instructors on www.ratemyprofessors.com (see Silva et al., 2008 for an example of a content analysis of information about psychology professors). Present the results of your content analysis to the class.

REFERENCES

Allport, F. H. (1924). *Social psychology*. Boston: Houghton Mifflin.

Armstrong, M. L., Roberts, A. E., Owen, D. C., & Koch, J. R. (2004). Contemporary college students and body piercing. *Journal of Adolescent Health*, *35*, 58–61. doi:http://dx.doi.org/10.1016/j.jadohealth.2003.08.012

Arnett, J. J. (2008). The neglected 95%: Why American psychology needs to become less American. *American Psychologist*, *63*, 602–614. doi:http://dx.doi.org/10.1037/0003-066X.63.7.602

Barchielli, A., & Balzi, D. (2002). Nine-year follow-up of a survey on smoking habits in Florence (Italy): Higher mortality among non-responders. *International Journal of Epidemiology*, *31*, 1038–1042.

Cerrito, P. B., & Levi, I. (1999). An investigation of student habits in mathematics courses. *College Student Journal*, *33*, 584–588.

Cho, H., Hall, J. G., Kosmoski, C., Fox, R. L., & Mastin, T. (2010). Tanning, skin cancer risk, and prevention: A content analysis of eight popular magazines that target female readers, 1997–2006. *Health Communication*, *25*, 1–10. doi:http://dx.doi.org/10.1080/10410230903265938

Edwards, A. L. (1957). *The social desirability variable in personality assessment and research*. New York: Dryden.

Friedman, H. H., & Weiser Friedman, L. (1986). On the danger of using too few points in a rating scale: A test of validity. *Journal of Data Collection*, *26*, 60–63.

Gächter, S. (2010). (Dis)advantages of student subjects: What is your research question? *Behavioral and Brain Sciences*, *33*, 32–33. doi:http://dx.doi.org/10.1017/S0140525X10000099

Gosling, S. D., Sandy, C. J., John, O. P., & Potter, J. (2010). Wired but not WEIRD: The promise of the Internet in reaching more diverse samples. *Behavioral and Brain Sciences*, *33*, 34–35. doi:http://dx.doi.org/10.1017/S0140525X10000300

Graeff, T. R. (2003). Exploring consumers' answers to survey questions: Are uninformed responses truly uninformed? *Psychology & Marketing*, *20*, 643–667. doi:http://dx.doi.org/10.1002/mar.10090

Groves, R. M. (2006). Nonresponse rates and nonresponse bias in household surveys. *Public Opinion Quarterly*, *70*, 646–675.

Harris, R. J., Hoekstra, S. J., Scott, C. L., Sanborn, F. W., & Dodds, L. A. (2004). Autobiographical memories for seeing romantic movies on a date: Romance is not just for women. *Media Psychology*, *6*, 257–284. doi:http://dx.doi.org/10.1207/s1532785xmep0603_2

Henrich, J., Heine, S. J., & Norenzayan, A. (2010). The weirdest people in the world? *Behavioral and Brain Sciences*, *33*, 1–23. doi:http://dx.doi.org/10.1017/S0140525X0999152X

Herold, E. S., & Milhausen, R. R. (1999). Dating preferences of university women: An analysis of the nice guy stereotype. *Journal of Sex and Marital Therapy*, *25*, 333–343. doi:http://dx.doi.org/10.1080/00926239908404010

Huffman, S., Tuggle, C. A., & Rosengard, D. S. (2004). How campus media cover sports: The gender-equity issue, one generation later. *Mass Communication & Society*, *7*, 475–489. doi:http://dx.doi.org/10.1207/s15327825mcs0704_6

Jay, T., King, K., & Duncan, T. (2006). Memories of punishment for cursing. *Sex Roles*, *55*, 123–133. doi:http://dx.doi.org/10.1007/s11199-006-9064-5

Johnston, K. L., & White, K. M. (2002). Binge drinking: A test of the role of group norms in the theory of planned behaviour. *Psychology and Health*, *18*, 63–77. doi:http://dx.doi.org/10.1080/0887044021000037835

Judson, R., & Langdon, S. W. (2009). Illicit use of prescription stimulants among college students: Prescription status, motives, theory of planned behaviour, knowledge and self-diagnostic tendencies. *Psychology, Health & Medicine*, *14*, 97–104. doi:http://dx.doi.org/10.1080/13548500802126723

Keeter, S., Christian, L., & Dimock, M. (2010, November 22). *The growing gap between landline and dual frame election polls*. Retrieved from www.pewresearch.org/2010/11/22/the-growing-gap-between-landline-and-dual-frame-election-polls/

Kulick, D., & Rosenberg, H. (2000). Assessment of university students' coping strategies and reasons for driving in high-risk drinking-driving situations. *Accident Analysis and Prevention*, *32(1)*, 85–94. doi:http://dx.doi.org/10.1016/S0001-4575(99)00060-3

Lambert, T. A., Kahn, A. S., & Apple, K. J. (2003). Pluralistic ignorance and hooking up. *Journal of Sex Research*, *40*, 129–133. doi:http://dx.doi.org/10.1080/00224490309552174

Lavrakas, P. J. (2008). *Encyclopedia of survey research methods*. Thousand Oaks, CA: Sage.

Likert, R. (1932). A technique for the measurement of attitudes. *Archives of Psychology*, *140*, 55.

Lund, H. G., Reider, B. D., Whiting, A. B., & Prichard, J. R. (2010). Sleep patterns and predictors of disturbed sleep in a large population of college students. *Journal of Adolescent Health Care*, *46*, 124–132. doi:http://dx.doi.org/10.1016/j.jadohealth.2009.06.016

Maldonado, C. C., Bentley, A. J., & Mitchell, D. (2004). A pictorial sleepiness scale based on cartoon faces. *Sleep*, *27*, 541–548.

McCarthy, J. (2016). Americans' support for gay marriage remains high, at 61%. Retrieved from www.gallup.com

McKetin, R., Chalmers, J., Sunderland, M., & Bright, D. A. (2014). Recreational drug use and binge drinking: Stimulant but not cannabis intoxication is associated with excessive alcohol consumption. *Drug and Alcohol Review*, *33*, 436–445. doi:http://dx.doi.org/10.1111/dar.12147

Newport, F., Jones, J. M., & Saad, L. (2008). Update: Little evidence of surge in youth vote. Retrieved from www.gallup.com

Nowlis, S. M., Kahn, B. E., & Dhar, R. (2002). Coping with ambivalence: The effect of removing a neutral option on consumer attitude and preference judgments. *Journal of Consumer Research*, *29*, 319–334. doi:http://dx.doi.org/10.1086/344431

Roberts, L. C., & White Blanton, P. (2001). "I always knew mom and dad loved me best": Experiences of only children. *Journal of Individual Psychology*, *57*, 125–140.

Robinson, J. P., Shaver, P. R., & Wrightsman, L. S. (1991). *Measures of social psychological attitudes*. San Diego, CA: Academic Press.

Sears, D. O. (1986). College sophomores in the laboratory: Influences of a narrow data base on social psychology's view of human nature. *Journal of Personality and Social Psychology*, *51*, 515–530. doi:http://dx.doi.org/10.1037/0022-3514.51.3.515

Sheldon, P., & Bryant, K. (2016). Instagram: Motives for its use and relationship to narcissism and contextual age. *Computers in Human Behavior*, *58*, 89–97. doi:http://dx.doi.org/10.1016/j.chb.2015.12.059

Silva, K. M., Silva, F. J., Quinn, M. A., Draper, J. N., Cover, K. R., & Munoff, A. A. (2008). Rate my professor: Online evaluations of psychology instructors. *Teaching of Psychology*, *35*, 71–80. doi:http://dx.doi.org/10.1080/00986280801978434

Stone, R. W., & Baker-Eveleth, L. (2013). Students' expectation, confirmation, and continuance intention to use electronic textbooks. *Computers in Human Behavior*, *29*, 984–990. doi:http://dx.doi.org/10.1016/j.chb.2012.12.007

Sutfin, E. L., McNamara, R. S., Blocker, J. N., Ip, E. H., O'Brien, M. C., & Wolfson, M. (2012). Screening and brief intervention for tobacco use by student health providers on college campuses. *Journal of American College Health*, *60*, 66–73. doi:http://dx.doi.org/10.1080/07448481.2011.572325

Tellis, G. J., & Chandrasekaran, D. (2010). Extent and impact of response biases in cross-national survey research. *International Journal of Research in Marketing*, *27*, 329–341. doi:http://dx.doi.org/10.1016/j.ijresmar.2010.08.003

8 Experimentation with One Independent Variable

LEARNING OBJECTIVES

- Define experimental design.
- Differentiate between extraneous variables and confounds.
- Differentiate between a within-subjects design and a between-subjects design.
- Summarize the different techniques for manipulating an independent variable.
- Explain the different ways to measure a dependent variable.
- Differentiate between ceiling and floor effects.
- Compare a posttest only design with a before–after design.
- Differentiate between descriptive statistics and inferential statistics.

FIGURE 8.1 Guéguen et al. (2010) used a cookie-rating task as a cover story; it was just a ploy to get the participants to interact.

Imagine you are a female college student participating in an experiment and your task is to taste cookies and discuss them with a male study participant. Now imagine that after this task is over, the other participant asks you for your phone number. Do you provide it?

Guéguen, Jacob, and Lamy (2010) were, in fact, quite curious about whether female participants would provide their phone numbers (they didn't really care what people thought of the cookies – that was just a way to get the participants to talk to each other). Here's what Guéguen et al. did and what they found. They randomly assigned female participants to two groups, and they found that participants in one of the groups were almost twice as likely as participants in the other group to provide their phone numbers. What was different about these two groups?

In fact, everything was the same for these two groups of females except for one thing. The one difference between the groups was that Guéguen et al. varied the type of music (romantic, neutral) playing in the background when the female college students were waiting for the study to begin. Those who heard the romantic music were almost twice

as likely to provide their phone number as were those who heard the neutral music. It was the type of music that caused the difference in responding.

How can we know the type of music *caused* people to respond differently to a request for a phone number? You're about to find out in this chapter about experimentation – the one research technique that allows us to conclude cause and effect. We'll start by examining what makes a study an experiment, and why we can establish cause and effect with it.

Experimental Design

Experimental design is the plan or strategy you use when conducting an experiment. To illustrate the relevant terminology we'll start with the simplest kind of experimental design: experiments with one independent variable.

When conducting the simplest kind of experiment, researchers manipulate (vary) one variable, called the independent variable, and observe the effects of that manipulation on a response measure called the dependent variable. The independent variable is considered to be the cause, and the dependent variable is considered to be the effect.

To establish cause and effect between an independent and a dependent variable, your experiment needs to fulfill two requirements:

1. It must have theoretically equivalent groups.
2. It must have *at least* two groups of study participants.

How do you make your groups theoretically equivalent? The answer depends on what kind of experimental design you have. Let's say you have one independent variable with two groups and you want to make those two groups theoretically equivalent. You could randomly assign your study participants to the two groups – this results in a **between-subjects**

Within-subjects
A group of people
sees both pictures.

Between-subjects
One group of people sees one set
of pictures, and a different
group sees another set.

FIGURE 8.2 A comparison of
within-subjects and between-
subjects designs.

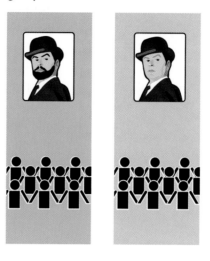

design. For example, if you wanted to see the effect of men's facial hair on women's ratings of attractiveness, you can randomly assign your participants to two different groups and then have one group rate a photo of a male with a full beard and the other group rate a clean-shaven male.

Let's look at another way to make your two groups theoretically equivalent. Again, we'll continue with the idea of an experiment with one independent variable with two groups. Your groups would be considered theoretically equivalent if you tested the same people in both groups – this results in a **within-subjects design**. Using my earlier facial hair example, all participants in this case would rate both a male with a full beard and a clean-shaven male.

Both these techniques, randomly assigning participants to groups and testing the same people in both groups, create theoretically equivalent groups (see Figure 8.2 for an illustration of the two techniques).

We'll discuss both types of designs in more detail later in this chapter. First we need to address an additional component that is important to ensuring our groups are theoretically equivalent.

Controlling Extraneous Variables/ Confounds

In a well-designed experiment, the only difference between your groups is the independent variable, the variable you purposely manipulate. All extraneous variables are held constant. **Extraneous variables** are all the uncontrolled variables that are not purposely manipulated but that could potentially affect our groups (for example, lighting in the room). We do not want extraneous variables to affect our participants' responses, so we eliminate their impact by keeping the extraneous variables constant across groups. Let's take a look at a more detailed example.

Assume Guéguen et al.'s experiment is slightly different, so that as the women wait for the cookie discussion to begin, there is music in the waiting room that varies for the different participants – the independent variable – but there is also some

FIGURE 8.3 If participants can hear construction noise during your study, and you, as the researcher, did not intend for this noise to be present, this noise is considered an extraneous variable.

construction noise nearby. Now Guéguen et al. didn't intend for this to happen. They didn't purposely manipulate construction noise, but for the purpose of this example assume it was present for some of the participants in *both* groups (those who heard romantic music and those who heard neutral music). Could this construction noise affect the participants' likelihood of giving the confederate their phone numbers? Possibly. Noise can affect mood (see for example, Smith, Whitney, Thomas, Perry, & Brockman, 1997), and that might affect one's willingness to be social. In this example, construction noise is an extraneous variable. The experimenter was not responsible for the presence of that noise, but it could still affect the participants in each of the two groups. Ideally, we want that construction noise to be equivalent across all groups – either present for everyone or present for no one.

The worst kind of extraneous variable, a **confound**, varies *systematically* with the independent variable. Let's look at how construction noise in this example can be a confound. Now instead of some of the participants in both groups hearing the construction noise, only those who hear neutral music in the waiting room hear the construction noise.

When the romantic music is playing, there isn't any construction noise at all. The noise is varying systematically with the type of music. So now, in this pretend example, if Guéguen et al. found that those who heard the romantic music were almost twice as likely to provide their phone number, they could not say the type of music *caused* that difference because there is a confound, the construction noise. It could be that the presence of the construction noise caused the difference in responding. (Note that if the construction noise is present only for all who hear the romantic music, and not those who hear the neutral music, again, you have a confound.)

Quite simply, when a confound is present, you are not able to establish cause and effect. Confounds decrease your **internal validity**, the extent to which you can determine that your independent variable caused your results. What is the moral of this story? Keep everything the same for all your experimental groups except for the independent variable manipulation(s), and you will be able to establish cause and effect.

Between-Subjects Designs

As you recall, in a between-subjects design with one independent variable, different people are placed into different groups and exposed to different levels of the independent variable. How do we determine who goes into what group? We randomly assign people to different groups. Next we'll discuss how to do that.

Random Assignment of Participants to Groups

Let's again talk about a situation in which you have one independent variable with two groups. Your goal is to have only one thing differ between your two groups: your independent variable manipulation. Remember how Guéguen et al. presented different types of music to their two different groups? They could conclude that the type of music caused the difference in the number of females offering their phone numbers because the only thing different for their two groups was the type of music presented in the waiting room. Everything else was the same. The confederate was the same guy in all cases. The room was the same in all cases. Each of the women had the same "single" relationship status (relationship status had been ascertained a week earlier). And while there were indeed different women in the two groups, the groups were considered overall to be equal. Why?

Because Guéguen et al. had randomly assigned their participants to the two groups. Therefore each participant was equally likely to be a member of each group, and all potential biases between groups are theoretically distributed in equal proportions. This will be discussed further below. Let's first talk about how to randomly assign participants to groups.

Researchers can randomly assign participants to groups by using a random number generator (see www.randomizer.org) or a random numbers table. We discussed using a random numbers table in Chapter 7 when we talked about choosing a *random sample*. Now we can use this same table (see Appendix B) to help us *randomly assign* participants to groups. Use this table alongside your list of participants in order to assign each of the participants a random number. Place your finger on one of the random numbers in the table; in a moment you'll be reading one digit numbers off the table. Assign the first person on your list that first number. Then go to the adjacent number. You may move up or down, right or left, but once you start in a direction, you must continue in that same direction. Continue down your list of participants assigning each a random number. Once every participant has a number assignment, make up a rule for group assignment. For example, if you want two groups, then you can put all odd numbers into group 1 and all even

numbers into group 2. When you are done you will have two theoretically equivalent groups.

I've indicated that when you randomly assign participants to groups, your groups become theoretically equal. Let's talk about what this means, using Guéguen et al.'s study as an example. Think about the kinds of things that might affect a woman's willingness to provide her phone number. Perhaps she already has someone special in her life. Recall that each woman in Guéguen et al.'s experiment had each acknowledged a week earlier that she did not have "someone in her life at the moment" (p. 304). If someone's relationship status had changed since then, using random assignment means you are just as likely to find those with relationship status changes in one group as in the other.

Perhaps the woman unwilling to give her number doesn't find the confederate attractive. Since participants were randomly assigned to groups, there will likely be approximately the same number of people in both groups who do not find him attractive. Maybe she's gay, and that's why she doesn't offer her number. Randomly assigning participants to the two groups means that you are likely to find gay women in equal proportions in the two groups. Maybe she's not feeling well, and that's why she doesn't offer her number. Again, random assignment of participants to groups means the likelihood of people not feeling well is approximately equal in both groups. If your groups are equal, then all uncontrolled variables (even those you can't even imagine) are just as likely to affect one group as another group. Thus, when participants are randomly assigned to groups, the groups are considered equal.

Matched-Groups Design

Occasionally researchers will take an additional step before randomly assigning participants to groups. They will match participants to each other on some variable, and then randomly assign the matched participants to groups. This results in what is known as a **matched-groups design**, and the groups are again considered equivalent. When you match participants, you should match on variables you think might affect your dependent variable. Let's look at an example.

Remember that Guéguen et al. were interested in whether women would say "yes" in response to a request for their phone number. Let's pretend that Guéguen et al. thought that a woman's level of social ability might affect the likelihood of her offering her phone number. So Guéguen et al. could therefore decide to give the participants a test to measure their level of social ability (it would be best to separate this test from the rest of the experiment so the goals of the experiment would not be obvious). Once each participant's level of social ability has been measured, the researchers can match participants on this characteristic.

Assign each participant a random number as we discussed earlier. Then look at the social ability score for the first participant on the list (let's call this person "Participant A"). Go down the list until you find a participant with a matching score. Then use a rule for group assignment (for example, in a two-group design, odd numbers go into group 1). This time however, you will place "Participant A" in the group that corresponds to his or her random number and his or her match will automatically go into the other group. You would then continue this matching procedure for each of the participants. So random assignment is still a part of your process, but the groups ultimately will be matched in terms of their social ability. Researchers can use this technique when they want to be as certain as possible that their groups are equivalent on one or more characteristics, but it is actually not often used because random assignment to groups on its own is generally thought to be an adequate way to create equivalent groups.

Within-Subjects Designs

All the experiments discussed in this chapter so far have been between-subjects experiments in that, for each, participants were randomly assigned to groups. Now let's look at a within-subjects design.

Again we'll start with the simplest kind of experiment, one with a single independent variable. Because this time we are using the same people for different levels of our independent variable, this design is often referred to as a **repeated-measures design**, reflecting the fact that we are repeatedly measuring the same people. Essentially, each person is his or her own control. Let's look at an example.

Engle-Friedman et al. (2003) used a repeated-measures design to determine how sleep loss would affect the amount of effort undergraduates made on a math test the next day. After an introductory session, they had 50 undergraduates come to the lab twice, once after a night of no sleep (participants had to call in to the lab every half-hour so they would stay awake), and once after a complete night of sleep. Some participants experienced the sleep loss first while others experienced the complete night of sleep first (these experiences were separated by a period of two weeks). So each person in this experiment was tested twice (repeatedly measured); each person was his or her own control.

So what happened? Participants tended to select less-challenging math problems after sleep loss as opposed to after a full night's sleep. In addition, participants who solved problems after a night of no sleep solved fewer problems correctly than those who solved problems after a complete night's sleep. So the next time you are studying for a test, remember this and get some sleep!

Order Effects and Counterbalancing. Recall that when you have a within-subjects variable, all participants experience each level of the independent variable. So it is extremely important that you control the order in which you present the levels. As an example, let's use something you're probably familiar with.

Remember taking the Scholastic Aptitude Test (SAT)? Many take this exam in preparation for applying to colleges. While the SAT has undergone periodic changes, it always has had separate sections for different areas of study. Let's pretend for this example that the SAT has only two sections: English and math (that's what it had when I took it – a hint to how old I am). Everyone has to be tested on both parts, so it's important to control the order of presentation. Think about it this way. If everyone does the English section first and the math section last, it is possible they will be tired (or bored or distracted) by the time they get to the math section, and therefore their math performance will suffer. We call this the **fatigue effect**. It is also possible that by the time people get to the second section, the math section in this case, the butterflies in their stomach will be gone and they will be getting the hang of the test. Their performance therefore improves during the second half. We call this the **practice effect**.

You also need to control for carryover effects when you are using a within-subjects design. **Carryover effects** occur when performance in one condition affects performance in another condition. This can be an issue when, for example, you are presenting different drug treatments to participants. Residual effects from prior treatments can affect later treatments. Or take the example of a soda taste test. The taste of one soda can affect the taste of sodas presented later. In both examples, one possible solution is to put ample time between the treatments.

Another concern with a within-subjects design is that participants can more readily determine the purpose of your study and/or your hypothesis since they are privy to all the levels of your independent variable. This result is known as a **sensitization effect**. If participants are able to figure out the

purpose of your study and what you are expecting to find, they may just act in line with what they think you expect to see. We discussed this in Chapter 3 as a problem of demand characteristics. As you may recall, demand characteristics are cues in the study that inform the participants about the study's true purpose and hypotheses. One way to avoid the sensitization problem is to develop a plausible cover story for your research. Provide this cover story before your experiment begins and then debrief once the experimental session is over.

Practice, fatigue, carryover, and sensitization effects are called **order effects** and they need to be controlled. One way to control them is to change the order of presentation. This is called **counterbalancing** and it is especially recommended as a way to control for practice, fatigue, and carryover effects. If you use **complete counterbalancing**, you make sure all possible orders of presentation are used. With a two-group presentation like the one I've described here with the SAT, it's simple. Some people get the English section first, and some get the English section last. So *both* the English section *and* the math section will be subject to fatigue and practice effects. When counterbalancing is used, order effects will not affect any reported average scores (like those presented by graduate schools' admissions offices).

There are more advanced ways to counterbalance when you have more than two groups; what is important to remember is that when you have a within-subjects design, counterbalancing is vital.

Which Design to Choose: Between-Subjects or Within-Subjects?

Both within-subjects and between-subjects designs have advantages and disadvantages (see Table 8.1). Within-subjects designs require fewer study participants than between-subjects experiments. If you determine that you need 30 participants per group

Table 8.1   Advantages and disadvantages of within-subjects and between-subjects designs.

| Within-subjects designs | | Between-subjects designs | |
Advantages	Disadvantages	Advantages	Disadvantages
Increased statistical power	Order effects are a possibility	Participants not privy to what other groups experience	Less statistical power than within-subjects designs
Needs fewer participants than between-subjects designs	Needs counterbalancing	Order effects are not a concern	Needs more research participants than within-subjects designs

and you have two groups, a within-subjects experiment will require 30 participants overall, while a between-subjects experiment will require 60. A within-subjects experimental design can also be a good choice when the participants need to be specialized in some way, such as having a specific skill, as you'll need to locate fewer participants overall.

Another advantage of a within-subjects design is their increased statistical **power**. This means that within-subjects designs have a greater ability to detect significant findings. The disadvantages of a within-subjects experiment are the issues I noted above such as order effects, but these can be controlled with counterbalancing.

The between-subjects design has the advantage of avoiding problems such as order effects by placing different people in the different groups. Quite simply, those in between-subjects design will not know what the other groups experience. And of course, the disadvantage of the between-subject design over the within-subjects design is that you need more participants in your experiment overall.

Manipulating Independent Variables

Now that you're familiar with the basics of experimental design, let's delve deeper into the ways independent variables can be manipulated.

Have you ever been concentrating in class only to be jolted by the sound of a phone ringing? End, Worthman, Mathews, and Wetterau (2010) decided to use an experiment to investigate whether a ringing cell phone could cause impaired academic performance. Participants were randomly assigned to two groups, shown a video, and later tested on the material. Some were not interrupted during the video presentation, while at predetermined times others heard a phone ringing that belonged to a confederate in the room. The ringing of the phone was the independent variable, and there were two levels of variation (presence of a ringing phone, absence of a ringing phone).

Let's pause for a minute to clarify some terms. When you are reading a journal article you will often see an independent variable stated with its levels of variation presented in parentheses like this: *a ringing phone (presence, absence)*. What you choose to call the independent variable and the levels have to make sense together. The independent variable label is an overall summary of what was manipulated. The names of the levels, also referred to as groups or conditions, describe the way it was manipulated. Figure 8.4 shows another way to represent End et al.'s independent variable manipulation.

The dependent variable in End et al.'s (2010) experiment was the score on a test of the information

IV: A Ringing Phone ← Independent Variable Label

1) presence
2) absence

Levels

FIGURE 8.4 End et al. (2010) varied the *presence/absence* of an independent variable (IV).

shown in the presented video. The question of interest for End et al. was: Did the presence of a ringing phone (as opposed to the absence of a ringing phone) cause a change in test performance? The answer was yes. Participants who watched a video interrupted by a ringing phone performed worse on the test than those whose video was not interrupted.

Why can we conclude from End et al.'s (2010) experiment that a ringing phone *caused* the poorer test performance? The experimenters fulfilled both of the requirements needed to establish cause and effect. They had two groups (you need at least two groups in an experiment), those who heard a phone ringing during the video and those who did not. In addition, these two groups were theoretically equivalent in that participants were randomly assigned to conditions. In other words, each participant was equally likely to be in the group that heard a ringing phone or not. Since the two groups are considered equivalent and there was only one thing different between them (there was either a ringing phone present or not), that one thing has to be responsible for any differences observed in the dependent variable (the test score). This is why we can say that we have a cause and effect relationship.

Thus, End et al. (2010) established a cause and effect relationship between the ringing phone and test performance. Participants who were in the ringing phone group performed significantly worse on the test than those who were in the non-ringing

phone group. So turn off those phones when you're in class or you (and your classmates) may miss something!

Presence/Absence of a Variable

In the above section I used an example that had one independent variable with two levels, the presence or absence of some treatment (a ringing phone). The presence/absence manipulation is common in experimentation. In some cases, a **placebo**, an inactive substance, represents the absence condition. For example, Ahluwalia et al. (2006) conducted an experiment in which the effects of nicotine gum versus a placebo were tested. The placebo was a gum that did not contain nicotine.

The condition in which the treatment is present is commonly referred to as the **experimental condition**, while the condition in which the treatment is absent is commonly called the **control condition**. However, a control condition is not necessarily the absence of something. There are other ways to vary your independent variable; you just always need something to compare to. Let's now look at other techniques of variation.

Amount of a Variable

Sometimes researchers choose to vary the amount of a variable. For example, Watson et al. (2000) varied the amount of caffeine (10 mg, 76 mg) ingested by a sample of women who had been off caffeine for 48 hours and off all food for 8 hours. Figure 8.5 shows another way to represent this independent variable.

IV: Amount of Caffeine ← Independent Variable Label

1) 10 mg
2) 76 mg

Levels

FIGURE 8.5 Watson et al. (2000) varied the *amount* of an independent variable.

All participants in this experiment were randomly assigned to drink 2 cans of Diet Coke either with or without caffeine, and all ate a Mars chocolate bar so that they would not suffer from hypoglycemia. Those who had Diet Coke with caffeine took in 76 mg of caffeine and those who had Diet Coke without caffeine took in 10 mg.

Note that when you have a manipulation like Watson et al.'s (2000) amount of caffeine manipulation, you still can name your conditions (levels) as "experimental" and "control" groups. Again, a control group doesn't necessarily mean the absence of something; it just reflects the idea that you are using a comparison group. In this case, since Watson et al. were interested in seeing the effects of varying amounts of caffeine, it seems reasonable to call the group that ingested more caffeine the experimental group, while the group that ingested less caffeine was the control group.

Watson et al. wanted to know whether the participants would feel and show different effects of the different amounts of caffeine. In fact, the level of caffeine intake did have an impact on some dependent variables, but not all. For example, those who drank the regular Diet Coke as opposed to the caffeine-free Diet Coke reported feeling more energy and having an improved mood, although there were no differences between the two groups in terms of intellectual function.

So were the differences caused by the differential caffeine intake? We do know that the groups were theoretically equivalent because the participants were randomly assigned, and there were at least two groups – so the requirements for causality have been fulfilled. Thus, the one thing that was different between the two groups, the amount of caffeine, was responsible for the observed differences.

Type of Variable

Sometimes, given your topic of study, it doesn't make sense to vary the amount of a variable or

FIGURE 8.6 Guéguen et al. (2010) varied the *type* of independent variable.

the presence and absence of a variable. Sometimes researchers choose to vary the *type* of variable. Think back to the work of Guéguen et al. who wondered whether the presence of romantic music could influence dating behavior. They chose to vary the type of music presented to female college students (romantic, neutral). So Guéguen et al. had one independent variable with two levels. Figure 8.6 shows how we can represent this independent variable.

There are many ways to manipulate the type of variable. For example, Guéguen (2015b) varied the type of hairstyle worn by women to see if this would affect the likelihood of being helped. Zucco, Aiello, Turuani, and Köster (2012) sought to assess whether the type of odor would affect memory tasks, and Oncken, Litt, McLaughlin, and Burki (2015) varied the type of e-cigarette flavor to identify its impact on smoking preferences.

Thus, we've covered three general ways to manipulate an independent variable – presence/absence, amount, and type.

Instructional versus Event Manipulations

Beyond thinking about whether to vary the type of variable, the amount of a variable, or the presence and absence of a variable, you can also decide whether you want to alter the instructions you provide the participants, thus using an **instructional manipulation** or alter the experiences they encounter, thus using an **event manipulation**. Event manipulations have some advantages over instructional manipulations. Let's look at an example of each.

Erhel and Jamet (2013) were interested in investigating the conditions under which a computer-based activity would be more effective in promoting learning. In one of their experiments, they varied the type of instructions by presenting the activity as either a learning module or a game.

After the instructions were provided, the participants completed the computer activity and then were tested on what they had learned (they had not known they would be tested). Those who had been told they were completing a learning module as opposed to a game showed more understanding of the presented material. This suggests that the strategy of "learning through playing" may not be the most effective approach to gaining information.

You may have noted that Erhel and Jamet used a "type of variable" manipulation. They varied the type of instructions provided to participants. And did it have an impact? Yes, we can conclude that the type of instruction caused the difference seen in the test results. However, although we can conclude cause and effect with an instructional manipulation, this technique has limitations. For one thing, participants can easily miss the instructions because they are not paying attention or don't hear them. If the researchers use an instructional manipulation and the participants miss the instructions, the researchers will not be providing the manipulation as intended. An event manipulation, on the other hand, is much more difficult for participants to miss; the events participants undergo are what changes. Let's look at a classic social psychology example that used an event manipulation.

In 1964 bystanders did not immediately aid a young woman in Queens, New York named Kitty Genovese even though she was attacked within earshot or sight of others. Although some have recently questioned the veracity of the originally reported details of Kitty's attack (see for example, Lurigio, 2015; Manning, Levine, & Collins, 2007), there is no doubt that her death led researchers to ask an important question: what factors could influence the likelihood of bystanders intervening in emergencies? In one of these early studies of bystander intervention, Latané and Darley (1968) set up a staged "emergency" in front of each participant, and they varied the type of companion present (no one, two nonreacting others [confederates], two other naïve participants). Note that in this case, there was one independent variable and it had three levels.

Here is what Latané and Darley did. Participants were brought to the lab and asked to fill out a questionnaire. While they were doing so, smoke began billowing into the room through a vent (the "emergency"), but the confederates in the room just shrugged and continued working on their questionnaires. The researchers wondered: Would the participant leave the room to report this smoke within 6 minutes or just ignore it? What would you do? Latané and Darley found that participants in the room alone were much more likely to report the smoke than those in the room with two nonreacting confederates or those in the room with two other naïve participants.

Recall that I provided this as an example of an event manipulation. Compare this to the instructional manipulation example that I provided earlier. An event manipulation is much more difficult for participants to miss than an instructional manipulation as the participants are typically deeply involved in the events that are occurring (again picture the situation set up by Latané and Darley with smoke filling up the room – it would be tough for experimental participants to miss this). It is for this reason that an event manipulation is often considered superior to an instructional manipulation.

An event manipulation often is said to be high in experimental realism. **Experimental realism** refers to the degree to which a research experience psychologically involves the experimental participants.

Certainly, having high experimental realism can be beneficial, but I do have one caveat. While it is often ideal to have your participants highly engaged in your created event, you do not want your manipulation to be obvious. You do not want your participants just acting the way they think you want them to act; you want true behavior. So design your independent variable manipulation so that it *can* influence your participants, but design it so that their behavior is not merely changed because participants are intentionally responding the way they think you want them to respond.

Individual Difference Manipulation

I want to mention one more way to vary an independent variable: the **individual difference manipulation**. This is a special kind of manipulation; it differs from the manipulations that we've talked about thus far in this chapter. In the earlier examples, the experimenter had complete control over the independent variable manipulation. Each group experienced a different level of the independent variable and the experimenter randomly determined who was in each group. When an experimenter uses an individual difference manipulation, the experimenter is not putting people into groups randomly, but instead is putting people into groups based on some personal characteristic that the individual has (such as gender, religion, education level, shyness level, self-esteem level). This personal characteristic is something that the participants had before being in the experiment. For example, I can put people in groups based on whether they are a first born or a "middle" child, but I can't experimentally manipulate these characteristics and say, "for the purpose of this experiment, you will be a first-born child." I, as the experimenter, have no control over whether someone is a first-born child or not.

You might recall that we have to fulfill two requirements in order to be able to say that we have a cause and effect relationship: theoretically equivalent groups and at least two groups. When we are using an individual difference manipulation, our groups are not going to be equivalent. In other words, if we put different people into groups on the basis of some individual difference characteristic, and not by using random assignment, the groups are not equivalent. Maybe first-born children vary from middle children in other ways beyond birth order and those other variables could affect the dependent variables. The point is: when you are using an individual difference manipulation, your groups are not equivalent; thus, you can't state cause and effect with certainty. Experiments with an individual difference manipulation are not "true" experiments but are quasi-experiments ("quasi" means "resembling"). We'll discuss quasi-experiments further in Chapter 10.

Increasing the Number of Levels of an Independent Variable

As indicated above, when we use an independent variable, we always have to have at least two groups, because we always need something to compare to. However, as you saw with Latané and Darley's smoky room experiment, we can manipulate an independent variable and provide more than just two levels of variation. Latané and Darley used three levels of variation when they varied the type of companion present (no one, two nonreacting others (confederates), two other naïve participants). The number of independent variable levels that you decide to include in your experiment depends on the number of comparisons that you wish to make, although there are practical limits to this. For one thing, the more comparisons we make, the more study participants we will need. Researchers rarely use more than four levels for a given independent variable.

Let's look at a couple of examples. Here's another example of research in which the type of variable

IV: Type of Store ← Independent Variable Label

1) flower
2) shoe
3) cake

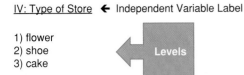

FIGURE 8.7 Guéguen (2012) used a *type* of variable manipulation with three levels.

IV: Heel Size ← Independent Variable Label

1) 0 cm
2) 5 cm
3) 9 cm

FIGURE 8.8 Guéguen (2015b) used an *amount* of variable manipulation with three levels (the 0 cm can be considered an absence manipulation).

was manipulated with three levels of variation. In this example, Guéguen (2012) again asks the question: Under what conditions are women more likely to say "yes" in response to a request for their phone number? In this experiment, Guéguen had an attractive male approach women who were approximately 18–25 years of age, and he randomly varied the type of store where they were approached among three options (flower store, shoe store, cake store). See Figure 8.7 for another way to represent Guéguen's (2012) independent variable.

Guéguen hypothesized that females approached in front of a flower store as opposed to the other stores would be more likely to agree to provide their phone number. His reason for this hypothesis stemmed from the work of Haviland-Jones, Hale Rosario, Wilson, and McGuire (2005) who found that flowers elicited positive moods in a variety of situations. Guéguen's findings were consistent with that obtained in Haviland-Jones et al.'s work.

Another possibility is to manipulate the amount of a variable and choose three or even more amounts of a variable. Researchers who do this often include an "absence" condition (you could think of Latané and Darley's [1968] "no companion present" condition as an "absence" condition). Let's look at another example from Guéguen. In this case, Guéguen (2015a) randomly varied the height of a female confederate's shoe heel (0, 5, 9 cm) to determine whether it would affect helping behavior by others. The condition in which the heel was 0 cm could be considered the "absence" of a heel condition. Figure 8.8

shows another way to represent this independent variable and its levels.

In one of the experiments in Guéguen's (2015a) article, the female confederate in her varying heel heights asked males passing by to answer a survey. Males were more likely to help when the confederate wore the highest heel than when she wore a flat heel.

Measuring Dependent Variables

There are a variety of ways to measure dependent variables; they generally fall into three categories: self-report measures, behavioral measures, and physiological measures. We'll discuss each of these types of measures in turn.

Self-Report Measures

Self-report measures are just what they sound like – you are asking people to report on themselves: what they think, what they feel, what they've done, and what they think they would do in a given situation. Self-reports can be responses to either open-ended or closed-ended questions. In fact, much of what we discussed in Chapter 7 regarding survey questions is relevant here; the difference between a survey and an experiment is that an experiment includes one or more independent variables. We've seen some examples of self-report measures in the research presented in this chapter. For example, Watson et al. (2000) asked people to report on their energy level and mood after ingesting caffeine.

While asking people to report on their thoughts and feelings can provide researchers with interesting insights, self-reports can also have limitations. People are not always inclined to tell the truth about what they think, how they feel, what they've done, or what they would likely do. They may not even know! In addition, sometimes just knowing their thoughts and feelings are being assessed can make people change their responses, a phenomenon known as reactivity (a concept we discussed in Chapter 5).

One form of reactivity comes from the idea that people have a tendency to want to present themselves in a favorable light, which means you may not get responses that represent the truth. This form of reactivity is known as social desirability (see Chapter 7 for more on this topic). Another potential problem with self-reports can occur if you are asking people to report on past events; they may not report accurately because they may not remember the event as it happened. Despite these concerns, self-reports can be quite helpful and are often used, sometimes in conjunction with other types of dependent variables.

Behavioral Measures

One of the problems that sometimes occurs with self-reports is that people will incorrectly report what they think they would do. They aren't necessarily lying; it's just that it's sometimes difficult to know how you would act unless you are actually in the particular situation. Putting people in a situation and seeing how they would act can solve this problem. Behavioral measures are also less likely to be compromised by reactivity if, for example, participants are not aware their behavior is being assessed. However, there are disadvantages to using behavioral responses. For example, knowing someone's behavioral response does not give you any information about why he or she acted that way (using a self-report in conjunction with a behavioral response could come in handy under these circumstances).

There are many ways to incorporate behavioral measures into an experiment. Consider the behavioral measures noted in this chapter to get an idea of the wealth of possibilities. For example, Guéguen et al. (2010) counted the percentage of females who provided their phone numbers. Guéguen (2015a) counted the percentage of males who answered a survey. Latané and Darley counted the percentage of people who reported smoke billowing into the room. Engle-Friedman et al. assessed the level of difficulty of math problems that people selected and completed. The choice of behaviors to measure is limited only by the imagination of the researchers (and ethical considerations, of course).

Physiological Measures

There are many different types of physiological measures. Researchers can record bodily responses such as heart rate, blood pressure, and respiration rate. These types of bodily responses are often used as indicators of, for example, increased stress. They can also record participants' brain activity using an electroencephalogram (EEG), muscle tension using an electromyogram (EMG), and the electrical conductance of the skin (an indicator of general emotional arousal). More recently, researchers have been using tools such as positron emission topography (PET) scans and functional magnetic resonance imaging (fMRI) for knowledge of what areas of the brain are active while participants work on particular tasks. Since I have not offered examples of physiological measures thus far in this chapter, I'll mention a few here so you can get a sense of how physiological measures can be used.

- Aiello, DeRisi, Epstein, and Karlin (1977) were interested in assessing how people were affected when their personal space was violated. They

FIGURE 8.9 Undergraduates had lower blood pressure readings when they petted a dog rather than when they read a book or talked with others (Grossberg & Alf, 1985).

found that those placed in closer physical proximity experienced higher skin conductance levels (an arousal stress response) than those who were less crowded.

- Grossberg and Alf (1985) found that undergraduates had lower blood pressure readings when they petted a dog rather than when they read a book or talked with others. Heart rate and blood pressure readings were lowest at rest.

- Ramsay, Yzer, Luciana, Vohs, and MacDonald (2013) had teenagers undergo brain scans (fMRI) while watching different types of commercials (strongly convincing antidrug ads, weakly convincing antidrug ads, nondrug ads). The convincing ads produced more brain activation than weak ads in areas of the brain responsible for both arousal and executive processes, suggesting that both affective and cognitive processing play a role in persuasiveness.

Physiological measures have the advantage of reducing reactivity because individuals are often not able to directly control these types of responses. A disadvantage is that some physiological responses, such as brain activation, need to be assessed with expensive equipment that may not be readily available to researchers.

A Few Final Points about Dependent Variables

Before you decide on your choice of dependent variables for your experimentation, there are still a few things you should know.

Which Dependent Variables Should You Choose?

As the paragraphs above suggest, there are many choices of dependent variables. Which one should you choose? Well, first of all, recognize that most experiments utilize more than one dependent variable, and you can also use more than one *type* of dependent variable in any one experiment (self-report, behavioral, physiological). Experimenters often do this in an effort to develop converging evidence, evidence from multiple dependent variables that paint a more complete picture of the topic of interest. So given all this information, what dependent variables should you choose? You want to choose the variable or variables that you expect to be sensitive to your independent variable manipulation. You are anticipating that your independent variable will have an impact on your dependent variable, so do your best to choose dependent variables that will likely show that impact. The existing literature on a topic can give you information regarding what dependent variables measures have worked (or not worked) successfully before.

Ceiling and Floor Effects

When you are creating your dependent variables, you need to be concerned with ceiling effects and floor effects. Let's talk about ceiling effects first.

If your dependent variable is *too* easy, participants are likely to do really well on the task. If everyone does really well, your independent variable manipulation will appear to have no effect on your dependent variable only because the dependent variable was too easy and thus participants reached maximum performance. This is a **ceiling effect**. We don't want a ceiling effect to occur. Think about it this way. Let's say we want to know how crowding affects memory, and our memory task is to recall the following three words: cat, dog, mouse. So we randomly assign participants to two rooms (crowded, non-crowded) where they learn the words to be recalled, and then we give them the memory test. The problem here is that everyone does well because the test is too easy. That's the ceiling effect. Everyone gets 100% or close to 100% on the test. It may be that crowding does affect memory, but we won't be able to tell from this test because everyone, no matter what group they are in (crowded or not) will do well. The way to fix this is to make the dependent variable task more difficult.

Now let's consider the floor effect. **Floor effects** occur when the dependent variable is too difficult. Just as you saw with ceiling effects, we also want to avoid floor effects. So let's say we want to see whether crowding affects memory, but this time our dependent variable is recalling all the details on an unstudied penny (see Nickerson & Adams [1979] for details on how difficult this test is). We randomly assign participants to two rooms (crowded, non-crowded) where they recall what they can about an unstudied penny. The problem here is that everyone does pretty poorly because the test is too difficult. It may be that crowding does affect memory, but again we won't be able to tell from this test because everyone does poorly, no matter what group they are in (crowded or not). The way to fix this is to make the dependent variable task easier.

Manipulation Checks

Oftentimes in experiments, researchers use a special kind of dependent variable called a manipulation check. A **manipulation check** is just what it sounds like – a way you can check to see whether your manipulation worked. If your manipulation didn't work, you need to go back, figure out how to improve your manipulation, and test new study participants with the improved manipulation. Then you need to check to see whether that new manipulation worked. Once you have determined that your manipulation worked, you can analyze your results and prepare your work for presentation and/or publication.

An example will help to illustrate the importance of the manipulation check. Morrison, Noel, and Ogle (2012) were interested in whether angry females were more likely to choose alcohol than those who were not angry. Let's go over some of the pertinent details.

Female participants arrived at the lab anticipating that they were going to be part of two experiments. A confederate pretending to be the second study participant arrived at the same time. For the first experiment, participants were given a series of anagrams to solve and were randomly assigned to the "anger" or "non-anger" conditions. In the "anger" condition, the confederate solved her anagrams quickly, then criticized the participant while she struggled to solve her set of anagrams (the participant's anagrams were rigged to be unsolvable). In the "non-anger" condition, the two participants worked on their solvable anagrams side by side for 8 minutes. Then participants in both conditions were asked to fill out questionnaires that assessed their current emotions.

After answering the questionnaires, the participant and the confederate were told they would now be a part of a second experiment, a taste test. A new experimenter who had no knowledge of the previous experiment's group assignments had the participant and confederate sit on opposite sides of the room to rate beverages. Two cups were labeled "beer" (it was really non-alcoholic beer) and two were labeled "ginger ale." Participants were given 20 minutes to do the ratings and were told they could "finish any or all of the beverages" (p. 910). The experimenters later calculated how much of the beer and ginger ale the true participant had consumed.

Now here's where I get to explain why a manipulation check is so important. Morrison et al. were interested in whether angry females would drink more alcohol than non-angry females. Thus, it was *vital* for them to know that their anger manipulation worked, that they had actually gotten those in the "angry" condition angry while those in the "non-anger" condition were not angry. When they assessed the emotions of the participants by asking them to rate how angry they were feeling on a scale from 1 (not at all) to 7 (extremely) angry, they found the participants were indeed feeling what the experimenters had anticipated. Once they were certain they had successfully made those in the "anger" condition angry, they could determine whether being angry caused more alcohol to be consumed. They did find that those who were angry consumed more "beer" than those who were not.

Morrison et al. had to assess their participants' emotions in a way that did not give away their hypothesis. Telling participants they were completing two separate experiments (with two different experimenters) helped to disconnect the anagram experience from the drinking experience. The experimenters were also able to confirm the effectiveness of the deception during the debriefing process.

If an experimenter is concerned that conducting the manipulation check will somehow affect the results, there are ways to avoid this problem. For example, one strategy is to conduct the manipulation check after the dependent variables have been measured and collected; this way your results cannot be tainted by any knowledge of the manipulation participants might gain from the manipulation check itself.

Avoid Experimenter Expectancies

No matter what type of dependent variable you use, be careful to avoid the influence of experimenter expectancies. The term **experimenter expectancies** refers to the influence of an experimenter's expectations on the results of an experiment. Quite simply, if an experimenter knows the hypotheses and/or the group assignments, this information can be conveyed to the participants (perhaps inadvertently), and potentially affect participants' responses or the way the experimenter interprets the responses provided. How do we guard against this? One possible remedy is to use a double-blind experiment. A **double-blind experiment** is one in which the participants and the researchers interacting with the participants (research assistants) do not know the group assignments and what responses are expected from the participants.

Another method that can be used to reduce the possibility of experimenter expectancies from affecting the results of the research is to limit the interaction between researchers and participants. One way to do this is to automate the experiment. For example, instead of having an experimenter verbally provide the instructions to the participants, participants could read the instructions on a computer screen. The more you automate the experimental session, the less opportunity the researcher has to let their expectations influence the results.

The Posttest Only Design versus the Before–After Design

Thus far, all the experiments we've discussed have been **posttest only** experiments. In other words, the

IV: Manipulation	Posttest (DV)
(1) Experimental	Y
(2) Control Group	Y

FIGURE 8.10 Diagram of a posttest only design.

Pretest (DV)	IV: Manipulation	Posttest (DV)
Y	(1) Experimental Group	Y
Y	(2) Control Group	Y

FIGURE 8.11 Diagram of a before–after design.

dependent variables were measured only after the independent variable had been manipulated and not before. Most experiments are posttest only experiments. If your groups are considered equivalent (because of random assignment or because you use the same people in your groups), there is generally no need for you to measure the dependent variable before you manipulate the independent variable; you just need to measure it after. Figure 8.10 is a diagram of this type of experiment with one between-subjects independent variable and two levels. Note that the dependent variable, symbolized as Y, is measured once for each group. In this case, after the manipulation of the independent variable, researchers would analyze statistically how much the groups differed from each other.

Occasionally researchers will include a pretest in their experiment just to ensure that the groups were equivalent from the start (non-equivalence can be an issue, even if you use random assignment, if your group size is smaller than 10 people or if some people drop out of your study early). This design is often referred to as a **before–after** design or **pretest–posttest** design. Figure 8.11 shows this type of experiment with one between-subjects independent variable and two levels. Note that the dependent variable, again symbolized as Y, is measured for both groups as both a pretest and a posttest. In this case, researchers would consider how much the groups changed from pretest to posttest in an effort to answer the question: Which group showed the greater amount of change?

Let's look at an example of a pretest–posttest design. Lull, Çetin, and Bushman (2015) wondered whether exposure to videos containing violence and sex would impair a task involving attention and memory (a test of foreign-language vocabulary). They randomly assigned Turkish university students to watch either a video that contained sex and violence or a neutral video. Randomly assigning the students to the video conditions should theoretically have resulted in the two groups being essentially equal in terms of their foreign-language performance. But Lull et al. wanted to make sure the groups were equal, so before they watched the video, all participants took a pretest to assess their foreign-language vocabulary. The pretest scores did not differ for the two groups. However, after watching the videos, those who saw the video with violence and sex did less well on the test than those who saw the neutral video.

The very act of taking a pretest can cause a change in the participants. For example, if you give the participants the same test twice, they can benefit from the repeated presentation. The solution to this problem is to make the pretest and posttest similar but different. Lull et al. (2015) accomplished this by having participants generate English words from 20 alphabet letters (10 for the pretest, 10 for the posttest – letters for the two tests were randomly determined). So, in the end, Lull et al. were able to conclude that the content of the videos affected the participants' foreign-language performance.

A Consideration of the Results

Before we finish this chapter, I want to discuss how researchers think about results from experiments with one independent variable. First I'll talk about the process generally, and then I'll go over a few examples. This discussion will not include calculations (often the calculations will be done using a computerized statistics program such as SPSS), but if you want to learn more about how to calculate the noted statistics, you should be able to find what you need in an introductory statistics textbook.

One of the first steps that researchers complete after collecting data is to calculate **descriptive statistics** to summarize the data they collected from each group. In order to do this, the researchers will typically calculate the average (mean) responses for each group. Once descriptive statistics have been calculated, researchers often use **inferential statistics** to determine whether the mean responses for the groups were significantly different from each other. In theoretical terms, inferential statistics are called "inferential" because you can infer information about a population based on what you have determined with your sample. In more practical terms, inferential statistical tests allow one to determine whether the obtained results are statistically significant or likely due to chance. Do we want our results to be due to chance? No, we want our results to be due to the effects of the independent variable. So when we compute inferential statistics we keep the likelihood of chance very low. Typically, if there is a less than 5% probability that chance could be responsible for the results, then the results are considered statistically significant. Inferential statistical techniques allow us to determine whether the responses between the different groups are likely due to the effects of the independent variable or likely just a chance occurrence. What kind of inferential tests do we use? How many groups you have and what kind of design you have (between-subjects, within-subjects) help you determine which type of statistic you need to use. There are, in fact, a variety of ways to analyze any given set of data. We'll review a few of the possibilities next.

Analysis for One Independent Variable with Two Groups

Let's first consider experiments with one independent variable with two levels. **T-tests** are commonly used to determine whether the difference between the mean scores of two groups is statistically significant. If your two-group experiment uses a between-subjects design (one independent variable with different participants in the two different groups), then you will use a **t-test for independent samples**, and if your two-group experiment uses a within-subjects design (one independent variable with the same participants in the two different groups), then you will use a **t-test for dependent samples**.

Between-Subjects. Let's look at an example of the analysis of data from a between-subjects design. Strohmetz, Rind, Fisher, and Lynn (2002) were interested in whether providing a fancy piece of candy with a restaurant check would increase the size of the tip. Here's what they did. They had experienced waiters work as confederates, randomly determining whether to provide candy or no candy when delivering the check. The waiters served 92 dining parties, and then calculated the tip percentage received for each condition. When candy was provided with the check, the tip percentage was 17.84%, and when candy was not provided with the check, the tip percentage was 15.06%. These percentages are the descriptive statistics for the two groups in this sample. A *t*-test for independent samples determined that the difference between these two percentages was statistically significant. In other words, providing candy led to a higher tip percentage. Here's one way to write up this result:

Restaurant patrons who were given candy with their check left a larger tip percentage ($M = 17.84$, $SD = 3.06$) than restaurant patrons who

were not given candy with their check
($M = 15.06$, $SD = 1.89$), t (90) = 5.25, p < .001,
effect size $r = .48$.

Let's talk briefly about the specifics of this result write-up. First read the sentence without reading what's in the parentheses. Note that these words make sense, and that's how it should be. The information in parentheses is not an integral part of the sentence, and the sentence should make sense when that information isn't included. Also note that the sentence is a parallel sentence. It makes the needed comparison between the two groups (those who were provided candy versus those who were not). The mean (average) and standard deviation (an indicator of variability) of the responses for each condition are provided in parentheses, abbreviated and italicized, stated immediately after each condition is identified. Finally, the details at the end of the sentence give information regarding the inferential statistic that was used: t (90) = 5.25, p < .001, effect size $r = .48$. The "t" indicates that a t-test was used. The "(90)" represents the degrees of freedom for this test (in very general terms, this is a reflection of sample size). The "p < .001" represents the probability value that was calculated for this comparison. The APA *Publication Manual* requires that researchers report exact p values (such as $p = .03$) unless the p value is less than .001; then just report it as p < .001. What this p value means is that it has been determined that the likelihood of this result being due to chance (as opposed to being due to the independent variable) is very, very small (less than .1%). The effect size notation provides information regarding the magnitude of the result. An indication of effect size is now required in many publications; note that there are different ways to represent effect size (r, Cohen's d). Now let's pretend that Strohmetz et al. (2002) had found that the two group percentages were not significantly different from each other.

In this case they would have had to report that the presence of candy did not affect the tip percentages. In this case, the write-up would look something like this:

> Those that received candy with their check left approximately the same tip percentage ($M = 17.84$, $SD = 3.06$) as those who were not given candy with their check ($M = 15.06$, $SD = 1.89$), t (90) = 5.25, $p = .08$, effect size $r = .48$.

In this pretend case, the words in the sentence reflect the idea that the tip percentages for the two groups were not significantly different from each other. The probability value also reflects this as the probability is greater than .05. This means that the probability that this finding is due to chance is greater than 5%. We typically do not want the likelihood of chance to be that high, thus when we obtain a probability that is greater than 5%, we consider that result to be statistically non-significant. (Remember that the current standard is to report exact p values. In this pretend "non-significant" situation I've written $p = .08$ in the sentence below just to provide you with an example of a probability value greater than .05.)

Within-Subjects. Now let's say that you have one independent variable with two levels, but this time all experimental participants experience both levels; in other words, a within-subjects design. This is the kind of design that Cockerton, Moore, and Norman (1997) used when they wanted to know if test performance would differ as a function of the background sounds present during testing. So they had undergraduates take one part of an IQ test in silence and another part of the test while classical background music was playing. Just as we saw above, Cockerton et al. (1997) had two groups to compare. Let's take a look at one of Cockerton et al.'s dependent variables. Cockerton et al. counted the number of correct answers in each condition. When there was music playing, the participants answered 16.10 questions correctly, and when there was no music playing, the participants answered 18.50 questions correctly. So the question is: Did the music have an impact on the test scores? In order words, was there a significant difference between 16.10 and 18.50? Cockerton et al. used a *t*-test for dependent samples to make this comparison, and found that yes, there was a statistically significant difference between those two numbers. When participants were listening to music as opposed to silence while taking the test, the participants answered more questions correctly (18.50 was found to be significantly more than 16.10). Here's one way to write this up with the statistical notation included:

> When classical music was playing in the background, participants answered more questions correctly ($M = 18.50$, $SD = 4.70$) than when no music was playing in the background ($M = 16.10$, $SD = 4.60$), $t(29) = 2.71$, $p < .05$.[1]

Note that if Cockerton et al. had found that the two numbers were not significantly different from each other, they would have had to report that the background sounds (music, silence) did not affect levels of correct responding.

We can also talk about a pretest–posttest situation in which two groups need to be compared. Let's use Lull et al.'s research as an example. Recall that Lull et al. had all participants randomly assigned to two groups. They all first took a foreign language vocabulary pretest and then either watched a video that contained sex and violence or watched a neutral video. Then Lull et al. counted the mean number of foreign words generated by the participants in each group. It was important to first compare the pretest scores to each other to ensure that the groups did not differ prior to the independent variable manipulation. Those that saw the violence and sex tape generated a pretest score of 96.03 while those that saw the tape with no violence and sex generated a pretest score of 93.63. A *t*-test was used to compare the two groups' scores to each other. The pretest scores for the two groups did not differ.

However, as you may recall, after watching the videos, there was a difference in the performance on the foreign language tests. Again, a *t*-test was used to compare the performance of the two groups. Those who saw the video with violence and sex did less well on the test (an average of 76.80 words generated) than those who saw the neutral video (an average of 90.94 words). Here's one way to write this up with the statistical notation:

> Those who were presented with a video that had violence and sex generated fewer foreign words on the posttest ($M = 76.80$, $SD = 27.93$) than those who were presented with a video that did not contain violence and sex ($M = 90.94$, $SD = 24.81$), $t(68) = 2.24$, $p = .03$, $d = .54$.

Analysis for One Independent Variable with More than Two Groups

When your experiment has *more* than two groups to compare, then you should no longer use a *t*-test. In this chapter we have considered experiments that fit into this category; we covered experiments that had one independent variable with three levels. Typically, in this sort of situation, we use an inferential statistical technique called a **one-way analysis of variance (ANOVA)**. It is called a *one-way* ANOVA because we have one independent variable. A one-way ANOVA

---

1 Note that at the time that Cockerton et al.'s (1997) article was published, the tradition was not to report exact *p* values, but instead provide values that rounded to $p < .10$, $p < .05$, $p < .01$ and so on. In addition, at the time the article was published, researchers did not typically provide an effect size.

will allow you to determine whether there are significant differences between any of the group means. If the ANOVA does not reveal that significant differences exist among the three groups, then you would conclude that your independent variable did not affect your dependent variable. In other words, despite treating your three groups differently, the three groups responded similarly on the dependent variable.

If however, the ANOVA reveals that the overall pattern of results includes at least two group means that are significantly different from each other, then researchers typically use an additional statistical test, a **post-hoc test**, to determine exactly which of the three groups differ from each other. (A post-hoc test is not needed in a two-group experiment because, if the ANOVA reveals significant differences, the differences can only be between the two groups that you are comparing.) Let's take a look at a three-group experiment as an example.

Between-Subjects. Dixon, Trigg, and Griffiths (2007) wondered whether background music (slow tempo, fast tempo, no music) would affect the behavior of those playing online roulette while in a university gaming laboratory. After being randomly assigned to groups, the undergraduates were briefed on how to play roulette, and then played a series of 10 games. The amount of money spent, the speed at which betting occurred, and the amount of risk undertaken were all assessed. For the purpose of this example, I'll just go over a couple of these dependent variables. Dixon et al. used an ANOVA to determine that the music did impact the time it took the participants to place a bet. In this case, the researchers were comparing the betting speed for the three groups (slow tempo, fast tempo, no music). A significant ANOVA indicated that the betting speed means for at least two of these groups were different from each other. This is a way to write this result up:

An ANOVA revealed that the music did impact the time it took the participants to place a bet, $F(2, 257) = 30.07, p < .001, r = .71$.

As we saw with the *t*-tests, the details at the end of the sentence provide information regarding the statistical test that was performed (an "*F*" test refers to an ANOVA), and the numbers in parentheses refer to the degrees of freedom for this test. For an ANOVA, the first number of the degrees of freedom is the number of groups being compared minus one, while the second number is the number of participants in the study minus the number of groups being compared. The probability value indicates the likelihood that this result is due to chance, and the "*r*" here is the effect size.

As noted above, when you are comparing more than two groups, an additional test is needed to determine which means are significantly different from each other. In this case Dixon et al. used something called **planned contrasts** to compare means. In other words, they decided in advance which means they would compare. They found that those who listened to fast tempo music had faster betting speeds ($M = 1.49, SD = .04$) than those who did not listen to music ($M = 1.98, SD = .46$) and those who listened to a slower tempo of music ($M = 2.53, SD = .39$). In addition, the betting speed observed during the slower tempo music was significantly slower than the betting speed observed during the condition with no music (this means that the mean of 2.53 was significantly different from the mean of 1.98).

I also want to review another of Dixon et al.'s (2007) results. In this case, we're going to look at one that was not significant. Dixon et al. found that the mean amount of money spent was similar for all of the groups, $F(2, 55) = 1.03, p = .36$. Notice that the p value here is greater than .05, which traditionally indicates a finding that is not significant.

Within-Subjects. Recognize that if you have a within-subjects experiment with more than two groups, you again can use an ANOVA to determine if there are significant differences between any of the groups. In this case, you would use a **repeated-measures ANOVA**. If your ANOVA revealed that there are significant differences overall, then, as before, you would need an additional statistical test to determine exactly which groups were significantly different from each other.

SUMMARY

Experimental research designs allow the researcher to determine cause and effect relationships between independent and dependent variables. The ability to state cause and effect comes from the use of theoretically equivalent groups (created by randomly assigning participants to groups in a between-subjects design or by testing the same participants in different groups in a within-subjects design) and the use of one or more control (comparison) groups. It is also important that researchers control the influence of extraneous variables, thus enabling researchers to conclude that the independent variable, rather than any uncontrolled factors, is the cause of the response on the dependent variable.

To manipulate an independent variable, researchers can vary the presence/absence of a variable, the amount of a variable, or the type of a variable. Researchers can also decide whether to provide their participants with a change in the instructions that they provide (an instructional manipulation) or a change in the events that participants experience (an event manipulation). In some cases researchers place people into groups based on some personal characteristic that the individual has. This "individual difference manipulation" decreases one's ability to establish cause and effect because participants are no longer randomly placed in groups.

Dependent variables can be self-reports, behavioral measures, and physiological measures. Researchers choose the dependent variables that they expect will be sensitive to their independent variable manipulation. Researchers also have a choice of using a posttest only design (the dependent variable is tested only once – after the independent variable manipulation) or a before–after design (the dependent variable is tested twice).

After collecting data, researchers typically calculate descriptive statistics to summarize the data they collected from each group and inferential statistics to determine whether the mean responses for the groups were significantly different from each other.

GLOSSARY

Before–after design (pretest–posttest design) – an experiment in which the dependent variable is measured both before and after the independent variable manipulation.

Between-subjects design – an experiment in which different participants are assigned to the different groups.

Carryover effects – performance in one condition affects performance in another condition. Counterbalancing is needed to guard against this.

Ceiling effect – the independent variable appears to have no effect on the dependent variable only because the dependent variable task was too easy.

Complete counterbalancing – all possible orders of presentation are controlled in a within-subjects design.

Confound – an extraneous variable that varies systematically with the independent variable. Affects internal validity.

Control condition – in an experiment, performance in the control condition is compared to performance in the experimental condition. A control condition often is characterized by an absent treatment.

Counterbalancing – controls the order of presentation in an experiment. Necessary for within-subjects designs.

Double-blind experiment – the participants and the researchers interacting with the participants do not know the group assignments and what responses are expected from the participants.

Event manipulation – the experiences that participants encounter are varied to see how this affects participants.

Experimental condition – in an experiment, the experimental condition is the group in which the treatment is present.

Experimental design – the plan or strategy used when conducting an experiment.

Experimental realism – the degree to which a research experience psychologically involves the experimental participants.

Experimenter expectancies – the influence of an experimenter's expectations (hypotheses) on the results of an experiment.

Extraneous variables – uncontrolled variables that are not purposely manipulated but that could theoretically affect the participants.

Fatigue effect – performance deteriorates as the participant becomes tired, bored, or distracted. Fatigue effects are a concern in within-subjects designs.

Floor effect – the independent variable appears to have no effect on the dependent variable only because the dependent variable task was too difficult.

Individual difference manipulation – participants are placed into different groups as a function of personal characteristics (such as gender, religion, education level, shyness level, self-esteem level).

Instructional manipulation – the instructions that participants are provided are varied to see how this affects participants.

Manipulation check – a dependent variable that enables one to determine whether an independent variable manipulation worked as intended.

Matched-groups design – pairs of participants are matched on a measure related to the dependent variable before being randomly assigned to groups.

One-way analysis of variance (ANOVA) – a one-way ANOVA allows you to determine whether there are significant differences between any of the group means. Appropriate to use for an experiment with one independent variable with more than two groups.

Order effects – in a within-subject design, the repeated testing of participants could yield better (practice effect) or worse (fatigue effect) performance. These order effects need to be controlled with counterbalancing.

Placebo – an inactive substance used as a comparison in an experiment.

Planned contrasts – comparisons between group means that are specified before the data are gathered.

Post-hoc test – after an ANOVA reveals that statistical differences exist among groups, a post-hoc test used to determine which specific groups are statistically different from each other.

Posttest only – an experiment in which dependent variables are measured only after the independent variable had been manipulated and not before.

Power – a study's ability to detect significant differences.

Practice effect – performance improves as the participant benefits from practice. Practice effects are a concern in within-subjects designs.

Pretest–posttest design (before–after design) – an experiment in which the dependent variable is measured both before and after the independent variable manipulation.

Repeated-measures analysis of variance (ANOVA) – an ANOVA allows you to determine whether there are significant differences between group means. Appropriate to use for a within-subjects experiment.

Repeated-measures design (within-subjects design) – the same people experience different levels of an independent variable.

Sensitization effect – knowledge of all levels of an independent variable in a within-subjects design may lead participants to figure out the study's purpose and/or hypothesis.

T-tests – used to determine whether the difference between the mean scores of two groups is statistically significant.

T-test for dependent samples – used to determine whether the difference between the mean scores of two groups in a within-subjects design is statistically significant.

T-test for independent samples – used to determine whether the difference between the mean scores of two groups in a between-subjects design is statistically significant.

Within-subjects design – an experiment in which the same people experience all levels of variation.

1   Define experimental design.
2   State the conditions necessary to establish cause and effect.
3   Differentiate between extraneous variables and confounds.
4   Explain what random assignment of participants to groups accomplishes.
5   Differentiate between a within-subjects design and a between-subjects design.
6   Explain order effects and counterbalancing.
7   Summarize the different techniques for manipulating an independent variable.
8   Differentiate between instructional versus event manipulations.
9   Explain the different ways to measure a dependent variable.
10 Differentiate between ceiling and floor effects.
11 Explain why a manipulation check is helpful.
12 Define experimenter expectancies.
13 Compare a posttest only design with a before–after design.
14 Differentiate between descriptive statistics and inferential statistics.

The following cited articles provide examples of experimental research. For each, obtain the article and answer the questions provided to learn more about how experimental research is conducted.

1   Neave, N., & Shields, K. (2008). The effects of facial hair manipulation on female perceptions of attractiveness, masculinity, and dominance in male faces. *Personality and Individual Differences, 45*, 373–377. doi:http://dx.doi.org/10.1016/j.paid.2008.05.007

2   Neighbors, C., Spieker, C. J., Oster-Aaland, L., & Lewis, M. A. (2005). Celebration intoxication: An evaluation of 21st birthday alcohol consumption. *Journal of American College Health, 54*, 76–80. doi:http://dx.doi.org/10.3200/JACH.54.2.76-80

3 Greitemeyer, T., Osswald, S., & Brauer, M. (2010). Playing prosocial video games increases empathy and decreases schadenfreude. *Emotion, 10*, 796–802. doi:http://dx.doi.org/10.1037/a0020194

    a. List all of the variables (independent and dependent). Include all levels with your identification of the independent variables.

    b. Were the independent variables between-subjects or within-subjects variables?

    c. Were the variables experimental manipulations or individual difference manipulations?

    d. If the researchers used a manipulation check, indicate what it accomplished.

    e. Summarize the main results in your own words.

SUGGESTED ACTIVITIES

1 Design your own experiment! Obtain and read a primary source journal article that is of interest to you. Then propose a follow-up experiment. What will you have as your independent variable? What will its levels be? Will your design be between-subjects or within-subjects? What will your dependent variable measure(s) be? What are your expected results?

2 Please answer the questions that follow the research summaries below.

    a. Garwood, Cox, Kaplan, Wasserman and Sulzer (1980) were presented with six photos, prejudged equivalent in physical attractiveness, and were asked to select a beauty queen. Half the photographs were labeled with a "desirable" first name and half were assigned an "undesirable" first name (p. 431). All participants viewed all six photos and voted for their choice.

    i. Name the independent variable and its levels.

    ii. Name the dependent variable.

    iii. Was this independent variable presented within-subjects or between-subjects?

    b. Trudel, Argo, and Meng (2016) were interested in whether linking people's identities to items affects how people dispose of those items. In one of their experiments they told their participants that they were interested in determining whether people could differentiate between tap water and bottled water (a cover story). They expected that linking one's identity to the product would lead to a participant being more likely to recycle as opposed to trashing the product (the latter would be seen as equivalent to trashing oneself). Participants then participated in a water taste test with either a blank cup, a cup with their name on it (identity linked), or a cup with their name spelled incorrectly (identity not linked). After the taste test, participants were told to "dispose of your cup on the way out" (p. 250). As expected, when participant identity was correctly represented, participants were significantly more likely to recycle.

    i. Name the independent variable and its levels.

    ii. Name the dependent variable.

    iii. Was this independent variable presented within-subjects or between-subjects?

REFERENCES

Ahluwalia, J. S., Okuyemi, K., Nollen, N., Choi, W. S., Kaur, H., Pulvers, K., & Mayo, M. S. (2006). The effects of nicotine gum and counseling among African American light smokers: A 2 × 2 design. *Addiction, 101*, 883–891. doi:http://dx.doi.org/10.1111/j.1360-0443.2006.01461.x

Aiello, J. R., DeRisi, D. T., Epstein Y. M., & Karlin, R. A. (1977). Crowding and the role of interpersonal distance preference. *Sociometry*, *40*, 271–282. doi:http://dx.doi.org/10.2307/3033534

Cockerton, T., Moore, S., & Norman, D. (1997). Cognitive test performance and background music. *Perceptual and Motor Skills*, *85*, 1435–1438. doi:http://dx.doi.org/10.2466/pms.1997.85.3f.1435

Dixon, L., Trigg, R., & Griffiths, M. (2007). An empirical investigation of music and gambling behaviour. *International Gambling Studies*, *7*, 315–326. doi:http://dx.doi.org/10.1080/14459790701601471

End, C. M., Worthman, S., Mathews, M. B., & Wetterau, K. (2010). Costly cell phones: The impact of cell phone rings on academic performance. *Teaching of Psychology*, *37*, 55–57. doi:http://dx.doi.org/10.1080/00986280903425912

Engle-Friedman, M., Riela, S., Golan, R., Ventuneac, A. M., Davis, C. M., Jefferson, A. D., & Major, D. (2003). The effect of sleep loss on next day effort. *Journal of Sleep Research*, *12*, 113–124. doi:http://dx.doi.org/10.1046/j.1365-2869.2003.00351.x

Erhel, S., & Jamet, E. (2013). Digital game-based learning: Impact of instructions and feedback on motivation and learning effectiveness. *Computers & Education*, *67*, 156–167. doi:http://dx.doi.org/10.1016/j.compedu.2013.02.019

Garwood, S. G., Cox, L., Kaplan, V., Wasserman, N., & Sulzer, J. L. (1980). Beauty is only "name" deep: The effect of first-name on ratings of physical attraction. *Journal of Applied Social Psychology*, *10*, 431–435. doi:http://dx.doi.org/10.1111/j.1559-1816.1980.tb00721.x

Greitemeyer, T., Osswald, S., & Brauer, M. (2010). Playing prosocial video games increases empathy and decreases schadenfreude. *Emotion*, *10*, 796–802. doi:http://dx.doi.org/10.1037/a0020194

Grossberg, J. M., & Alf, E. F. (1985). Interaction with pet dogs: Effects on human cardiovascular response. *Journal of the Delta Society*, *2*, 20–27.

Guéguen, N. (2012). "Say it … near the flower shop": Further evidence of the effect of flowers on mating. *Journal of Social Psychology*, *152*, 529–532. doi:http://dx.doi.org/10.1080/00224545.2012.683463

(2015a). High heels increase women's attractiveness. *Archives of Sexual Behavior*, *44*, 2227–2235. doi:http://dx.doi.org/10.1007/s10508-014-0422-z

(2015b). Women's hairstyle and men's behavior: A field experiment. *Scandinavian Journal of Psychology*, *56*, 637–640. doi:http://dx.doi.org/10.1111/sjop.12253

Guéguen, N., Jacob, C., & Lamy, L. (2010). "Love is in the air": Effects of songs with romantic lyrics on compliance with a courtship request. *Psychology of Music*, *38*, 303–307. doi:http://dx.doi.org/10.1177/0305735609360428

Haviland-Jones, J., Hale Rosario, H., Wilson, P., & McGuire, T. R. (2005). An environmental approach to positive emotion: Flowers. *Evolutionary Psychology*, *3*, 104–132.

Latané, B., & Darley, J. M. (1968). Group inhibition of bystander intervention in emergencies. *Journal of Personality and Social Psychology*, *10*, 215–221. doi:http://dx.doi.org/10.1037/h0026570

Lull, R. B., Çetin, Y., & Bushman, B. J. (2015). Violent and sexual media impair second-language memory during encoding and retrieval. *Journal of Experimental Social Psychology*, *56*, 172–178. doi:http://dx.doi.org/10.1016/j.jesp.2014.10.001

Lurigio, A. (2015). Crime narratives, dramatizations, and the legacy of the Kitty Genovese murder. *Criminal Justice and Behavior*, *42*, 782–789. doi:http://dx.doi.org/10.1177/0093854814562954

Manning, R., Levine, M., & Collins, A. (2007). The Kitty Genovese murder and the social psychology of helping: The parable of the 38 witnesses. *American Psychologist*, *62*, 555–562. doi:http://dx.doi.org/10.1037.0003-066X.62.6.555

Morrison, P. M., Noel, N. E., & Ogle, R. L. (2012). Do angry women choose alcohol? *Addictive Behaviors*, *37*, 908–913. doi:http://dx.doi.org/10.1016/j.addbeh.2012.03.018

Neave, N., & Shields, K. (2008). The effects of facial hair manipulation on female perceptions of attractiveness, masculinity, and dominance in male faces. *Personality and Individual Differences*, *45*, 373–377. doi:http://dx.doi.org/10.1016/j.paid.2008.05.007

Neighbors, C., Spieker, C. J., Oster-Aaland, L., & Lewis, M. A. (2005). Celebration intoxication: An evaluation of 21st birthday alcohol consumption. *Journal of American College Health*, *54*, 76–80. doi:http://dx.doi.org/10.3200/JACH.54.2.76-80

Nickerson, R. S., & Adams, M. J. (1979). Long-term memory for a common object. *Cognitive Psychology*,

11, 287–307. doi:http://dx.doi.org/10.1016/0010-0285(79) 90013-6

Oncken, C. A., Litt, M. D., McLaughlin, L. D., & Burki, N. A. (2015). Nicotine concentrations with electronic cigarette use: Effects of sex and flavor. *Nicotine & Tobacco Research*, *17*, 473–478. doi:http://dx.doi.org/10.1093/ntr/ntu232

Ramsay, I. S., Yzer, M. C., Luciana, M., Vohs, K. D., & MacDonald III, A. W. (2013). Affective and executive network processing associated with persuasive antidrug messages. *Journal of Cognitive Neuroscience*, *25*, 1136–1147. doi:http://dx.doi.org/10.1162/jocn_a_00391

Smith, A., Whitney, H., Thomas, M., Perry, K., & Brockman, P. (1997). Effects of caffeine and noise on mood, performance and cardiovascular functioning. *Human Psychopharmacology*, *12*, 27–33. doi:http://dx.doi.org/10.1002/(SICI)1099-1077(199701/02)12:1 < 27::AID-HUP827 > 3.0.CO;2-Y

Strohmetz, D. B., Rind, B., Fisher, R., & Lynn, M. (2002). Sweetening the till: The use of candy to increase restaurant tipping. *Journal of Applied Social Psychology*, *32*, 300–309. doi:http://dx.doi.org/10.1111/j.1559-1816.2002.tb00216.x

Trudel, R., Argo, J. J., & Meng, M. D. (2016). The recycled self: Consumers' disposal decisions of identity-linked products. *Journal of Consumer Research*, *43*. doi:http://dx.doi.org/10.1093/jcr/ucw014

Watson, J. M., Lunt, M. J., Morris, S., Weiss, M. J., Hussey, D., & Kerr, D. (2000). Reversal of caffeine withdrawal by ingestion of a soft beverage. *Pharmacology Biochemistry and Behavior*, *66*, 15–18. doi:http://dx.doi.org/10.1016/S0091-3057(00)00233-1

Zucco, G. M., Aiello, L., Turuani, L., & Köster, E. (2012). Odor-evoked autobiographical memories: Age and gender differences along the life span. *Chemical Senses*, *37*, 179–189. doi:http://dx.doi.org/10.1093/chemse/bjr089

9 Factorial Designs: Experiments with More than One Independent Variable

The Terminology of the Factorial Design
Using a 2 × 2 Design
Between-Subjects Designs
Within-Subjects Designs
Possible Outcomes in a 2 × 2 Design
Individual Difference Manipulation
Using a 2 × 3 Design
Using a 3 × 3 Design
Mixed Designs
Higher-Order Factorial Designs
Summary
Glossary
Review Questions
Suggested Activities
Articles as Illustration

LEARNING OBJECTIVES

- Define the terms factorial design, factor, main effect, and interaction.

- Summarize how to decide whether you have main effects and a significant interaction in a 2 × 2 design.

- Differentiate between a 2 × 2 between-subjects design and a 2 × 2 within-subjects design.

- Differentiate between a 2 × 2, a 2 × 3, and a 3 × 3 design.

- Define a mixed design.

- Explain what a higher-order factorial design is.

Have you ever been bumped from an overbooked flight? Typically, when a flight is overbooked, the airline will offer passengers a monetary incentive and a ticket for a later flight. But what happens when no one volunteers to take the airline up on the offer? United Airlines was recently in the news because of the way their employees handled this circumstance. When no one accepted an offer of a $1,000 voucher and a ticket for a later flight, United Airline representatives selected passengers to remove from the flight (four United employees needed the seats). One of the chosen passengers refused to leave the plane, and thus he was forcibly dragged off, while videotaped by fellow passengers (Victor & Stevens, 2017).

Overbooking a flight is a common phenomenon and you can be removed from a flight without your approval; however airlines set their own policies regarding who gets bumped (for example, some airlines use the order in which the passengers checked in as a guide for who to bump). United Airlines was heavily criticized for the particular way they handled the removal of this passenger. People were upset not only about the physical manner in which this passenger was removed, but also that United chose to bump passengers after they boarded the plane, an unusual occurrence (Horowitz & Ostrower, 2017).

After videos of this event went viral, some competing airlines put forth ads reminding potential passengers of what happened on this United Airlines flight while promoting their own cause. For example, Emirates Airlines tweeted "Fly the Friendly Skies … THIS TIME FOR REAL." Royal Jordanian Airlines tweeted "We would like to remind you that drags on our flights are strictly prohibited by passengers and crew" ("drags" here refer to both the Airline's non-smoking policy and what had occurred on that United flight). Spirit Airlines took a different approach with an ad that emphasized how gentle they are with your bags, and then proclaiming, "Here at Spirit, we treat your bags as well as we treat you" (Shropshire & Channick, 2017). These ads are using humor in an effort to inform people about a serious and potentially frightening issue, the possible repercussions of airline overbooking. But is an ad of this sort, and others that take a similar approach, effective? Let's take a look at research that considered this general question.

Researchers have generally found that when ads present topics that are frightening, people often have defensive responses to them (such as "Oh, that's scary – I won't think about that"), thus rendering the ad less persuasive (see for example, Keller & Block, 1996). Mukherjee and Dubé (2012) wondered whether using humor to convey frightening information in ads could reduce the defensive response and increase the persuasiveness of the ad.

To do this Mukherjee and Dubé conducted an experiment in which they manipulated both the amount of fear arousal elicited by an ad (moderate, high) *and* the presence of humor in the ad (present, absent). You may have noticed that Mukherjee and Dubé had two independent variables: (1) fear arousal and (2) humor. Researchers often design research studies that include more than one independent variable in an effort to determine how multiple variables individually and together affect dependent variables of interest. In other words, with this experiment Mukherjee and Dubé were able to determine whether fear arousal *alone* would affect the effectiveness of the ad. They were also able to assess whether humor *alone* would affect the effectiveness of the ad and whether the two variables, fear and humor, would *together* affect the effectiveness of the ad. This ability to ask questions about both the individual and the combined impact of variables is a key feature of these multi-variable research designs.

I'll briefly go over Mukherjee and Dubé's method and results here so you get a feel for why a multi-variable design can be helpful. All their participants saw an ad promoting the importance of using sunscreen, but the ads varied in the level of fear arousal (moderate, high) and presence of humor (present, absent). Participants then answered questions regarding their views of the ad. Manipulation checks enabled Mukherjee and Dubé to determine that both the fear and the humor manipulations elicited the intended reactions (for example, more fear was elicited in the high fear-arousing condition than in the moderate fear-arousing condition).

Mukherjee and Dubé assessed persuasion by measuring participants' attitude toward the brand of sunscreen presented in the ad. First we can consider how fear alone affected ratings. The amount of fear aroused didn't affect ratings of the ad. We can also consider how humor alone affected ratings. Participants provided more favorable ratings about the ad when humor was present as opposed to absent. Now let's consider fear and humor together. There was a significant interaction between fear and humor, as depicted in Figure 9.1. Humor had an impact on ratings, *but only* when fear was high. When fear was moderate, the presence versus absence of humor did not affect ratings.

It is clear from using this multi-variable design that the relationship between humor and the attitude

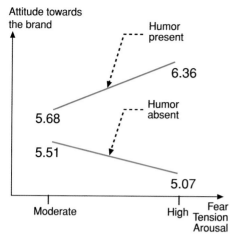

FIGURE 9.1 Interaction of fear arousal and humor in Mukherjee and Dubé's (2012) experiment on rated attitudes.

toward the ad is best understood by considering the independent variables together. We can't just say humor had an impact on attitudes toward the ad. That's not the whole story, because humor affected attitudes only when fear was high.

Now that you've had an introduction to a design that uses more than one independent variable, let's look at this kind of design in more depth.

All the experiments we reviewed in Chapter 8 had just one independent variable (with 2 or more levels). We've been asking the question: Did the independent variable manipulation affect the dependent variable response? In the current chapter, we're asking an analogous question, but as you saw in the sunscreen ad example, we now will be discussing designs in which more than one independent variable is manipulated in a single experiment. Let's start with some terms.

The Terminology of the Factorial Design

A **factorial design** is an experiment that has more than one independent variable. Each independent variable can also be referred to as a **factor** and each factor has to have at least two levels. We sometimes

refer to experiments according to how many independent variables (or factors) are used. A factorial design with two independent variables is called a two-way design, one with three independent variables is a three-way design, and so on. The independent variables in a factorial design can be between-subjects variables (different people in the different groups), within-subject variables (same people in the different groups), or a combination of between- and within-subject variables (a mixed design).

There are benefits to using these multi-factor designs. In the real world, our behavior is likely affected by multiple variables all acting at once. If I do well on a test, it is probably because I studied hard, slept well before the test, and ate a good breakfast. The absence of any one of those variables would affect my score – or would it? Wouldn't that be interesting to determine? How about knowing whether medicines work best on their own or better (or worse) when paired with another? Again, this would be valuable information. So researchers often aim to mirror the complexity of the real world by including more than one independent variable in a single experiment, so they can assess whether and how variables together affect a given response.

As you saw above, when we have more than one independent variable, we need to ask the following questions: Did *each* independent variable affect the dependent variable response, and how did the combination of the independent variables together affect the dependent variable response? So when we have a factorial design, we want to determine the effects of each of the independent variables on the dependent variable. These are called the **main effects**. We also want to determine whether the **interaction** of those independent variables had an impact on the dependent variable; these are **interaction effects**. An interaction occurs when the effect

Thank you message on the check

FIGURE 9.2 Diagram of a 2 × 2 design.

Smiley face on the check

of one independent variable changes over the levels of another independent variable.[1] Let's go over some examples.

Using a 2 × 2 Design

The simplest kind of factorial design is a design that has two independent variables, each with two levels. Once we have at least two independent variables in our experimental design, we have a shorthand way to refer to the design according to the number of levels each independent variable has. So a design with two independent variables, each with two levels, is referred to as a 2 × 2 (pronounced "two by two"). You may notice that if you do the math suggested by this design name, you get the number of groups or **cells** in the design (2 × 2 = 4).

As I mentioned above, the independent variables in a factorial design can be between-subjects variables (different people in the different groups). Let's look at a between-subjects design first.

Between-Subjects Designs

Have you ever had a job working for tips in a restaurant? I did this when I was in high school (I was not good at it; if the man I spilled drinks on is reading this, I'm still sorry). I've often wondered how I could increase my average tip percentage. Researchers have investigated this. My former student Liubove ("Liu") Bjorklund and I were also interested in this

topic, because although Liu works in a law office each weekday, on Sundays she works as a waitress at a national chain restaurant.

Liu and I decided to investigate whether writing a thank you message (Liu wrote "thank you, Liu") on the check or drawing a smiley face on the check would affect the tips she received, measured as the average percentage of the overall bill. We considered the tip percentage (such as, the tip was 15% of the overall bill) rather than the actual amount of money given, because tip percentage is a better measure of what people think of the service. In the United States (where we did this experiment), it is customary to tip 15% of the total bill before taxes; anything more is assumed to be a thank you for superior service, and less can be read as a belief that the service was relatively poor. So will people think more highly of her service if Liu writes a thank you message and/ or draws a smiley face on their check? You're about to find out.

Let's first talk about the design Liu and I created. One of our independent variables – writing a thank you message on the check – had two levels (presence, absence) and the other independent variable – drawing a smiley face on the check – had two levels (presence, absence). Again, this is a 2 × 2 design, and it has four cells. We can diagram this design as show in Fig. 9.2.

As you can see from this design, one of our independent variables with its levels is represented across

1 Note that when a main effect is said to be present, this is equivalent to stating that the main effect is significant (the independent variable affected the dependent variable) and when an interaction is said to be present, this is equivalent to stating that the interaction is significant (the effect of one independent variable changes over the levels of another independent variable). If a main effect or an interaction is not significant, this will be stated directly (for example, "the main effect was not significant").

the top, and the other independent variable with its levels is represented along the left side. It doesn't matter which independent variable you put where, as long as you keep each independent variable with its correct levels. You can also see from this diagram that I've labeled each of the four groups with a number. We always number the groups in this way, starting from the top left and going from left to right on each line. So as you can see from this diagram:

- Group 1 in our experiment had both a thank you message and a smiley face on their checks,
- Group 2 got a smiley face but not a thank you message,
- Group 3 received a thank you message but no smiley face
- Group 4 received neither a thank you message nor a smiley face.

Each table Liu served was randomly assigned to a group. Here's how we did this. Liu had shuffled index cards in her apron, each corresponding to a different group. When it was time to write the check, Liu reached into her apron pocket and pulled out an index card, which indicated the group assignment. As a result of this group assignment, Liu knew whether to write a thank you message on the check, draw a smiley face, both, or neither.

When we have two independent variables in an experiment, we have three questions to answer, and I'll ask these questions within the context of our experiment. I'll concentrate on the dependent variable, average tip percentage. Let's first consider the main effects. Note that the number of main effects is always equal to the number of independent variables, so in the case of our experiment we have two main effects to consider.

The first question is: "Did the first independent variable, the thank you message (presence, absence), have an effect on the average tip percentage?" This is a main effect question, in that we are considering

FIGURE 9.3 Researchers have studied how restaurant servers can increase their average tip percentage.

only one of the variables at this moment and ignoring the other.

The second question is: "Did the second independent variable, drawing a smiley face on the check (presence, absence), have an effect on the average tip percentage?" This is another main effect question, in that we are again considering only one of the variables at this moment and ignoring the other.

Statistical analyses are used to determine whether there are significant differences between the means for each of the groups (each group's average response). Let's take a look at where the means for each of these main effect questions come from. Consider the first main effect question: Did writing a thank you message on the check have an effect on the average tip percentage? To assess this, we need to compare marginal means for this main effect. **Marginal means** are the overall means for each

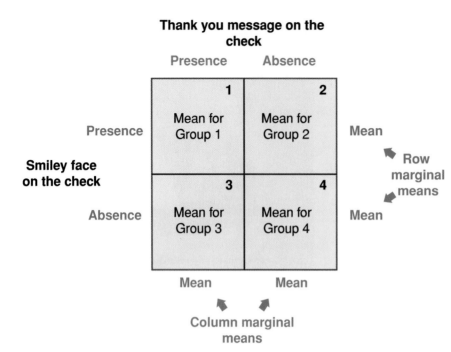

FIGURE 9.4 Diagram of a 2 × 2 design with column marginal means and row marginal means noted.

level of an independent variable, and they are found in the "margins" of a diagram of the design – outside the cells. If the sample sizes in the relevant cells are equal, the marginal means are just the average of the means for those cells. If the samples in the relevant cells are unequal, a weighted mean is used (the larger cell sample counts more).

In Figure 9.4 the marginal means for the main effect of writing a thank you message on the check are the column marginal means (picture grand building columns rising to the sky – see the red highlighted areas in Figure 9.4). These are the means we will compare to see whether writing a thank you message on the check affects the average tip percentage.

Now consider the other main effect: Will drawing a smiley face on the check affect the average tip percentage? To assess this, we need to compare the marginal means for the main effect of drawing a smiley face on the check. In Figure 9.4, the marginal means for drawing a smiley face on the check are the row marginal means (picture the horizontal rows in a movie theater) – see the green highlighted areas

in Figure 9.4. These are the means that will be compared to determine if drawing a smiley face on the check affects the average tip percentage. Figure 9.5 provides another way to think about this design and where the relevant means for each main effect are.

The third question is: Did the two independent variables, together, have an effect on the average tip percentage? This is an interaction question, in that we are considering the effect of the variables together (look at the cell means in this case). In other words, is the effect of one of the independent variables the same at different levels of the other independent variable? This point should become clearer later when I discuss a research example that has a significant interaction (as you'll see in a moment, the experiment I'm currently describing does not).

We had an introduction to the concept of significance in Chapter 8. That discussion is relevant here too. Recall that we make decisions about what kind of statistic to use by asking ourselves how many groups we have in the overall design, and what kind of design we used (within-subjects,

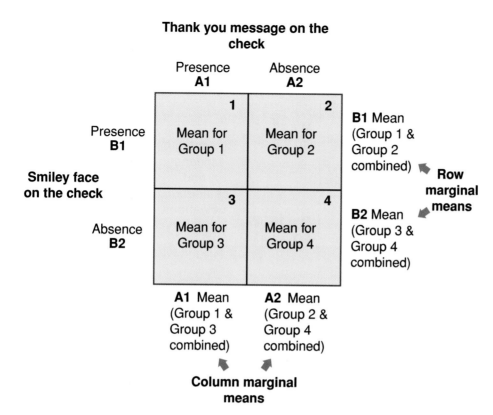

Thank you message on the check

	Presence **A1**	Absence **A2**
Presence **B1**	1 Mean for Group 1	2 Mean for Group 2
Absence **B2**	3 Mean for Group 3	4 Mean for Group 4

Smiley face on the check

B1 Mean (Group 1 & Group 2 combined)

B2 Mean (Group 3 & Group 4 combined)

Row marginal means

A1 Mean (Group 1 & Group 3 combined)

A2 Mean (Group 2 & Group 4 combined)

Column marginal means

FIGURE 9.5 Diagram of a 2 × 2 design with the column marginal means and row marginal means explained.

between-subjects, or both). In our tipping experiment, there are four groups overall (equal to the total number of cells in the experiment), and the design was between-subjects in that there were different people (in this case, different tables) in the different groups. You've already had an introduction to a statistic that can be used with this design, an ANOVA (see Chapter 8). When we are using an ANOVA for a factorial design, we name this ANOVA using the levels from each independent variable. So here we used a 2 × 2 ANOVA to analyze our data. This ANOVA indicated, for each of the two main effects, and the interaction, whether the result was likely due to chance or likely due to the impact of the independent variable(s).

Let's look again at our design with actual numbers. The first main effect question was: Did writing a thank you message on the check affect the average tip percentage? As I indicated above, we

have to compare the relevant marginal means for this main effect: the column marginal means. In this case the means to be compared are 18.49 and 14.54 as illustrated in Figure 9.6. The ANOVA made this comparison and revealed that these two means were significantly different from each other. You can tell which condition led to a larger average tip percentage by looking at the means themselves. As you can see, when Liu wrote a thank you message on the checks she earned a higher tip percentage (18.49%) than when she didn't write a thank you message on the checks (14.54%). For this first example, I'll provide information regarding where to find the means to compare and how to write up the results. We'll revisit how to write up results in Chapter 14.

Here's one way to write this finding more formally (for instance, if you were writing the results section of a publication):

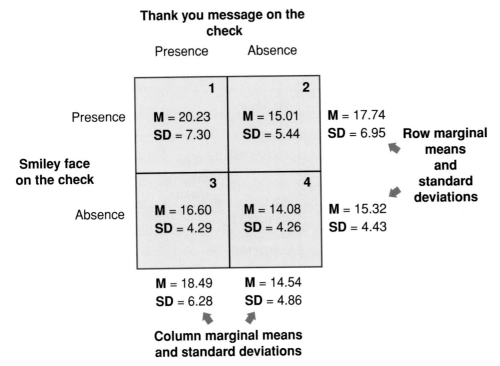

FIGURE 9.6 Heath and Bjorklund's tipping experiment: average tip percentages and standard deviations.

Writing a thank you message on the checks generated a larger tip percentage ($M = 18.49$, $SD = 6.28$) than not writing a thank you message on the checks ($M = 14.54$, $SD = 4.86$), F (1, 128) $= 16.25$, $p < .001$, partial $\eta^2 = .11$.

Now let's look more closely at the way this result was written. I'll color code the sentence so that you can see what part of the sentence I am referring to. Here is the sentence again:

Writing a thank you message on the checks generated a larger tip percentage ($M = 18.49$, $SD = 6.28$) than not writing a thank you message on the checks ($M = 14.54$, $SD = 4.86$), F (1, 128) $= 16.25$, $p < .001$, partial $\eta^2 = .11$.

- Each condition being compared has a mean and a standard deviation presented.
- The words in this stated result indicate that there is a difference between the two means,

and the sentence indicates the direction of the difference (which condition led to a larger tip percentage).

- The details provided at the end of the sentence give the reader information about the statistic that was conducted.
  - The "*F*" refers to the ANOVA value that was computed.
  - The numbers in parentheses refer to the degrees of freedom for this test. The first number of the degrees of freedom is the number of groups being compared minus one, while the second number is the number of participants in the study minus the number of groups being compared.
  - The probability value indicates the likelihood that this result is due to chance. In this case, "*p*" is less than .05, which is interpreted to indicate that the means being compared are significantly different from each other (not

likely due to chance). In other words, the independent variable had an impact on the average tip percentage.

- o The "partial η^2" (partial eta squared) at the end of the sentence refers to the effect size, a measure of the magnitude of the finding.
- o Note that all statistical notation (F, M, SD, p) is in italics.

Some writers prefer to indicate explicitly that the main effect was significant (or not) before offering the details of the finding. So here's an example of this alternative way to write up this finding:

The main effect of writing on the check was significant, $F(1, 128) = 16.25$, $p < .001$, partial $\eta^2 = .11$. Writing on the checks generated a larger tip percentage ($M = 18.49$, $SD = 6.28$) than not writing on the checks ($M = 14.54$, $SD = 4.86$).

Now let's look at the second main effect with the actual means we obtained. Recall the question we are asking with this main effect: Did drawing a smiley face on the check affect the average tip percentage? To assess this, we need to compare the marginal means for the main effect of drawing a smiley face on the check: the row marginal means. The same ANOVA analysis referred to above also made this comparison and revealed that the two relevant means (17.74 and 15.32) were significantly different from each other. Here's one way to write this:

When a smiley face was drawn on the checks, the average tip percentage was larger ($M = 17.74$, $SD = 6.95$) than when a smiley face was not drawn on the checks ($M = 15.32$, $SD = 4.43$), $F(1, 128) = 5.64$, $p = .02$, partial $\eta^2 = .05$.

Note that in the significant main effects noted above, each sentence was written to indicate that a difference exists and the direction of the difference was noted.

This is important to do when you are writing up a significant effect. If your result is not significant, you need to represent the means as equal to each other.

Let's pretend for a moment that drawing a smiley face on the check didn't have an impact. We would have to express that non-significant effect in our sentence. We do this with words and with an indication that $p > .05$. That is, the probability of obtaining this finding by chance is greater than 5%. Note that you would report the actual probability value – I've written $p = .11$ in the sentence below just to provide you with an example of a probability value greater than .05. So for example, we could write something such as the following:

Those who had a smiley face on their checks left a similar tip percentage ($M = 17.74$, $SD = 6.95$) to those who did not have a smiley face on the checks ($M = 15.32$, $SD = 4.43$), $F(1, 128) = 5.64$, $p = .11$, partial $\eta^2 = .05$.

The third question to be addressed in our tipping experiment concerns the interaction between the two independent variables. Did the two independent variables, together, have an effect on the average tip percentage? In other words, we are now asking the question: Is the effect of one of the independent variables the same at different levels of the other independent variable? In this case the ANOVA compared each of the cell means to each other and did not find significant differences. Here is a way to write up this non-significant interaction:

The interaction between writing a thank you message on the check and drawing a smiley face on the check on the average tip percentage was not significant, $F(1, 128) = 2.00$, $p = .16$, partial $\eta^2 = .02$.

Note that the write-up shown immediately above used this pattern: The interaction of *independent*

		Type of Career	
		Low-Status (Receptionist)	High-Status (Manager)
Type of Dress	Sexy	1	2
	Neutral	3	4

FIGURE 9.7 Diagram of Glick et al.'s (2005) 2 × 2 design.

variable A and *independent variable B* on *dependent variable of interest* was not significant. This is a very common way to write up a non-significant interaction.

Now let's discuss further the results we obtained. The main effect of writing on the check was significant. When Liu wrote her thank you message on the check, she received a larger average tip percentage than when she did not. So if you are waiting tables, this result suggests you should write a thank you message on your checks. The main effect of drawing a smiley face on the check was also significant. When Liu drew a smiley face on the check, she received a larger tip percentage than when she did not. This research suggests that you too can enjoy a higher tip percentage if you draw a smiley face on your checks as opposed to not drawing a smiley face. However, note that the interaction of the two variables was not significant. The group that saw a thank you message and a smiley face did tip the largest amount (20.23%); however, that percentage was not significantly higher than that obtained in the other three groups. In other words, there was no added advantage (or disadvantage) of providing *both* a thank you message *and* a smiley face.

Let's look at another example of a factorial design; this time our example will have a significant interaction. While it's often inappropriate and unfortunate, sometimes people come to conclusions based on stereotypes, and this includes stereotypes regarding women. Glick, Larsen, Johnson, and Branstiter (2005) were interested in what people think of sexy women who have low- versus high-status jobs. To investigate this, they had college students provide their perceptions of a female shown in a videotape. Participants were randomly assigned to groups, and before seeing the videotape they first read about the female who had either a low-status job (receptionist) or a high-status job (manager). In the video, the way the female was dressed was varied (sexy or neutral). Thus, Glick et al. conducted a 2 × 2 experiment, diagrammed as shown in Figure 9.7.

Let's concentrate on the results Glick et al. obtained when they asked participants to rate the females with regard to competence. As in the tipping example, we have three questions to address:

1. Did the type of dress have an impact on ratings of competence? (a main effect question)
2. Did the type of career have an impact on ratings of competence? (a main effect question)
3. Did the interaction of the two independent variables have an impact on ratings of competence? (an interaction question)

You are already familiar with what means to compare in this kind of design (row marginal means, column marginal means, cell means) because we went over this information with our tipping design. So let's go right to a discussion of Glick et al.'s results.

Glick et al. used an ANOVA to analyze the results. They found that although the main effect of type of career was not significant (participants rated the receptionist as being as competent as the manager),

FIGURE 9.8 How one is dressed can affect perceptions in some situations! Participants saw a *receptionist* as equally competent no matter how she was dressed (sexy versus neutral), but they saw the *manager* as less competent when she was presented in a sexy manner versus a neutral manner (Glick et al., 2005).

the main effect of type of dress was significant. Specifically, participants saw the female as more competent when she was dressed in a neutral manner than in a sexy manner. This main effect is qualified by the obtained interaction. That is, the means for the interaction revealed that participants saw the *receptionist* as equally competent no matter how she was dressed (sexy versus neutral), but they saw the *manager* as less competent when she was presented in a sexy manner versus a neutral manner.

Figure 9.9 illustrates the interaction obtained by Glick et al. Until now we've been looking at line graphs displaying interactions. I chose to use a bar graph to display their interaction. A bar graph is typically used to display the relationship between categorical variables, while a line graph typically shows the relationship between continuous variables.

Notice that above I said the "main effect is qualified by the obtained interaction." This is an important point. Whenever we have a significant interaction, we must interpret any main effects involving the same factors with the understanding that the

main effects do not tell the whole story. Recall that, for instance, Glick et al. obtained a significant main effect for type of dress in that participants saw the female as more competent when she was dressed in a neutral manner than in a sexy manner. However, the interaction showed that this result held *only* when the participants were rating the manager, *not* when they were rating the receptionist. So when reporting these results, we would say that the main effect of type of dress is *qualified* by the interaction between the type of dress and the type of career.

The moral of Glick et al.'s research is that if a female wants a high-status job she may need to recognize that the way she dresses can have an impact on people's perceptions of her level of competence. However, recognize that this research is potentially limited in its application because the people making the judgments were undergraduates. Business professionals may view people differently, although there is evidence that business professionals do apply stereotypes on the basis of physical attraction (Tews, Stafford, & Zhu, 2009).

Within-Subjects Designs

The experiments discussed above were 2 × 2 between-subjects designs. Of course, you can also conduct an experiment that uses a 2 × 2 within-subjects design. We talked about within-subjects designs in Chapter 8, and what you learned previously about these designs still holds (for example, order effects are potentially a problem). In Chapter 8 our within-subjects designs only had one independent variable. Here we'll talk about a 2 × 2 within-subjects design. So here we have four groups and all the participants are in each and every group. Let's look at an example.

If someone asked you where you were last night, do you think it would take longer for you to respond with a lie or with the truth? Why? These are the

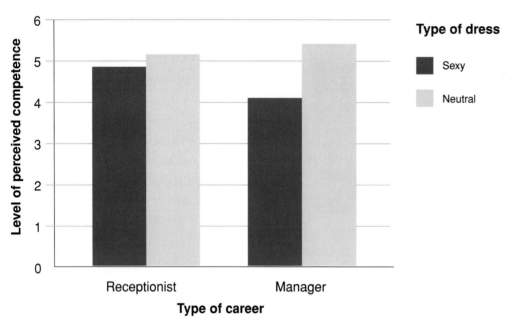

FIGURE 9.9 Glick et al.'s (2005) interaction of type of career and type of dress on competence ratings.

basic questions that interested Williams, Bott, Patrick, and Lewis (2013). Here's what they did in their third experiment. They presented red, green, or blue squares to participants and asked them to name the color. But sometimes Williams et al. told participants to lie and sometimes they told participants to tell the truth. In addition, sometimes participants had to decide which color choice to use as their lie, and sometimes there was only one lie choice. So there were two independent variables: (1) type of response (lie, truth) and (2) number of lie response possibilities (1, 3), and they were both within-subjects variables. In other words, all participants went through each of the four conditions presented in the

design shown in Figure 9.10. The order in which the conditions were presented to each participant was counterbalanced to avoid order effects (as discussed in Chapter 8).

The dependent variable in this experiment was how long it took participants to provide a verbal response. So let's talk about the results. Again, Williams et al. had two independent variables, so they had two main effects to consider. Did the type of response required affect response time? Did the number of possible lie responses affect response time? The answer to both questions was yes. A repeated-measures ANOVA revealed that the type of response had a significant impact on response

		Type of Response	
		Lie	Truth
Number of Lie	1	1	2
Response Possibilities	3	3	4

FIGURE 9.10 Diagram of Williams et al.'s (2013) within-subjects design.

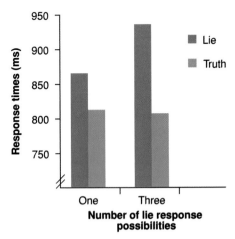

FIGURE 9.11 Bar graph illustrating Williams et al.'s (2013) interaction between the number of lie response possibilities and the type of response on response times.

time; true responses were provided more quickly than lie responses. The number of lie response possibilities also affected response time. When more lie responses were available to participants, they took longer on average to respond.

Williams et al. also needed to assess whether the interaction of their two independent variables was significant. The repeated-measures ANOVA they conducted revealed that the obtained main effects were qualified by a significant interaction. When participants had to lie, they took longer to respond when they had more lie options rather than fewer, but when they had to tell the truth, the number of lie options had no impact on the time needed to respond. You can see this interaction in Figure 9.11.

You can see in Figure 9.11 that there is little difference in the response times for truthful responses (the green bars are basically at the same level). You can also see that there appears to be a difference in the response times for lie responses (see the difference in the heights of the red bars?).

You can sometimes detect the presence of a significant two-way interaction by looking at a bar graph like the one in Figure 9.11 or a line graph. The key

is to check for nonparallel lines. For example, in Figure 9.11, imagine drawing a line to connect the tops of each of the matching bars (connect the two green bars and connect the two red bars). Now look at the lines you have drawn; are these lines parallel to each other or not? If they are parallel, then you do not have a significant interaction. If the lines are not parallel, then you *could* have a significant interaction. The analysis that you compute, in this case an ANOVA, will confirm whether or not your interaction is significant.

Now let's go back to the questions Williams et al. asked. Does it take longer to respond with a lie or with the truth? Williams et al. found that a lie takes longer, and that answer is consistent with what others have found. What about why this happens? The experiment I've discussed here provides one possible answer (they address other possibilities with additional experimentation). When people have more lie options to consider, they have to make a choice, and this requires time.

Possible Outcomes in a 2 × 2 Design

With the above examples, we have reviewed what to consider when you have a 2 × 2 factorial design:

1. Is there a main effect for the first independent variable?
2. Is there a main effect for the second independent variable?
3. Is there an interaction between the two independent variables?

The beauty of the factorial design is its ability to tease apart the separate and combined influences of the independent variables. Remember the tipping experiment? The factorial design allowed us to determine whether it's writing a thank you message on the check, drawing a smiley face on the check, or the combination of those two things that affects tipping percentages.

In the tipping example, we had two main effects and we did not find a significant interaction. In Glick et al.'s example on dress and careers, we had one main effect and a significant interaction. In Williams et al.'s work on lies, we saw two main effects and an interaction. Thus, we've seen three different 2 × 2 designs, each with a different set of outcomes. In fact, there are actually eight possible outcomes in a 2 × 2 design. Let's look at this more closely. For the moment, let's call one independent variable "factor A" and the other independent variable "factor B" in our two-variable design. Using these terms we can list the possible set of results in a 2 × 2 design.

Outcomes without a Significant Interaction. We'll start with the results that do not include a significant interaction. There are four of those (significant findings are in bold):

1. no main effects, no interaction
2. **a main effect for factor A** only, no interaction
3. **a main effect for factor B** only, no interaction
4. **main effects for both factor A and factor B**, no interaction

Think for a moment: Which pattern did we find in the tipping example? Recall that the main effect of writing on the check was significant, and the main effect of drawing a smiley face on the check was also significant. However, the interaction of the two variables was not significant. This corresponds to the fourth option listed above: main effects for both factor A and factor B, and no interaction.

Figure 9.12 shows these four patterns of results with a set of hypothetical data. For this set of hypothetical data, I have pretended to manipulate the presence of exercise (presence, absence) and

breakfast (presence, absence) on a measure of cognitive performance (number of digit combinations correctly detected in an array of numbers). All four patterns in Figure 9.12 represent a 2 × 2 design without a significant interaction.

Let's go over how to read Figure 9.12. The data for each of the four examples are represented in both a table and a line graph (the four cell means for each 2 × 2 are plotted in each line graph). Factor A (exercise/no exercise) is represented along the x-axis (the horizontal axis) in the graph. The legend in the graph indicates the colors used to illustrate factor B (breakfast/no breakfast). The dependent variable is represented on the y-axis (the vertical axis); in this case, the number of correct responses ranges from 0 to 10. The row marginal means reflect the main effect of exercise (factor A shown in red), and the column marginal means reflect the main effect of breakfast (factor B shown in green).

In the summary below, I review each of the outcome patterns shown in Figure 9.12. In addition, I have indicated one possible way to write up each result (each result could be represented in a variety of ways although the general meaning would remain the same).

- Figure 9.12/**Example 1**:
  ○ In this example, the main effect of exercise (exercise/no exercise) was not significant (5 is not significantly different from 5).[2] Those who exercised performed similarly to those who didn't.
  ○ The main effect of breakfast (breakfast/ no breakfast) was not significant (5 is not significantly different from 5). Those who ate breakfast performed similarly to those who didn't.

2 Recognize that numbers can be different values and still be considered as not *significantly* different from each other. The same numerical values are being compared here (5 compared to 5) to make the similarity between the numbers overly obvious.

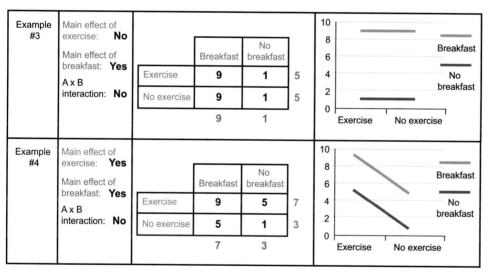

FIGURE 9.12 These four outcome possibilities reflect 2 × 2 designs with no interaction between exercise (variable A) and breakfast (variable B). Dependent variable: cognitive performance (number of digit combinations correctly detected).

- o The interaction was not significant (the cell means were not significantly different from each other).
- o The fact that one line in this graph is directly on top of the other line reflects the overall lack of differences in these findings.
- Figure 9.12/**Example 2:**

- o The main effect of exercise is significant (10 is significantly different from 4). Those who exercised showed a stronger performance than those who didn't.
- o The main effect of breakfast was not significant (7 was not significantly different from 7). Those who ate breakfast

performed as well as those who didn't eat breakfast.

- o The interaction was not significant.
- o The graph of the four cell means reflects the overall pattern of outcomes: Exercise was beneficial over no exercise regardless of whether participants ate breakfast or not.

- Figure 9.12/**Example 3**:
  - o The main effect of exercise is not significant (5 is not significantly different from 5). Those who exercised performed as well as those who didn't exercise.
  - o The main effect of breakfast is significant (9 is significantly different than 1). Those who ate breakfast had a better performance than those who didn't.
  - o The interaction is not significant.
  - o The graph of the four cell means reflects this overall pattern of outcomes: Participants showed better performance when they ate breakfast regardless of whether or not they exercised.

- Figure 9.12/**Example 4**:
  - o The main effect of exercise is significant (7 is significantly different from 3). Those who exercised showed a stronger performance than those who didn't.
  - o The main effect of breakfast is significant (7 is significantly different from 3). Those who ate breakfast showed a stronger performance than those who did not eat breakfast.
  - o The interaction is not significant.
  - o The graph illustrates this overall outcome. Those who exercised showed a stronger performance than those who didn't (the lines are higher on the exercise side of the graph rather than on the non-exercise side) and those who ate breakfast showed stronger performance than those who didn't (the blue "breakfast" line is above the purple "no breakfast" line).

Outcomes with a Significant Interaction. There are also four patterns of outcomes in a 2×2 design that each include a significant interaction. Again I've bolded the significant findings. Here's a list of these outcomes:

1. no main effects, **an interaction only**
2. **a main effect for factor A** only, **an interaction**
3. **a main effect for factor B** only, **an interaction**
4. **main effects for both factor A and factor B**, **an interaction**

Before we go over these outcomes with my hypothetical data, let's talk about what we need to do when we obtain a significant interaction.

When you obtain a significant interaction, you should examine the means that created the interaction as this will help you understand the interaction. One common approach is to conduct a simple main effects analysis (we'll discuss this conceptually – a statistics textbook can provide details on how to conduct the analyses).

A **simple main effect** is the effect of one independent variable at only one level of another independent variable. To conduct a simple main effects analysis for a 2×2 interaction, you would compare the four possible simple main effects. This will allow you to determine which group means differ from each other. Figure 9.13 illustrates the comparisons that need to be made (see the green Xs in the figure) when you have a significant interaction in a 2×2 design.

Now let's think about simple main effects with my hypothetical data. We'll use Example 5 from Figure 9.14 as my hypothetical dataset. When you conduct a simple main effects analysis you would statistically determine which cell means are significantly different from each other. The list below represents the four comparisons I would make if I had a significant interaction in this 2×2 design.

Tests the difference between
A1B1 and A2B1

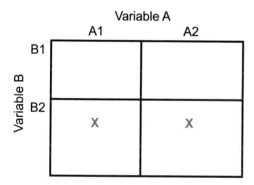

Simple main effect of A at B1:
Do the means for conditions
A1 and A2 differ for those
who received condition B1?

Tests the difference between
A1B1 and A1B2

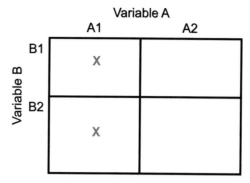

Simple main effect of B at A1:
Do the means for conditions
B1 and B2 differ for those
who received condition A1?

Tests the difference between
A1B2 and A2B2

Simple main effect of A at B2:
Do the means for conditions
A1 and A2 differ for those
who received condition B2?

Tests the difference between
A2B1 and A2B2

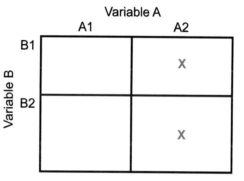

Simple main effect of B at A2:
Do the means for conditions
B1 and B2 differ for those
who received condition A2?

FIGURE 9.13 Illustration of the means to be compared in a simple main effects analysis when you have a significant interaction in a 2 × 2 design.

1. For those who exercised, compare the performance for those who had breakfast (mean = 9) with those who didn't have breakfast (mean = 1).
2. For those who had breakfast, compare the performance for those who exercised (mean = 9) with those who didn't exercise (mean = 1).
3. For those who didn't exercise, compare the performance for those who had breakfast (mean = 1) with those who didn't have breakfast (mean = 9).

227

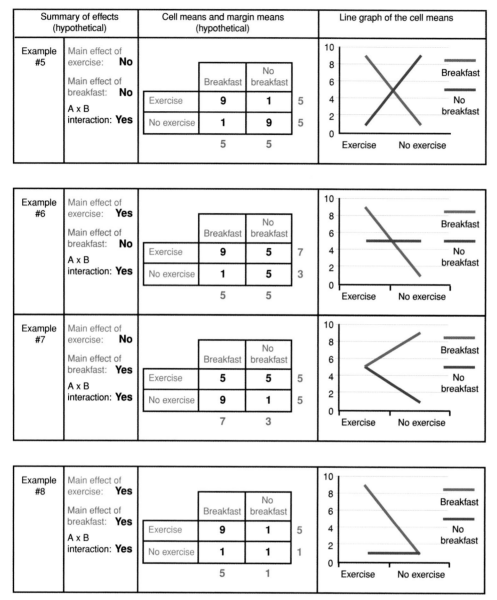

	Summary of effects (hypothetical)		Cell means and margin means (hypothetical)		Line graph of the cell means
Example #5	Main effect of exercise: **No** Main effect of breakfast: **No** A x B interaction: **Yes**		Breakfast / No breakfast / Exercise: 9, 1 → 5 / No exercise: 1, 9 → 5 / margins 5, 5		graph
Example #6	Main effect of exercise: **Yes** Main effect of breakfast: **No** A x B interaction: **Yes**		Breakfast / No breakfast / Exercise: 9, 5 → 7 / No exercise: 1, 5 → 3 / margins 5, 5		graph
Example #7	Main effect of exercise: **No** Main effect of breakfast: **Yes** A x B interaction: **Yes**		Breakfast / No breakfast / Exercise: 5, 5 → 5 / No exercise: 9, 1 → 5 / margins 7, 3		graph
Example #8	Main effect of exercise: **Yes** Main effect of breakfast: **Yes** A x B interaction: **Yes**		Breakfast / No breakfast / Exercise: 9, 1 → 5 / No exercise: 1, 1 → 1 / margins 5, 1		graph

FIGURE 9.14 These four outcome possibilities reflect 2 × 2 designs with an interaction between exercise (variable A) and breakfast (variable B). Dependent variable: cognitive performance (number of digit combinations correctly detected).

4. For those who didn't have breakfast, compare the performance for those who exercised (mean = 1) with those who didn't exercise (mean = 9).

That was a glimpse of the comparisons you need to make when you have a significant interaction in your 2 × 2 design. As I mentioned, and as you see in Figure 9.14, there are four possible outcomes with a significant interaction that can occur in a 2 × 2 design. Since each of these outcomes includes a significant interaction, I will take a moment to remind you that, when you have a significant interaction, you must interpret main effects involving the same factors with the understanding that the main effects do not tell the whole story. In the four examples that include a significant interaction (summarized below), I will point out that any obtained significant main effects are qualified by the obtained interaction. Again, I have indicated one possible way to write up each result.

- Figure 9.14/**Example 5**:
  - There is not a main effect of exercise (5 is not significantly different from 5).
  - There is not a main effect of breakfast (5 is not significantly different from 5).
  - There is an interaction. The graph illustrates this outcome, which is called a **crossover interaction** because the lines in the graph intersect each other. This graph shows that those who exercised did better when they also ate breakfast while those who didn't exercise did better when they didn't eat breakfast.
- Figure 9.14/**Example 6**:
  - There is a main effect of exercise (7 is significantly different from 3). Those who exercised correctly identified more digit combinations than those who didn't exercise.
  - There is not a main effect of breakfast (5 is not significantly different from 5).
  - There is a significant interaction that qualifies the main effect of exercise. As you can see in the graph, for those who didn't eat breakfast, the presence or absence of exercise didn't make a difference. However, for those who ate breakfast, exercise gave participants a cognitive boost.
- Figure 9.14/**Example 7**:
  - There is not a main effect of exercise (5 was not significantly different from 5).
  - There is a main effect of breakfast (7 was significantly different from 3). Those who

ate breakfast correctly detected more digit combinations than those who didn't eat breakfast.
  - A significant interaction qualifies the main effect of breakfast. The graph illustrates this outcome, which we call a **spreading interaction**. The lines are not parallel and they do not cross each other. In this case, exercise led to the same level of performance regardless of whether one ate breakfast or not. However, when one did not exercise, eating breakfast led to stronger performance than not eating breakfast.
- Figure 9.14/**Example 8**:
  - There is a main effect of exercise (5 is significantly different from 1). Participants who exercised detected more digit combinations than those who didn't exercise.
  - There is a main effect of breakfast (5 is significantly different from 1). Participants who ate breakfast detected more digit combinations than those who didn't eat breakfast.

There is an interaction that qualifies the main effects. For those who didn't exercise, the presence or absence of eating breakfast didn't make a difference to participants' cognitive performance. However, for those who exercised, eating breakfast provided a cognitive boost.

As you can see, statistically evaluating the differences between the cell means can provide you with insights regarding your interaction. In addition, visualizing an interaction by graphing it can also help you understand an interaction.

Individual Difference Manipulation

In Chapter 8 I introduced the individual difference manipulation as another way to vary an independent variable. Recall that when an experimenter uses an individual difference manipulation, he or she is

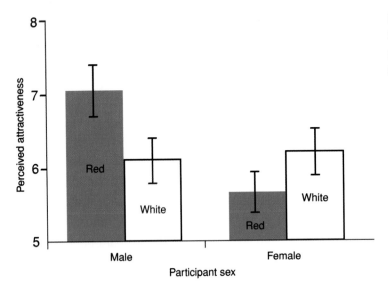

FIGURE 9.15 Elliot and Niesta's (2008) interaction of background color and participant sex on ratings of perceived attractiveness.

putting people into groups not randomly, but based on some personal characteristic such as gender. I mention this again because researchers often use individual difference manipulations in factorial designs. Let's look at an example of a 2 × 2 that incorporates an individual difference manipulation.

Elliot and Niesta (2008) used a series of experiments to investigate the idea that the color red boosts men's attraction to women. In one of these experiments they had male and female undergraduates randomly assigned to view a photo of a woman pictured either on a red background or on a white background. After seeing this photo the participants rated the woman's attractiveness. Thus, this is a 2 × 2 design in which the background color (red, white) and gender of participant (male, female) were manipulated. Elliot and Niesta conducted an ANOVA and determined that there was an interaction between background color and gender of participant. They used planned contrasts (discussed in Chapter 8) to help them interpret the interaction pictured in Figure 9.15.

As you can see in Figure 9.15, males perceived the woman as more attractive when she was photographed against a red rather than a white background.

Females did not rate the woman differently as a function of the background color (Elliot and Niesta's overlapping vertical lines in this part of the graph reveal that this difference was not significant). In addition, when the background was red, males rated the woman as more attractive than females did. When the background was white, there was no difference in ratings between males and females.

Remember that when you are using an individual difference manipulation, your groups are not equivalent. Participants were not randomly assigned to groups, but instead were placed into groups based on gender. Thus, you can't state cause and effect with certainty. As you might recall, experiments with an individual difference manipulation are considered quasi-experiments, a topic we'll discuss further in Chapter 10.

Using a 2 × 3 Design

Thus far in this chapter, we've discussed between-subjects 2 × 2 designs, and a within-subjects 2 × 2 design. They provide good examples for learning the basics. However, factorial designs can easily become more complex than a 2 × 2. For instance, we can increase the number of levels in any of the independent variables. Most published articles do take this more complex approach, utilizing experimental designs that have more than four groups. We'll turn to one of these kinds of designs next. I'll give you a couple of examples from the research literature, and for each we'll discuss how to think about the results conceptually.

We'll start with a 2 × 3 between-subjects design. You can tell from the name that there are two independent variables because there are two numbers present (2 and 3). The first independent variable has 2 levels and the second has 3 levels. You can also tell how many groups the experiment has: 2 × 3 = 6 groups.

The article containing Koernig and Page's (2002) 2 × 3 experiment caught my eye because of the first part of its title: "What if your dentist looked like Tom Cruise?" An interesting question indeed! The impetus for this question came from research on advertising demonstrating that using an attractive spokesperson to advertise a product often enhances consumers' attitudes toward the product. However, researchers have found that this enhancement tends to happen only if the product being endorsed is related to attractiveness. Hair dye is a product related to attractiveness, for instance, while cheese is not. Researchers (such as Kamins, 1990) have called this connection the match-up hypothesis: An attractive spokesperson will enhance a product only when the product has an association with beauty.

Koernig and Page wondered whether the match-up hypothesis applied to the service industry. To address this question, they varied the type of service (related to attractiveness: hairdresser, unrelated to attractiveness: dentist) and the attractiveness of a service provider (low, moderate, high); they randomly assigned their participants to groups. Figure 9.16 shows their 2 × 3 design.

Koernig and Page asked people to make various decisions about the presented service providers, including how much they liked the service provider and how much expertise they perceived the provider to have. Let's briefly review a portion of their results. Koernig and Page had two independent variables so they had two main effects to consider. One main effect concerned the type of service offered (related to attractiveness: hairdresser; unrelated to attractiveness: dentist). Did the type of service have a significant impact on perceived expertise? It didn't; an ANOVA revealed that people generally felt the same way about the dentist versus the hairdresser.

The other main effect asks whether the attractiveness of a service provider (low, moderate, high) had a significant impact on ratings of the service providers' expertise. Using the same ANOVA, Koernig and Page found that differences did exist among the three means; since there are three means to consider for this independent variable, a post-hoc test is needed to determine which means are significantly different from each other (we discussed post-hoc tests in Chapter 8). However, instead of considering where

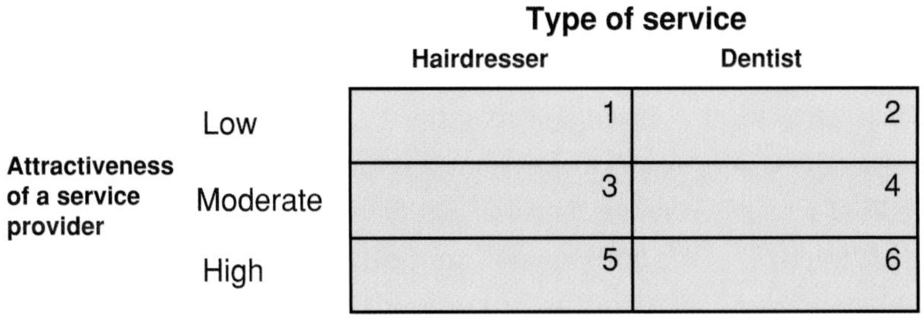

FIGURE 9.16 Diagram of Koernig and Page's (2002) 2 × 3 experiment.

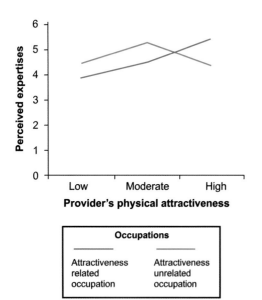

FIGURE 9.17 Line graph illustrating Koernig and Page's (2002) interaction between provider physical attractiveness and type of occupation on perceived expertise ratings.

FIGURE 9.18 Researchers sometimes use a mirror to heighten participants' self-awareness.

the differences are among these three means, I will concentrate, as Koernig and Page did, on the significant interaction that was revealed by the ANOVA, because this qualifies the main effect results. Specifically, when participants were rating the perceived expertise of the hairdresser, higher levels of the attractiveness of the hairdresser led to higher ratings of perceived expertise. On the other hand, when participants were evaluating a dentist (the provider of a service relatively unrelated to attractiveness), it was the moderately attractive provider, not the highly attractive one, who got the highest ratings of perceived expertise. You can see this significant interaction in Figure 9.17.

So it appears from this research that people have expectations for the appearance of their dentists and hairdressers, and that violating these expectations can affect attitudes toward these providers. In other words, if your dentist looks like Tom Cruise (or whomever it is that you find highly attractive), you might decide to seek dental care elsewhere in an effort to obtain what you see to be the highest level of perceived expertise.

We've now considered a 2 × 2 between-subjects design, a 2 × 2 within-subjects design, and a 2 × 3 between-subjects design. The 2 × 3 between-subjects design is commonly found in publications, but the within-subjects version of this design is rare. Thus, I'd like to turn now to an illustration of another commonly used design, the between-subjects 3 × 3.

Using a 3 × 3 Design

Let's talk about a 3 × 3 design. What do we know about this design just by seeing the "3 × 3" name? We know it has two independent variables and they each have 3 levels (there are 2 numbers and they are both 3). We also know the design has 9 groups (3 × 3 = 9). Our example will be a between-subjects design, so you also know there are different people in the different groups.

Psychologists have long been interested in what would make someone more or less likely to help another person. Berkowitz (1987) was interested in how mood and self-awareness would affect participants' likelihood of helping. He used a between-subjects 3 × 3 design in which he varied mood and self-awareness. To vary mood, Berkowitz used a method called the Velten mood induction procedure (Velten, 1968). With this procedure, participants read a series of 50 statements that are increasingly more positive (inducing a positive mood), increasingly more negative (inducing a negative mood), or relatively bland (inducing a neutral mood). A mood questionnaire was used to verify that participants' moods were as intended.

For the self-awareness manipulation, one-third wrote about geography as they faced a mirror (mirror-heightened awareness). One-third wrote about themselves as they faced the back of the mirror (writing-heightened awareness), while one-third wrote about geography as they faced the back of the mirror (low self-awareness). After the participants completed their tasks, the researcher said the experiment was over. Then the experimenter asked for some help adding up scores on data sheets for another study. The number of pages scored was the

dependent variable. So first, let's take a look at a diagram of this design (see Figure 9.19).

We have two independent variables, so we have two main effects to consider. Let's consider the type of mood main effect first. Did the type of mood affect the amount of help provided? Compare the column marginal means in the figure. Berkowitz ran a 3 × 3 ANOVA to make this comparison and determined that the type of mood main effect was significant. In other words, participants' mood had an impact on the number of data sheets they summed. However, since there are three mood means to consider, the ANOVA can't tell the whole story. It reveals only that there are *at least* two means that are significantly different from each other. A post-hoc test is needed to determine which of the relevant means are significantly different from each other. Berkowitz's post-hoc test showed that participants who were feeling positive summed more data sheets than those feeling negative or neutral (8.97 was significantly different from 5.72 and 6.78).

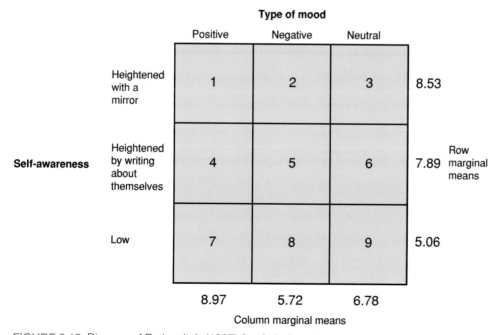

FIGURE 9.19 Diagram of Berkowitz's (1987) 3 × 3 design showing number of data sheets summed (row marginal means and column marginal means).

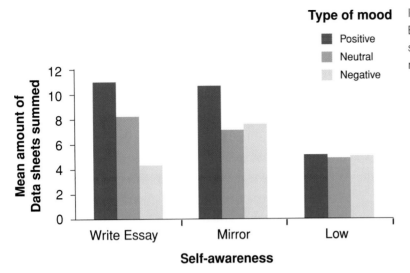

Type of mood
- ■ Positive
- ■ Neutral
- ■ Negative

FIGURE 9.20 A bar graph showing Berkowitz's (1987) interaction between self-awareness and mood on the mean number of data sheets summed.

As for the second main effect in this experiment, the question is whether heightened self-awareness led to more help than a low level of self-awareness. The ANOVA revealed that the awareness manipulation had a significant impact on helping behavior. However, a post-hoc test was needed here too, because there are three means (row marginal means) to compare in this main effect. This post-hoc test revealed that participants whose awareness was heightened by either the mirror or the essay helped more than those experiencing low self-awareness (8.53 and 7.89 were significantly different from 5.06). Both these main effects are qualified by an interaction between type of mood and level of self-awareness.

This interaction is illustrated in Figure 9.20. The means in this case indicate that when self-awareness was low, the type of mood didn't affect the amount of help that was offered; the amount of help offered was minimal no matter what mood was experienced (when self-awareness is low, all the bars in the figure are about the same height). However, when self-awareness was heightened with a writing assignment or a mirror, the experience of a positive versus a negative or neutral mood increased the amount of help the participants provided.

Mixed Designs

Recall our discussion of between-subjects and within-subjects variables. Now that I've reviewed both types of variables, it's time to review an experiment that contains both within- and between-subjects variables. When you do this, you have a **mixed design**. This is, in fact, a common approach. Let's go over an example.

Oh, Chung, and Han (2014) were interested in movie trailers. In recent years, movie trailers have become on-the-web entertainment (people seek out, download, and watch them), and they are sometimes combined with user-control abilities. In this context, user control refers to the "degree to which users can control the flow of information, including the order, path, or process by which users go through the content provided by the media" (p. 82). Oh et al. wondered how the availability of user control (high user control, low user control) would affect how much people become "immersed"

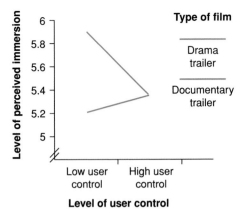

FIGURE 9.21 Oh et al.'s (2014) interaction between user control and content type on ratings of perceived immersion.

(deeply engaged) in the trailers for different types of movies (drama, documentary) (p. 86). The type of movie was manipulated within-subjects, and the user control variable was manipulated between-subjects. What this means is that all participants saw both types of movie trailers, but they had either high or low ability to control the way they went through the content.

What happened? While neither the main effect of user control nor type of film was significant, Oh et al. found that the two independent variables interacted when they considered how immersed people said they were while watching. This significant interaction is depicted in Figure 9.21.

As Oh et al. expected, the participants were more immersed in the trailer when they had less control rather than more, but only when watching the trailer for the drama. When watching a documentary, the amount of user control did not matter. Additional analyses revealed that feeling immersed in the experience was a good predictor of how much participants enjoyed the trailers. So next time you have an opportunity to watch a movie trailer for a drama online, you may wish to stick to those trailers that allow you to be a passive observer as opposed to an active participant. The difference could affect your enjoyment of the experience.

Higher-Order Factorial Designs

Thus far, we've seen a variety of two-factor designs. We can make an experimental design still more complex by including a higher number of independent variables (for example, $2 \times 2 \times 2$), though this also increases the number of groups we need to test. In addition, as the number of independent variables increases, the number and potential complexity of possible interactions between them also increases.

Let's look briefly at an example of a higher-order factorial design.

Have you ever overheard a male in a group make a sexist remark? Let's now say a female in the group responded to that remark. What would you think of that female? Would you like and respect her more if she confronted the male or stayed silent? Well, these are questions that Dodd, Giuliano, Boutell, and Moran (2001) asked. They had male and female participants read a transcript of a conversation between three friends in which one of the two males makes a comment (sexist, ambiguous). The female in the conversation then either ignores the comment or confronts the issue.

If you look carefully at my description of this experiment, you can detect three independent variables, each with two levels: gender of participant (male, female), type of comment (sexist, ambiguous), and type of response to comment (ignore, confront). So this is a $2 \times 2 \times 2$ design, and participants were randomly assigned to one of four groups (the gender variable is an individual difference variable, so assignment to groups for this variable is not random). You can diagram this design as shown in Figure 9.22. Notice that if you do the math indicated

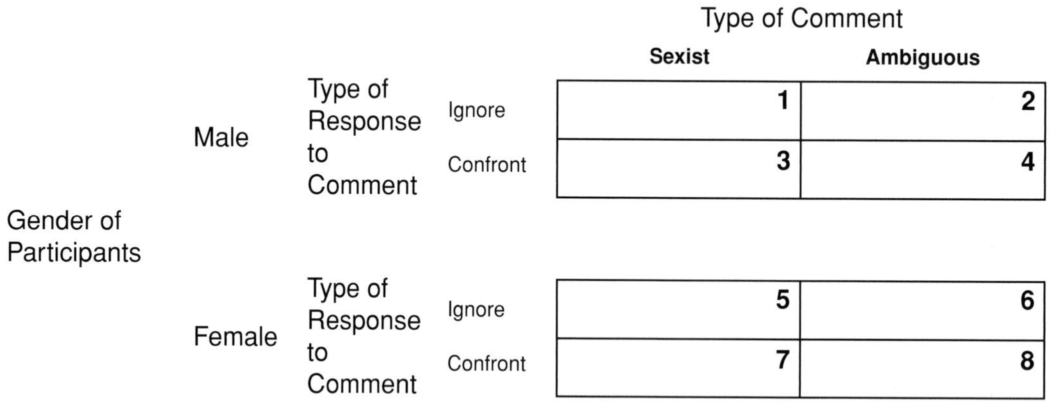

Type of Comment

			Sexist	Ambiguous
Male	Type of Response to Comment	Ignore	1	2
		Confront	3	4
Female	Type of Response to Comment	Ignore	5	6
		Confront	7	8

Gender of Participants

FIGURE 9.22 Diagram of Dodd et al.'s (2001) 2 × 2 × 2 design.

by a 2 × 2 × 2, the result will be the number of cells in the design: 8.

Now let's talk about Dodd et al.'s results conceptually. I'll concentrate on the results with regard to the question of how much participants respected the target woman. Dodd et al. had three independent variables so they have three main effects to investigate. Specifically, one main effect asks the question: Did the gender of the participant (male, female) have a significant impact on how much the participants respected the woman?

A second main effect concerned the type of comment made (sexist, ambiguous). Did the type of comment made have a significant impact on how much the woman was respected?

The third main effect concerned the type of response to the comment (ignore, confront). Did the type of response the woman made to the comment have a significant impact on how much the participants respected the woman?

In addition to the main effects, each of these independent variables can interact with another independent variable in two-way interactions to affect decisions regarding respectability, and they could all interact together in a three-way interaction.

As we discussed previously, statistical analyses will let you know whether you have significant main effects and interactions. Remember that you can sometimes detect a two-way interaction by looking at a bar graph or a line graph. Are the drawn lines parallel to each other? If so, then you do not have a significant interaction. If the lines are not parallel, then you could have a significant interaction.

The same reasoning holds for a line graph. Note that even if your bar graph or line graph suggests that a significant interaction is present, you'll still need to conduct a statistical test (for example, an ANOVA) to know for sure.

You can also examine line graphs for a significant three-way interaction. Having a significant three-way interaction means you have a two-way interaction (non-parallel lines) for one level of the third independent variable, and a differently patterned two-way interaction (or no interaction) for the other level of that variable. Three-way interactions are typically graphed using two different graphs. If the interactions depicted in the two line graphs appear different from each other, you may have a significant three-way interaction. You can learn more about higher-order factorial designs in textbooks that cover statistical methods or advanced research methods.

SUMMARY

A factorial design is an experiment that has more than one independent variable. The independent variables in a factorial design can be between-subjects variables (different people in the different groups), within-subject variables (same people in the different groups), or a combination of between- and within-subject variables (a mixed design). When we have a factorial design, we want to determine the effects of each of the independent variables on the dependent variable – these are main effects. We also want to determine whether the interaction of those independent variables had an impact on the dependent variable. The presence of a significant interaction means that one independent variable changes over the levels of another independent variable. The beauty of the factorial design is its ability to tease apart the separate and combined influences of the independent variables.

The simplest kind of factorial design is a design that has 2 independent variables, each with 2 levels – a 2×2 design. There are eight possible outcomes for a 2×2 design, four with and four without an interaction. When we obtain a significant interaction, we need to interpret the interaction; simple main effects analyses help us do this. Visually depicting an interaction in a line or bar graph also helps one to understand one's results. If the lines in a line graph are parallel, for example, then you do not have a significant interaction. If the lines are not parallel, then you *could* have a significant interaction; a statistical analysis will confirm this.

Many researchers use factorial designs that are more complex than a 2×2. For instance, we can increase the number of levels in any of the independent variables, producing, for example, a 2×3 design or a 3×3 design. We can make an experimental design still more complex by including a higher number of independent variables (for example, a $2 \times 2 \times 2$), though this also increases the number of groups we need to test. In addition, as the number of independent variables increases, the number and potential complexity of possible interactions between them also increases.

GLOSSARY

Cells – the number of groups in a factorial design.

Crossover interaction – a line graph pattern in which the lines of the graph cross each other.

Factor – an independent variable.

Factorial design – an experiment that has more than one independent variable.

Interaction effect (interaction) – a result in a factorial design in which the effect of one independent variable changes over the levels of another independent variable.

Main effect – the effect of one independent variable on a dependent variable in a multi-variable design.

Marginal means – the overall means for each level of one independent variable.

Mixed design – an experiment that contains both within- and between-subjects variables.

Simple main effect – the effect of one independent variable at only one level of another independent variable.

Simple main effects analysis – asks the question: Are the differences between means at one level of the independent variable the same as the differences between means at another level of the independent variable?

Spreading interaction – a pattern of data in a line graph in which the lines are not parallel and they do not cross each other.

REVIEW QUESTIONS

1   Explain the following terminology: factorial design, factor, main effect, interaction.

2 Demonstrate how to diagram a 2 × 2 design.

3 List the three questions that need to be asked when conducting a 2 × 2 design.

4 Explain how column marginal means and row marginal means are relevant to main effects.

5 Differentiate between a 2 × 2 between-subjects design and a 2 × 2 within-subjects design.

6 Explain what it means to say that an interaction "qualifies" a main effect.

7 Describe the eight possible outcomes in a 2 × 2 design.

8 Explain how simple main effects help to explain an interaction.

9 Differentiate between a 2 × 2, a 2 × 3, and a 3 × 3 design.

10 Define a mixed design.

11 Explain what a higher-order factorial design is.

ARTICLES AS ILLUSTRATION

Read one or more of the following articles, and answer the questions that follow.

1 Wang, S. S., Moon, S., Kwon, K. H., Evans, C. A., & Stefanone, M. A. (2009). Face off: Implications of visual cues on initiating friendship on Facebook. *Computers in Human Behavior, 6*, 226–234. doi:http://dx.doi.org/10.1016/j.chb.2009.10.001

2 Guéguen, N. (2015). Women's hairstyle and men's behavior: A field experiment. *Scandinavian Journal of Psychology, 56*, 637–640. doi:http://dx.doi.org/10.1111/sjop.12253

    a. List all of the variables (independent and dependent). Include all levels with your identification of the independent variables.

    b. Were the independent variables between-subjects or within-subjects variables?

    c. Were the variables experimental manipulations or individual difference manipulations?

    d. If the researchers used a manipulation check, indicate what it accomplished.

    e. Summarize the results in your own words (main effects and interactions).

SUGGESTED ACTIVITIES

1 A couple of summaries are presented below. Please answer the questions that follow each summary.

    a. Would you take a drink from a stranger's water bottle? Martin and Leary (1999) asked this very question with their research. They varied whether or not the participants were challenged to drink from the bottle. In addition, the researchers varied what they referred to as "social image-concern" (p. 1092). To create this manipulation, they asked each participant to fill out a personality profile. Then those in the "high image-concern" condition read that they scored as "average" on dimensions of agreeableness and "atypically high" on dimensions such as cautiousness, one who avoids risk. Those in the "low image-concern" condition read that they scored as "average" on all dimensions, thus they were generally well adjusted. With the help of a clever cover story, a confederate offers each participant a drink from his water bottle. Those who were challenged to take a drink drank more of the water than those who were not challenged. In addition, those who were led to believe that they avoid risk (high image-concern) drank more water than those who were in the low image-concern condition.

    b. Harakeh and Vollebergh (2012) had smokers aged 16–24 complete a 30 minute music task with a confederate (the music task was a cover story). During the music task the experimenters varied the number of cigarettes the confederate smokes (none, 3) and the peer pressure condition (confederate offers the participant 3 cigarettes during the half-hour or does not offer any). The experimenters measured the number of cigarettes smoked by the study participants during the music task. Peer pressure did not affect the number of cigarettes smoked, but the presence of a confederate smoking did impact the number of cigarettes smoked by study participants.

  (i)   Name the design.

  (ii) Name the independent variables and their levels.

  (iii) Name the dependent variable.

  (iv) Were these independent variables presented within-subjects or between-subjects?

2 For this activity you will find a primary source journal article in which the authors used a factorial design for their experimentation. You can tell when researchers used a factorial design if they refer to their experimental design using the levels of their independent variables (such as 2 × 3). Diagram the design.

3 Design your own multi-variable experiment! Obtain and read a primary source journal article of interest to you. Then propose a follow-up factorial design. What will you have as your independent variables? What will their levels be? Will your design be between-subjects, within-subjects, or a mixed design? What will your dependent variable measure(s) be? What are your expected results?

4 Consider this list of factorial designs:

  a. 2 × 2
  b. 2 × 2 × 3
  c. 3 × 4
  d. 2 × 2 × 2 × 2
  e. 3 × 3
  f. 3 × 2 × 2

For each of the above designs, indicate the number of independent variables in the experiment, the number of levels of each independent variable, and the number of cells in the experimental design.

REFERENCES

Berkowitz, L. (1987). Mood, self-awareness, and willingness to help. *Journal of Personality and Social Psychology, 52*, 721–729. doi:http://dx.doi.org/10.1037/0022-3514.52.4.721

Dodd, E. H., Giuliano, T. A., Boutell, J. M., & Moran, B. E. (2001). Respected or rejected: Perceptions of women who confront sexist remarks. *Sex Roles, 45*, 567–577. doi:http://dx.doi.org/10.1023/A:1014866915741

Elliot, A. J., & Niesta, D. (2008). Romantic red: Red enhances men's attraction to women. *Journal of Personality and Social Psychology, 95*, 1150–1164. doi:http://dx.doi.org/10.1037/0022-3514.95.5.1150

Glick, P., Larsen, S., Johnson, C., & Branstiter, H. (2005). Evaluations of sexy women in low- and high-status jobs. *Psychology of Women Quarterly, 29*, 389–395. doi:http://dx.doi.org/10.1111/j.1471-6402.2005.00238.x

Guéguen, N., (2015). Women's hairstyle and men's behavior: A field experiment. *Scandinavian Journal of Psychology, 56*, 637–640. doi:http://dx.doi.org/10.1111/sjop.12253

Harakeh, S., & Vollebergh, W. A. M. (2012). The impact of active and passive peer influence on young adult smoking: An experimental study. *Drug and Alcohol Dependence, 121*, 220–223. doi:http://dx.doi.org/10.1016/j.drugalcdep.2011.08.029

Horowitz, J., & Ostrower, J. (2017, April 10). The often-overlooked reason United can kick you off your flight. Retrieved from money.cnn.com/2017/04/10/news/united-overbooking-policy/index.html

Kamins, M. A. (1990). An investigation into the "match-up" hypothesis in celebrity advertising: When beauty may be only skin deep. *Journal of Advertising, 19(1)*,

4–13. doi:http://dx.doi.org/10.1080/00913367.1990.10673175

Keller, P. A., & Block, L. G. (1996). Increasing the persuasiveness of fear appeals: The effect of arousal and elaboration. *Journal of Consumer Research, 22*, 448–459.

Koernig, S. K., & Page, A. L. (2002). What if your dentist looked like Tom Cruise? Applying the match-up hypothesis to a service encounter. *Psychology & Marketing, 19*, 91–110. doi:http://dx.doi.org/10.1002/mar.1003

Martin, K. A., & Leary, M. R. (1999). Would you drink after a stranger? The influence of self-presentational motives on willingness to take a health risk. *Personality and Social Psychology Bulletin, 25*, 1092–1100. doi:http://dx.doi.org/10.1177/01461672992512003

Mukherjee, A., & Dubé, L. (2012). Mixing emotions: The use of humor in fear advertising. *Journal of Consumer Behavior, 11*, 147–161. doi:http://dx.doi/org/10.1002/cb.389

Oh, J., Chung, M., & Han, S. (2014). The more control, the better? The effects of user control on movie trailer immersion and enjoyment. *Journal of Media Psychology, 26*, 81–91. doi:http://dx.doi.org/10.1027/1864-1105/a000114

Shropshire, C., & Channick, R. (2017, April 12). Some United competitors taking jabs at airline, but ridicule is not without risk. Retrieved from www.chicagotribune.com

Tews, M. J., Stafford, K., & Zhu, J. (2009). Beauty revisited: The impact of attractiveness, ability, and personality in the assessment of employment suitability. *International Journal of Selection and Assessment, 17*, 93–100. doi:http://dx.doi.org/10.1111/j.1468-2389.2009.00454.x

Velten, E. (1968). A laboratory task for induction of mood states. *Behaviour Research and Therapy, 6*, 473–482. doi:http://dx.doi.org/10.1016/0005-7967(68)90028-4

Victor, D., & Stevens, M. (2017, April 10). United Airlines passenger is dragged from an overbooked flight. Retrieved from www.nytimes.com

Wang, S. S., Moon, S., Kwon, K. H., Evans, C. A., & Stefanone, M. A. (2009). Face off: Implications of visual cues on initiating friendship on Facebook. *Computers in Human Behavior, 26*, 226–234. doi:http://dx.doi.org/10.1016/j.chb.2009.10.001

Williams, E. J., Bott, L. A., Patrick, J., & Lewis, M. B. (2013). Telling lies: The irrepressible truth? *PLOS ONE, 8*(4), e60713. doi:http://dx.doi.org/10.1371/journal.pone.0060713

10 Quasi-Experimental Designs

LEARNING OBJECTIVES

- Explain when to use a quasi-experimental design.

- Explain how to use an individual difference manipulation in a quasi-experimental design.

- Identify possible threats to internal validity in a quasi-experimental design.

- Explain how internal validity can be threatened in a true experimental design.

Would you be more likely to lie for a friend than a stranger? That was one of the questions asked recently by Marion and Burke (2015). They had pairs of friends and pairs of strangers come to their lab to work on a series of tasks. Shortly after their arrival, the two participants were separated and one was recruited to be a confederate (the other remained naïve to the true purpose of the study). Then the two participants came together to work on a task. The researcher left them alone while they were working, saying she was briefly leaving the building. Before completing the collaborative task, the confederate briefly left the testing room "to use the restroom." The confederate returned and the two participants finished the task.

The researcher returned shortly thereafter and said some money had been taken from an adjoining room. She asked the participants whether they had seen or heard anyone enter that room. As pre-arranged, the confederate claimed they were both in the testing room with the door closed during the entire session. This, of course, was a lie. The

FIGURE 10.1 Money has disappeared and you know that the person you are with (either a friend or a stranger) had an opportunity to take it. When questioned will you reveal your knowledge of this opportunity or lie? Marion and Burke (2015) found that those who were friends with the suspect were significantly more likely to lie than those who were not.

confederate had left the room. Each naïve participant was later questioned separately about whether they had both been in the room the whole time. The question of interest was: Would naïve participants be equally likely to lie for a friend as for a stranger? Would the naïve participant say the other participant had never left the room?

Marion and Burke found that those who were friends with the confederate were significantly more likely to lie (41%) than those who were not (18%). They cannot conclude that the reason for this result was solely friendship however. As Marion and Burke acknowledge, what is missing from their design is random assignment to groups. They chose to work with students who were *already* friends and with students who had never met. They did not randomly assign people to groups and say, "Forget whether you know each other or not; for the purpose of this research, you will be friends" or "you will be strangers." The independent variable of relationship (friends, strangers) was out of the researchers' control. Thus, Marion and Burke needed to use a

quasi-experimental design. Since the groups are not considered equivalent, something inherently different about the groups (beyond the independent variable) could be responsible for the results.

In this chapter, we'll first discuss further what a quasi-experimental design is. Then we'll cover different types of quasi-experimental designs. Finally we'll discuss the different reasons why quasi-experimental designs cannot allow us to state cause and effect with certainty.

What Is a Quasi-Experimental Design?

You may recall from Chapter 8 that in order to establish cause and effect when conducting an experiment, you need at least two groups and the groups have to be equivalent. There are two ways to violate these requirements: (1) You can have fewer than two groups and (2) you can have at least two groups but the groups are not equivalent. Quasi-experimental designs commit these violations. Some have only one group of participants, and some have more than one group but the groups are not equivalent. In all cases these quasi-experimental designs *resemble* true experimental designs (in fact, "quasi" means "resembling"); both true and quasi-experimental designs have independent and dependent variables. However, all quasi-experimental designs violate the requirement of having two or more equivalent groups; thus our ability to establish cause and effect is definitively diminished.

Why use quasi-experimental designs at all if we can't use them to establish cause and effect? Well, as you'll see, sometimes putting together a true experiment with equivalent groups just isn't possible. Researchers sometimes do not have a reasonable control group available and thus can test only one group of participants. In other cases, they can create multiple groups, but random assignment to those groups is not possible and they test preformed groups. As you can see, there are two main categories of quasi-experimental designs: (1) those without a control group and (2) those with nonequivalent groups. In the next section we look more closely at these two major categories of quasi-experimental designs by examining different types within them. Note that for the research designs covered in this chapter, the terms "treatment" and "intervention" are synonymous with the term "independent variables."

Quasi-Experimental Designs without a Control Group

First we'll discuss quasi-experimental designs that do not have a control group. As you'll see, despite the differences in these designs, they share a feature: they do not allow us to make causal claims with certainty.

One-Group Posttest-Only Design. The first type of quasi-experimental design we'll discuss is the **one-group posttest-only design**. The name indicates that this design has only one group and only a posttest. In other words, the group will be tested once (that's the dependent variable) and this test will occur only after the treatment has occurred. This design is diagrammed as shown in Figure 10.2. Note that in this and all subsequent diagrams in this chapter, x = the treatment (think of this as similar to an independent variable condition) and O = observation (the dependent variable). Thus O1 = the first observation or posttest.

The one-group posttest-only design is not a popular design because of its limitations. Whenever

FIGURE 10.2 Diagram of a one-group posttest-only design. X = treatment and O = observation.

you hear the term "one group," you know something vital is missing from the design – a comparison group. Without a group to compare to, you have no ability to discern whether your "independent variable" affected the results. I put quotation marks around the term independent variable for a reason. Recall the meaning of independent variable; it's a variable you manipulate or vary between groups. But if you have only one group, you are not varying anything. Let's look at an example.

Morgan (2001) used a one group posttest-only design to assess the potential benefits of educating military personnel about the hazards of tobacco use (smoking, chewing tobacco). She provided a one-hour presentation on the dangers of using tobacco, and a month later she gave participants a post-intervention survey; 40% of the original sample responded, and 80% indicated an intention to quit tobacco use.

Morgan acknowledged that her one group posttest-only design had limitations. Specifically, without an equivalent control group, we cannot say definitively that the presentation regarding the hazards of tobacco use caused Morgan's results. Quite simply, it is possible that similar results could have been obtained in the absence of the tobacco hazard education.

A **one-group pretest–posttest design** can be considered a slight improvement over a one-group posttest-only design. In the one-group pretest–posttest design, we measure the dependent variable twice, once before and once after a treatment occurs. Thus, we can determine how people were doing with regard to the dependent variable before the treatment was provided and establish whether they have shown any change from pretest to posttest (that's why it's an improvement over the one-group pretest–posttest design). However we cannot know with certainty what is responsible for that change. This design is shown in Figure 10.3.

FIGURE 10.3 Diagram of a one-group pretest–posttest design. X = treatment and O = observation.

Here's an example. Carney, McGehee, Lee, Reyes, and Raby (2010) used a one-group pretest–posttest design to investigate whether providing video feedback could reduce the number of driving errors made by newly licensed adolescent drivers. The researchers first collected pretest data for a six-week period. Carney et al. consider this period their first observation, O1, recording the number of driving errors and related information such as proper seat belt use. Then the researchers provided a 40-week intervention. Participants were given both immediate and delayed feedback on any driving error or safety violation they committed, such as braking abruptly. The immediate feedback was a light blinking on the dashboard, and the delayed feedback was a written report and a DVD showing the errors. Both forms of delayed feedback were mailed to the driver's parents, who were asked to review the errors with the drivers.

FIGURE 10.4 Carney et al. (2010) used a one-group pretest–posttest design to investigate whether providing video feedback could reduce the number of driving errors made by newly licensed adolescent drivers.

The 40-week intervention was followed by a six-week period in which errors were assessed without intervention; this was the second observation period, O2. The dependent variable in both cases was the number of driving errors per 1,000 miles driven. The number was highest during the pretest, decreased during the intervention, and did not significantly increase during the posttest.

Carney et al.'s analyses suggests that the intervention may have had an impact (there were fewer driving errors during and after intervention than before). That is one possible explanation for the results; however, it is not possible to determine definitively whether the intervention was responsible for the drop in driving errors. The biggest problem here, as the researchers acknowledged, was the absence of a control group. It's possible these new drivers would have become better drivers and made fewer errors without the intervention. Without having an equivalent control group, we cannot know with certainty what's responsible for these results.

Simple Interrupted Time Series Design. The **simple interrupted time series design** is a quasi-experimental design in which the dependent variable is repeatedly measured before and after a treatment. The design can be diagrammed, as shown in Figure 10.5. This design is an improvement over the one-group pretest–posttest design described above in that the repeated observations we make allow us to see how much fluctuation there is in participants' responses. (Recall that the one-group pretest–posttest design has only one pretest and one posttest measure.) We'll look at an example of an interrupted time series design in a moment, but first, let's reminisce.

Are you familiar with the *Teenage Mutant Ninja Turtles*? It's a pretty brutal example of children's media (television, movies), and I have found

FIGURE 10.5 Diagram of a simple interrupted time series design. X = treatment and O = observation.

myself wondering whether watching these ninjas fight would somehow affect viewers. Perhaps Hawton et al. (1999) had a similar thought. They used an interrupted time series design to investigate whether seeing a drug overdose on a television hospital drama had an impact on viewers (see Figure 10.6 for a description of the hospital episode in question). Hawton et al. tabulated the number and type of overdose cases brought to area hospitals for three weeks before and three weeks after the televised showing. They found 17% more overdoses in the first week after the broadcast, and 9% more in the second week (in the third week overdoses were equivalent to pre-broadcast rates). In the two weeks after the broadcast there was also an increase in overdoses using the same drug compound as shown in the broadcast.

You might reasonably ask whether those who overdosed had actually seen the televised overdose. Only 24% of the 4,403 overdose patients answered a questionnaire, and only 3% of those who overdosed in the first week reported seeing the episode. Of these, 15% indicated that the episode influenced their decision to overdose, while another 15% indicated that the episode influenced their drug choice. On the other hand, some had reported deliberately avoiding the drug used in the TV program because liver damage was portrayed as a possible lasting effect of such an overdose. An additional 10% indicated that what they had seen on the episode influenced the speed with which they sought help after their overdose.

So can Hawton et al. claim that the broadcast of interest caused the overall increase in observed overdoses? The questions the study participants answered suggest that the broadcast did lead a few to overdose, but remember that, since this design does not have an equivalent control group, we have to acknowledge that there could be other possible reasons for the observed increase in overdoses. Perhaps something else occurred during the time frame of interest that influenced the likelihood of overdoses in the area. Without a similar control group potentially affected by the same influences, we cannot conclude definitively that only the independent variable affected the participants.

Depiction of Paracetamol Overdose in Episode of *Casualty*

The overdose storyline involved an RAF pilot in his 30s who have having difficulty returning to work after the aircraft he was flying accidentally crashed, killing a colleague. His sense of guilt and fear that he might have epilepsy led to excessive drinking and marital conflict. He was taken to the accident and emergency department after collapsing, and, after a dramatic scene in which he vomited blood, it was discovered that his blood levels of paracetamol were high. Two nurses were shown urgently questioning him about a possible overdose, and when he admitted to taking about 50 paracetamol over two days earlier they looked very concerned. The dialogue emphasised the danger:
Nurse: "You should have come in earlier. Paracetamol just keeps on working, steadily destroying the liver."
Patient's wife: "What are you saying? It's too late?"
The message was repeated in the final scene of the story:
Doctor: "Your husband is suffering from severe liver damage caused by the paracetamol. It's disturbing his blood's ability to clot. We've got to transfer him to a specialist unit now...It doesn't look very good."

FIGURE 10.6 Description of the hospital episode used by Hawton et al. (1999).

Quasi-Experimental Designs with a Nonequivalent Control Group

Now we'll turn to a discussion of the quasi-experimental designs that incorporate a control group. Again, recognize that all these designs have nonequivalent groups. You'll see as we go along why random assignment is not possible in these cases.

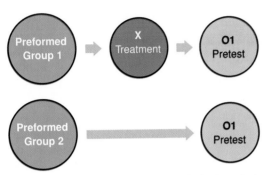

FIGURE 10.7 Diagram of a nonequivalent control group posttest-only design.

Nonequivalent Control Group Posttest-Only Design. The **nonequivalent control group posttest-only design** does incorporate a control group, but that control group is not equivalent to the experimental group (there is no random assignment). In addition, the dependent variable is assessed only once, after the treatment. This design can be diagrammed as shown in Figure 10.7.

Let's look at an example.

If you are like many psychology majors, you will probably enroll for a course on abnormal psychology during your college career. In this course, you'll learn about various psychological disorders, including how to determine whether someone has a particular disorder. Rahman and Zeglin (2014) were interested in whether students would benefit from using comic book characters when assessing and diagnosing psychological disorders. (As you may recall, Bruce Wayne, who became Batman, was no more than 10 when he saw both his parents murdered. Did witnessing such a scene leave a psychological mark on this young boy?)

In an effort to determine whether analyzing comic book characters would be an effective way to master the material (as compared to lecture only), Rahman and Zeglin tested undergraduates enrolled in two sections of an abnormal psychology course. Both sections received the standard lecture on how to diagnose various psychological disorders. However,

FIGURE 10.8 Did early childhood trauma affect Batman?

students in one of the sections were told to select a graphic novel and diagnose a character from it. The other section was the control group. Thus, diagnosis of a comic book character (present, absent) was the independent variable. However, note that the groups were not equivalent. The researchers had no control over who was in which section of the course; students decided that for themselves. These students were in preformed groups.

Both sections of the course were later given a quiz testing their knowledge of diagnosing psychological disorders. Their quiz score was the dependent variable. What did Rahman and Zeglin find? Those who had diagnosed the comic book character performed significantly better on the quiz than those who had not. Can we then conclude that the comic book activity caused the better quiz outcome? Not necessarily. The groups were not known to be equivalent at the start; thus we cannot say definitively that the independent variable (the presence/absence of the comic book activity) was the cause of the difference in quiz scores. Perhaps there was something inherently different about the students in the two sections. Maybe one section took place in the morning, and maybe those who decide to take morning classes are more conscientious students. This is just one possibility. It may be that the two sections are different in other ways; just the fact that they are not equivalent means that we are unable to establish cause and effect.

Nonequivalent Control Group Pretest–Posttest Design. In the **nonequivalent control group pretest–posttest design**, as the name suggests, pre- and posttest scores are obtained for a treatment group and for a control group, but again the groups are not equivalent. This design can be represented as shown in Figure 10.9.

As we saw with the one group pretest–posttest design, adding a pretest does give us the advantage of knowing how our groups perform before any treatment is provided. So even though they are not theoretically equivalent in every way (as they would be if we randomly assigned participants to groups), we can know whether the groups are equivalent on the response measure of interest. Let's look at an example.

Workman, Bloland, Grafton, and Kester (1986–1987) used a nonequivalent control group pretest–

posttest design to investigate the effects of assertiveness training on various indices such as the levels of assertiveness, anxiety, and self-concept in female community college students. The students themselves decided which group they wanted to be part of: an assertiveness training group or a discussion group (the control group). Pretests assessing assertiveness and related characteristics occurred during the first meeting. Meetings were then held once a week for nine weeks; posttests were given in the ninth week (Workman et al. modified the noted design slightly by also using posttests after 18 weeks to establish whether any changes had been maintained after the training ended).

Workman et al. did not find any differences between the two groups on the pretests. So the groups had been determined to be the same on the dependent variables prior to any intervention. There were, however, differences on the posttests. Those in the assertiveness training group showed more assertiveness, a stronger self-concept, and less anxiety than the discussion group, and these changes persisted over the 18 weeks.

As suggested above, we cannot know that the assertiveness training is what caused the differences between the two groups in Workman et al.'s research. Because the students themselves chose which group they wanted to be a part of, there may have been inherent differences between the students in the two groups beyond what was assessed. For example,

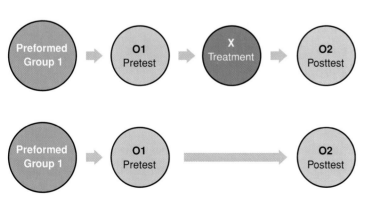

FIGURE 10.9 Diagram of a nonequivalent control group pretest–posttest design. X = treatment and O = observation.

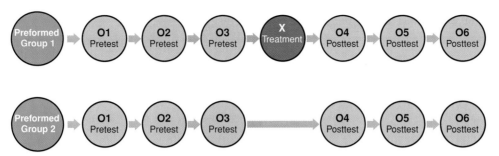

FIGURE 10.10 Diagram of an interrupted time-series design with a nonequivalent control group. X = treatment and O = observation.

those who signed up for assertiveness training may have been very motivated to change their level of assertiveness, and that heightened level of motivation may have been what was driving the results. In fact, Workman et al. acknowledge that students in the assertiveness training group may have specifically worked to fulfill the experimenters' expectations (recall that the goal of the study was known to the participants).

Interrupted Time-Series Design with a Nonequivalent Control Group. In an **interrupted time-series design with a nonequivalent control group**, a series of pre- and posttest scores are obtained for an experimental and a nonequivalent control group. This design can be diagrammed as shown in Figure 10.10.

Vingilis et al. (2005) used this design to investigate the possibility that extended drinking hours in Ontario, Canada affected motor vehicle fatalities in which the driver had a positive blood alcohol concentration (BAC) reading. More specifically, in May 1996, the Canadian Liquor License Act approved a change in closing times for drinking establishments in Ontario; they were now able to close at 2 a.m. nightly instead of 1 a.m. A quasi-experimental design is ideal for evaluating the potential impact of this Act, because the shift was not under the control of the experimenters but was a policy change

made by government authorities. Vingilis et al. used a quasi-experimental design to compare the number of BAC-positive motor vehicle fatalities in Ontario and in two neighboring US states used as control populations for a period before and after the change in closing times, for a total of 84 monthly observations between 1992 and 1998. In other words, Vingilis et al. used a slight modification of the design shown in Figure 10.10 in that they used a series of pre- and posttest scores for an experimental and *two* nonequivalent control groups.

FIGURE 10.11 Vingilis et al. (2005) used an interrupted time-series design with two nonequivalent control groups to investigate the possibility that extended drinking hours in bars in Ontario, Canada affected motor vehicle fatalities in which the driver had a positive blood alcohol concentration reading.

Did Vingilis et al. find an increase in the number of BAC-positive motor vehicle fatalities in Ontario after May 1996? They did not. In fact, they found that the control states had lower BAC rates and more motor vehicle fatalities, which led them to speculate that these states may not have been good choices for control groups. The researchers propose a number of possible reasons for the lack of increase. Certainly, it could be that extending alcohol availability for just an hour a night is not enough to make an impact. The researchers also note that while the Liquor License Act approved a change in closing times, not all establishments complied; thus the availability of alcohol may not have substantially changed. In addition, other policy changes that took place within the same time span may have affected the results. For example, in November 1996, Ontario instituted a 90-day driver's license suspension for those caught driving under the influence. The quasi-experimental nature of this work does not allow the researchers to know which if any of these and/or other changes had an impact on their results.

More on Testing Preformed Groups

Each of the nonequivalent control group designs we've discussed above tested participants who were assigned to groups without random assignment. Instead, the groups were preformed. For example, Rahman and Zeglin compared the quiz scores of two different sections of an abnormal psych class. Students themselves decided which class section they would be a part of; the researchers did not randomly assign the students to sections. We are now going to discuss cases in which study participants are assigned to groups based on their own individual characteristics. Putting people into groups as a function of their own characteristics is a relatively common research strategy. We'll refer to it as using an

individual difference manipulation (you may recall that the individual difference manipulation was discussed in Chapter 8).

Designs Using an Individual Difference Manipulation

When a researcher uses an individual difference manipulation, he or she is not putting people into groups randomly but instead is grouping them based on some personal characteristic they possess like gender, sexual orientation, religion, education level, shyness level, self-esteem level, or a diagnosis (such as schizophrenia). For example, I can put people in groups based on a mental health diagnosis, but I can't experimentally manipulate these characteristics and say, "For the purpose of this experiment, you will be schizophrenic." The researcher has no control over whether someone is schizophrenic or not.

Let's take a look at an example. McGuirk and Pettijohn (2008) were interested in the relationship between birth order and attitudes toward romantic relationships. They wondered whether, for example, being a jealous middle child might potentially lead to jealousy in later romantic relationships. So birth order was McGuirk and Pettijohn's individual difference manipulation. The college students in their sample were assigned to groups not randomly but based on their birth order (oldest, middle, youngest, or only children). They found that middle children did report more jealousy in their romantic relationships than those born first. Could they conclude that the jealousy middle children experienced early in life led to more jealousy in their later relationships? No, because those who differ with regard to birth order potentially differ on many other characteristics as well. So, as with all quasi-experimental research, there could be something other than the independent variable that influenced the later relationships of these individuals.

Designs Using Age as an Individual Difference Manipulation

One individual difference manipulation, age, deserves a special mention because it is so frequently used. Researchers sometimes want to see how people change over time, but of course they cannot randomly assign people to be a certain age. However, they can put people in groups based on their age. There are two general ways to do this.

When researchers use a **longitudinal design**, they study a single group of participants over a long period of time, sometimes years or decades (for instance, Mischel et al., 2011). Because this textbook focuses on research pertinent to college students' lives, we'll look at a longitudinal research example relevant to that general population.

Galambos, Vargas Lascano, Howard, and Maggs (2013) tracked the sleep experiences of a sample of students over the course of four years of college. Beyond considering information such as sleep quantity, Galambos et al. also considered how sleep varied with variables such as stress and academic performance. Males were sleeping more than females when they started college, but by the end of the four years females were sleeping more than males. In addition, as the years went by, students slept later in the morning. Perhaps those who had earned more credits were increasingly able to be first in line to register for courses that met later in the day.

What about the interplay of sleep and stress? You will probably not be surprised to learn that students slept better when their stress levels were lower and when they had a stronger support system. As for the relationship between academic performance and sleep, grade point averages did tend to be higher when students went to bed earlier. As in all quasi-experimental designs, we cannot definitively establish a cause and effect relationship. So we can't know for sure that going to bed earlier causes higher grades. It is one possibility, but there are other explanations.

For example, those who are better performers academically might just prefer earlier bedtimes.

Longitudinal designs are a good way to study changes that occur as people age. However, since they tend to require so much time to conduct (4 years in Galambos et al.'s example), researchers sometimes use a cross-sectional design as an alternative. Instead of testing the same people year after year as they do with longitudinal designs, researchers using **cross-sectional designs** test people of different ages, and they test each age group only once. Here is an example.

Hookah use, also known as water pipe smoking, is an experience in which users inhale tobacco smoke and charcoal fumes, often with others inhaling from the same pipe. Braun, Glassman, Wohlwend, Whewell, and Reindl (2012) were interested in investigating hookah use for college students, and they chose a cross-sectional design to do it. They sent a survey to a randomly selected sample of students. Thirty percent of those who responded were first-year students, 23% were sophomores, 24% were juniors, and 23% were seniors. (Do not confuse random selection and random assignment. These students were randomly *selected* from the entire student population at one university. They were not randomly *assigned* to be first years, sophomores, and so on, so this still qualifies as a quasi-experimental design.)

Fifteen percent had smoked hookah at least once; only 6% of those sampled had smoked hookah in the 30 days prior to answering the questionnaire. Of those who smoked, 42% smoked at least once a month, usually with friends. Braun et al. also questioned the participants about their perceptions of risks associated with hookah use. The students underestimated the health risks of hookah use (respiratory effects and cancer – Centers for Disease Control and Prevention, 2016). Interestingly, 98% believed they could quit hookah use at any time; they did not recognize that smoking hookah is addictive. The researchers also found a relationship between hookah use and other high-risk behaviors such as tobacco use, marijuana use, and binge drinking. For example, those who smoked cigarettes or marijuana were more likely to smoke hookah.

The experiences of college students give us a great illustration of an advantage of using a cross-sectional design. You can use a longitudinal design and spend 4 years following the same students, or you can use a cross-sectional design and just give one test to students who are at different points in their college careers. A cross-sectional design saves time and money.

There are disadvantages to using the cross-sectional approach, especially in research that spans long time periods. The concern here is that people who are of different ages can also be of different generations, or **cohorts**, and thus differ in their attitudes and experiences. For instance, most of today's students have probably known since they were young how to communicate with each other by texting, snapchatting, and instagramming. However, those who were born much earlier didn't grow up with those same types of experiences. How might this difference affect the participants, and would it affect research results? Researchers who conduct cross-sectional research with large age gaps need to be aware of possible cohort effects.

Possible Threats to Internal Validity

Now we're going to discuss the possible threats to internal validity that can occur when you do not have a true research design (at least two equivalent groups). Recall that when you can confidently state that your independent variable caused the difference observed in your dependent variable, your experiment is said to have high internal validity. Quasi-experimental designs do not allow us to state

definitively that the independent variable caused the change in the dependent variable, so in these designs, internal validity is compromised.

Five of the threats we'll discuss below (maturation, history, instrumentation, regression toward the mean, and attrition) are possible threats to internal validity in one-group designs and in designs that incorporate more than one group. The sixth threat, selection, is a threat to internal validity *only* when you have more than one group and the groups are not equivalent (random assignment was not used). For each threat, we'll discuss what researchers can do to recognize and/or eliminate it.

Maturation

Maturation refers to changes (developmental, physical, psychological) in your participants over time. For example, maturation could have been the reason Carney et al. saw changes in the number of driving errors their adolescent participants made in the year they were studied. Maybe the adolescents matured over the course of the study, leading them to make better decisions, and that's why their driving improved.

In fact maturation can come up as a threat to internal validity any time you are conducting a study of a relatively long duration. Take the work of Cornell, Callahan, and Loyd (1991). They conducted a study of females who had entered college early and enrolled in an accelerated residential program. Cornell et al. assessed the personality of these females at the beginning and at the end of their first year in college. Any changes over this year could reasonably be due to the residential program or to the students' natural maturation over the course of the year (or even to other unnamed variables). Cornell et al. anticipated maturation as a threat to internal validity; thus they had a control group. They compared the results of their experimental group to those of a group of intellectually similar students who were still in high school. Those in the residential program (the experimental group) showed more changes in psychological growth than those who remained in high school. With the addition of this control group, Cornell et al. eliminated maturation as a viable reason for the observed differences in those having the college experience (because both groups were expected to mature at the same rate). However, the lack of random assignment meant there were potentially other factors that were different between the two groups that could be responsible for the observed changes in psychological growth.

History

When a study includes a pretest and at least one posttest, other events outside your intended manipulation(s) can occur between tests that can affect your results. When this happens, a **history effect** is the culprit. Carney et al.'s work with adolescent drivers again gives us an illustration of history as a possible reason for results. Can you conclude that the monitoring and feedback intervention Carney et al. used caused these new drivers to improve? Not necessarily, because other things going on outside the intervention could have affected people's driving skills. Maybe people in the town knew someone who had just experienced a dangerous car accident. Perhaps the Students Against Drunk Driving chapter in the community had just created a mock car crash scene at the local high school. If you are testing only one group, you will never know definitely what is responsible for any changes seen.

To eliminate history as a threat to your internal validity, you need to have a control group of similar participants in your study. Ideally, of course, you would want to randomly assign participants to groups, but when that is not possible, having a control group as similar as possible to your experimental study participants can help you to eliminate history as a reason for your results. If you do this, both

groups are equally likely to experience history, and history is eliminated as a possible threat to internal validity.

Instrumentation

If changes occur in the instruments you use to measure participants' performance, you have a threat to validity known as **instrumentation**. This could mean that something went wrong with the equipment you are using (for example, a computer malfunctions). Sometimes it means that those measuring performance are, over time, changing how they measure performance. Perhaps they are getting better because of practice, or they are getting worse because of fatigue. Ideally, you want the measurement of performance to be consistently accurate. In an effort to avoid instrumentation as a threat to your internal validity, you should include a control group in your research study. If the groups are similar to each other, then both are similarly likely to experience instrumentation, and instrumentation potentially can be eliminated as a possible threat to internal validity.

Regression toward the Mean

Regression toward the mean is a potential threat to internal validity if you are using a design that includes multiple observations (as quasi-experimental designs often do), and the measures for your initial observations are extremely high or low. More specifically, when performance on an earlier test is extreme (either extremely good or extremely poor), the next time the test is taken, the score is likely to be less extreme and therefore closer to the mean (the average performance of the group).

Suppose you take the Scholastic Aptitude Test (SAT) and get an extremely high score or extremely low score. If you take the test again, chances are you will get a score slightly closer to the mean SAT score for the overall population of SAT test takers. That is regression toward the mean.

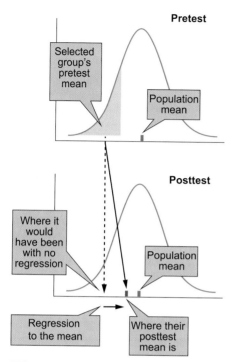

FIGURE 10.12 Regression toward the mean.

Why does regression toward the mean occur? The reason is that the measures themselves are not perfectly reliable. A perfectly reliable test would give you the same result every time you take it, revealing exactly what you know. But tests are not just a reflection of what you know. Your score also reflects how you feel – tired, anxious, hungry, inattentive. An extremely high score means it was likely that everything was going your way; you weren't tired or inattentive, overly anxious, or hungry. What's the likelihood that all these factors would be on your side when you take the test a second time? Any deviation from this ideal set of influences would likely yield a lower score. The same applies to an extremely low score. Say you took the SAT after partying late the night before, and then you forgot to eat breakfast before beginning the test, and – you know where this is going. That score is not likely to be your best performance. But the next time you take it, you'll likely learn from your earlier experience. This time, there won't be any partying the

night before, and you'll make sure to have a hearty, healthy breakfast before the day begins. So you're likely to do better and get a score that is closer to the mean score.

Regression toward the mean may play a role when researchers select their study participants *because* their scores on a variable of interest are extreme. Baseball's "sophomore slump" provides us with a good illustration. The sophomore slump is a large decline in performance during a baseball player's second year after an outstanding first season. To study it, researchers consider the records of players who had an extreme score in their first year in terms of batting, pitching, and so on. Among a variety of reasons offered for the second-year slump is regression toward the mean (see Taylor & Cuave, 1994).

The bottom line is that whenever a sample of participants undergoes repeated testing, initially achieving extreme scores and later achieving scores closer to the mean, the reason could be your intervention or it could just be regression toward the mean. Again, as with the other threats to internal validity, including a similar control group in your research study can potentially eliminate regression toward the mean as a possible threat to internal validity.

Attrition

Attrition, also known as **mortality**, refers to a loss of participants in your research study. The problem here is that those who remain may somehow be different from those who dropped out, and this difference may be affecting your results. Let's look at an example.

Wong et al. (2012) implemented and evaluated the benefits of a school-based program designed to help alleviate depression in adolescents. Thirteen classes across four schools were assigned to either an experimental group (those who participated in the depression reduction program) or a control group (those who were on the waiting list). School administrators made the class assignments, so participants were not assigned to groups randomly. Professionals (two social workers and a clinical psychologist) led approximately half the classes through the program, while the other half were led by teachers. Overall, the program did not appear to be effective in reducing the symptoms of depression in the targeted adolescents. Wong et al. note that one possible reason for the failure of the intervention was the high and variable attrition rates in the various groups. In some cases, those who dropped out were merely absent from school; in other cases, attrition was the result of an inability to match up individuals' pre-and posttest results (students were given code numbers to use instead of their names and these numbers were sometimes copied incorrectly). Whatever the reason for the attrition, we must ask whether those who dropped out were somehow different from those who stayed. If those who left had instead stayed, the overall results could have been different.

Whenever you experience the loss of participants from your groups, especially if you experience a differential loss (a loss of different amounts in the different groups), you need to take a serious look at what may be causing those participants to drop out, and consider how your results may be affected by the loss. If you do not lose participants, you can rule attrition out as a potential threat to the internal validity of your work.

As you can well imagine, attrition is often a concern when researchers are conducting longitudinal research. Following study participants over the course of many years can become difficult, because people sometimes move without leaving a forwarding address, or they lose interest in the research project, or they die. Researchers who conduct longitudinal work expend a lot of effort on trying to keep the contact information of their participants current, because any loss of participants can be a concern.

Let's look at an example of attrition in a longitudinal study. Recall the work of Galambos et al. in assessing sleep in college students over the course of four years. The researchers began by recruiting 198 first-year students, and then on five occasions over the next four years, they assessed all those still enrolled at the time. That number varied from 164 to 92 depending on the year. Galambos et al. recognized that attrition might be a limitation in their research, meaning those who left might somehow be different from those who remained, so at the end of the fourth year they took a closer look at data collected during the first assessment, comparing those who were still present and those who were now absent. They determined that these two groups were similar in almost all assessed ways, such as in terms of sleep quantity, stress levels, alcohol use, and academic performance. They concluded that attrition likely did not affect their results.

Selection

Selection effects are a potential problem any time you are using a between-subjects design (different people in different groups) and your participants are distributed into groups in a manner that was not random. In these circumstances a systematic bias might be present, making the participants in the different groups different from each other in ways beyond the independent variable.

We saw selection as a potential threat to internal validity in Workman et al.'s (1986–1987) research cited above. Recall that Workman et al. had the students themselves choose whether to be a part of an assertiveness training group or a discussion group; the participants were not randomly assigned to the groups. When participants themselves determine their group assignment, they are said to be **self-selected**. The study participants in these two groups may already be different in terms of characteristics that could influence the results. Thus, as with all the other quasi-experimental designs, we cannot state that the treatment caused the results.

Selection can also interact with other threats to internal validity. Let's look at an example in which both selection *and* attrition were threats to the internal validity of a research project. Kostic, Groomes, and Yadon (2015) wondered whether students in a research methods class could benefit from using a game show format when reviewing material for a test. Kostic used his own research methods classes to test this idea. In one semester he used a practice exam format before each of the four exams. He presented "retired" multiple-choice questions on his PowerPoint slides, and for each question, students raised their hands to indicate their chosen response (p. 351). After students had made their choices, each question/answer combination was discussed.

In the next semester's class Kostic used the same retired questions before each exam, but this time he presented the questions in game show format, using a different format before each of the four exams:

1. "Who Wants to Be an Experimental Psychologist?" In a format patterned after the television program "Who Wants to Be a Millionaire?" students worked in teams, taking turns answering multiple-choice questions worth increasing amounts of pretend game show money. Those of you familiar with the show will not be surprised to learn that the teams had "lifelines" they could turn to if they were stuck on a question. Instead of "calling a friend" or polling the audience as contestants do on the TV show, they were allowed to refer to their textbooks, notes, or phones for help on a question. Students also had an opportunity to use a "50/50 option" on a question; this would make answering the question easier by eliminating two of the four multiple-choice

options available. The team with the most "money" at the end of the class won.

2. "Are You Smarter than an Experimental Psychologist?" This format was patterned after the television program "Are You Smarter than a 5th Grader?" Teams of students took turns deciding whether the "experimental psychologist" (the instructor) was correct in his answers to the questions (he was deliberately incorrect half the time). Teams could earn an extra point each time they said an answer was incorrect and provided the correct answer in its place. The team that earned the most points by the end of the class won.

3. "The Experimental Psychology Is Right" was based on "The Price Is Right." The instructor called individual students to "come on down" to the front of the classroom to be a contestant and answer a multiple-choice question. Just as in the show, others in the class were free to aid the contestant by shouting out what they thought was the answer. If the student-contestant answered the question correctly, he or she was free to stay for the bonus round. Those who didn't answer correctly had to rejoin the audience. Once five contestants had answered a question correctly, it was time for the bonus round: a "Research Methods Showdown." The five contestants answered showdown questions without any aid from the audience. The first to answer a question correctly won.

4. "JEOPexperimentalpsychologY" was based on the long-running game show "Jeopardy!" In the TV version, a Jeopardy! board is presented, and players choose from a variety of clues on this board and then respond to the clue with a question. In Kostic's version, teams of players took turns choosing and then attempting to answer a multiple-choice question from a Jeopardy-like board shown on a PowerPoint

slide. The board contained a few question categories, each with questions that had different point values. Answering the question correctly earned the corresponding point value; an incorrect answer led to that point value being subtracted from the team's point total. Toward the end of the class period, a Final Jeopardy question allowed teams to wager points from their total. At the end of the class, the team with the most points won.

Before I tell you what Kostic et al. found, I want to point out that no one really won anything. Also, as in the practice test sessions in the preceding semester, in each game show format students were allowed to discuss the answers after they had answered the questions. In addition, students in both the practice exam and game show conditions had electronic access to the retired questions and answers prior to each exam. Both classes took the same four exams over the course of their semester (the exams covered the same content but used different questions from those used in the review sessions). So did the two types of review experiences differentially affect course evaluations and test grades? The practice-test takers and the game show contestants did differ in terms of their course evaluations. For example, those who reviewed test material using the game show strategy gave higher ratings of overall course quality than the other group. However, the grades earned by the two groups did not differ.

Can Kostic et al. conclude that the use of the game show format caused the increase in course evaluation ratings? Not necessarily, because this research was quasi-experimental. Kostic used the practice test in one semester and the game show format in the next, and there were different students in the class each semester. But Kostic et al. did not determine who was in each class; the students decided that for themselves. They were self-selected. Perhaps

there was something inherently different about the two classes that had nothing to do with the type of review session they received. This could mean that selection is a potential threat to the internal validity of this work.

Researchers often try to eliminate known threats in an effort to increase internal validity. Kostic et al. pointed out, for example, that the two groups' achievement of similar grades suggests the two samples were comparable and that the results were not necessarily affected by selection. However, Kostic et al. had an additional concern. Their research was potentially affected by attrition in that 79% of students in the first semester filled out the course evaluations, while in the second semester, only 52% did so. This is a real concern because those who filled out the evaluations may have had different views of the course from those who didn't.

As a postscript to this tale, I want to mention that Kostic et al. ran a second study, an experiment in which they randomly assigned students to using either a practice exam or a game show format to review test items. They found results similar to those obtained in their first study: rated attitudes were affected but grades were not. Under these experimental conditions, we could say that the game show format *caused* an increase in the rated attitudes.

A Final Point about Threats to Internal Validity

It is also possible to have threats to internal validity in true experimentation; attrition is the most likely concern. Let's talk about how this can happen.

Zhou and Fishbach (2016) created a clever way to demonstrate how attrition can affect your results even when you have a control group and your study participants are randomly assigned to groups. They conducted an online experiment in which randomly

Table 10.1   Potential threats to internal validity.

Type of threat	
Maturation	Changes in your participants over time can affect your results, independent of your intended manipulation(s).
History	When a study includes a pretest and at least one posttest, other events outside your intended manipulation(s) can occur between tests that can affect your results.
Instrumentation	Changes can occur in the instruments used to measure participants' performance (such as computers or humans) that affect your results.
Regression toward the mean	When performance on an earlier test is extreme (either extremely good or extremely poor), the next time the test is taken, the score is likely to be less extreme, closer to the mean.
Attrition	If participants do not complete the study and those who remain are different from those who dropped out, this difference may affect the results.
Selection	If participants are distributed into groups in a nonrandom manner, those in different groups may be different from each other in ways beyond the independent variable.

assigned participants were asked either to "imagine applying eyeliner" or to "imagine applying aftershave" (p. 498). For the dependent variable, Zhou and Fishbach asked participants to report their weight. Now Zhou and Fishbach did not expect that imagining applying eyeliner versus aftershave would affect reported weights. However, they did expect that some participants would drop out of their experiment, and as a result of that attrition, there would *appear* to be a relationship between these variables.

In other words, Zhou and Fishbach expected that males would not feel comfortable imagining putting on eyeliner and so wouldn't answer the question, essentially dropping out of the study. This would leave more females in the eyeliner condition than males. Because females tend to weigh less than males, it would *appear* that reported body weight was lower for those asked to apply eyeliner than aftershave. What happened when they ran this experiment?

As expected, attrition occurred: 32% dropped out of the eyeliner condition and 24% dropped out

of the aftershave condition (these numbers are not significantly different from each other). After participants dropped out, there were more females in the eyeliner condition than males, and the eyeliner group weighed significantly less than the aftershave group. However, we should not conclude that what participants were asked to imagine caused the difference in weight. If participants had not dropped out, the results would have likely been different. Random assignment of participants to groups would have likely led to similar weights for both groups. Furthermore, while researchers are often especially concerned when they experience a differential loss across groups, Zhou and Fishbach's work illustrates that even an equivalent loss across groups can be damaging to internal validity (recall that the attrition rates were comparable). Khou and Fishbach's research illustrates how important it is to be aware of attrition and its potential threat to internal validity, regardless of the type of design you use.

As for the other potential threats, remember that selection is a threat only if you have nonequivalent groups. As for maturation, history, instrumentation, and regression toward the mean, as mentioned previously, if you have at least two equivalent groups, these concerns are probably not threats to internal validity because your groups are equally likely to be affected by them. For a review of the threats to internal validity covered in this chapter, see Table 10.1.

SUMMARY

When it is not possible to conduct a true experiment in which equivalent groups can be compared, researchers can use a quasi-experimental design. Quasi-experimental designs can either lack a control group or test nonequivalent groups.

When researchers test nonequivalent groups, the participants are sometimes assigned to groups based on their own individual characteristics, such as gender, sexual orientation, and religion. This is an individual-difference manipulation. When researchers wish to see how people change with time, they use age as an individual difference manipulation. In this case, they will either use a longitudinal design in which they study a single group of participants over a long period of time, or use a cross-sectional design in which they test people from different age groups all at the same time.

All quasi-experimental designs are limited in their ability to establish cause and effect because of their lack of equivalent groups. When your groups are equivalent with the exception of the independent variable, then any change in the dependent variable must be due to the one element that is different between the groups: the independent variable. However, when your groups are not equivalent, something other than the independent variable could cause a change in the dependent variable. In these situations, internal validity is compromised. Maturation, history, instrumentation, regression toward the mean, and attrition can be a threat to designs that incorporate one group or more than one group. The sixth threat, selection, is a threat to internal validity only when you have more than one group and random assignment to groups is not used.

Researchers often strive to eliminate known threats in an effort to increase the internal validity of their research. When they succeed, they can make a stronger argument for the internal validity of their research findings. When a threat to internal validity cannot be ruled out, researchers must acknowledge that an alternative explanation exists for their research findings.

GLOSSARY

Attrition (mortality) – a loss of participants in a research study. Those who remain in the study may somehow be different from those who dropped out, and this difference may affect the results, thus attrition can be a threat to internal validity.

Cross-sectional designs – designs in which people of different ages are tested and compared.

History effect – When a study includes a pretest and at least one posttest, other events outside your intended manipulation(s) can occur between tests that can affect your results. This is a threat to internal validity.

Instrumentation – if changes occur in the instruments used to measure participants' performance (such as computers or humans), this is a threat to internal validity.

Interrupted time-series design with a nonequivalent control group – a quasi-experimental design in which a series of pre- and posttest scores are obtained for an experimental and a nonequivalent control group.

Longitudinal design – a design in which a single group of participants is studied over a long period of time.

Maturation – when changes in your participants over time (independent of the independent variable manipulation) influence your results, it is a threat to your internal validity.

Nonequivalent control group posttest-only design – a quasi-experimental design that incorporates a control group, but that control group is not equivalent to the experimental group. This design only uses a posttest.

Nonequivalent control group pretest–posttest design – a quasi-experimental design in which pre- and posttest scores are obtained for a treatment group and for a control group, but the groups are not equivalent.

One-group posttest only design – a quasi-experimental design that has only one group and only a posttest. This design does not have a control group.

One-group pretest–posttest design – a quasi-experimental design in which the dependent variable is measured twice, once before and once after a treatment occurs. This design does not have a control group.

Regression toward the mean – in designs that include multiple observations, when performance on an earlier test is extreme (either extremely good or extremely poor), the next time the test is taken, the score is likely to be less extreme and therefore closer to the mean (the average performance of the group). This can be a threat to internal validity.

Selection – if you are using a between-subjects design and your participants are distributed into groups in a nonrandom manner, the participants in the different groups may be different from each other in ways beyond the independent variable. This can be a threat to internal validity.

Self-selected – When participants themselves determine their group assignment, they are said to be self-selected.

Simple interrupted time series design – a quasi-experimental design in which the dependent variable is repeatedly measured before and after a treatment. This design does not have a control group.

REVIEW QUESTIONS

1 Explain why a quasi-experimental design would be used.
2 Summarize the different quasi-experimental designs that do not have a control group.
3 Summarize the different quasi-experimental designs that have a nonequivalent control group.
4 Explain and give examples of an individual difference manipulation.
5 Differentiate between a longitudinal design and a cross-sectional design.
6 Describe the six possible threats to internal validity that can occur with quasi-experimental designs.
7 Explain how attrition can threaten internal validity in a true experimental design.

ARTICLES AS ILLUSTRATION

Below you will find examples of articles that use the techniques we've discussed in this chapter; each article is accompanied by a series of questions.

1 More communities are using a public bicycle share program in an effort to increase physical

activity. Fuller, Sahlqvist, Cummins, and Ogilvie (2012) used a simple interrupted time series design to investigate whether the use of a bike share program increased in London when the public transportation system (the "Tube") went on strike. Read Fuller et al.'s article and answer the questions that follow.

Fuller, D., Sahlqvist, S., Cummins, S., & Ogilvie, D. (2012). The impact of public transportation strikes on use of a bicycle share program in London: Interrupted time series design. *Preventive Medicine, 54*(1), 74–76. doi:http://dx.doi.org/10.1016/j.ypmed.2011.09.021

a. What was the independent variable in this study?
b. What were the dependent variables in this study?
c. Was the presence of the transportation strikes associated with a change in the use of the shared bike program? If so, describe this relationship.
d. Can we conclude that the transportation strike caused a change in the use of bicycles in the shared bike program? Why or why not?

2 Clapp et al. (2005) use a nonequivalent control group pretest–posttest design to evaluate the effectiveness of a campaign to reduce the occurrence of college students driving under the influence (DUI) of alcohol. Read their article and answer the questions that follow.

Clapp, J. D., Johnson, M., Voas, R. B., Lange, J. E., Shillington, A., & Russell, C. (2005). Reducing DUI among US college students: Results of an environmental prevention trial. *Addiction, 100*, 327–334. doi:http://dx.doi.org/10.1111/j.1360-0443.2004.00917.x

a. Why was this study considered a quasi-experimental design?
b. Describe the two groups.
c. Describe the pretest.
d. Describe the intervention.
e. What were the main dependent variables?
f. Describe the results. Did the intervention appear to be successful? Can the researchers conclude that the intervention *caused* the results? Why or why not?

3 Kasperski et al. (2011) conducted a longitudinal study to investigate how college students' use of cocaine changed during four years of college.

Kasperski, S. J., Vincent, K. B., Caldeira, K. M., Garnier-Dykstra, L. M., O'Grady, K. E., & Arria, A. M. (2011). College students' use of cocaine: Results from a longitudinal study. *Addictive Behaviors, 36*(4), 408–411. doi:http://dx.doi.org/10.1016/j.addbeh.2010.12.002

a. Why was this study considered a longitudinal design as opposed to a cross-sectional design?
b. What are the advantages and disadvantages of a longitudinal design?
c. How would you turn this study into a cross-sectional design?
d. Provide a summary of the results. How did use of cocaine change over the four years of assessment?

SUGGESTED ACTIVITIES

1 Marion and Burke (2013) conducted an experiment in which they randomly assigned study participants to one of two relationship conditions ("friendship-enhancing condition" or "stranger-maintaining condition"). In the friendship-enhancing condition, participants were told they were assigned to work with one other because they had similar personalities. In the stranger-maintaining condition, they were told that they were assigned to work with the other because they had different personalities. Compare the quasi-experimental study conducted by Marion and Burke (2015) described at the beginning of this chapter to the earlier study published by Marion and Burke (2013) described here. Explain why the 2013 version of this research is a true research design while the 2015 version is considered a quasi-experimental design. Can we establish a cause and effect relationship in both? Why or why not?

2 In quasi-experimental designs, random assignment to groups is not possible. Generate a list of five individual difference manipulations that would necessitate using a quasi-experimental design. I'll start: birth order. As the experimenter, I cannot randomly assign people to a specific birth order (I cannot say: "For the purpose of this study, you'll be a middle child"), although I can put people into groups on the basis of their previously identified birth order. What other independent variables can you think of that do not allow for random assignment to groups?

3 For each of the following scenarios, identify one or more alternate reasons for the results (a threat to the study's internal validity).

a. A group of college students on academic probation are placed in a special program to help them acquire appropriate study skills. At the end of the 6-month program, the students' grade point averages rise significantly. Is the study skill program responsible for these results?

b. One of the trainers at the university gym wants to help students lose weight. Toward

that end, she devises a new workout technique that she thinks will help (jazz dancing on a treadmill). She tells the students who have expressed interest in losing weight that she's going to create two groups: one group will use the new technique, and one group will use another technique (walking on a treadmill). She asks students to decide what group they want to be in. As the study progresses, some participants in the jazz dancing treadmill group drop out because of the difficulty of mastering the intricate footwork. At the end of the study, those in the dancing treadmill group have lost more weight than those in the walking treadmill group. Based on these results, would you recommend that others take up jazz dancing on the treadmill?

REFERENCES

Braun, R. E., Glassman, T., Wohlwend, J., Whewell, A., & Reindl, D. M. (2012). Hookah use among college students from a Midwest university. *Journal of Community Health, 37,* 294–298. doi:http://dx.doi.org/10.1007/s10900-011-9444-9

Carney, C., McGehee, D. V., Lee, J. D., Reyes, M. L., & Raby, M. (2010). Using an event-triggered video intervention system to expand the supervised learning of newly licensed adolescent drivers. *American Journal of Public Health, 100,* 1101–1106. doi:http://dx.doi.org/10.2105/AJPH.2009.165829

Clapp, J. D., Johnson, M., Voas, R. B., Lange, J. E., Shillington, A., & Russell, C. (2005). Reducing DUI among US college students: Results of an environmental prevention trial. *Addiction, 100,* 327–334. doi:http://dx.doi.org/10.1111/j.1360-0443.2004.00917.x

Centers for Disease Control and Prevention. (2016). Hookahs. Retrieved from www.cdc.gov/tobacco/data_statistics/fact_sheets/tobacco_industry/hookahs/

Cornell, D. G., Callahan, C. M., & Loyd, B. H. (1991). Personality growth of female early college entrants: A controlled, prospective study. *Gifted Child Quarterly*, *35*, 135–143. doi:http://dx.doi.org/10.1177/001698629103500305

Fuller, D., Sahlqvist, S., Cummins, S., & Ogilvie, D. (2012). The impact of public transportation strikes on use of a bicycle share program in London: Interrupted time series design. *Preventive Medicine*, *54*(1), 74–76. doi:http://dx.doi.org/10.1016/j.ypmed.2011.09.021

Galambos, N. L., Vargas Lascano, D. I., Howard, A. L., & Maggs, J. L. (2013). Who sleeps best? Longitudinal patterns and covariates of change in sleep quantity, quality, and timing across four university years. *Behavioral Sleep Medicine*, *11*, 8–22. doi:http://dx.doi.org/10.1080/15402002.2011.596234

Hawton, K., Simkin, S., Deeks, J. J., O'Connor, S., Keen A., Altman, D. G., Philo, G., & Bulstrode, C. (1999). Effects of a drug overdose in a television drama on presentations to hospitals for self poisoning: Time series and questionnaire study. *British Medical Journal*, *318*, 972–977.

Kasperski, S. J., Vincent, K. B., Caldeira, K. M., Garnier-Dykstra, L. M., O'Grady, K. E., & Arria, A. M. (2011). College students' use of cocaine: Results from a longitudinal study. *Addictive Behaviors*, *36*(4), 408–411. doi:http://dx.doi.org/10.1016/j.addbeh.2010.12.002

Kostic, B., Groomes, D. R., & Yadon, C. A. (2015). Game shows as review activities: The impact on course evaluations and student perceptions. *Scholarship of Teaching and Learning in Psychology*, *1*(4), 349–361. doi:http://dx.doi.org/10.1037/stl0000039

Marion, S. B., & Burke, T. M (2013). False alibi corroboration: Witnesses lie for suspects who seem innocent, whether they like them or not. *Law and Human Behavior*, *37*(2), 136–143. doi:http://dx.doi.org/10.1037/lhb0000021

Marion, S. B., & Burke, T. M. (2015). Lying witnesses: The effect of relationship on the corroboration of a false alibi. Presented at the American Psychology-Law Society conference. San Diego, CA.

McGuirk, E. M., & Pettijohn II, T. F. (2008). Birth order and romantic relationship styles and attitudes in college students. *North American Journal of Psychology*, *10*, 37–52.

Mischel, W., Ayduk, O., Berman, M. G., Casey, B. J., Gotlib, I. H., Jonides, J., … Shoda, Y. (2011). "Willpower" over the life span: Decomposing self-regulation. *Social Cognitive and Affective Neuroscience*, *6*, 252–256. doi:http://dx.doi.org/10.1093/scan/nsq081

Morgan, B. J. (2001). Evaluation of an educational intervention for military tobacco users. *Military Medicine*, *166*, 1094–1098.

Rahman, R. O., & Zeglin, R. J. (2014). Holy psychopathology Batman: The pedagogical use of comic books in the teaching of abnormal psychology. *Psychology Teaching Review*, *20*, 59–65.

Taylor, J., & Cuave, K. L. (1994). The sophomore slump among professional baseball players: Real or imagined? *International Journal of Sport Psychology*, *25*(2), 230–239.

Vingilis, E., McLeod, A. I., Seeley, J., Mann, R. E., Beirness, D., & Compton, C. P. (2005). Road safety impact of extended drinking hours in Ontario. *Accident Analysis and Prevention*, *37*(3), 549–556. doi:http://dx.doi.org/10.1016/j.aap.2004.05.006

Wong, P. W. C., Fu, K., Chan, K. Y. K., Chan, W. S. C., Liu, P. M. Y., Law, Y., & Yip, P. S. F. (2012). Effectiveness of a universal school-based programme for preventing depression in Chinese adolescents: A quasi-experimental pilot study. *Journal of Affective Disorders*, *142*(1–3), 106–114. doi:http://dx.doi.org/10.1016/j.jad.2012.03.050

Workman, J. F., Bloland, P. A., Grafton, C. L., & Kester, D. (1986–1987). Changes in self-concept, locus of control, and anxiety among female college students as related to assertion training. *Educational Research Quarterly*, *11*(2), 21–28.

Zhou, H., & Fishbach, A. (2016). The pitfall of experimenting on the web: How unattended selective attrition leads to surprising (yet false) research conclusions. *Journal of Personality and Social Psychology*, *111*, 493–504. doi:http://dx.doi.org/10.1037/pspa0000056

11 Small-*N* Designs

LEARNING OBJECTIVES

- Explain what a small-N design is.
- Summarize the history of small-N designs.
- Explain why it is important to establish a stable baseline.
- Describe how the two reversal designs can be used to elicit behavior change.
- Differentiate between the three types of multiple-baseline designs.
- Explain what a changing-criterion design can accomplish.

Do you ever have trouble getting to class on time or even at all? Some students certainly do, and, perhaps not surprisingly, they may find this difficulty affects their grade (Friedman, Rodriguez, & McComb, 2001). The reason I bring this up is that a group of researchers, Bicard, Lott, Mills, Bicard, and Baylot-Casey (2012), set out to help four college athletes attend class and get there on time. These particular students were in danger of failing out of school, so there was a real need to curb their problem behavior.

What did Bicard et al. do to help? Before they could try to fix the problem, they had to find out just how bad it was. They needed to know how often these students were missing class and how often they were late. As we'll discuss below, this is called establishing the baseline. Once the baseline has been established, then it is time to provide an intervention to attempt to change the behavior. Bicard et al. instructed the students to text their academic counselor right before they entered the classroom each day. This requirement improved attendance and punctuality for all the students. In fact, as a test of how well it worked, Bicard et al. stopped requiring the texts at the start of a new semester, and the students tended to revert back to their old ways, missing class or arriving late. Once the texting requirement was put back into place, they once again showed improved behavior.

What I have just described was the use of a small-*N* design. In this chapter we explore what small-*N* designs are, their history, and how they work.

What Are Small-N Designs?

Small-*N* designs, also referred to as single-participant or single-subject designs, are designed to aid participants in changing behavior. We call them small-*N* designs because they use small sample sizes (*N* refers to the size of your sample); only one participant or just a few participants are tested. We'll talk about how this works in a moment, but first note that in almost all the research we've discussed thus far in this textbook (except the case study technique), we've compared the performances of groups to each other. In small-*N* designs, in contrast, we assess the effect of an independent variable in an experiment that has, in many cases, just one participant. Yes, there's an independent variable, and yes, it's still considered an experiment, but there's usually only one participant or just a few participants.

Note that while small-*N* designs often concern only one participant, they are different in some ways from case studies, which can also be completed with just one participant (see Chapter 5 for more on case studies). Both are a method of choice when you could not reasonably gather together a large group of people who share the characteristics of interest. However, case studies are in-depth *descriptions* of one participant, while small-*N* designs are experimental. As you'll see, in small-*N* designs the behavior of a single

person (or just a few people) is examined under well-controlled conditions to assess the effectiveness of a particular treatment on one or more target behaviors. Research with a small-*N* is much more than just description; under the appropriate conditions, it can establish cause and effect. Cause and effect cannot be established with a case study.

History of Small-N Designs

Psychology is a relatively young science. Many sources date the start of modern psychology to work done in Germany by Wilhelm Wundt beginning in 1879 (see Hunt, 1993), and the earliest researchers in psychology often studied single individuals, presenting the results for each rather than combining the data from multiple individuals. Additional individuals were tested to see whether the results would be replicated.

A classic example of research with a very small sample is the work of Hermann Ebbinghaus, who had just one participant: himself! Ebbinghaus, a German psychologist, created 2,300 nonsense syllables (meaningless consonant/vowel/consonant combinations) and used these to study his own memory. He would, for example, memorize lists of nonsense syllables, of varying length, and then record how many he could recall, often graphing the results (Ebbinghaus, 1885/1913). As you can see in the forgetting curve shown in Figure 11.1, less information is retained as time goes by. Ebbinghaus' intensive work on memory has remained influential (see Murre & Dros [2016] for a single-participant replication of Ebbinghaus' forgetting curve).

Ebbinghaus' work is just one example of the small-*N* work that was done in the early days of psychology. You may also be familiar with Pavlov's (1927) work with dogs. Does that name ring a bell? Ivan Pavlov, a Russian physiologist who studied psychological phenomena, worked with just one animal

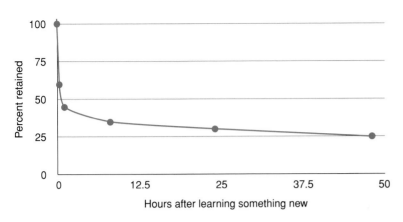

at a time. He and his colleagues found that a dog would salivate when seeing food, not just when the food was present in the dog's mouth. The dogs even learned to associate previously unrelated stimuli, such as a tone, with the promise of food and would salivate to these stimuli as well.

So conducting small-*N* research was a common approach early on. However, soon a tremendous change occurred in psychology with the development of inferential statistics, most notably the ANOVA statistical technique created by the English statistician Ronald Fisher (1925). By the early 1950s, the ANOVA had become the most often used technique in psychological research (Rucci & Tweney, 1980). Researchers were now routinely testing large groups of people, manipulating more than one independent variable, and testing for differences between the groups. Small-*N* designs generally fell out of favor, and it even became difficult for those using small-*N* designs to get their work published. As B. F. Skinner (1983) noted, "The editors of the standard journals … were uneasy about the small number of subjects" (p. 138).

FIGURE 11.2 Hermann Ebbinghaus.

FIGURE 11.3 Ivan Pavlov's famous experiments on classical conditioning were conducted with one dog at a time.

FIGURE 11.4 B. F. Skinner conducted experiments with small samples using animals such as pigeons.

Skinner, a US psychologist, was the best known among those who continued to work with very small samples. Skinner was interested in studying the behavior of animals such as rats and pigeons and determining how the consequences that followed behavior influenced subsequent behavior. Thus, from his work we know, for example, how behavior can be changed with reinforcement and punishment. The impact of this work is far reaching.

Skinner had been publishing steadily since 1930 and was frustrated by the new lack of recognition by journal editors. Thus, in 1958, he and his colleagues founded their own society, the Society for the Experimental Analysis of Behavior, and a journal, the *Journal of the Experimental Analysis of Behavior* (Skinner, 1983). In 1968, the Society created another new journal, the *Journal of Applied Behavior Analysis*, "primarily for the original publication of experiments relevant to the behavior of individual organisms." The society (Division 25 of the American Psychological Association) and its two journals still exist and are flourishing.

Today, small-*N* designs are often used in applied settings to assess whether an experimental treatment affects one or more target behaviors. Small-*N* designs are well recognized for their ability to allow us to see how a *particular individual* reacts to a

given intervention (in group experimentation you find out only how people *generally* react to a given intervention). Thus, researchers are once again doing small-*N* research; however, they generally are not studying themselves as Ebbinghaus did. There now is a clear separation between the experimenter and the study participant (Goodwin, 2010). And many journals now accept manuscripts detailing experimentation performed on small samples. In fact, you'll read about some of this work as you go through this chapter.

Small-N Designs: General Details

We'll cover a variety of small-*N* designs in this chapter. Some are called **reversal designs** or **withdrawal designs**. Both names refer to the fact that in these designs we take the treatment away to see whether, without it, the behavior will revert to its naturally occurring state.

In some cases, it is inappropriate or even unethical to use a reversal design. In other words, in some cases the treatment should not be removed because the behavior in question (such as drug use) should not be reversed. In this kind of situation, we should use a different kind of small-*N* design, such as a multiple-baseline design; this kind of design never incorporates a withdrawal of treatment, but it does require an assessment of multiple behaviors, participants, or settings, as you will see later.

Finally, a third general type of small-*N* design we'll discuss is the **changing-criterion design**. The goal in this design is for the participant(s) to reach increasingly demanding goals over time. This design can also work as an alternative to a reversal design because it does not include a withdrawal of treatment.

Regardless of what kind of small-*N* design you are using, there are a couple of commonalities you should be aware of. First, for each of these designs, you need to establish a baseline. Second, you cannot assume a treatment that works for any given participant will work for others. To obtain evidence that the treatment is externally valid, we must replicate the work with other study participants. We will discuss each of these points below.

The Importance of Establishing a Baseline

To assess how a participant will be affected by an intervention, the researcher needs to assess the target behavior(s) repeatedly both before and after the treatment. Assessing behavior *prior* to the presentation of the treatment is what is referred to as establishing the **baseline**.

Here's an example of establishing a baseline. Let's say you want to help a new employee operating a cash register to avoid cash shortages at the end of each day (see Rohn, Austin, & Lutrey, 2002). Before you provide an intervention to help this employee, you have to first determine how much of a shortage he or she typically experiences on a daily basis. To establish this baseline, you will assess the size of the cash shortage each day over a series of days.

Determining how the participant is performing prior to any treatment you provide is vital. Behavior can fluctuate; people exhibit better behavior at some times than at other times. So we must observe the behavior in question for an extended period prior to treatment in order to have a representative view of what it is like in its non-treated state. Think about it this way: How can we know whether our treatment had an impact if we don't know how well the person was doing before we tried to intervene? You need to determine baseline performance before you provide a treatment, and this baseline needs to be as stable as possible.

Researchers who use small-*N* designs typically use graphs to keep track of the behavior(s) in question. Graphing the behavior(s) will help you determine when the behavior you are observing is stable (the line on a line graph should be as horizontal

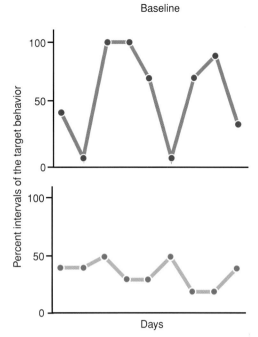

FIGURE 11.5 Data showing a relatively large amount of variability (top panel) and a relatively small amount of variability (bottom panel) (Kazdin, 2011). It is far easier to evaluate the effects of treatment when your baseline has little variability.

as possible). It is far easier to evaluate the effects of treatment when your baseline has little variability. See Figure 11.5 for illustrations of baseline data showing a relatively large amount of variability (top panel of the figure) and a relatively small amount (bottom panel).

If the line on your graph is trending up or trending down or alternating between up and down, as opposed to looking relatively flat, you need to continue making observations until the behavior you are observing stabilizes. See Figure 11.6 for examples of a relatively stable baseline (top panel), one trending up (middle panel), and one trending down (bottom panel).

If your baseline isn't stable, try to identify the source of the variability – consider what might be affecting your participant's behavior – and then try

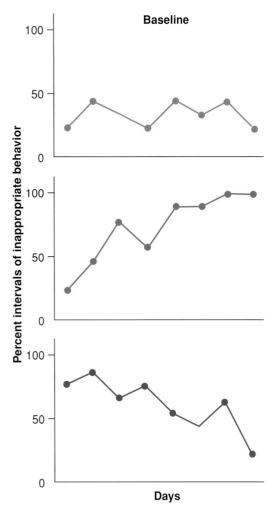

FIGURE 11.6 Hypothetical data showing the disruptive behavior of a hyperactive child (Kazdin, 2011). The top panel shows a stable rate of behavior. The middle panel illustrates a systematic trend with behavior becoming worse over time (trending up in this case means more disruptive behavior). The bottom panel illustrates a systematic trend with behavior becoming better over time (trending down in this case means less disruptive behavior).

to control that influence. Let's look at a hypothetical example. Think back to Bicard's research in which he and his colleagues wanted to help four college student athletes attend class and be on time. For the purpose of this example, let's concentrate on just one of those athletes. Let's say that when you are

measuring the baseline performance of this one athlete, you find a lot of variability in his attendance and punctuality. He sometimes comes to class, and when he does, he is sometimes on time, sometimes a little late, and sometimes very late. In other words, his target behaviors are extremely variable. Before you intervene, you need to figure out what is influencing this behavior. Is he sometimes up late partying the night before class? Does he eat breakfast only some of the time? Is he having trouble sleeping? Is he fighting with his roommate, girlfriend, parents? Identify the source(s) of the variability and then try to control the influences in his environment that could be affecting his behavior. Once you have controlled these environmental influences, you will have a better sense of how often your subject gets to class on time under typical circumstances.

Once your baseline is stable, it's time to provide the treatment. Again, researchers will generally use graphs to help them determine whether the treatment has influenced the behavior in question. Specifically, researchers want to see a change from baseline to treatment represented on a graph by a lack of data point overlap from one phase to the next (the lines from one phase to the next are not close to touching each other). This pattern is evidence that the treatment is responsible for the change in behavior. However, it is the *repeated* illustration of this pattern that gives us confidence the behavior change was caused by the treatment and was not a result of an uncontrolled variable, such as history or maturation. And as you'll see below, some of the small-*N* designs do allow for a repeated assessment of how behavior is responding to treatment.

External Validity of Small-*N* Designs

While it is possible to establish that a treatment caused the observed change in behavior using a small-*N* design, we cannot necessarily jump to the conclusion that the same treatment will work for all those with similar goals. To obtain evidence that the treatment is externally valid, we must replicate the work with other study participants. The more the results are replicated with additional individuals, in different settings, and at different times, the more we are confident in their generalizability.

Now that you are familiar with some of the shared characteristics of small-N designs, let's look more closely at the features of the different design types.

Reversal Designs

As noted above, some small-*N* designs are referred to as reversal or withdrawal designs, because researchers using these designs provide treatment and then remove it to determine whether behavior will revert to its naturally occurring state. Let's look at two main types of reversal design.

ABA Designs

The simplest reversal design is the **ABA design**. "A" refers to the baseline condition – the target behavior in its naturally occurring state before the intervention. "B" refers to the treatment designed to alter the target behavior, and the second "A" refers to the baseline again. If the treatment was responsible for altering the target behavior, then taking it away should eliminate the behavior change.

We've noted the need to make multiple observations during the baseline phase until the target behavior has stabilized. The same is true during the treatment phase; we want the behavior that is being treated to also stabilize so we have a good understanding of the level of performance that is possible with the provided treatment. Thus, we need to make multiple observations over an extended period during the treatment phase.

Small-*N* designs have often been used to help athletes achieve a goal. Let's look at one of those examples.

Pates, Maynard, and Westbury (2001) wanted to investigate the effects of using hypnosis to improve the jump- and set-shooting performance of basketball players. Someone who is hypnotized is in a very relaxed state and tends to be very responsive to suggestions. Pates et al. reasoned that a hypnotic intervention could be introduced through the use of triggers. "Triggers are words, sounds, images or a natural part of a routine that one can do or think about in order to induce a response" (p. 87). So Pates et al. decided to use an ABA design to test the idea that a hypnosis trigger could alter the performance of three male basketball players at a community college in London.

For the purpose of this example, we will concentrate on Pates et al.'s examination of jump-shooting. To make a jump shot, the participants had to run across the court, stop at a certain point, and attempt to make a basket. The observers rated the quality of each shot on a 5-point scale: 1 = miss, 2 = hit the rim and out, 3 = hit the backboard and in, 4 = hit the rim and in, 5 = nothing but net. Pates et al. began by determining what the naturally occurring jump shot behavior was for each of the three players. To establish a stable baseline, each was observed during multiple shot attempts. You can see a visual depiction of this baseline for participant 2 in the first phase of the graph in Figure 11.7.

Once the stable baseline had been established, Pates et al. began preparing the participants for the intervention. This required hypnotizing them and setting up the trigger for each that referred to his ideal performance state. When they had come out of the hypnotic state, the participants were told they could access their ideal performance by using their trigger.

The players were next asked to listen to an audio recording of the hypnosis intervention every day for 7 days. Then the tracking of the intervention began. The players each went back to the basketball court and attempted their jump shots using their triggers

Participant 2

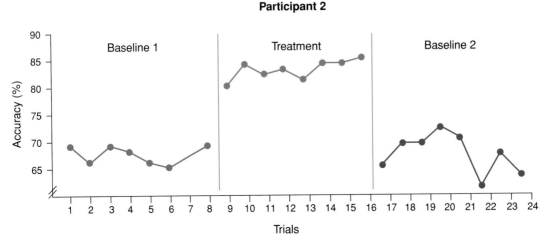

FIGURE 11.7 Pates et al. (2001) used an ABA design in an effort to improve the jump- and set-shooting performance of basketball players. This figure illustrates the jump-shooting performance for one of the participants.

(the treatment phase in Fig. 11.7). Finally, in the reversal portion of the study (the second baseline phase in Figure 11.7), the players' performances were tracked as they made their jump shots without using their triggers.

As you can see from the graph, there is a stable baseline in the first phase, performance improves in the treatment or intervention phase, and then it returns to baseline level in the third phase. As mentioned previously, researchers reviewing the results of small-*N* research often do not use statistics to determine whether the intervention had an impact but instead review the visual evidence. Pates et al. point out that the intervention appeared to have an immediate effect, without any overlapping data points from phase to phase.

ABAB Designs

The **ABAB design** is another reversal design, and, as before, "A" stands for baseline and "B" for treatment. While the ABA design finishes with the participant back at baseline, the ABAB design finishes with the participant in the treatment phase (that is certainly a benefit). To illustrate the use of an ABAB

design, we'll look at a study of someone with special needs. Small-*N* designs are often used to establish whether a particular intervention will work with someone who has such needs, for instance because of a developmental disability.

Hart and Whalon (2012) were interested in whether the iPad could help Austin, a 16-year-old male student with autism and a cognitive disability, improve academically. The specific goal was to get him to respond correctly to a science teacher's questions without being prompted. The researchers specifically chose the ABAB design because, if the intervention worked, they wanted to leave Austin and his teacher with the technology they needed for him to continue at an improved performance level.

Video self-modeling stimuli were created on an iPad in the following way. A video began with the following words on the screen that were read aloud: "Austin pays attention in class. He always answers the teacher's questions. Watch Austin answer questions" (p. 441). Then Austin was filmed answering questions correctly in response to his teacher's prompts, and the prompting was edited out of the video. So in its

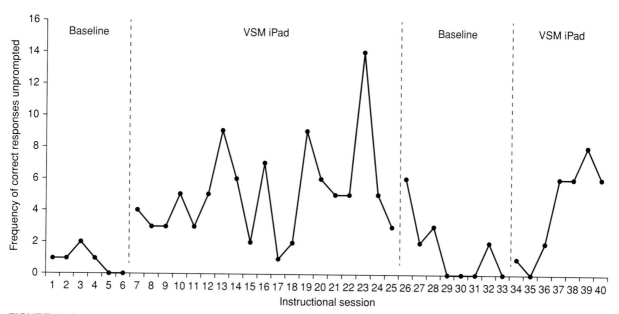

FIGURE 11.8 Hart and Whalon (2012) used an ABAB design. Here is an illustration of their participant's unprompted, correct responses across phrases. VSM = Visual Self-Modeling.

entirety, the video stimuli consisted of the quote noted above, followed by Austin successfully answering three questions seemingly without being prompted.

Hart and Whalon began the study by establishing a stable baseline of Austin's correct responding; data were collected for six class sessions. Then the researchers provided the intervention by having Austin watch the video three times just before each day's science class. They next collected data on correct responding for 20 class sessions. After the treatment phase had been completed, Austin attended science class without seeing the video first; data were collected for this second baseline phase for 8 class sessions. Finally, Austin completed a second treatment phase. In each phase, the number of unprompted correct responses Austin provided was counted (see Figure 11.8 for a visual representation of the results of this ABAB design). After reviewing the graphs for each phase, Hart and Whalon concluded that video self-modeling worked to help Austin improve his rate of correct, unprompted responding to his teacher's questions.

A Few Points to Note about Reversal Designs

The goal with small-N designs is to change behavior and ascertain that the treatment was responsible for that change. How do we know whether a treatment is responsible for a behavior change? If every time the treatment is provided, behavior changes, and every time the treatment is taken away, behavior reverts back to baseline, then you can be confident the treatment was responsible for the behavior change. Confidence grows the more you see this pattern. Thus, an ABAB design is preferred to an ABA design because, in an ABAB design, there are two opportunities to see behavior change as a result of the provided treatment. We can think of an ABAB design as a replication of the experiment for a single participant; the second AB combination is a repeat of the first. And, as noted above, the ABAB design also has the advantage of finishing the research study with the treatment still in place as opposed to leaving the participant at baseline. If a treatment is provided and behavior changes, but the change is due to a factor other than the treatment such as maturation or history, then it is unlikely it will revert to baseline when the treatment is taken away.

There are some situations in which a reversal design should *not* be used. If you are looking at a behavior that cannot be reversed, such as learning to ride a bicycle, for instance, do not use a reversal design. Once you learn how to ride a bike, it's tough to unlearn, so even when an intervention to help you is stopped, you will still know how (your behavior won't revert to baseline). There are also behaviors that *should not* be reversed, namely any kind of dangerous behavior such as the taking of illicit drugs. So, for example, you should not use a reversal design to stop someone from taking heroin. It is unethical to put someone in danger, and having someone restart a heroin addiction is putting someone in danger. So when you have a behavior that poses a risk to the participant or cannot be reversed, do not use a reversal strategy. Let's now turn to alternate techniques.

Multiple-Baseline Designs

A **multiple-baseline design** is a good choice of small-*N* design if you are studying behaviors that cannot or should not be reversed, because in these designs the treatment is never withdrawn. There are actually several types of multiple-baseline designs. In a **multiple-baseline design across behaviors**, researchers provide treatments for several different behaviors for a single individual, targeting one behavior at a time. Once the treated behavior stabilizes, the intervention is then applied to the next target behavior. In a **multiple-baseline design across participants**, researchers provide a treatment for different individuals who have the same target behavior change as a goal. And finally, in a **multiple-baseline design across settings**, researchers provide treatments for one individual in multiple settings, targeting one setting at a time. We'll look at each of these in turn.

Multiple-Baseline Designs across Behaviors

Let's start by thinking about the types of behaviors that are usually a part of a conversation: maintaining eye contact, smiling, and making comments. People on the autism spectrum typically have trouble with these behaviors. Scattone (2008) wanted to improve the conversational skills of a 9-year-old male, Matthew, who had been diagnosed with Asperger's syndrome (an autism spectrum disorder). Scattone used a combination of *Social Stories*™ and video modeling as the treatment. *Social Stories* are instructional readings that provide details about what should be done in particular social events. In Hart and Whalon's video modeling discussed above, the video was of the participant himself responding correctly (video *self*-modeling). In Scattone's research, the reading of each *Social Story* was videotaped, and then two adults were shown having a conversation and modeling the target skill. Scattone used a multiple-baseline design across behaviors to assess the effectiveness of the intervention.

In a multiple-baseline design across *behaviors*, researchers will first get a baseline for all the targeted behaviors, then introduce the treatment for one behavior at a time. If the target behavior that is exposed to the treatment changes while all the other behaviors that are being watched remain at baseline, this provides evidence for the effectiveness of the treatment for that behavior. Once the behavior being treated shows a change, you can move to treating the next behavior. (If there is no change, a new treatment needs to be considered.) This pattern is repeated until an intervention has been applied to each targeted behavior.

Scattone used this approach when working with Matthew, her study participant. During the

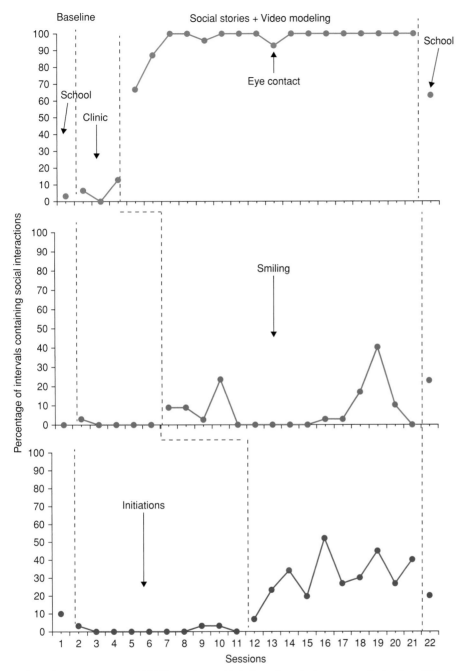

FIGURE 11.9 Scattone (2008) used a multiple-baseline design across behaviors. This figure illustrates the percentage of intervals containing social interactions.

intervention phases of this research, Matthew reviewed the *Social Story* in the lab with Scattone. Then he watched the relevant video at home each evening. See Figure 11.9 for a graph showing Matthew's baselines and intervention results. The vertical dotted line in the graph indicates the point in time at which each behavior was targeted; as you can see, the treatment targeted only one behavior at a time, in this case eye contact, smiling, and initiating conversation in that order. Scattone performed a visual inspection of the graphed results and concluded that, while the eye contact and initiation behaviors improved, the results were far less promising for smiling.

Scattone saw her results as showing promise for the use of *Social Stories* plus video modeling as a treatment for those with autism. However, note that, as Scattone acknowledged, we cannot know from this research whether it was the *Social Story* or the video modeling that changed Matthew's behavior. It is possible that each treatment in isolation could have had the same impact as the two had together. Future research can, of course, be designed to address that question.

Multiple-Baseline Designs across Participants

Let's now take a look at how one set of researchers used a multiple-baseline design across *participants* to alter behavior. Luke and Alavosius (2011) used a multiple-baseline design across participants to see whether providing feedback to medical workers regarding proper hand-washing would increase adherence to stated hand-washing rules. Their participants were a nurse practitioner, a physician assistant, and a medical assistant, all of whom had frequent contact with hospital patients.

The US Centers for Disease Control and Prevention (CDC) provides eight steps to follow for hand-washing, and three for hand-sanitizing (Fig. 11.10); hands had to be washed or sanitized "before contact with patient's skin, after contact with patient's skin, before donning gloves, after removing gloves, or after contact with inanimate objects in the immediate vicinity of the patient to be considered adherence to the operational definition" (Luke & Alavosius, 2011, p. 968).

Each time a participant was observed, his or her adherence to the rules was scored. Luke and Alavosius first assessed how well the participants were adhering

---

Hand washing

Wet hands with water
Apply one full pump of soap
Hands wet before getting soap
Rub hands for at least 15 seconds
Soap covers backs of hands, palms, and
    wrists with hands below elbows
Rinse hands until all visible soap has
    been rinsed off
Dry hands with new paper towel
Use new paper towel to turn off faucet

Hand sanitizing

Apply product to hand
Rub hands together
Cover all visible parts until dry

FIGURE 11.10 The US Centers for Disease Control and Prevention's rules for hand-washing and hand-sanitizing. (Adapted from Luke & Alavosius, 2011.)

to the rules without any instruction. After recording baseline levels for each participant, the researchers provided intervention in the form of periodic verbal and written feedback after a participant was observed with a patient. After participants mastered the rules (100% adherence to the rules for five consecutive observations), feedback stopped and adherence to the rules was checked periodically for two months.

As you can see from Figure 11.11, all participants showed an increase in adherence to the hand-washing/sanitizing rules after the baseline phase. Specifically, Participant 1 followed the rules 44% of the time, on average, during baseline, 87% of the time during the intervention phase, and 97% during the maintenance phase. The second participant also improved, showing an average adherence rate of 57% during baseline, 86% during intervention, and 100% during the maintenance period. The third participant showed similar gains (59% during baseline, 95% during the intervention period, and 96% during maintenance). The authors concluded that the feedback provided had led to this increase in adherence to the rules.

You may notice from Figure 11.11 that the treatment is staggered, successively provided to each

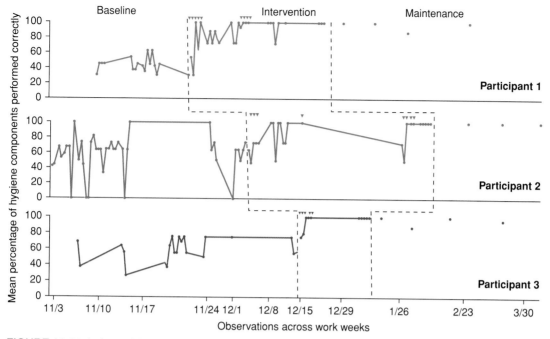

FIGURE 11.11 Luke and Alavosius (2011) used a multiple-baseline design across participants to improve adherence to hand hygiene rules in three medical staff members. This figure illustrates the mean percentage of hand hygiene components performed correctly over the course of successive work weeks.

individual. In other words, the researchers provided the intervention to one participant at a time. If the individual exposed to the treatment changes while those who have not yet undergone the intervention remain at baseline, this provides evidence for the effectiveness of the treatment.

You may have also noticed that the multiple-baseline design across participants has a built-in test of the generalizability of treatment effects. In other words, this design can demonstrate that a particular treatment worked to change behavior in different individuals, and that knowledge can increase your confidence in the generalizability of the findings.

Multiple-Baseline Designs across Settings

Now let's turn to an example illustrating the use of a multiple-baseline design across *settings*. In this example, Dalton, Martella, and Marchand-Martella

(1999) used a self-management program to reduce the off-task behavior in three different school settings (science class, language arts class, and study hall) for two male adolescents with learning disabilities. Teachers noted that these two students, Peter and Brian, were frequently disruptive in class, and their academic performance in these general education classes was suffering.

Dalton et al. used a multiple-baseline design across settings for each of the two students. First they assessed "off-task" baseline behavior for each student. Off-task behavior was defined as (a) not being in a seat, (b) talking, (c) interrupting others, (d) not working on assigned task, and (e) engaging in bodily movements non-congruent with assigned task (such as playing with a pencil). They observed the students every 30 seconds in the same 10-minute time slot 4 days a week. If an off-task behavior occurred at all in a 30-second period,

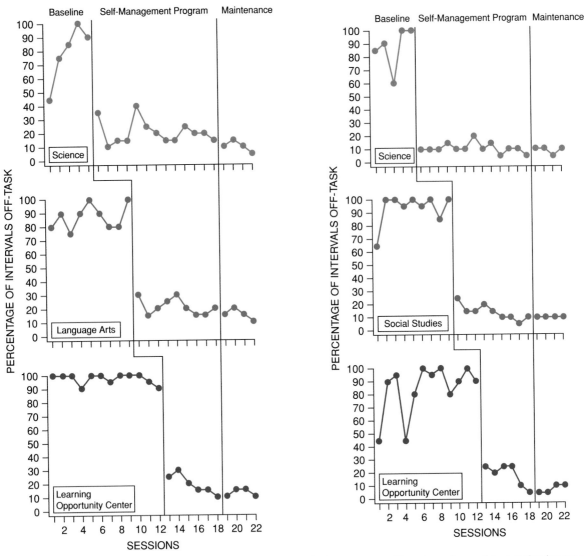

FIGURE 11.12 Dalton et al. (1999) used a multiple-baseline design across settings to reduce off-task behavior across three settings in two adolescents, Peter and Brian. The percentage of time spent off task for Peter is illustrated in the figure on the left and for Brian on the right.

it was counted. As you can see from Figure 11.12, both Peter and Brian spent a large percentage of time doing off-task behaviors during the baseline period.

After baseline behavior had been assessed in all three settings, Peter and Brian were trained to monitor their own behavior. Then this intervention was introduced successively in each setting. Let's take a closer look at the intervention.

The students were first taught how to recognize off-task behavior and then were tested on this knowledge. They were praised when they were correct in their assessment. After training, Brian and Peter were ready to self-monitor. They were taught how to assess their own behavior every 5 minutes, circling "yes" if on task and "no" if not on a form that said "Are you working?" at the top. Below were 9 or 10 boxes (depending on the setting), each with a question such as "Did you get started on time?" Brian and Peter received points for correctly filling out the self-monitoring form, and if they earned enough points over 4 days, they could exchange those points for things they wanted.

As you can see from the figure, after the intervention off-task behavior decreased for both Peter and Brian according to their own assessments, and this decrease held through the maintenance period. Now it is certainly reasonable to wonder whether Peter and Brian were representing their behavior accurately. In fact, teachers also rated the students' behavior after each class/study hall session, and these ratings did also reflect the desired decrease in off-task behavior. The authors concluded that the students had been able to assess their behavior independently and accurately. Interestingly, Peter and Brian also showed some improvement in academic performance, and they ended up in detention less. Thus Dalton et al. concluded that the self-management program was successful in all three settings.

A Few Points to Note about Multiple-Baseline Designs

In each type of multiple-baseline design, the treatment is staggered, successively provided to each target behavior, individual, or setting. If the target behavior, individual, or setting exposed to the treatment changes while all other targets stay at baseline levels, this provides evidence for the effectiveness of the treatment. If *only* the target behavior changes, it becomes increasingly implausible that something other than the treatment is driving the change. Knowing your treatment is creating the change in the target behavior is indeed the goal.

Changing-Criterion Designs

A third type of small-N design is the changing-criterion design, in which, as we mentioned above, a participant has to reach increasingly demanding goals over time. Once baseline performance has been established, a target behavior (the criterion) is set and the participant is encouraged to meet that goal, with reinforcement to provide motivation. Once behavior has reached the targeted level, the goal is advanced to a new level. Thus, with this design, a participant can become increasingly more adept at performing a target behavior. Let's take a look at an example.

Larwin and Larwin (2008) used a changing-criterion design in which the participant, a 14-year-old female, was required to walk increasingly greater distances on a treadmill in order to earn time on her phone and on the Internet. In fact, the goal of this research was twofold – to increase physical activity and to decrease media time. The research began as other small-N research does – by measuring the target behavior at baseline. For the purpose of illustration, I'll concentrate on the physical activity requirement. As you can see in Figure 11.13, the 2-week long baseline stage shows that initially the participant was not walking on the treadmill at all. In phase I, she received 1 hour of Internet time (beyond that needed for school) for every mile walked on the treadmill per day. The figure shows how the number of miles walked increased over baseline.

In phase 2, Larwin and Larwin required the participant to walk an even greater distance – 1.5 miles per day – to earn a greater reinforcement – 1.5 hours of phone and Internet time (with additional time given for walking beyond the required distance). (Note that Larwin and Larwin changed the reinforcer from just Internet time in phase 1 to Internet and phone time in phase 2 because they determined that Internet time alone was not as powerful a reinforcer as they needed.) As you can see from the graph, the participant tended to walk greater distances in response to this change in the criterion. The main goal for the project overall was to get the participant

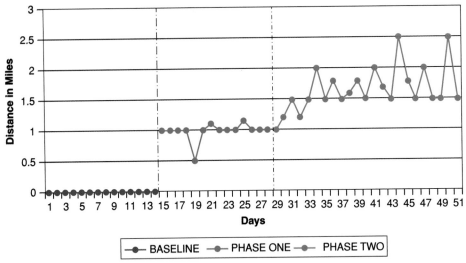

FIGURE 11.13 Larwin and Larwin (2008) used a changing-criterion design to increase physical activity and to decrease media time for an adolescent. This figure illustrates the overall miles walked during baseline and two treatment phases.

to walk at least 1.5 miles per day for at least 5 days a week; the secondary goal was to decrease her phone and Internet use. Both goals were met. The changing-criterion design was ideally suited for this participant because it allowed her to work up to achieving the goals.

SUMMARY

In research using small-*N*s, we assess the effect of an independent variable from an experiment that often has just one participant. Three of the major types of small-*N* designs are reversal designs, multiple-baseline designs and changing-criterion designs. In all, a stable baseline must first be established as a record of the target behavior before intervention.

Small-*N* design studies do allow researchers to establish cause and effect relationships, although you cannot assume that a treatment found to work for one participant will work for others. As with all research, the more the results are replicated with additional individuals, in different settings, and at different times, the more we are confident in their generalizability.

In the two reversal designs, ABA and ABAB, "A" stands for baseline and "B" for the intervention. "Reversal" refers to taking away the treatment to see whether behavior will revert to its naturally occurring state. Providing the treatment again, as in the ABAB design, should lead to behavior change once more, if the treatment is working as expected.

Multiple-baseline designs are typically used when studying behaviors that cannot or should not go back to baseline, because in these designs the treatment is never withdrawn. In a multiple-baseline design across behaviors, researchers provide treatments for several different behaviors for a single individual, targeting one behavior at a time. In a multiple-baseline design across participants, researchers provide a treatment for different individuals who have the same target behavior change as a goal. In a multiple-baseline design across settings, researchers provide treatments for one or more individuals in multiple settings, targeting one setting at a time. In each of these designs, the effectiveness of a treatment is demonstrated by showing that a targeted behavior changes when a treatment is provided.

A third type of small-N design is the changing-criterion design, in which a participant has to reach increasingly demanding goals over time. As with multiple-baseline designs, this type of small-N design does not include a withdrawal of treatment.

GLOSSARY

ABA design – a small-N reversal design in which "A" refers to the baseline condition and "B" refers to the treatment designed to alter the target behavior. This design ends at baseline.

ABAB design – a small-N reversal design in which "A" refers to the baseline condition and "B" refers to the treatment designed to alter the target behavior. This design ends with treatment.

Baseline – level of performance in the absence of treatment.

Changing-criterion design – a small-N design in which a participant has to reach increasingly demanding goals over time. Once baseline performance has been established, a target behavior (the criterion) is set. Once behavior has reached the targeted level, the goal is advanced to a new level.

Multiple-baseline design – a small-N design in which the treatment is never withdrawn.

Multiple-baseline design across behaviors – a small-N design in which researchers provide treatments for several different behaviors for a single individual, targeting one behavior at a time. The treatment is never withdrawn.

Multiple-baseline design across participants – a small-N design in which researchers provide a treatment for different individuals who have the same target behavior change as a goal. The treatment is never withdrawn.

Multiple-baseline design across settings – a small-N design in which researchers provide treatments for one individual in multiple settings, targeting one setting at a time. The treatment is never withdrawn.

Reversal designs (withdrawal designs) – small-N designs in which the treatment is provided and then taken away to see whether, without it, the behavior will revert to its naturally occurring state.

REVIEW QUESTIONS

1 Explain what a small-N design is.
2 Summarize the history of small-N designs.
3 Explain why it is important to establish a stable baseline.
4 Describe how to establish a stable baseline.
5 Explain how the external validity of small-N designs is increased.
6 Differentiate between the ABA and the ABAB design.
7 Describe the conditions in which a reversal design should not be used.
8 Differentiate between the three types of multiple-baseline designs.
9 Explain what a changing-criterion design can accomplish.

ARTICLES AS ILLUSTRATION

1 Could increasing the opportunities to respond in a fifth-grade classroom help a child respond accurately and be less disruptive? Haydon, Mancil, and Van Loan (2009) use an ABA design to investigate. Read Haydon et al. and answer the questions that follow.

Haydon, T., Mancil, G. R., & Van Loan, C. (2009). Using opportunities to respond in a general education classroom: A case study. *Education and Treatment of Children*, *32*, 267–278. doi:http://dx.doi.org/10.1353/etc.0.0052

a. Describe the study participant.

b. Describe the intervention.

c. What were the dependent variables?

d. Look at the graphs and use these to describe the results.

e. Would an ABAB design have been better for the study participant? Explain your answer. Why was an ABAB design not used?

2 Could an iPad application work effectively to help students manage their recreational activities? Uphold, Douglas, and Loseke (2014) use an ABAB design to answer this question. Read Uphold et al. and answer the questions shown below.

Uphold, N. M., Douglas, K. H., & Loseke, D. L. (2014). Effects of using an iPod App to manage recreation tasks. *Career Development and Transition for Exceptional Individuals*, 39, 1–11. doi:http://dx.doi.org/ 10.1177/2165143414548572

a. Describe the sample.

b. Describe the intervention.

c. What were the dependent variables?

d. Describe the baseline and intervention phases of this ABAB design.

e. How did they establish a stable baseline?

f. Briefly describe the results for each participant.

g. The researchers added a generalization phase to the end of the ABAB design. What was the specific purpose of this phase and what did this phase reveal?

h. What are the researchers' overall conclusions?

3 Downs, Miltenberger, Biedronski, and Witherspoon (2015) tested whether video self-evaluation could be successfully used to help

two university students learn yoga poses. They used a multiple-baseline design across behaviors with each of the two students. Read Downs et al. and then answer the questions below.

Downs, H. E., Miltenberger, R., Biedronski, J., & Witherspoon, L. (2015). The effects of video self-evaluation on skill acquisition with yoga postures. *Journal of Applied Behavior Analysis*, 48, 930–935. doi:http://dx.doi.org/10.1002/jaba.248

a. Describe the two study participants. Why do you think it was important that the students had no yoga experience prior to the start of the research study?

b. Describe the new skills the participants were trying to achieve.

c. Describe the intervention.

d. Look at the graphs and use these to describe the results for each of the two participants.

4 Could a personal digital assistant, a handheld device used to manage personal information, help a 14-year-old male become more independent at home and at school? Ferguson, Smith Myles, and Hagiwara (2005) used a multiple-baseline design across settings to answer this question. Read Ferguson et al. and then answer the questions below.

Ferguson, H., Smith Myles, B., & Hagiwara, T. (2005). Using a personal digital assistant to enhance the independence of an adolescent with Asperger syndrome. *Education and Training in Developmental Disabilities*, 40, 60–67.

a. Describe the study participant.

b. Describe the intervention.

c. What were the dependent variables?

d. Describe the baseline and intervention phases of this design.

e. Briefly describe the results.

f. What does the vertical line in Ferguson et al.'s graphs indicate and why was this line staggered from graph to graph?

5 Often teachers are interested in obtaining not just correct responding from a student, but correct and rapid responding (referred to as fluency). In Fienup and Doepke's (2008) research study, a changing-criterion design was used to evaluate an intervention designed to increase fluent responding in a young boy with autism. Read Fienup and Doepke's article and then answer the questions below.

Fienup, D. M., & Doepke, K. (2008). Evaluation of a changing criterion intervention to increase fluent responding with an elementary age student with autism. *International Journal of Behavioral Consultation and Therapy*, 4, 297–303. doi:http://dx.doi.org/10.1037/h0100859

a. Why was a changing-criterion design appropriate for this particular evaluation?

b. Describe the study participant.

c. Describe the intervention.

d. What was the dependent variable?

e. Describe the baseline and intervention phases of this design. Why did the researchers include a baseline reversal in their study?

f. Briefly describe the results.

SUGGESTED ACTIVITIES

1 Students can perform their own ABA study and graph the results. See Carr and Austin (1997) for an idea using exercise as an independent variable and pulse rate as the dependent variable.

2 For each of the following scenarios, design an intervention, explain your choice of design, and graph your hypothetical results.

a. You're doing an internship at an elementary school and a teacher has asked you to help her with one of her students. This student, Lindsay, is having great difficulty with her spelling homework. How will you attempt to improve her performance?

b. A student at an elementary school, Courtney, constantly forgets to wash her hands after using the restroom. Her mother reports that Courtney shows the same behavior at home. What do you propose to do to get Courtney to wash her hands when appropriate at both school and at home?

c. Three members of your college soccer team could improve their passing skills. How can you help?

REFERENCES

Bicard, D. F., Lott, V., Mills, J., Bicard, S., & Baylot-Casey, L. (2012). Effects of text messaged self-monitoring on class attendance and punctuality of at-risk college student athletes. *Journal of Applied Behavior Analysis*, 45, 205–210. doi:http://dx.doi.org/10.1901/jaba.2012.45-205

Carr, J. E., & Austin, J. (1997). A classroom demonstration of single-subject research designs. *Teaching of Psychology*, 24, 188–190. doi:http://dx.doi.org/10.1207/s15328023top2403_7

Dalton, T., Martella, R. C., & Marchand-Martella, N. E. (1999). The effects of a self-management program in reducing off-task behavior. *Journal of Behavioral Education*, 9(3/4), 157–176. doi:http://dx.doi.org/10.1023/A:1022183430622

Downs, H. E., Miltenberger, R., Biedronski, J., & Witherspoon, L. (2015). The effects of video self-evaluation on skill acquisition with yoga postures. *Journal of Applied Behavior Analysis*, 48, 930–935. doi:http://dx.doi.org/10.1002/jaba.248

Ebbinghaus, H. (1885). *Memory: A contribution to experimental psychology*. Trans. H. A. Ruger and C. E. Bussineus (1913). New York: Teachers College.

Ferguson, H., Smith Myles, B., & Hagiwara, T. (2005). Using a personal digital assistant to enhance the independence of an adolescent with Asperger syndrome. *Education and Training in Developmental Disabilities*, 40, 60–67.

Fienup, D. M., & Doepke, K. (2008). Evaluation of a changing criterion intervention to increase fluent responding with an elementary age student with autism. *International Journal of Behavioral Consultation and Therapy*, 4, 297–303. doi:http://dx.doi.org/10.1037/h0100859

Fisher, R. A. (1925). *Statistical methods for research workers*. London: Oliver & Boyd.

Friedman, P., Rodriguez, F., & McComb, J. (2001). Why students do and do not attend classes: Myths and realities. *College Teaching*, 49, 124–133.

Goodwin, C. J. (2010). Using history to strengthen a research methods course. *History of Psychology*, 13, 196–200. doi:http://dx.doi.org/10.1037/a0019395

Hart, J. E., & Whalon, K. J. (2012). Using video self-modeling via iPads to increase academic responding of an adolescent with autism spectrum disorder and intellectual disability. *Education and Training in Autism and Developmental Disabilities*, 47, 438–446.

Haydon, T., Mancil, G. R., & Van Loan, C. (2009). Using opportunities to respond in a general education classroom: A case study. *Education and Treatment of Children*, 32, 267–278. doi:http://dx.doi.org/10.1353/etc.0.0052

Hunt, M. (1993). *The story of psychology*. New York: Anchor Books.

Kazdin, A. E. (2011). Single-case research designs: Methods for clinical and applied settings (2nd ed.). Oxford: Oxford University Press.

Larwin, K. H., & Larwin, D. A. (2008). Decreasing excessive media usage while increasing physical activity: A single-subject research study. *Behavior Modification*, 32, 938–956. doi:http://dx.doi.org/10.1177/0145445508319668

Luke, M. M., & Alavosius, M. (2011). Adherence with universal precautions after immediate personalized performance feedback. *Journal of Applied Behavior Analysis*, 44, 967–971. doi:http://dx.doi.org/10.1901/jaba.2011.44-967

Murre, J. M. J., & Dros, J. (2016). Replication and analysis of Ebbinghaus' forgetting curve. *PLOS ONE*, 10(7), 1–23. doi:http://dx.doi.org/10.1371/journal.pone.0120644

Pates, J., Maynard, I., & Westbury, T. (2001). An investigation into the effects of hypnosis on basketball performance. *Journal of Applied Sport Psychology*, 13, 84–102. doi:http://dx.doi.org/10.1080/10413200109339005

Pavlov, I. P. (1927). Conditioned reflexes: An investigation of the physiological activity of the cerebral cortex. Trans. G. V. Anrep. Oxford: Oxford University Press.

Rohn, D., Austin, J., & Lutrey, S. M. (2002). Using feedback and performance accountability to decrease cash register shortages. *Journal of Organizational Behavioral Management*, 22, 33–46. doi:http://dx.doi.org/10.1300/J075v22n01_03

Rucci, A. J., & Tweney, R. D. (1980). Analysis of variance and the "second discipline" of scientific psychology: A historical account. *Psychological Bulletin*, 87(1), 166–184. doi:http://dx.doi.org/10.1037/0033-2909.87.1.166

Scattone, D. (2008). Enhancing the conversation skills of a boy with Asperger's Disorder through *Social Stories*™ and video modeling. *Journal of Autism and Developmental Disorders*, 38, 395–400. doi:http://dx.doi.org/10.1007/s10803-007-0392-2

Skinner, B. F. (1983). *A matter of consequences*. New York: Knopf.

Uphold, N. M., Douglas, K. H., & Loseke, D. L. (2014). Effects of using an iPod App to manage recreation tasks. *Career Development and Transition for Exceptional Individuals*, 39, 1–11. doi:http://dx.doi.org/10.1177/2165143414548572

12 External Validity

LEARNING OBJECTIVES

- Define external validity.
- Differentiate between internal validity and external validity.
- Define population validity.
- Define ecological validity.
- Define temporal validity.

I'd like to start this chapter by describing an experiment designed to investigate whether drinking alcohol affects self-disclosure. To do this Sayette (1994) brought male social drinkers to his lab and, given their informed consent, gave them either enough alcohol to be legally drunk or just a placebo (those who drank the placebo thought they were drinking alcohol). Then he asked each participant to speak for 3 minutes on the following topic: "What I like and dislike about my body and physical appearance" (p. 129). After that, undergraduates working for the experimenter listened to audiotapes of these speeches. They counted the number of negative, positive, and neutral items in each speech as well as the amount of time each speaker spent presenting each type of information.

What did Sayette find? The participants who were intoxicated disclosed fewer negative pieces of information about themselves than those who were sober. The intoxicated participants also spent marginally less time disclosing negative information than those who were sober. On the other hand, there was no difference

FIGURE 12.1 Sayette (1994) found that males who were intoxicated disclosed fewer negative pieces of information about themselves than those who were sober.

in the amount of positive information participants in the two groups disclosed about themselves.

So what does this mean? Does Sayette's research suggest that a drunk person you meet in a bar is likely to disclose less negative information than a sober person? In other words, "Do people behave in real life as they behave in our experimental laboratories?" (Bem & Lord, 1979, p. 833). This question is an example of those we ask when we are concerned with *external validity*, and that's the topic of this chapter.

What Is External Validity?

When we want to assess external validity, we ask, "Will the results generalize?" More specifically, as noted in Chapter 1, external validity is the extent to which results of a study (experimental or non-experimental research) can be generalized to other people, places, and times. Considering the issue of external validity is often but not always important. It depends on what your goals are for your research (Mook, 1983).

For instance, sometimes we conduct research designed to answer questions that have direct and obvious relevance to the real world. When you are

conducting this kind of applied research, the external validity of your results is likely important to you.

Basic research, on the other hand, tests theories for which there isn't a direct or immediately obvious application to everyday life. For example, in the early days of memory research, participants would often be asked to memorize and recall long lists of digits. What real-life situation calls for us to do this? I can't think of one, but we certainly did learn a lot about basic memory processes from this work. We learned, for example, that longer lists take more time to memorize and are more difficult to recall (see for example, Robinson & Darrow, 1924). While research examining the recall of long lists of digits does not seem to resemble real-life experiences, understanding generally how memory can work can be important in a variety of circumstances, including studying for a test. So, in basic research, establishing external validity may or may not be a goal.

After a brief review of the relationship between internal validity and external validity, we'll talk about three major kinds of external validity. First, we'll look at **population validity**, which asks the question, "Will the results obtained with the tested sample generalize to other people?" Then we'll consider **ecological validity**, which asks, "Will the results obtained hold in other settings?" Finally we'll turn to a consideration of **temporal validity**, which asks, "Will the results obtained hold at other times?"

What Is the Relationship between Internal Validity and External Validity?

As we discussed in Chapter 1, internal validity is the extent to which we can say our independent variable caused our dependent variable's results. Thus, internal validity is an issue only when we are doing an experiment and want to establish cause and effect (we are trying to establish whether our

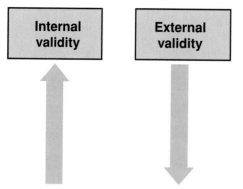

FIGURE 12.2 As internal validity increases, external validity typically decreases.

independent variable(s) caused our dependent variable to change). Internal validity is not relevant for non-experimental work, in which there is no independent variable and thus no possibility for cause and effect.

Experimentation is often conducted in a laboratory because there it is relatively easy for the researcher to control all that is presented to participants and to vary just the independent variable(s). Let's look back at Sayette's research as an example. Sayette conducted his research in a lab where it is easy to control who drinks and how much they drink. Results in the lab typically have high internal validity because of this high degree of control. However, an experiment completed in the lab doesn't often resemble real-life experiences. Considering Sayette's work again, it is certainly odd to be drinking in a lab while discussing what you like and don't like about your body. Thus, the external validity of research conducted in the lab is sometimes relatively low. In fact, internal and external validity tend to be inversely related (negatively correlated). As one kind of validity increases, the other tends to decrease (Figure 12.2).

When experimenters want to try to increase external validity, they sometimes conduct their experimentation in the real world. This is called doing **field experimentation**. The research still has all the

components of experimentation – including independent and dependent variables – but it is conducted in the real world instead of in a lab. Because field experimentation does a better job of resembling real life, results are more likely to generalize to real life. However, internal validity in field experimentation is sometimes lower than in the lab, because it's often much more difficult to have as much control over what your experimental participants experience in the real world.

Researchers who conduct non-experimental research also sometimes conduct their research in the real world. In this case, the work is often called **field research** (as opposed to field "experimentation"). Again, doing your research in the field can help increase the study's external validity. So while internal validity is relevant only for experiments, external validity can be a valid issue for both experimental and non-experimental research. In both cases, if your research is relevant to the real world, then it is appropriate to want to know whether your research findings are valid only for the study you conducted, or whether they hold true beyond your study. Because external validity is relevant to both experimental and non-experimental research, we will be discussing both types of research in this chapter.

It is also worth pointing out that sometimes one type of validity takes priority over another. Again, it depends on what your goals are for your research. If your goal is to determine whether you have a cause and effect relationship, then a high level of internal validity is a priority. If, however, previous research has already established that a cause and effect relationship exists, then you might be interested in determining whether the relationship demonstrated in the lab will hold in the real world, with other people, in other settings, or at other times. In these cases, external validity will be a priority.

Most importantly, as with all research, researchers have the responsibility to recognize the limitations

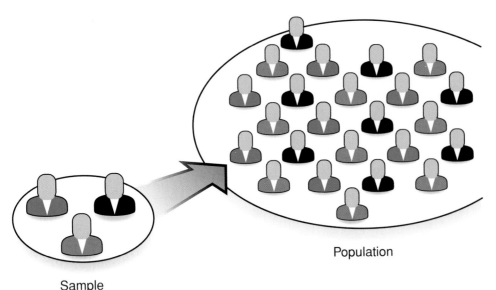

Sample

Population

FIGURE 12.3 Population validity allows us to say that the results obtained from the sample of participants who were tested hold for the larger population of interest.

of their work, and, where appropriate, to include a discussion of generalizability in any presentation of their research.

The rest of this chapter will be concerned with external validity. We'll start by talking about specific types of external validity.

Population Validity

Population validity allows us to say that the results obtained from the sample of participants who were tested hold for the larger population of interest (see Figure 12.3). Before we go any further, let's discuss what I mean when I refer to a "population of interest" or a "target population."

Defining your Target Population

When researchers conduct experimentation, they are typically interested in finding out something about people (we can have a comparable conversation about conducting research with animals, but I am concentrating on people in this text). The research

question will help them identify what their target population is. For example, let's say the researchers want to find out how undergraduate students at a particular university feel about their campus food service choices. In this case, the target population or the population of interest is undergraduate students at that particular university.

Or let's say a researcher wants to determine how undergraduate students in the US feel about their campus college food service choices. Now the target population has changed; it is *all* US undergraduate students. Let's look at a third example. Suppose a researcher wants to find out how US adults tend to feel about recycling. Now the target population is all US adults. Again, the research question helped identify the population of interest.

How Characteristics of the Sample Affect Population Validity

Now let's say you've determined what your target population is. Chances are you can't conduct research with everyone from your target population.

It's too time-consuming and expensive, and all the people in that population may not be easily accessible to you. So instead we collect data from just a sample, a relatively small group of people. In fact, the ideal situation is to determine who your target population is and then randomly sample from that target population. If you do this, you can generalize your results beyond your sample to the target population, and your experimentation will be high in population validity.

Unfortunately, we seldom have the luxury of randomly sampling from the actual population of interest. It can be relatively difficult and time-consuming to do this, so we often just test a convenience sample. As you may recall from Chapter 7, a typical convenience sample is psychology undergraduates who participate in research studies in exchange for extra class credit or as a requirement for a class. In fact, researchers have found that in some areas within psychology, approximately 75% of the research published had undergraduates as participants (Sears, 1986).

Let's say, for example, that I'm interested in determining how undergraduates at my university feel about campus food service options. Specifically, say my university is choosing between two different food service providers and I decide students should be asked which pizza they prefer –Company A's or Company B's. I decide, for convenience purposes, to test a sample of psychology majors at my university and ask them for their views. I find out that Company A's pizza is preferred. Should I recommend that Company A be hired? In other words, can we generalize the results obtained with my convenience sample to the overall population of interest, in this case all my university's undergraduates? It's difficult to say. There may be something inherently different about these psychology majors, compared to the undergraduate students at my University as a whole (see King, Bailly, & Moe, 2004). If I had taken the

ideal route and *randomly* sampled from all undergraduates at my university, I could then assume that the views of my sample do represent the views of that population.

Now take this a step further. Often when psychology researchers test their undergraduate convenience samples, they are not just thinking of their university population as their population of interest. Often psychology researchers would like to target a population beyond their university. However, as I just suggested, those who sample from the convenient college student population are limited in their ability to generalize their results. We know, for example, that undergraduates differ from the general population in a variety of ways. For example, undergraduate samples have been found to be relatively young, intelligent, and more responsive to authority, and they tend to change their minds more often than those who are older (Sears, 1986). We must express caution before generalizing the results collected from a convenient college student sample.

Now let's think about this issue in a slightly different way. Let's say the sample you test is primarily US Caucasians. Will your results pertain to people in other countries and/or of other ethnicities? In fact, as I mentioned in Chapter 7, researchers have recently been urged (see, for example, Arnett,

FIGURE 12.4 Can we generalize the results collected from convenient college student samples?

2008) to make more efforts to recognize cultural differences. The importance of this point is apparent when you consider that the samples tested in six major US journals had a tendency to focus on US adults (Arnett, 2008). Henrich et al. (2010) noted that psychological research in the world's top journals tends to be based on WEIRD samples (Western, Educated, Industrialized, Rich, and Democratic). This is a narrow slice of the world. How much could we generalize the results of this research to the rest of the world?

Henrich et al. asked this specific question with their review of multiple areas of research in which results from WEIRD samples could be compared to those from other cultures; they often found differences. As a result, Henrich et al. maintain that college students are not appropriate samples from which to make claims about human psychological processes, and they encourage researchers to conduct research with more diverse populations.

Let's now take a look at a couple of research projects in which a conscious effort was made to collect data that allowed for an extension of population validity. We'll start with the work of Suminski, Petosa, Utter, and Zhang (2002).

Suminski et al. were interested in the rates of physical activity of college students. One of their goals was to aid colleges in designing physical activity programs for students. Here's what Suminski et al. did. They tested students at a college that has a required health and fitness course for all. Across three semesters, they collected data from virtually all in this required course (almost all students in these courses consented to be a part of this research).

There are multiple advantages of gathering data from a sample in this way. First, data were essentially gathered from virtually all students at this university. Thus, this research likely did not suffer from a self-selection problem. As you may recall from

Chapter 10, self-selection occurs when your research is restricted to those who chose to be in your study; when this happens, you have to wonder whether those who consented to be in the study are somehow different from those who did not consent. Second, Suminski et al. gathered data across multiple semesters. If they had collected data from students in only one semester, we might wonder whether there was something different about the students in the health and fitness class in that semester versus other semesters (maybe a new fitness craze hit the nation during that semester, and it has temporarily changed the way students are exercising?!). The resulting sample represented all majors of study, was composed of both males and females, and was ethnically diverse. These details are important when we are considering whether we can generalize to college students outside our sample.

Overall, Suminski et al. found that almost half their sample did not participate in *vigorous* physical activity in the preceding month, with almost 20% indicating they were completely inactive. When Suminski et al. compared physical activity patterns across genders and ethnicities, they found, for example, that female minority students were especially likely to be inactive. As a result, they recommended that those designing physical activities at colleges should consider ethnic differences when designing programs.

To summarize, Suminski et al.'s target population was college students in general, and their sample was composed of college students who varied in terms of their majors, genders, and ethnicities. So can we generalize Suminski et al.'s results to other college students? In this case, we can feel confident generalizing these results to those at similar types of colleges in the same geographic region (a large metropolitan university in the south central United States). However, as Suminski et al. appropriately acknowledge, it is advisable to use caution when

FIGURE 12.5 How physically active are college students? Suminski et al. (2002) gathered data from college students who varied in terms of their majors, genders, and ethnicities in an effort to make their answers to this question more generalizable.

FIGURE 12.6 The Global Deception Research Team (2006) asked people in 58 countries, "How can you tell when people are lying?" Gaze aversion was the most common response. This "worldwide" approach to answering this question has high population validity.

generalizing the results to those at other types of colleges.

Let's look at another study, the best example of extending population validity I have ever seen. First let me introduce the topic. How do you know when someone is lying to you? This question was asked in the United States, and a common answer was that those who are lying tend to avert their gaze (Zuckerman, Koestner, & Driver, 1981). People in other Western countries have also been shown to expect that eye contact will decrease while someone is lying (for example, see Akehurst, Köhnken, Vrij, & Bull, 1996). A group of researchers collectively known as the Global Deception Research Team (2006) wondered whether believing that gaze aversion was an indicator of deception was a Western norm or one that would be expressed worldwide. So the group set out to investigate the population validity of this belief. In order to do this, they asked 20 males and 20 females in each of 58 countries, "How can you tell when people are lying?" Although other cues were mentioned, gaze aversion was the most common response. Thus, with this work, the Global Deception Research Team heightened the population

validity of this finding. (By the way, gaze aversion is *not* a good indicator of whether someone is lying to you [DePaulo et al., 2003]; people just tend to think it is.)

Replication to Extend Population Validity

It is rare for any one study to satisfy all questions about external validity (most research does not even come close to covering the world to the extent the Global Deception Research Team did). What often happens instead is that evidence for or against external validity accumulates over time as researchers conduct additional studies. In other words, the population validity of research is often extended through replication.

As we discussed in Chapter 1, replication is the process of conducting a study again and getting the same pattern of results (in other words, the findings are reproduced). There are two kinds of replication. An **exact replication** refers to the idea that one completes a study in virtually the same way it was originally conducted, but with a new set of participants and often in a new setting (such as another researcher's laboratory). A **conceptual replication** is when one completes a study in a way that is similar to but not exactly the same as the way it was completed before. Whether they are exact or conceptual, replications that yield similar results provide evidence for the generalizability for the results – that is, the likelihood the results would hold for others. Let's first take a look at an exact replication that was conducted in an effort to explore the population validity of the original research.

Have you ever had an opportunity to download content from the Internet that wasn't yours to download? Krawczyk, Tyrowicz, Kukla-Gryz, and Hardy (2014) were interested in determining how people feel about various online piracy situations. Researchers have generally sought to ask easily accessible samples of college students what their views are on this topic. Krawczyk et al. wanted to discover whether the typical views of college students would be similar to the views of a different type of sample. So they conducted a survey twice, once with a sample of college students and once with a sample of Facebook users who "openly endorse protection of intellectual property rights for cultural goods" (p. 32). Krawczyk et al. reasoned that, if differences in views about online piracy exist, they would likely be most evident between these two extreme types of samples.

For each of their two studies, the researchers provided participants with a set of scenarios and asked them to judge the actions described on a scale ranging from 1 = totally unacceptable to 4 = fully acceptable. Here's one of the scenarios: "Johnny found and downloaded from a site allowing sharing and downloading files without their authors' knowledge, the newest season of a high budget, American TV series" (p. 38).

The second study was an exact replication of the first, using the same methodology in an attempt to determine whether the results of the first study generalized to the new population. In fact, they did.

FIGURE 12.7 Krawczyk et al. (2014) found that a sample of college students and a sample of Facebook users who endorsed protection of intellectual property rights had similar views of online piracy. Asking people from these two different types of groups for their views increased the population validity of the results.

Despite differences in the populations, the two samples had similar views of online piracy. For example, both groups recognized the act of unauthorized distribution of goods as unethical, but saw this behavior as worse when a peer as opposed to a company was the creator of the material. Interestingly, both groups downloaded and shared unauthorized content equally often. Therefore, with this work, Krawczyk et al. now have more confidence that their results have high population validity.

Now we turn to a conceptual replication designed to extend population validity. Picture this: You meet your friend for lunch and ask her how she is. She says she's fine, but her face looks sad and you guess that something is upsetting her. Sounds plausible, right? In fact, our ability to read emotion in other people's faces has been studied for decades. Is it a universal ability? In other words, does a smiling face mean the same to everyone, everywhere?

In a classic series of studies, Ekman (1971) presented study participants from 5 "literate" countries (Brazil, United States, Argentina, Chile, and Japan) 30 photos of Caucasians showing facial expressions.

In each case, the participants were asked to identify the emotion shown in each face by choosing a word describing one of a selection of basic emotions (happiness, sadness, surprise, fear, anger, disgust/contempt). Participants were also asked to rate the intensity of each emotion on a 7-point scale.

Ekman found strong consensus, with most participants agreeing on the emotions shown in 28 of the 30 presented photos. Furthermore, he found no differences among the different cultures in terms of emotion intensity.

Ekman's results from the study noted above do provide evidence for the universality of facial expressions of emotion. However, as Ekman notes, there is another possible reason for the results. Perhaps people from different countries agree on the recognition of facial expressions of emotion because they've all seen these expressions portrayed in the media – television, movies, magazines. Thus, in response to this possibility, Ekman conducted another study, testing two isolated cultures that were not privy to the media influences noted above. This next study is a conceptual replication designed to extend the population validity of Ekman's original study. It is a conceptual replication because the methodology was different, although the goals were the same – to help determine whether there is universality in the facial expression of emotion.

Here's what Ekman did in this next study. He traveled to New Guinea to test members of the Fore and Dani cultures, isolated populations that did not have access to the same media influences that those in his first study had. I'll just describe Ekman's procedure with the Fore culture. Because this culture was "preliterate" (citizens did not read or write), a different procedure was needed. In this case, instead of presenting 30 photos of Caucasians displaying emotions and asking participants to choose a word corresponding to the displayed emotion, Ekman showed three photos of Caucasians displaying

different emotions, told a short story ("His friends have come and he is happy"), and then asked the participants to choose which photo fit the story (p. 271).

What did Ekman find? He found that people from the Fore culture chose the same emotions for the scenarios as participants from the "literate countries." Generally speaking, the research with the Fore culture provided additional evidence of the universality of facial expressions. Thus, with this study, Ekman completed a conceptual replication of his earlier work, and with it he extended the population validity of his results.

Ecological Validity

Now let's discuss another form of external validity, ecological validity, that concerns our ability to generalize to additional settings. We'll start with a consideration of one type of setting, lab spaces. Psychological research is often conducted in psychology laboratories. These are usually spaces at colleges and universities; they likely have desks, chairs, file cabinets, computers, and perhaps some assorted psychological equipment. They don't really resemble the types of spaces where most people live their lives. Does what happens there tell us anything about life outside of these lab spaces? Again, that's a question of external validity. In this case, the type of external validity that is relevant is ecological validity, the ability to generalize across settings.

Let's take a closer look at this issue with an example. Spangenberg, Grohmann, and Sprott (2005) were interested in how the scent and music presented in a retail environment can affect views of the shopping experience. First they pretested a variety of scents and ultimately chose one that a group of participants rated as closely associated with Christmas. Then, for the main experiment, they prepped the lab to have either a Christmas scent or no ambient scent.

They also had a recording of a musical artist singing Christmas music or non-Christmas music. Some participants experienced Christmas music and a Christmas scent; some experienced Christmas music and no scent; some experienced non-Christmas music and a Christmas scent, while others experienced non-Christmas music and no scent. When participants arrived at the lab, the music and scent conditions were already present. The participants were asked to view a series of slides showing typical department store merchandise and answer questions about the retail environment.

Spangenberg et al. found that in an environment with both Christmas music and a Christmas scent (as opposed to no scent and non-Christmas music), participants had more favorable attitudes toward the "store" and the merchandise. Inconsistency between the music and scent presentation generally led to less favorable ratings.

Spangenberg et al. proposed that their results suggest that presenting consistent environmental cues can potentially lead to favorable outcomes for those in the retail environment. Their work does have the advantage of being high in internal validity. They had complete control over the presence and absence of both the music and the scents. Everything else was the same for all the participants. So we can know that, for this experimentation, the results are due to the music and scent manipulations. However, as Spangenberg et al. acknowledge, the generalizability of the results may be limited. Sitting in a psychology lab while viewing merchandise on slides does not really resemble the real-life shopping experience in a department store. Thus, we cannot know that the results Spangenberg et al. obtained are what we would see in the real world; we can only speculate. Further research (a conceptual replication!) could be conducted in an environment that more closely resembles real life in an effort to extend the generalizability of this work.

Because Spangenberg et al.'s experiment does not really resemble the real-life experience of shopping in a department store, it is considered low in what we call mundane realism. **Mundane realism** is the extent to which an experiment resembles the real world. Experiments conducted in the lab are often relatively low in mundane realism. If you want to generalize from a specific laboratory study to the real world, you will make less of a conceptual leap if your study already resembles the real-world experience.

One possibility to increase the mundane realism of Spangenberg et al.'s experiment is to create a "department store" environment in the lab. Instead of presenting merchandise on slides, experimenters could bring merchandise into the lab and display it as if it were in the store itself. This could increase the mundane realism, although you would still have the question of whether the results have ecological validity. Would you obtain the same results in a setting outside the lab? This is an empirical question that future research will have to answer.

Generalizing from the Lab to the Field

As we saw earlier, in an effort to heighten external validity, we sometimes actually conduct our research, experimental or non-experimental, in the real world. This "field research" has a tendency to increase the mundane realism – and our confidence in generalizing our results to the real world. Let's take a look at research that started in a lab and then was replicated in the real world in an effort to increase its ecological validity.

Swami and Furnham (2007) conducted an experiment to determine how undergraduates in Britain viewed blonde and brunette women with and without tattoos. The women were presented to study participants in 16 different cartoon-like drawings projected on a large screen (comparable to the sample drawings shown in Figure 12.8). The drawings incorporated a variation in hair color (blonde, brunette) as well as 8 levels of body art (no tattoo present, tattoos present at 1, 2, or 3 locations [arm, hip, ankle]). Swami and Furnham presented the drawings in random order to a sample of students in Britain and asked them to rate the women on a variety of characteristics using a 9-point scale (such as 1 = not at all physically attractive/sexually promiscuous; 9 = very physically attractive/sexually promiscuous). Specifically, they were interested in who would be rated as more physically attractive, more sexually promiscuous, and more likely to consume a large amount of alcohol.

What did Swami and Furnham find? First of all, brunettes were rated as more attractive, less promiscuous, and lighter drinkers than blondes. In addition, women with tattoos were seen more negatively than those without tattoos. Those with tattoos were seen as less attractive, more promiscuous, and heavier drinkers than those without. Those with more versus fewer tattoos were seen even more negatively.

Can we generalize these results to the real world? First, let's consider the level of mundane realism. Swami and Furnham had their study participants rate drawings of women that were projected on a screen. Does that sound like a real-life experience? I would say no, it doesn't. The mundane realism was indeed low. In the real world, we do not generally judge women from mere drawings or rate their promiscuity on a 9-point scale. This lack of resemblance to the real world suggests that the external validity of Swami and Furnham's work is low.

But there is a way to increase the external validity of Swami and Furnham's experimentation, and that is just what Guéguen (2013) set out to do. Guéguen did a conceptual replication of Swami and Furnham's research, but in Guéguen's case the experimentation was conducted in the field. Because Guéguen's research was actually conducted in the real world,

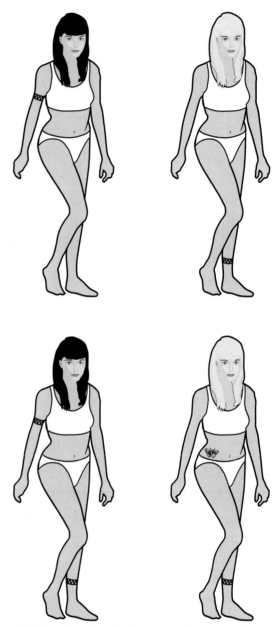

FIGURE 12.8 The 16 drawings in Swami and Furnham's (2007) experiment varied in terms of hair color (blonde, brunette) as well as body art (no tattoo present, tattoos present at one, two or three locations [arm, hip, ankle]) comparable to that shown here.

it has high mundane realism, and we have far more confidence that the obtained results will generalize to the population of interest. Let's take a closer look at what Guéguen did.

Guéguen approached the issue from an evolutionary point of view. This perspective promotes the idea that males have the goal of ensuring their genetic material survives. To achieve this goal, they are motivated to increase their number of female sexual partners. We would then expect them to be responsive to cues that reveal females' level of receptivity to sexual advances. Guéguen indicated that Swami and Furnham's research suggests tattoos might act as one of those cues. Guéguen surmised that if tattoos indicate a woman is more sexually promiscuous as Swami and Furnham's results suggest, then males would be more likely to approach a woman with a tattoo than one without.

Guéguen conducted his study on a beach, and the participants were men who just happened to be on the beach at the time. He had 11 female confederates, each previously rated as attractive and all wearing red two-piece bathing suits. When it was time for a confederate to take part in the experiment (they took turns), she would walk alone to an area of the beach with a lot of men present. Then she would spread out a beach towel, lie on her stomach, and appear to read a book. In half these instances the confederate wore a butterfly tattoo on her lower back. In the other half, the confederate did not. Each confederate went to multiple beaches, and each experienced both tattoo and non-tattoo conditions.

A male confederate sitting nearby was designated as an observer. Specifically, he would time how long it took, once the woman settled on the towel and opened her book, for a man to approach and talk to her. If a man approached and spoke to the woman, her response was, "Hello, I am waiting for my boyfriend who is likely to arrive in 1 or 2 min" (p. 1520). At that point the male confederate would approach, and the two confederates would leave the beach together.

What did Guéguen find? More men made contact with the women who had tattoos, and men approached the women with tattoos faster than they approached the women without tattoos.

So now Guéguen has evidence that men will more readily approach women with tattoos. But did they do so because they saw these women as more attractive than those without tattoos (inconsistent with Swami and Furnham's work), or because they saw them as sexually promiscuous (consistent with Swami and Furnham's work)? Guéguen did a second study to investigate this issue more directly. The procedure was similar in that the female confederate again lay on a beach towel and read while on her stomach. In half of the cases, she had a butterfly tattoo on her lower back. But for this study, instead of waiting for men to approach the woman, the male confederate approached nearby males and asked them to look at the woman carefully and rate (1) the probability of having a date with her if the opportunity presented itself, (2) the likelihood of the woman's agreeing to have sex on the first date, and (3) how attractive the woman was.

So now what happened? Table 12.1 provides these results. In this case the men indicated that they thought they were more likely to have a date with the tattooed woman (6.82 was determined to be significantly different from 5.48), and that the tattooed woman would be more likely to have sex on that first date (6.29 was determined to be significantly different from 4.53).

These results are consistent with what Swami and Furnham found. The results of Guéguen's two studies extend the external validity of Swami and Furnham's research findings with regard to promiscuity. More specifically, the ecological validity of these results has been extended; these findings were consistent from the lab to the real world.

However, Guéguen did not find results consistent with Swami and Furnham with regard to the question of attractiveness; the woman was rated equally attractive with and without the tattoo (refer back to

Table 12.1 Mean of women's physical attractiveness, probability of having a date, and probability of having sex on the first date. Each question was rated on a scale of 1–9.

Measure	Tattoo n = 220		No tattoo n = 220	
	Mean	Standard Deviation	Mean	Standard Deviation
Probability of a date	6.82	1.65	5.48	1.71
Probability of having sex on the first date	6.29	1.35	4.53	1.22
Physical attractiveness	7.22	1.94	6.94	2.07

Source: Guéguen, N. (2013). Effects of a tattoo on men's behavior and attitudes towards women: An experimental field study. *Archives on Sexual Behavior, 42,* 1517–1524. doi:10.1007/s10508-013-0104-2.

Table 12.1: 7.22 was not determined to be significantly different from 6.94). In other words, Guéguen did not replicate Swami and Furnham's results with regard to levels of perceived attractiveness. Why the difference in results? Well, there were methodological differences in the research studies, and this could account for the differences in results. Recall that Swami and Furnham had people judge the attractiveness of drawings while Guéguen had people judge real women (the realistic testing situation in Guéguen's work does make it more externally valid). However, Swami and Furnham used different tattoos than Guéguen and put them in different places on the body than Guéguen did. This too could be important to perceived attractiveness ratings. It is up to future researchers to continue to refine these results, to do more research so they can understand what can happen in the lab and what is likely to happen in the real world.

Generalizing to Multiple Settings

Sometimes when we talk about ecological validity, we're concerned not with whether the results obtained in the lab setting will generalize to just *one* real-world setting but with whether they will hold in multiple settings. Let's look at a series of examples.

Many researchers have considered what the impact of crowding is to various psychological measures such as negative affect. Think about this for a moment. Have you ever been in a classroom that is overcrowded – every desk is taken and they are arranged such that every desk touches those next to it? If you concentrate hard, you can probably feel the person behind you breathing on your neck! I'm exaggerating, but the underlying question is valid. How does a crowded environment affect people differently from how a more spacious environment does?

Researchers have found evidence in the laboratory that people experience more negative affect in a crowded condition than in a less crowded one (Griffitt & Veitch, 1971). But do people tend to feel more negative affect in a crowd when they are in real-life settings? Although the results are not entirely consistent (see Epstein, 1981 for a review), researchers have obtained evidence of the relationship between crowding and negative affect in a variety of settings, thus extending the ecological validity of these results. I'll give you a few examples. We'll start by looking at different types of settings on college campuses.

Over a period of 4 years Sommer and Becker (1971) had college students rate how they felt about their classroom (they tested students in the same classroom in every case). They found a positive correlation between the number of people in a class and the number of complaints; that is, the more crowded condition was associated with more complaints.

Aiello, Baum, and Gormley (1981) looked at another type of campus setting. They found that undergraduates who had three in their dorm room as opposed to two reported more negative affect (the rooms were similar in size). Zuckerman, Schmitz, and Yosha (1977) also considered the effects of crowding in dorms; however, instead of considering the room itself, they considered the amount of crowding in the overall dorm. One dorm was categorized as more crowded than the other because it had smaller rooms, more rooms on each floor, and public spaces that more people shared. Zuckerman et al. compared survey responses from random respondents in the two dorms. Those in the less crowded dorm indicated that they were in a better mood than those in the more crowded dorm. These results, a relationship between crowding and affect, are consistent with what others have found.

Researchers have also tested the relationship between crowding and affect outside of university settings to extend the ecological validity even further. For example, Paulus, Cox, McCain, and Chandler (1975) found that those in crowded prison environments (with more individuals in their housing units) had more negative affective responses. Thus, by testing prisoners as opposed to undergraduates, Paulus et al. extended both the ecological validity and the population validity of the finding that crowded conditions tend to be associated with negative affect. Other researchers have considered the effects of crowding at still more settings, including psychiatric hospitals (Nijman & Rector, 1999), oil-drilling platforms (Cox, Paulus, McCain, & Schkade, 1979), and trains (Evans & Wener, 2007). Each time the impact

of crowding is investigated in a new setting is an opportunity to increase the ecological validity of the results.

Replication to Extend Ecological Validity

As you can see, replication is an important component of extending ecological validity. But not all work needs to be ecologically valid. Think about your research question. Is it important to know whether your results will hold in multiple settings? If so, then extending the ecological validity would be a goal. But it is not necessarily a goal for just one researcher or just one research team. Each research team could reasonably build on what others have done before. That's the way research works.

Temporal Validity

Temporal validity refers to the extent to which we can generalize the results of a research study across time. Some results have not been shown to be stable over long periods. For example, in recent years, smoking behaviors and attitudes toward smoking have been changing (for example, Ashley et al., 1998). I remember when professors smoked in their offices, talk-show hosts smoked on television, and people smoked in elevators! Can you imagine any of those behaviors happening now? Attitudes toward smoking and behaviors related to smoking that were assessed in the 1950s would not have temporal validity; the results would not stand the test of time.

Temporal validity can also be considered in other ways. Instead of looking at time as the passage of years, we can consider time in different ways. We'll talk about two issues relevant to temporal validity: (1) seasonal variation, and (2) cyclical variation.

Seasonal Variation

When considering temporal validity, you may need to consider **seasonal variation**. It is an acknowledgment that some psychological phenomena vary from season to season.

Let's take a look at research on a phenomenon that has often been noted to have seasonal variation: mood. Many researchers have found that perceived mood can fluctuate with the seasons (for example, Haggag, Eklund, Linaker, & Götestam, 1990, although see Traffanstedt, Mehta, & LoBello, 2016). So those who conduct research on topics related to mood (such as depression) have often considered possible seasonal variation. Here is an example.

Kristjánsdóttir, Olsson, Sundelin, and Naessen (2013) were interested in studying the seasonal variation in self-reported health and depression in adolescent girls, with a specific interest in how hormonal contraception might affect that relationship. To investigate these relationships, they collected data over a 1-year period from a portion of those visiting a youth health center in Sweden. Kristjánsdóttir et al. found, as others also had, that depression in adolescents varied across seasons, with higher levels in the winter than in the summer months. In other words, they replicated the work of previous researchers when they found seasonal variation in self-reported mental health.

What did Kristjánsdóttir et al. find out about those on hormonal contraception? These participants generally reported that their physical and mental health were as good as or in some cases better than that of those taking other medications (such as for physical ailments or depression and anxiety) or no medication at all. What's important for our purposes is recognizing that had Kristjánsdóttir et al. confined their study to testing during only one season instead of four, their results would have been an incomplete picture of the state of health in these adolescent participants. Gathering data in a way that reveals seasonal variation was important in this kind of research.

Sometimes it's not previous research that suggests possible seasonal variation; it's the research question that prompts researchers to look across a number of seasons. Let's take a look at an example of this.

Smart and Bisogni (2001) were interested in what influenced the food choices of male college hockey players. It's a reasonable question, but the answer differs depending on when we ask it. Thus, Smart and Bisogni surveyed and observed their participants for 10 months broken into 4 periods: (1) dry-land training, (2) in season, (3) off season, and

FIGURE 12.9 Temporal validity refers to the extent to which we can generalize the results of a research study across time. In some cases we need to consider the possibility of seasonal variation in results.

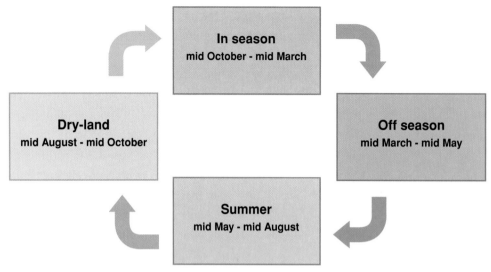

FIGURE 12.10 The 10-month observation period in Smart and Bisogni's (2001) study.

(4) summer (Figure 12.10). Smart and Bisogni found distinct differences in the types of food preferred as a function of these periods. For example, during the off season, participants tended to indulge more in preferred foods such as cookies, while during dry-land training and the hockey season they were more careful to eat a healthy diet. Thus, again, if the researchers had asked the hockey players to describe their diet at only one point during the year, they would have derived a less-complete picture of how the diets of these players can change throughout the year.

Let's take a look at one more example of a research topic in which a consideration of seasonal variation is worthwhile. First, I have a question for you. Does the amount of exercise you do vary at different times of the year? If it does, think about possible reasons why. Now let's look at how a group of researchers considered the same question.

McCormack, Friedenreich, Shiell, Giles-Corti, and Doyle-Baker (2009) surveyed adult males and females of various ages in Calgary, Canada on the amount of walking and moderate and/or vigorous physical activity they typically do in a week. They

recognized that seasonal conditions such as weather and daylight can affect physical activities (imagine walking outside in the middle of a Canadian winter!); thus, they conducted their survey during months from all seasons. Their goal was to measure physical activity in a random sample of Calgarian participants, determine whether there were differences among ages and genders, and then make recommendations regarding ways to encourage physical activity across all seasons.

What did McCormack et al. find? First, they replicated the work of others in finding that, overall, the amount of physical activity was lower in winter than in other seasons. In addition, they did find differences in the amount of physical activity as a function of gender and age. For example, males and middle-aged participants overall were more likely to take part in *vigorous* physical activity during the summer than in the winter. As a result of their research, McCormack et al. recommended a variety of actions to increase activity during the colder months, such as encouraging walking in indoor venues, removing snow and ice from sidewalks, and ensuring that outdoor lighting is adequate during shorter days.

If McCormack et al. had asked study participants about their level of physical activity at only one point in time, as opposed to asking about activities across all seasons, they would not have as complete a picture of how much this Canadian population exercises. Note that our earlier discussion of population validity is also relevant to McCormack et al.'s research. As McCormack et al. acknowledge, their results are "likely more generalizable to regions that have similar demographic and socio-cultural profiles and climate conditions" (p. 1015).

Cyclical Variation

Cyclical variation is another concept relevant to temporal validity. **Cyclical variation** refers to a regular variation that can occur within study participants themselves. Researchers may not have to worry about cyclical validity if their research topic is unlikely to be affected by it. Let's look at a research example that included a cyclical variation widely known to exist within female participants – the menstrual cycle. Approximately every 28 days, females' bodies go through a cyclical pattern of fluctuating hormones. Females are typically fertile only during a 6-day window about midway through this cycle. Many researchers have documented ways in which the menstrual cycle affects females' lives (see Farage, Osborn, & MacLean, 2008 for a review). We're going to look more closely at one such investigation.

Saad and Stenstrom (2012) considered the effects of the menstrual cycle from an evolutionary perspective. They expected, for example, that during the more fertile days of their cycle, females would "maximize their attractiveness to potential mates" (p. 105). In order to assess this, they had females track their spending patterns over a 35-day period (which was likely to encompass one complete menstrual cycle for participants). They found, for example, that females spent more money on increasing their attractiveness (such as by making clothing purchases) during the fertile phase of their menstrual cycle. In comparison, the amount of money spent on items unrelated to beauty did not fluctuate with the phases of the menstrual cycle. Thus, Saad and Stenstrom's research question required the gathering of data across the complete menstrual cycle.

Replication to Extend Temporal Validity

Temporal validity is not always a concern. Much research will not show a variation in results as a function of when the study was conducted. However, for those topics that have shown variation, it is important to recognize that *when* you do the research can affect your results.

One of the ways that you can determine whether temporal validity is a possible concern for your topic is to do a thorough review of the literature on your topic before you begin your investigation. Has collecting data over time been important in previous investigations on your topic? Alternatively, perhaps researchers have not yet considered collecting data over time, but you suspect that it might be important to your investigation. Let's look at an example. Pretend that multiple research teams had considered the dietary habits of hockey players, some asked for responses in the winter and some in the summer, and they found very different results. One idea for future research is to try to determine why the results have been mixed. Could temporal validity be a reason for the discrepancies? Look at the details of these investigations. Were they conducted at different times of the year? Were the investigations with congruent results completed at a similar time of the year? If so, temporal validity could be an explanation for the different results from investigation to investigation. You can then conduct a study to investigate this possibility – collecting data across multiple seasons to determine if this more complete picture of a hockey player's diet over time explains the previously mixed results.

SUMMARY

External validity can be important when you wish to generalize your research results. There are three major kinds of external validity: (1) population validity, which asks the question, "Will the results obtained with the tested sample generalize to other people?" (2) ecological validity, which asks, "Will the results obtained hold in other settings?" and (3) temporal validity, which asks, "Will the results obtained hold at other times?" Temporal validity can be further broken down into seasonal variation, an acknowledgment that some psychological phenomena vary from season to season, and cyclical variation, which refers to a regular variation that can occur within study participants themselves.

External validity is potentially a goal for those performing both experimental and non-experimental research, while internal validity, the extent to which we can say our independent variable caused our dependent variable's results, is only relevant for experimentation. External and internal validity tend to be inversely related. Results from experimentation in the lab typically have high internal validity because of the high degree of control. However, an experiment completed in the lab doesn't often resemble real-life experiences, thus the external validity of research conducted in the lab is sometimes relatively low. When researchers want to try to increase external validity, they sometimes conduct their research in the field.

Replication of research is a large part of the effort to extend external validity. Obtaining similar results with other samples, in other settings, at other times can help researchers to know how generalizable their results are.

GLOSSARY

Conceptual replication – one completes a study in a way that is similar to but not exactly the same as the way it was completed before.

Cyclical variation – a type of temporal validity. Cyclical variation refers to a regular variation that can occur within study participants themselves.

Ecological validity – asks the question "Will the results obtained hold in other settings?"

Exact replication – one completes a study in virtually the same way it was originally conducted.

Field experimentation – experimentation conducted in the real world.

Field research – a term often used to refer to non-experimental research conducted in the real world.

Mundane realism – the extent to which an experiment resembles the real world. Experiments conducted in the lab are often relatively low in mundane realism while those conducted in the real world tend to be high in mundane realism.

Population validity – asks the question, "Will the results obtained with the tested sample generalize to other people?"

Seasonal variation – a type of temporal validity that is an acknowledgment that some psychological phenomena vary from season to season.

Temporal validity – asks the question "Will the results obtained hold at other times?"

REVIEW QUESTIONS

1 Define external validity.
2 Differentiate between internal validity and external validity.

3 Define population validity.

4 Explain how a research question can help you define your target population.

5 Explain how the characteristics of a sample can affect population validity.

6 Differentiate a convenience sample from a WEIRD sample.

7 Define ecological validity.

8 Discuss how generalizing from the lab to the field can increase mundane realism.

9 Explain why a researcher would want to determine if results generalized to multiple settings.

10 Define temporal validity.

11 Explain why a researcher might need to consider a seasonal variation.

12 Explain why a researcher might need to consider a cyclical variation.

ARTICLES AS ILLUSTRATION

1 Read Danhauer et al.'s (2012) survey regarding high school students' views about iPod use and hearing health, and answer the questions that follow.

Danhauer, J. L., Johnson, C. E., Dunne, A. F., Young, M. D., Rotan, S. N., Snelson, T. A., Stockwell, J. S., & McLain, M. J. (2012). Survey of high school students' perceptions about their iPod use, knowledge of hearing health, and need for education. *Language, Speech, and Hearing Services in Schools*, *43*, 14–35. doi:http://dx.doi.org/10.1044/0161-1461(2011/10-0088)

a. Describe the sample and the procedure.
b. What are the limitations of the tested sample?

c. Briefly describe the results.
d. Propose three ways to extend the population validity of this work.

2 Read the article on tattoos and risky behavior by King and Vidourek (2013) and answer the questions that follow.

King, K. A., & Vidourek, R. A. (2013). Getting inked: Tattoo and risky behavioral involvement among university students. *Social Science Journal*, *50*, 540–546. doi:http://dx.doi.org/10.1016/j.soscij.2013.09.009

a. Describe the sample and the procedure.
b. Briefly describe the results.
c. Can we assume that the results obtained hold for all college students? Why or why not? What are the limitations of the tested sample?
d. Propose a way to extend the population validity of this work.

3 Read Want's (2014) article about the ecological validity of research on the impact of viewing thin-ideal media images and answer the questions.

Want, S. C. (2014). Three questions regarding the ecological validity of experimental research on the impact of viewing thin-ideal media images. *Basic and Applied Social Psychology*, *36*, 27–34. doi:http://dx.doi.org/10.1080/01973533.2013.856783

a. Lab researchers have repeatedly investigated how women are impacted by exposure to attractive media images. Summarize these general findings.
b. The author argues that there are three reasons why these laboratory findings may not generalize to the real world. Summarize these three reasons.

c. Indicate why Want's article is a discussion of *ecological* validity (information provided in this chapter will help you answer this question).

4 Read Cockerton, Moore, and Norman's (1997) article on cognition and music and answer the questions.

Cockerton, T., Moore, S., & Norman, D. (1997). Cognitive test performance and background music. *Perceptual and Motor Skills*, *85*, 1435–1438. doi:http://dx.doi.org/10.2466/pms.1997.85.3f.1435

a. Describe the sample and the procedure.
b. Briefly describe the results.
c. Propose a replication to extend the population validity of this research.
d. Propose a replication to extend the ecological validity of this research (be careful to propose a new type of setting, not just another college).

5 Read Spangenberg et al.'s (2005) research on the effects of scent and music in a retail setting and answer the questions.

Spangenberg, E. R., Grohmann, B., & Sprott, D. E. (2005). It's beginning to smell (and sound) a lot like Christmas: The interactive effects of ambient scent and music in a retail setting. *Journal of Business Research*, *58*, 1583–1589. doi:http://dx.doi.org/10.1016/j.jbusres.2004.09.005

a. Describe the sample and the procedure.
b. Briefly describe the results.
c. Propose a way to extend the temporal validity of this research beyond Spangenberg et al.'s idea for the Fourth of July.

1 Use Danhauer's (2012) survey (available in the article) regarding high school students' views on iPod use and hearing health to test a new (and different type of) sample in an effort to extend the population validity.

2 In the section in this chapter on ecological validity, a series of articles on crowding was presented. Propose a study to investigate and potentially extend further the ecological validity of the general relationship between crowding and affect.

3 Choose one of the following topics and find journal articles that reveal earlier and more recent attitudes regarding: (1) smoking, (2) same-sex marriage, (3) the death penalty, and (4) tattoos. Discuss the temporal validity of the obtained results. Are there similarities/differences?

REFERENCES

Aiello, J. R., Baum, A., & Gormley, F. P. (1981). Social determinants of residential crowding stress. *Personality and Social Psychology Bulletin*, *7*, 643–649. doi:http://dx.doi.org/10.1177/014616728174021

Akehurst, L., Köhnken, G., Vrij, A., & Bull, R. (1996). Lay persons' and police officers' beliefs regarding deceptive behavior. *Applied Cognitive Psychology*, *10*, 461–471. doi:http://dx.doi.org/10.1002/(SICI)1099-0720(199612)10:6 < 461::AID-ACP413 > 3.0.CO;2-2

Arnett, J. J. (2008). The neglected 95%: Why American psychology needs to become less American. *American Psychologist*, *63*, 602–614. doi:http://dx.doi.org/10.1037/0003-066X.63.7.602

Ashley, M. J., Cohen, J., Ferrence, R., Bull, S., Bondy, S., Poland, B., & Pederson, L. (1998). Smoking in the home: Changing attitudes and current practices. *American Journal of Public Health*, *88*, 797–800. doi:http://dx.doi.org/10.2105/AJPH.88.5.797

Bem, D. J., & Lord, C. G. (1979). Template matching: A proposal for probing the ecological validity of experimental settings in social psychology. *Journal of Personality and Social Psychology*, *37*, 833–846. doi:http://dx.doi.org/10.1037/0022-3514.37.6.833

Cockerton, T., Moore, S., & Norman, D. (1997). Cognitive test performance and background music. *Perceptual and Motor Skills*, *85*, 1435–1438. doi:http://dx.doi.org/10.2466/pms.1997.85.3f.1435

Cox, V. C., Paulus, P. B., McCain, G., & Schkade, J. K. (1979). Field research on the effects of crowding in prisons and on offshore drilling platforms. In J. R. Aiello and A. Baum (eds.), *Residential crowding and design* (pp. 95–106). New York: Plenum Press.

Danhauer, J. L., Johnson, C. E., Dunne, A. F., Young, M. D., Rotan, S. N., Snelson, T. A., Stockwell, J. S., & McLain, M. J. (2012). Survey of high school students' perceptions about their iPod use, knowledge of hearing health, and need for education. *Language, Speech, and Hearing Services in Schools*, *43*, 14–35. doi:http://dx.doi.org/10.1044/0161-1461(2011/10-0088)

DePaulo, B. M., Lindsay, J. J., Malone, B. E., Muhlenbruck, L., Charlton, K., & Cooper, H. (2003). Cues to deception. *Psychological Bulletin*, *129*, 74–118. doi:http://dx.doi.org/10.1037/0033-2909.129.1.74

Ekman, P. (1971). Universal and cultural differences in facial expressions of emotion. *Nebraska Symposium on Motivation*, *19*, 207–283.

Epstein, Y. M. (1981). Crowding stress and human behavior. *Journal of Social Issues*, *37*(1), 126–144. doi:http://dx.doi.org/10.1111/j.1540-4560.1981.tb01060.x

Evans, G. W., & Wener, R. E. (2007). Crowding and personal space invasion on the train: Please don't make me sit in the middle. *Journal of Environmental Psychology*, *27*, 90–94. doi:http://dx.doi.org/10.1016/j.jenvp.2006.10.002

Farage, M., Osborn, T. W., & MacLean, A. B. (2008). Cognitive, sensory, and emotional changes associated with the menstrual cycle: A review. *Archives of Gynecology and Obstetrics*, *278*(4), 299–307. doi:http://dx.doi.org/10.1007/s00404-008-0708-2

The Global Deception Research Team (2006). A world of lies. *Journal of Cross-Cultural Psychology*, *37*(1), 60–74. doi:http://dx.doi.org/10.1177/0022022105282295

Griffitt, W., & Veitch, R. (1971). Hot and crowded: Influences of population density and temperature on interpersonal affective behavior. *Journal of Personality and Social Psychology*, *17*, 92–98. doi:http://dx.doi.org/10.1037/h0030458

Guéguen, N. (2013). Effects of a tattoo on men's behavior and attitudes towards women: An experimental field study. *Archives of Sexual Behavior*, *42*, 1517–1524. doi:http://dx.doi.org/10.1007/s10508-013-0104-2

Haggag, A., Eklund, B., Linaker, O., & Götestam, K. G. (1990). Seasonal mood variation: An epidemiological study in northern Norway. *Acta Psychiatrica Scandinavica*, *81*, 141–145. doi:http://dx.doi.org/10.1111/j.1600-0447.1990.tb06467.x

Henrich, J., Heine, S. J., & Norenzayan, A. (2010). The weirdest people in the world? *Behavioral and Brain Sciences*, *33*, 61–83. doi:http://dx.doi.org/10.1017/S0140525X0999152X

King, A. R., Bailly, M. D., & Moe, B. K. (2004). External validity considerations regarding college participant samples comprised substantially of psychology majors. In S. P. Shohov (ed.). *Advances in Psychology Research*, *29*, 71–85.

King, K. A., & Vidourek, R. A. (2013). Getting inked: Tattoo and risky behavioral involvement among university students. *Social Science Journal*, *50*, 540–546. doi:http://dx.doi.org/10.1016/j.soscij.2013.09.009

Krawczyk, M., Tyrowicz, J., Kukla-Gryz, A., & Hardy, W. (2014). "Piracy is not theft!" Is it just students who think so? *Journal of Behavioral and Experimental Economics*, *54*, 32–39. doi:http://dx.doi.org/10.1016/j.socec.2014.11.003

Kristjánsdóttir, J., Olsson, G. I., Sundelin, C., & Naessen, T. (2013). Self-reported health in adolescent girls varies according to the season and its relation to medication and hormonal contraception: A descriptive study. *European Journal of Contraception and Reproductive Health Care*, *18*, 343–354. doi:http://dx.doi.org/10.3109/13625187.2013.821107

McCormack, G. R., Friedenreich, C., Shiell, A., Giles-Corti, B., & Doyle-Baker, P. K. (2009). Sex- and age-specific seasonal variations in physical activity among adults. *Journal of Epidemiology and Community Health, 64,* 1010–1016. doi:http://dx.doi.org/10.1136/jech.2009.092841

Mook, D. G. (1983). In defense of external invalidity. *American Psychologist, 38,* 379–387. doi:http://dx.doi.org/10.1037/0003-066X.38.4.379

Nijman, H. L. I., & Rector, G. (1999). Crowding and aggression on inpatient psychiatric wards. *Psychiatric Services, 50,* 830–831. doi:http://dx.doi.org/10.1176/ps.50.6.830

Paulus, P., Cox, V., McCain, G., & Chandler, J. (1975). Some effects of crowding in a prison environment. *Journal of Applied Social Psychology, 5,* 86–91. doi:http://dx.doi.org/10.1111/j.1559-1816.1975.tb00674.x

Robinson, E. S., & Darrow, C. W. (1924). Effects of length of list on memory for numbers. *American Journal of Psychology, 35,* 235–243. doi:http://dx.doi.org/10.2307/1413826

Saad, G., & Stenstrom, E. (2012). Calories, beauty, and ovulation: The effects of the menstrual cycle on food and appearance-related consumption. *Journal of Consumer Psychology, 22,* 102–113. doi:http://dx.doi.org/10.1016/j.jcps.2011.10.001

Sayette, M. (1994). Effects of alcohol on self-appraisal. *International Journal of the Addictions, 29,* 127–133. doi:http://dx.doi.org/10.3109/10826089409047373

Sears, D. O. (1986). College sophomores in the laboratory: Influences of a narrow data base on social psychology's view of human nature. *Journal of Personality and Social Psychology, 51,* 515–530. doi:http://dx.doi.org/10.1037/0022-3514.51.3.515

Smart, L. R., & Bisogni, C. A. (2001). Personal food systems of male college hockey players. *Appetite, 37,* 57–70. doi:http://dx.doi.org/10.1006/appe.2001.0408

Sommer, R., & Becker, F. D. (1971). Room density and user satisfaction. *Environment and Behavior, 3,* 412–417.

Spangenberg, E. R., Grohmann, B., & Sprott, D. E. (2005). It's beginning to smell (and sound) a lot like Christmas: The interactive effects of ambient scent and music in a retail setting. *Journal of Business Research, 58,* 1583–1589. doi:http://dx.doi.org/10.1016/j.jbusres.2004.09.005

Suminski, R. R., Petosa, R., Utter, A. C., & Zhang, J. J. (2002). Physical activity among ethnically diverse college students. *Journal of American College Health, 51,* 75–80. doi:http://dx.doi.org/10.1080/07448480209596333

Swami, V., & Furnham, A. (2007). Unattractive, promiscuous and heavy drinkers: Perceptions of women with tattoos. *Body Image, 4,* 343–352. doi:http://dx.doi.org/10.1016/j.bodyim.2007.06.005

Traffanstedt, M. K., Mehta, S., & LoBello, S. G. (2016). Major depression with seasonal variation: Is it a valid construct? *Clinical Psychological Science, 4,* 825–834. doi:http://dx.doi.org/10.1177/2167702615615867

Want, S. C. (2014). Three questions regarding the ecological validity of experimental research on the impact of viewing thin-ideal media images. *Basic and Applied Social Psychology, 36,* 27–34. doi:http://dx.doi.org/10.1080/01973533.2013.856783

Zuckerman, M., Koestner, R., & Driver, R. (1981). Beliefs about cues associated with deception. *Journal of Nonverbal Behavior, 6,* 105–114. doi:http://dx.doi.org/10.1007/BF00987286

Zuckerman, M., Schmitz, M., & Yosha, A. (1977). Effects of crowding in a student environment. *Journal of Applied Social Psychology, 7,* 67–72. doi:http://dx.doi.org/10.1111/j.1559-1816.1977.tb02418.x

13 Online Research

LEARNING OBJECTIVES

- Identify three ways researchers can use online data collection.

- Explain the ethical responsibilities of the online researcher.

- Demonstrate how to place a survey and experiment online.

- Identify ways to recruit online participants.

- Explain what *Mechanical Turk* is.

- Describe how special populations can be studied online.

- Identify advantages and disadvantages of online data collection.

Do you remember your dreams? Ever dream of flying? Researchers have long been interested in dream content and have generally found that some dream themes, such as flying, are relatively common. Furthermore, these themes have been found to be consistent across various sample populations (see for example, Schredl, Ciric, Götz, & Wittman, 2004). Mathes, Schredl, and Göritz (2014) decided to take this investigation online, to see whether the typical dream themes found by earlier researchers would be reported by a large sample asked about the content of their most recent dreams.

First Mathes et al. found a large percentage of dreams reported as happening very recently, within the last week (see Table 13.1). The dream themes were generally consistent with what others had

FIGURE 13.1 Do you remember your dreams? Mathes et al. (2014) found common themes in dream content when they asked a sample of online participants to report on their recent dreams.

Table 13.1 Time interval between study participants and dream occurrence as reported by Mathes, Schredl, & Göritz (2014).

Last recent dream of ($N = 2,828$)	Percent
Last week	79.00
Last month	15.31
Last year	5.06
> 1 year	0.64

Source: Mathes, J., Schredl, M., & Göritz, A. S., (2014). Frequency of typical dream themes in most recent dreams: An online study. Dreaming, 24, 57–66. doi:http://dx.doi .org/10.1037/a0035857.

Table 13.2 Top 10 typical dream themes as reported by Mathes, Schredl, & Göritz (2014).

Dream themes	Ranking
Flying or soaring thorough the air	1
Trying something again and again	2
Being chased or pursued	3
Sexual experiences	4
School, teachers, studying	5
Arriving too late	6
A person now dead being alive	7
A person now alive being dead	8
Being physically attacked	9
Swimming	10

Source: Mathes, J., Schredl, M., & Göritz, A. S. (2014). Frequency of typical dream themes in most recent dreams: An online study. Dreaming, 24, 57–66. doi:http://dx.doi .org/10.1037/a0035857.

found. The 10 most common themes from Mathes et al.'s study are shown in Table 13.2. How many of these have you experienced?

Mathes et al. are just one of many research teams that have decided to collect data online. The practice is becoming increasingly common. Skitka and Sargis (2006) found that only about 2% of articles in a 2003/2004 sample of American Psychological Association journals used the Internet to collect data. A few years later, Sargis, Skitka, and McKeever (2013) found that an average of 11% of articles in a 2009/2010 sample of journals used Internet methodology. In fact, Internet research was present in 16% of the 2009/2010 articles in the top-tier social psychology journal *Journal of Personality and Social Psychology*. What was considered a "new methodological frontier" in 2005 (Skitka & Sargis, 2005, p. 1) is rapidly becoming mainstream.

In this chapter we'll look at examples of online research, the ethics of using the Internet for data collection, and the advantages and disadvantages of collecting data online. We will also discuss how to prepare a survey and look at an experiment for online data collection.

How Do Researchers Use Online Data Collection?

As suggested above, many researchers now use online data collection, and they do so in a variety of ways. Some have published work that focused on comparing the viability of this methodology to that of traditional, offline research. Others have explored new questions, perhaps attracted by easy access to potentially large and relatively diverse samples. Still others have chosen to use online data collection to examine how we interact with technology. We'll discuss each of these purposes in turn.

Perhaps because online research is still relatively new, many researchers have been studying the viability of this technique. How do the results of online testing compare to those of traditional offline research? Are the samples more diverse, or less? Mathes et al. had an assessment of viability as one of their goals. Let's take a look at another example.

Boynton and Smart Richman (2014) asked their online respondents to keep a daily diary of their alcohol use, an often-used technique for assessing alcohol consumption. See Figure 13.2 for an example of daily alcohol consumption measures comparable to that used by Boynton and Smart Richman.

Boynton and Smart Richman found that their final sample was indeed more diverse (older, richer, and more ethnically diverse) than a typical college student sample, yet it yielded results generally comparable to those of offline investigations of college students. For example, beer was the most common type of alcohol consumed by this US sample, and more drinking took place on the weekends.

In some cases researchers choose to test online for reasons other than to compare online and offline results. Perhaps they are enticed by the possibility of increasing the diversity of their sample, or by the relative ease with which study participants can be obtained. Let's look at an example. Hefner (2016) wondered why people watch wedding reality TV shows such as "Say Yes to the Dress," and whether their tendencies to watch had any relationship to their views about romance. In one of her studies, Hefner recruited participants to fill out an online questionnaire by advertising on Twitter, Facebook,

LinkedIn, and Craigslist. She asked respondents how much wedding reality TV they watched and why, as well as questions about their romantic beliefs. She found that viewing wedding reality TV was associated with the belief that love conquers all. Earlier researchers had not considered whether an association existed between viewing wedding reality shows and romantic beliefs, so Hefner didn't compare her results to any others.

As the use of technology increases in our lives, it is reasonable to expect that researchers will also design studies to explore its impact, and at least some of this research will take place online. For example, think about smartphones. As of 2015, 64% of people in the United States owned a smartphone, and almost 20% of them relied exclusively on their phone to go online (Smith, 2015). Researchers have considered how smartphones have changed our lives. Some have been interested in how much people text, and whether the frequency changes with, for example, age (Lenhart, 2015). Some have looked more into *why* people text. Let's briefly go over an example of this kind of study.

Harrison and Gilmore (2012) were interested in when and why college students text. So they created an online survey presenting 29 social situations and asked a sample of students at their university to indicate whether they texted in such situations. The results were fascinating (see Table 13.3). For example, almost 30% said they have texted while in the shower. Approximately 33% have texted during a religious service, and 13% have texted while having sex. The "why" results were also intriguing. For example, almost 26% used a text to break up with someone, and almost 46% texted someone they were romantically interested in while they were on a date with someone else. Texting has definitely infiltrated many aspects of the lives of these college students.

Another approach researchers have been taking is to conduct an analysis of the content of texts,

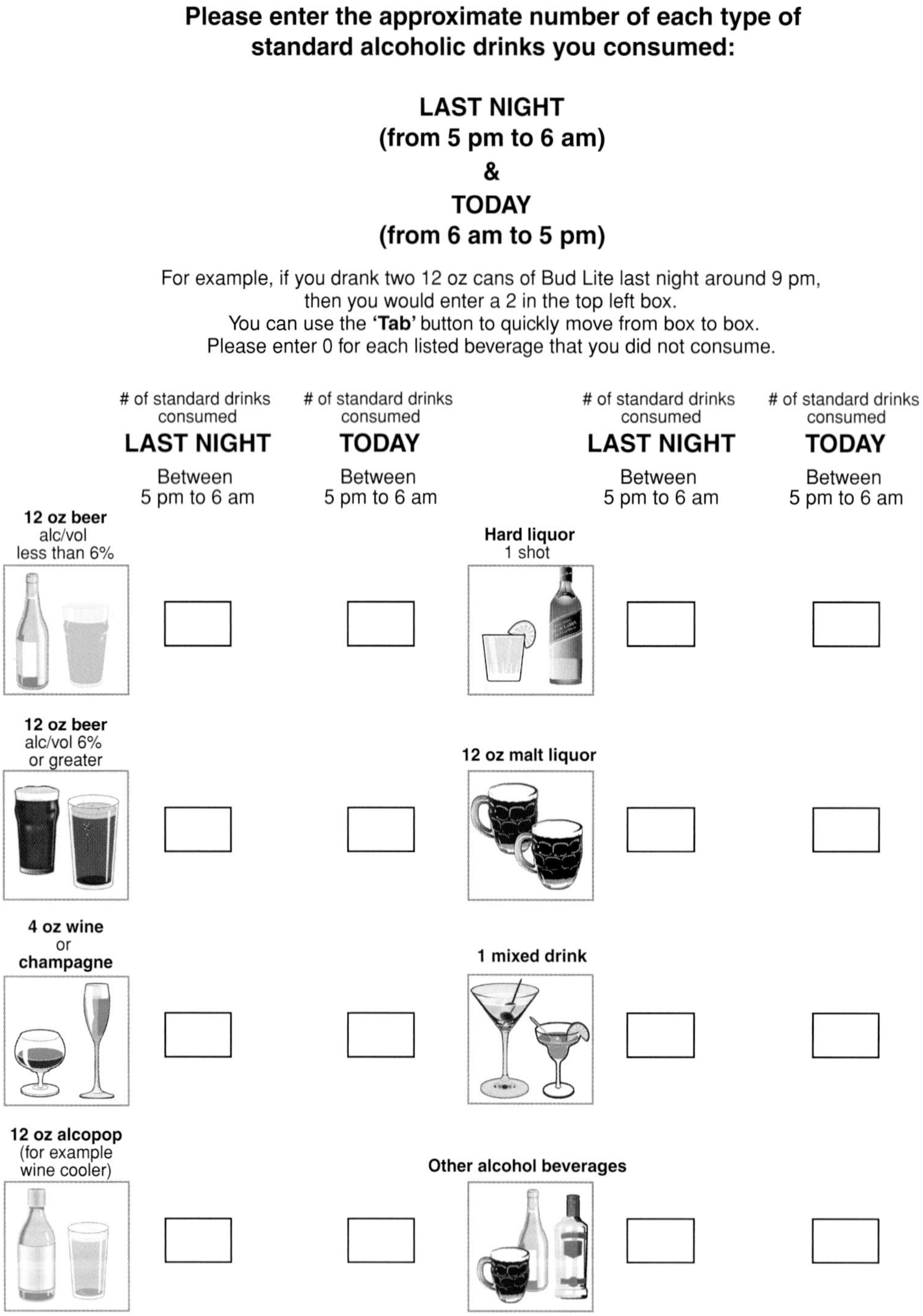

Please enter the approximate number of each type of standard alcoholic drinks you consumed:

LAST NIGHT
(from 5 pm to 6 am)

&

TODAY
(from 6 am to 5 pm)

For example, if you drank two 12 oz cans of Bud Lite last night around 9 pm,
then you would enter a 2 in the top left box.
You can use the **'Tab'** button to quickly move from box to box.
Please enter 0 for each listed beverage that you did not consume.

	# of standard drinks consumed **LAST NIGHT** Between 5 pm to 6 am	# of standard drinks consumed **TODAY** Between 5 pm to 6 am		# of standard drinks consumed **LAST NIGHT** Between 5 pm to 6 am	# of standard drinks consumed **TODAY** Between 5 pm to 6 am
12 oz beer alc/vol less than 6%	☐	☐	**Hard liquor** 1 shot	☐	☐
12 oz beer alc/vol 6% or greater	☐	☐	**12 oz malt liquor**	☐	☐
4 oz wine or **champagne**	☐	☐	**1 mixed drink**	☐	☐
12 oz alcopop (for example wine cooler)	☐	☐	**Other alcohol beverages**	☐	☐

FIGURE 13.2 Boynton and Smart Richman's (2014) daily alcohol consumption measures.

Table 13.3   Percentage of respondents engaging in text messaging in various situations.

Have you used text messaging …	% ever engaging in behavior
Romance	
To flirt with someone?	80.00
To ask someone out?	47.00
To be romantic?	86.10
To tell someone you love him or her?	88.10
Staying connected	
To report to your family where/how you are?	91.10
To report to your significant other where/how you are?	90.00
To check on your family?	91.00
Escaping the present	
While you were at work and supposed to be working?	84.00
While drunk?	73.70
While you were going to the bathroom?	85.10
During a movie/show/sporting event you paid to see?	84.00
While you were in the shower?	29.70
From an airplane during flight?	21.80
During a religious service?	32.60
While having sex?	13.00
While eating?	92.10
Social breaches	
While speaking to someone else on the phone?	77.20
While speaking to someone else in person?	93.10
While on a date?	71.30
While service personnel are trying to wait on you (for example in a restaurant)?	91.00
To one friend while you were hanging out with another?	91.10
To talk to someone you're romantically interested in while on a date with someone else?	45.90
To break up with someone?	25.70
To cheat on your significant other?	19.00
Maleficence	
To fight with someone?	73.30
After someone told you to STOP texting them?	27.70
To insult someone?	53.00
Sexting	
That contains sexually explicit material?	65.30
To describe your sexual intent/actions ("sexting") to someone?	57.40

Source: Harrison, M. A. & Gilmore, A. L. (2012). U txt when? College students' social contexts of text messaging. *Social Science Journal, 49*, 513–518. doi:http://dx.doi.org/10.1016/j.soscij.2012.05.003

Facebook posts, tweets, and so on. There are many ways to gather content to analyze for a study like this. For example, to analyze tweets from Twitter, you can get a 3-day trial subscription to **Tweetarchivist** (www.tweetarchivist.com/) or pay for a longer one. Tell *Tweetarchivist* what term(s) you wish to search for, and the program will gather relevant tweets for later analysis (see Lachlan, Spence, & Lin, 2014 for an example).

Some researchers have conducted analyses of Facebook content. For example, Beullens and Schepers (2013) were interested in the way alcohol use was portrayed on Facebook in a sample of students at their university in Belgium. How did they get access to Facebook profiles? One of the study authors created a Facebook profile and sent a friend request to students at the university that included a message about recruiting study participants. When they had access to the desired number of Facebook profiles, the researchers analyzed the photos and text contained in these profiles, looking for content that indicated alcohol use.

They found, for example, that most of the Facebook profiles contained at least one photo that referenced alcohol use, while 40% had at least one Facebook post referencing alcohol. However, when they considered the overall number of photos and status updates, the percentage depicting alcohol use was rather small. Only 6.5% of the photos showed alcohol being used, and only about 3% of the total status updates referred to alcohol. In a majority of the cases, the references to alcohol, both in photos and in text, were positive, and friends' reactions to these posts were also quite positive.

Beullens and Schepers note that the portrayal of alcohol use in the Facebook profiles of their participants was far more prevalent than what other researchers have generally found. Was the reason that these researchers were looking at Belgians' profiles while much of the earlier research considered Facebook profiles in the United States? Was it that Beullens and Schepers' sampling technique did not generate a representative sample? Only future research can answer these questions.

Ethics of Online Research

Many of the same ethical considerations we discussed in Chapter 3 are also relevant for online research; you are still responsible for abiding by the APA Ethics Code (APA, 2002). You still have to submit your research plans to the IRB. The APA Ethics Code generally states that informed consent may not be needed if the study is anonymous and does not cause the participants any harm. But since the Code does not cover online research directly, you should err on the side of caution and get your participants' informed consent. Your participants can indicate their consent by clicking a button on an online informed consent form. See Figure 13.3 for an example of one of the informed consent forms I used in an online research study.

In addition to obtaining informed consent, you still need to protect your study participants from harm, use deception only when deemed absolutely necessary, and in most cases debrief. When would you *not* debrief? The APA Ethics Code states that there may be cases in which the risk of harm to participants is minimal and in which "scientific or humane values justify withholding" a debriefing (APA, 2002, p. 1070). Again, the Code was written with offline participants in mind, though we can extrapolate its concepts to online research. I recommend debriefing whenever it is feasible (your participants can read an explanation of the purpose of your research once they have finished the study); however, ultimately it is up to the researcher(s) and the IRB to decide how to handle these ethical issues.

Doing research online can bring special challenges (see Bohannon, 2016; Emery, 2014). The researcher is not there to answer questions for

FIGURE 13.3 Sample informed consent form for online research.

Informed Consent

You are being invited to participate in research being conducted by Dr. Wendy Heath of Rider University.

Purpose of the Study:

This study is designed to explore people's perceptions of a defendant.

Risks Involved in the Study:

There are no known risks involved in participating in this research. This study received approval from the Rider University Human Subjects Committee in June 2016. The contact information for this Committee is as follows: Chair of the Human Subjects Committee, Rider University Psychology Department, Lawrenceville, NJ 08648.

Benefits Involved in the Study:

This brief questionnaire will help us understand how individual jurors view someone who is on trial.

What Will Be Asked of You:

You will be asked to read a brief scenario and to answer a series of questions. Overall, participation in this study should take no more than ten minutes. You will not be contacted for any reason, unless you request it.

Your Rights as a Participant:

Your participation is completely voluntary, and you may choose to end the study at any time. If you have any questions or concerns you may contact:
Dr. Wendy Heath
Rider University
Psychology Department
2083 Lawrenceville Road
Lawrenceville, NJ08648
heath@rider.edu

Confidentiality and Anonymity:

Your identity remains completely anonymous. Your responses will never be matched to your identity, and no one will know how you personally chose to answer a question.

If you have read the above statement and agree to continue, then click on the "Continue to Next Page" button below. If you would rather not participate, then close the web page.

online participants, either during the study or later at the debriefing. The researcher should, of course, provide his or her contact information during the informed consent process, but it is up to the participants to reach out and make that contact if they have any questions or comments. You may choose to encourage participants to make a note of the researcher's contact information in case it is needed.

Another possible concern for those doing online research is the obligation to keep participants' identification confidential. One way to lessen the risk to your participants when you are collecting data online is not to ask for identifying information like names (Kraut et al., 2004).

Online Research: Surveys and Experiments

As you saw above, researchers are using the Internet to collect data in a variety of ways and on a variety of topics. In this section, I'll talk about creating an online survey and an online experiment and provide published examples of each.

Creating an Online Survey

There are many ways to create an online survey. I'll talk first about how to create or modify a survey for administration online using *SurveyMonkey*, and then I'll give an example of an online survey created with *SurveyMonkey*.

SurveyMonkey is easily available (www.survey-monkey.com). The free basic version allows you to create an unlimited number of surveys, each with up to 10 questions and up to 100 responses (you can upgrade to accommodate more questions/responses for a fee). There are certainly other online survey builders beyond *SurveyMonkey*; see www.survey-gizmo.com and www.questionpro.com, for example. Many follow the same general procedures.

Before you can create a survey you need to sign up for a *SurveyMonkey* account. For a free account, click "Sign Up Free" on the *SurveyMonkey* home page. You'll have to choose a username and a password and provide your email address. Once you have signed up, answer the brief questions that follow. Then choose "Create Survey," and click "Start from Scratch." Enter a name for your survey, and then click "Create Survey." This will bring you to a new page.

Let's now talk about preparing a survey for online use. We've already discussed how to write questions for a survey (see Chapter 7). Now we'll discuss the mechanics of putting those questions into an online survey builder. The first thing you'll likely want to put in your survey is an informed consent form. To do this, click on the down arrow next to the "New Question" button, select "Text," and then enter your informed consent form information (see Figure 13.3 for a sample form). When you are done entering this information, click on "Save."

Now we'll start entering questions. As you'll see in *SurveyMonkey*, there are various response formats you can use in online research. Let's start by going back to the down arrow next to the "New Question" button and choose "multiple choice." This is a very common question format; some survey builders call it a "radio button" format. It allows respondents to choose one or sometimes multiple responses from a series of options.

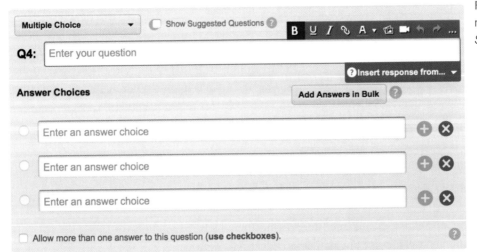

FIGURE 13.4 A common multiple-choice format in *SurveyMonkey*.

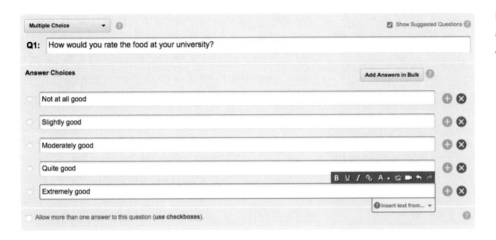

FIGURE 13.5 Filling in a blank question page in *SurveyMonkey*.

1. How would you rate the food at your university?

○ Not at all good

○ Slightly good

○ Moderately good

○ Quite good

○ Extremely good

FIGURE 13.6 This question is ready for respondents!

For example, in Figure 13.4, you can see what a vertical multiple-choice question looks like in *Survey-Monkey* before you insert your desired information.

You'll see that everything in *SurveyMonkey* is very easy to modify. To create a question and provide answer choices, just insert the information in the available spaces as shown in Figure 13.5 and click "Save."

This question will ultimately look like that shown in Figure 13.6.

It is also possible to place multiple-choice items horizontally on a page (see Figure 13.7). *Survey-Monkey* calls this type of question a "matrix/rating scale" question and recommends it when you want to use the same rating scale for multiple questions. Whether you choose vertical or horizontal placement, it's a good idea to label each answer.

Drop-down menus (see Figure 13.8) are often used to record demographic information such as age or country of residence. As *SurveyMonkey* notes, drop-down menus are useful when you want to save space in a survey. However, they have been found to have higher non-response rates than questions using radio buttons (Healey, 2007).

You can also collect data using an open-ended response format. As we discussed in Chapter 7, in an open-ended survey question, respondents do not have response options to choose from; instead they answer by writing their own response in a "single

2. How would you rate each meal at your university?

	Not at all good	Slightly good	Moderately good	Quite good	Extremely good
Breakfast	○	○	○	○	○
Lunch	○	○	○	○	○
Dinner	○	○	○	○	○

FIGURE 13.7 A horizontal or matrix/rating scale question in *SurveyMonkey*.

3. What is your age?

FIGURE 13.8 A sample drop-down menu in *SurveyMonkey*.

4. What is your favorite food item in your university cafeteria?

FIGURE 13.9 An open-ended survey question in *SurveyMonkey*.

text box" (see Figure 13.9). You can choose to limit the length of the response to only a few characters or allow for a much longer essay-like response.

When you have finished your last question, use the "Text" option to provide a debriefing statement. Then click "Done." Once you have completed preparing your survey, click "Preview & Test" so you can see what it will look like to your respondents. Then you should pilot the survey (as we discussed in Chapter 1) by doing a few practice sessions to make sure your participants will easily understand all the questions. In other words, give the survey to a few people you can question afterward. Then it's time to recruit participants. You have some choices here. *SurveyMonkey* will assign your survey a link and you can email this link to prospective participants. Alternatively, you can put this link on a blog or website or add it to a Facebook, LinkedIn, or Twitter page.

Once you have finished collecting your data, *SurveyMonkey*'s basic plan allows you to view the first 100 responses for each of your surveys. These data can be viewed individually or in summary form so you can easily see how people overall responded to your questions. Seeing a summary of 100 responses might be all that you need. The basic

SurveyMonkey plan will not allow you to export your data for further analysis (an upgraded plan will). However, since you can view your data, you can transcribe it onto a data sheet and then input the data into a statistical program for further analysis (details regarding how to analyze the data are beyond the scope of this text).

An Online Survey: A Published Example

Let's now take a look at an example of a research survey that was used to collect data online. For the sake of consistency, the following example utilized *SurveyMonkey*.

But first, I have a confession. I am one of those people who cannot go a day without checking Facebook. I know I'm not alone. According to Facebook, as of July 2015, more than 1.13 billion people were daily Facebook users (Facebook reports second quarter 2016 results, 2016).

Park and Lee (2014) wanted to know how students at their college felt about Facebook. They used a survey to assess college students' motivations for using Facebook and how this use related to their feelings about campus life. To assess this information, Park and Lee used multiple-choice questions, asking students to choose their level of agreement on a 7-point scale (options ranged from "strongly disagree" to "strongly agree") with statements such as "I feel out of touch when I haven't logged onto Facebook for a while" (p. 608).

Park and Lee wanted to know why and how much students on their campus used Facebook, so they selected a random sample of students from their student directory and sent them a link to their *SurveyMonkey* survey. Almost 20% of these students answered their survey (since so many did not respond, a non-response bias may be a concern here). What did Park and Lee find? The students were generally avid Facebook users, spending an average of over 7 hours per week on the site. Many found it enjoyable as a form of entertainment, and a means of maintaining relationships ("I am using Facebook in order to communicate with friends and family") and impression management ("I want other users in Facebook to perceive me as likable," p. 608). On the other hand, the students were generally not using Facebook to stay aware of campus activities, so this motivation did not directly contribute to their satisfaction with campus life. Consider using an online survey to see whether and why students on your campus use Facebook (or Twitter, or SnapChat, or Instagram …). See the Suggested Activities section for more about this idea.

Creating an Online Experiment

When we conduct an experiment, as you know, we manipulate one or more independent variables and observe the effects of that manipulation on a response measure called the dependent variable. If we are doing a between-subjects experiment, we want to randomly assign participants to different groups. If we are doing a within-subjects experiment, we want to randomly determine the order in which the participants receive the stimuli. Either way, randomization will be needed, so how do we do that online? Unfortunately, the basic version of *SurveyMonkey* is not capable of randomization, but if you upgrade your account, you can use it for this purpose. Because I want to show you how to randomize for free, we'll talk about a different survey building tool this time.

Qualtrics is a survey builder like *SurveyMonkey*, but its free version has the capability of randomization. In fact, *Qualtrics'* free version provides access to many of its features, but it allows you to have only one active survey with 100 responses (as opposed to *SurveyMonkey*'s unlimited number of surveys). Still it is a popular choice. In a recent survey of researchers, a majority of the respondents indicated that they use *Qualtrics* for their online surveys (Gureckis et al., 2016).

Urbaniak and Kilmann's (2003) experimentation on the "nice guy paradox" is my inspiration for the following experiment (p. 413). The nice guy paradox is the idea that "although women often portray themselves as wanting to date kind, sensitive, and emotionally expressive men … when actually presented with a choice between such a 'nice guy' and an unkind, insensitive, emotionally closed, 'macho man' or 'jerk,' they invariably reject the nice guy in favor of his more macho competitor" (p. 413). Urbaniak and Kilmann decided to determine whether they could find evidence of this stereotype in the lab (spoiler alert: they generally didn't). Let's walk through how to set up a variation of Urbaniak and Kilmann's experiment as if we were planning to put the experiment online.

This experiment will have one independent variable (level of dating partner's niceness), and that variable will have two levels (high, low); participants will be randomly assigned to conditions. That's the experimental design. Now let's talk about how to set it up.

First you need to register at the *Qualtrics* website; go to www.Qualtrics.com and register for a free

FIGURE 13.10 Do women prefer to date a nice guy or a jerk? Urbaniak and Kilmann (2003) investigated the 'nice guy paradox.'"

account. Once you have signed up for the account and verified your email address, you can login. After you login, click "Create Project," choose "New Blank Project," then name your project. Then click "Create Project" again. Then you have choices. You can work from an existing survey or from *Qualtrics'* library of survey questions. Since we don't have our own existing survey in *Qualtrics*, we can either create a survey from scratch (like *SurveyMonkey*, *Qualtrics* has many question formats to choose from) or use questions from the *Qualtrics* library. I'm going to do a little of both. Let's go through the following steps:

- Enter the *Qualtrics* survey library by clicking the "Import Questions From" icon.
- Select "*Qualtrics* Library" and then "Survey Library."
- Choose "Higher Education" and then "Informed Consent."
- Click the informed consent text (on the left) and then click "Import 1 Question."

This leads you to a new page with an informed consent form on it. In a moment I'm going to change this informed consent form to reflect the experiment I'm planning, and then I'll be ready to add more information. But first I want to name the section I'm working on; *Qualtrics* does this by allowing you to create "blocks."

Blocks will come in handy later when we need to incorporate random assignment into our *Qualtrics* plan. What are blocks? Well, you can think of blocks thematically. Pages that can be thought of as "belonging together" can generally be placed in one block. So first I'll work on an "informed consent" block. On the upper left of the informed consent form, you'll see a box in which you can enter the words "Informed Consent Block." Now you're ready to make the changes in the informed consent form. Changing the informed consent form is very easy in *Qualtrics* because everything is point and click. For

example, I want to change the introduction to reflect that "The purpose of this study is to collect information regarding women's views of dating. Only women who are 18 years of age or older can participate." Make the other changes to the form as needed (look back at Figure 13.3 for a sample informed consent form).

After the consent form, we need a page break. Click "Add Page Break" on the right-hand side of the screen. Now I'm ready to create a new block. I will click "Add Block" at the bottom of the screen. Click "Block 1" to change the name of this block. Since the next thing participants will see is the instructions, I'll call this next block "Instruction Block."

I will be providing a variation of the instructions given by Urbaniak and Kilmann. I click on the pull-down arrow on the "Create a New Question" button in this Instruction Block and then click the "Descriptive Text" option. I will click in this space and type the following:

On the following page, you will be provided with a scenario in which a woman named Susan is participating in a dating game show. Susan will be presented with the opportunity to date one of the two male contestants. She must choose between them based on their answers to her question. Please read the information provided and answer all the questions that follow.

Now it's time to put in the experimental stimuli. This information is very similar to one of the exchanges used by Urbaniak and Kilmann (p. 416) except, for simplicity sake, my version has only two levels of "niceness" instead of three. I'm going to break my experimental stimuli into several blocks because this will help me when it's time to indicate which conditions should be randomly distributed. I start by clicking "Add Block" on the bottom of the screen. I name this block: "Scenario Block 1." I click on the "Create a New Question" pull-down menu in this block and choose "Descriptive Text." Then I write the following:

> Susan: "Okay, Bachelor #1: What is your definition of a 'Real Man?' And are you one yourself?"

That's all I want in this first scenario block. All my participants will see this information immediately after the instructions. Now I want to create my first block of information about Todd. I will ultimately have two blocks of information pertaining to Todd (nice guy/jerk), and participants will each see only one of these blocks. So I click "Add Block" on the bottom of the screen, name it "Todd 1," and then click on the "Create a New Question" pull-down menu in this block and choose "Descriptive Text." I'll then put the following text in this block.

> TODD: "A real man is someone who is in touch with his feelings and those of his partner. Someone who is kind and attentive and doesn't go for all that macho stuff. He's also great in the bedroom and puts his partner's pleasure first. I'd definitely say I'm a real man."

The information above describes a Todd who is a nice guy. But I need my comparison Todd, the jerk. So I click "Add Block," and call it "Todd 2." Then I click on the "Create a New Question" pull-down menu and choose "Descriptive Text." Then I enter the following text in this Todd 2 block.

> TODD: "A real man knows what he wants and he knows how to get it. Someone who knows who he is but keeps other people guessing and on their toes – he doesn't go in for all that touchy-feely stuff. He's also great in the bedroom and can tell his partner what he likes. I'd definitively say I'm a real man."

So now I have information about both Todds, the nice guy and the jerk. But I still need to give participants another bachelor to choose from, someone to compare to Todd. So I click "Add Block" on the bottom of the screen, call it "Scenario Block 2," click on the "Create a New Question" pull-down menu, and choose "Descriptive Text" and enter the following text.

> SUSAN: "Bachelor #2, same question."
> MICHAEL: "A real man is relaxed. He doesn't let the world get him down. He's confident, solid, and keeps a positive attitude at all times. He's also a great kisser – and I'm definitely one of those!"

I also want to include my dependent variables in this experiment, and I will put them all in the same "dependent variable" block. So I click "Add Block" on the bottom of the screen, call it "Dependent Variable Block" and add in my questions to this block, one at a time. First I want to ask demographic questions. I have decided to use a text entry question to ask respondents what gender they are (I want to use this to double-check that only females have responded). So I will click the "Create a New Question" pull-down menu and choose "Text Entry." I will replace "Click to write the question text" with the words "What is your gender?" Then I will go through the same procedure to create a "text entry" question to ask for their age.

The next question I want to ask is: "Should Susan choose to date Todd or Michael?" The two response options will be Todd and Michael. To do this I will click on the "Create a New Question" pull-down menu and choose "Multiple Choice." I will click in the appropriate spaces to fill in this information. Since I only want two response options for this question, I will click on the third response option and use the pull-down menu to choose "remove choice." Then I want to ask: "Which of the men would you choose to date?" So I choose the "Multiple Choice" question again and fill in the information I need.

Again, the response options will be Todd or Michael so I will delete the third response option.

I have 6 more questions to include, and I want each to be created with 5-point scales. Since *Qualtrics* automatically has placeholders for 3 answer options, I need to add 2 more response options for each question. You can add response options for each question by increasing the number of answer choices on the right-hand side of the screen. These are the questions I want:

- How desirable would Todd be as a marriage partner? (1 = not at all desirable, 2 = a little desirable, 3 = somewhat desirable, 4 = very desirable, 5 = extremely desirable)
- How desirable would Michael be as a marriage partner? (1 = not at all desirable, 2 = a little desirable, 3 = somewhat desirable, 4 = very desirable, 5 = extremely desirable)
- How desirable would Todd be as a one-night-stand? (1 = not at all desirable, 2 = a little desirable, 3 = somewhat desirable, 4 = very desirable, 5 = extremely desirable)
- How desirable would Michael be as a one-night-stand? (1 = not at all desirable, 2 = a little desirable, 3 = somewhat desirable, 4 = very desirable, 5 = extremely desirable)
- How nice is Todd? (1 = not at all nice, 2 = a little nice, 3 = somewhat nice, 4 = very nice, 5 = extremely nice)
- How nice is Michael? (1 = not at all nice, 2 = a little nice, 3 = somewhat nice, 4 = very nice, 5 = extremely nice). (These last two questions are manipulation checks – see Chapter 8).

When you are done putting in your questions, put in a page break by choosing a "page break" option on the right-hand side of the page. The next block I want to include is a debriefing block. Choose "Add Block" on the bottom of the screen and name it "Debriefing Block." Click the "Create a New

Question" pull-down menu and choose "Descriptive Text." Place the following text in this block:

The purpose of this study was to determine whether participants would make choices in line with the "nice guy paradox" and reject the nice guy in favor of his more macho competitor. If you have any questions please contact Dr. Wendy Heath at heath@rider.edu.

See Figure 13.11 for an overview of the study.

If you now click on "survey flow" at the top of the *Qualtrics* screen you will see all your blocks listed. You can see my list of blocks in Figure 13.12.

There are a few steps I need to take in "Survey Flow" before this experiment is ready. Recall that at the bottom of the consent form people will be provided an option to consent or not. If they do not consent they need to be "skipped" to the end of the survey. Here's how we'll do that.

- Go to the "Informed Consent Block" in "Survey Flow" and click "Add Below."
- Click "Branch," then click "Add a Condition."
- Select the consent question (Q1).
- Select "I do not consent."
- Click "Okay."
- Click "Add a New Element Here."
- Click "End of Survey."
- Click "Save Flow" to save what you've just done.
- Click "Preview Survey" to see what happens when you click "I consent" or "I do not consent." The former should take you to the instructions. The latter should take you to the end of the survey.

Now that I've entered all the information for this experiment, it's time to tell *Qualtrics* that I want each participant to see information about only one of the Todds and that I want *Qualtrics* to randomly determine which Todd they see. I can arrange for

You will be provided with a scenario in which a woman named Susan is participating in a dating game show. Susan will be presented with the opportunity to date one of the two male contestants. She must choose between them based on their answers to her question. Please read the information and answer all the questions that follow.

Susan:"Ok, Bachelor #1: What is your definition of a "real man?" And are you one yourself?"
(Participants will see one of the next two "Todd" versions.)

Todd: "A real man knows what he wants and he knows how to get it. Someone who knows who he is but keeps other people guessing and on their toes - he doesn't go in for all that touchy-feely stuff.
He's also great in the bedroom and can tell his partner what he likes.
I'd definitely say I'm a real man."

Todd: "A real man is someone who is in touch with his feelings and those of his partner.
Someone who is kind and attentive and doesn't go for all that macho stuff.
He's also great in the bedroom and puts his partner's pleasure first.
I'd definitely say I'm a real man."

Susan: "Bachelor #2, same question."

Michael: "A real man is relaxed. He doesn't let the world get him down.
He's confident, solid, and keeps a positive attitude at all times.
He's also a great kisser-
and I'm definitely one of those!"

1. **What is your gender?** _____
2. **What is your age?** _____
3. **Should Susan choose to date Todd or Michael?** Todd Michael
4. **Which of the men would you choose to date, Todd or Michael?** Todd Michael
5. **How desirable would Todd be as a marriage partner?**
   (1 = not at all desirable, 2 = a little desirable, 3 = somewhat desirable, 4 = very desirable, 5 = extremely desirable)
6. **How desirable would Michael be as a marriage partner?**
   (1 = not at all desirable, 2 = a little desirable, 3 = somewhat desirable, 4 = very desirable, 5 = extremely desirable)
7. **How desirable would Todd be as a one-night-stand?**
   (1 = not at all desirable, 2 = a little desirable, 3 = somewhat desirable, 4 = very desirable, 5 = extremely desirable)
8. **How desirable would Michael be as a one-night-stand?**
   (1 = not at all desirable, 2 = a little desirable, 3 = somewhat desirable, 4 = very desirable, 5 = extremely desirable)
9. **How nice is Todd?** (1 = not at all nice, 2 = a little nice, 3 = somewhat nice, 4 = very nice, 5 = extremely nice)
10. **How nice is Michael?** (1 = not at all nice, 2 = a little nice, 3 = somewhat nice, 4 = very nice, 5 = extremely nice)

Debriefing: The purpose of this study was to determine if participants would make choices in line with the "nice guy paradox", and reject the nice guy in favor of his more macho competitor. If you have any questions please contact
Dr. Wendy Heath at heath@rider.edu.

FIGURE 13.11 Overview of the "nice guy paradox" study.

Show Block: **Informed Consent Block** (2 Questions)	Add Below	Move	Duplicate	Delete
Show Block: **Instruction Block** (1 Question)	Add Below	Move	Duplicate	Delete
Show Block: **Scenario Block 1** (1 Question)	Add Below	Move	Duplicate	Delete
Show Block: **Todd 1** (1 Question)	Add Below	Move	Duplicate	Delete
Show Block: **Todd 2** (1 Question)	Add Below	Move	Duplicate	Delete
Show Block: **Scenario Block 2** (1 Question)	Add Below	Move	Duplicate	Delete
Show Block: **Dependent Variable Block** (10 Questions)	Add Below	Move	Duplicate	Delete
Show Block: **Debriefing Block** (1 Question)	Add Below	Move	Duplicate	Delete

FIGURE 13.12 List of survey blocks in a sample *Qualtrics* survey.

this randomization while I'm in the "Survey Flow" view. Here's what I need to do.

- Click on "Survey Flow."
- My two Todd conditions need to come right after Susan's first question. So on the "Scenario Block 1" line I click on "Add Below," and then I will click on "Randomizer." I will replace the "0" in this randomizer box to "1" so the randomizer will "randomly present 1 of the following elements." Since I want true randomization, I elect *not* to check the "evenly present elements" option, because this would just *evenly* assign people to groups.
- Right below the "Randomizer" box, I will choose "Add a New Element Here" and then choose "Embedded Data."
- In the area that says "Enter Embedded Data Field Name Here" write in "Todd." Then click on "Set a Value Now" and type in a "1" to replace the words "Custom Value" (as shown in Figure 13.13).
- Now we will do what is necessary to represent the second Todd condition. Underneath the "Set Embedded Data" box, choose "Add a New

Element Here" and then choose "Embedded Data."

- In the area that says "Enter Embedded Data Field Name Here" write in "Todd." Then click on "Set a Value Now" and type in a "2" to replace the words "Custom Value" (as shown in Figure 13.13).
- Now click on "Add a New Element Here" and then click on "Branch." Click anywhere inside the "Branch" box to activate it, and then use your keyboard's down arrow to move the Branch box out of the randomizer (click the down arrow once).
- Click on "Add a Condition" in the Branch box. Use the "Question" pull-down menu to choose "Embedded Data." In the box, type "Todd" and then type a 1 so that this section reads, "If Todd is Equal to 1." Click "OK."
- Activate the "Show Block: Todd 1" block by clicking on it, and then use the up arrow on your keyboard (click once) to move the Todd 1 block right under the Branch box.
- Now we need to do the same thing for the Todd 2 condition. Click on "Add a New Element Here" under the Todd 1 box, and then click

on "Branch." Click inside the "Branch" box to activate it, and then use your keyboard's down arrow to move the Branch box out of the randomizer (click the down arrow once).

- Click on "Add a Condition" in the Branch box. Use the "Question" pull-down menu to choose "Embedded Data." In the box, type "Todd" and then type a 2 so that this section reads, "If Todd is Equal to 2." Click "OK."

- Activate the "Show Block: Todd 2" block by clicking on it, and then use the up arrow on your keyboard (click once) to move the Todd 2 block right under the Branch box.

- I have now set up *Qualtrics* to randomly assign one of the two conditions to each participant; this randomizing section looks like that shown

in Figure 13.13. If you have more than two groups in the research you are preparing, you would expand this procedure to include each of the groups you wish to randomly assign. Finally, remember to click "Save Flow" before leaving this screen so this randomizing command is maintained.

Once you've done all this, preview your research document by clicking "Preview Survey." When you are satisfied with your document, it's time to recruit participants. Click "Distributions." *Qualtrics* will ask you how you want to distribute the survey. If you wish you can make a selection here, such as email or social media. You can also choose to get an "anonymous link" that you can use later if you wish to send to prospective participants. I will refer to the link

FIGURE 13.13 Randomizing section of a sample *Qualtrics* survey.

later. Let's now talk about what to do once you have collected the data.

When it is time to view your results in *Qualtrics*, follow the steps below.

- Log in to www.Qualtrics.com and click on the project of interest.
- Click the "Reports" tab that is near the top of the screen.
- Choose "Printed Reports."
- Choose "Create New Report" and then click "Create."
- At this point you have choices as to how you want to display your data. I recommend choosing the option on the right, which gives you all available options: title, graph, table, and stats. Click "Generate Report."
- We want to see how those who received information about the two different Todds responded. In the upper right-hand side of the screen, you will see a number that represents the number of study participants you have tested. Click the wrench icon next to it and choose "Edit Drill Down." You will then be asked to choose what you want to "Drill-Down By"; choose "Todd" because you want to split your data according to the two Todds. This will provide you with the results for each type of Todd. Click "Apply to Report."
- Click "Share" to export these results to PDF, Excel, PowerPoint, or Word. You can also choose to "Print" these results.

Note that you cannot download the raw data from *Qualtrics* if you have only a free account. You also cannot analyze the data within *Qualtrics* with a free account. However, many universities have *Qualtrics* licenses and you may be eligible for an account under your university's license, which would allow you to export your data. In any case, it is possible to view the data for analysis in an outside program like Excel or SPSS. Here's what you need to do.

- Click on the research project you want to work with.
- Pull down the "Tools" menu and choose "Export Survey to Word." Make sure all the options are checked ("Show Question Numbers," "Show Logic," "Show Coded Values," and "Strip HTML Tags from all Questions and Answers"). Click "Export."
- Create a spreadsheet within your statistics software. Create one or more columns for whatever identifying information you have collected (such as IP address). Create a column that will reflect what "Todd" group each respondent received (Todd 1, Todd 2). Then make a column for each question of the survey.
- Go to the "Data & Analysis" pull-down menu in *Qualtrics*. Then, on each line, click the "Actions" pull-down menu and choose "Export" as a PDF.
- Each respondent (and thus each PDF) will make up a row in the spreadsheet. Export a PDF for each respondent. Copy these data onto a data sheet and input the data into a statistical program for further analysis (again, details regarding how to analyze the data are beyond the scope of this text).

Note that *Qualtrics* occasionally makes minor changes to their website, thus what I've described may not be an exact match for what you see. If you need help while in *Qualtrics*, visit the *Qualtrics* "Support" Department to contact *Qualtrics* directly.

An Online Experiment: A Published Example

Let's now go over an example of an experiment that was conducted using *Qualtrics* so you can get more of a feel for what is possible. Have you ever watched a television program that had a Twitter feed of viewers' comments crawling along the bottom of the screen? Cameron and Geidner (2014) were interested in whether the content of that crawling information affected people's views of what they were watching. Perhaps it's a political debate and viewers will later have to vote for their candidate of choice. Perhaps it's an entertainment program, such as "Dancing with the Stars," and those at home can vote for their favorite dance team. Would the comments in the crawl affect those views? That's what Cameron and Geidner were determined to find out.

For their first experiment, Cameron and Geidner made three different versions of two videos from the television show "American Idol." Each video showed a top-10 but non-winning male idol contestant singing. One version of each video was manipulated to show 70% positive Twitter comments crawling along the bottom of the screen; the remaining comments were neutral or negative. A second version of each video was manipulated to show 70% negative Twitter comments crawling along the bottom of the screen; the remaining comments were neutral or positive. A third version of each video was created to act as a control; no Twitter comments were present. Participants were randomly assigned to conditions.

Cameron and Geidner used *Qualtrics* to create their online experiment (you can use *Qualtrics* to present your participants with video content). They sent undergraduates in journalism courses at their university a letter requesting their participation and included a link to the online experiment. Those who elected to participate were shown online videos of two contestants and were asked to rate both the quality of the singer (1 = very negative, 7 = very positive) and their level of agreement with the statement, "I think [name of performer] could be the winner of *American Idol*" (1 = strongly disagree, 7 = strongly agree).

What did Cameron and Geidner find? In general, those who saw the videos with the positive Twitter feed had significantly more positive views of the singers and thought it was more likely these singers would win than did those who saw the negative or control videos. These results suggest that broadcasters should be advised that the content of the crawling message may indeed affect the thoughts and behaviors of their viewers, and that these techniques should be used with caution whenever television viewers vote.

How Do I Recruit Participants?

We've now discussed putting both survey and experimental research online. As alluded to above, survey and experiment builders, such as *SurveyMonkey* and *Qualtrics*, generally generate a web link (a URL) that you can make available to prospective survey respondents. Both Park and Lee and Cameron and Geidner chose to test undergraduates at their home universities by sending them the generated link. However, there are times when researchers may wish to test those outside their universities. For example, you may choose to recruit potential respondents through email or social media. You may also choose to post your link on a website that lists available research studies (such as Hanover College's "Psychological Research on the Net" available at http://psych.hanover.edu/research/exponnet.html).

If you have funding, you may choose to pay a survey-builder company such as *SurveyMonkey* to recruit participants from its vast database of survey respondents. If you decided to do this, you would be able to target specific types of people by naming the demographic criteria you need (say, females over 30). However, since significant funding can be difficult to obtain, you might consider *Mechanical Turk (MTurk)* as a way to obtain large samples from around the world for relatively little money. After an introduction to *MTurk*, I'll show you how to link research studies created on *Qualtrics* to *MTurk*.

The reason I'm concentrating on describing how to link *Qualtrics* to *MTurk* and not describing linking *SurveyMonkey* to *MTurk* is that, as of this writing, *SurveyMonkey* doesn't have an officially sanctioned way of generating the random code needed for *MTurk* as proof of research participation.

Mechanical Turk

In the eighteenth and nineteenth centuries, a human-sized puppet dressed in Turkish robes, an apparent automaton, astounded crowds across Europe as it demonstrated its chess-playing skills, easily beating most opponents (Figure 13.14). It was later revealed that a chess master was hidden in the table beneath, moving the chess pieces with magnets (Folbre, 2013). The automaton was not capable of playing chess at all. This story was the inspiration behind *Amazon's* **Mechanical Turk** (**MTurk**), a website launched in 2005 to engage large numbers of humans in tasks computers cannot do (Baz, 2014).

Today *MTurk* is known as a flourishing online labor market. Amazon calls those who participate in tasks **Workers** and says there are more than half a million Workers on *MTurk*, although the number of unique individuals participating in research has been estimated to be far less (Bohannon, 2016). While a majority of them live in the United States or India (Paolacci, Chandler, & Ipeirotis, 2010), their overall diversity is impressive; Workers from as many as 190 countries have been documented (Amazon, n.d.).

Before I go further to explain how *MTurk* works, I want to note that there is an ethical concern regarding *MTurk* and its use of identification numbers to track its Workers. It has recently been revealed (Lease et al. [2013]) that the ID used in the *MTurk* marketplace is also the ID you use as an Amazon customer, so identifying information may be available through this route. In response to this potential problem, Lease et al. suggest that Amazon assign unique ID numbers to *MTurk* Workers that will not also be used at other Amazon sites. Until that occurs, they recommend that researchers replace the *MTurk* Worker IDs with a new set of IDs and eliminate any link between the two. Unfortunately, many researchers are under the impression that *MTurk* Workers are anonymous because explicit identifying information like names is not collected. Now we know that a conscious effort must be made when using *MTurk* to protect online participants' privacy.

How Can I Become an *MTurk* Worker?

Before launching your own study on *MTurk*, you might wish to see how others use *MTurk* to conduct their research. If so, go on www.mturk.com to see what it is like to be an *MTurk* Worker. You first need to register as a Worker and get approved by Amazon (this process takes about 48 hours). Once you have been approved, go to *MTurk* and click "Find HITs now." HITs are Human Intelligence Tasks, and you can search for these by keyword (such as psychology) and amount of pay. You then can complete almost any task that interests you (some require that you get "qualified" first). Once you submit your data

FIGURE 13.14 The Mechanical Turk, a chess-playing automaton.

and your submission has been approved by those offering the task, money is paid into your Amazon payment account. It's that simple!

How Do I Put My Research on *MTurk*?

Those who list tasks to be performed are called **Requesters**. To list a task on *MTurk*, that is, to upload your survey or experiment, you must first register for an *MTurk* Requester Account (you must have a US billing address). Social science researchers are increasingly using *MTurk* to collect data, so we will go over the process of putting your research study on *MTurk*. We'll start by focusing on how you can link *Qualtrics* to Amazon. There are two major steps you need to take in order to prepare your *Qualtrics* research for *MTurk*: (1) get *Qualtrics* to generate a random number for each participant, (2) link *Qualtrics* to *MTurk*. We'll cover each of these procedures in turn.

Get* Qualtrics *to Generate a Random Number for Each Participant. In *MTurk*, Workers are paid only for completed work that was done correctly. So researchers need to be able to know which participants finished the work as directed. You can program *Qualtrics* to generate a randomly determined code and then compare it to the list of Worker-entered codes on *MTurk*. If the two codes match, this means the Worker received the code by completing the task (getting to the final page). You can then approve the work and the participant will get paid.

Let's now talk about how to generate a random code in *Qualtrics* for an already-created survey or experiment.

- Go to www.Qualtrics, choose the project you want to link to *MTurk*.
- Scroll down to the "Debriefing Block."
- Click on the words in your Debriefing Block. Add the words "Your participation code is:" to this block.

- Go to "Survey Flow."
- Scroll down to the "Debriefing Block."
- Click "Add Below."
- Click "Embedded Data."
- Replace the words "Enter Embedded Data Field Name Here" with the phrase: ParticipantCode.
- Click "Set a Value Now." We're now going to tell *Qualtrics* that we want a random number between 100,000 and 999,999 to be generated for each participant. Click "Custom Value" and insert the following: ${rand://int/100000:999999}
- Click anywhere in the embedded data element box to activate it and then hit your keyboard's up arrow once to move the Embedded Data Element box right above the Debriefing block. See Figure 13.15 for a partial view of your Survey Flow.
- Click outside the "Debriefing Block" to deactivate it.
- Click "Save Flow."
- You should now be back in the "Survey" area. Scroll down to the "Debriefing Block."
- Click on your words in the "Debriefing Block."
- Click "Piped Text."
- Click "Embedded Data Field." Replace the words "Embedded Data Field" with the phrase: ParticipantCode
- Make sure that the words "Your participant code is:" come before the random number place holder (the random number place holder looks like: ${e://Field/ParticipantCode}). You can move the phrase "Your participant code is:" if you need to.
- Click "Insert."
- You have now added a random number generator to *Qualtrics*. Now your participants will each get a unique random number at the end of their session.
- You can click "Preview Survey" and review the survey to ensure that there is a random number generated at the end.

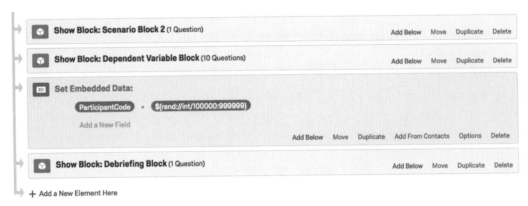

FIGURE 13.15 A partial view of a sample *Qualtrics* survey flow.

- Note that when you host your survey or experiment on a third party site such as *Qualtrics*, you should include a question in your questionnaire that asks for this Worker ID code. This will enable you to match codes from your questionnaire to codes at the *MTurk* site. If you determine that someone didn't complete the task adequately, you can then reject their payment.

Link *Qualtrics to* MTurk. Recall that when we created the research in *Qualtrics* we ended up generating a web link (a URL) that is basically the Internet address for your study. If you decide that *MTurk* is your participant pool of interest, you will be using this URL in *MTurk*. Let's talk specifically how to set this up.

Go to https://requester.mturk.com and get ready to click.

- First click "Create."
- Then sign in to create your project. Now it's time to fill in information regarding your study. Give your project a name; this name is not shown to your workers (I chose "Dating Project"). Give your study a title (say, "Answer a survey about your opinions on dating"), and describe your task ("Give us your opinion about a dating situation"). Be careful not to use terms that could affect participants' responses. For example, I wouldn't want to title my dating

study "Would you be willing to date a jerk?" Then put in some keywords (such as "dating," "game show"). Note that Workers often use keywords to find tasks they want to do, so you need to think of keywords that could lead people to your task. See Figure 13.16.

- In the next section, you will indicate the details, such as how much "reward" you intend to pay your Workers (I decided on $0.25 per task completed), how many Workers you want (say, 50), and how long they have to complete your task (say, 1 hour). You will also need to indicate how long your task will be available to Workers (such as 7 days), and how long you have to review and reject work before it is automatically approved (say, 3 days). See Figure 13.17.

- At this point you are going to set the qualifications for your Workers. Do you want your Workers to be Masters? Master Workers have already shown that they are good at a specific kind of task. If you want only Master Workers to complete your task, you should expect to pay more. If you are not going to require Master Workers, click "no." You can also specify any additional qualifications for your prospective Workers here. You can, for example, specify whether you want Workers who have an approval rate over a specific level. An *MTurk* Worker with a high approval rating

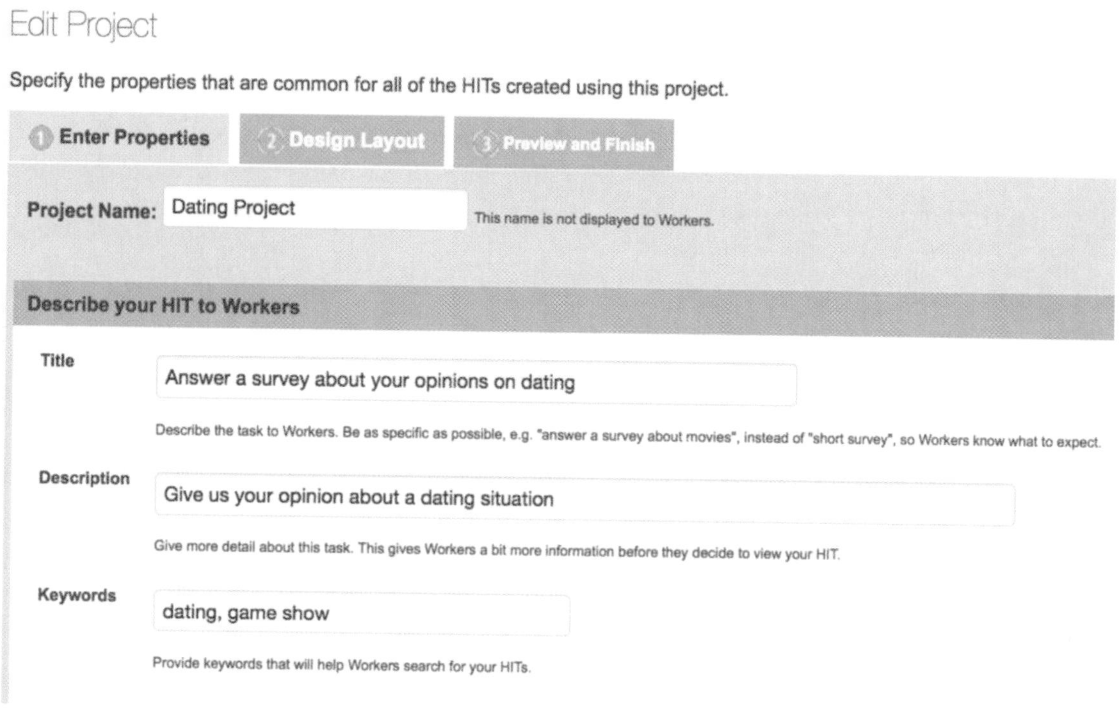

Edit Project

Specify the properties that are common for all of the HITs created using this project.

| ① Enter Properties | ② Design Layout | ③ Preview and Finish |

Project Name: Dating Project   This name is not displayed to Workers.

Describe your HIT to Workers

Title

Answer a survey about your opinions on dating

Describe the task to Workers. Be as specific as possible, e.g. "answer a survey about movies", instead of "short survey", so Workers know what to expect.

Description

Give us your opinion about a dating situation

Give more detail about this task. This gives Workers a bit more information before they decide to view your HIT.

Keywords

dating, game show

Provide keywords that will help Workers search for your HITs.

FIGURE 13.16 *MTurk* sample edit project page.

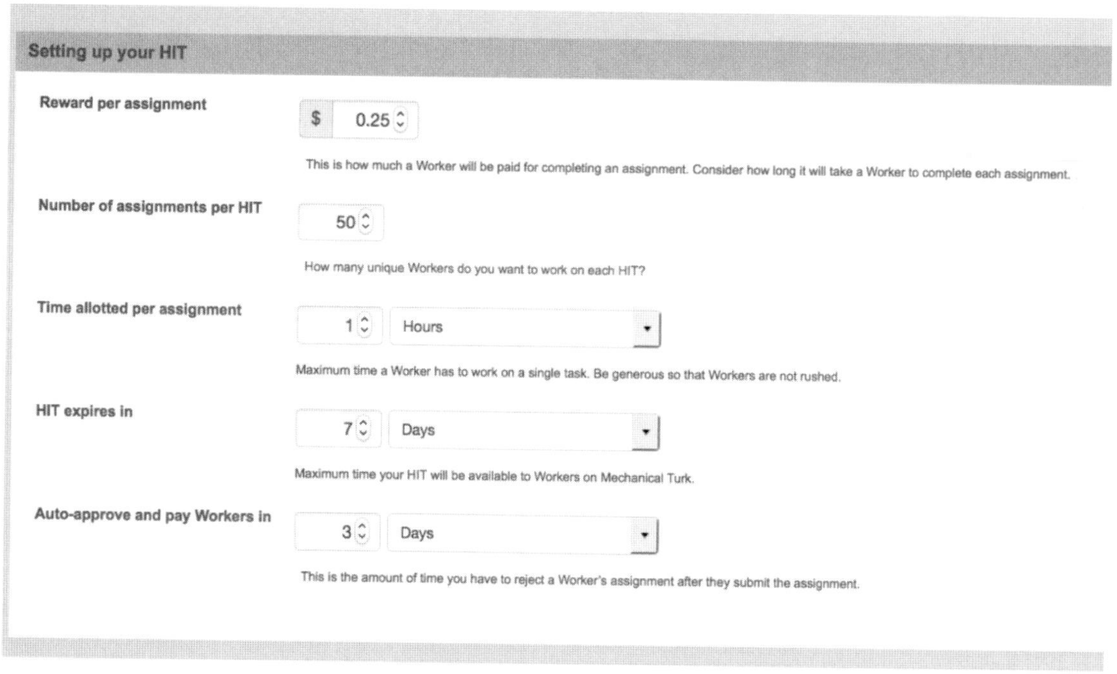

Setting up your HIT

Reward per assignment

$ 0.25 ⌄

This is how much a Worker will be paid for completing an assignment. Consider how long it will take a Worker to complete each assignment.

Number of assignments per HIT

50 ⌄

How many unique Workers do you want to work on each HIT?

Time allotted per assignment

1 ⌄   Hours ▾

Maximum time a Worker has to work on a single task. Be generous so that Workers are not rushed.

HIT expires in

7 ⌄   Days ▾

Maximum time your HIT will be available to Workers on Mechanical Turk.

Auto-approve and pay Workers in

3 ⌄   Days ▾

This is the amount of time you have to reject a Worker's assignment after they submit the assignment.

FIGURE 13.17 *MTurk* sample setting up HIT page.

(such as 95%) is one who has consistently submitted high-quality work.

- Click "Save" to save your preferences.
- Click "Design Layout." At this point you should highlight the instructions and replace them with instructions that make sense given your study. I put in the following: "You will read a scenario about a dating game show. Please read the scenario carefully and answer the questions that follow. At the end of the task, you will receive a code to paste into the box below. Make sure to leave this window open as you complete the survey. When you are finished, you will return to this page to paste the code into the box."
- Go to www.Qualtrics.com. Click on the survey you want to link to *MTurk*. Click "Distributions" then click "Anonymous Link." This will yield your *Qualtrics* URL. Place your *Qualtrics* URL into the *MTurk* "survey link" area and then click "Preview."
- Click "Finish" on the next page, and then click "Publish Batch" on the page that follows. You will then see what your "HIT" or Human Intelligence Task will look like to potential Workers.
- Click "Next." Amazon will then ask for a credit card to cover the cost of your payments to participants as well as your *MTurk* fees (Amazon will do these calculations for you). Provide your credit card information. Click "Purchase & Publish." Your project has been launched!
- Once you have participants, you can review your data from *Qualtrics*.
- Go to your Amazon account, click on the "Manage" tab, compare the code for each participant to the codes shown in *Qualtrics*, and decide whether to approve the work of each participant. If you check "approve," the participant gets paid.

An Alternate Way to Conduct an Online Experiment

I chose to use *Qualtrics* to design a between-subjects online experiment, because it will allow you to randomly assign participants to groups without incurring a cost. And if you use *MTurk* to collect data, it prevents respondents from completing the same task more than once, which is ideal because, in a between-subjects experiment, you do not want the same person in more than one condition. Thus, the approach I've covered so far can work well. However, some researchers have suggested a different approach to conducting between-subjects experimentation in *MTurk* (see Johnson & Borden, 2012).

Instead of listing one link in *MTurk* that contains an instruction for random assignment, you can create different groups (experimental and control groups) that are each given a separate link. In fact, you could create these different groups using *SurveyMonkey* or *Qualtrics* or even use *MTurk*'s templates to create your different groups. Then you would place the multiple links in *MTurk*. You need to make sure you change the HIT project name so you know one group from another (participants do not see these names), but use the same HIT title for each link (participants do see this name). You also need to take an extra step. You need to go over the *MTurk* Worker IDs to ensure that Workers did not participate more than once (and if they did, make sure you accept only the first time they participated, because later participation may be affected by earlier participation).

Why Are *MTurk* Workers Willing to Work for so Little Money?

When I first was introduced to *MTurk*, I was astounded by how little Requesters were willing to pay Workers to complete their tasks. Most were paying mere pennies per task, and rarely was anyone offering more than a dollar. The amount of compensation has been shown to affect participation rate, but participants have been shown to be willing to complete short tasks for very little money (Buhrmester, Kwang, & Gosling, 2011). For example, Buhrmester et al. asked *MTurk* respondents to reply to two questions (age and gender) in exchange for one cent. They received 500 responses in just a little over a day. Why would people take time out of a presumably busy day to do a task for so little money?

Researchers have considered that very question. Paolacci et al. (2010) found that some respondents were indeed motivated by the money. Interestingly, approximately 14% of those sampled revealed that completing *MTurk* tasks was their primary source of income, and over 61% indicated they were motivated by the additional income that working on *MTurk* tasks provides. On the other hand, a significant percentage of their respondents indicated that they used *MTurk* tasks for entertainment (40.7%) and killing time (32.3%). Almost 70% said working on *MTurk* tasks was a "fruitful way to spend free time" (p. 413). Couple this with the idea that people can elect to do this work whenever they want, and you have a marketplace that works!

How do you decide how much to pay your Workers? One recommendation is to look at what others are paying for similar tasks. Certainly you'll want to consider your budget too and remember that you will need to both pay your workers and cover your *MTurk* fees. *MTurk* charges 20% of the amount you pay workers, with additional charges if you use Master Workers. Some (for example, Barger, Behrend, Sharek, & Sinar, 2016) have suggested using the current minimum wage to calculate a fair wage for your Workers. For example, currently the federal minimum is $7.25/hour (approximately $0.12/min). If your task is estimated to take 10 minutes, you can offer $1.21 for successful completion of the task, and higher pay rates for more complex tasks or tasks that require specialized skills.

You can ask for your Workers to be qualified in a particular way (for example, you can request that they be parents). This type of "premium qualification" will cost a one-time additional fee (see https://requester.mturk.com/pricing).

How Do the Data from *MTurk* Compare to Data Collected Elsewhere?

Many researchers have sought to determine how participants assessed through *MTurk* differ from those in more traditional samples (such as university students). This is an important question. Psychological science has, at times, been criticized for its heavy reliance on college students for testing. Are *MTurk* samples more diverse, and perhaps more representative of the general population, than are samples of college students? Some researchers have found that *MTurk* samples are more diverse than typical college samples (see for example, Buhrmester et al.), although not everyone has found this level of diversity (see Bohannon, 2016). Paolacci et al. (2010) found that their US sample of *MTurk* Workers was "at least as representative of the U.S. population as traditional subject pools, with gender, race, age and education of Internet samples all matching the population more closely than college undergraduate samples and Internet samples in general" (p. 414).

Researchers have evaluated the quality of data obtained on *MTurk* in a variety of ways, and the general conclusion is favorable. For example, one way to assess attentiveness in a sample is to include attention checks in the survey questions. An **attention check** is a question included in a series of questions to test whether participants are paying attention. Hauser and Schwarz (2016) found that *MTurk* Workers with high approval ratings were more attentive to attention checks than were their resident college students responding online (see Figure 13.18 for an example of an attention check used by Hauser and Schwarz).

Crump, McDonnell, and Gureckis (2013) also examined the quality of *MTurk* data; they looked at a series of classic cognitive tasks to evaluate whether

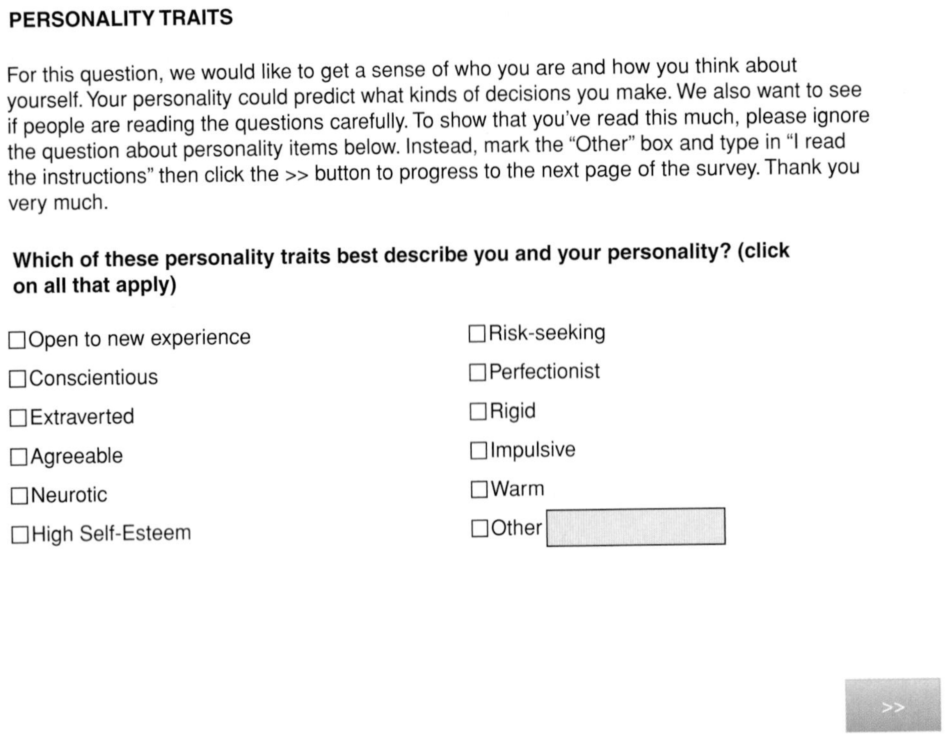

PERSONALITY TRAITS

For this question, we would like to get a sense of who you are and how you think about yourself. Your personality could predict what kinds of decisions you make. We also want to see if people are reading the questions carefully. To show that you've read this much, please ignore the question about personality items below. Instead, mark the "Other" box and type in "I read the instructions" then click the >> button to progress to the next page of the survey. Thank you very much.

Which of these personality traits best describe you and your personality? (click on all that apply)

☐ Open to new experience   ☐ Risk-seeking

☐ Conscientious   ☐ Perfectionist

☐ Extraverted   ☐ Rigid

☐ Agreeable   ☐ Impulsive

☐ Neurotic   ☐ Warm

☐ High Self-Esteem   ☐ Other [＿＿＿＿＿＿＿]

[>>]

FIGURE 13.18 Example of an attention check used by Hauser and Schwarz (2016). Used with permission of David Hauser (djhauser@umich.edu).

the results obtained with *MTurk* were similar to those obtained in previous research. In most cases, they were. In addition, *MTurk* Workers have shown the same cognitive biases as those in traditional samples – that is, they make the same kinds of errors (Goodman, Cryder, & Cheema, 2013).

Another way researchers have checked the viability of *MTurk* research is by recruiting people from different sources and then comparing the obtained results. For example, Paolacci et al. (2010) recruited participants from (1) *MTurk*, (2) a university, and (3) online discussion boards. The comparison revealed some interesting points. Those recruited from the online sources were older than the college sample. Paolacci et al. also considered the percentage of respondents who started the survey but then dropped out. Over 90% of those from the college sample and from *MTurk* completed the study; only

67% of participants from the online discussion boards did. Moreover, Paolacci et al. concluded that the results obtained using the *MTurk* sample "did not substantially differ" from those obtained with the college sample (p. 416).

Some researchers might be hesitant to test online because it is difficult to know whether the respondents are telling the truth about themselves. This too has been tested in a variety of ways, with good results. For example, Shapiro, Chandler, and Mueller (2013) checked the reported location of respondents (by confirming it with an Internet protocol [IP] address) and found they generally told the truth about where they were. Some might argue that people don't have much motivation to lie about their location. However, note that researchers have also checked for truth telling by looking for consistency in the reporting of demographics (such as age) over time. Again the results have been reassuring (see Mason & Suri, 2012; Shapiro et al., 2013).

Can Special Populations Be Studied Online?

Some have wondered whether collecting data from specialized populations will also benefit from online data collection. If you have a sample of potential respondents you already know about and can contact (such as a support group at a hospital or members of a Facebook group that targets a specific disorder), you can email them your study web link and they can choose whether to participate in your study. But what if you do not have a ready sample of a special population? What if instead you need to look for people who fit your criteria? Shapiro et al. decided to consider that very question using *MTurk*.

Shapiro et al. collected data from a sample of *MTurk* Workers and determined whether they were viable candidates for the study of various clinical issues (such as depression). To do this, they asked *MTurk* Workers who were US citizens to answer a series of questions that assessed their mental health and their personal experience of clinically relevant events like traumas. Since the requested information was of a sensitive nature, Shapiro et al. were concerned that Workers might be inclined to lie. So they collected data in two waves. A week after the first assessment, they invited the participants (identified only by an ID number) back to answer a second survey with many of the same questions. Shapiro et al. were able to determine whether a participant was likely fabricating information by comparing each person's demographic responses from week one and week two (very few had inconsistent responses).

Shapiro et al. found the prevalence of depression, general anxiety, and exposure to traumatic events to be generally equal to the prevalence previously found in the general population when tested offline. A substantial number of respondents also reported problems in areas of substance abuse. Overall they indicated feeling relatively more comfortable revealing information about their mental health online than in a face-to-face interview situation.

This data collection technique had additional benefits; it was amazingly quick and relatively inexpensive. The first wave of 530 participants were each paid $0.75 for the 20-minute task, and the data were collected in only two days! The second wave of participants ($N = 397$) were paid $0.80 each; these data were collected in five days. There were concerns, however. For example, a surprisingly large number of respondents reported experiencing symptoms that should be extremely rare, raising the possibility that they were falsifying information. Given these concerns, Shapiro et al. suggested ways to address data quality issues. For example, they recommended pre-screening Workers and having only those who meet predefined criteria complete the study. Ultimately Shapiro et al. concluded that *MTurk* was indeed a viable way to access various clinical populations.

Advantages and Disadvantages of Online Research

As a result of reading this chapter you may have a sense of the advantages and disadvantages of online data collection. Let's review these now. One of the advantages of collecting data online is that it can be done relatively quickly. When I was in graduate school, I remember being quite dismayed that it took me 11 months to collect the data for my dissertation. I needed a total of 300 participants but could test, at most, only four at a time. I daydreamed about graduating a year earlier if only I could collect data from larger groups. Imagine what my daydreams would have been like if I had read about a research team collecting data for their study in a matter of hours (see Emanuel, 2014). We rarely design our studies based on how fast we can collect data, but the world of data collection has changed tremendously in recent years, and collecting data relatively quickly has become a reality.

Another advantage of online testing is the prospect of large samples, which can be especially important for those, such as researchers at small colleges, who do not have easy access to large pools of prospective study participants (Johnson & Borden, 2012). Yet another advantage was revealed by Shapiro et al. Recall that their respondents indicated feeling more comfortable revealing information about their mental health online than in a face-to-face interview. Thus, if you are collecting data of a very personal nature, you may wish to take the online route.

A further advantage of online data collection is that online samples have been found by some to be more diverse than traditional college samples (for example, Gosling, Vazire, Srivastava, & John, 2004). The ability to test a more diverse population can increase the external validity of the work (see, for example, Daftary-Kapur & Greathouse, 2011; Wiener Krauss, & Lieberman, 2011). You may recall from Chapter 7 that psychological research in the world's top journals tends to be based on WEIRD samples (Western, Educated, Industrialized, Rich, and Democratic). As a result of this bias, Henrich et al. (2010) encouraged researchers to conduct research with more diverse populations; the Internet could help make that happen.

There are potential disadvantages to online research. For example, a computer could crash or malfunction while the participant is in the middle of an online session. The researcher loses data and the participant is left hanging, without the benefit of debriefing. If the data collected are of a particularly sensitive nature, or if a deceptive cover story must be revealed, debriefing is vitally important. In fact, some (such as Buchanan & Williams, 2010) have said that deception should be avoided for online research because of the risk that debriefing might not take place. If the participant has questions to ask or wishes to indicate being unable to complete the study, the hope is that he or she can refer back to the researcher's contact information on the informed consent form to do so. As you can see, this potential snag is uniquely an online problem.

Another problem that can occur with online testing is that you don't really know whether people are misrepresenting who they are (for instance, a minor might represent him- or herself as someone who is at least 18). It can be difficult to spot falsified demographic information. One possible way to deal with this problem is to do as Shapiro et al. did. They attempted to determine whether participants were likely fabricating information by comparing their demographic responses from two online sessions conducted a week apart. The assumption here is that those falsifying information will be unlikely to be consistent in their lies. It isn't a fail-proof method, but it can help. Deceptive participants are often less of an issue in traditional offline samples.

A further challenge is participants who drop out of the study. While dropouts are not unique to online research, they sometimes are more prevalent than in offline testing. There might be a computer crash or other technical problem, or there may be a host of other reasons more directly under the participant's control. He or she may be bored, hungry, or tired and decide to quit, and just closing your browser is easier than getting up and leaving in the presence of the researchers. Online participants who decide to quit during a testing session typically do not get the benefit of debriefing, again truly a concern for those conducting online data collection.

SUMMARY

Researchers are increasingly using online data collection for various purposes. Regardless of the reason, however, they still have a responsibility to treat their participants ethically.

Surveys and experiments can both be conducted online. For example, both *SurveyMonkey* and *Qualtrics* generate a web link after you create your research project, and this link can be sent to potential participants through email or social media. We can access samples that are more traditional in nature (just sending an email link to our university students) or that are more global in nature. *Qualtrics* and *SurveyMonkey* can also be used with *MTurk*, an online labor market where Requesters can make their research projects available for *MTurk* Workers to do in exchange for nominal pay. *MTurk* samples have generally been found to be more diverse than typical college student samples, and large samples can often be collected quickly and easily, even from special populations. As always, your choice of a survey or an experiment, and of a local or global sample, depends on your decisions about the best way to answer your research questions.

GLOSSARY

Attention check – a question presented in the middle of a survey designed to assess the attentiveness of the respondents.

Mechanical Turk (MTurk) – a website that engages large numbers of humans in tasks computers cannot do. Researchers can collect data through this site.

Qualtrics – an online survey builder. The free version is capable of randomization, which allows for random assignment of groups for experimentation.

Requesters – those who place tasks on *Mechanical Turk*.

SurveyMonkey – an online survey builder.

Tweetarchivist – an online source of archived Tweets.

Workers – those who participate in tasks on *Mechanical Turk*.

REVIEW QUESTIONS

1 Identify three ways that researchers can use online data collection.
2 Explain the ethical responsibilities of the online researcher.
3 Demonstrate how to place a survey and experiment online.
4 Identify ways to recruit online participants.
5 Explain what *MTurk* is.
6 Distinguish between an *MTurk* Worker and a Requester.
7 Explain why people participate in *MTurk* tasks.
8 State how data collected using *MTurk* compare to data collected elsewhere.
9 Describe the viability of studying special populations online.
10 Identify advantages and disadvantages of online data collection.

ARTICLES AS ILLUSTRATION

The articles presented below provide examples of topics covered in this chapter. The questions that follow each of the articles will help you focus on the important points of each.

1 Blomquist, B. A., & Giuliano, T. A. (2012). Do you love me, too? Perceptions of responses to *I Love You*. North American Journal of Psychology, 14(2), 407–418.

Ever said "I love you" to someone who then doesn't say it back? Or ever been on the receiving end of those fateful words and not felt the same in return? What have you said? There are lots of things that can be said in response to "I love you." Blomquist and Giuliano were interested in determining how women and men react when different responses to "I love you" occur. They conducted two studies. The first study tested an *MTurk* sample, the second tested a college sample. Answer the following questions for the first study:

a. Describe the design.

b. What is their hypothesis?

c. Describe the sample.

d. Describe the methodology.

e. Describe the results.

Answer the following questions for the second study.

a. Describe the design of this second study. How is the purpose of the second study different from the purpose of the first study?

b. Describe the sample. How does the sample of this second study differ from the sample of the first study?

c. Describe the methodology.

d. Describe the results. Could the type of sample affect the obtained results? If so, how?

2 Gardner, R. M., Brown, D. L., Boice, R. (2012). Using *Amazon*'s Mechanical Turk website to measure accuracy of body size estimation and body dissatisfaction. *Body Image, 9,* 532–534. doi:http://dx.doi.org/10.1016/j.bodyim.2012.06.006

Gardner et al. uses *MTurk* in a new way. Please answer the following questions.

a. What was the purpose of Gardner et al.'s research?

b. Describe Gardner et al.'s sample.

c. Describe Gardner et al.'s methodology.

d. How do the results obtained by Gardner et al. generally compare to the results from previous researchers who have considered similar questions?

e. Did Gardner et al. conclude that using *MTurk* was a viable avenue for research on satisfaction with body image?

SUGGESTED ACTIVITIES

1 As I mentioned earlier, consider using an online survey on your campus to see if and why the students on your campus use Facebook (or Twitter, or SnapChat, or Tinder). You can refer to Park and Lee's article for ideas on what questions to ask.

2 Another idea for a survey is to do a conceptual replication of Harrison and Gilmore's study on the "social contexts of text messaging" (p. 513). Harrison and Gilmore provide ample information regarding their study to enable you to easily create a similar survey. Think about how you would like to extend their work. Do you want to ask questions of students at a different kind of college (for example religious)? Do you want to test a non-college sample to see if the results are comparable to what Harrison and Gilmore found? Note that Harrison and Gilmore provide great ideas for future research; perhaps one of those would be of interest.

REFERENCES

Amazon (n.d.). *Service summary tour*. Retrieved from https://requester.mturk.com/tour

American Psychological Association. (2002). Ethical principles of psychologists and code of conduct. *American Psychologist, 57,* 1060–1073. doi:http://dx.doi.org/10.1037/0003-066X.57.12.1060

Barger, P., Behrend, T. S., Sharek, D. J., & Sinar, E. F. (2016). I-O and the crowd: Frequently asked questions about using Mechanical Turk for research. Retrieved from www.siop.org/tip/oct11/03barger.aspx

Baz, E. (2014). MTurk Amazon Mechanical Turk review: Earn some extra cash. Retrieved from beginatzero.com

Beullens, K., & Schepers, A. (2013). Display of alcohol use on Facebook: A content analysis. *Cyberpsychology,*

Behavior, and Social Networking, *16*, 497–503. doi:10.1089/cyber.2013.0044

Blomquist, B. A., & Giuliano, T. A. (2012). Do you love me, too? Perceptions of responses to *I love you*. *North American Journal of Psychology*, *14*, 407–418.

Bohannon, J. (2016, June 7). Psychologists grow increasingly dependent on online research subjects. Retrieved from www.sciencemag.org/

Boynton, M. H., & Smart Richman, L. (2014). An online daily diary study of alcohol use using Amazon's Mechanical Turk. *Drug and Alcohol Review*, *33*, 456–461. doi:http://dx.doi.org/10.1111/dar/12163

Buchanan, T., & Williams, J. E. (2010). Ethical issues in psychological research on the Internet. In S. D. Gosling & J. A. Johnson (eds.), *Advanced methods for conducting online behavioral research*. Washington, DC: American Psychological Association. doi:http://dx.doi.org/10.1037/12076-016

Buhrmester, M., Kwang, T., & Gosling, S. D. (2011). Amazon's Mechanical Turk: A new source of inexpensive, yet high-quality, data? *Perspectives in Psychological Science*, *6*, 3–5. doi:http://dx.doi.org/10.1177/1745691610393980

Cameron, J., & Geidner, N. (2014). Something old, something new, something borrowed from something blue: Experiments on dual viewing TV and Twitter. *Journal of Broadcasting & Electronic Media*, *58*, 400–419. doi:http://dx.doi.org/10.1080/08838151.2014.935852

Crump, M. J. C., McDonnell, J. V., & Gureckis, T. M. (2013). Evaluating Amazon's Mechanical Turk as a tool for experimental behavioral research. *PLOS ONE*, *8(3)*, 1–18.

Daftary-Kapur, T., & Greathouse, S. (2011). Forensic psychological research and the Internet. In B. Rosenfeld & S. D. Penrod (eds.), *Research methods in forensic psychology*. Hoboken, NJ: John Wiley & Sons.

Emanuel, G. (2014, March 5). Post a survey on Mechanical Turk and watch the results roll in. Retrieved from www.npr.org

Emery, K. (2014). So you want to do an online study: Ethics considerations and lessons learned. *Ethics and Behavior*, *24*, 293–303. doi:http://dx.doi.org/10.1080/10508422.2013.860031

Facebook reports second quarter 2016 results. (2016, July 27). Retrieved from https://investor.fb.com/investor-news/press-release-details/2016/Facebook-Reports-Second-Quarter-2016-Results/default.aspx

Folbre, N. (2013, March 18). The unregulated work of Mechanical Turk. *The New York Times*. Retrieved from www.nyt.com

Gardner, R. M., Brown, D. L., & Boice, R. (2012). Using Amazon's Mechanical Turk website to measure accuracy of body size estimation and body dissatisfaction. *Body Image*, *9*, 532–534. doi:http://dx.doi.org/10.1016/j.bodyim.2012.06.006

Goodman, J. K., Cryder, C. E., & Cheema, A. (2013). Data collection in a flat world: The strengths and weaknesses of Mechanical Turk samples. *Journal of Behavioral Decision Making*, *26*, 213–224. doi:http://dx.doi.org/10.1002/bdm.1753

Gosling, S. D., Vazire, S., Srivastava, S., & John, O. P. (2004). Should we trust web-based studies? A comparative analysis of six preconceptions about Internet questionnaires. *American Psychologist*, *59*, 93–104. doi:http://dx.doi.org/10.1037/0003-066X.59.2.93

Gureckis, T. M., Martin, J., McDonnell, J., Rich, A. S., Markant, D., Coenen, A., Halpern, D., Hamrick, J. B., & Chan, P. (2016). psiTurk: An open-source framework for conducting replicable behavioral experiments online. *Behavior Research Methods*, *48*, 829–842. doi:http://dx.doi.org/10.37758/s13428-015-0642-8

Harrison, M. A., & Gilmore, A. L. (2012). U txt WHEN? College students' social contexts of text messaging. *Social Science Journal*, *49*, 513–518. doi:http://dx.doi.org/10.1016/j.soscij.2012.05.003

Hauser, D. J., & Schwarz, N. (2016). Attentive Turkers: MTurk participants perform better on online attention checks than do subject pool participants. *Behavior Research Methods*, *48*, 400–407. doi:http://dx.doi.org/10.3758/s13428-015-0578-z

Healey, B. (2007). Drop downs and scroll mice: The effect of response option format and input mechanism employed on data quality in web surveys. *Social Science Computer Review*, *25*, 111–128. doi:http://dx.doi.org/10.1177/0894439306293888

Hefner, V. (2016). Tuning into fantasy: Motivations to view wedding television and associated romantic beliefs. *Psychology of Popular Media Culture*, *5*, 307–323. doi:http://dx.doi.org/10.1037/ppm0000079

Henrich, J., Heine, S. J., & Norenzayan, A. (2010). The weirdest people in the world? *Behavioral and Brain Sciences*, *33*, 61–83. doi:http://dx.doi.org/10.1017/S0140525X0999152X

Johnson, D. R., & Borden, L. A. (2012). Participants at your fingertips: Using Amazon's Mechanical Turk to increase student–faculty collaborative research. *Teaching of Psychology*, *39*, 245–251. doi:http://dx.doi.org/10.1177/0098628312456615

Kraut, R., Olson, J., Banaji, M., Bruckman, A., Cohen, J., & Couper, M. (2004). Psychological research online: Report of Board of Scientific Affairs' Advisory Group on the conduct of research on the Internet. *American Psychologist*, *59*, 105–117. doi:http://dx.doi.org/10.1037/0003-066X.59.2.105

Lachlan, K. A., Spence, P. R., & Lin, X. (2014). Expressions of risk awareness and concern through Twitter: On the utility of using the medium as an indication of audience needs. *Computers in Human Behavior*, *35*, 554–559. doi:http://dx.doi.org/10.1016/j.chb.2014.02.029

Lease, M., Hullman, J., Bigham, J. P., Berstein, M., Kim, J., Lasecki, W. S., Bakhski, S., Mitra, T., & Miller, R. C. (2013). Mechanical Turk is not anonymous. Available at https://papers.ssrn.com/sol3/papers.cfm?abstract_id=2228728

Lenhart, A. (2015, April 9). Mobile access shifts social media use and other online activities. Retrieved from www.pewinternet.org/

Mason, W., & Suri, S. (2012). Conducting behavioral research on Amazon's Mechanical Turk. *Behavior Research Methods*, *44*, 1–23. doi:http://dx.doi.org/10.3758/s13428-011-0124-6

Mathes, J., Schredl, M., & Göritz, A. S. (2014). Frequency of typical dream themes in most recent dreams: An online study. *Dreaming*, *24*, 57–66. doi:http://dx.doi.org/10.1037/a0035857

Paolacci, G., Chandler, J., & Ipeirotis, P. (2010). Running experiments on Amazon Mechanical Turk. *Judgment and Decision Making*, *5*, 411–419.

Park, N., & Lee, S. (2014). College students' motivations for Facebook use and psychological outcomes. *Journal of Broadcasting & Electronic Media*, *58*, 601–620. doi:http://dx.doi.org/10.1080/08838151.2014.966355

Sargis, E. G., Skitka, L. J., & McKeever, W. (2013). The Internet as psychological laboratory revisited: Best practices, challenges, and solutions. In Y. Amichai-Hamburger (ed.), *The social net: Understanding our online behavior*. Oxford: Oxford University Press. doi:http://dx.doi.org/10.1093/acprof:oso/9780199639540.003.0013

Schredl, M., Ciric, P., Götz, S., & Wittman, L. (2004). Typical dreams: Stability and gender differences. *Journal of Psychology: Interdisciplinary and Applied*, *138*, 485–494. doi:http://dx.doi.org/10.3200/JRLP.138.6.485-494

Shapiro, D. N., Chandler, J., & Mueller, P. A. (2013). Using Mechanical Turk to study clinical populations. *Clinical Psychological Science*, *1*, 213–220. doi:http://dx.doi.org/10.1177/2167702612469015

Skitka, L. J., & Sargis, E. G. (2005). Social psychological research and the Internet: The promise and peril of a new methodological frontier. In Y. Amichai-Hamburger (ed.), *The social net: The social psychology of the Internet*. Cambridge: Cambridge University Press.

(2006). The Internet as psychological laboratory. *Annual Review of Psychology*, *57*, 529–555. doi:http://dx.doi.org/10.1146/annurev.psych.57.102904.190048

Smith, A. (2015). U.S. smartphone use in 2015. Retrieved from www.pewinternet.org

Urbaniak, G. C., & Kilmann, P. R. (2003). Physical attractiveness and the "nice guy paradox": Do nice guys really finish last? *Sex Roles*, *49*, 413–426. doi:http://dx.doi.org/10.1023/A:1025894203368

Wiener, R. L., Krauss, D. A., & Lieberman, J. D. (2011). Mock jury research: Where do we go from here? *Behavioral Sciences and the Law*, *29*, 467–479. doi:http://dx.doi.org/10.1002/bsl.989

14 Writing About and Presenting Your Research

LEARNING OBJECTIVES

- Describe what goes into each of the major sections of a psychology research paper.

- Define plagiarism.

- Differentiate between the two ways to present research at a conference.

- Describe ways to achieve clarity in your writing.

- Describe the peer review process.

If a tree falls in the forest and no one is around to hear it, does it make a sound? I never liked that question, but I do like an analogous one: If you do research and you never tell anyone about it, have you contributed to science? I know the answer to that one! The answer is no. We have a responsibility to disseminate our research, to tell others what we have done and what we have found, so that together we can move toward finding answers to our questions.

There are a few different ways to disseminate information about our research. We can present a paper or a poster at a conference, and we can publish our work. We'll cover all these approaches in this chapter.

The sixth edition of the *Publication Manual of the American Psychological Association* (APA, 2010) governs the way we present our work (see Figure 14.1), and so we will refer to the relevant sections of the APA *Publication Manual* throughout this chapter. If

FIGURE 14.1 Front cover image of *Publication Manual of the American Psychological Association*, 6th edition.

you have questions regarding APA style that are not addressed here, you can consult the current *Publication Manual* or the APA style blog (blog.apastyle.org). Tutorials showing the basics of APA style are also available at the APA website (www.apa.org).

We'll start by looking at how a psychology research paper is organized.

The Organization of a Psychology Research Paper

A typical psychology research paper will contain the following sections:

1. Title page
2. Abstract
3. Introduction
4. Method
5. Results
6. Discussion
7. References
8. Tables and figures (these are optional).

As we progress through this chapter, I will cover the kind of information contained in each section. Later, we will talk about the specific formatting of each section, and you'll see examples of the different sections of a research paper, which will be annotated so you can see exactly where and how different information is represented. At this stage, while you are writing the paper, it's called a **manuscript**. Writing in APA style is a learned skill that takes practice. Reading through this chapter and referring to the sample manuscript in Appendix A will help you write your own manuscript.

Title Page

A title page of a manuscript contains | See section 2.01 of the *Publication Manual*.

the title of the article and information about who did the research and where. As the APA *Publication Manual* (2010) indicates, a title should "summarize the main idea of a manuscript simply and, if possible, with style" (p. 23). The *Manual* recommends that you do all this using no more than 12 words.

If you are writing up an experiment, you can represent your independent variables and at least a summary of your dependent variables in your title. Below is a common format for this type of title, for an experiment with one independent variable: "Effects of Independent Variable on Dependent Variable."

Here's an example of a title that uses this format: "Effects of Social Skills Training on Attitudes toward Dating." This title tells you that the researchers varied social skills training (presence, absence) in an effort to see how it would affect attitudes toward dating (a summary of the dependent variables).

If you have two independent variables, you can still use this format for your title. Here's an example: "Effects of Social Skills Training and Date Location on Dating Attitudes." In this case, I varied two independent variables, social skills training (presence, absence) and date location (movie theater, bowling alley), and I wanted to see how these variables would affect attitudes toward dating. Adding a second independent variable meant possibly going over the APA limit of 12 words in a title. In an effort to cut down the number of words used, I shortened "attitudes toward dating" to "dating attitudes."

How do you write the title with style? Often researchers will use a two-part title, using the first part to catch readers' interest and adding a descriptive subtitle. Here's one from Wright and Sinclair (2012): "Pulling the Strings: Effects of Friend and Parent Opinions on Dating Choices." You can see that Wright and Sinclair (2012) still used the "Effects of the Independent Variables on the Dependent Variables" approach. The second part of their title tells you specifically about the article's content. They added a first part to the title because it's catchy and might attract a reader's interest. Wright and Sinclair investigated whether friends and parents can have an impact on the dating choices of undergraduates playing an online dating game. It turns out that the opinions only of friends, not of parents, predicted who the undergraduates wanted to date (is this surprising?). So it's actually the friends, not parents, who are "pulling the strings."

Let's look at a few more examples of titles. Sometimes authors use the title to reveal the main results. For example, Kang and Williamson (2014) used the title "Background Music Can Aid Second Language Learning." You know instantly from this title what their research revealed.

Of course, sometimes authors write up research that is non-experimental, so the format described above ("Effects of the IV on the DV") is not appropriate. One possibility in this kind of case is to reveal the type of research in the title. So for example, Jakeman, Silver, and Molasso (2014) used the following title to describe their survey: "Student Experiences at Off-Campus Parties: Results from a Multicampus Survey." Also note that there are ways to write a title describing survey research without using the word "survey" in the title. For example, Van Volkum (2008) titled her work "Attitudes toward Cigarette Smoking among College Students."

Another type of article researchers write is a review article. A review article is a secondary source, because its authors are describing research that was already published in primary sources. Review articles often reveal their nature in the title. For example, Jacobi's (1991) title "Mentoring and Undergraduate Academic Success: A Literature Review" describes both the topic and the approach.

As for formatting the title page, as you'll see in Appendix A, APA style requires that your title be centered on the page and placed on the upper half of the page. It is in upper and lower case letters (capitalize all significant words that are four letters or more as well as all nouns, adjectives, adverbs and pronouns). The title page also will contain the author or authors' name(s) and institutional affiliation(s). Authors' names typically follow the "first name, middle initial, last name" format. Thus, on all my publications, I am "Wendy P. Heath." Underneath each author's name on the title page, you'll put the author's affiliation. That's the place where the author conducted the research. My institutional affiliation is Rider University.

A researcher should be listed as an author only if he or she actually worked on the project in a

> See section 4.15 of the *Publication Manual*.

> See section 2.02 of the *Publication Manual*.

substantial way. Since completing and writing up a research project includes so many steps, there are many ways to substantially participate, such as coming up with the research idea and hypotheses, writing a lot of the manuscript, or analyzing the results.

Lesser contributions such as collecting data should be acknowledged in an author note; these contributors are not usually listed as authors. The *Publication Manual* also dictates the order of the authors' names on a manuscript. The first author is the person who contributed the most, while the second author contributed less than the first but more than the third, and so on. The placement of the authors on the title page corresponds to their contribution order.

Finally, the title page of a manuscript should also include an **author note**. The APA *Publication Manual* lists the kind of information you can find in an author note, such as where to contact an author for further information.

See section 2.03 of the *Publication Manual*.

Abstract

On the second page of the manuscript you will find the abstract. The abstract is a brief summary of the article, and it should be able to stand alone and be readily understood. Think back to our discussion of doing a literature search on *PsycINFO* (see Chapter 2). Remember that when you search for journal articles about your topic, the information you see first is the title and the abstract, which allows you to decide whether you want to read the full article. So you want an abstract that is informative, providing the major aspects of your article in a short and clearly understandable fashion.

See section 2.04 of the *Publication Manual*.

In fact, journals usually set a word limit for the length of abstracts, typically no more than 250 words. There are also formatting requirements. The abstract is alone on the second page of your paper with the word Abstract centered at the top. The abstract is typed in block format; it's a single block of text with no paragraph indentation.

Even though the abstract appears on the second page of your manuscript, it is the part of your manuscript you will write last. Why? Because only after you have completed the entire manuscript will you know what information you'll need to summarize. Anything mentioned in the abstract has to be represented in the manuscript itself.

What goes in an abstract? The following information is typically found, in this order:

- purpose of the research (the "purpose statement")
- number and type of participants
- brief description of the methodology
- brief description of the main results
- a statement of the implications (what your results can mean for the real world)

Let's look at how these components can get incorporated into an abstract. I'll use King and Vidourek's (2013) abstract as my example.

The purpose of the study is to assess university students' involvement in tattooing and examine associations between tattooing and risky behaviors. University students enrolled

The purpose statement is presented first.

Next you should provide information regarding the number and type of study participants tested and provide brief details on the methodology used.

in physical education and health classes at one Midwestern university are study participants, and a survey is used to examine 998 university students' involvement in tattooing. The results indicate that 29% of respondents have a tattoo. The most common locations for tattoos are the chest (37.6%), foot (26.8%), arm (15.8%), and back (14.4%).

Females are more likely than males to have a tattoo. Tattooed students are significantly more likely than non-tattooed students to engage in alcohol and marijuana use and risky sexual behaviors. Suicidal behaviors and suicidal ideation are not related to tattoo status among university students. Therefore, college health professionals should be aware of associations between tattooing and risky behavioral involvement. Educational programs are needed to increase student awareness of body modification and associated risk behaviors. (p. 540)

The next part of your abstract should be a brief summary of your major results.

Abstracts often end with a statement of the implications of the results.

As you can see from their abstract, King and Vidourek conducted a survey. Let's now look at an abstract that provides information about an experiment. This example comes from Howell and Giuliano's (2011) study of how people view the use of profanity by those coaching teams of male athletes and female athletes.

Although many sports fans believe that expletive use is a typical part of coaching, there is a dearth of research on the perceptions of such behavior. As such, the present study was designed to test the hypothesis that expletive use by coaches is more accepted when it is directed at a male team than when it is directed at a female team. As part of a 2 (Expletive Use: Present or Absent) × 2 (Team Gender: Female or Male) between-subjects design, 60 participants (30 women, 30 men) read and gave reactions to a fictitious speech ostensibly given by a male basketball coach to his team. Consistent with predictions, participants rated the speech to be less effective when it contained expletives than when it did not. Furthermore, when the speech was directed at a female team, male participants considered it even less effective if it contained expletives than if it did not. By contrast, when the speech was directed at a male team, male participants rated the speech to be equally effective, regardless of whether or not it contained expletives. Female participants did not exhibit this effect. The present study suggests that expletive use in coaching may be an ineffective strategy and reveals that males and females have different expectations and opinions of expletive use in coaching. Thus, coaches should be aware of the possible negative ramifications of their use of profanity, particularly with female athletes.

These authors first provide a rationale for their research.

The authors provide a "purpose statement." They also chose to provide a hypothesis, which is not a necessary part of an abstract.

Provide information regarding the number and type of study participants tested and provide brief details on the methodology used. Here the authors note the type of design (between-subjects) as well as the names and levels of each independent variable (the dependent variables were summed up earlier: perceptions of the coaches). Also note that the authors considered how male versus female participants viewed the coaches. This is a quasi-experimental variable.

The authors provide a summary of the major results.

Here are the implications of the results. Basically, someone can get in trouble using profanity when coaching a team, especially a team of females!

As you can see in Howell and Giuliano's abstract, they provide information regarding their independent variables along with each variable's levels (expletive use: present, absent; team gender: male, female). It's important to include this level of detail. Note that the authors capitalized the names of their independent variables and levels; APA style dictates that, in some cases, variables should be capitalized when they appear with a multiplication sign (see the APA *Publication Manual* for more information).

There's one more point I want to mention about the manuscript's abstract page. When you prepare a manuscript, place a list of keywords under the abstract. **Keywords** are words or phrases that represent main concepts from the manuscript. These keywords can be seen as suggestions that will help those searching *PsycINFO* to find your article. Look at article citation pages in *PsycINFO* to find examples of keywords. For example, according to *PsycINFO*, the following keywords are relevant to Howell and Giuliano's work: *coach expletive use, team gender perception, coaching effectiveness, sports*. Using these search phrases/terms in *PsycINFO* will elicit Howell and Giuliano's article as well as others that share those keywords.

The Introduction

The purpose of the introduction is to: (1) provide information about what others have done on the topic of interest, (2) develop a rationale for doing the present research, and (3) provide general details regarding the present research. The introduction begins on the third page of the manuscript. The first thing you write on that third page is your title, centered, at the top of that page. Then you are ready to write your introduction.

See section 2.05 of the *Publication Manual*.

Psychologists typically write their papers by starting with a very broad introduction to their general topic. From there they get more and more specific as they move through the introduction, until finally, in the *last* paragraph of the introduction, they present the purpose of the current research. In the sections provided below, I will describe how to write an introduction, giving examples along the way.

The First Paragraph of the Introduction

As noted above, a psychology research paper typically begins with a broad introduction to the general topic. Sometimes researchers choose to cite a real-life example as a way to introduce the overall topic, a 'hook' to draw people in. For example, take a look at this opening paragraph from Howell and Giuliano's (2011) article:

> In February of 2009, Oklahoma State University's men's basketball coach Travis Ford was caught by a live television feed screaming expletives at one of his players (Associated Press, 2009). The media was flooded with coverage of the incident and incited public outcry about Ford's behavior. In fact, both the OSU athletic director and the head of the Big-12 athletic conference went on record as disapproving of Ford's behavior. Nevertheless, no action was taken against Ford because, as the Associated Press (2009) acknowledged, Ford is not the only coach to use such language, but was merely one of the unlucky ones to be caught doing so. Replying to the news story online, many sports fans, players, and coaches commented that profanity use by a coach is a "normal [behavior] in competitive sports" and that Ford was simply "doing what works." (Howell & Giuliano, 2011, p. 70)

As you can see, Howell and Giuliano use their first paragraph to introduce the topic of using profanity when coaching by citing a real instance of this behavior.

Alternatively, you can choose to go directly from your opening sentence – the general introduction – to the literature review without citing a real-life analogy. Here's an example of a first paragraph I wrote that takes this approach:

> *Researchers have considered the kinds of factors that can influence whether or not females will accept a male's offer for a date.*

Open with a relatively general statement.

> *Some have found evidence of a female preference for a mate who is financially*

Get more specific.

> *secure. For example, female college students stated that a male's earning capacity was an important characteristic for potential mates (Stewart, Stinnett, & Rosenfeld, 2000). Harrison and Saeed (1977) also found evidence for this preference when they examined newspaper ads written by females seeking male partners. Females were more likely than males to include their desire for financial security in their ad. Guéguen and Lamy (2012)*

Focus on a topic of interest with literature as relevant as possible. Make sure you transition from sentence to sentence. Use connectors such as "for example."

> *took a different approach to the question and also found evidence for a female's preference for higher financial status in a male. Specifically, they found that females were more likely to give their phone number to a male who was in a high-status car as opposed to a lower-status car.*

The above examples illustrated two ways to introduce your general research topic to your audience.

In the first example the authors used an anecdote to introduce the general topic. Anecdotes, if used at all, are used sparingly in a research paper. Most if not all of the background information you provide in your paper will be evidence from peer-reviewed journal articles, an approach illustrated in the second example shown above.

The Middle Paragraph(s) of the Introduction. After your brief introduction to your general topic of interest, you should use the middle section of your introduction to provide information about previous research on your topic. It may be that no one has completed research on your exact topic, and that's not a problem. Your goal is to make sure you summarize the *most relevant* research there is.

When presenting information regarding a source, note the author's/authors' last name(s) and the year the source was published, and provide information regarding the methodology and variables studied. For example, one reasonable guideline to use if you are citing an experiment from an article is to note all the independent variables manipulated by the author(s), but note only the dependent variables relevant to your research that the author(s) in question considered. Then emphasize the pertinent findings of the previous research. Don't include trivial details about what someone else has done. Do not include the title of their work, the number of study participants, the types of statistical tests, or the design that they used. This means each source could reasonably be addressed in one or two sentences, as you see in my example.

There are two ways to include citations in your work. The citation can be an integral part of the sentence or it can be tacked on to the sentence. If the citation is an integral part of the sentence, give the last name(s)

See section 6.11–6.12 of the *Publication Manual.*

of the author(s) and, in parentheses, the year in which the work was published. For example:

Grossberg and Alf (1985) found that under-graduates had lower blood pressure readings when they petted a dog rather than read a book or talked with others.

If the citation is tacked on to the sentence, enclose the entire citation in parentheses and use an ampersand (&) to indicate "and." For example:

Undergraduates had lower blood pressure readings when they petted a dog rather than read a book or talked with others (Grossberg & Alf, 1985).

If the source you are citing has only one or two authors, name all of them each time you cite the source. If the source has between three and five authors, name all authors the first time they appear in your paper, and then you use "et al." (this means "and others"):

Glick, Larsen, Johnson, and Branstiter (2005) were interested in what people think of sexy women who have low- versus high-status jobs. To investigate this, Glick et al. (2005) had college students provide their perceptions of a female presented on videotape.

If the source you are citing has six or more authors, name the first author and use "et al." the first time and every time you cite the source in the body of the paper. Then list all the authors in your reference section at the end of the paper.

When should you cite a source? Anytime you use someone else's ideas or words, you need to give them credit for the information. Doing otherwise is plagiarism (see more on plagiarism below). But you don't need to cite a source in every sentence. If it is clear that you are still talking about the same source

you cited earlier in that same paragraph, you do not need to cite it again.

Aiello, DeRisi, Epstein, and Karlin (1977) were interested in determining how people would be affected when their personal space is violated. They found that those experiencing closer physical proximity experienced higher skin conductance levels (an arousal stress response) than those who were less crowded.

I did not have to cite Aiello et al. in the second sentence above because it was clear that I was still referring to the same source I cited in the earlier sentence. Also recognize that in the above example I could use "they" to refer to Aiello et al. in the second sentence only if the earlier reference citation was an integral part of the sentence. Think about it this way. When you are writing your sentences, try reading your work aloud but don't read anything in parentheses. This means you can't refer to a tacked-on citation later as "they" because it is as if the citation in parentheses was not even there, and it wouldn't be clear who "they" referred to.

You also need to make sure you have transitions from paragraph to paragraph, and from sentence to sentence. For example, you can start a paragraph with an

See section 3.05 of the *Publication Manual.*

introductory statement that addresses the topic you will cover in that paragraph ("One of the variables of interest is …"). Then you can write, "For example," and give an example of research that addresses that topic. This helps ensure that your work "flows." You can see examples of transitional words in my paragraph that discussed the influences researchers have considered with regard to whether females will accept a male's offer of a date. You will also see other examples in the sample manuscript presented in Appendix A.

The Last Paragraph of the Introduction. The last paragraph of the introduction is where you provide details about your specific research study. One way to do this is to use a purpose statement. For example, when you are writing up an experiment, the purpose statement will include the independent variables (with their levels) and a statement of (or a summary of) your dependent variables. Here's a suggested format for a purpose statement for an experiment with one independent variable:

The purpose of the present experiment is to investigate the effects of [state first independent variable here with the levels in parentheses] on [state dependent variable summary here].

Here's a suggested format for a purpose statement for an experiment with two independent variables:

The purpose of the present experiment is to investigate the effects of [state first independent variable here with the levels in parentheses] and [state second independent variable here with the levels in parentheses] on [state dependent variable summary here].

Your purpose statement should be followed, in the same paragraph, by your hypothesis or hypotheses. Hypothesis formation will be discussed more fully below. Finally, this paragraph will end with a brief mention of your general methodology; this can usually be accomplished in one or two sentences. An example is presented below. In this example, I have provided information regarding the study that concerned whether females will accept a male's offer of a date; this experiment has one independent variable as noted in the paragraph. You can also see an example of a last paragraph of the introduction in the sample manuscript in Appendix A. That example will provide you with information regarding an experiment completed with two independent variables.

In an effort to investigate further the appeal of a male's financial security in the dating decisions of females, the purpose of the present experiment is to determine the effects of the type of clothing (designer, non-designer) on the likelihood of date acceptance. If the male is wearing designer clothing as opposed to

> Provide a rationale for doing the present work.

> Here is the purpose statement. The independent variable and its levels are provided in this statement. The dependent variable, likelihood of date acceptance, is also in this purpose statement.

> The hypothesis(es) are provided after the purpose of the research is stated. Note that the hypotheses are derived from the previous literature whenever possible.

non-designer clothing, then females are expected to be more likely to accept a date offer. Females will be brought to the lab under the pretense of working with another study participant (a confederate)

> Here is a brief mention of the methodology. It should be the last sentence of your introduction.

on a task. The male confederate will be dressed in designer clothing or non-designer clothing, and at the end of the task will ask the female for her phone number.

You can also write up a purpose statement when you are writing up non-experimental research. For example, consider the survey research conducted by Harrison, Bealing, and Salley (2015). Here is the statement they made to describe their research: "The present study investigates college students' use of text messaging in various social situations to determine whether they consider such actions socially appropriate or think such actions are indeed social breaches."

As I mentioned above, one of the goals of the literature review is to establish the rationale for the current study. Remember from Chapter 2 that published research typically offers something original to the field, something that has not been done before. Perhaps you are doing the research to test a theory. Perhaps you are investigating something that has not been considered by previous researchers. Perhaps you are investigating a topic that others have considered, but you are using a different methodology or a different type of sample. You need to indicate how and why you are doing the research you are doing.

I'll give you an example. We've already discussed Howell and Giuliano's study on the use of profanity in coaching. Here's how Howell and Giuliano explained the rationale for their study:

> *The research reviewed thus far suggests that expletive use by a coach should decrease his or her perceived effectiveness, especially in situations involving a male coach and a female team. However, there is a dearth of research empirically investigating the effects of expletive use as a function of gender in a coaching context. As such, the present study sought to integrate previous research on profanity use with research on coaching techniques by measuring men's and women's perceptions of cursing behavior as a function of team gender. To explore this question, the current study varied the content of a hypothetical halftime speech (i.e., it did or did not contain expletives), as well as the gender of the team (i.e., female or male) at whom the speech was directed, in order to determine the extent to which these factors influenced the perceived effectiveness of a coach's cursing behavior. (Howell & Giuliano, 2011, p. 71)*

As mentioned earlier, another possible rationale for a study is to test a theory or test competing theories. Let's look at an example. Say you arrive at class early. Do you have a tendency to choose

FIGURE 14.2 Karev (2000) found that university students showed a preference for the left side of classrooms.

a seat on a particular side of the room? Harms, Poon, Smith, and Elias (2015) were interested in this very question. They indicated that researchers have studied seating in movie-theater settings and found a tendency for people to sit on the right side of the theater (facing the screen). Two competing theories have been offered to account for this finding. One theory, endorsed by Weyers, Milnik, Müller, and Pauli (2006), suggests that this tendency to go to a particular side of the room is due to "basic behavioural tendencies" (p. 181). On the other hand, Karev (2000) suggests that an expectation of processing demand influences this bias. Karev's theory is tied to knowledge of how the brain typically processes information. For most, the left side of the brain is mainly responsible for language and analytical content while the right side of the brain is mainly responsible for non-language actions, such as spatial and emotional content (see Badzakova-Trajkov, Corballis, & Häberling, 2016, for a review). Understanding this theory also requires that one know that the brain has contralateral control (Whitehead & Banihani, 2014). What you see in your right visual field will be processed on the left side of the brain. Thus, if one sits on the right side of the movie theater, then the screen will be mainly on the left side of the visual field and the information coming in will be processed on the right side of the brain. Karev argued that people at the movies expect emotional content so they have a tendency to sit on the right to enable an efficient processing of that content and he found evidence for this.

Harms et al. decided to test for a seating bias in university classrooms and compare these results to those previously found in movie theaters. If students showed a tendency to prefer the right side of the classroom, Harms et al. said this would support Weyers et al.'s theory; people just tend to turn to the right. However, if university students showed a tendency to prefer the left side of the classroom, this would support the idea that students are anticipating a different processing demand in the classroom than people expect in a theater. Why? If you anticipate a high processing demand from, for example, hearing a lecture, then you would benefit from placing the instructor in your right visual field; this would allow information to move efficiently into the left hemisphere of the brain where language is typically processed. So what happened? The university students showed a preference for the left side of the classrooms; Karev's theory was supported.

As I mentioned before, after you state the purpose of your research, you need to state your hypothesis(es). Typically your hypotheses come from your reading of the literature. For example, take the research I referred to above. Since others had investigated what influences females' preferences for a date and found that monetary issues were important, I could hypothesize that I would find something comparable, even though no one had done the exact same research I had done. There are a few guidelines to follow when you create your hypotheses. Take another look at this hypothesis; I'll color code it so you can see what the guidelines refer to.

If the male is wearing designer clothing as opposed to non-designer clothing, then females are expected to be more likely to accept a date offer.

Your hypothesis should:

1. be a parallel statement,
2. state direction,
3. state that this is an expectation, prediction, or hypothesis,
4. include the dependent variable,
5. reflect that the hypothesized outcome is relevant for more than one study participant (unless you are running a single-subject design [see Chapter 11]).

I chose to write the above hypothesis using an "if/then" statement; however, there are other ways to write a hypothesis. You could, for example, write the above hypothesis in this alternative way: Females are expected to accept date offers more often from men wearing designer as opposed to non-designer clothing.

Let's say you want to run a study on the topic of dating attitudes. Before you plan anything, you'll want to become familiar with what has already been done on the topic, for several reasons: (1) you can see what methodologies have worked, (2) you can learn what others have done so that you can potentially make an original contribution to the literature, and (3) you can learn what others have done to help you determine what to expect from your work – that is, you can formulate your hypothesis(es).

Note that it is important that you state your hypotheses before you conduct your study.

If you state your hypotheses after you see how the data come out, instead of before you conduct the study, you are "HARKing" ("hypothesizing after the results are known)" which is not an appropriate scientific procedure (see Kerr, 1998, p. 196). This doesn't mean you have to read everything that has been done on a particular topic; there may be hundreds or even thousands of studies on a given topic. But it does mean you need to become familiar with the state of the literature at that moment in time. Read some recent publications on your topic; since all articles will begin with information on the literature that led up to their plans for their research, you can learn from their experiences. This is a good start. However, once you have isolated the works that are most pertinent to your plans, you need to seek out the original sources for that work. Do not just trust that the summaries you read represented the work correctly. Secondary sources are great when you are at the beginning of your search for literature. They can help you become familiar with your topic and help you generate ideas for your own research. Whenever possible, though, obtain original sources when you are writing.

Sometimes, forming your hypotheses is difficult. Perhaps the previous research on a topic has been mixed. For example, let's pretend the research considering the value of financial stability in a male partner is mixed; assume some studies demonstrate that females have a preference for a financially stable male and some studies don't. In this case, you can try to figure out what underlies the two types of results. Is there a difference in methodology? Is there a difference in the type of sample? If you see a pattern, you can devise a research study to investigate the conditions in which each result is more likely. Again, it helps to have a good understanding of the existing literature.

Method

Your Method section is usually divided into a Participants subsection, a Materials or Apparatus subsection, and a Procedure subsection. Some papers

See section 2.06 of the *Publication Manual.*

combine the Materials and Procedure section, and some

include additional sections, such as a Design subsection that describes the experimental design used or a Measures subsection that provides details about the different measures participants filled out. The subsections you choose to use are up to you and your co-authors.

As for formatting, the Method heading is bold, capitalized, and centered. The subheadings are bold, capitalized, and flush left. I'll discuss a variety of these subsections below.

The Participants Subsection. In the Participants subsection, you will provide information about the participants such as the number of participants tested, information about their characteristics (say, undergraduates at a small northeastern university), and incentives, if any, that were provided in exchange for participation (such as money or extra class credit). You should also indicate any other information you collected regarding your participants. For example, it is common for researchers to collect demographic information such as age (provide the mean and standard deviation) and gender. You can also use this subsection to indicate whether participants were tested individually or in groups; if you tested in groups, state the range of group size.

The Design Subsection. A design subsection is appropriate when you have conducted an experiment. In this section, you will provide information about your independent variable(s) and levels, and indicate whether your research was a between-subjects, within-subjects, or mixed design. Let's take a look at an example of a Design subsection:

A 2 × 2 between-subjects design was used with victim age (5 years old, 40 years old) and defendant gender (male, female) as the independent variables. Participants were randomly assigned to groups.

Notice that I named my design by its levels as discussed in Chapter 9, and I have indicated that participants were randomly assigned to groups. Indicating that you randomly assigned participants to groups is a common way to indicate that you used a between-subjects design.

Let's take a look at a mixed design example. Jones, Jones, Thomas, and Piper (2003) conducted an experiment to investigate how drinking a moderate amount of alcohol would affect males' and females' ratings of unknown males' and females' faces. Here is an excerpt from their Design subsection:

A 2 × 2 × 2 three-factor design was employed with repeated measures on one factor. The within-participants factor was sex of face (two levels: male and female). Between-participants factors were sex of rater (two levels: male and female) and alcohol consumption status (two levels: some and none).(Jones et al., 2003, p. 1071)

Jones et al. also name their design by its levels (2 × 2 × 2) and indicate which variables were between-participants (I refer to this as "between-subjects") and which variable were within-participants ("within-subjects"). The within-subjects factor was sex of face, so this means all participants in Jones et al.'s experiment rated both male and female faces. The between-subjects factors were the sex and alcohol consumption status of the rater. This means every participant was either a male or a female and either had some alcohol to drink or not. While including this information in the Method section is appropriate, having a separate Design subsection is not absolutely necessary. Many authors include it when conducting an experiment so readers can quickly refer to this section to find out details about the design used.

The Apparatus/Materials Subsection. Typically researchers utilize either an Apparatus or a Materials subsection. I'll discuss each one here.

An Apparatus subsection provides information about the instruments that provided stimuli to your participants. Say you presented stimuli to your participants using a computer. Your Apparatus subsection would offer information about the type and model of the computer you used. This section provides enough essential detail so that anyone wishing to replicate the work would have a good understanding as to how it was originally done. As an example, let's look at part of an Apparatus section from Jones et al.'s work on drinking and the ratings of unknown males' and females' faces.

An Apple Powerbook G3 laptop computer running SuperLab 1.75 (Cedrus Corporation) was used to present 118 (59 male) facial stimuli to participants in a preview phase and a rating phase. The computer screen was 24 × 18 cm, the facial stimuli were 18 × 12 cm. The viewing distance was approximately 50 cm. (Jones et al., 2003, p. 1071)

A Materials subsection is often used to describe visual or verbal stimuli. So, for example, if you used vignettes to present information to participants, you can describe the vignettes in a Materials section. If you used a questionnaire, either questions you wrote yourself or a previously published scale, you can describe these measures in the Materials section (include information about what the response options were). Let's look at an example of a Materials section. This example comes from the work of Harrison, Shortall, Dispenza, and Gallup (2011) who wondered if those who are seen as more attractive babies would be seen as more attractive adults (spoiler alert: they were not). Here's how they described their stimuli:

Photographs of infants and adults were obtained from high school yearbooks dating from 1977 to 1993 from three different US regions. To maximize facial visibility, we did not include photographs of babies wearing blankets around their heads or head adornments, adults with facial hair, and individuals wearing hats or glasses. The stimulus material consisted of both an infant photograph and an adult photograph of the same individual, and the resulting target sample consisted of 40 individuals (20 males, 20 females). All of the adult photographs belonged to White students that were high school seniors, making them approximately 18 years old ... Because all of the infant photographs were presented in gray scale in yearbooks, all adult images originally presented in color were changed to gray scale. (Harrison et al., 2011, p. 611)

Some choose to use a Measures section to provide information about questions they asked of their study participants. For example, in a study of ethnic and racial differences in body satisfaction, Kronenfeld, Reba-Harrelson, Von Holle, Reyes, and Bulik (2010) presented varied drawings of a woman's silhouette and then asked participants questions about them. Kronenfeld et al. stated the following in a Measures section:

Each woman was asked the following questions: "Which silhouette is closest to what you currently look like?" and "Which silhouette would you prefer to look like?" (Kronenfeld et al., 2010, p. 132)

(Kronenfeld presented the silhouettes in an Appendix in their article.)

Others use a Measures section to provide reliability and validity information regarding a scale or test that they used to measure a particular construct (see Chapter 4). For example, in an investigation of a possible link between depression in undergraduates and solitary drinking, Keough, O'Connor, Sherry, and Stewart (2015) provided information about the multiple measures they used. I'll provide information about one as an example.

The Rutger's Alcohol Problem Index (RAPI; White & Labouvie, 1989) is a 23-item measure of alcohol-related problems. Participants indicated how often they experienced each problem in the past 6 months. Reponses were made on a 5-point scale (0 = never; 4 = 8 times). Sum scores were calculated. Previous research supports good internal consistency, test–retest reliability, and concurrent validity of the RAPI in undergraduates (Miller, Miller, Verhegge, Linville, & Pumariega, 2002). The present alpha was .90, which is excellent. (Keough et al., 2015, p. 218)

The Procedure Subsection. In this subsection you will describe all the major procedural steps in the order in which they occurred for your participants. Also include information about the steps you took to ensure your participants were treated ethically, such as informed consent and debriefing. Be careful not to repeat details you provided in other sections. For example, if your experiment involves presenting scenarios to participants and then asking them questions, provide details about the scenarios and the questions in the Materials section, but in the Procedure section indicate simply that participants read scenarios and answered questions. In Keough et al.'s research on depression and drinking they simply reported "participants completed self-report measures in the lab and were compensated with course credit or money ($10/hour)" (p. 2.17). You can also see an example of a Procedure section in the sample manuscript provided in Appendix A.

Results

The Results section, and only the Results section, is where you will give your readers information about your statistical analyses. If the research was an experiment, reveal how different groups performed relevant to each other. If the research was not an experiment, describe how participants performed overall. We typically do not reveal how *individual* participants performed (except perhaps in a small-*N* design as discussed in Chapter 11).

See section 2.07 of the *Publication Manual.*

Clarity is of upmost importance in a Results section. One way to achieve clarity is to divide your Results section into subsections and label each with a heading. Authors often choose to present results one dependent variable at a time, using the name of the dependent variable as the heading. I also recommend tying your results to your hypotheses so readers can easily see whether your hypotheses were supported.

Within each Results subsection, start with your simpler results and move toward the more complex results. If you did an experiment, report main effects first, followed by interactions. If you did a correlational study, report simple correlations first, followed by more complex results such as from multiple regression analyses.

Start your Results section with information about any manipulation checks you performed. Manipulation checks allow you to establish whether your experimental manipulation worked. So report this first, and then move from dependent variable to dependent variable, reporting on your results as you go.

Think back to the presentation of results in Chapter 8 in which experimental results were compared.

For each condition being compared, a mean and a standard deviation were presented. In addition, statistical information was presented that revealed whether the means being compared were significantly different from each other. This is the sort of information that goes into a Results section.

You probably won't be surprised to learn that the APA *Publication Manual* has specific guidelines regarding the way you present your data. Virtually all statistical notation is presented in italics (for example,

See section 4.45 of the *Publication Manual.*

F, M, SD, p), and there is a space on either side of any equal sign. Every number is rounded to two decimal places. The APA *Publication Manual* also has rules for reporting probability values. You need to report exact probability values ($p = .02$), although there is an exception. If you generate probability values less than .001, report that value as $p < .001$.

Now let's take a look at a specific example of how to read an ANOVA summary table and write up a result. You may recall, from Chapter 9, the tipping experiment I conducted with my former student in which we varied whether writing a thank you message on a restaurant check (presence, absence) and drawing a smiley face on the restaurant check (presence, absence) affected the average tip people left. You also may recall that we obtained the following result:

When a smiley face was drawn on the checks, the average tip percentage was larger ($M = 17.74$, $SD = 6.95$) than when a smiley face was not drawn on the checks ($M = 15.32$, $SD = 4.43$), $F (1, 128) = 5.64$, $p = .02$, partial $\eta^2 = .05$.

Now let's look and see where these numbers came from. We used a 2 × 2 Analysis of Variance (ANOVA) to analyze our data. This ANOVA indicated, for each of the two main effects and the interaction, whether the result was likely due to

Table 14.1 ANOVA summary table of dependent variable: Tip percentage.

Source	Type III sum of squares	df	Mean square	F	Sig.	Partial eta squared
Corrected model	750.097	3	250.032	8.249	.000	.162
Intercept	35794.455	1	35794.455	1180.906	.000	.902
Smiley face	170.864	1	170.864	5.637	.019	.042
Thank you	492.464	1	492.464	16.247	.000	.113
Smiley face * Thank you	60.469	1	60.469	1.995	.160	.015
Error	3879.808	128	30.311			
Total	40764.615	132				
Corrected total	4629.905	131				

chance or likely due to the impact of the independent variable(s).

When you conduct an ANOVA, you get what is known as an ANOVA summary table. The ANOVA summary table in our case looked like Table 14.1.

The ANOVA summary table, plus a table of the means and standard deviations relevant to this dependent variable (Table 14.2), gives us the information we need to write up this result.

Now let's look at that result again and I'll color code it so you can see where the numbers came from.

When a smiley face was drawn on the checks, the average tip percentage was larger ($M = 17.74$, $SD = 6.95$) than when a smiley face was not drawn on the checks ($M = 15.32$, $SD = 4.43$), $F (1, 128) = 5.64$, $p = .02$, partial $\eta^2 = .05$.

The smiley face main effect is one of the main effect results from this experiment. This ANOVA summary table has a total of two main effects (one for each independent variable) and an interaction, and all this information can be described in your Results section. (Note that we typically do not

Table 14.2 Dependent variable: Means and standard deviations for tip percentage.

Smiley face	Thank you	Mean	Standard deviation	N
Absent	Absent	14.0842	4.26052	33
	Present	16.5953	4.28834	32
	Total	**15.3205**	**4.42541**	65
Present	Absent	15.0067	5.44364	32
	Present	20.2269	7.29671	35
	Total	**17.7336**	**6.94610**	67
Total	Absent	14.5384	4.86267	65
	Present	18.4924	6.27739	67
	Total	16.5453	5.94498	132

include ANOVA Summary tables in a manuscript.) You will see a complete Results section in the sample paper presented in Appendix A.

Discussion

There are multiple things to accomplish in the Discussion section, and a particular order in which to do so. We'll go paragraph by paragraph. These are general guidelines, and there are a variety of ways to meet them. I am providing you with information to allow you to meet these general goals.

See section 2.08 of the *Publication Manual*.

The First Paragraph of the Discussion. In the first paragraph, you first want to restate your hypotheses and say whether you obtained support or nonsupport for your hypotheses. Note that you will represent your results in the Discussion section without providing any numbers and without talking about statistical tests. Think about it this way. You wrote about your results in the Results section with the numbers attached; now remove those numbers. Here's an example. In the Results section you saw the following sentence:

When a smiley face was drawn on the checks, the average tip percentage was larger ($M = 17.74$, $SD = 6.95$) than when a smiley face was not drawn on the checks ($M = 15.32$, $SD = 4.43$), $F (1, 128) = 5.64$, $p = .02$, partial $\eta^2 = .05$.

That sentence can now be:

When a smiley face was drawn on the checks, the average tip percentage was larger than when a smiley face was not drawn on the checks.

I've provided this example just so you can see how your sentence would look without the statistics. However, note that you shouldn't necessarily use the same wording that you used in the Results section. I can, for example, rewrite the example shown above in the following way:

Participants tipped more, on average, when a smiley face was drawn as opposed to not drawn on the checks.

List your hypotheses and indicate concisely whether your data are consistent with your hypotheses. If none of your hypotheses were supported, for example, you can state them all and then indicate just once that none was supported instead of saying so for each of them. After reviewing your hypotheses and the findings related to those hypotheses, indicate any other findings that you consider to be important.

The Middle Paragraph(s) of the Discussion. In the middle paragraphs of the Discussion section you want to discuss your obtained results in light of previous research. Did you obtain results that are consistent with what others have found? Were your results consistent with what relevant theory predicted? Cite previous research in this discussion. You can revisit articles presented in the introduction. You can also use additional literature to explain why obtained results were inconsistent with earlier work.

After you review your results in light of the previous literature, start a new paragraph. You'll use this paragraph to provide a critique of the current research. Are there any methodological issues that should be addressed? If you did an experiment, was there a confound that affected your internal validity? If you conducted a correlational study, acknowledge that a statement of causality is not possible and postulate what other influences there may be on your variables. Another possible area to address is the external validity of your results. Are you limited in your ability to generalize your results to your population of interest, perhaps because of the way you obtained your study participants? For example, if you tested university undergraduates, you may not be able to generalize your results beyond that type of population.

The information you provide in your critique paragraph should lead you to ideas for future research. You can put these in the same paragraph as your critique or in a new "future research" paragraph. Think about what you now know after doing your research; what would you recommend future researchers do differently? You might suggest testing a different population (to increase external validity) or making changes in methodology. Provide a reason for each recommended change.

Researchers also often include at least one idea that isn't just a recommendation that comes out of a critique of your current work. Now that you've done your research study, what would be a reasonable next step? Did your results fit presented theory? If not, perhaps the theory needs to be revised and a new study proposed to test the revision. Any future ideas you provide must be closely related to what you did in the current study. You can't just say, "Next time, just study something else!"

Let's take a look at an example of these two different kinds of future research ideas. Think back to Harrison et al.'s study of the stability of attractiveness from infancy to adulthood. One of their ideas for future research came out of a possible perceived limitation of this work. Recall that all their photos were presented in gray scale. They suggested that future researchers consider the possibility of using color photos to enable raters to rate attractiveness using these additional color cues. Harrison et al. also had a suggestion for future research that was not precipitated by a perceived limitation in their current work. Here's what they said:

> It is important to note that estrogen and progesterone levels mediate young women's sensitivity toward infants' faces (Sprengelmeyer et al., 2009). While we did not take into account the menstrual/hormonal status of female raters in the present study, this would be an interesting direction for future research. (Harrison et al., 2011, p. 615)

I hope you can see how this idea, measuring the estrogen and progesterone level of raters, is a reasonable next step for future research in this area, but it was not directly motivated by a limitation of the current work.

The Last Paragraph of the Discussion. Finally, you need to end your discussion. The last paragraph can state the implications of your findings – what they mean for the real world – and then end with a conclusion. Do not leave your reader hanging. A common way for writers to close their Discussion section is to indicate that more research is needed. If you did an experiment, your concluding sentence could take the following form:

> More research on the effects of [put independent variables here] is needed before definitive conclusions can be made.

References

Every paper has a Reference section in which you place citations for all the references *you cited in your paper*. This is an important point. It is possible that you read an article and found that it wasn't going to work for your paper. If you do not cite a source in the body of your paper, you should not cite it in the reference section.

The Reference section starts on a new page and is headed by the centered, bold and capitalized word

See sections 2.11, 6.22–6.32, and 7.01–7.11 of the *Publication Manual*.

References. All references are listed in alphabetical order; the last name of the first author of each source is what you'll use to decide where in the alphabetical list your source citation belongs. All references will use a hanging indent in which the first line of each reference is flush left while subsequent lines are indented.

The APA *Publication Manual* specifies how to write up each type of source. I'll go over the most common types of sources. Below is the general format for a journal article with one author followed by a specific example. I'll point out a few things. Note that every time there is a space, it is only one space. Also the first word of the title of the journal article is capitalized, but the rest of the title is not. The exception to this, as you'll see in the example, is that the first word of any subtitle in the journal article title is also capitalized. The name of the journal is treated differently. When you are writing the name of the journal, all major words (except prepositions) are capitalized. You'll also see the title of the journal is in italics from the start of the journal title until the comma after the volume and issue number. The issue number needs to be present only if each issue of the journal (or other type of periodical such as a newsletter) begins on page 1. How do you determine whether each issue of a journal begins with page 1? Krupa (2011) recommends that you go to the journal's website and look over the table of contents of past issues. If each issue begins on page 1, include the issue number in parentheses in your reference citation (see the citation below).

Last name, Initial of first name. Initial of middle name. (Date of publication). Title of journal article. *Name of Journal, Volume (Number)*, pages. doi:xxxxxxxxx

Heath, W. P. (2009). Arresting and convicting the innocent: The potential role of an "inappropriate" emotion level in the accused. *Behavioral Sciences & the Law, 27*, 313–332. doi:http://dx .doi.org/10.1002/bsl.864

Below is an example of a journal article citation with two authors. As you see, there is an ampersand joining the two authors, and there is a comma and a space before that ampersand. Add more authors and you'll use the same format; an ampersand is placed right before the last author's name.

Kraemer, D. L., & Hastrup, J. L. (1988). Crying in adults: Self-control and autonomic correlates. *Journal of Social and Clinical Psychology, 6(1)*, 53–68. doi:http://dx.doi.org/10.1521/ jscp.1988.6.1.53

Here is an example of a book citation:

Izard, C. E. (1977). *Human emotions*. New York: Plenum Press.

Here is an example of a citation from a website:

Peters, J. (2013). *When ice cream sales rise, so do homicides. Coincidence or will your next cone murder you?* Retrieved from www.slate.com

When you are citing a source from the web, ideally you should indicate the author, date, title and source. See the APA style blog (http://blog.apastyle.org/) or Lee (2010) for more on citing from a website.

You may have noticed that some of the reference citations shown above have a digital object identifier (DOI). This DOI is a unique sequence of letters and numbers that can be used to find an article in a search at CrossRef.org. Try it. Take this DOI: http://dx.doi. org/10.1002/bsl.864, and place it (without spaces) in the metadata search field found at Crossref.org. You should see a citation for one of my articles.

The publisher assigns a DOI when an article is published. You need to provide it for all references for which it is available, and you find it in *PsycINFO* citations (older references do not always have a DOI). You can see an example of a *PsycINFO* citation page in Figure 14.3; the DOI is available toward the bottom of this figure.

Publication Type: Journal; Peer Reviewed Journal

Publication History: Accepted: Jul 29, 1993; Revised: Jun 20, 1993; First Submitted: Dec 12, 1991

Release Date: 19940801

Copyright: American Psychological Association. 1994

Digital Object Identifier: http://dx.doi.org/10.1037/0022-3514.66.2.287

FIGURE 14.3 An excerpt from a page in *PsycINFO* that shows a Digital Object Identifier.

When possible, copy and paste the DOI from *PsycINFO* into your reference citation on the References page to avoid making errors in transcription. You may need to change the DOI's font and font size when you do that so it is consistent with the rest of your paper.

Another place to find a DOI is on the actual article itself. See an example from one of my articles in Figure 14.4.

Tables and Figures

Recall the following sentence: When a smiley face was drawn on the checks, the average tip percentage was larger ($M = 17.74, SD = 6.95$) than when a smiley face was not drawn on the checks ($M = 15.32, SD = 4.43$), $F (1, 128) = 5.64, p = .02$, partial $\eta^2 = .05$.

> See sections 5.01–5.30 of the *Publication Manual*.

In the above sentence, I was comparing two means. Researchers tend to use sentences when referring to up to three means. However, when we need to compare more than three means, we tend to use a table or a figure to provide the information. You will probably not be surprised this time either to learn that the APA *Publication Manual* has lots of rules regarding how to present tables and figures. We'll talk about general guidelines for each.

First let's take a look at a table from a manuscript I wrote about being questioned for jury duty. I asked my respondents about the kinds of questions they were asked; the results are presented in Table 14.3.

Behavioral Sciences and the Law
Behav. Sci. Law 27: 313–332 (2009)
Published online 21 April 2009 in Wiley InterScience
(www.interscience.wiley.com) DOI: 10.1002/bsl.864

Arresting and Convicting the Innocent: the Potential Role of an "Inappropriate" Emotional Display in the Accused

Wendy P. Heath, Ph.D.*

FIGURE 14.4 An excerpt from an article that shows a Digital Object Identifier.

You usually cite a table in the body of your manuscript when you are writing up your Results section. However, your tables will appear not in the body of your manuscript (as Table 14.3 appears to do); each table will appear on a separate page, immediately after the References section (see sample manuscript in Appendix A).

When you are writing your Results section, you can refer to one or two of the numbers from the table, but do not list all of them in your text. If you did that, there would be no point in using a table. There are other rules. For example, as you see above in Table 14.3, APA tables have only horizontal lines, never vertical lines. You can also see that tables have titles. Each table is named consecutively (Table 1, Table 2 …) in plain text, and then a description of the table's contents is provided in italics.

Now let's talk about figures. Figures are often used to illustrate statistical interactions. You saw

Table 14.3   What kinds of information were you asked to provide during voir dire? (N = 181).

Name	Exact address	Town	Phone number	Email address	Education	Occupation
86%	53%	72%	41%	17%	67%	84%
Place of Employment	Marital Status	Names of Family Members	Occupation of Spouse	Information about Children	Personal Experiences	Likes and Dislikes
52%	66%	8%	30%	20%	39%	17%

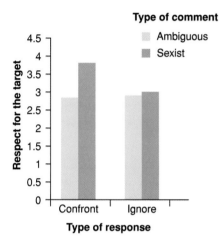

FIGURE 14.5 A bar graph illustrating Dodd et al.'s (2001) interaction between the type of comment and the type of response on perceived level of respectability for the target.

examples of both line graphs and bar graphs in Chapter 9. A line graph is typically used to show the relationship between continuous variables, while a bar graph is typically used to show the relationship between categorical variables. Figure 14.5 is another look at a figure from Dodd et al.'s (2001) experiment on perceptions of females who confront sexist comments.

Number your figures consecutively (*Figure 1, Figure 2*, and so on) and put this number in italics. When you present a figure in your manuscript, usually in your Results section, write a quick

summary of what the figure illustrates. For Figure 14.5, for example, you would indicate in your text that the figure indicates that when the male made a sexist comment, participants respected the woman more when she confronted rather than ignored the comment. However, when the male made an ambiguous comment, participants generally had the same level of respect for the woman regardless of whether she ignored or confronted the speaker.

APA rules govern how figures look and where they appear too. As with tables, you refer to the figures in your text, again usually when you are writing up your Results section. And as with tables, figures do not appear in the body of the manuscript. Each figure appears on a separate page, at the end of the manuscript, after any tables (see the sample manuscript in Appendix A). They need to have clearly labeled axes, with the *y* axis (the vertical axis) representing the dependent variable.

Plagiarism

Plagiarism occurs when a writer uses someone else's *words or ideas* without giving credit to the original source of the information. In general, you should

See section 1.10 of the *Publication Manual*.

both put information into your own words (paraphrase it) *and* cite the author(s) and year of the original source.

If you take an exact quote from another writer, anything from a single distinctive word to whole sentences, APA format requires that you place the quoted words in quotation marks and cite the author(s), year, and page number from which the quotation was taken. Use exact quotations sparingly. After all, if you are using quote after quote in your paper, *you are not actually writing the paper.* Use direct quotations only when the words in the original source used are so special that you cannot think of any other words to express the thought.

FIGURE 14.6 Attending a conference is a great way to present your research and/or learn about the research that others are doing.

How to Give a Research Presentation

Attending a professional conference is a wonderful way to become familiar with research that is relatively current. It is usually only about 6 months between the time someone submits research for possible inclusion in a conference and the time he or she actually presents it (the time from submission to actual publication in a journal tends to take much longer).

Within psychology there are many conferences to choose from. The largest is the APA convention, held each year in August (see www.apa.org for more information). APA is actually organized into divisions; there are over 50, each focusing on a different aspect of psychology (Division 41 is the American Psychology-Law Society, for example), and many divisions have their own conferences. There are also psychology conferences that do not have direct ties to APA. For example, there are regional psychology conferences (like the Eastern Psychological Association), and an Association for Psychological Science conference held in May each year (see www.psychologicalscience.org). Try

to attend at least one conference while you are a student, especially if you are thinking of making psychology your career. Each of these conferences provides opportunities for students to present their research. Of course, you can attend even if you are not presenting your work; it's a great way to be exposed to what's new in the field, and the way this work is presented.

Conferences typically provide two ways to present research: (1) researchers present their work on a poster, and/or (2) researchers speak to an audience. These two options will be discussed below.

Poster

In a conference poster session, presenters and their posters line a room, usually for an hour or two, while an audience circulates among the posters. Presenting your work with a poster provides you with an extended opportunity to talk with people who are interested in your research.

The text on your poster will be sufficiently large so that people can see your work from a distance. Typically this means your title and headings should be at least 30-point font, while the remaining text

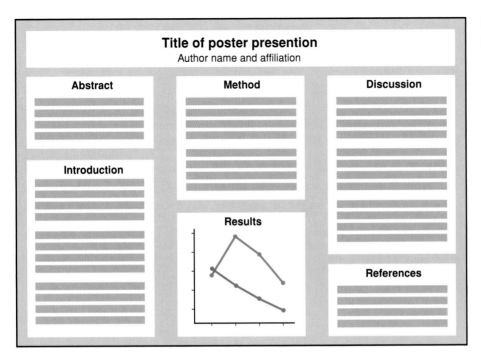

FIGURE 14.7 Sample poster configuration.

Sample poster configuration

should be at least 20-point font. That does mean that space will be quite limited on your poster, so you want to pare your work down to its most essential details and present them as clearly as you can. As you can see in Figure 14.7, the major components of a paper are present in a poster and follow the same sequence. (Note that you can use "Introduction" as a heading in a poster.) Including visual displays of data by using tables and/or figures is also often recommended.

You can use *PowerPoint* to create your poster; just insert multiple text boxes into one slide. Then you can print that one slide on large paper using a special printer. Typically your poster will be pinned to a 4 ft high × 8 ft long bulletin board, so you need a poster that comes close to filling that space without spilling over.

Beyond talking with those interested in your poster, it also helps to have a handout available so people can take information about your research with them when they leave. If you use *PowerPoint* to create your poster, as suggested above, you can easily just print it on an 8½ × 11 inch page.

Presentation

When you are providing a verbal presentation of your research, it is a good idea to have a visual component to your talk, such as *PowerPoint* slides. When preparing your slides, make sure that they are not too dense with content. Each slide should have a few bullet points in at least a 24-point font, and you should not just read from your slides or from your notes. Prepare additional information so you will have something to say to accompany your slide presentation. The sound of your voice is important too. Show your enthusiasm for your topic by varying the tone of your voice as the content varies. If appropriate and practical, consider incorporating a demonstration or a hands-on activity for the audience. All this should be polished; rehearse your talk in front of a mirror or before a friend or two so you will be comfortably prepared. Rehearsal will also allow you to ensure that your talk fits the allotted time slot (at a conference this slot can be as short as 10 minutes). Finally, remember to make eye contact with audience members and enjoy yourself. Public speaking is a skill; like so many things, it gets better with practice.

A Few Words about Writing

You will want to write your research paper clearly and concisely, and the *Publication Manual* has guidelines on how best to accomplish this. I'll mention a few of the major points here (also see Figure 14.8 for recommendations).

Clarity in writing is crucial, and you can achieve it in different ways. Use headings to organize your manuscript; headings can help you and your reader keep track of your main points. Avoid abrupt shifts in your writing by using transitions (such as *since, therefore, in addition, furthermore*) from sentence to sentence, and from paragraph to paragraph. Keep verb tense consistent within a given section. The *Publication Manual* recommends using past tense ("patrons gave more favorable tips") or present perfect ("researchers have found") in the Introduction, the Method section, and the Results section, and using present tense ("the results reveal") in the Discussion section to present the implications of the results and your conclusions.

Avoid biased writing. Bias can be present in various forms (gender, sexual orientation, racial and ethnic identity, disabilities, and age), and the

See section 3.02 of the *Publication Manual*.

See section 3.06 of the *Publication Manual*.

Publication Manual has guidelines regarding each of these. For example, the *Publication Manual* indicates that it is acceptable to refer to North American people of African ancestry as *Black* or *African American*. Note that these terms are capitalized proper nouns. Your work would be biased if you referred to one racial or ethnic group using a capitalized proper noun and to another using a lower case presentation.

See 3.12–3.16 of the *Publication Manual* for information on reducing bias.

The *Publication Manual* is also available as a resource for recommendations on the use of grammar. For example, the *Publication Manual* recommends that writers use active voice rather than passive voice. Here are examples of each:

See sections 3.18–3.22 of the *Publication Manual* for information on grammar and usage.

Active voice: The server approached the table.
Passive voice: The table was approached by the server.

The Peer Review Process

I mentioned above that we have a responsibility to disseminate our research, but not every research study will be worthy of that dissemination. In most cases,

See sections 8.01–8.02 in the *Publication Manual*.

the work we want to present at a conference or publish in a journal will undergo peer review. That means others familiar with our topic of research, usually three people, will evaluate it. They will evaluate the quality of our research and the importance of our findings.

Peer reviews are often "blind." This means two things. The first is that those who are doing the reviewing do not know who did the research. Thus any feelings the reviewer might have toward the

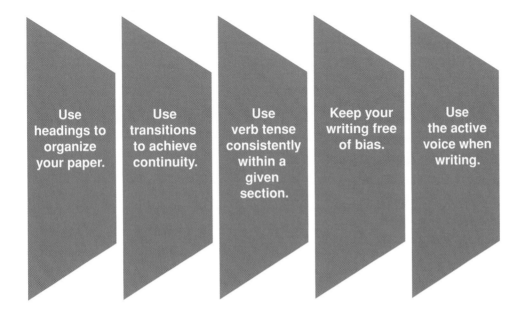

FIGURE 14.8 Recommendations for writing your manuscript.

researcher(s) can't influence the evaluation. The second meaning of "blind" in this context is that those who did the research do not know who is doing the reviewing. That way, if the review is negative, the researcher can't hold it against the reviewer.

Most conferences and journals use peer review, and while the likelihood of rejection varies from conference to conference and from publication to publication, it is a reality. Next I will discuss the review process for conferences and journals in turn.

Submitting your work for possible conference presentation usually requires submitting an abstract and sometimes a short version of the work to be presented (say, 1,000 words). As mentioned before, there are traditionally a couple of ways to present your work at a conference. You can speak in front of an audience; this is usually in a talk of about 15 minutes. This is the toughest level of acceptance to achieve in a conference. Or you can present your work in the form of a poster. It is usually easier to get a poster accepted. In fact, it is often possible to submit your work to a

conference with the instruction that if it doesn't get accepted for a talk, you would like it to be considered for a poster. Acceptance rates for conferences vary, but decisions are usually "accept as a paper," "accept as a poster," or "reject."

Rejection rates, especially for top-tier journals, can be 75% or even higher. To get an idea of sample rejection rates for APA journals, you can consult the journal *American Psychologist* (see www.apa.org/pubs/journals/statistics.aspx); this journal lists the yearly rejection rates for all APA journals.

The decisions handed down by a journal editor are usually "accept," "accept with minor revisions," "accept with major revisions," "revise and resubmit," and "reject." If you get an "accept with minor/major revisions" or "revise and resubmit," then you need to consider the recommendations of the reviewers and change the manuscript in line with them or explain to the editor the reason(s) you are not willing to make a recommended change. Even if your manuscript was rejected, you may still wish to make some of the suggested changes to improve it before submitting it somewhere else (you can submit to only one journal at a time).

If your manuscript does get rejected, try to submit it elsewhere as quickly as possible. Don't be too despondent when you receive a manuscript rejection. It happens to us all. Actually some rejections ended up being pretty humorous. One of my favorites is a rejection letter that said the researcher didn't seem to understand the topic being discussed and recommended the researcher "read some of Antonucci's work to get a better feel for it." Who received this recommendation? Toni C. Antonucci ("Rotten reviews," 2015)!

The Research Paper Checklist

I have mentioned some elements of APA style as we progressed through this chapter. Would it surprise you to learn there are still more? I find that using a checklist can help ensure that you do not neglect important formatting requirements. Below is a research paper checklist that covers the main formatting requirements. There are also items on this checklist that refer to content rather than APA style, to help you uncover areas of your manuscript that need work.

Check entries off once you have completed them.

General Questions
Is the paper double-spaced throughout? (The one exception to this rule is that tables and figures can have single spacing.)

Does each page have a running head followed by a page number (all on one line?) (Note that the words "Running head:" are only on the first page.)

Are all titles and headings in upper and lower case letters (except for the running head)?

Are all margins at least 1 inch on all sides?

Is past tense used to indicate actions that have previously occurred (reports of previous research)?

Title Page
Is the length of the title 12 words or less?

Are the title, the author's (or authors') name(s), and affiliation(s) centered on the page?

Is the running head no longer than 50 characters, including spaces and punctuation?

Is the running head flush left on the top of the title page and on all subsequent pages?

Are the words "Running head" written correctly (only the "R" in caps)?

Is the running head itself all caps?

Is an author note present on the title page?

Abstract
Is the abstract in block format (no indentation)?

Is the abstract headed by the centered word "Abstract"?

Is the abstract no more than 250 words long?

Does the abstract include the important elements of the report including: the problem to be investigated, the number of participants tested, the method (including independent and dependent variables [if applicable]), a statement of the results, and a statement of implications?

Is a list of keywords provided after the abstract?

Introduction
Is the introduction headed by the paper's title, not by the word "Introduction"?

Did you start the introduction with a general introduction to the overall topic?

Is previous research described in your own words with the sources properly cited?

Are reference citations complete, accurate, and correctly formatted?

Is there a rationale established for the present research?

Is the description of the study's purpose and hypotheses at the end of the introduction, after the literature review?

Is there a clear statement of the hypotheses to be tested?

Is there a brief mention of the method used in the present research?

Method
Is the method section headed by the centered and bold word "Method"?

Does the method section start immediately after the end of the introduction (on the same page)? (This is the proper format unless the heading would be alone at the end of a page without at least another line to follow it.)

Is the method section organized into the appropriate subsections, each with a bold and flush left heading (for example, Participants, Materials/Apparatus, Procedure)?

Participant Subsection
Is there a statement of how many participants there were and how they were selected and compensated?

Are all the demographic details you collected regarding your sample presented in the Participant subsection?

Materials/Apparatus Subsection
Are the essential details regarding the materials and/or the apparatus provided?

Procedure Subsection
Are all ethical procedures adequately stated (such as informed consent, debriefing)?

Are the essential features of the procedure stated?

Results
Is the results section headed by the centered word "Results"?

Does the results section immediately follow the end of the method section (on the same page)? (This is the proper format unless the heading would be alone at the end of a page without at least another line to follow it.)

Are all descriptive statistics (such as means and standard deviations) provided in the appropriate places?

Is all statistical notation (such as F, df, p, M, SD) italicized?

Are the relevant effect sizes noted?

Are the results presented in APA style?

Is the reader appropriately directed to each table and appendix?

Discussion
Is the discussion section headed by the centered word "Discussion"?

Does the discussion section immediately follow the end of the results section (is it on the same page)? (This is the proper format unless the heading would be alone at the end of a page without at least another line to follow it.)

Does the discussion section begin with a restatement of the hypotheses with support/non-support noted?

Are the results discussed in light of previous research and theory?

Is there a critique of the present research?

Have you presented at least one future research idea? (Note that your research idea has to be related to the current research.)

References
Does the reference section begin on a new page?

Is the reference section headed by the centered word "References"?

Are the references listed in alphabetical order by the first author's last name?

Does each reference have a hanging indent? (Subsequent lines of each reference are indented.)

Is an issue number provided for all journals (and other types of periodicals such as newsletters) paginated by issue (each issue begins with page 1)?

Are italics used when appropriate (use italics from the journal name through to comma after volume number/issue number)?

Is the DOI provided for every reference that has a DOI available?

Is there a citation listed on the reference page for every source cited in the paper?

Tables and Figures

Is each table and figure typed on a separate page?

Are all lines in the tables horizontal?

Are the table columns lined up?

Is each table and figure identified by the appropriate heading ("Table X" or *Figure #*) and a title?

In the body of the table, does each column have a heading?

Expression and Style (see APA *Publication Manual* chapters 2, 3, & 4)

Is the paper clearly written with complete sentences and correct grammar?

Is the paper well organized?

Is there a transition from paragraph to paragraph?

Are spelling, punctuation, and capitalization correct?

Is the writing unbiased?

The above checklist will help you determine if you have followed APA style. However, there is still more to do, beyond the checklist, before your manuscript should be considered complete. You need to proofread! Again and again! I like to read my manuscript aloud to check for flow and clarity. I do a separate read just for spelling, punctuation, and grammar and a spell check through my word processing program. However, I recognize that sometimes my word processing program does not recognize all of the psychology jargon I use, so at times I need to override what the word processing program says. In summary, reviewing your writing is an extremely important step.

SUMMARY

To disseminate information regarding our research, we can present a paper or a poster at a conference, and/or we can publish our work. The APA *Publication Manual* governs the way we present our work.

A typical psychology research paper contains: (1) a title page, (2) an abstract (a short summary of the work), (3) an introduction (provides information about previous research on the topic and general details about the present research including a rationale and hypotheses), (4) a method section (provides details regarding the participants, materials, and or apparatus used and the procedure followed), (5) a results section (provides information regarding statistical analyses used), (6) a discussion section (reviews findings in light of previous literature, provides a critique and future research ideas), (7) a references section, and (8) tables and/or figures (optional).

To avoid plagiarizing, put information in your own words and cite your sources. Write clearly and concisely; the *Publication Manual* provides guidelines.

Any work we submit for presentation or publication will undergo a peer review. Reviewers will evaluate the quality of the research and the importance of the findings; they decide whether the research still needs work, is accepted, or is rejected.

Writing an APA style paper is a learned skill. While it does get easier with experience, the need to "write and revise" will always be part of the process.

GLOSSARY

Author note – notation on the title page of a manuscript that includes information such as where to contact an author for further information.

Keywords – words or phrases that represent main concepts from the manuscript. These keywords are placed under the abstract in a manuscript.

Manuscript – an author's original text in its prepublication form.

Plagiarism – occurs when a writer uses someone else's words or ideas without giving credit to the original source of the information.

REVIEW QUESTIONS

1 Describe what goes into each of the major sections of a psychology research paper.
2 Explain how to write a hypothesis.
3 Demonstrate how a DOI is used at CrossRef.org.
4 Define plagiarism and indicate how it can be avoided.
5 Differentiate between the two ways to present research at a conference.
6 Describe ways to achieve clarity in your writing.
7 Describe the peer review process.

ADDITIONAL SOURCES TO CONSIDER

Cooper, H. (2011). *Reporting research in psychology: How to meet journal article reporting standards*. Washington, DC: American Psychological Association.

Landrum, R. E. (2008). *Undergraduate writing in psychology: Learning to tell the scientific story*. Washington, DC: American Psychological Association.

Nicol, A. A. M., & Pexman, P. M. (2010). *Displaying your findings: A practical guide for creating figures, posters, and presentations*. Washington, DC: American Psychological Association.

Nicol, A. A. M., & Pexman, P. M. (2010). *Presenting your findings: A practical guide for creating tables*. Washington, DC: American Psychological Association.

Sternberg, R. J., & Sternberg, K. (2010). *The psychologist's companion: A guide to writing scientific papers for students and researchers*. (5th ed.). Cambridge: Cambridge University Press.

SUGGESTED ACTIVITIES

The suggested activities for this chapter involve writing a full or partial manuscript. After you decide on a topic (see Chapter 2 for ideas on how to come up with a topic), you need to decide whether you are going to write a complete manuscript or a partial one. There are a variety of ways to write partial papers that give you some experience writing before you embark on writing a complete manuscript. For example, you can write just a literature review. This would be equivalent to writing the introduction to a paper except that you will not have a final paragraph that details the study you are about to describe. Someone reading your literature review should be able to answer the following questions:

a. What is your topic?
b. What do we know about this topic from previous research?

Alternatively, you can write a research proposal. This would include a literature review and the last paragraph of the introduction would introduce the study you are proposing. Someone reading your literature review should be able to answer the following questions:

a. What is your topic?
b. What do we know about this topic from previous research?
c. What is the purpose of your proposed study? If experimental, the purpose statement should indicate your independent and dependent variables.
d. What are your hypotheses?
e. What is your proposed methodology?

A research proposal can also have a Method section in which you write (in future tense) what you are planning to do. All method subsections can be included here. Someone reading your method section should be able to answer the following questions:

a. What type of study participant are you planning on testing?

b. What compensation will you be offering your study participants?

c. What materials will you be using for testing?

d. What is your procedure?

e. How will you ensure that your study participants will be treated ethically?

Finally, you can create an entire research paper that provides information about a study that you've already completed. Add a Results and a Discussion section to that noted above. Someone reading your Results section should be able to answer the following questions:

a. What type of statistics were calculated?

b. What did the statistics reveal?

Someone reading your Discussion section should be able to answer the following questions:

a. What were the hypotheses and were they supported?

b. Were the obtained results consistent with previous research?

c. What were the limitations of the current research?

d. What are the recommended next steps for future research?

Include a title page, a reference page, and an abstract. Use the checklist provided in this chapter to help ensure that you provided the needed information in APA style. Finally, remember that you need to read and revise, read and revise.

REFERENCES

Aiello, J. R., DeRisi, D. T., Epstein Y. M., & Karlin, R. A. (1977). Crowding and the role of interpersonal distance preference. *Sociometry*, *40*, 271–282.

American Psychological Association. (2010). *Publication Manual of the American Psychological Association*. (6th ed.). Washington, DC: American Psychological Association.

Associated Press. (2009). Oklahoma State coach Ford apologizes for cursing at player. Retrieved from http://usatoday30.usatoday.com/sports/college/mensbasketball/big12/2009-02-10-oklahoma-state-ford_N.htm

Badzakova-Trajkov, G., Corballis, M. C., & Häberling, I. S. (2016). Complementarity or independence of hemispheric specialization: A brief Review. *Neuropsychologia*, *93*, 386–393. doi:http://dx.doi.org/10.1016/j.neuropsychologia.2015.12.018

Cooper, H. (2011). *Reporting research in psychology: How to meet journal article reporting standards*. Washington, DC: American Psychological Association.

Dodd, E. H., Giuliano, T. A., Boutell, J. M., & Moran, B. E. (2001). Respected or rejected: Perceptions of women who confront sexist remarks. *Sex Roles*, *45*, 567–577. doi:http://dx.doi.org/10.1023/A:1014866915741

Glick, P., Larsen, S., Johnson, C., & Branstiter, H. (2005). Evaluations of sexy women in low- and high-status jobs. *Psychology of Women Quarterly*, *29*, 389–395. doi:http://dx.doi.org/10.1111/j.1471-6402.2005.00238.x

Grossberg, J. M., & Alf, E. F. (1985). Interaction with pet dogs: Effects on human cardiovascular response. *Journal of the Delta Society*, *2(1)*, 20–27.

Guéguen, N., & Lamy, L. (2012). Men's social status and attractiveness: Women's receptivity to men's date requests. *Swiss Journal of Psychology*, *71*, 157–160. doi:http://dx.doi.org/10.1024/1421-0185/a000083

Harms, V. L., Poon, L. J. O., Smith, A. K., & Elias, L. J. (2015). Take your seats: Leftward asymmetry in classroom seating choice. *Frontiers in Human Neuroscience*, *9*, 1–7.

Harrison, A. A., & Saeed, L. (1977). Let's make a deal: An analysis of revelations and stipulations in lonely hearts advertisements. *Journal of Personality and Social Psychology*, *35*, 257–264. doi:http://dx.doi.org/10.1037/0022-3514.35.4.257

Harrison, M. A., Bealing, C. E., & Salley, J. M. (2015). 2 TXT or not 2 TXT: College students' reports of when text messaging is social breach. *Social Science Journal*, *52*, 188–194. doi:http://dx.doi.org/10.1016/j.soscij.2015.02.005

Harrison, M. A., Shortall, J. C., Dispenza, F., & Gallup, G. G., Jr. (2011). You must have been a beautiful baby:

Ratings of infant facial attractiveness fail to predict ratings of adult attractiveness. *Infant Behavior & Development, 34,* 610–616. doi:http://dx.doi.org/10.1016/j.infbeh.2011.06.003

Heath, W. P. (2009). Arresting and convicting the innocent: The potential role of an "inappropriate" emotion level in the accused. *Behavioral Sciences & the Law, 27,* 313–332. doi:http://dx.doi.org/10.1002/bsl.864

Howell, J. L., & Giuliano, T. A. (2011). The effect of expletive use and team gender perceptions of coaching effectiveness. *Journal of Sport Behavior, 34,* 69–81.

Izard, C. E. (1977). *Human emotions.* New York: Plenum Press.

Jacobi, M. (1991). Mentoring and undergraduate academic success: A literature review. *Review of Educational Research, 61,* 505–532. doi:http://dx.doi.org/10.2307/1170575

Jakeman, R. C., Silver, B. R., & Molasso, W. (2014). Student experiences at off-campus parties: Results from a multicampus survey. *Journal of Alcohol and Drug Education, 58(2),* 64–85.

Jones, B. T., Jones, B. C., Thomas, A. P., & Piper, J. (2003). Alcohol consumption increases attractiveness ratings of opposite-sex faces: A possible third route to risky sex. *Addiction, 98,* 1069–1075. doi:http://dx.doi.org/10.1046/j.1360-0443.2003.00426.x

Kang, H. J., & Williamson, V. J. (2014). Background music can aid second language learning. *Psychology of Music, 42,* 728–747. doi:http://dx.doi.org/10.1177/0305735613485152

Karev, G. B., (2000). Cinema seating in right, mixed and left handers. *Cortex, 36(5),* 747–752. doi:http://dx.doi.org/10.1016/S0010-9452(08)70550-1

Keough, M. T., O'Connor, R. M., Sherry, S. B., & Stewart, S. H. (2015). Context counts: Solitary drinking explains the association between depressive symptoms and alcohol-related problems in undergraduates. *Addictive Behaviors, 42,* 216–221. doi:http://dx.doi.org/10.1016/j.addbeh.2014.11.031

Kerr, N. L. (1998). Harking: Hypothesizing after the results are known. *Personality and Social Psychology Review, 2,* 196–217. doi:http://dx.doi.org/10.1207/s15327957pspr0203_4

King, K. A., & Vidourek, R. A. (2013). Getting inked: Tattoo and risky behavioral involvement among university students. *Social Science Journal, 50,* 540–546. doi:http://dx.doi.org/10.1016/j.soscij.2013.09.009

Kraemer, D. L., & Hastrup, J. L. (1988). Crying in adults: Self-control and autonomic correlates. *Journal of Social and Clinical Psychology, 6(1),* 53–68. doi:http://dx.doi.org/10.1521/jscp.1988.6.1.53

Kronenfeld, L. W., Reba-Harrelson, L., Von Holle, A., Reyes, M. L., & Bulik, C. M. (2010). Ethnic and racial differences in body size perception and satisfaction. *Body Image, 7(2),* 131–136. doi:http://dx.doi.org/10.1016/j.bodyim.2009.11.002

Krupa, T. (2011). How to determine whether a periodical is paginated by issue [Blog post]. Retrieved from http://blog.apastyle.org/apastyle/2011/10/how-to-determine-whether-a-periodical-is-paginated-by-issue.html

Landrum, R. E. (2008). *Undergraduate writing in psychology: Learning to tell the scientific story.* Washington, DC: American Psychological Association.

Lee, C. (2010). How to cite something you found on a website in APA style [Blog post]. Retrieved from http://blog.apastyle.org/apastyle/2010/11/how-to-cite-something-you-found-on-a-website-in-apa-style.html

Miller, B. E., Miller, M. N., Verhegge, R., Linville, H. H., & Pumariega, A. J. (2002). Alcohol misuse among college athletes: Self-medication for psychiatric symptoms? *Journal of Drug Education, 32,* 41–52. doi:http://dx.doi.org/10.2190/JDFM-AVAK-G9FV-0MYY

Nicol, A. A. M., & Pexman, P. M. (2010). *Displaying your findings: A practical guide for creating figures, posters, and presentations.* Washington, DC: American Psychological Association.

(2010). *Presenting your findings: A practical guide for creating tables.* Washington, DC: American Psychological Association.

Peters, J. (2013). When ice cream sales rise, so do homicides. Coincidence or will your next cone murder you? Retrieved from www.slate.com

Rotten reviews (Oct. 2015). Association for Psychological Science Observer. Retrieved from www.psychologicalscience.org/publications/observer/2015/october-15/rotten-reviews.html

Sprengelmeyer, R., Perrett, D. I., Fagan, E. C., Cornwell, R. E., Lobmaier, J. S., Sprengelmeyer, A., … Young, A. W. (2009). The cutest little baby face: A hormonal link to sensitivity to cuteness in infant faces. *Psychological Science, 20,* 149–154. doi:http://dx.doi.org/10.1111/j.1467-9280.2009.02272.x

Sternberg, R. J., & Sternberg, K. (2010). *The psychologist's companion: A guide to writing scientific papers for students and researchers.* (5th ed.). Cambridge: Cambridge University Press.

Stewart, S., Stinnett, H., & Rosenfeld, L. B. (2000). Sex differences in desired characteristics of short-term and long-term relationship partners. *Journal of Social and Personal Relationships, 17,* 843–853. doi:http://dx.doi.org/10.1177/0265407500176008

Van Volkum, M. (2008). Attitudes toward cigarette smoking among college students. *College Student Journal, 42,* 294–304.

Weyers, P., Milnik, A., Müller, C., & Pauli, P. (2006). How to choose a seat in theatres: Always sit on the right side? *Laterality, 11,* 181–193. doi:http://dx.doi.org/10.1080/13576500500430711

White, H. R., & Labouvie, E. W. (1989). Towards the assessment of adolescent problem drinking. *Journal of Studies on Alcohol, 50,* 30–37. doi:http://dx.doi.org/10.15288/jsa.1989.50.30

Whitehead, L., & Banihani, S. (2014). The evolution of contralateral control of the body by the brain: Is it a protective mechanism? *Laterality: Asymmetries of Body, Brain and Cognition, 19,* 325–339. doi:http://dx.doi.org/10.1080/1357650X.2013.824461

Wright, B. L., & Sinclair, H. C. (2012). Pulling the strings: Effects of friend and parent opinions on dating choices. *Personal Relationships, 19,* 743–758. doi:http://dx.doi.org/10.1111/j.1475-6811.2011.01390.x

Appendix A: A Sample Manuscript

Here is an example of how a relatively simple experiment can be represented in manuscript form. This manuscript is annotated with information from the APA *Publication Manual* and tips for writing so you can see why I wrote what I did.

Note that while under normal circumstances it is inappropriate to falsify data, for the purposes of this Appendix I made changes to the results of the real experiment so I can illustrate what significant and non-significant main effects look like and what a significant interaction looks like. (In the actual results, the servers benefited from writing a thank you message and drawing a smiley face – that is, the two main effects were significant. However, the interaction was not significant.)

There is more than one way to write any given paper, but the format of the psychology research paper tends to be standard, as illustrated here.

Running head: TIPPING BEHAVIOR

1

How "Thank You" and a Smiley Face on Checks Affect Tipping Behavior

Wendy P. Heath and Liubove A. Bjorklund

Rider University

Author Note

Correspondence concerning this article should be addressed to Wendy Heath, Department of Psychology, Rider University, Lawrenceville, NJ 08648. E-mail: heath@rider.edu

---

The running head should be formatted as shown, with no more than 50 characters including spaces. It should be in all capitals and should use key words from the title. Note that the words "Running head" appear only on the first page. See section 8.03 of the Publication Manual for information on the running head.

The page number is on the upper right-hand side of the page.

The recommended length of the title is no more than 12 words. See section 2.01 of the Publication Manual for information on writing the title.

The title, the authors' names, and name of the institution are all centered in the upper half of the page. Capitalize all words that have four or more letters, all verbs, nouns, adjectives, adverbs and pronouns. See section 4.15 of the APA Publication Manual for information on capitalizing major words in titles.

It is customary to include each author's middle initial.

See section 2.02 of the Publication Manual for information on writing the author's name and institutional affiliation.

List the institution where the work was performed.

An author note contains contact information for the corresponding author and may also contain other information, such as the identification of any grants that supported the work. See section 2.03 of the Publication Manual for information on writing the Author Note.

The heading "Abstract" is capitalized and centered. The Abstract begins on a new page and is in block format (no indentation). The word limit for abstracts are set by journals, typically ranging from 150-250 words. See section 2.04 in the Publication Manual for information on the abstract.

Double space the manuscript and use 1-inch margins.

This is the purpose statement.

Provide basic information about the participants.

This is a summary of the results.

This is a statement of the implications of the results.

Provide keywords from your abstract. These words will help those searching PsycINFO find your work.

Abstract

The purpose of this experiment was to investigate whether a thank-you message written on a check (presence, absence) and whether a smiley face drawn on a check (presence, absence) affects the average tip percentage given to a female server. One hundred thirty-two tables were served during the course of this experiment. Immediately before delivering the checks, the server randomly determined whether or not to write a thank-you message and draw a smiley face on them. After payment was made, the server recorded the amount of the bill (before tax), the number of patrons, and the amount of the tip. When a smiley face was drawn on the checks, the average tip percentage was larger than when a smiley face was not drawn on the checks. However, the presence of both a smiley face and a thank-you message on the check led to the highest average tip percentage. It appears that a smiley face had to be present in order for the thank-you message to have an impact. On the basis of this research, servers should be advised to add both a smiley face and a thank-you message to their checks in order to maximize their tip income.

Keywords: restaurant tipping, servers, thank-you message, smiley face

TIPPING BEHAVIOR   3

How "Thank You" and a Smiley Face on Checks

Affect Tipping Behavior

Many United States (US) employers pay less than minimum wage to employees who receive tips for services they provide (US Department of Labor, 2016); the tips are expected to compensate for the lowered wage. Thus, tipped employees such as restaurant workers are likely motivated to discover how to increase the tips that they receive. Many books have offered advice on the topic (such as Sanchez, 2013), and researchers have been seeking answers as well.

Some researchers have found that changes to servers' appearance can affect tip percentages. For example, Jacob, Guéguen, Boulbry and Ardiccioni (2010) found that male, but not female, patrons gave more favorable tips to female servers wearing makeup (foundation, eye makeup, and lipstick) than to those not wearing makeup. Similarly, Guéguen (2012) found that a female server's hair color affected tipping behavior. In this case, male patrons (but not females) gave larger tips to a blonde server than to a server with black hair, brown hair, or red hair (wigs were used to create the hair color variation).

Other researchers have found that what the food server says while providing service can increase tipping behavior. For example, Garrity and Degelman (1990) found that when the food server provided her name when she first approached the patrons, they tipped more than when she did not. Seiter (2007) investigated how an interaction between patron and server beyond the initial introduction could affect tipping. He found that female servers who complimented patrons on their dinner choices received larger tip percentages than those who did not offer such compliments.

Writing messages on the check has also been shown to have an effect on tipping behavior. For instance, Rind and Bordia (1995) varied whether servers wrote "thank you," "thank you" and the server's name, or nothing at all on the back of the check. They found that the largest average tip percentage was obtained when the server wrote "thank you" on the back of the check. Writing "thank you" led to significantly larger tips than writing nothing or writing "thank you" plus the server's name. In a later study, Rind and Bordia (1996) tested whether drawing a smiley face on the back of a check would increase

The title of the paper is placed at the top of the introduction.

The introduction starts on a new page. See section 2.05 of the Publication Manual for information on writing the introduction.

This reference citation is "tacked on" as opposed to being an integral part of the sentence.

This is a very general introduction to the concept of tipping. The second sentence gets slightly more specific by introducing the topic of restaurant workers as a type of tipped employee.

The first sentence of the paragraph provides an introduction to the content of the paragraph.

"For example" is a transition statement that connects the first sentence to the later information.

Use past tense when discussing previous research.

"Similarly" is another transition phrase.

Notice how each research study can be summarized in 1-2 sentences.

tips. They found that tip percentages increased when a smiley face was drawn on the check by a female server, but not by a male server.

In each of the above examples, the servers could be said to be trying to alter the impression they are creating. According to Leary and Kowalski (1990), "impression management (also called *self-presentation*) refers to the process by which individuals attempt to control the impressions others form of them" (p. 34). Whether emphasizing their appeal through makeup and hair color or attempting to appear friendly through verbal or written messages, the servers are attempting to increase their likeability with the hope that this will translate into larger tips.

The purpose of the present study was to investigate whether a thank-you message written on the check (presence, absence) and whether a smiley face drawn on the check (presence, absence) affects the average tip percentage given to a female server. This work builds on that of Rind and Bordia (1995; 1996). Rind and Bordia did consider the impact of writing and drawing on checks; however, they did their research on a college campus serving campus employees and students. Would the results at a non-campus restaurant be comparable? It is possible that the patrons at a campus eatery are different from those at a non-campus restaurant, perhaps because those at a campus restaurant are repeat patrons. Lynn and Grassman (1990) have found that regular patrons tend to leave larger tips than non-regulars (although see Bodvarsson & Gibson, 1991), perhaps because they expect to have future interactions with the server. Thus, a goal of the present work was to determine whether writing a thank-you message and drawing a smiley face on the checks would affect tip percentages at a community-based restaurant. In accordance with impression management theory (Leary & Kowalski, 1990), we anticipated that our server's actions (writing and drawing on the checks) would be seen as attempts to increase her likeability with the hope that this would translate into larger tips. Thus, we hypothesized the following. If the server wrote a thank-you message on the check as opposed to not writing a thank-you message, then we expected patrons would leave a higher tip percentage. Similarly, if the server drew a smiley face on the check as opposed to not drawing on the check, then we expected patrons would leave a higher tip percentage. However, because these

When providing a direct quote, cite the author, year and page number. See section 6.03 of the Publication Manual for information on the direct quotation of sources.

This reference citation is an integral part of the sentence.

A theory has been offered to explain why the earlier results were obtained.

This is the purpose statement.

This passage establishes the rationale for the current experiment.

The presented theory was used to help form hypotheses.

two independent variables have not been investigated simultaneously in previous research, we are not hypothesizing a significant interaction.

Immediately prior to delivering the checks, a female server randomly determined whether or not to write a thank-you message and whether or not to draw a smiley face on them. After payment was made, the server recorded the amount of the bill (before tax), the number of patrons, and the amount of the tip. ●

Method ●

Participants ●

One hundred thirty-two tables were served during the course of this experiment (32–35 tables per group). See Table 1 for summary statistics regarding this sample.

Design ●

A 2 × 2 between-subjects design was used with a thank-you message written on a check (presence, absence) and a smiley face drawn on a check as the independent variables. Tables were randomly assigned to conditions by the server.

Materials and Procedure

One 27-year-old female was the server for every table. This server has nine years of experience waiting tables, four years at the current restaurant location. Data were collected over the course of six consecutive Sundays (September 27–November 1, 2015). The server was instructed to act the same way with all patrons except for the assigned variations. The restaurant is part of a casual-dining "grill and bar" chain located in central New Jersey.

● Each table was randomly assigned to a group. The server had shuffled index cards in her apron, each corresponding to a different group. When it was time to write the check, the server reached into her apron pocket and pulled out an index card that indicated the group assignment. As a result of this group assignment, the server knew whether to write a thank-you message and whether to draw a smiley face on the check. Both the writing and the drawing were placed on the front of the check.

After the patrons had left, the server recorded the amount of the bill before tax, the number of patrons, and the amount of the tip.

Results ●

As a first step, a tip percentage was calculated for each table. To calculate a table's tip percentage, we divided the amount of the tip by the size of the bill before tax and then multiplied the result by 100.

A brief mention of method was provided.

The "Method" heading is centered, capitalized and in bold. See section 2.06 of the Publication Manual for information on writing the Method section.

Subheadings (like "Participants") are flush left, capitalized, and bold.

Having a Design section is an option when the research is experimental.

This passage represents the procedure. You should provide enough of the details to enable a reader to conduct a replication of the study.

The Results heading is centered, capitalized, and bold. If you had a complex Results section, you could choose to have subheadings to separate your results by, for example, type of dependent variable.

See section 2.07 of the Publication Manual for information on writing the Results section.

You need to indicate what kind of analysis was conducted.

Indicate, where appropriate, that the result had been predicted.

Use italics for statistical notation (M, SD, F, p, η).

This is a significant finding, thus the sentence is written to reflect that there was a difference between the relevant means.

This is a non-significant finding; thus the sentence is written to reflect that there was not a difference between the relevant means.

Briefly tell your reader what the important message is in the Figure.

This part of the Results paragraph concerns the interaction.

The "Discussion" heading is centered, capitalized, and bold.

See section 2.08 of the Publication Manual for information on writing the Discussion section.

Indicate whether there were any other important findings.

Comment on the results in light of earlier research.

Try to explain why the hypothesis wasn't supported.

A 2 × 2 Analysis of Variance was used to analyze the tip percentages and determine whether they were affected by the independent variable manipulations. As anticipated, when a smiley face was drawn on the checks, the average tip percentage was larger ($M = 18.69$, $SD = 6.76$) than when a smiley face was not drawn on the checks ($M = 14.54$, $SD = 4.94$), $F (1, 128) = 16.24$, $p < .01$, partial $\eta^2 = .11$. On the other hand, those who had a thank-you message on their checks left a similar tip percentage ($M = 17.46$, $SD = 7.00$) as those who did not have a thank-you message on the checks ($M = 15.80$, $SD = 5.34$), $F (1, 128) = 2.21$, $p = .14$, partial $\eta^2 = .02$. The significant main effect is qualified by a significant interaction between writing a thank-you message on the check and drawing a smiley face on the check, $F (1, 128) = 6.15$, $p = .01$, partial $\eta^2 = .05$. See Figure 1. Examination of the means reveals that when both a smiley face and a thank-you message were present, the server received the highest average tip.

Discussion

As hypothesized, when a smiley face was drawn on the checks, the average tip percentage was larger than when a smiley face was not drawn on the checks. However, the hypothesis that the server would benefit from just writing a thank-you message on the check was not supported. Tip percentages were similar when the thank-you message was present or absent. However, the two variables interacted such that when both were present, the server received the highest average tip percentage. It appears that a smiley face had to be present in order for the thank-you message to have an impact.

The hypotheses were created with impression management theory (Leary & Kowalski, 1990) in mind. We anticipated that writing and drawing on the checks would be seen as a server's attempt to increase the server's likeability and this would translate into larger tips. This did happen as expected with the smiley face manipulation, a finding consistent with what Rind and Bordia (1996) found. This replication suggests we can generalize the result to eating establishments beyond a college campus.

Why didn't the server's words alone on the check have an impact on tips as Rind and Bordia (1995) had found? The present work does differ methodologically from Rind and Bordia's (1995), and these differences may account for the differences in results. Specifically, in the present experiment, the written message was either "thank you" and the server's name or nothing at all. Recall that Rind and Bordia (1995) found that writing "thank you" led to larger tips than writing no message at all or writing "thank you" plus the server's name. Rind and Bordia (1995) postulated that writing "thank you" on the checks raised tips to a "ceiling" level, and thus the addition of the server's name did not affect tips that were already high (p. 749). Perhaps the type of eating establishment had an impact here. One possibility is that increased patron frequency at the campus establishment led to an increased level of familiarity and friendliness. In the present research there is no advantage to adding a "thank-you" message with the server's name over writing no message at all. The "thank-you" message does not have its impact unless a smiley face is there too. In the non-campus establishment perhaps the smiley face acts as a signal of friendliness, an extra boost to get to that increased level of likeability.

In any case, we can only speculate that adding writing and drawing to the checks increases server likeability. Future researchers may wish to have patrons evaluate the service and the server more directly, perhaps with a short questionnaire provided with the check, to determine what exactly underlies the tipping decisions.

Another potential limitation of the current experimentation is that the server was aware of the group assignment, and thus there could be a concern that she acted differently as a function of group assignment. However, each table was not assigned to a condition until the bulk of the interaction with the patrons was over. Thus, given this timing, it was unlikely the results were affected by any action by the server as a function of group assignment. One possibility for the future is to have group assignments made by those not engaged in serving the patrons.

The research presented here suggests that female restaurant servers should be advised to add both a smiley face and a thank-you message to their checks in order to maximize their tip income. Interestingly, Rind and Bordia (1996) found that adding a smiley face to a check did not benefit male servers, perhaps because of a perception that this action was not gender-appropriate for a male. Would other types of drawings affect tips for male servers? Future researchers may wish to add to the current investigation by exploring how various drawings and other types of messages affect the tips received by male and female servers.

Address potential limitations.

Make recommendations for future research.

This is a statement of the implications of the results.

Conclude by looking forward at the additional research that is needed.

Appendix A

See section 2.11, 6.22-6.32 and 7.01-7.11 in the Publication Manual for information on creating a References section.

Start the References section on a new page.

Each reference citation uses a hanging indent format (first line is flush left and subsequent lines of the reference are indented).

List each author's last name first, followed by the author's initials. An ampersand separates the last author from those who come before.

An issue number is provided here because the issues of this journal each start with the number 1.

The first word in the title of the journal article and the first word in the subtitle of the journal article are capitalized.

All words in the title of the journal (except prepositions) are capitalized.

This is an example of a book citation. See section 7.02 in the Publication Manual for information on providing book citations.

When you are citing a source from the web, ideally you should indicate the author, date, title and source. See Lee (2010).

References

Bodvarsson, Ö. B., & Gibson, W. A. (1994). Gratuities and customer appraisal of service: Evidence from Minnesota restaurants. *Journal of Socio-Economics, 23*(3), 287–302. doi:http://dx.doi.org/10.1016/1053-5357(94)90005-1

Garrity, K., & Degelman, D. (1990). Effect of server introduction on restaurant tipping. *Journal of Applied Social Psychology, 20*, 168–172. doi:http://dx.doi.org/10.1111/j.1559-1816.1990.tb00405.x

Guéguen, N. (2012). Hair color and wages: Waitresses with blond hair have more fun. *Journal of Socio-Economics, 41*(4), 370–372. doi: http://dx.doi.org/10.1016/j.socec.2012.04.012

Jacob, C., Guéguen, N., Boulbry, G., & Ardiccioni, R. (2010). Waitresses' facial cosmetics and tipping: A field experiment. *International Journal of Hospitality Management, 29*(1), 188–190. doi:http://dx.doi.org/10.1016/j.ijhm.2009.04.003

Laurenson, J. (2014, August 16). France's waiters watch their tips decline. Retrieved from www.bbc.com/news/world-europe-28793677

Leary, M. R., & Kowalski, R. M. (1990). Impression management: A literature review and two-component model. *Psychological Bulletin, 107*(1), 34–37. doi:http://dx.doi.org/10.1037/0033-2909.107.1.34

Lee, C. (2010). How to cite something you found on a website in APA style [Blog post]. Retrieved from http://blog.apastyle.org/apastyle/2010/11/how-to-cite-something-you-found-on-a-website-in-apa-style.html

Lynn, M., & Grassman, A. (1990). Restaurant tipping: An examination of three "rational explanations." *Journal of Economic Psychology, 11*(2), 169–181. doi:http://dx.doi.org/10.1016/0167-4870(90)90002-Q

Rind, B., & Bordia, P. (1995). Effect of server's "thank you" and personalization on restaurant tipping. *Journal of Applied Social Psychology, 25*, 745–751. doi:http://dx.doi.org/10.1111/j.1559-1816.1995.tb01772.x

Rind, B., & Bordia, P. (1996). Effect on restaurant tipping of male and female servers drawing a happy, smiling face on the backs of customers' checks. *Journal of Applied Social Psychology, 26*, 218–225. doi:http://dx.doi.org/10.1111/j.1559-1816.1996.tb01847.x

Sanchez, R. R. (2013). *How to increase your tips waiting tables*. Bloomington, IN: Trafford.

Seiter, J. S. (2007). Ingratiation and gratuity: The effect of complimenting customers on tipping behavior in restaurants. *Journal of Applied Social Psychology, 37*, 478–485. doi:http://dx.doi.org/10.1111/j.1559-1816.2007.00169.x

US Department of Labor (2016). Minimum wages for tipped employees. Retrieved from www.dol.gov/whd/state/tipped.htm

Table 1

Summary statistics (based on 132 observations)

Variables	Minimum	Maximum	Mean	Standard deviation
Number of customers per table	1.00	6.00	2.80	1.20

See sections 5.07-5.19 of the Publication Manual for information on creating tables.

One could choose to put this information in the text. I chose to put it in a table so that I could illustrate what a table would look like in an APA style manuscript. Note that only horizontal lines are used.

Appendix A

The lines that each look like a capital "I" on each of the red and blue bars are called "error bars" and they represent confidence intervals. I choose to show the confidence intervals so that you can get a better sense of potential differences between groups. You can compare the confidence intervals from bar to bar. If the intervals do not overlap, we can be confident that the means you are comparing differ. So in the bar graph shown, it appears that the tip percentages for the smiley face conditions differ but only when the thank you message is present.

The figure starts on a new page headed by a caption. Note that the phrase "Figure 1" is in italics.

See sections 5.20-5.30 of the Publication Manual for information on creating figures.

Single spacing is allowed in tables and figures.

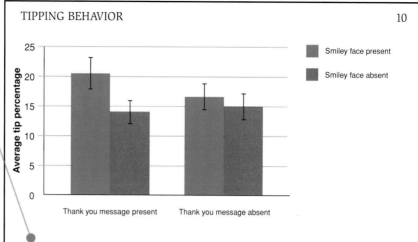

Figure 1. Average tip percentage as a function of whether a smiley face and a thank-you message are present or absent on patrons' restaurant check. Error bars designate 95% confidence intervals.

Appendix B: Table of Random Numbers

Line/column	(a)	(b)	(c)	(d)	(e)	(f)	(g)	(h)
1	43936	15097	01616	15501	73844	25374	97343	28319
2	87730	57159	48873	26846	66367	47804	30051	56754
3	44341	87325	11488	39000	03347	36864	09756	17638
4	57418	01211	43273	90530	01875	94398	16829	22978
5	22574	79185	09352	45409	84121	21101	10161	89866
6	46736	33255	47141	05484	30455	28983	59958	67031
7	88798	53954	58486	98007	52886	61690	88394	08284
8	18965	16570	70640	34987	68504	41396	49277	99075
9	32851	74912	22169	06956	99479	21910	54618	83053
10	10824	14433	77049	15760	26183	41800	21506	82389
11	64895	78780	37123	62095	60622	91598	98670	04011
12	85594	90125	29646	84526	93330	20033	13365	80253
13	48209	02279	40068	00143	46477	80917	30714	81321
14	06552	27251	38596	31119	53550	86257	14692	29387
15	46073	08688	20842	57822	73440	53145	14029	04820
16	10420	42205	93734	92262	23237	03752	09093	93071
17	95207	34728	16165	98411	25115	45005	11892	11229
18	33919	71708	31782	78117	12556	35796	12961	08024
19	58890	70235	62758	85189	17897	19774	61027	63826
20	40328	52482	89462	05079	84785	45668	36460	37528
21	73844	25374	97343	28319	35391	40732	24710	72776
22	66367	47804	30051	56754	76644	43532	42868	18301
23	03347	36864	09756	17638	67435	44600	39664	27914
24	01875	94398	16829	22978	51413	92666	95466	13624
25	84121	21101	10161	89866	50750	68099	69167	65963
26	30455	28983	59958	67031	72372	56350	04416	33660
27	52886	61690	88394	08284	48613	74508	49941	23642
28	68504	41396	49277	99075	49682	71303	59554	94802
29	99479	21910	54618	83053	24306	00548	18706	64231
30	26183	41800	21506	82389	99738	00807	97602	07215
31	60622	91598	98670	04011	87989	36055	65299	51009
32	35391	34323	71303	18965	12297	13624	43273	24046
33	76644	28578	00548	32851	56090	65963	09352	37932
34	67435	92002	00807	10824	39259	33660	47141	42464
35	51413	63163	36055	64895	25778	23642	58486	96534
36	50750	32591	55022	85594	90934	94802	70640	17233
37	72372	75576	91193	24710	15097	64231	22169	79848
38	48613	19369	50345	42868	57159	07215	77049	38191
39	49682	75980	02684	39664	87325	51009	37123	77712
40	24306	89057	96939	95466	01211	07620	28578	15501
41	99738	54213	86921	69167	79185	94139	92002	26846
42	87989	51818	31523	04416	33255	85853	63163	39000
43	06147	20438	27510	49941	53954	83457	32591	90530
44	02943	40732	43936	59554	16570	52077	75576	45409
45	32187	43532	87730	18706	74912	55686	19369	05484
46	05888	44600	44341	97602	14433	69572	75980	98007
47	41137	92666	57418	65299	78780	47545	89057	34987
48	86662	68099	22574	55281	72776	01616	54213	06956
49	96275	56350	46736	26442	18301	48873	51818	15760
50	81985	74508	88798	95870	27914	11488	20438	62095

Index